# Pro JSP 2
## Fourth Edition

Simon Brown, Sam Dalton, Daniel Jepp,
David Johnson, Sing Li, and Matt Raible
Edited by Kevin Mukhar

Apress®

**Pro JSP 2, Fourth Edition**

**Copyright © 2005 by Simon Brown, Sam Dalton, Daniel Jepp, Dave Johnson, Sing Li, and Matt Raible**

ISBN (pbk): 1-59059-513-0

Printed and bound in the United States of America 9 8 7 6 5 4 3 2 1

Trademarked names may appear in this book. Rather than use a trademark symbol with every occurrence of a trademarked name, we use the names only in an editorial fashion and to the benefit of the trademark owner, with no intention of infringement of the trademark.

Lead Editors: Steve Anglin and Kevin Mukhar
Technical Reviewers: Scott Davis and Dilip Thomas
Editorial Board: Steve Anglin, Dan Appleman, Ewan Buckingham, Gary Cornell, Tony Davis,
    Jason Gilmore, Jonathan Hassell, Chris Mills, Dominic Shakeshaft, Jim Sumser
Associate Publisher: Grace Wong
Project Manager: Beckie Brand
Copy Edit Manager: Nicole LeClerc
Copy Editor: Sharon Wilkey
Assistant Production Director: Kari Brooks-Copony
Production Editor: Ellie Fountain
Compositor: ContentWorks
Proofreader: Sue Boshers
Indexer: Julie Grady
Artist: Kinetic Publishing Services, LLC
Interior Designer: Van Winkle Design Group
Cover Designer: Kurt Krames
Manufacturing Director: Tom Debolski

Distributed to the book trade worldwide by Springer-Verlag New York, Inc., 233 Spring Street, 6th Floor, New York, NY 10013. Phone 1-800-SPRINGER, fax 201-348-4505, e-mail orders-ny@springer-sbm.com, or visit http://www.springeronline.com.

For information on translations, please contact Apress directly at 2560 Ninth Street, Suite 219, Berkeley, CA 94710. Phone 510-549-5930, fax 510-549-5939, e-mail info@apress.com, or visit http://www.apress.com.

The source code for this book is available to readers at http://www.apress.com in the Source Code section.

# Contents at a Glance

# Contents

## ■CHAPTER 6    Tag Files and Simple Tags

## ■CHAPTER 7    Classic Tags

# About the Authors

**SIMON BROWN** works in London as a technical architect and has been using Java since its early beginnings, working in roles ranging from developer and architect to mentor and trainer. When not working with Java, he can usually be found speaking or writing about it. In the past few years, Simon has spoken at the JavaOne Conference and has authored or coauthored several books, including his own, entitled *Professional JSP Tag Libraries* (Peer Information, 2002). Simon maintains an active involvement within the Java community as a bartender (moderator) with JavaRanch and his open-source JSP custom tag-testing framework called TagUnit.

Simon graduated from the University of Reading in 1996 with a First Class BSc (Hons) degree in Computer Science and is a Sun Certified Enterprise Architect for J2EE, Web Component Developer for J2EE, and Developer for the Java 2 Platform.

For information about what Simon is currently up to, you can point your browser to his web log at `http://www.simongbrown.com/blog/`.

*I would like to thank my wife, Kirstie—you're always there for me.*

**SAM DALTON** has worked with Java and related technologies in London for a number of years, and has coauthored two titles, *Professional Java Servlets 2.3* (Peer Information, 2002) and *Professional SCWCD Certification* (Wrox Press, 2002). Sam is an active contributor to TagUnit, an open-source custom tag-testing framework (`http://www.tagunit.org`) and is also pursuing other open-source interests. He has embarked on the next stage of his career adventure by joining ThoughtWorks (`http://www.thoughtworks.co.uk`).

Sam graduated from the University of Reading in 1997 with a 2:1 honors degree in Computer Science. He has also achieved various certifications, including Sun Certified Web Component Developer and Sun Certified Developer. Please feel free to e-mail any questions or comments about this book and related topics to `books@samjdalton.com`.

*Well, here we are again! Who would have thought I would ever be involved in three books? Not me, that's for sure! There are a number of people that I would like to thank for supporting/putting up with me while I was contributing to this book. First of all, as ever, I would like to thank my darling wife, Anne, without whom I would not have the energy to do half of the things that I do. I would also like to thank my Mum and Dad; it means a great deal to me to see how proud my work makes you—thanks! Enjoy the book, and happy reading!*

■**DANIEL JEPP** is a senior developer at Dresdner Kleinwort Wasserstein, based in London. He has been working with the Java platform and related technologies for a number of years and has spoken at several sessions at the JavaOne Conference. Dan coauthored *Professional SCWCD Certification* with Sam Dalton in 2002.

Dan graduated from the University of Kent, in Canterbury, England, where he attained a 2:1 honors degree in Computer Science, and has since gained the following Sun Certifications: Sun Certified Programmer, Developer, and Web Component Developer for the Java 2 Platform.

> *Dedicated to my fiancée, Kelly, whose love, support, and encouragement will leave me forever grateful.*

■**DAVID JOHNSON** is an experienced software developer who has worked in the commercial software development, telecommunications, and Geographic Information Systems industries. David has been working with Java since before the dawn of Java 1.0. Since then, he has been involved in the development of a number of Java-based commercial products, including the HAHTsite Application Server, HAHT eSyndication, Venetica's Jasper document viewer, and Rogue Wave Software's Object Factory IDE. David is also an active weblogger and the original developer of the open-source Roller Weblogger (http://www.rollerweblogger.org) software. David works at HAHT Commerce and lives in Raleigh, North Carolina, with his wife and three children.

> *First and foremost, I must thank my beautiful wife, Andi, for giving me the encouragement and time needed to work on this book. She kept my three little boys, Alex, Linus, and Leo, happy and quiet while I toiled away in the back room on my chapters. I should also thank fellow Roller Weblogger developers Lance Lavandowska and Matt Raible. Lance helped me to get started with this project, and Matt helped to improve and perfect my example code. Finally, I would like to thank Bill Barnett and the whole HAHTsite Application Server team at HAHT Commerce for teaching me just about everything I know about web-application performance and scalability and for inspiring me to learn more.*

■**SING LI** was first bitten by the computer bug in 1978 and has grown up with the microprocessor revolution. His first PC was a $99 do-it-yourself COSMAC ELF computer with 256 bytes of memory and a 1-bit LED display. For more than two decades, Sing has been a developer, author, consultant, speaker, instructor, and entrepreneur. His wide-ranging experience spans distributed architectures, web-application and service systems, computer telephony integration, and embedded systems. Sing is a regular book contributor, has been working with and writing about Java, Jini, and JXTA since their very first alpha releases, and is an evangelist of P2P technology and a participant in the JXTA community.

**MATT RAIBLE** is a Montana native who grew up in a log cabin without electricity or running water. After hiking to school a mile and a half every day (and skiing in the winter), he would arrive home to a very loving family. "The Cabin" is a beautiful and awesome place that will always be near and dear to Matt's entire family. Even without electricity, his father, Joseph, connected them to the Internet by using a 300 baud modem, a Commodore 64, and a small generator. CompuServe was the name, slow was the game. Matt became inspired by the Internet in the early 1990s, and has been developing websites and web applications ever since. He graduated from the University of Denver in 1997 with degrees in Russian, International Business, and Finance. To learn more about Matt and his life as a J2EE Developer, visit him at http://raibledesigns.com.

*I'd like to thank my beautiful wife, Julie, and adorable daughter, Abbie, for their love and support while writing these chapters. Abbie was born three weeks before I was asked to write my chapters, and her smiles and giggles were an incredible inspiration. Chris Alonso, thanks for motivating me to go into computers as a profession and for being such a good friend. Thanks to my dad for passing along his knack for computers and great memory, and to my Mom for giving me a passion for life, happiness, and humor. Kalin—you're the best sister in the world and you make this world a better place with your smiles and laughter. Last but not least, thanks to Matt Good for letting me write Java, and to Martin Gee and Brian Boelsterli for their mentoring.*

# About the Editor

**KEVIN MUKHAR** is a software developer from Colorado Springs, Colorado. For the past seven years, he has worked on various software systems using different Java Enterprise technologies. He has coauthored several other books, including *Beginning Java EE 5: From Novice to Professional* (Apress, 2005), *The Ultimate Palm Robot* (Osborne/McGraw-Hill, 2003), and *Beginning Java Databases* (Wrox Press, 2001). In addition to developing software during the day, he is working on a master's degree in computer science. His web page is http://home.earthlink.net/~kmukhar/.

# About the Technical Reviewers

■**SCOTT DAVIS** is a senior software engineer at OpenLogic. He is passionate about open-source solutions and agile development. In addition to serving as technical editor for several Apress titles including *Pro Jakarta Tomcat 5* and *Beginning JSP 2: From Novice to Professional*, he coauthored *JBoss At Work* (O'Reilly Media, 2005). He is the author of the upcoming book *Pragmatic GIS* (Pragmatic Bookshelf, 2006), which focuses on free/open-source geography software solutions such as Google Maps and GeoServer.

Scott is a frequent presenter at national conferences (such as No Fluff, Just Stuff) and local user groups. He was the president of the Denver Java Users Group in 2003 when it was voted one of the top-ten JUGs in North America. Since a quick move north, he has been active in the leadership of the Boulder Java Users Group. Keep up with him at http://www.davisworld.org.

■**DILIP THOMAS** is an open-source enthusiast who keeps a close watch on LAMP technologies, open standards, and the full range of Apache Jakarta projects. He is coauthor of *PHP MySQL Website Programming: Problem - Design - Solution* (Apress, 2003) and a technical reviewer/editor on several open-source/open standard book projects. Dilip is an editorial director at Software & Support Verlag GmbH.

Dilip resides in Bangalore, India, with his beautiful wife, Indu, and several hundred books and journals. Reach him via e-mail at dilip.thomas@gmail.com.

# Acknowledgments

When we started this revision, it was going to be just a simple update: change a few things here and there to make sure the book was consistent with JSP 2.1. Along the way, it turned into a much bigger task. Part of the reason for that was our desire to make this the best possible book about JSP 2.1 that we could. So I want to acknowledge everyone at Apress who helped make this the book it is, especially Sharon Wilkey, Beckie Brand, Ellie Fountain, Ami Knox, Steve Anglin, and the technical reviewers Scott Davis and Dilip Thomas.

While I worked on this book, my wife and I experienced a lot of changes and challenges in our lives. I'd like to thank some of the many people who helped us through that time: Tom and Marg Gimmy, Dave and Kris Johnson, my family, Anne's family, and Dawn Girard. And of course, no thanks would be complete without thanking my family, Anne and Christine, for letting me spend the time away from them needed to do this project.

Kevin Mukhar

# Introduction

**W**elcome to the fourth edition of *Professional JSP*, designed to help new and experienced Java developers alike discover the power (and even the joy) of creating Java-based server-side solutions for the Web by using **JavaServer Pages**, or **JSP** for short. If you've programmed with JSP before, you'll find that the new features in JSP 2.1 make developing JSP pages easier than ever before. If you only know a little Java, this is your chance to add JSP to your toolbox skills.

**JSP** is a server-side technology that takes the Java language, with its inherent simplicity and elegance, and uses it to create highly interactive and flexible web applications. In today's unsure economic climate, having the Java language as the cornerstone of JSP makes JSP particularly compelling for business: Because Java is an open language (meaning it doesn't require expensive licenses), JSP solutions can be highly cost-effective.

The founding premise of JSP is that HTML can be used to create the basic structure of a web page, and Java code can be mixed in with the HTML to provide the dynamic components of the page that modern web users expect. If you understand the concepts of HTML and web pages, JSP provides an unbeatable way to learn about creating innovative, interactive content as well as coming to grips with the popular language of Java. This book will be your guide as you step into this exciting new world.

## Who Is This Book For?

This book is aimed at anyone who knows the Java language and core APIs and wants to learn about web programming with the latest versions of the JSP and Servlet APIs.

Familiarity with HTML is required; however, no prior knowledge of server-side Java programming is necessary. Having said that, this book does not claim to be exhaustive in all areas, particularly in relation to other Java Enterprise Edition APIs such as Enterprise JavaBeans.

## What's Covered in This Book

This book covers the latest versions of the JSP and Servlet specifications—versions 2.1 and 2.5 respectively, both of which are new specifications developed through the **Java Community Process** (http://www.jcp.org/).

---

**Note** At the time this book was being published, the JSP specification was in Proposed Final Draft stage. It's possible that some small changes might be made before the specification reaches final release; however, any modifications are likely to be minor and the new specifications are already being implemented by a number of products such as Tomcat 5.5.

---

Those who have read previous editions of this book will notice that this edition is a revision of *Professional JSP, 3rd Edition*. Because the third edition covered JSP 2.0, most of the information was still current for this book, which covers JSP 2.1. However, we've gone through the entire book and ensured that the material is still correct for JSP 2.1. We've gone through every chapter and updated the text to make it clearer and more concise. Finally, we've added an entire new chapter on JavaServer Faces, one of the newest Java web-application technologies.

If you already have some exposure to server Java web development, you should pay attention to any changes in the technologies that are indicated throughout the book, or skip ahead to the sections that interest you the most. On the other hand, if you're new to JSP, servlets, and JSTL, and this is somewhat confusing, you've come to the right place; the early chapters in this book, especially, were written with you in mind.

Here is what you can expect to find in each chapter:

Chapter 1, *The Anatomy of a JavaServer Page*, looks at the JSP life cycle, JSP application architecture, and the fundamentals of JSP pages, and provides a feel for where JSP technology fits within the Java EE 5 and other web components such as servlets, tag libraries, and JavaBeans, which exist in the Java EE 5 web tier for providing dynamic web-based content.

Chapter 2, *Servlets and Deployment*, delves into what Java servlets are, and looks at the development and deployment of Java servlets. The Servlet and JSP specifications are developed in parallel, and this chapter is up to date for the latest release of JSP 2.1 and Servlets 2.5 (as is the rest of the book).

We discuss one of the new features of the JSP 2.1 specification in Chapter 3, *The JavaServer Pages Expression Language*. The JSP expression language is what you'll be using most often in JSP pages, an intentionally simple language that is, to a large extent, independent of JSP.

Chapter 4, *JavaServer Pages Standard Tag Library*, looks at the reasons for the creation of the JSTL, its details (it is in fact four different tag libraries), and how to install the JSTL.

Chapter 5, *JavaServer Faces*, is an introduction to JavaServer Faces (JSF), a framework for creating component-based user interfaces. You'll learn how to use JSF with JSP pages to create feature-rich user interfaces.

*Tag Files and Simple Tags* is the title of Chapter 6. Tags contained within JSTL are extremely valuable for improving the readability and maintainability of a JSP page. You can also build custom tags to enable your own functionality to be reusable and easily maintained. Tag files and simple tags are both new mechanisms for writing custom tags introduced as a part of the JSP 2.1 specification.

Chapter 7, *Classic Tags*, takes a look at the facilities provided by former versions of the JSP specification for writing custom tags. As you'll see throughout the chapter, these previous methods, now called classic tags, provide a great deal more flexibility and therefore are still useful in some scenarios.

After you learn the basics of building custom tags, Chapter 8, *Custom Tag Advanced Features and Best Practices*, wraps up your understanding by looking at some more advanced features and the best way to use custom tags.

Chapter 9, *Data Access Options for Web Applications*, discusses how best to access your back-end data from your JSPs and servlets. No matter what type of JSP application you're writing, you'll need to either store the data that is created by your application, or use data from an external source, and this chapter looks at examples using a MySQL database.

In Chapter 10, *Introduction to Filtering*, you'll look at filtering, a standard feature of all Servlet 2.5–compliant containers. You'll explore the life cycle of a filter as managed by the container, discuss the very important concept of filter chaining, and then create and deploy two simple filters.

Chapter 11, *Advanced Filtering Techniques*, is a cookbook for the application of filters, as you turn your attention to the more advanced techniques involved in applied filter programming by looking at five examples that can be used as the basis for your own filter implementation.

Chapter 12, *Security in Web Applications*, looks at making your web applications secure and explores different methods of authentication and authorization.

Chapter 13, *Improving Web-Application Performance and Scalability*, is your guide to a number of well-known tools and techniques such as page caching and database connection pooling that you can use to improve performance and stability, even after you've designed and coded your application.

Chapter 14, *Web-Application Design and Best Practices*, brings together the techniques covered in the earlier chapters and shows how to build maintainable, extensible Java-based web applications. It looks at the importance of good design and how it can help you build high-quality web applications that are easier to maintain and extend in the future.

In Chapter 15, *Using Struts, XDoclet, and Other Tools*, you'll develop a résumé building and viewing web application called `struts-resume`, by using a variety of third-party products. All of the products used in `struts-resume` are open source and help to facilitate and speed up various stages of the development process.

# What You Need to Use This Book

The first thing you'll need to use this book is a computer that supports the Java programming language. This includes computers that run Microsoft Windows, Sun Solaris, or Linux.

We don't use any proprietary software, and all code runs on open-source products, available free of charge over the Internet. Consequently, an Internet connection is pretty much essential in order to get hold of this software.

The primary piece of software you'll need is a web container that supports the JSP 2.1 and Servlet 2.5 specifications. Although there are a number of options to choose from, we've elected to use the Jakarta Tomcat web container throughout the whole book because it's the officially designated reference implementation. Version 5.5 is the latest and greatest, which supports the specs we require. You can get the latest release information about Tomcat 5.5 from `http://jakarta.apache.org/tomcat/index.html`.

As you need further software components during the course of the book, we'll indicate clearly where to download them from.

# Conventions

We've used several styles of text and layout in this book to differentiate between different kinds of information. Here are examples of the styles used and an explanation of what they mean.

Code has several fonts. If we're talking about code in the text, we use a nonproportional font like this: for...next. If it's a complete code listing that can be entered and used as part of an application, then it will appear in a nonproportional font with a caption like this:

**Listing 1-2.** *date.jsp*

```
<html>
  <body>
    <h2>Greetings!</h2>
    <p>The current time is <%=new java.util.Date()%> precisely</p>
  </body>
</html>
```

Code that is an extract or snippet from a larger listing will appear without a caption, like this:

```
import javax.servlet.http.*;

public class SessionTracker2 extends HttpServlet {
  public void doGet(HttpServletRequest req, HttpServletResponse res)
```

Sometimes you will need to type in commands on the command line, which we display using the following style:

```
> set classpath=.;%Java EE_HOME%\lib\j2ee.jar
\projsp> javac -d . client\*.java
```

We show the prompt using a > symbol or \\*dirname*> (where *dirname* is a directory name) and then the commands you need to type. As you can see, we tend to use the Windows directory separator character when showing directory paths. We do this because we expect that a lot of readers will be using a Windows platform when they try out the code. But we also develop on Linux or Solaris platforms, and if you do too, then you should use the directory separator that is correct for your platform.

---

**■Note** Advice, hints, and background information come in this type of font offset by borders. Important pieces of information also come in this format. Depending on the type of information, we preface the text with the word Note, Tip, or Caution. Notes consist of incidental information of one type or another that defines, explains, or elaborates on the main discussion. Tips will make your programming easier. For instance, a Tip might point out another way to use a certain feature that's not obvious from the main discussion. Cautions indicate a potential hazard. For example, a Caution might be a method that if misused could crash your application server.

---

Bullets appear indented, with each new bullet marked as follows:

- **Important Words** are in a bold type font.
- Words that appear on the screen or in menus, such as `File` or `Window`, are in a monospaced font.

Numbered lists are similar to bulleted lists:

1. Do this action first.
2. Do this action next.

# What to Do If You Encounter Problems

Despite all our best efforts, and despite this book's numerous sharp-eyed editors, there is a possibility that errors managed to sneak through. It has been known to happen. If you are having problems with any of the text or code examples, the first place to go for corrections is the web page for the book (`http://www.apress.com/book/bookDisplay.html?bID=464`). If any errata have been identified, you will find a link for Corrections on the book's web page. If you click this link, you will find a page that lists known errors with the code or book text, and corrections for those problems.

If you can't find your problem listed on the Corrections page, you will find a link to Submit Errata on the main book page. If you've double-checked and triple-checked your problem and still can't get the code to work or the text to make sense, use the Submit Errata link to send us a description of the problem. We can't promise a speedy response, but we do see all submissions and post responses to the Corrections page after we've had a chance to check out the problem.

# CHAPTER 1

# The Anatomy of a JavaServer Page

The Java Platform, Enterprise Edition 5 (Java EE 5) has two different but complementary technologies for producing dynamic web content in the presentation tier—namely **Java Servlet** and **JavaServer Pages (JSP)**.

Java Servlet, the first of these technologies to appear, was initially described as extensions to a web server for producing dynamic web content. JSP, on the other hand, is a newer technology but is equally capable of generating the same dynamic content. However, the way in which a servlet and a JSP page produce their content is fundamentally different; servlets embed content into logic, whereas JSP pages embed logic into content.

JSP pages contain markup interlaced with special JSP elements that provide logic for controlling the dynamic content. Servlets are built using Java classes that contain statements to output markup code. Of these two paradigms, JSP pages are preferred for presenting dynamic content in the presentation tier due to their greater readability, maintainability, and simplicity. Further increasing the simplicity and ease of use of JSP pages was one of the main objectives of the JSP 2.0 specification, which included several new features to make it easier than ever to embrace JSP technology, especially for developers who aren't fluent in the Java syntax.

The inclusion of a new **expression language (EL)** enables JavaScript-style JSP code to be embedded within pages, which makes it much easier for web developers not familiar with the Java syntax to understand the JSP logic. A library of standard actions known as the **JavaServer Pages Standard Tag Library (JSTL)** is also included to provide a host of useful, reusable actions such as conditional statements, iteration, and XML integration to name a few. These actions are applicable in some shape or form to most JSP web applications, and their use will greatly improve the reliability and ease of development for JSP page authors. Custom actions (also known as custom tags) also benefit from changes in the JSP specification, and it's now possible to write a custom action entirely in JSP syntax instead of Java syntax!

JSP 2.1 further eases the development of JSP pages by unifying the JSP expression language with the JavaServer Faces (JSF) expression language. These new features will help make JSP pages easier to write and maintain and are discussed in detail in the following chapters:

- The JSP 2.1 expression language (EL) (see Chapter 3)

- The JavaServer Pages Standard Tag Library (JSTL) (see Chapter 4)

- The JavaServer Faces custom tags (see Chapter 5)

- JSP custom tags (see Chapters 6, 7, and 8)

In this chapter, you'll take a look at some of the fundamental concepts based around JSP technology, such as the following:

- The mechanics of a JSP page

- Typical JSP architectures

- Core JSP syntax

- Tag libraries

The aim of this chapter is to help you gain a grounding in the basics of JSP technology so you can make full use of the rest of the chapters in this book that build on these basic principles.

# Before You Begin

To begin examining the basics of JSP technology, it's essential that you have a cursory familiarity with the alternative and complementary presentation-tier web component, Java servlets. The next chapter will discuss servlets in more detail.

## Java Servlets

As mentioned earlier, servlets can most simply be described as custom web-server extensions, whose jobs are to process requests and dynamically construct appropriate responses. In practice, such responses are usually returned in the form of HTML or XML and are the result of a user making an HTTP request via a web browser. Servlet technology has been an extremely popular choice for building dynamic web applications such as e-commerce sites, online banking, and news portals, for reasons of simplicity, extensibility, efficiency, and performance over alternative technologies such as Common Gateway Interface (CGI) scripts.

Some of the most basic advantages of servlet technology are as follows:

- **Simplicity:** Servlets are easy to write, and all the complicated threading and request delegating is managed by the servlet container.

- **Extensibility:** The Servlet API is completely protocol independent.

- **Efficiency:** Unlike CGI scripts, the execution of a servlet doesn't require a separate process to be spawned by the web server each time.

- **Performance:** Servlets are persistent, and their life cycle extends beyond that of each HTTP request.

Servlets are simply Java classes that inherit from the `javax.servlet.Servlet` interface. These servlets are compiled and deployed inside a servlet container, which is a Java environment that manages the life cycle of the servlet and deals with the lower-level socket-based communication. The servlet container may be part of an existing Java-enabled web server itself or may be used as a stand-alone product that is integrated with a third-party web server. The servlet Reference Implementation container, Apache Jakarta Tomcat for example, may be used as a stand-alone web server or as a separate servlet container inside a larger commercial web server such as the Apache web server.

Servlets are typically used for returning text-based content such as HTML, XML, WML, and so on. However, they are equally at home returning binary data such as images or serialized Java objects, which are often used by further servlets to generate some appropriate dynamic response.

# JSP Under the Hood

A JSP page is simply a regular text file that contains markup (usually HTML) suitable for display inside a browser. Within this markup are special JSP elements that you'll learn more about later. These are used to provide processing logic that enables dynamic content to be produced on a request-by-request basis.

In JSP terms, any markup that isn't a JSP element is known as template text, and this really can be any form of text-based content such as HTML, WML, XML, or even plain text! Of course the mixture of JSP elements and template text cannot simply be sent to the browser without any form of processing by the server. We mentioned earlier how JSP technology is an extension of servlet technology, and so you probably won't be surprised to learn that each JSP page is, in fact, converted into a servlet in order to provide this processing logic. Figure 1-1 shows a JSP page being translated and compiled into a servlet in response to a request. This servlet is known as the JSP **implementation servlet**.

**Figure 1-1.** *The JSP container translates and compiles the JSP source into an implementation class, which is used to process all requests.*

A request for a JSP page is handled initially by the web server, which then delegates the request to the JSP container. The JSP engine will translate the contents of the JSP into its implementation servlet, which the container then uses to service the request. Usually a JSP container will check whether the contents of a JSP page have changed before deciding if it needs to retranslate the page in response to a request. This feature can make on-the-spot changes to JSP pages easy because the next request will automatically cause a retranslation and the most up-to-date content will be returned. Compare this with a purely servlet-based approach, which would require the servlet container to be shut down in order to have the necessary changes made, such as recompilation, testing, and finally, a restart!

Let's take a closer look at the process of taking a plain JSP text file and turning it into a dynamic web component; this process is also known as the JSP life cycle.

## The JSP Life Cycle

As you've just seen, JSP pages don't directly return content to the client browser themselves. Instead, they rely on some initial server-side processing that converts the JSP page into the JSP page implementation class (see Figure 1-2), which handles all requests made of the JSP.

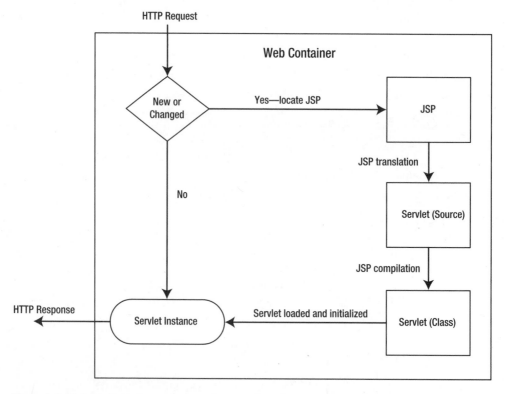

**Figure 1-2.** *Before processing a request, the container determines whether the JSP source is new or has changed. If so, the container translates and compiles the JSP page into a servlet class, or page implementation class, before passing the request to the servlet for processing.*

As you can see in Figure 1-2, the JSP servlet container decides whether the JSP page has been translated before. If not, the JSP container starts the translation phase to generate the JSP page implementation servlet, which is then compiled, loaded and initialized, and used to service the request. If the JSP container detects that a JSP page has already been translated and hasn't subsequently changed, the request is simply serviced by the implementation servlet that already exists inside the container.

The life cycle of a JSP page can be split into four phases: translation, initialization, execution, and finalization.

## Translation

The first stage in the life cycle of a JSP page is known as the translation phase.

When a request is first made for a JSP page (assuming it hasn't been precompiled), the JSP engine will examine the JSP file to check that it's correctly formed and that the JSP syntax is correct. If the syntax check is successful, the JSP engine will translate the JSP page into its page implementation class, which takes the form of a standard Java servlet. After the page's implementation servlet has been created, it will be compiled into a class file by the JSP engine and will be ready for use.

Each time a container receives a request, it first checks whether the JSP file has changed since it was last translated. If it has, it's retranslated so that the response is always generated by the most up-to-date implementation of the JSP file.

## Initialization

After the translation phase has been completed, the JSP engine will need to load the generated class file and create an instance of the servlet in order to continue processing the initial request. Therefore, the JSP engine works very closely with the servlet container and the JSP page implementation servlet and will typically load a single instance of the servlet into memory. This single instance will be used to service all requests for the JSP page. In a real-world web application, those requests will most likely happen concurrently, so your JSP page must be multithreaded.

Prior to the Servlet 2.5 specification, the Java Servlet specification provided two separate threading models that could be used for a servlet. The models determine whether single or multiple instances of a servlet can exist. The default threading model for any servlet is the multithreaded one that requires no additional work for the developer. In this model, the container creates only a single instance of the servlet class and sends multiple requests to the instance concurrently.

To select the single-threaded model for your JSP, you must set an attribute of the `page` directive called `isThreadSafe` to `false` to serialize all requests to the implementation servlet behind the JSP:

```
<%@ page isThreadSafe="false" %>
```

In the past, containers would support this feature by creating an implementation page that implements the `SingleThreadModel` interface. When the implementation page implements this interface, the JSP container creates multiple instances of the implementation class; each instance handles a single request at any given time. However, note that the JSP 2.1 specification advises developers against using `isThreadSafe="false"` because the Servlet 2.5 specification has deprecated `SingleThreadModel`.

---

■**Caution**  A JSP page that sets the page attribute `isThreadSafe` to `false` may contain deprecated code in the implementation class. In addition, it does not guarantee thread safety in all cases. Do not rely on `isThreadSafe="false"` to protect your JSP page from concurrency problems.

---

After the servlet class is loaded, the container initializes the servlet instance with a call to an initialization method. For a JSP implementation servlet, that method is the `jspInit()` method. As the name suggests, this method is used for initializing the implementation servlet in an identical manner to the standard servlet `init()` method, which is used to initialize a servlet. The behavior of both methods can be regarded as identical, and each is called exactly once. Although `jspInit()` is automatically generated during the translation phase, it's possible to override this method in the JSP page by using a declaration. The method can be used for initializing application-level variables or resources, for example:

```
<%! AppVar appvar = null; %>
<%!
  public void jspInit() {
    try {
      appvar = initAppVar(...);
    } catch (Exception e){
      //handle exception
    }
  }
%>
```

## Execution

After the web container has loaded and initialized the implementation servlet, the initial request can be serviced. To service the request, the web container calls the `_jspService()` method of the implementation servlet. As we mentioned, each request to the JSP page results in a separately threaded call to the `_jspService()` method.

The `_jspService()` method provides all the functionality for handling a request and returning a response to the client. All the scriptlets and expressions end up inside this method, in the order in which they were declared inside the JSP page. Notice that JSP declarations and directives aren't included inside this method because they apply to the entire page, not just to a single request, and therefore exist outside the method. The `_jspService()` method may not be overridden in the JSP page.

## Finalization

The last phase in the life cycle is the finalization phase. As with the previous two phases, there is a corresponding method in the implementation servlet for this phase. The method is named `jspDestroy()`. Like the `destroy()` method found in a standard servlet, this method is called by the servlet container when the page implementation servlet is about to be destroyed. This destruction could be for various reasons, such as the server being low on memory and wanting to free up some resources, but the most common reason is that the servlet container is shutting down or being restarted.

After this method has been called, the servlet can no longer serve any requests. Like the destroy() method, jspDestroy() is an excellent place to release or close application-level resources when the servlet is shutting down. To do this, simply provide an implementation of this method via a JSP method declaration. For example, to release the application resource you opened inside the jspInit() method, you would use the following:

```
<%!
  public void jspDestroy() {
    try {
      appVar.release();
    } catch (Exception e){}
    appVar = null;
  }
%>
```

# JavaServer Pages Best Practices

One of the design goals of this book, apart from the obvious introduction to the concepts and mechanics of JSP technology, is to teach right from the start the best practices learned from experience. Of all the best practices that have been established around JSP, one of the most important suggests that there should be as little Java code as possible embedded inside a JSP page. Experience has shown us that three key factors benefit from this practice:

- Reusability

- Readability

- Maintainability

Let's look at each of these and see how their use can benefit your JSP applications.

## Reusability

A common goal associated with using any programming language is that of reuse, whether it involves structuring code inside modules, classes, or some other language-specific construct. Reusing code leads to increased maintainability and productivity, and higher quality because changes to such common functionality need to be made in only a single place. Although the concept of building web-based applications is relatively new, this goal applies equally to building Java-based web applications with JSP.

Web-based applications are typically built up around the pages or screens from which the application is comprised. For example, in an online bookstore, you might build a welcome page first, followed by a page that shows a list of books, and then a page that displays the information about a single book. With the ability to embed Java code inside JSP pages, there can be a tendency to simply reuse code on a source-code level by copying and pasting it between JSP pages. Although this does achieve some reuse, it brings with it a dramatic decrease in the maintainability of such code as changes and bugs slowly creep in and around the system. Ideally, you're looking for reusability at the class or component level.

Throughout this book, you'll see many techniques for aiding reusability provided by the JSP specification—such as JavaBeans components, custom tags, and tag libraries. A **tag library** (commonly known as a **taglib**) is simply a collection of one or more custom tags that are generally related in some way. For example, as we said earlier, the JSP 2.0 specification introduced a standard tag library known as the JSTL. The JSP 2.1 specification refines the JSTL. The JSTL's core library contains tags that solve many of the common and recurring problems encountered when building JSP-based web applications. After the tags are bundled into a tag library, that tag library can be reused across the following:

- A single page

- The pages of a web application

- Different web applications

The ability to easily reuse custom tags across more than a single page illustrates the true potential of tag libraries when building web applications. This is something that you'll be seeing when you examine the best practices for designing and building custom tags in later chapters.

## Readability

Another important best practice is that of readability. Embedding too much Java code in the page can easily lead to pages that are unreadable as content (typically HTML) is mixed with JSP tags and Java code wrapped up as scriptlets. In addition to the confusion caused by the various syntaxes that each of these "languages" uses, one clear problem with embedding Java code inside JSP pages is that it's hard to correctly indent your source code. Writing and indenting code is trivial when dealing with regular class files, but trying to correctly indent Java code that is mixed with HTML and JSP elements is a different story.

Wrapping up reusable functionality as custom tags or JavaBeans components removes this code from the page, therefore making it cleaner, shorter, and more readable. Also, choosing appropriate names for your custom tags can make a page more readable by page designers—those who are responsible for the look and feel of a page rather than the mechanics of how it works. This, as you'll see when we talk about some of the best practices associated with custom tags, is very important and often overlooked.

## Maintainability

Having a system that promotes reusability and readability is great, but what does that mean in the real world? The maintainability of an application is how well the system can be modified and fixed during its lifetime, which for a given application is typically hard to measure. However, in looking at any system, several signs help us to identify whether that system will be easy or difficult to maintain. In reality, this is dictated by reuse and the need to ensure that the code is as readable as possible—the two goals that custom tags can help you achieve.

# JavaServer Pages Application Architecture

All the factors mentioned in this chapter—reusability, readability, maintainability—are improved by a good design or architecture; therefore, it's worth ensuring that sufficient time is taken early in your project life cycle to select the architecture that best suits your environment and technologies. Although architecture and design can seem a little daunting at first (especially when you're new to the technology and all you really want to do is cut code), with a little effort you'll soon start to understand the benefits that are to be gained by using tried and tested patterns.

As you're no doubt aware, the Java EE 5 presentation tier consists of several components—for example, servlets, JSP pages, tag libraries, and JavaBeans—which may be used to create a presentation layer for a web application. All these components have their relative strengths and weaknesses, particularly when used in different combinations. Good design, therefore, is concerned not only with selecting the correct component for a task but also with ensuring that the component is used in the correct manner.

In recent times, two popular web-application architectures have been repeatedly used for web-application design, and there are strengths and weaknesses to consider with both. Let's discuss the simpler of these two architectures first.

## Model 1 Architecture

The simplicity of the Model 1 architecture is that each JSP page is entrusted to deal with its request entirely by itself, thereby generating a response and sending it back to the client, and for this reason it's often known as page-centric. Usually such JSP pages will use some form of **model** to represent the business logic of the application. JavaBeans components are often used to model business logic. The JavaBean neatly encapsulates the business logic for reusability and at the same time keeps the amount of processing logic in the page to a minimum.

Figure 1-3 shows a JSP page entrusted with handling a client request and building an appropriate response all by itself. It is also using a JavaBean to encapsulate business logic.

**Figure 1-3.** *In a Model 1 architecture, all the application processing occurs in a single tier of the application.*

Each JSP page has the potential to contain a lot of processing logic. However, as long as the application is relatively small with few pages, the Model 1 architecture is a good choice because it's quick and simple to put together. However, such a page-centric architecture can begin to introduce problems when used with larger, more complex applications. Some of the more common problems are outlined here.

### Maintainability Problems

Because each JSP page is solely responsible for handling a client request, it will often have to directly interact with a business layer. This can result in the application structure being embodied within the pages themselves. This obviously makes the pages more complicated and more likely to contain lots of scriptlet code, which ultimately makes them far harder to maintain.

### Reusability Problems

When most of the processing logic is embedded into the JSP pages, it becomes much more difficult to reuse common functionality because it's usually implemented using scriptlets. Often this results in a lot of cutting and pasting of code that isn't only bad from a reusability perspective but is also likely to introduce errors and decrease productivity.

### Security Problems

Because each JSP page is responsible for handling all of its processing, it's possible that any actions that require a user to be logged in or that access password-protected resources such as databases could end up exposing sensitive information by embedding it in the page. It's therefore important to make sure that any such logic is encapsulated into JavaBeans components or custom actions to prevent this possible security hole.

Of course it would make far more sense to provide such security controls via a single, centralized access point, and you will see how the next architecture up for discussion does exactly this.

## Model 2 Architecture (Model-View-Controller)

As you might expect, the Model 2 architecture builds on the Model 1 architecture you've just seen, and it overcomes many of the problems identified earlier.

The Model 2 architecture is a server-side implementation of the popular **Model-View-Controller (MVC)** design pattern. This pattern enforces the separation of the way application data is modeled (hence, the **model**) from the way it's presented (the **view**), and it also requires a separate component to handle the processing in between (the **controller**). Separating these responsibilities into components gives the developer a good opportunity to select the right type of component for each based on its suitability to the task.

As mentioned earlier, JSP pages are best used for presenting content and aren't particularly good for providing complex business processing because readability and maintainability would decline. Servlets, on the other hand, are particularly good components for providing business processing but aren't best suited to generating content. Most applications implementing the Model 2 architecture therefore utilize a controller servlet to handle all the request processing and delegate requests to separate JSP components to provide the presentation, thereby making the best use of both technologies. Remember that the Model 1 architecture you saw earlier forced the controller and the view to coexist inside the same component, which accounts for a lot of its shortcomings.

As you can see in Figure 1-4, all requests made of the web application are handled by a single controller servlet. Depending on the type of request received, the controller servlet is responsible for populating the model component with data that it has obtained, usually by interacting with the business layer. The controller then forwards the request to the JSP view component, which constructs a suitable response to the request based on the data stored in the model component.

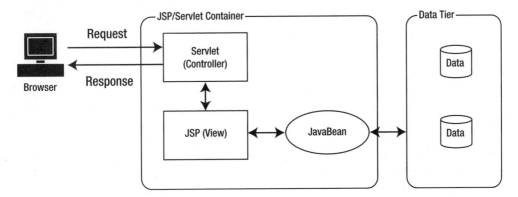

**Figure 1-4.** *In a Model 2 architecture, different components handle the application processing and the presentation of data.*

There are, as always, varying versions of this architecture, such as providing multiple controllers to distribute the request-handling functionality across multiple servlets. Although not recommended, it's also possible to provide JSP-based controllers and servlet-based view components; the choice is yours! Remember that the best designs select a component based on its suitability for its job. JSP pages make poor controllers because they're designed to render content, whereas servlets are best suited to request processing and computations instead of generating content.

Whatever components you select, you cannot fail to appreciate how much cleaner this architecture is than the Model 1 architecture; each component has a definite, well-defined role.

Let's revisit some of the problems that the Model 1 architecture faced and see how this new design helps solve some of them.

## Maintainability

Many of the maintainability problems associated with the Model 1 architecture were a direct result of implementing a controller and view as part of the same component: the JSP page. Because all the business processing and content generation were forced together, the result was messy pages that could be hard to maintain. By separating your application's logic from its presentation by using MVC components, it's far easier to develop cleaner code that focuses specifically on the job at hand, resulting ultimately in a more flexible and maintainable application.

## Security

By providing an initial single point of access for potential requests, a servlet-based controller component is an excellent place to provide some form of authentication. If the user making the request can pass the authentication mechanism (perhaps a username or password test), the controller can continue with the request as usual or alternatively forward it to an appropriate page (perhaps a login page!) where the error can be dealt with.

Because the controller component is responsible for handling every request, security checks have to exist in only a single place, and of course any changes to the security mechanism have to be made only once. By implementing your security constraints in a single place, it's far easier to take advantage of declarative security mechanisms. Recall that the Model 1 architecture required each page to provide similar security checks by itself, which provides a significant security hole if the developer forgets to provide it!

### Extensibility

One of the best points about the Model 2 architecture is that all the processing logic is centralized. No longer does such code have to be placed in a scriptlet located deep within a JSP page, where it's so much more difficult to access.

This centralization helps to provide a more component-based solution. By utilizing JavaBeans components and custom or standard actions, and enabling software components to be reused and extended, you greatly reduce the chance of making a change that causes a "ripple" effect to other dependent components.

# JSP Fundamentals—Hands On

Before you take an in-depth look at the individual components that compose a JSP page, you should have a basic idea of how JSP applications are deployed and structured inside a JSP container.

## Basic Deployment

Although all JSP and servlet containers have their own specific deployment processes, generally the basic techniques are still the same: you copy your web application (JSP pages, servlets, and static HTML) in a predefined structure into a special deployment directory specified by the container.

The Java Servlet specification defines a special structure that all web applications must follow so that servlet/JSP containers know exactly where to find the resources that compose the web application. Most containers allow web applications to be deployed in one of the following two forms:

- **Expanded directory format**: The web application in its predefined structure is simply copied into the container's deployment directory.

- **Web ARchive file (WAR)**: The web application in its predefined structure is archived into a compressed WAR before being copied to the container's deployment directory.

The web-application structure defines the exact locations inside your web applications to locate deployment descriptors, HTML and JSP pages, and compiled Java classes as well as third-party Java ARchive (JAR) files that are required by your web applications. We won't explain the intricacies of the web-application structure because this will be covered in far greater detail in later chapters. For now we will explain the structure of a minimal but fully functional web application that you can use to test the simple JSP examples you will learn about throughout this chapter.

Because Tomcat 5 for the Apache Jakarta project is the reference implementation of the Servlet 2.5 and JSP 2.1 specifications and will therefore be featured heavily throughout this book, it makes sense to base the deployment introduction around the Tomcat 5 container; but feel free to use the container of your choice. When we refer to Tomcat 5, you can take that to mean Tomcat 5.0 or Tomcat 5.5. Both versions support the latest servlet and JSP specifications. However, Tomcat 5.5 has numerous improvements over 5.0; the potential obstacle you face is that Tomcat 5.5 requires the use of J2SE 5.0 whereas Tomcat 5.0 needs only J2SE 1.4. If you can, we recommend you use Tomcat 5.5.

If you haven't yet done so, you should download and install Tomcat 5.0 or 5.5. Tomcat can be downloaded from `http://jakarta.apache.org`. The installation is automated for simplicity, and instructions for installing Tomcat can be found on the Tomcat home page. If you are using some other web container, such as JBoss, BEA WebLogic, or the Sun Application Server, install your container according to the documentation with your container.

Notice, in Figure 1-5, that Tomcat has been installed beneath the `C:\Program Files\Apache Software Foundation\Tomcat 5.5` directory, which will be referred to as the `%TOMCAT_HOME%` directory from now on. If you have Tomcat installed on Mac OS X or a Unix variant, you will have a directory structure that is similar, but appropriate for your operating system.

**Figure 1-5.** *A typical Tomcat installation has numerous subdirectories that contain different parts of the system.*

As you can see, there are a fair number of subdirectories and each has a specific purpose. For example, the `bin` directory contains all the necessary scripts required to start the container, and the `conf` directory contains all the XML-based configuration files used by Tomcat. Don't worry about understanding all the complex configuration files and directory structures; this exercise is designed to get a working web application for you to test the examples you'll see later in the chapter.

We mentioned earlier that most servlet containers have a special deployment directory in which developers can place web applications as either WAR files or in exploded directory format. You may have guessed by now that in Tomcat it's the %TOMCAT_HOME%\webapps directory where you'll be creating the test application ready for deployment. Ignoring the subdirectories that already exist beneath the webapps directory (yes, they too are web applications in case you were wondering!), first create a directory to house the web application called test and then another directory inside this one called WEB-INF. Now you have the structure shown in Figure 1-6.

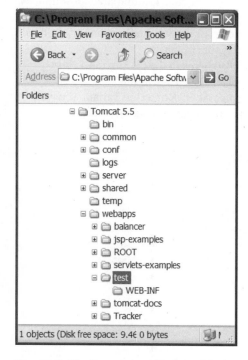

**Figure 1-6.** *The Tomcat installation with the newly created test and WEB-INF subdirectories*

This standard web-application structure is defined in the Servlet specification. This structure is also used as the format for the contents in WAR files. We refer to this structure as the exploded directory format.

As you may be aware, all web applications must have a deployment descriptor in order to work, and yours is no different. Copy and paste the minimal deployment descriptor in Listing 1-1 into a file called web.xml and save it beneath the WEB-INF directory you just created.

**Listing 1-1.** *web.xml*

```
<?xml version="1.0"?>

<web-app xmlns="http://java.sun.com/xml/ns/javaee"
```

```
        xmlns:xsi="http://www.w3.org/2001/XMLSchema-instance"
        xsi:schemaLocation="http://java.sun.com/xml/ns/javaee/web-app_2_5.xsd"
        version="2.5">
</web-app>
```

A point worth remembering is that the name of the test directory that you're using to house the web application is known as the **context** of the web application; you'll need to be aware of this context to request the resources of your test web application. You'll see this in action shortly.

Now that you've set up the required web-application structure, let's create a dynamic web component (that's a JSP page to you and me!) that will return the current time of day along with a greeting. Copy Listing 1-2 into a file called %TOMCAT_HOME%\webapps\test\date.jsp.

**Listing 1-2.** *date.jsp*

```
<html>
  <body>
    <h2>Greetings!</h2>
    <p>The current time is <%=new java.util.Date()%> precisely</p>
  </body>
</html>
```

Again, don't worry about understanding the syntax of this JSP; you'll learn all about JSP syntax later.

The next step is to start your server (if it isn't already running). With Tomcat 5.0 and earlier versions, you can start the server by using a script or a menu option. With Tomcat 5.5 for Microsoft Windows, the startup scripts have been removed and you will start Tomcat from the menu.

With Tomcat 5.0 and earlier, you can start Tomcat by running the %TOMCAT_HOME%\bin\ startup.bat script (or startup.sh if running Tomcat on Linux or Solaris). When Tomcat is running, you should see a prompt with messages like those shown in Figure 1-7.

**Figure 1-7.** *When starting Tomcat by using a script, you will see output in the console window.*

If you are starting Tomcat from the Windows Start menu, select the Monitor Tomcat option from the Apache menu item. After the monitor has started, right-click the monitor icon in the system tray and select Start Service from the menu.

To test that Tomcat is running successfully, load the Tomcat welcome page by opening a web browser and typing the following link:

```
http://localhost:8080
```

Note that this assumes you installed Tomcat on its default port 8080, so you should change it as needed.

Figure 1-8 shows the Tomcat welcome page, which indicates that all is well.

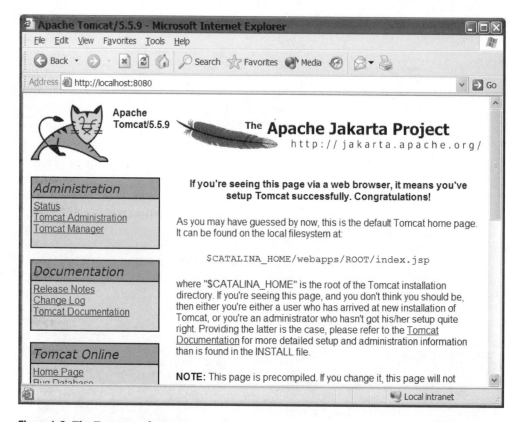

**Figure 1-8.** *The Tomcat welcome page*

If for some reason you don't see this welcome screen, make sure that you have Tomcat running and are accessing the correct port. Consult the Tomcat documentation if problems persist.

Now you're at last ready to access the test web application. Do this by typing the following URL:

```
http://localhost:8080/test/date.jsp
```

Notice how you use the context of the web application (test) to inform the servlet container that it's your application whose date.jsp file you wish to access. You should now see output similar (not the same though—remember it's dynamic!) to the screen shot shown in Figure 1-9.

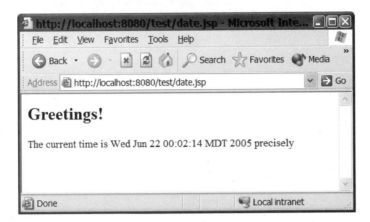

**Figure 1-9.** *The response from date.jsp*

That's it; congratulations! Creating and deploying a JSP web-based application wasn't so hard after all, was it? For the remainder of this chapter, you'll see lots of JSP code examples that you're encouraged to copy and paste into JSP files beneath the webapps\test directory (and change the link accordingly) to see the code in action. Note that you may need to stop and start Tomcat to see some changes in action.

## JavaServer Pages

As mentioned earlier, the sole purpose of JSP technology is to produce dynamic, web-based content. This capability is implemented by embedding programmatic logic among template data (usually markup such as HTML, XML, and so on) which together produces the dynamic content on a request-by-request basis. This programmatic logic may be classified into the following JSP elements:

- Scripting elements

- Directives

- Action elements

In a moment you'll look at each of the elements so you can see how they combine to produce the dynamic content required by today's web applications. First let's look at the template text.

## Template Text

As we said earlier in the chapter, any non-JSP code located inside a JSP page is known as **template text**. Template text can take any form as long as it's text based. The most common form of template text is markup such as HTML or XML. For example, if your web design team were to develop an HTML page that you were required to convert into a JSP page in order to add some form of dynamic processing, then all the HTML markup would be referred to as template text (see Listing 1-3).

**Listing 1-3.** *template_text.jsp*

```
<%@ taglib uri="http://java.sun.com/jstl/core" prefix="c" %>
<%@ page import="com.apress.projsp.CalendarBean"%>

<html>
  <head>
  <title>My JSP Example</title>
  </head>
  <body>
    <jsp:useBean id="cal" class="com.apress.projsp.CalendarBean"/>
    <c:set var="hour" value="${cal.hour}" scope="request" />

    <c:choose>
      <c:when test="${hour > 0 && hour <=11}">
        Good Morning!
      </c:when>
      <c:when test="${hour >= 12 && hour <=17}">
        Good Afternoon!
      </c:when>
      <c:otherwise>
        Good Evening!
      </c:otherwise>
    </c:choose>
  </body>
</html>
```

This is a JSP page that dynamically produces a greeting depending on the time of day. (This JSP page won't compile and run without the CalendarBean class. We will deploy this JSP page with the CalendarBean class in Chapter 4.) For now, don't worry about understanding the syntax of the various JSP elements but notice that the bolded static HTML is referred to as template text. The reason for this term is simply that a JSP page can be thought of as a "template" for producing some output. It's the JSP logic embedded inside this template text that is responsible for producing the output based upon this template.

During the translation phase, all the template text found in the original JSP page is converted into Java statements in the page implementation servlet. The Java statements simply output the template text in the correct order as part of the response.

# Scripting Elements

Scripting elements are used within a JSP page to manipulate objects and perform computations that enable the generation of dynamic content. Scripting elements can be classified into the following categories:

- Comments

- Declarations

- Scriptlets

- Expressions

- Expression language expressions

We will discuss each scripting element in turn.

## Comments

JSP comments are a good way of explaining any complicated logic that may arise for whatever reason—perhaps a comment could be used to flag a piece of scripting code to be simplified at a later date with a custom tag. Alternately, comments provide non-Java-speaking HTML users or web designers some clues as to what a piece of "magic" JSP code does.

JSP comments may be declared inside a JSP page as follows:

```
<%-- This is a JSP comment --%>
```

Comments in JSP pages get stripped out during the translation phase and aren't sent to the client as part of the response. HTML comments, on the other hand, such as the one shown next, do get sent to a client's browser, and any client can view the comments by using the View Source options that most modern browsers provide:

```
<!-- This is an HTML comment -->
```

Having JSP comments stripped and not part of a client response is beneficial because it not only keeps the size of the response as small as possible, thereby aiding performance, but also removes clues about the technology used to implement a web-based application that a hacker could target.

There is of course no reason why JSP expressions and HTML comments cannot work together:

```
<!-- HTML comment generated <%= new java.util.Date() %> -->
```

You'll learn the meaning of this JSP expression shortly, but suffice it to say the previous comment produces the following in the content returned to a client:

```
<!- HTML comment generated Fri Jan 03 12:37:09 GMT 2005 -->
```

## Declarations

JSP pages allow both methods and variables to be declared in a similar manner to the way in which they're declared inside standard Java classes. As with standard methods and variables, after they are declared inside a JSP page, they're available to subsequent scriptlets and expressions and so on for reference.

During the translation phase, any JSP declarations (methods or variables) found inside the page are actually created outside the _jspService() method in the JSP page implementation servlet and therefore are available to any scripting elements throughout the page.

JSP declarations must be placed between <%! and %> declaration delimiters. The general form of a declaration is shown here:

```
<%! declaration; [declaration;]+...%>
```

For example:

```
<%! Date now = new Date(); %>
```

```
<%!
  private int calculate(int a, int b) {
    ...
  }
%>
```

The previous examples demonstrate two simple JSP declarations. The first generates a java.util.Date instance that is available to the rest of the JSP page (and therefore to the servlet), whereas the second declares a stand-alone method that again is available to the rest of the page.

---

**■Caution**  When declaring a page-level variable via a JSP declaration, you should ensure that its access is thread-safe. Multiple threads can execute the same servlet (JSP implementation class) simultaneously, and any page-level variables are accessible by each thread.

---

## Scriptlets

Quite simply, scriptlets are small blocks of source code contained within the <% and %> delimiters that can be used to provide programming-style language functionality around a page's content, thus making their output dynamic.

For example:

```
<%
  User user = (User)request.getAttribute("User");
  if (user != null) {
%>
  Welcome, you have successfully logged in!
<%
  }
%>
```

You can see from the previous example how a simple piece of dynamic content can be created with a scriptlet. If an object attribute called user exists in the request, a welcome message is generated; otherwise, one isn't! Admittedly, this piece of dynamic content isn't the most complex, but hopefully you can see how scriptlets add logic between the markup of your JSP page to control the output.

The supported scripting languages available for use inside scriptlets are defined by the page directive's language attribute. In all specifications, from JSP 1.0 to the current JSP 2.1, the only defined value for this attribute is Java. Unlike declarations, all scriptlet code will be inserted into the _jspService() method of the generated servlet, which is used to handle the request and generate the response. When multiple scriptlets are included in any page, they're included into the compiled servlet in the order in which they appear in the JSP. Unlike JSP declarations, any variables declared in a scriptlet aren't available to the rest of the JSP page because they're treated as local variables inside the _jspService() method.

When JSP 1.0 first arrived, scriptlets were quickly adopted as the most popular way of adding dynamic features to JSP. Unfortunately, scriptlets became too popular and soon JSP page authors were embedding too much business logic among their markup. This caused several problems.

In multideveloper projects, it's quite common for a web designer with no Java or JSP skills to produce an HTML UI for an application that is then passed to Java developers to convert their work into JSP by adding dynamic content and hooking together business logic along the way. This caused delays and frustrations in the JSP 1.0 days due to the dependencies formed between the UI and Java developer. Also problems arose because UI designers would struggle to maintain their pages, as they would need to understand the scriptlet code surrounding their markup properly in order to change it. On top of these difficulties, adding too many scriptlets to a JSP file also makes it incredibly difficult to read and hence maintain. Anyone who has had to spend hours debugging a JSP page only to find a closing brace is missing will testify how much more difficult it is to fix a page with too many scriptlets in it.

Thankfully, the early experiences of UI and JSP developers haven't been wasted, and other methods are now considered better alternatives. For example, using standard JSP actions to manipulate JavaBeans (which contain business logic) and encapsulating logic inside custom actions (also known as custom tags) are two alternatives that solve many of the problems mentioned earlier. Most noticeably, both solutions use XML-style tags that can be used in harmony with the tools of a UI designer.

JSP 2.0 introduced another two candidates that further facilitate scriptless JSP code. The first of these new features comes in the form of the **JSTL,** which provides standard actions for many of the simple tasks required of a modern dynamic web application. Second, for the first time an **expression language (EL)** is available, which can be used to help reduce or even eradicate scriptlets.

As we mentioned at the start of this chapter, further information on JavaBeans, JSTL, and custom actions can be found later in this book. For now you just need to understand what scriptlets can do along with their limitations.

## Expressions

Expressions are similar to scriptlets, but as their name suggests they evaluate a regular Java expression and return a result. This result must be a string or be convertible to a string; otherwise, an exception will be raised during the translation phase or at runtime. Expressions are evaluated by the JSP implementation servlet and are returned to the client as part of the response.

As with the other tag types, expressions must be placed between <%= and %> expression delimiters so that the JSP engine is aware of the developer's intent to return the value of the expression in the response. The general syntax is as follows:

```
<%= expression %>
```

Two simple JSP expressions can be seen here. They could be part of any regular JSP page that generates nonstatic HTML.

```
<h1>Welcome Back : <%= user.getName() %></h1>
```

```
<b>Today's date is <%= new java.util.Date()%></b>
```

Apart from producing dynamic content as part of the client response, JSP expressions can be used to pass request-time parameters and values to other JSP actions that may appear on the page. You'll look at an explanation of this later in this chapter, and again when we look at JSP standard actions (Chapter 4) and custom actions (Chapters 6 and 7).

---

**Note**  Unlike declarations and scriptlets, JSP expressions don't require a closing semicolon (in fact they won't compile with one) because they evaluate the result of a single expression.

---

## Expression Language Expressions

JSP 2.0 introduced an EL that is based on ECMAScript and XML Path Language (XPath), and that has been designed to be simple to use and more user-friendly than Java.

The new EL has built-in support for JavaBean access and manipulation, collections of objects, and automatic type conversion, to name but a small part of its extensive feature list. If you're familiar with JavaScript, you should have no problem understanding the syntax of the EL, which insists that all expressions must be enclosed within ${ and } delimiters.

Unfortunately, another Java technology, JavaServer Faces (JSF), was implementing an expression language at approximately the same time as JSP 2.0, and the two versions are incompatible in some respects. JSP 2.1 unifies the two expression languages and provides an additional syntax for expression language statements, allowing the use of #{} to enclose expression language statements.

EL expressions can be used in any attribute that accepts a runtime expression, usually a standard or custom action, or even in plain template text. The addition of the EL further facilitates the writing of scriptless JSP pages, that is, pages that don't contain any Java scriptlets, expressions, or declaration elements.

Although it's the subject of Chapter 3, here are a couple of examples to give you a flavor of the new EL:

```
${anObject.aProperty}
```

```
<c:if test="${user.salary > 10000}" >
  ...
</c:if>
```

You can see from the first example just how simple it is to access the property of any JavaBean object, with no Java knowledge required at all! The second example demonstrates one of the core actions from the JSTL that is used to provide conditional processing of JSP code. Here an EL expression is used to provide the Boolean test for the action.

# JSP Implicit Objects

All JSP scripting elements have access to a number of useful objects that are provided by the JSP container and are known as implicit objects. Each of these implicit objects are classes or interfaces as defined by either the Servlet or JSP specifications and are described in greater detail in this section.

## request

The most notable of the implicit objects is the `request` object, which is an instance of the `javax.servlet.http.ServletRequest` interface. The `request` object provides access to all the available information about the user request (such as request parameters and headers) and may be used in exactly the same way that the `HttpServletRequest` parameter is used in the `service()` method of a servlet.

Let's consider an example. Imagine a simple JSP page that expects a single-request parameter called `userName` and constructs a personalized response to the user:

```
<html>
<head><title>A Simple Example</title></head>
<body>
<h2>Hello <%=request.getParameter("userName")%>, Have a nice day!</h2>
</body>
</html>
```

This simple JSP page extracts a request parameter called `userName` from the implicit request object and constructs an appropriate greeting. To send a request parameter to a JSP page like the one outlined previously, either use an HTML form or add the parameter to the query string of your request as follows:

```
http://localhost:8080/test/Request.jsp?userName=Dan
```

## response

Like the `request` object seen earlier, there's also an accompanying implicit `response` object that represents the current response to be returned to the user. The `response` object is an instance of the `javax.servlet.http.HttpServletResponse` interface. Again, this object can be used in exactly the same way as the `HttpServletResponse` parameter received by the `service()` method of a servlet.

## out

The implicit `out` object represents an instance of the `javax.servlet.jsp.JspWriter` class that can be used to write character data to the response stream in a similar manner to that seen by the `java.io.PrintWriter` class. Although methods provided by the `JspWriter` such as `print()`

and `println()` can be used to write text to the body of the response, it's usually sufficient to rely on plain template text and JSP action elements instead of explicitly writing to the out implicit object.

### session

The implicit `session` object provides a reference to an implementation of the client's individual `javax.servlet.http.HttpSession` object, which can be used to store and retrieve session data. Although `HttpSession` can be used explicitly, it should be noted that several action elements that interact with the session are available and can be used instead.

### config

The `config` object simply provides the JSP developer with access to the `ServletConfig` object that is used by the web container to configure the JSP page. The `ServletConfig` interface is most commonly used to provide access to any initialization parameters that have been configured for the JSP page via the deployment descriptor of the web application.

### application

The implicit `application` object provides a reference to the `javax.servlet.ServletContext` interface of the web application. The `ServletContext` object is used by a web container to represent an entire web application, and therefore any data that is stored inside it will be available to all resources included in the application.

As with the `session` object, several action elements exist that interact with the `ServletContext` so it may not be necessary to interact directly with the object itself.

### page

The implicit `page` object references an instance of the JSP's page implementation class and is declared of type `Object`. The `page` object is rarely used in scripting elements and simply serves as a link between the JSP page and its implementing servlet.

### pageContext

The `pageContext` object is slightly different in its functionality from the rest of the available implicit objects. A `pageContext` instance provides the JSP developer with access to all the available JSP scopes and to several useful page attributes, such as the current request and response, the `ServletContext`, `HttpSession`, and `ServletConfig` to name but a few.

Perhaps the most useful piece of functionality provided by the `pageContext` variable is its ability to search for named attributes across multiple scopes. Therefore, if you were unsure in which scope a particular attribute is located, the `pageContext` can be used to traverse all available scopes until the attribute is found.

The `pageContext` variable provides this cross-scope functionality because it exists at a level of abstraction higher than the lower-level JSP implementation classes. The JSP container will create a new, unique instance of this class for each request received and assign it to the pageContext variable.

## exception

The implicit `exception` object is available only to those JSP pages that declare themselves as error pages by using the following page directive. (You'll learn more about directives shortly!)

```
<%@ page isErrorPage="true" %>
```

The `exception` object itself is an instance of `java.lang.Throwable` and will represent a run-time error that occurred during the request process.

Any scripting elements inside a JSP page that reference the implicit `exception` object when that page hasn't been declared as an error page will cause a fatal error at translation time.

# JSP Directives

Directives are used for passing important information to the JSP engine. Although directives generate no output, they provide a powerful mechanism for providing page-level information that is typically used during the compilation and translation phases.

JSP page authors have the following three types of directives at their disposal:

- page directives

- include directives

- taglib directives

Each type of directive provides different information to the JSP engine or signifies some required behavior of the generated servlet. The information contained inside a directive is totally independent of any user request and is of use only to the JSP engine. All three directive types must be declared between `<%@` and `%>` directive delimiters and take the following form:

```
<%@ directive {attribute="value"}* %>
```

Generally speaking, directives should be placed at the top of the JSP page; however, the `include` directive, which you'll see later, is an exception to this rule. Let's examine each directive type in turn.

## The page Directive

The first directive type is the `page` directive, which is used to define any page-dependent properties that a JSP page may have, such as library dependencies, buffering, or error-handling requirements.

The syntax of a page directive is as follows:

```
<%@ page page_directive_attr_list %>
```

where the `page_directive_attr_list` is used to define the name of any page attribute along with its value in the form `attributeName=attributeValue`.

Each page directive applies to the entire compilation unit (that is, the JSP page in which the page directive appears, plus any included JSP pages). Although multiple page directives may occur, it should be noted that each attribute can occur only once in the page with the exception of the `import` attribute.

Table 1-1 shows the permitted attributes and their possible values as defined by the
page_directive_attr_list.

**Table 1-1.** *Attributes for the page Directive*

| Attribute | Permitted Value | Description |
|---|---|---|
| language | Java | The scripting language used in scriptlets, expressions, and declarations in the JSP. Currently, JSP 2.1 supports only a value of Java, and any other value would cause a fatal translation error. |
| extends | className | The name of a fully qualified Java class that will form the superclass of the JSP page's implementation servlet. This attribute should not be used lightly because its use prohibits the JSP container from using its own specially optimized classes. |
| import | importList | Indicates the classes available for use within the scripting environment. Any import values must be fully qualified Java class names and result in a standard Java import statement in the page implementation servlet. Note that an import attribute may be a fully qualified package name followed by a ".*" or a list of comma-separated classes. The default import list is java.lang.*, javax.servlet.*, javax.servlet.jsp.*, and javax.servlet.http.*. |
| session | true\|false | Indicates that the page requires an HttpSession object. If a value of true is provided, an implicit scripting variable named session, which references the current HttpSession object, is available to the page. If a value of false is used, any references to the implicit session variable will cause a fatal translation error. The default value is true. |
| buffer | none\|sizekb | Specifies the buffering model for the initial JspWriter used to handle the response generated by the page. A value of none indicates no buffering is required and all output is written immediately. A value of nkb, where n is some positive integer (e.g., 16kb), is the size of the buffer. The size of the buffer can be declared only in kilobytes, and the kb suffix is required. If a buffer size is specified, all output is buffered with a buffer not smaller than the one specified. The default is to buffer output with a buffer of at least 8 KB (the actual size is container dependent). |

| Attribute | Permitted Value | Description |
| --- | --- | --- |
| autoFlush | true\|false | Indicates whether the output buffer should be flushed automatically when full (specified by a value of true) or whether an exception should be raised indicating buffer overflow (specified by a value of false).<br>Note that it's illegal to set autoFlush=true when buffer=none. The result is a translation-time error.<br>The default value is true. |
| isThreadSafe | true\|false | Indicates the threading model to be used by the web container when dispatching requests to the page implementation servlet.<br>A value of true ensures that the JSP container may choose to dispatch multiple requests to the page simultaneously. A value of false indicates that the JSP container must serialize multiple requests to the page one at a time.<br>Note that if a value of true is passed, the JSP page author must ensure that access to any shared variables is synchronized to protect thread safety.<br>The default value is true. |
| info | info_text | Can be used to provide any arbitrary string, which is returned via a call to the page implementation servlet's getServletInfo() method. |
| isErrorPage | true\|false | Indicates whether the current page is intended to be an error page, which may be referenced by the errorPage attribute of another JSP page. If a value of true is specified, an implicit scripting variable exception is made available that references the offending Throwable from another JSP page.<br>The default value is false. |
| errorPage | error_url | Defines the URL to a resource that any throwable objects not caught by the page implementation are forwarded to for error processing.<br>When an error page for a web application is defined in its deployment descriptor (web.xml), the JSP's error page is tried ahead of the one defined by the deployment descriptor. |
| contentType | ctInfo | Defines the character encoding for the JSP page and its response as well as the Multipurpose Internet Mail Extensions (MIME) type of the response.<br>The default value for the type is text/html and for the charset it's ISO-8859-1. |
| pageEncoding | peInfo | Defines the character encoding for the JSP page. The default value is ISO-8859-1. |

*Continued*

**Table 1-1.** *Continued*

| Attribute | Permitted Value | Description |
|---|---|---|
| isELIgnored | true\|false | Defines whether the EL expressions are evaluated for the JSP page. If true, any EL expressions are simply ignored by the JSP container. The default value is false. |
| DeferredSyntaxAllowedAsLiteral | true\|false | Indicates whether the character sequence #{ is allowed when used as a string literal in this page and translation unit. If false (the default value), a translation error occurs when the character sequence is used as a string literal. |
| trimDirectiveWhitespaces | true\|false | Indicates how whitespaces in template text should be handled. If true, template text that contains only whitespaces is removed from the output. The default is not to trim whitespaces. |

The following are some examples of the page directive in action:

```
<%@ page language="Java" %>
```

Here the scripting language to be used on the page is set to Java (the only permitted value).

```
<%@ page import="java.util.Date, java.text.*" %>
```

The java.util.Date class, along with all the classes from the java.text package, are available for use on the page.

```
<%@ page isThreadSafe="false" buffer="20kb" %>
```

Notice that it's possible to provide multiple attributes in the one page directive; here the JSP container is advised that multiple requests may not access the page simultaneously and that the page buffer should not be smaller than 20 KB.

## The include Directive

You've just seen how the page directive can be used to pass information to the JSP engine during the translation phase, to control how the page implementation class is generated. The include directive also executes at translation time and enables the contents of a separate resource to be statically merged inside the original page, thus radically affecting the generated servlet.

After translation, the generated JSP servlet contains the content and logic as defined by the two separate resources, in the order that they were specified in the original JSP. This makes it seem as though they were from a single JSP file.

The following is the syntax for the include directive:

```
<%@ include file="relativeURL" %>
```

The directive accepts a single `file` attribute that is used to indicate the resource whose content is to be included in the declaring JSP. The `file` attribute is interpreted as a relative URL: if it starts with a slash, it's interpreted as relative to the context of the web application (namely a context-relative path); otherwise, it's interpreted as relative to the path of the JSP page that contains the `include` directive (namely a page-relative path). The included file may contain either static content, such as HTML or XML, or another JSP page.

For example:

```
<%@ include file="/copyright.html"%>
```

As you can see from the previous example, a static HTML file located at the root of the web-application context will be statically included in the JSP page that declares the directive. The included file in this case contains important legal copyright information that must be included on all pages of a web application. The `include` directive is an excellent mechanism for reusing a predefined component, such as the `copyright.html` file, to save the duplication of code on each page. This makes the JSP pages smaller, easier to read, and more maintainable, as changes need to be applied in only one place but are reflected throughout the application.

---

■**Caution** When using the `include` directive, remember that the combined contents of the original JSP page and all its included resources are translated into the same implementation servlet. Therefore, the original JSP page will share its scripting variables and declarations with those inside the included resources, and any duplication of variable or method names will result in a fatal JSP translation error, because the merged file won't be syntactically correct.

---

The `include` directive is slightly different from the other JSP directives, which are typically declared only once at the top of each JSP page. A JSP page may contain any number of `include` directives at any position in the page to indicate the exact positions where the content from the included resource should be inserted. Therefore, the `include` directive is well suited to implement simple template mechanisms that are so commonly used in today's modern web applications. This enables all the commonly used resources of a web application (such as a header, footer, or navigation page) to be encapsulated as separate components (for example, JSP pages or static HTML pages) included throughout the application.

Let's consider a real-world example of such a templating mechanism that utilizes the `include` directive to provide a consistent page layout for a web application.

Consider the following two JSP pages, `Header.jsp` (Listing 1-4) and `Footer.jsp` (Listing 1-5).

**Listing 1-4.** *Header.jsp*

```
<html>
  <head><title>A Very Simple Example</title></head>
  <body style="font-family:verdana,arial;font-size:10pt;">
    <table width="100%" height="100%">
      <tr bgcolor="#99CCCC">
        <td align="right" height="15%">Welcome to this example...</td>
      </tr>
      <tr>
        <td height="75%">
```

**Listing 1-5.** *Footer.jsp*

```
        </td>
      </tr>
      <tr bgcolor=" #99CC99">
        <td align="center" height="10%">Copyright ACompany.com 2005</td>
      </tr>
    </table>
  </body>
</html>
```

`Header.jsp` declares the starting elements of an HTML table that is to be 100 percent of the page size and has two rows, whereas `Footer.jsp` simply declares the closing elements for the table. Used separately, either page will result in partial HTML code that will look strange to a user, but when they're combined by using the `include` directive, it's easy to create consistent pages as part of a web application.

Let's see just how simple this basic template mechanism is to use. Listing 1-6 shows a JSP page that uses the `include` directive.

**Listing 1-6.** *Content.jsp*

```
<%@ include file='./Header.jsp'%>
<p align="center">The Content Goes Here...!!!</p>
<%@ include file='./Footer.jsp'%>
```

`Content.jsp` looks like a simple page with only three lines of code: the two `include` directives and the actual body of the page. Notice how the body of the page is between the two directives. This ensures that all of this page's body content is included inside the table declared in `Header.jsp`.

To run this example, simply copy the three files `Content.jsp`, `Header.jsp`, and `Footer.jsp` beneath the `test` web application directory you created earlier and go to the following URL:

```
http://localhost:8080/test/Content.jsp
```

You should see something like Figure 1-10.

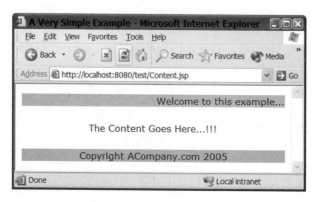

**Figure 1-10.** *A common header and footer can easily be included in all JSP pages.*

To demonstrate just how effective this basic template mechanism is, use Listing 1-7 to construct another page (`MoreContent.jsp`) and see how easy it is to maintain the same look and feel.

**Listing 1-7.** *MoreContent.jsp*

```
<%@ include file="./Header.jsp"%>
<p align="center">Here is some more content...!!!</p>
<%@ include file="./Footer.jsp"%>
```

To open it, do exactly the same as you did for the `Content.jsp` page, only this time point to the following URL:

```
http://localhost:8080/test/MoreContent.jsp
```

You should see something like Figure 1-11.

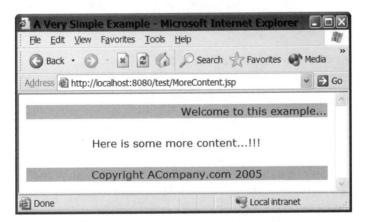

**Figure 1-11.** *This JSP page uses the same common header and footer. Thus, no matter how many pages are in your application, a change to only two files will change the header and footer for all the pages.*

This example demonstrates how useful the `include` directive is for constructing component-based web applications that share a consistent look and feel throughout, are extremely maintainable, and do not suffer from problems caused by code duplication.

## The taglib Directives

A tag library contains a collection of actions (also known as tags) that can be grouped together to perform some form of logic. These actions are XML based, so their use is considerably easier for a non-Java-speaking UI designer. Of course another major benefit is that they can encapsulate large amounts of programmatic logic into a single line of code, which is a much better solution in terms of readability and maintainability and of course reuse, when compared to the ugly scriptlet-based approach you saw earlier.

Tag libraries come in two flavors these days. The first is custom tag libraries, which have generally been put together by a development team or acquired from another team or project or even the Internet—and as of JSP 2.0, from the JSTL, which contains a set of useful actions that are applicable in some form to almost every web application in use today.

To use a custom tag library, the web container needs to be made aware of specific information about the library itself. A special file called a **tag library descriptor** (TLD) is used for this purpose. The XML-based TLD file is used to provide general descriptive information about the custom tag library, such as a description of its usage and the JSP version that the tag supports. More important, the TLD file contains essential information about each of the custom actions or tags that are included inside the tag library, such as which attributes are permitted by which tags, whether the tags accept body content, and so on.

After the JSP container is made aware of the TLD for a particular custom tag library, the JSP developer can use any of the tags declared inside the library. Like custom Java classes (in fact, any class that doesn't reside in the core `java.lang` package), tag libraries must be imported into the page before they can be used. You've seen that Java classes are imported into a JSP page by using a JSP page directive, and in a similar fashion, tag libraries are imported by using the `taglib` directive.

The syntax for the `taglib` directive is as follows:

```
<%@ taglib {uri="/tagLibraryURI" | tagdir="/WEB-INF/tags/dirname"
          prefix="tagPrefix" %>
```

The attributes are shown in Table 1-2.

**Table 1-2.** *Attributes for the taglib Directive*

| Attribute | Description |
|---|---|
| uri | Can be either an absolute or a relative Uniform Resource Identifier (URI) that identifies the TLD, and therefore, the tag library that is associated with the prefix. |
| tagdir | Indicates this prefix is to be used to identify tag extensions installed in the WEB-INF\tags directory or a subdirectory. An implicit tag library descriptor is used. A translation error must occur if the value does not start with WEB-INF\tags. A translation error must occur if the value does not point to a directory that exists. A translation error must occur if used in conjunction with the uri attribute. |
| prefix | Indicates a uniquely identifiable string, which is used in the <prefix:tagname> declaration to identify the particular tag in use. Note that prefixes that start with any of the following aren't allowed because they're reserved by Sun: jsp, jspx, java, javax, servlet, sun, and sunw. All prefixes must follow the naming convention as specified in the XML namespaces specification. The current version of the JSP specification doesn't support empty prefixes. |

There are, in fact, four ways that the `taglib` directive can be used to make a tag library available to JSP page authors, and you'll see each in turn.

### Option 1—Absolute URI

The first option for using the `taglib` directive passes an absolute value in the `uri` attribute that represents the location of the TLD file:

```
<%@ taglib uri="/WEB-INF/tlds/myTaglib.tld" prefix="myPrefix" %>
```

The location of the TLD file is explicitly given by the `uri` attribute. In this example, the `WEB-INF\tlds\myTaglib.tld` file describes the tag library, and any references to any of the tags inside this library must be prefixed with `myPrefix` to distinguish the tag from any other tag library that may be available.

For example, if a tag named `displayImage` were included in the library, its use would look something like this:

```
<myPrefix:displayImage file="logo.jpg" />
```

The `taglib` directive is typically used in this form during development, when the locations of resources, such as images and TLDs, haven't been finalized. Perhaps the application hasn't been packaged into a WAR file and still exists in exploded directory format; therefore, an absolute value for the TLD file is usually the most convenient.

Leaving your `taglib` directives in this form after the development process has finished is perhaps not the most flexible option available. Every tag library used in the application would, therefore, have its TLD location hard-coded into the JSP source. If the location of a TLD had to change for some reason, each JSP page would have to be altered, which could potentially be a long-winded, error-prone exercise.

### Option 2—Relative URI

The second form of the `taglib` directive uses a relative URI to indicate the location of the TLD file. If a relative URI is to be used, a relative mapping must be configured in the web application's deployment descriptor by using the `<taglib>` element. So, to use a relative URI in the `taglib` directive, we would provide a mapping in the deployment descriptor as shown in this example:

```
<webapp>
  <taglib-uri>/myTaglib</taglib-uri>
  <taglib-location>/WEB-INF/tlds/myTaglib.tld</taglib-location>
</webapp>
```

The `<taglib-uri>` element provides an alias to the TLD at the location given by the `<taglib-location>` element. If the deployment descriptor for a web application declared the relative URI as shown, any JSP pages contained in the web application could import the available tag library by using the `/myTaglib` URI:

```
<%@ taglib uri="/myTaglib" prefix="myPrefix" %>
```

The `taglib` directive no longer explicitly declares the location of the TLD file, but instead relies upon the existence of a relative URI mapping in the application's deployment descriptor. This form of the directive is the most popular because of the flexibility it provides. For example, by enabling the relative URI mapping to be set in the deployment descriptor, the location of the TLD files can effectively be set at deployment time, and any changes to the location can be made very simply in the one place.

### Option 3—Packaged JAR

The third use of the `taglib` directive provides an absolute path to an external JAR file. As the name suggests, a JAR file is simply a way of packaging compiled Java classes and resources into a compressed archive file that can be placed into your application's class path for use.

Often when you use a third-party software component, it will be distributed as a JAR file. JAR files are created by using the %JAVA_HOME%\bin\jar.exe utility. Further information on its usage may be found by simply running the jar command without any parameters.

As mentioned, the taglib directive can accept an absolute path to a JAR file as the value of the uri attribute. This form requires that the JAR file contain all the tag handler classes as well as the TLD file, which must be located inside the META-INF directory of the JAR file.

This particular form of packaging is most commonly used when tag libraries are being used from external sources, perhaps when they're purchased from a third party or from another application. It provides a good way to encapsulate all the necessary aspects of a tag library into one distributable component.

Let's look at an example:

```
<%@ taglib uri="/WEB-INF/lib/myTaglib.jar" prefix="myPrefix" %>
```

The entire tag library is stored in a single component inside the WEB-INF\lib directory, where it will be added to the web application's class path, from where it's available.

The one downside to packaging your tag libraries into an external JAR file is that the TLD file is difficult to access. Any change to the TLD elements requires the JAR to be extracted first and then repackaged. Of course, the advantage of this method is that your tag libraries are self-contained and easy to distribute and reuse.

### Option 4—Tag Files

The final use of the taglib directive provides a path to a directory that contains tag files. Tag files are special JSP files that end with the suffix .tag or .tagx. They can contain the same kinds of JSP elements as in a JSP page, with some exceptions. In other words, a tag file implements a tag by using JSP code rather than Java code. The container creates an implicit TLD for the files contained in the directory and makes the custom tags available to the JSP author. See the "Tag Files" chapter in the JSP 2.1 specification for more details on syntax and usage of tag files.

## Action Elements

We mentioned earlier how difficult it is to read and maintain JSP pages that are full of scriptlet code. Not only are such pages "ugly," but they're almost meaningless to a web developer unless that developer also happens to be a Java developer who may have written the scriptlet code in the first place.

A better alternative is to use existing actions (tags) provided by a tag library that encapsulate pieces of functional logic. These actions make JSP pages much cleaner and more readable. Also, because they're XML tag-based, they are usable by a non-Java UI developer. In JSP 2.1 there are three types of action elements:

- Standard actions

- Custom actions

- JSTL actions

Let's take a brief look at each one.

## Standard Actions

The JSP standard actions have been in existence since the first release of the JSP 1.0 specification and provide the JSP page author with a (relatively small) selection of useful actions. The majority of the provided functionality is based on the manipulation of JavaBeans components as well as the dynamic inclusion of files at request time and URL forwarding.

Let's look at some of the more popular standard actions to get a "flavor" of their functionality.

### The <jsp:include> Action

You saw earlier how the `include` directive provides a simple mechanism for including the contents of a separate web component into the declaring JSP page at translation time. The `<jsp:include>` action provides a similar facility but with some subtle differences. The `<jsp:include>` action is actually executed at request time, thereby enabling the inclusion of both static and dynamic content and thus providing a more flexible approach.

Another major difference is that the `<jsp:include>` action doesn't include the actual content from the included resource in the same manner as the `include` directive. Instead, the `<jsp:include>` action will include any output generated by the included resource directly to the `JspWriter` assigned to the implicit `out` variable. This means that you can specify any different type of web resource, such as another JSP page or servlet, as long as it produces content of the same type as the calling JSP page.

The syntax for using the standard `include` action is as follows:

```
<jsp:include page="relativeURL" flush="true"/>
```

Here you can see the action has two attributes. The `page` attribute is mandatory and contains a relative URL to the resource to be included, in the same way that the `file` attribute was interpreted by the `include` directive. The second attribute, `flush`, specifies whether the body of the response should be "flushed," or sent to the client browser before the page inclusion. The `flush` attribute is optional and defaults to `false` if not specified.

Because the `flush` attribute can cause buffered content to be returned to a client before the included resource is executed, any included resources may not set any response headers.

We mentioned earlier that the `<jsp:include>` action allows static as well as dynamic content to be included, and we hinted that this ability offers flexibility that isn't achievable by using the `include` directive. One example of such flexibility is that the page attribute can be specified via a request parameter, because the `<jsp:include>` action isn't executed until the main page is requested:

```
<jsp:include page="${param.nextPage}" />
```

Here you can see how the value of the `page` attribute isn't known until the main JSP page containing the `<jsp:include>` is requested and the value is obtained by extracting a request parameter by using EL. In other words, it's possible to create dynamic content that is so dynamic, its content isn't known until request time!

You can include additional request parameters with the request that is passed to the included page. You do that with the `<jsp:param>` element:

```
<jsp:include page="includedPage">
  <jsp:param name="userName" value="Dan" />
</jsp:include>
```

The `<jsp:param>` tag has two attributes: `name` and `value`. The attribute `name` gives the name of the parameter, which can be used by the included page to access the parameter. The attribute `value`, which can be a request-time expression, gives the value of the attribute.

### The <jsp:useBean> Action

Before any JavaBeans component can be manipulated from a JSP page, it's first necessary to obtain an instance of the JavaBean, either by retrieving a preexisting JavaBean from one of the available JSP scopes or by creating a new instance. Either option could take several lines of scripting code, especially if the JavaBean needs to be initialized before use, which as you've seen, can clutter the JSP page.

The `<jsp:useBean>` action is specifically designed to simplify this process. This standard action associates an instance of a Java object (our JavaBean) that is defined with a given `scope` and `id` and makes it available as a scripting variable of the same `id`. The `<jsp:useBean>` action is highly flexible, and its exact functionality is controlled by the attributes passed to the action. When used correctly, this action can greatly reduce the amount of scriptlet code that would otherwise be required.

The syntax for the `<jsp:useBean>` action is as follows:

```
<jsp:useBean id="name" scope="page|request|session|application" typeSpec/>
```

where

```
typeSpec ::= class="className"                          |
             class="className" type="typeName"          |
             type="typeName" class="className"          |
             beanName="beanName" type="typeName"        |
             type="typeName" beanName="beanName"        |
                             type="typeName"
```

Before you see an example of the action at work, first consider Listing 1-8, a scriptlet-based alternative that will print the current time of day (`dateScriptlet.jsp`):

**Listing 1-8.** *dateScriptlet.jsp*

```jsp
<%@ page import="java.util.Date, java.text.DateFormat"%>
<html>
  <head>
    <title>Professional JSP 2.1</title>
  </head>
  <body style="font-family:verdana;font-size:10pt;">
    <%
       DateFormat df = DateFormat.getInstance();
       Date today = new Date();
    %>

    <h2>Today's Date is <%= df.format(today) %></h2>
  </body>
</html>
```

This JSP page simply imports the `java.util.Date` and `java.text.DateFormat` classes for use and uses a scriptlet to initialize the `Date` and `DateFormat` objects. Some simple template text is used to construct an HTML page, and finally a JSP expression is used to format the `Date` object.

Enter the code in Listing 1-8 into a file called `dateScriptlet.jsp` beneath the `test` web-application folder in the normal manner. Open the following URL in your browser:

```
http://localhost:8080/test/dateScriptlet.jsp
```

The output should be similar to Figure 1-12, displaying the correct date and time.

**Figure 1-12.** *This JSP page uses a scriptlet to display the date and time.*

Although the previous example is perfectly functional, you can see the problems a web designer with no Java skills would have understanding even these simple scriptlets. Another possible problem could be that the JSP page won't be compatible with the tools used by the web designer because she's used to XML-type languages. In a more complex example, you can imagine how the problem gets worse and worse.

Let's now see how you can encapsulate the previous date-formatting functionality into a JavaBeans component and use the `<jsp:useBean>` action to solve the problems mentioned earlier (see Listing 1-9).

**Listing 1-9.** *DateFormatBean.java*

```java
package com.apress.projsp;

import java.util.Date;
import java.text.*;

public class DateFormatBean {
  private DateFormat dateFormat;
  private Date date;

  public DateFormatBean() {
    dateFormat = DateFormat.getInstance();
```

```java
    date = new Date();
  }

  public String getDate() {
    return dateFormat.format(date);
  }

  public void setDate(Date date) {
    this.date = date;
  }

  public void setFormat(String format) {
    this.dateFormat = new SimpleDateFormat(format);
  }
}
```

This simple JavaBeans component (DateFormatBean.java) initializes itself with a default date and format on initialization as well as providing custom methods to set a different date format or time. When all the initialization is completed, the getDate() method simply returns the predefined date in the given date format.

You can see in Listing 1-10 how simple it is to use <jsp:useBean> to initialize an instance of DateFormatBean as opposed to the scriptlet approach.

**Listing 1-10.** *dateBean.jsp*

```html
<html>
  <head>
    <title>Professional JSP 2.1 </title>
  </head>
  <body style="font-family:verdana;font-size:10pt;">
    <jsp:useBean id="date" class="com.apress.projsp.DateFormatBean"/>

    <h2>Today's Date is <%= date.getDate()%></h2>
  </body>
</html>
```

The <jsp:useBean> action creates an instance of the JavaBean class and stores a reference to it in a scripting variable, which is called date. All this without a single scriptlet! A simple JSP expression is used to call the getDate() method to retrieve the formatted date. It should be no surprise to learn that the output is exactly the same as in the earlier example—only the implementation is different.

### The <jsp:getProperty> and <jsp:setProperty> Actions

You saw from the <jsp:useBean> action how simple it is to work with JavaBeans from inside the JSP pages. It should probably be of little surprise to learn that there are also standard actions designed to manipulate and retrieve the attributes of these JavaBeans, again without the need for scriptlets or expressions!

As the name suggests, the `<jsp:getProperty>` tag is used to retrieve or access the existing properties of a JavaBean instance. Any JavaBean properties that are retrieved by using this tag are automatically converted to a string and are placed into the implicit out variable, as output.

The syntax for this tag is as follows:

```
<jsp:getProperty name="name" property="propertyName" />
```

The `<jsp:getProperty>` tag has two attributes: name and property, both of which must be present. The name attribute references the name of the JavaBean instance on which the property attribute exists. This attribute will search all available JSP scopes until the named JavaBean is found. Should the tag fail to locate the requested JavaBean, a suitable exception will be thrown at request time.

This tag is relatively simple in the functionality that it provides, but to use it in a JSP, you must ensure that the JavaBean has already been made available to the JSP engine through a `<jsp:useBean>` tag. Without the inclusion of this extra tag, neither the `<jsp:getProperty>` nor the `<jsp:setProperty>` tag will function as expected.

Although the previous example you saw was a great improvement over the earlier scriptlet-based example, you still relied on the use of a JSP expression to access the date property from DateFormatBean. You can use the `<jsp:getProperty>` action instead of the expression so that the entire JSP page is XML based.

Look at Listing 1-11 to see the changes to the earlier example that would be necessary (dateBean_getProperty.jsp).

**Listing 1-11.** *dateBean_getProperty.jsp*

```
<html>
  <head>
    <title>Professional JSP 2.1 </title>
  </head>
  <body style="font-family:verdana;font-size:10pt;">
    <jsp:useBean id="date"
            class="com.apress.projsp.DateFormatBean"/>
    <h2>Today's Date is <jsp:getProperty name="date"
                                  property="date"/></h2>
  </body>
</html>
```

Again, this is a better solution. Yet you still haven't changed the content returned, just its implementation.

To complement the `<jsp:getProperty>` action, the `<jsp:setProperty>` tag can be used to set the value of an attribute inside a JavaBean. The `<jsp:setProperty>` action is somewhat more flexible and provides the ability to set properties based on request attributes, and so on. In its simplest form, the action may be used as follows:

```
<jsp:setProperty name="beanName" property="property" value="value"/>
```

The name and property attributes are used in exactly the same way as with the `<jsp:getProperty>` action; the additional value attribute simply indicates the new value to set the JavaBean property to.

In addition to the preceding simple syntax, you can use the `<jsp:getProperty>` action in a number of other ways:

```
<jsp:setProperty name="beanName" property="*" />
```

When using this syntax, the JSP page will attempt to find request parameters in the request with the same names as the JavaBean properties. The JavaBean properties will be set with the value of the matching request parameter.

```
<jsp:setProperty name="beanName" property="property"
                 param="paramName"/>
```

When using the `param` attribute, the JSP page will set the value of the property that has the given property name to the value of the parameter given by `paramName` in the set of request parameters.

```
<jsp:setProperty name="beanName" property="property" />
```

When using only the `property` attribute, the JSP page will attempt to set the value of the property by matching the property name to the parameter with the same name in the set of request parameters.

Although the `<jsp:setProperty>` action can be used anywhere within a JSP page, it's often used as a nested action inside the body content of the `<jsp:useBean>` action. The consequence of this is that the nested `<jsp:setProperty>` action will be executed only the first time the `<jsp:useBean>` instantiates a JavaBean. If an existing JavaBean is located in any one of the JSP scopes, the nested action won't be called.

In Listing 1-9 earlier, there were two methods that additionally set the date and the date format properties to custom values. Let's use the `<jsp:setProperty>` action to set the date format to a different value from that in the previous example (see Listing 1-12).

**Listing 1-12.** *dateBean_setProperty.jsp*

```
<html>
  <head>
    <title>Professional JSP 2.1</title>
  </head>
  <body style="font-family:verdana;font-size:10pt;">
    <jsp:useBean id="date" class="com.apress.projsp.DateFormatBean">
      <jsp:setProperty name="date" property="format"
          value="EEE, d MMM yyyy HH:mm:ss z"/>
    </jsp:useBean>
    <h2>Today's Date is <jsp:getProperty name="date" property="date"/></h2>
  </body>
</html>
```

If you want to use a compiled JavaBean in a JSP web application, the JSP engine (for example, Tomcat) needs to know where to look for it. By default Tomcat (and any other servlet container) checks for classes in the `WEB-INF\classes` directory under the web-application directory, and then in JAR files in the `WEB-INF\lib` directory. So, for our test web application we'll put the JavaBeans in the `webapps\test\WEB-INF\classes` directory. Use the following steps to create the web application:

1. Create the directory structure `webapps\test\WEB-INF\classes\com\apress\projsp`.

2. Create a new file called `DateFormatBean.java` and enter the code from Listing 1-9 earlier in this section and compile it.

3. Create the `dateBean.jsp`, `dateBean_getProperty.jsp`, and `dateBean_setProperty.jsp` pages beneath the `test` web-application folder (Listings 1-10, 1-11, and 1-12).

Start Tomcat, open a browser, and run the `dateBean.jsp`, `dateBean_getProperty.jsp`, and `dateBean_setProperty.jsp` pages as you did earlier. Notice that this time, when you use the `dateBean_setProperty.jsp` page, you have changed the date format that the JSP page generates (see Figure 1-13)!

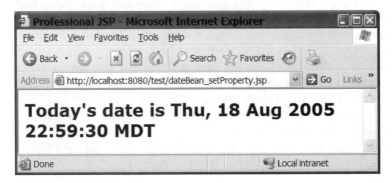

**Figure 1-13.** *The JSP page uses a JavaBean with a setProperty element to format the date in a particular format.*

### The <jsp:forward> Action

Another handy action available to JSP page authors is the `<jsp:forward>` action, which not surprisingly is used to forward the current request to another resource such as a static resource, a JSP page, or a servlet in the same context as the containing JSP, for processing.

The syntax for the action is as follows:

```
<jsp:forward page="relativeURL" />
```

Any buffered content that was written before the call to the `<jsp:forward>` action will be ignored. If any buffered content has already been flushed (sent to the client), the call will result in an `IllegalStateException`.

Note that nested `<jsp:param>` actions may be used in the `<jsp:forward>` action in the same way as with the `<jsp:include>` action to pass additional request parameters to the new resource.

For example:

```
<jsp:forward page="/pages/login.jsp">
  <jsp:param name="userName" value="Dan" />
</jsp:forward>
```

## Custom Actions

Earlier you learned about the potential problems created by introducing too much (if any at all!) scriptlet code into a JSP page. Overuse of scriptlets complicates the lives of JSP developers and non-Java-speaking UI designers alike.

You've also seen how many of the problems associated with scriptlet code can be alleviated by encapsulating some of the ugly scriptlet code into JavaBeans components and manipulating them by using some of the standard actions. Although this approach is far superior to the scriptlets approach, it's not the only available solution.

Custom actions are another mechanism for encapsulating functionality into reusable components for use inside JSP pages. Unlike JavaBeans components, custom actions have full access to their environment (such as the request and session objects), which makes it far easier to provide functionality suitable for a website. A good example of a custom action is performing calculations where the result is locale sensitive, such as being dependent on the language or number format. A JavaBeans component has no idea about the environment in which it's run, and therefore a developer would have to work a little harder to get the same functionality. That isn't to say that JavaBeans components have no advantages. For one, they're by far the best mechanism for representing business objects and storing state, because they don't care about their environment!

Custom actions are packaged together (usually with several similar or complementary actions) into a tag library that must be registered with a JSP container via its TLD file, which advertises the services provided by the tag library. After a tag library is successfully installed inside a JSP container, the library must be imported by using the taglib directive you saw earlier before any of the action it provides may be used.

The following example demonstrates the use of a custom action called foo from a tag library configured by a web application's deployment descriptor called myTagLib:

```
<%@ taglib uri="/myTagLib" prefix="myPrefix" %>

<myPrefix:foo>
   ...
</myPrefix:foo>
```

You can see how a tag library must be imported before any of the actions it provides (in this case the foo action) may be used on the page. Notice how a prefix is used to provide a namespace for actions from one tag library to another.

You'll learn more about creating and using custom actions, including some of the new features for simplifying their creation, in Chapters 6, 7, and 8.

## JavaServer Pages Standard Tag Library Actions

You saw previously how useful the standard actions included in the JSP specification are to page authors; well, the JSTL takes this idea a step further and signifies a new phase for JSP page authors.

The JSTL specification was first released in June 2002 with the sole purpose of making JSP pages easier to write. The JSTL provides four new tag libraries that may be used in a similar manner to the standard tags you saw earlier:

- Core

- Internationalization (I18n) and Formatting

- XML

- SQL

As the names suggest, each library contains a host of useful actions that are suitable for many tasks that JSP page authors are continually having to code manually, such as conditional statements and looping, formatting based on locales, XML manipulation, and database access.

The JSTL also uses the EL, which makes the actions even easier to use, especially for a developer unfamiliar with Java syntax. For a more in-depth look at the JSTL and how its tags can be controlled, take a look at Chapter 4.

# Summary

Hopefully this chapter has provided you with a general feel for where JSP technology fits within the Java Platform, Enterprise Edition 5, and how it fits with regard to the other web components such as servlets, tag libraries, and JavaBeans, which exist in the web tier for providing dynamic web-based content.

You were also introduced to some of the most popular JSP architectures that are regularly used for designing modern web applications so that you can see the bigger picture next time you're confronted with design choices. Or maybe this chapter will help you analyze an existing application.

Last, and most important, you were introduced to all the core syntax-level attributes that are available to a JSP page author, including custom actions and the JSTL. This grounding will give you a head start when approaching some of the more complex chapters, which will build on the JSP basics that you've learned so far.

# CHAPTER 2

■ ■ ■

# Servlets and Deployment

In this chapter, you'll look at the development and deployment of Java servlets. The Servlet and JSP specifications are developed in parallel for each major release of the specifications; the current releases are Servlet 2.5 and JSP 2.1. In this chapter, we'll cover the following areas:

- An introduction to developing Java servlets, including a history of servlets

- Key features of the Java Servlet API

- Developing HTTP servlets

- Deploying Java Servlet 2.5–based web applications

This chapter isn't a definitive guide to Java servlets; instead it provides an overview of the Servlet API and the deployment of applications based on this API.

## What Is a Servlet?

As you learned in the previous chapter, JSP pages are translated into servlets before the web container executes them. This chapter presents the anatomy of a Java servlet and the Servlet model that supports such servlets, and thus JSP pages.

A servlet is a server-side component that is capable of dynamically processing requests and constructing responses in a protocol-independent manner. Figure 2-1 shows the classes that are involved in developing servlets.

All the classes and interfaces shown in Figure 2-1 are in either the `javax.servlet` or `javax.servlet.http` package. The `javax.servlet` package provides the contract between the servlet or web application and the web container. This allows the vendors of web containers to focus on developing the container in the manner most suitable to them, assuming they provide implementations of the standard interfaces for the web application to use. From the developer's perspective, the package provides a standard library to process client requests and develop servlet-based web applications.

At the center of the package is the `javax.servlet.Servlet` interface. This interface defines the core structure of *all* servlets; however, in developing most servlets, you inherit from a defined implementation of this interface (such as `HttpServlet`).

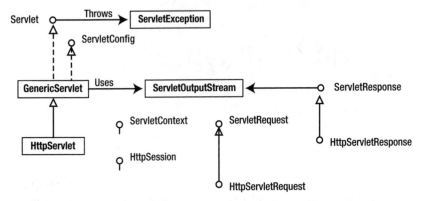

**Figure 2-1.** *This Unified Modeling Language (UML) diagram shows the interfaces and classes that form the Servlet API. Note that this diagram uses the convention of an open circle (also known as lollipop notation) to represent an interface. The interfaces and classes that you will use the most are the Servlet interface and its descendants, and the ServletRequest and ServletResponse interfaces and their descendants.*

The additional classes and interfaces that you can see in Figure 2-1 provide additional services to the web-application developer; for example, the web container provides access to the client request via a standard interface, ServletRequest, and provides access to the response via ServletResponse. The javax.servlet package provides the basis for developing cross-platform and cross-web-container web applications without worrying about the implementation of each web container.

## Why Servlets?

Why use servlets at all? After all, you have JSP pages, which are far easier to create than servlets. While this is definitely true, there are times when using a servlet is much more appropriate than using a JSP page. One such occasion is in the JSP Model 2 architecture; this was discussed in Chapter 1.

Servlets are best used in situations where a great deal of programmatic control is required, such as decision making, database querying, or accessing other enterprise resources. If you attempt to perform these types of operations within a JSP page, you'll encounter the following problems:

- **Maintainability:** Because access to resources will be spread over a number of different JSP pages and interspersed with HTML display information, your pages will be hard to maintain. The code will also be hard to read because it is interspersed with the HTML code and indentation becomes tricky.

- **Reusability:** When most of the processing logic is embedded into the JSP pages, it becomes much more difficult to reuse common functionality because it's usually implemented by using scriptlets. Often this results in lots of cutting and pasting of code that isn't only bad from a reusability perspective but is also likely to introduce errors and of course decrease productivity.

However, there are also many times when using a servlet isn't appropriate. These situations occur primarily when a lot of display formatting is required. For example, it would be best not to use a servlet to present the front page of a website. If you were to use a servlet, it would contain lots of lines such as the following:

```
out.println("<a href=\"cart.jsp\">Cart</a>");
```

This is both messy and hard to maintain; every quotation mark must be escaped, and you get no feel for the nesting in the page because the ubiquitous `out.println` statements surround everything.

## JavaServer Pages Are Servlets!

As mentioned in Chapter 1, JSP pages are translated to servlets before they are run. The web container performs this translation transparently when a user makes a request for a given JSP page. For example, say you were to code the following JSP page and save it as `simple.jsp`:

```
<html>
  <body>
    This is a very nice JSP page. Today's date is <%=new java.util.Date()%>
  </body>
</html>
```

If you make a request for it, a servlet such as the following would be generated:

```
package org.apache.jsp;

import javax.servlet.*;
import javax.servlet.http.*;
import javax.servlet.jsp.*;

public final class simple_jsp
    extends org.apache.jasper.runtime.HttpJspBase
    implements org.apache.jasper.runtime.JspSourceDependent {

  private static java.util.Vector _jspx_dependants;

  public java.util.List getDependants() {
    return _jspx_dependants;
  }

  public void _jspService(HttpServletRequest request,
                          HttpServletResponse response)
      throws java.io.IOException, ServletException {

    JspFactory _jspxFactory = null;
    PageContext pageContext = null;
    HttpSession session = null;
    ServletContext application = null;
    ServletConfig config = null;
```

```
    JspWriter out = null;
    Object page = this;
    JspWriter _jspx_out = null;
    PageContext _jspx_page_context = null;


    try {
      _jspxFactory = JspFactory.getDefaultFactory();
      response.setContentType("text/html");
      pageContext = _jspxFactory.getPageContext(this, request, response,
                                      null, true, 8192, true);
      _jspx_page_context = pageContext;
      application = pageContext.getServletContext();
      config = pageContext.getServletConfig();
      session = pageContext.getSession();
      out = pageContext.getOut();
      _jspx_out = out;

      out.write("<html>\r\n");
      out.write("  <body>\r\n");
      out.write("    This is a very nice JSP page. Today's date is ");
      out.print( new java.util.Date() );
      out.write("\r\n");
      out.write("  </body>\r\n");
      out.write("</html>");
    } catch (Throwable t) {
      if (!(t instanceof SkipPageException)){
        out = _jspx_out;
        if (out != null && out.getBufferSize() != 0)
          out.clearBuffer();
        if (_jspx_page_context != null)
            _jspx_page_context.handlePageException(t);
      }
    } finally {
      if (_jspxFactory != null)
          _jspxFactory.releasePageContext(_jspx_page_context);
    }
  }
}
```

---

■**Note** This servlet was generated by Tomcat 5.5 running on Windows XP and was written to the %TOMCAT_HOME%\work\Catalina\localhost\jsp-examples\org\apache\jsp directory. The servlet generated by your container will vary by container and operating system. Locations for these generated servlets will also vary among web containers.

---

As you can see, the servlet generated performs a whole lot of initialization, such as getting hold of the servlet context, session, and page context objects that might be used by your JSP. After this has been done, the servlet outputs the template text and JSP elements by using a series of `write` and `print` statements. If you look at the generated servlet and compare it to the JSP, it's easy to see why it's better to write JSPs to perform display formatting operations rather than servlets.

## The javax.servlet Interfaces

The `javax.servlet` package is composed of fourteen interfaces. The web container implements these seven interfaces:

- `ServletContext`

- `ServletConfig`

- `ServletResponse`

- `ServletRequest`

- `RequestDispatcher`

- `FilterChain`

- `FilterConfig`

These are objects that the container must provide to the servlets within it. The developer uses the interfaces to develop servlets, and the web-container vendors can decide the most suitable way to implement these interfaces. The remaining seven interfaces are implemented by the web-application developer to provide the application's functionality:

- `Servlet`

- `ServletContextListener`

- `ServletContextAttributeListener`

- `ServletRequestAttributeListener`

- `ServletRequestListener`

- `SingleThreadModel`

- `Filter`

As we have mentioned, the `Servlet` interface is key in developing servlets. This interface defines the life-cycle methods of a basic servlet: initialization, service, and destruction. The interface definition is shown here:

```
package javax.servlet;

import java.io.IOException;

public interface Servlet {
```

```
    public void init(ServletConfig servletconfig)
                        throws ServletException;
    public ServletConfig getServletConfig();
    public void service(ServletRequest servletrequest,
                        ServletResponse servletresponse)
                throws ServletException, IOException;
    public String getServletInfo();
    public void destroy();
}
```

This interface also provides a method to obtain an instance of the ServletConfig interface. The container uses the ServletConfig interface to pass initialization information to a
servlet. The ServletConfig interface also has a way to get hold of an instance of ServletContext
for the current web application (via the getServletContext() method). The ServletContext
interface is the web application's view on the web container. This allows a web application to
use the services of the container, such as logging and request dispatching. You can see the
ServletConfig interface definition here:

```
package javax.servlet;

import java.util.Enumeration;

public interface ServletConfig {
    public String getServletName();
    public ServletContext getServletContext();
    public String getInitParameter(String s);
    public Enumeration getInitParameterNames();
}
```

The ServletContext interface definition is shown here:

```
package javax.servlet;

import java.io.InputStream;
import java.net.MalformedURLException;
import java.net.URL;
import java.util.Enumeration;
import java.util.Set;

public interface ServletContext {
    public ServletContext getContext(String s);
    public int getMajorVersion();
    public int getMinorVersion();
    public String getMimeType(String s);
    public Set getResourcePaths(String s);
    public URL getResource(String s)
                            throws MalformedURLException;
    public InputStream getResourceAsStream(String s);
    public RequestDispatcher getRequestDispatcher(String s);
```

```
  public RequestDispatcher getNamedDispatcher(String s);
  /**
   * @deprecated Method getServlet is deprecated
   */
  public Servlet getServlet(String s)
                        throws ServletException;
  /**
   * @deprecated Method getServlets is deprecated
   */
  public Enumeration getServlets();
  /**
   * @deprecated Method getServletNames is deprecated
   */
  public Enumeration getServletNames();
  public void log(String s);
  /**
   * @deprecated Method log is deprecated
   */
  public void log(Exception exception, String s);
  public void log(String s, Throwable throwable);
  public String getRealPath(String s);
  public String getServerInfo();
  public String getInitParameter(String s);
  public Enumeration getInitParameterNames();
  public Object getAttribute(String s);
  public Enumeration getAttributeNames();
  public void setAttribute(String s, Object obj);
  public void removeAttribute(String s);
  public String getServletContextName();
}
```

The ServletContextListener interface is a life-cycle interface that programmers can implement to listen for changes to the state of the ServletContext object. This means that programmers can choose to be informed of events such as the destruction or creation of a ServletContext object. This allows the developer to perform application startup- and shut-down-type functionality (for example, logging creation or destruction of the resource, or initializing application-level constants) within a web applications. The ServletContextListener interface definition is shown here:

```
package javax.servlet;

import java.util.EventListener;

public interface ServletContextListener extends EventListener {
  public void contextInitialized(ServletContextEvent
                               servletcontextevent);
  public void contextDestroyed(ServletContextEvent
                               servletcontextevent);
}
```

Implementations of the ServletContextAttributeListener interface can perform similar functionality, but the events that they are notified about relate to the modification (adding, changing, deleting) of attributes on the servlet context. This interface definition is shown here:

```
package javax.servlet;

import java.util.EventListener;

public interface ServletContextAttributeListener extends EventListener {
  public void attributeAdded(ServletContextAttributeEvent
                             servletcontextattributeevent);
  public void attributeRemoved(ServletContextAttributeEvent
                               servletcontextattributeevent);
    public void attributeReplaced(ServletContextAttributeEvent
                                  servletcontextattributeevent);
}
```

The RequestDispatcher interface manages client requests by directing them to the appropriate resources on the server. The developer can use this interface to redirect the application to different pages and servlets. The definition of this interface is shown here:

```
package javax.servlet;

import java.io.IOException;

public interface RequestDispatcher {

  public void forward(ServletRequest servletrequest,
                      ServletResponse servletresponse)
                          throws ServletException, IOException;
  public void include(ServletRequest servletrequest,
                      ServletResponse servletresponse)
                          throws ServletException, IOException;
}
```

The ServletRequest interface encapsulates all the information that is transmitted to a servlet through its service() method during a single client request. A ServletRequest object created by the container provides methods to access parameter names, parameter values, and attributes, as well as an input stream. The source for this interface is shown here:

```
package javax.servlet;

import java.io.*;
import java.util.*;

public interface ServletRequest {

  public Object getAttribute(String s);
  public Enumeration getAttributeNames();
```

```
    public String getCharacterEncoding();
    public void setCharacterEncoding(String s)
                throws UnsupportedEncodingException;
    public int getContentLength();
    public String getContentType();
    public ServletInputStream getInputStream()
                                    throws IOException;
    public String getParameter(String s);
    public Enumeration getParameterNames();
    public String[] getParameterValues(String s);
    public Map getParameterMap();
    public String getProtocol();
    public String getScheme();
    public String getServerName();
    public int getServerPort();
    public BufferedReader getReader()
                            throws IOException;
    public String getRemoteAddr();
    public String getRemoteHost();
    public void setAttribute(String s, Object obj);
    public void removeAttribute(String s);
    public Locale getLocale();
    public Enumeration getLocales();
    public boolean isSecure();
    public RequestDispatcher getRequestDispatcher(String s);
    public String getRealPath(String path);
    public int getRemotePort();
    public String getLocalName();
    public String getLocalAddr();
    public int getLocalPort();
}
```

You can access parameters passed to the request via the following methods:

```
public String getParameter(String name)
public String[] getParameterValues(String name)
public java.util.Enumeration getParameterNames()
public java.util.Map getParameterMap()
```

The getParameter() method will return the parameter value with the given name, or null if the parameter does not exist. If this method is used with a multivalued parameter, the value returned will be equal to the first value in the array returned from the getParameterValues() method. The getParameterNames() method is used to retrieve a java.util.Enumeration of String objects containing the names of all the parameters found in the request. If the request does not contain any parameters, an empty Enumeration will be returned. Finally, the getParameterMap() method returns a java.util.Map containing all the parameters found in the request. The parameter names form string-based keys to individual parameter values that are stored as string arrays.

## The javax.servlet Classes

In addition to the interfaces that you've seen, there are nine classes contained within the javax.servlet package. They are as follows:

- GenericServlet

- ServletContextEvent

- ServletContextAttributeEvent

- ServletInputStream

- ServletOutputStream

- ServletRequestEvent

- ServletRequestAttributeEvent

- ServletRequestWrapper

- ServletResponseWrapper

The GenericServlet abstract class can be used to develop protocol-independent servlets and requires only that subclasses implement its service() method. For servlets intended to function in a web context, it's more common to extend the HttpServlet abstract class (which you'll look at in a later section).

The two event classes, ServletContextEvent and ServletContextAttributeEvent, are used for notification about changes to the ServletContext object and its attributes.

The two event classes, ServletRequestEvent and ServletRequestAttributeEvent, are used for notification about changes to the ServletRequest object and its attributes.

The ServletInputStream and ServletOutputStream abstract classes provide the ability to read and write binary data from and to the client. Classes that extend either of these abstract classes must provide an implementation of the java.io.InputStream.read() and java.io.OutputStream.write() methods, respectively.

Last, the wrapper classes ServletRequestWrapper and ServletResponseWrapper provide useful implementation of the ServletRequest and ServletResponse interfaces. These can be used or subclassed to give developers the ability to adapt the standard behavior of these objects for their own applications' needs.

## The Life Cycle of a Servlet

The javax.servlet.Servlet interface defines the methods that all servlets must implement and, among others, three methods that are known as **life-cycle methods**:

```
public void init(ServletConfig config) throws ServletException
public void service(ServletRequest req, ServletResponse res)
            throws ServletException, IOException
public void destroy()
```

These life-cycle methods are each called at separate times during the life span of a servlet, from the initial creation to the moment it's removed from service and destroyed. These methods are called in the following order:

1. When the servlet is constructed, it is initialized with the init() method.

2. Any requests from clients are handled initially by the service() method before delegating to the doXxx() methods in the case of an HttpServlet. The service() method is responsible for processing the request and returning the response.

3. When the servlet needs to be removed from service, it's destroyed with the destroy() method, then garbage collected and finalized. When the container decides to take a servlet out of service, it first ensures that any service() method calls have been completed.

Figure 2-2 shows this sequence of events.

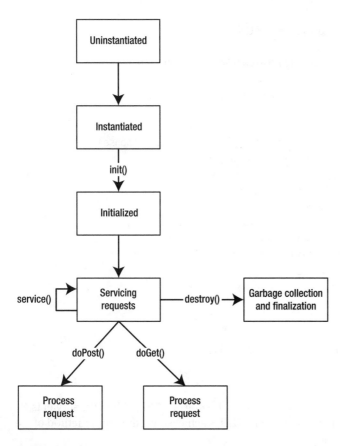

**Figure 2-2.** *The servlet life cycle moves from instantiation and initialization to the servicing of requests. At the end of the servlet life cycle, the container will stop sending requests to the servlet and remove the servlet intance.*

# A Simple Servlet

In this section, you'll look at an example of a simple generic servlet. This servlet will extend the class GenericServlet that provides a basic implementation of the Servlet interface. You'll implement the service() method of this class in our subclass, which will do the work of our servlet. You'll also override the init() and destroy() methods of the GenericServlet abstract base class. The code for our servlet is shown in Listing 2-1 (written as a standard .java file).

**Listing 2-1.** *MyServlet.java*

```java
package com.apress.projsp;

import java.io.*;
import java.util.Date;

import javax.servlet.*;

public class MyServlet extends GenericServlet {

  public void init(ServletConfig config) throws ServletException {
    super.init(config);
    log("MyServlet initialized at:" + new Date());
  }

  public void service(ServletRequest request, ServletResponse response)
                      throws ServletException, IOException {

    response.setContentType("text/html");
    PrintWriter out = response.getWriter();
    out.println("<html><head><title>BasicServlet</title></head>");
    out.println("<body><h2>" + getServletName() + "</h2>");
    out.println("This is a basic servlet.<br>");
    out.println("<hr></body></html>");
    out.close();
  }

  public void destroy() {
    log("MyServlet was destroyed at:" + new Date());
  }
}
```

This servlet performs a very simple job: it outputs a string of HTML. When the servlet is initialized, it will print a message to the servlet log. This is achieved via the log() method of the GenericServlet base class as follows:

```java
log("MyServlet initialized at:" + thisDate);
```

You'll also use this method to print a message when the servlet is destroyed. To deploy the servlet to a web container, you'll need to provide a **deployment descriptor** (web.xml) and arrange the files in the appropriate directory structure for Java web applications. The deployment descriptor gives the container information about the components that you are deploying to it. Deployment descriptors are thoroughly explained later in this chapter. For now it suffices to see the deployment descriptor that will allow you to deploy your servlet:

```xml
<?xml version="1.0" encoding="ISO-8859-1"?>

<web-app xmlns="http://java.sun.com/xml/ns/javaee"
         xmlns:xsi="http://www.w3.org/2001/XMLSchema-instance"
         xsi:schemaLocation="http://java.sun.com/xml/ns/javaee/web-app_2_5.xsd"
         version="2.5">

    <servlet>
        <servlet-name>MyServlet</servlet-name>
        <servlet-class>com.apress.projsp.MyServlet</servlet-class>
    </servlet>

    <servlet-mapping>
        <servlet-name>MyServlet</servlet-name>
        <url-pattern>/MyServlet</url-pattern>
    </servlet-mapping>
</web-app>
```

Our files must be arranged as shown in Figure 2-3.

```
□ ☞ Tomcat 5.5
   □ ☞ webapps
      □ ☞ servletExamples
         □ ☞ WEB-INF
            □ ☞ classes
               □ ☞ com
                  □ ☞ apress
                     ⊞ ☞ projsp
```

**Figure 2-3.** *The directory structure for the examples in the servlet chapter*

- servletExamples is the name of our web application.

- WEB-INF is the directory indicating that this is a web application—the directory name is case sensitive.

- web.xml is the deployment descriptor, which sits inside the WEB-INF folder.

- classes is the directory where you store the classes—in appropriate subdirectories for the package structure, for example, com\apress\projsp (as shown here) might contain MyServlet.class and MyServlet.java.

Although the web container will generate the JSP implementation servlet and compile it, you need to compile servlets that you write. To do this, you need the `javax.servlet` API classes in your class path. Depending on your web container, these might exist either as a separate Servlet JAR file or as part of a greater Java EE 5 JAR. In the case of Tomcat 5, the file is `servlet-api.jar` located in the `common\lib` directory. Using your favorite build method or integrated development environment (IDE), you need to add the library with the servlet API to your class path. If you are using some container other than Tomcat, consult the documentation to determine the JAR file that contains the Servlet API classes.

There are two ways you can deploy a web application into Tomcat:

- Copy your application's files and directories directly into Tomcat's `webapps` directory.

- Create a distributable Web ARchive (WAR) file.

For simplicity, you'll use the former here, but use the latter with the more complete example at the end of this chapter.

So to deploy the application within Tomcat, you can place this directory structure within the `%TOMCAT_HOME%\webapps` directory; the application will now be available at the following URL: `http://localhost:8080/servletExamples/MyServlet`. You'll get the page shown in Figure 2-4 in your browser.

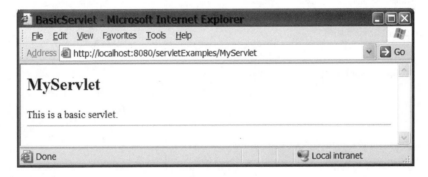

**Figure 2-4.** *The output from MyServlet displays a simple message in the browser.*

If you were to look at your web container's log file (for Tomcat this is located at `%TOMCAT_HOME%\logs\localhost.YYYY-MM-DD.log`) you'll see the message shown in Figure 2-5 toward the end of the file.

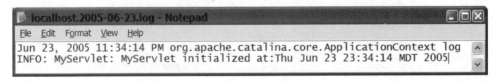

**Figure 2-5.** *When the servlet container calls the init() method of MyServlet, it prints a message to the container's log file.*

If you now stop the web container and look at the log again, you'll see that the servlet has been destroyed and the text shown in Figure 2-6 will be present in the log.

**Figure 2-6.** *When the servlet container calls the destroy() method, MyServlet prints another message to the log.*

# HTTP Servlets

As we have mentioned, the javax.servlet package provides generic interfaces and classes to service clients' requests independent of the protocol used. This means that any behavior that is specific to a particular package has to be implemented within the application by the developer. For this reason, the javax.servlet package is extended to provide a mechanism to handle requests in a protocol-dependent manner. This allows protocol-specific functionality to automatically be provided to the developer.

In this section, you'll look at one such extension: the javax.servlet.http package. This package provides classes that can be used and extended to develop servlets that provide HTTP-specific functionality.

The main class in the javax.servlet.http package is the HttpServlet abstract class. This class extends from the javax.servlet.GenericServlet class. This means that all functionality provided by this class is available to HTTP servlets. The first point to note about the HttpServlet class is that it has several new methods that provide protocol-specific functionality. Instead of the single service() method as in the GenericServlet class, you now have methods such as doGet() and doPost() that allow your servlet to perform a different task depending upon the manner in which it's being called. However, this rarely happens in practice.

The request-handling methods that are provided are as follows:

```
protected void doGet(HttpServletRequest req, HttpServletResponse resp)
                        throws ServletException, IOException
```

The doGet() method is intended to retrieve an entity from the server as referenced by a request URL.

```
protected void doHead(HttpServletRequest req, HttpServletResponse resp)
                                throws ServletException, IOException
```

The doHead() method is simply a GET request that is intended to return only the HTTP header information.

```
protected void doPost(HttpServletRequest req, HttpServletResponse resp)
                                throws ServletException, IOException
```

The doPost() method is intended to allow posting of information (forms and so on) to the server.

```
protected void doPut(HttpServletRequest req, HttpServletResponse resp)
                              throws ServletException, IOException
```

The doPut() method is used to upload a file to a server in a manner similar to the FTP.

```
protected void doOptions(HttpServletRequest req, HttpServletResponse res)
                              throws ServletException, IOException
protected void doTrace(HttpServletRequest req, HttpServletResponse resp)
                              throws ServletException, IOException
```

The doOptions() and doTrace() methods allow you to override the behavior of HTTP. There is almost no reason to override either of these methods unless the servlet implements functionality beyond the HTTP 1.1 specification.

To handle a request of a given type, you simply override the appropriate method.

# HTTP Responses and Requests

As well as providing the HttpServlet class, the javax.servlet.http package also provides HTTP-specific versions of the ServletRequest and ServletResponse objects. These are named HttpServletRequest and HttpServletResponse, respectively.

## HttpServletRequest

You can use the HttpServletRequest interface to access the HTTP-specific information of the request to your HttpServlet (such as the HTTP request parameters). Since the HttpServletRequest interface extends the ServletRequest interface, you can perform all the functions of ServletRequest as well, such as retrieving request parameters. Some of the useful operations that you can perform on your request are covered in the following sections.

### Retrieving HTTP Request Header Information

HTTP headers store a wide range of information about the user and the request, and they are transmitted between a user (usually a browser) and a web server during each request. HTTP header information is separate from the body of a request and provides some useful information that can be used by a web component (servlet or JSP page) when constructing a response.

A few of the more common headers are shown in Table 2-1 to give you an idea of the information passed between the browser and web server.

**Table 2-1.** *HTTP Header Names and Their Usage*

| Header | Usage |
|---|---|
| Date | The date and time the request was served |
| Accept | The media types accepted by the client |
| Accept-Encoding | The types of data encoding that the browser knows how to decode |
| Connection | Whether the client can handle persistent HTTP connections |
| Content-Length | The length of the body in bytes, or –1 if the length is unknown |

| Header | Usage |
|--------|-------|
| Cookie | The cookies returned by the client browser to the server |
| Host | The host and port of the original URL |
| Referrer | The URL of any referring web page |
| User-Agent | The client or browser making the request |

The `HttpServletRequest` interface defines several methods that provide access to the available headers:

```
public String getHeader(String name)
public java.util.Enumeration getHeaders(String name)
public java.util.Enumeration getHeaderNames()
public String getMethod()
```

The available methods for accessing HTTP headers take a similar form to those methods used for accessing HTML form parameters. The `getHeader()` method is used to access a given header's value. The `getHeaders()` method returns an enumeration of string objects that represent all the values of a given request header; this method can be used for headers that may have multiple values, such as the `Accept-Language` header. The name parameter passed to the `getHeader()` or `getHeaders()` methods isn't case sensitive.

When you are unsure of the available headers, the `getHeaderNames()` method may be used to obtain an enumeration of available header names. Finally, the `getMethod()` method can be used to retrieve the HTTP method used, such as `GET`, `POST`, or `PUT`.

`HttpServletRequest` also provides a couple of utility methods that can be used to convert the return type of specific header values.

```
public long getDateHeader(String header)
```

The `getDateHeader()` method will return a given header as a long value that represents a `Date` object. This method could be used with the `If-Modified-Since` or `Date` headers.

```
public int getIntHeader(String header)
```

The `getIntHeader()` method returns a given header as an integer value.

Both of these methods will return –1 if the given header isn't available. The reason to use these over the alternative `getHeader()` method is that you won't have to perform any casting on the value returned. This produces neater and more reliable code.

### Retrieving Path Information

You can also extract a lot of information relating to the path used to request your servlet. The following methods return information about this path:

```
public String getQueryString()
```

The `getQueryString()` method returns the query string of a request, or `null` if there was no query string. For example, for the following URL, `http://localhost:8080/servletExamples/TestServlet?name=sam`, the method would return `name=sam`.

```
public String getContextPath()
```

The getContextPath() method returns the first part of the URL after the first "/"after the server and port (localhost:8080 in the example URL). For the example URL, this would return servletExamples.

```
public String getServletPath()
```

The getServletPath() method returns the path to your servlet. In the URL mentioned earlier, this would return /TestServlet.

```
public String getPathInfo()
```

The getPathInfo() method returns any additional path information after your servlet path and before your query string. In our example, there is no such information present, so null would be returned.

```
public String getRequestURI()
```

The getRequestURI() method returns the complete URI for the request; for example, this would be /servletExamples/TestServlet?name=sam for the URL mentioned earlier.

```
public String getRequestURL()
```

The getRequestURL() method returns the full URL that the client entered into the browser to make the request to your servlet. For example, this is http://localhost:8080/servletExamples/TestServlet?name=sam, for the URL mentioned earlier (yes that is correct, it's the whole URL!).

## HttpServletResponse

You can use the HttpServletResponse interface to provide a response to the request to your servlet. Because this class extends the ServletResponse interface, you can perform all the functions of that class as well. Some of the useful operations that you can perform on your response are covered here.

### Setting an HTTP Response Header and Setting the Content Type of the Response

You've seen how the HttpServletRequest interface provides methods to access any HTTP headers set by a client's browser when requesting a web resource. Similarly, the HttpServletResponse interface provides methods to set headers in the response that is sent back to the browser from the web server. These methods are as follows:

```
public void addHeader(String name, String value)
public void addDateHeader(String name, long date)
public void addIntHeader(String name, int value)
public void setHeader(String name, String value)
public void setDateHeader(String name, long value)
public void setIntHeader(String name, int value)
```

Here you can see two similar types of methods: the addXxxHeader() and setXxxHeader(). Although similar in functionality, the two method types have distinctly different behavior. The addHeader(), addDateHeader(), and addIntHeader() methods all simply add a named header value to the response. The result of calling any of these three methods is that multivalue headers can be created in the response.

The setHeader(), setDateHeader(), and setIntHeader() methods will actually check for the existence of a header or headers with the same name already in the response. If the methods find an existing header or headers, they are simply replaced with the new value; otherwise, a new header is created.

It's important to note that for any headers to take effect, they obviously must be set before the response is committed and sent back to the client.

The HttpServletResponse interface also inherits the following two methods from its superclass, javax.servlet.ServletResponse:

```
public void setContentLength(int length)
public void setContentType(String type)
```

The setContentLength() method, used for persistent HTTP connections, sets the length of the content body returned to the client. If this value is set too low, the client may stop reading the response prematurely. Likewise, setting this value too high may leave clients hanging around, needlessly waiting for more data. When this method is called from an HTTP servlet, it has the effect of setting the Content-Length header.

The setContentType() method is used to set the Multipurpose Internet Mail Extensions (MIME, RFC 2045 and 2046) type of the response. The effect of calling this method from an HTTP servlet is that the Content-Type header is set accordingly.

In an HTTP servlet that serves HTML content, the content type is set as follows:

```
response.setContentType("text/html");
```

text/html is the most common type of content returned from servlets. It should also be noted that MIME types are used in many protocols other than HTTP (such as Simple Mail Transfer Protocol, or SMTP, e-mail) to indicate the type of the response and to show that many different content types exist.

Another method that is worth mentioning in this context is the setLocale(java.util.Locale) method that is provided by the javax.servlet.ServletResponse interface. This method automatically sets the Content-Language header with the locale. If the servlet has defined a content type, setLocale() will also set the charset component of the Content_Type header.

### Acquiring a Text Stream for the Response

The ServletResponse interface is responsible for the response that is sent back to a client after the request for some form of resource (HTML, XML, file, and so on). This interface makes a java.io.PrintWriter available to any servlet that returns text-based markup such as HTML, XML, or WML to a client.

The PrintWriter object enables character data to be sent back to the client. Therefore, the following method is provided by the ServletResponse interface:

```
public java.io.PrintWriter getWriter() throws java.io.IOException
```

---

■**Note** This method returns a `PrintWriter` object that uses the character encoding as specified when calling the `setContentType()` method. The `setContentType()` method must be called before calling the `getWriter()` method.

---

The `ServletResponse` interface also provides a `flushBuffer()` method, which will force any content stored in an internal buffer to be written to the client. Calling the `flush()` method of the `PrintWriter` will also have a similar effect.

### Acquiring a Binary Stream for the Response

As mentioned earlier, servlets do not just have to return character data such as HTML to clients. The `ServletResponse` interface also provides access to a `javax.servlet.ServletOutputStream` object, which can be used for returning binary information such as a GIF image to a client and is obtained with the following method:

```
public javax.servlet.ServletOutputStream getOutputStream()
                    throws java.io.IOException
```

The `ServletOutputStream` class, as the name suggests, is a subclass of `java.io.OutputStream`, so the normal techniques of chaining may be employed: `ServletOutputStream` can be wrapped inside a `java.io.BufferedOutputStream` or `java.io.ObjectOutputStream`.

Calling `flush()` on `ServletOutputStream` or `flushBuffer()` on `ServletResponse` will commit the response to the client.

### Redirecting an HTTP Request to Another URL

It's often desirable for a servlet to redirect the request to another URL. The reasons for doing this are many—for example, a user may not have logged in to an application and needs to be redirected to a login page, or a site may have moved and users need to be pointed toward an alternative URL.

As the name suggests, the redirect mechanism involves a server informing the client that they must request another URL. Most modern browsers support this functionality automatically, and it causes the user only a slightly longer waiting period before their request is served.

It should be noted that there is a distinct difference between redirecting and forwarding a user to an alternative URL. Forwarding is totally invisible to the client, and the resource that was forwarded to is returned as if it were the output from the original request. This is a powerful mechanism; generally, forwarding is used to hide the implementation details of components that make up a web application.

The `sendRedirect()` method is provided by the `javax.servlet.http.HttpServletResponse` interface:

```
public void sendRedirect(String location)
```

The location URL passed into the `sendRedirect()` method may be an absolute or relative URL. Absolute URLs must start with a "/" and are interpreted as relative to the servlet container root. Relative URLs do not start with a "/" and are interpreted as relative to the current request URI.

It's important to note that if the response has already been committed when the sendRedirect() method is called, an IllegalStateException is thrown.

Another important point to note is that if URL rewriting is being used to maintain client sessions and a redirect is required, the encodeRedirectURL() method of the HttpServletResponse interface should be used to add the session information to the redirect URL so that the client's session state is maintained. There are multiple types of redirect headers, which are detailed in the section "Error Pages" later in this chapter.

## HttpServlet Example

This section presents a simple example of an HttpServlet. This servlet will simply obtain the headers from the HttpRequest and respond by outputting these to the requesting browser. Here, you do not implement duplicate functionality in both the doGet() and doPost() methods; instead you call one from the other (doPost() calls doGet()) so that the servlet responds identically regardless of whether the request is a GET or a POST. The code for the servlet is shown in Listing 2-2.

**Listing 2-2.** *HttpServletHeaders.java*

```java
package com.apress.projsp;

import java.io.*;
import java.util.*;
import javax.servlet.*;
import javax.servlet.http.*;

public class HttpServletHeaders extends HttpServlet {

  public void doGet(HttpServletRequest request,
                    HttpServletResponse response)
                    throws IOException, ServletException {

    response.setContentType("text/html");

    PrintWriter out = response.getWriter();
    out.println("<html>");
out.println("<head>");

    out.println("<title>Here are the headers</title>");
    out.println("</head>");
    out.println("<body>");

    out.println("<h3>Headers</h3>");
    out.println("<table border=0>");
    Enumeration e = request.getHeaderNames();
    while (e.hasMoreElements()) {
      String headerName = (String)e.nextElement();
```

```
        String headerValue = request.getHeader(headerName);
        out.println("<tr><td>");
        out.println(headerName);
        out.println("</td><td>");
        out.println(headerValue);
        out.println("</td></tr>");
      }
      out.println("</table>");
  out.println("</body>");
  out.println("</html>");
    }

  public void doPost(HttpServletRequest request,
                     HttpServletResponse response)
                     throws IOException, ServletException {
    doGet(request, response);
  }
}
```

You'll deploy the servlet by using the deployment descriptor shown in Listing 2-3 (see the following "Deploying Java Servlet–Based Web Applications" section). As you can see, it's quite similar to the one you used earlier.

**Listing 2-3.** *web.xml*

```
<?xml version="1.0" encoding="ISO-8859-1"?>

<web-app xmlns="http://java.sun.com/xml/ns/javaee"
         xmlns:xsi="http://www.w3.org/2001/XMLSchema-instance"
         xsi:schemaLocation="http://java.sun.com/xml/ns/javaee/web-app_2_5.xsd"
         version="2.5">

  <servlet>
      <servlet-name>HttpServletHeaders</servlet-name>
      <servlet-class>com.apress.projsp.HttpServletHeaders</servlet-class>
  </servlet>

  <servlet-mapping>
      <servlet-name>HttpServletHeaders</servlet-name>
      <url-pattern>/HeaderServlet</url-pattern>
  </servlet-mapping>

</web-app>
```

Now compile the servlet file and copy it with the deployment descriptor into the directory structure shown in Figure 2-7. To compile the servlet, you will need to add the appropriate JAR file to your class path. For Listing 2-2, you will need the Servlet API JAR file. If you are using

Tomcat, this file is `servlet-api.jar` in the `common\lib` directory. If you are using some other web container, consult the documentation to determine the appropriate JAR file to use.

**Figure 2-7.** *The directory structure used for the example HttpServletHeaders*

- `servletExamples` is the name of your web application.

- `WEB-INF` is the directory indicating that this is a web application—the directory name is case sensitive.

- `web.xml` is the deployment descriptor, which sits inside the `WEB-INF` folder.

- `classes` is the directory where you store the classes—in appropriate subdirectories for the package structure, for example, `com\apress\projsp\` (as shown here) will contain `HttpServletHeaders.class` and `HttpServletHeaders.java`.

Figure 2-8 shows what you'll see in your browser when making a request for `http://localhost:8080/servletExamples/HeaderServlet`.

**Figure 2-8.** *The HttpServletHeaders servlet echoes the request headers to the client.*

# Deploying Java Servlet–Based Web Applications

In this section, you'll look at the deployment of Java servlet–based web applications. You'll focus on the deployment of servlets. We've already created and used **deployment descriptors** (the file named web.xml) several times. As we mentioned earlier, the deployment descriptor describes the web application to the container. The deployment descriptor file is perhaps the single most important item of your web application.

For the deployment descriptor to be valid for web applications using the Servlet 2.5 specification, several things must be true:

- The file must conform to the web application XML Schema, shown here:

```
<web-app xmlns="http://java.sun.com/xml/ns/javaee"
         xmlns:xsi="http://www.w3.org/2001/XMLSchema-instance"
         xsi:schemaLocation="http://java.sun.com/xml/ns/javaee/➥
web-app_2_5.xsd"
         version="2.5">
```

- The deployment descriptor must be a well-formed XML file.

- The deployment descriptor must be named web.xml.

- The deployment descriptor must reside at the top level of the WEB-INF directory of your web application.

Now that you know what a deployment descriptor is, you may ask what it does. In a nutshell, the deployment descriptor conveys the elements and configuration information of a web application to developers, assemblers, and deployers. All manner of information is defined in the deployment descriptor: from information about the web application itself to information about its constituent parts, and most important, how those parts are assembled into a complete web application. This section discusses the elements of the deployment descriptor that are important for most web applications. The way in which a deployment descriptor is written is often the key to how well a web application fits its purpose. It's simple to write the components of a web application, but how it's assembled is a difficult and often neglected task.

The sections of the deployment descriptor that we are going to focus on are those that relate to the deployment and configuration of servlets and JSP pages. This does not include the deployment of tag libraries and expression language (EL) functions because these are covered elsewhere in this book. The sections that you'll focus on here are as follows:

- Servlet definitions and mappings

- Servlet context initialization parameters

- Error pages

- JSP configuration elements

To illustrate the parts of the deployment descriptor, we'll show you the following simple (but complete) example and then explain its constituent parts:

```xml
<?xml version="1.0" encoding="ISO-8859-1"?>

<web-app xmlns="http://java.sun.com/xml/ns/javaee"
         xmlns:xsi="http://www.w3.org/2001/XMLSchema-instance"
         xsi:schemaLocation="http://java.sun.com/xml/ns/javaee/web-app_2_5.xsd"
         version="2.5">

  <display-name>Test Web Application</display-name>
  <description>A test web application</description>

  <context-param>
    <param-name>adminEmail</param-name>
    <param-value>admin@apress.com</param-value>
  </context-param>

  <servlet>
    <servlet-name>Servlet1</servlet-name>
    <servlet-class>com.apress.projsp.Servlet1</servlet-class>
     <init-param>
      <param-name>version</param-name>
      <param-value>0.1b</param-value>
     </init-param>
  </servlet>

  <servlet>
    <servlet-name>Servlet2</servlet-name>
    <servlet-class>com.apress.projsp.Servlet2</servlet-class>
  </servlet>

  <servlet-mapping>
    <servlet-name>Servlet1</servlet-name>
    <url-pattern>/home.html</url-pattern>
  </servlet-mapping>
  <servlet-mapping>
    <servlet-name>Servlet2</servlet-name>
    <url-pattern>/AnotherServlet</url-pattern>
  </servlet-mapping>

  <jsp-config>
    <jsp-property-group>
      <url-pattern>*.jsp</url-pattern>
      <el-ignored>false</el-ignored>
      <scripting-enabled>false</scripting-enabled>
      <include-prelude>/header.jsp</include-prelude>
```

```
        <include-coda>/footer.jsp</include-coda>
        <page-encoding>UTF-8</page-encoding>
      </jsp-property-group>
    </jsp-config>

    <error-page>
      <exception-type>java.lang.ArithmeticException</exception-type>
      <location>/error.html</location>
    </error-page>

    <error-page>
      <error-code>404</error-code>
      <location>/404.html</location>
    </error-page>

</web-app>
```

Although the previous deployment descriptor looks daunting because of its size and use of different, perhaps unfamiliar, tags, you'll soon see that it's very simple.

At the start of the deployment descriptor, there are several tags that are not directly related to servlets but give information about the web application. These tags occur directly after the <web-app> tag, which denotes the start of the deployment descriptor. These tags are as follows:

```
<display-name>Test Web Application</display-name>
<description>A test web application</description>
```

The <display-name> tag allows you to specify a short name for the overall web application. This tag is designed to allow the name of the web application to be displayed by GUI tools. The <description> tag allows you to provide a short textual description of the purpose of this web application. This is a very simplistic form of documentation for the overall web application.

Now let's move on and look at the parts of the example deployment descriptor that relate directly to servlet deployment.

## Servlet Definitions

Looking at the deployment descriptor, you can see that it defines two servlets in the web application. You can see this by looking at the number of unique <servlet> tags. The first of our two servlets is defined here:

```
<servlet>
  <servlet-name>Servlet1</servlet-name>
  <servlet-class>com.apress.projsp.Servlet1</servlet-class>
  <init-param>
    <param-name>version</param-name>
    <param-value>0.1b</param-value>
  </init-param>
</servlet>
```

The <servlet> tag contains several child tags that give information about the declaration of the servlet. This information includes the unique name that the servlet is registered with in this web application, and the full name of the class that implements the servlet's functionality.

The <servlet-name> tag gives the servlet's unique name within the web application. In the case of our first servlet, you can see that it's called Servlet1.

The <servlet-class> tag gives the fully qualified class name of the class that implements the functionality of this servlet. In the case of our first servlet, you can see that Servlet1 is implemented in the class com.apress.projsp.Servlet1.

Looking at the <servlet> element for our first servlet, you can see that it contains more than just the name and class of the servlet. It also contains an <init-param> tag. This tag allows you to specify initialization parameters for our servlet.

```
<init-param>
  <param-name>version</param-name>
  <param-value>0.1b</param-value>
</init-param>
```

As you can see, our servlet has one parameter set. The <param-name> child tag gives the name that the parameter can be accessed by, and the <param-value> gives the starting value for the parameter. The parameter can be accessed from our first servlet by using the getInitParameter() method on the ServletConfig object. This method is

```
public String ServletConfig.getInitParameter(String name)
```

So to access the parameter defined for our first servlet, you can use the following code within the servlet's class:

```
...
  String version = getInitParameter("version");
...
```

Notice that you don't need to get the ServletConfig object explicitly, because the GenericServlet class implements the ServletConfig interface so that the method is available to you.

You won't be examining the definition of our second servlet in detail, because this is nearly identical to the first servlet. However, the second servlet's definition is simpler because it does not contain any initialization parameters.

## Servlet Mappings

After you've defined your servlet through the <servlet> tag, you need to map it to a particular URL pattern. This is necessary so that the web container knows which requests to send to a particular servlet. You may think, "Why can't I just pass all requests to the servlet with the same name as the end of the URL?" For example, http://localhost:8080/mywebapp/Servlet1 would be routed to the servlet defined with the name Servlet1. This would seem like a logical approach and is in fact the most common way of implementing the mappings between servlets and URLs. However, the approach isn't very flexible. Imagine if you wanted to map more than one URL to the same servlet, which could, for example, check that a user is logged in. This is where the <servlet-mapping> element comes in, and where it illustrates its power.

In the example deployment descriptor, you map servlets to some strange-looking URL patterns. Our first servlet is invoked every time any URL that ends with `home.html` is encountered. The unique servlet name that you defined in the `<servlet>` tag (referenced here as `<servlet-name>`) is mapped to a URL pattern referenced here in a `<url-pattern>` element:

```
<servlet-mapping>
  <servlet-name>Servlet1</servlet-name>
  <url-pattern>/home.html</url-pattern>
</servlet-mapping>
```

Again, we won't discuss our second servlet, because this is very similar to the first, except that it maps to any URL ending in `AnotherServlet`.

It's worth mentioning at this stage that servlets can be mapped to more than one URL through the use of wildcards in the `<url-pattern>` child tag of the `<servlet-mapping>` tag. For example, the following maps every URL encountered to the same servlet, which allows you to have a central servlet that handles all requests:

```
<servlet-mapping>
  <servlet-name>ValidatorServlet</servlet-name>
  <url-pattern>/*</url-pattern>
</servlet-mapping>
```

You can also have more than one `<servlet-mapping>` tag per defined servlet. This allows you to map completely disparate URLs to the same target.

## Servlet Context Initialization Parameters

Here we'll discuss the application (or servlet context) initialization parameters. You've already seen how to define initialization parameters for individual servlets; now you'll look at defining parameters for the whole web application.

To achieve this, you use the `ServletContext` object. The `ServletContext` is a servlet's view onto the web application that contains it. As such, if a parameter is set in the `ServletContext`, it's accessible from all servlets in the web application.

Through the deployment descriptor, you can provide the `ServletContext` with any number of initialization parameters. You could use such parameters to convey application information such as an administrator's e-mail address. These parameters are available to the servlets in the web application via the `getInitParameter()` and `getInitParameterNames()` methods of the `ServletContext` object:

```
public abstract String getInitParameter(String name)
public abstract Enumeration getInitParameterNames()
```

Note that because this is an interface, all methods are abstract and their implementations must be provided by the web container.

In the example, you define one initialization parameter for your web application by using a `<context-param>` element:

```
<context-param>
  <param-name>adminEmail</param-name>
```

```
      <param-value>admin@apress.com</param-value>
   </context-param>
```

This parameter represents the e-mail address of the application's administrator. This can be pulled into any servlet in the application so that the e-mail address used is consistent throughout the system. To obtain this parameter from any particular servlet, you can use the following code:

```
...
   String adminEmail = getServletContext().getInitParameter("adminEmail");
...
```

## Error Pages

In the bad old days of web development, if an error occurred in an application, you would see the familiar HTTP error 500, or worse still, a nasty stack trace on the browser. For example, if your servlet performed an operation that resulted in an exception, it was quite common to see the output shown in Figure 2-9 in the client browser.

**Figure 2-9.** *When your application does not define error handling, it is possible that the user could see stack traces or other user-unfriendly error messages.*

In a production system, this sort of page does not inspire much confidence in the end user of the application! You can prevent such pages from appearing through the use of error pages.

Error pages allow you to respond to problems with custom pages that offer specific information about the trouble at hand. These errors can include Java exceptions as well as HTTP errors (for example, the result of a page not being found).

Our sample deployment descriptor defines two error pages. The first error page is shown whenever the server encounters a `java.lang.ArithmeticException` (as shown previously). The tags to define this are shown here:

```
<error-page>
    <exception-type>java.lang.ArithmeticException</exception-type>
    <location>/error.html</location>
</error-page>
```

The `<error-page>` tag has two children: `<exception-type>` and `<location>`. The `<exception-type>` child tag defines the exception to catch, and `<location>` defines the page or resource to display on encountering the error defined.

After adjusting your deployment descriptor, if you were to run the same servlet that produced the earlier error, `error.html` would be called and displayed (Figure 2-10) instead of the nasty Java stack trace.

**Figure 2-10.** *By defining error handling in your application, you can control what the user sees when an error occurs.*

As most users will agree, they would rather be presented with a human-readable error page than a huge, meaningless (to some anyway!) Java stack trace.

---

**■Tip** In testing these error-handling examples with Microsoft Internet Explorer, you may find that Internet Explorer does not display the error pages properly. Instead it displays its own default error page. When Tomcat 5 encounters an error, it sends an HTTP status code of 500 along with the error page (see Table 2-2). When the error page that is sent is less than a certain size, Internet Explorer displays its own error page rather than the one sent by the server. Most often, the critical size is 512 bytes (although we have seen situations where 1024 bytes seems to be the critical size). So, if everything seems correct, but Internet Explorer won't display `error.html` or `404.html`, try adding an HTML comment so that the file size (and thus response size) exceeds 512 or 1024 bytes.

---

Your sample deployment descriptor also contains an error-page definition for an HTTP error. This is defined by using the following tags:

```
<error-page>
  <error-code>404</error-code>
  <location>/404.html</location>
</error-page>
```

This looks similar to the previous example, but note the use of the `<error-code>` child tag, instead of the `<exception-type>` child. This `<error-code>` child defines the HTTP error under which the defined error page will be shown. In this example, when the web container cannot find a file requested in the web application, it will show the page 404.html rather than the server's default error page. For example, when you try to call WrongServlet, which is obviously not a real servlet, you should get a customized error page like the one shown in Figure 2-11.

**Figure 2-11.** *Error pages can be sent to the user for HTTP status codes.*

A list of HTTP status codes and their meanings is given in Table 2-2.

**Table 2-2.** *HTTP Status Codes and Their Meanings*

| Status Code | Meaning | Status Code | Meaning |
| --- | --- | --- | --- |
| 100 | Continue | 404 | Not Found |
| 101 | Switching Protocols | 405 | Method Not Allowed |
| 200 | OK | 406 | Not Acceptable |
| 201 | Created | 407 | Proxy Authentication Required |
| 202 | Accepted | 408 | Request Time Out |
| 203 | Nonauthoritative Information | 409 | Conflict |
| 204 | No Content | 410 | Gone |
| 205 | Reset Content | 411 | Length Required |
| 206 | Partial Content | 412 | Precondition Failed |
| 300 | Multiple Choices | 413 | Request Entity Too Large |
| 301 | Moved Permanently | 414 | Request URL Too Large |

*Continued*

**Table 2-2.** *Continued*

| Status Code | Meaning | Status Code | Meaning |
| --- | --- | --- | --- |
| 302 | Moved Temporarily | 415 | Unsupported Media Type |
| 303 | See Other | 500 | Server Error |
| 304 | Not Modified | 501 | Not Implemented |
| 305 | Use Proxy | 502 | Bad Gateway |
| 400 | Bad Request | 503 | Out of Resources |
| 401 | Unauthorized | 504 | Gateway Time Out |
| 402 | Payment Required | 505 | HTTP Version Not Supported |
| 403 | Forbidden | | |

# JavaServer Pages Configuration Elements

A new feature of the Servlet 2.4 deployment descriptor is the addition of several JSP configuration elements inside a `<jsp-config>` element. These elements allow you to do the following:

- Enable or disable EL evaluation

- Enable or disable scripting elements

- Indicate page-encoding information

- Automatically include preludes and codas

You can perform some or all of these functions for individual pages or groups of pages. This grouping is controlled by the `<jsp-property-group>` element. This allows you to map URLs to groups of the properties mentioned earlier. As you can see in the previous example, you are applying several properties to *all* JSP pages in the application; this uses the following property group:

```
<jsp-config>
  <jsp-property-group>
    <url-pattern>*.jsp</url-pattern>
  </jsp-property-group>
</jsp-config>
```

## Enabling Expression Language Evaluation

To enable or disable the evaluation of the EL, you can use the `<el-ignored>` element. This can be used to easily set the `isELIgnored` property of a group of JSP pages. By default, the EL evaluation is enabled for web applications using a Servlet 2.4 or Servlet 2.5 `web.xml`. To disable evaluation for all the JSP pages in our application, you can use a fragment similar to the following:

```
<jsp-config>
  <jsp-property-group>
    <url-pattern>*.jsp</url-pattern>
    <el-ignored>true</el-ignored>
```

```
    </jsp-property-group
  </jsp-config>
```

You can also disable the EL for specific pages by using a snippet such as the following:

```
<jsp-config>
  <jsp-property-group>
    <url-pattern>noel.jsp</url-pattern>
    <el-ignored>true</el-ignored>
  </jsp-property-group
</jsp-config>
```

## Enabling Scripting Elements

To enable or disable the evaluation of scripting elements within a page, you can use the `<scripting-invalid>` element. By default, scripting is enabled. To disable scripting for all the JSP pages in your application, you can use a fragment similar to the following:

```
<jsp-config>
  <jsp-property-group>
    <url-pattern>*.jsp</url-pattern>
    <scripting-invalid>true</scripting-invalid>
  </jsp-property-group>
</jsp-config>
```

To disable scripting for a specific page, you can use a snippet such as the following:

```
<jsp-config>
  <jsp-property-group>
    <url-pattern>noscript.jsp</url-pattern>
    <scripting-invalid>true</scripting-invalid>
  </jsp-property-group>
</jsp-config>
```

## Indicating Page-Encoding Information

Using the `<page-encoding>` element, you can define the encoding for a group of JSP pages. The valid values of the `<page-encoding>` tag are those of the `pageEncoding` page directive. It's a translation-time error to define the `pageEncoding` of a JSP page through one value in the JSP configuration element and then give it a different value in a `pageEncoding` directive, but it's legal to give it the same value. You can use a snippet similar to the one shown here to control the page encoding:

```
<jsp-config>
  <jsp-property-group>
    <url-pattern>*.jsp</url-pattern>
    <page-encoding>ISO-8859-2</page-encoding>
  </jsp-property-group
</jsp-config>
```

### Automatically Including Preludes and Codas

Through the use of the `<include-prelude>` and `<include-coda>` elements, you can automatically include a page before and after the evaluation of a group of pages.

The `<include-prelude>` element is a context-relative path that must correspond to an element in the web application. When the element is present, the given path will be automatically included (as in an `include` directive) at the beginning of each JSP page in this `<jsp-property-group>`.

The `<include-coda>` element is a context-relative path that must correspond to an element in the web application. When the element is present, the given path will be automatically included (as in an `include` directive) at the end of each JSP page in this `<jsp-property-group>`.

The following fragment shows a file being included at the start and end of every JSP page in the web application:

```
<jsp-config>
  <jsp-property-group>
    <url-pattern>*.jsp</url-pattern>
    <include-prelude>/header.jsp</include-prelude>
    <include-coda>/footer.jsp</include-coda>
  </jsp-property-group>
</jsp-config>
```

# An Example Web Application

You are now in the position to pull together all the information in this chapter as a complete web-application example.

This section covers most of the code required to produce a sample web application, as well as the information needed to deploy the completed application to a web container (in this example, Tomcat 5.5). In the interest of space, not all the source files needed for this application are listed in the book. These files consist of one exception class, the error pages for the application, and two simple HTML pages. These files are simple enough that you should be able to develop them on your own. Alternately, you can download them as part of the code download for this book, at the Source Code area of the Apress website (http://www.apress.com).

## The Store

The example used in this section is the ubiquitous web-store application. You'll see a front page, a shopping cart, and a checkout page.

After you've looked at the code for the application, you'll examine the deployment descriptor for the application.

The application will be written in the JSP Model 2 style (see Chapter 1 for a detailed description of this), beginning with the controller.

---

**Note** Bear in mind that this is a very simplistic application. Over the course of this book, the examples will grow gradually more sophisticated.

---

## The Controller Servlet

The Controller servlet (FrontController.java in Listing 2-4) coordinates the behavior of our store.

**Listing 2-4.** *FrontController.java*

```java
package com.apress.projsp.store;

import java.io.*;
import java.util.*;
import javax.servlet.*;
import javax.servlet.http.*;

public class FrontController extends HttpServlet {

  public void init() throws ServletException {

    HashMap products = new HashMap();

    Product p = new Product(1, "Dog", "9.99");
    products.put("1", p);

    p = new Product(2, "Cat", "4.99");
    products.put("2", p);

    p = new Product(3, "Fish", "1.99");
    products.put("3", p);

    //Store products in the ServletContext
    getServletContext().setAttribute("products", products);

  }
  public void doPost(HttpServletRequest req, HttpServletResponse res)
      throws ServletException, IOException {

    // load the action
    String name = req.getPathInfo().substring(1);

    String viewName = "/error.jsp";
    try {
      name = "com.apress.projsp.store." + name;
      Class c = getClass().getClassLoader().loadClass(name);
      Action action = (Action) c.newInstance();
      viewName = action.process(req, res);

    } catch (ClassNotFoundException e) {
      e.printStackTrace();
```

```
    } catch (InstantiationException e) {
      e.printStackTrace();
    } catch (IllegalAccessException e) {
      e.printStackTrace();
    }

    RequestDispatcher dispatcher =
      req.getRequestDispatcher(viewName);
    dispatcher.forward(req, res);

  }

  public void doGet(HttpServletRequest req, HttpServletResponse res)
      throws ServletException, IOException {

    doPost(req, res);

  }

}
```

As you can see, this servlet is fairly simple. Its primary job is to receive a request, work out how to process it, delegate the processing to an appropriate class, and forward it to the next JSP page in the store. This is achieved by reading the request path and attempting to instantiate a class that matches the last part of it. For example, if the request is http://localhost:8080/store/servlet/DummyAction, the servlet will attempt to instantiate a class called DummyAction in the current package. After this class has been instantiated, it will call the method process on it, passing in the current request and response objects. This relies on the class implementing a known interface called Action. This interface (Listing 2-5) is simple, containing only one method.

**Listing 2-5.** *Action.java*

```
package com.apress.projsp.store;

import javax.servlet.ServletException;
import javax.servlet.http.HttpServletRequest;
import javax.servlet.http.HttpServletResponse;

public interface Action {

  /**
   * Peforms the processing associated with this action.
   *
   * @param request     the HttpServletRequest instance
   * @param response     the HttpServletResponse instance
   * @return  the name of the next view
   */
```

```
public String process(HttpServletRequest request,
                      HttpServletResponse response)
    throws ServletException;

}
```

It is the job of implementations of this interface to process the current request and return the name of the next page to forward it to. Our store has several implementations of this interface, which will all be shown and explained in this section.

Getting back to the controller, you can see that it also performs another job. The init() method of the servlet creates a collection of Product objects that are placed into the ServletContext. This would not normally be done, because the products would be obtained from somewhere such as a database or configuration file. We have done it this way to avoid cluttering up the code with data-access code. Product is just an object that holds the basic data for each item. See Listing 2-6.

**Listing 2-6.** *Product.java*

```
package com.apress.projsp.store;

public class Product {

  private String name;
  private String price;
  private int id;

  public Product(int id, String name, String price) {
    this.price = price;
    this.name = name;
    this.id=id;
  }

  public String getPrice() {
     return this.price;
  }

  public String getName() {
    return this.name;
  }

  public int getId() {
    return this.id;
  }

  public String toString() {
    return "Product:id=" + id + " name=" + name + " price=" + price;
  }

}
```

## The Store Actions and JavaServer Pages

Now we have the base for our actions and model, let's flesh it out by combining them with the view.

### MainAction

The main action in our store is implemented (surprisingly) by a class called MainAction. This class implements the Action interface that you saw earlier. This action, the code of which is shown in Listing 2-7, has no other purpose at this time than to forward onto the main page in this site, main.jsp.

**Listing 2-7.** *MainAction.java*

```
package com.apress.projsp.store;

import javax.servlet.http.HttpServletRequest;
import javax.servlet.http.HttpServletResponse;
import javax.servlet.ServletException;

public class MainAction implements Action {

  public String process(HttpServletRequest req, HttpServletResponse res)
      throws ServletException {

    return "/main.jsp";

  }
}
```

The main page for this site, main.jsp, is shown in Listing 2-8. This simple page displays the list of products available to purchase.

**Listing 2-8.** *main.jsp*

```
<%@ page import="java.util.*,com.apress.projsp.store.*" %>

<%
  HashMap products = (HashMap) application.getAttribute("products");

  // List the products, clickable to add to cart
  Iterator it = products.values().iterator();
  out.println("<table>");
  while (it.hasNext()) {
    out.println("<tr>");
    Product product = (Product) it.next();
%>
```

```
<td>
 <a href='CartAction?add=true&id=<%=product.getId()%>'>➥
<%=product.getName()%></a>
</td>
<td>
 <%=product.getPrice()%>
</td>

</tr>
<%}%>
</table>
```

You display the products by getting the previously created hash table from `ServletContext` (this was created by the controller servlet that you read about earlier). You then loop through the hash table, writing each product out into an HTML table row. Each product name is rendered as a hyperlink so you can add it to the shopping cart that you'll read about next.

This main page has a header and footer included so you can simply change the style of the page without changing the code that displays products. This is achieved by using the `<include-prelude>` and `<include-coda>` subelements of the `<jsp-config>` deployment-descriptor element. The following excerpt shows the deployment-descriptor elements that are required:

```
<jsp-config>
  <jsp-property-group>
    <url-pattern>*.jsp</url-pattern>
    <include-prelude>/header.jsp</include-prelude>
    <include-coda>/footer.jsp</include-coda>
  </jsp-property-group>
</jsp-config>
```

This includes the file `/header.jsp` as the page header and the file `/footer.jsp` as the page footer. These are included for every JSP page within the system.

The header simply contains a basic header and heading, as shown in Listing 2-9.

**Listing 2-9.** *header.jsp*

```
<html>
    <head>
        <title>The Store</title>
    </head>
    <body>
        <h1>Welcome to the Apress Store</h1>
        <br>
```

The footer closes the body and adds some navigation links, as shown in Listing 2-10.

**Listing 2-10.** *footer.jsp*

```
    <br>
        <table>
            <tr>
                <td><a href="CartAction?add=false">Display Cart</a></td>
                <td><a href="CheckOutAction">Check Out</a></td>
            </tr>
        </table>
    </body>
</html>
```

### CartAction

The cart in your store holds only one type of each product. This is primarily so that you can illustrate error pages for your sample application. The code that implements your cart is another action, CartAction.java, and a simple Java class, named Cart.java, shown in Listing 2-11.

**Listing 2-11.** *Cart.java*

```java
package com.apress.projsp.store;
import java.util.*;

public class Cart {

  private HashMap items = new HashMap();

  public Cart() {
  }

  public Iterator getItems() {
    return items.values().iterator();
  }

  public void addItem(Product product) throws ItemAlreadyAddedException {
    Integer id = new Integer(product.getId());
    if (this.items.containsKey(id)) {
      throw new ItemAlreadyAddedException();
    }
    this.items.put(id, product);
  }

}
```

The code in Listing 2-12 shows the action, called CartAction.java, that handles the web operations on the shopping cart.

**Listing 2-12.** *CartAction.java*

```java
package com.apress.projsp.store;

import java.io.*;
import java.util.*;

import javax.servlet.*;
import javax.servlet.http.*;

public class CartAction implements Action {

  public String process(HttpServletRequest req, HttpServletResponse res)
      throws ServletException {

    // Check to see if you are adding to the cart or
    // if you want to display the cart
    String adding = req.getParameter("add");

    // Get the cart if it exists
    HttpSession session = reqt.getSession();

    Cart cart = (Cart) session.getAttribute("cart");

    if (cart == null) {
      cart = new Cart();
    }

    if (adding.equalsIgnoreCase("true")) {
      // Add to it
      addToCart(req, cart);
    }
    return "/cart.jsp";

  }

  private void addToCart(HttpServletRequest request, Cart cart)
      throws ItemAlreadyAddedException {
    // Get the item to add from the request

    // Get the products from the ServletContext
    HashMap products = (HashMap)request.getSession().getServletContext().
                            getAttribute("products");

    // Find the one represented by the ID that you passed in
    try {
      String id = request.getParameter("id");
```

```
          Product p = (Product) products.get(id);

          System.out.println(p);
          // Add it to the cart
          cart.addItem(p);
          // Add the cart to the session
          request.getSession().setAttribute("cart",cart);

      } catch (NumberFormatException nfe) {
        throw new ItemAlreadyAddedException();
      }
    }
}
```

In this code, CartAction performs two tasks: it both adds to the shopping cart and displays the cart.

The first thing done in this action is to retrieve the shopping cart from the user's session. If there is no cart in the session, a new Cart object is created as follows:

```
Cart cart = (Cart) session.getAttribute("cart");

if (cart == null) {
  cart = new Cart();
}
```

Next, this method decides what to do to the cart based on a parameter (called adding) passed to the action in HttpServletRequest. If the parameter contains the value true, you call the method addToCart(). If the adding parameter is false, you simply redirect to the cart.jsp page. This method looks for another parameter in HttpServletRequest called id. It then looks for this product in the list of products that you placed into ServletContext in the initialization, and adds it to the cart object. As mentioned earlier, a cart can contain only one of each product. If the user tries to add more than one of the same item to the cart, an ItemAlreadyAddedException is thrown. As you'll see later, the web container catches this exception and a special page is shown.

---

■**Note** We do not show the listing for ItemAlreadyAddedException.java, nor the page sent in response to this exception, duplicateItem.html, in this book. Creation of these files is left as an exercise for you. Or, if you download the code for this book from the Source Code area of the Apress website (http://www.apress.com), you can find the source for ItemAlreadyAddedException.java and duplicateItem.html.

---

After the item is added to the cart (or if the adding parameter is false), the cart is written out to the user's browser by redirecting to the cart.jsp page. This page is shown in Listing 2-13.

**Listing 2-13.** *cart.jsp*

```
<%@page import="java.util.*,com.apress.projsp.store.Cart,
                com.apress.projsp.store.Product"%>

<%Iterator items = ((Cart)session.getAttribute("cart")).getItems();%>
    <h1>Current Cart Contents:</h1>
    <table>
    <%while (items.hasNext()) {%>

     <tr>
      <%Product p = (Product)items.next();%>

      <td><%=p.getName()%></td>
      <td><%=p.getPrice()%></td>
        </tr>
    <%}%>

    </table>
```

### CheckOutAction

A store is useful only if you can actually buy the products that you put into your cart. In the example store, the CheckOutAction handles this. Obviously, you cannot really buy the items because this is only an example. The checkout process in our store simply displays the contents of the cart and gives the user a Confirm button. Listing 2-14 shows the code for the CheckOutAction.

**Listing 2-14.** *CheckOutAction.java*

```
package com.apress.projsp.store;

import java.io.*;

import javax.servlet.*;
import javax.servlet.http.*;

public class CheckOutAction implements Action {

  public String process(HttpServletRequest req, HttpServletResponse res)
          throws ServletException {

      return "/checkout.jsp";

  }
}
```

The action simply redirects the user to the checkout.jsp page shown in Listing 2-15.

**Listing 2-15.** *checkout.jsp*

```
<jsp:include page="cart.jsp" />

<br>Please Click Confirm to check out<br>
<form action='ConfirmAction'><input type='submit' value='Confirm'></form>
```

This page includes the content of the cart.jsp page to display the cart to the user. The page also includes a Confirm button. When clicked, the button will invoke ConfirmAction.

### ConfirmAction

The confirm action in our store simply redirects to a confirmation page. In a real store, this action might process credit-card information or any number of other things. Listing 2-16 shows the code for this action.

**Listing 2-16.** *ConfirmAction.java*

```
package com.apress.projsp.store;

import javax.servlet.http.HttpServletRequest;
import javax.servlet.http.HttpServletResponse;
import javax.servlet.ServletException;

public class ConfirmAction implements Action {

  public String process(HttpServletRequest req, HttpServletResponse res)
      throws ServletException {
    return "/confirmed.html";
  }
}
```

ConfirmAction simply redirects you to an HTML file to tell the user that their order has been confirmed. In a real store, you would output a receipt or something like it at this stage.

Having seen all the important code for the simple store application, you'll now look at the deployment descriptor required to deploy this application.

## The Deployment Descriptor

Now it's time to deploy the application. Listing 2-17 shows the deployment descriptor that you'll be using to do this.

**Listing 2-17.** *web.xml*

```
<?xml version="1.0" encoding="ISO-8859-1"?>

<web-app xmlns="http://java.sun.com/xml/ns/javaee"
         xmlns:xsi="http://www.w3.org/2001/XMLSchema-instance"
```

```
        xsi:schemaLocation="http://java.sun.com/xml/ns/javaee/web-app_2_5.xsd"
        version="2.5">

  <servlet>
      <servlet-name>FrontController</servlet-name>
      <servlet-class>
          com.apress.projsp.store.FrontController
      </servlet-class>
      <load-on-startup>1</load-on-startup>
  </servlet>

  <servlet-mapping>
      <servlet-name>FrontController</servlet-name>
      <url-pattern>/servlet/*</url-pattern>
  </servlet-mapping>

  <jsp-config>
      <jsp-property-group>
          <url-pattern>/*</url-pattern>
          <include-prelude>/header.jsp</include-prelude>
          <include-coda>/footer.jsp</include-coda>
      </jsp-property-group>
  </jsp-config>

  <welcome-file-list>
      <welcome-file>index.html</welcome-file>
  </welcome-file-list>

  <error-page>
      <exception-type>
            com.apress.projsp.store.ItemAlreadyAddedException
      </exception-type>
      <location>/duplicateItem.html</location>
  </error-page>

</web-app>
```

This deployment descriptor contains all the elements to build the application and allow it to be deployed into a web container.

The first thing that you set up is the controller servlet. This servlet processes all requests beginning with /servlet that are received by the web application. This is achieved by using two different deployment descriptor elements, including the <servlet> element:

```
  <servlet>
      <servlet-name>FrontController</servlet-name>
      <servlet-class>
            com.apress.projsp.store.FrontController
```

```
    </servlet-class>
    <load-on-statup>1</load-on-statup>
</servlet>
```

and the `<servlet-mapping>` element:

```
<servlet-mapping>
    <servlet-name>FrontController</servlet-name>
    <url-pattern>/servlet/*</url-pattern>
</servlet-mapping>
```

This means that the controller servlet will be requested by using a path similar to the following:

```
http://localhost:8080/store/servlet/ActionName
```

where `ActionName` is the name of the class that implements the action that you wish to process your request.

After you've mapped the controller servlet, you declare the pages to be included as the header and footer of each page in the application. This is achieved by using the following elements:

```
<jsp-config>
    <jsp-property-group>
        <url-pattern>/*</url-pattern>
        <include-prelude>/header.jsp</include-prelude>
        <include-coda>/footer.jsp</include-coda>
    </jsp-property-group>
</jsp-config>
```

This says that for every page (shown by the /* in the `<url-pattern>` element) in the application, you'll include /`header.jsp` at the start and /`footer.jsp` at the end. This allows you to change the appearance of the site at deployment time.

You then have the `welcome` file for the application:

```
<welcome-file-list>
    <welcome-file>index.html</welcome-file>
</welcome-file-list>
```

This index page just ensures that you can direct the user to the `MainAction` without the user having to know the complex URL required.

Next you define an error page for the application. This page is invoked when a specified error occurs in any part of the application. The `<error-page>` element in the deployment descriptor that does this is shown here. More information about this mechanism can be found in the earlier discussion of error pages.

```
<error-page>
    <exception-type>
        com.apress.projsp.store.ItemAlreadyAddedException
    </exception-type>
    <location>/duplicateItem.html</location>
</error-page>
```

This definition says that whenever the exception com.apress.projsp.store.ItemAlready➡ AddedException is thrown, the page duplicateItem.html is shown. As you may you recall, we have said that only one item of a specific type can be added to the user's shopping cart. If this constraint is violated, the previous exception is thrown and the user is presented with a page indicating that no duplicate items can be added to the cart.

## Deploying the Application

Now we'll demonstrate how to deploy the completed and archived application to Tomcat.

---

■**Note** The files for this example and the earlier examples, along with the respective WAR files, are available for download from the Source Code area of the Apress website (http://www.apress.com).

---

First you must create a WAR file containing the application. A WAR file is just like a JAR file except that the files must be located in specific directories and it's created by using the jar utility. Therefore, before you can create the WAR file, you must place all the files in the correct directories as shown in Figure 2-12 (this is the same structure that you saw earlier when you deployed directly to Tomcat).

```
☐ 🗁 Tomcat 5.5
   ☐ 🗁 webapps
      ☐ 🗁 store
         ☐ 🗁 WEB-INF
            ☐ 🗁 classes
               ☐ 🗁 com
                  ☐ 🗁 apress
                     └ 🗁 projsp
```

**Figure 2-12.** *The directory structure for the store application*

- store is the root directory. When you deployed to Tomcat, this was the name of the web application, but when you deploy as a WAR, it's the name of the WAR file that becomes the application's name (in Tomcat). All the JSP files (main.jsp, cart.jsp, checkout.jsp, error.jsp, header.jsp, and footer.jsp) and HTML files (index.html, confirmed.html, and duplicateItem.html) should be located under this directory.

- WEB-INF is the directory indicating that this is a web application—the directory name is case sensitive.

- web.xml is the deployment descriptor, which sits inside the WEB-INF folder.

- classes is the directory where you store all the class files in appropriate subdirectories for the package structure, for example, com\apress\projsp\store\ (as shown here) will contain Action.class, Cart.class, CartAction.class, CheckOutAction.class, ConfirmAction.class, FrontController.class, ItemAlreadyAddedException.class, MainAction.class, and Product.class.

After the files are in their respective folders, run the following command from the command prompt from the root folder as follows:

```
\store>jar -cvf store.war.
```

This will create a WAR file in the same directory that contains all the items in the application.

### Deploying with Tomcat

Deploying this application with Tomcat is simplicity itself. For basic deployments, all you need to do is copy your WAR file into the webapps directory of your Tomcat installation. It's located at %TOMCAT_HOME%\webapps.

If this is the first time you have copied the WAR file to the webapps directory, Tomcat will detect the new file and automatically deploy the application. If you are attempting to redeploy the store application, Tomcat does not check for newer versions of existing WAR files; you can do a couple of things to get Tomcat to redeploy the application. We recommend that you go to the Tomcat Management page, which you can access through a link on the main Tomcat page, http://localhost:8080. Find the store application in the list and click the Undeploy link for the application. Then, copy the WAR file to the webapps directory and Tomcat will redeploy it.

To deploy the example in a more advanced way, you can follow these steps:

1. Copy your WAR file to the webapps directory of your Tomcat installation. This step is voluntary, but it's sensible to keep your web-application deployments in the same place.

2. Add an entry to the server.xml file. This file is located in the %TOMCAT_HOME%\conf directory. The line that you should add to deploy the store application is as follows:

   ```
   <Context path="/store" docBase="/store.war" reloadable="true"/>
   ```

   This line declares a context to exist with its base URI being /store (this can be any valid path). This context is fulfilled by the application at /store.war. You are passing another parameter when creating the context.

   If the reloadable parameter is set to true, Tomcat monitors classes in WEB-INF\classes and WEB-INF\lib for changes and automatically reloads the web application if a change is detected. This feature is useful during application development, but it requires significant runtime overhead and isn't recommended for use on deployed production applications.

   There are many other parameters that can be passed. Most of these are beyond the scope of this chapter, but it would be very useful to enable more control over how your application is deployed. Details of these parameters can be found at http://jakarta.apache.org/tomcat/.

3. Start Tomcat, and your application will be deployed. It can now be accessed at http://localhost:8080/store/. The home page contains a link that passes you through to the main page at http://localhost:8080/store/servlet/MainAction. Figure 2-13 shows the main store page accessed from the home page.

**Figure 2-13.** *The main store page, accessed from the home page*

4. If you make changes to the application, create a new WAR file, remove the old application by using the Tomcat Management page, copy the new WAR over the old one, and Tomcat will redeploy the new version. Alternately, if the only change is a change to a JSP, you can simply copy the new JSP to the appropriate location in the application directory under webapps. Tomcat will automatically detect the new JSP, translate and compile it, and use it for the next request for that JSP.

# Summary

This chapter has covered a very large subject area in a very short space. It is intended as an overview, and you are encouraged to explore more detailed texts on the subjects that it contains. You've seen that the Java Servlet API allows you to build platform-independent server-side Java components to handle user requests. You've also seen that servlets are protocol-independent but that they can be developed for specific protocols, particularly HTTP.

You've also looked at the deployment of servlet-based web applications, with particular attention paid to the deployment descriptor. You've seen how the deployment descriptor describes servlets to the container. You've learned about the new deployment-descriptor elements that support the configuration of JSP 2.1 pages. These elements provide the ability to enable and disable the EL and scripting as well as the ability to automatically include other pages at the start and end of a group of JSP pages.

# CHAPTER 3

■■■

# The JavaServer Pages
# Expression Language

**O**ne of the features of the JSP specification that you'll be using most often is the **JSP expression language**, an intentionally simple language that is, to a large extent, independent from JSP.

In previous incarnations of JSP, Java code was embedded into JSP pages in the form of scriptlets, for example:

```
<%
  MyBean bean = new MyBean();
  String name = bean.getName();
  out.println(name);
%>
```

This scriptlet creates a new instance of a class called MyBean, gets its name property, assigns this to a string variable, and then outputs this string to the page. Now you might be looking at this and thinking, "I can achieve the same thing by using the JSP standard actions (<useBean> and <getProperty>)."

Although this is certainly true, it was previously extremely hard to write a function-rich JSP-based web application without using a number of scriptlets within your pages. In fact, there are many problems associated with using Java code in the form of scriptlets in JSP pages. The first and most obvious of these is that it's very common for non-Java programmers to create the user interface for a system. This is because graphic designers are generally better than Java programmers at creating functional user interfaces. The second problem caused by the use of scriptlets is that of maintainability. Embedding large amounts of code into the user interface of a system makes the interface much harder to change and understand.

For all of these reasons, the JSP 2.0 specification introduced an expression language (EL) that can do pretty much everything that scriptlets can do. This language is far simpler to understand than Java and looks very similar to JavaScript. The following are good reasons for this similarity:

- JavaScript is something that most page authors are already familiar with.

- The EL is inspired by ECMAScript, which is the standardized version of JavaScript.

In fact, both ECMAScript and the XPath EL inspired the JSP EL. The EL specification states, "... the experts involved were very reluctant to design yet another expression language and tried to use each of these languages, but they fell short in different areas."

If you've been following the progress of JSP, and the JSP Standard Tag Library (JSTL), you're probably aware that the first expression language was released as part of the JSTL. The EL was then incorporated into the JSP 2.0 specification with JSTL 1.1.

At around the same time, the JavaServer Faces (JSF) expert group was developing an expression language for JSF. Because of JSF requirements, the JSF expression language had some differences from the JSP expression language. JSP 2.1 unifies the two versions so that there is a single expression language used for JSP, JSTL, and JSF.

In this chapter, you'll learn the following:

- The syntax and usage of the EL, including reserved words, disabling scriptlets in a page, and disabling the evaluation of the EL on a page or set of pages

- The operators within the EL, including arithmetic operators, comparison operators, logical operators, and other operators

- The use of JavaBeans with the EL

- The implicit objects within the EL

- The declaration and use of functions in the EL

# The Syntax and Use of the Expression Language

In this section, you'll look at the syntax of the EL, see how to use it on a JSP page, and learn the reserved words of the language. After you've looked at the basics, you'll move on to look at how and why you might disable the EL and Java scriptlets within a page or set of pages.

## Basic Syntax

No matter where the EL is used, it's always invoked in a consistent manner, via the construct ${expr} or #{expr}, where expr is the EL expression that you wish to have evaluated.

In the EL 2.1 specification, the syntax of ${expr} and #{expr} are equivalent and can be used interchangeably. However, when used with some other Java Platform, Enterprise Edition API, the other API may enforce restrictions on the use of ${expr} and #{expr}. Specifically, when used with JSP pages, the two forms cannot be used interchangeably. Within a JSP page, ${expr} is used for expressions that are evaluated immediately, whereas #{expr} is used for expressions for which evaluation is deferred. Deferred expressions are used with custom actions, which you will look at in Chapters 6 and 7.

A simple use of the EL is shown here. This piece of code creates a JavaBean and outputs its name property:

```
<jsp:useBean id="bean" class="MyBean"/>
${bean.name}
```

We'll discuss the detailed syntax of JavaBeans later in the "JavaBeans and the Expression Language" section.

Note that in the previous example you used the `<useBean>` standard action to create the object. This is the recommended way to do this, rather than instantiating the object in a scriptlet.

## Literals

Just as in any programming language, the EL provides several literals for developers to use. A literal can be of a Boolean, integer, floating point, string, or null type. The following are valid values for each literal type:

- **Boolean:** `true` or `false`.

- **Integer**: This is limited to values defined by the `IntegerLiteral` regular expression as follows:

```
IntegerLiteral ::= ['0'-'9']+
```

This regular expression says that an integer is any sequence of digits using the digits from 0 to 9. The specification also allows an integer literal to be preceded by a unary "-" symbol to form negative integer literals. For example, the following are valid integers:

```
-102
 0
 21
 21234
```

- **Floating point**: This is defined by the following `FloatingPointLiteral` expression:

```
FloatingPointLiteral ::= ((['0'-'9'])+ '.' (['0'-'9'])* Exponent?
                        | '.' (['0'-'9'])+ Exponent?
                        | (['0'-'9'])+ Exponent?
Exponent ::= ['e','E'] (['+','-'])? (['0'-'9'])+
```

This expression is more complex. As with integer literals, a floating-point literal can be preceded by a unary "-" symbol to produce negative floating-point literals. To help you understand this, here are some valid floating-point literals:

```
-1.09
-1.003
 1.0E10
 1.
-10.0
 0.1
```

- **String**: A string is any sequence of characters delimited with either single or double quotes. For example, `"a string"` and `'a string'` are both valid; however, `"as'` and `'as"` are not valid. If you want to represent quotes within a string, then you can use `\"` for double quotes, or `\'` for single quotes. Alternately, if the string is delimited by double quotes, you can use single quotes within the string without escaping the single quotes, and vice versa. To represent a `\` in a string, you use the escape sequence `\\`.

- **Null**: You can represent null by using the literal `null`.

# Default Values and the Expression Language

Experience suggests that it's most important to be able to provide as good a presentation as possible, even when there are simple errors in the page. To meet this requirement, the EL does not provide warnings, just "default values" and "errors." Default values are type-correct values that are assigned to a subexpression when there is a problem, and errors are exceptions to be thrown (and then handled by the standard JSP error-handling process). An example of such a default value is 'infinity'. This value is assigned to an expression that results in a divide by zero. For example, the following piece of EL will display infinity rather than causing an error:

```
${2/0}
```

The equivalent Java expression would throw an ArithmeticException.

# Using the Expression Language

You can use the EL in the same places as you would have used a scriptlet, for example:

- Within attribute values for JSP standard and custom tags

- Within template text (that is, in the body of the page)

### Using the Expression Language Within Custom Tags

Using the EL within the attributes of a custom tag in a JSP page allows you to dynamically specify the attribute values for a custom tag. This is an extremely powerful mechanism. The following code snippet shows how you might dynamically specify an attribute to a custom tag by using a scriptlet:

```
<myTagLibrary:myTag counter="<%= 1+1 %>" />
```

To achieve this dynamic behavior prior to the JSP 2.0 specification, you had to use scriptlets. As we've discussed, scriptlets are untidy and cause all sorts of problems with readability and maintainability. By using an EL statement, you can dynamically provide the values to a custom tag's attribute. If you were to repeat the previous tag example by using the EL, you would see that the code is much neater:

```
<myTagLibrary:myTag counter="${1+1}" />
```

You can see that the value 1+1 is being passed to the custom tag as an attribute named counter. The details of the creation of custom tags are discussed at length in Chapters 6 through 8.

You'll look at more advanced use of the language with JavaBeans, arithmetic, and comparisons later in this chapter.

### Using the Expression Language Within JSP Template Text

Now that you've seen how the EL can be used to provide the values of custom tag attributes, you'll learn how you can use the EL within the body of a JSP page so that you can produce dynamic content. Listing 3-1 shows an example of a JSP page with some dynamic content generated by the EL. This page displays the value of a parameter (passed to the page) called name. The user is then given a text field in which to enter a new name, and a button to submit the name back to the page for another greeting.

**Listing 3-1.** *templateText.jsp*

```
<html>
  <head>
    <title>EL and Template Text</title>
    <style>
      body, td {font-family:verdana;font-size:10pt;}
    </style>
  <head>
  <body>
    <h2>EL and Template Text</h2>
    <table border="1">
      <tr>
        <td colspan="2">Hello ${param['name']}</td>
      </tr>
      <tr>
        <form action="templateText.jsp" method="post">
          <td><input type="text" name="name"></td>
          <td><input type="submit"></td>
        </form>
      </tr>
    </table>
  </body>
</html>
```

To run this example, you need to deploy it into a JSP 2.0– or JSP 2.1–compliant web container. As with all examples in this book, we will be using Tomcat 5.5, so you'll need to create the deployment descriptor shown in Listing 3-2.

**Listing 3-2.** *web.xml*

```
<?xml version="1.0" encoding="ISO-8859-1"?>
<web-app xmlns="http://java.sun.com/xml/ns/javaee"
         xmlns:xsi="http://www.w3.org/2001/XMLSchema-instance"
         xsi:schemaLocation= ➥
"http://java.sun.com/xml/ns/javaee/web-app_2_5.xsd"
         version="2.5">

</web-app>
```

Here is the complete list of steps needed to create, deploy, and run this example:

1. Create the directory %TOMCAT_HOME%\webapps\expressionLanguage\WEB-INF.

2. Create the web.xml file shown in Listing 3-2. Save it to the webapps\expressionLanguage\ WEB-INF folder.

3. Create the JSP page in Listing 3-1 and save it to the `webapps\expressionLanguage` folder.

4. Start Tomcat, if needed, open your web browser, and go to `http://localhost:8080/expressionLanguage/templateText.jsp`.

Figure 3-1 shows the page that should appear in the web browser.

**Figure 3-1.** *The templateText.jsp displays the value submitted by the user.*

As you can see, this page is a very simple, personalized greeting. When the page first loads, there will be no request parameter, so the greeting will be only the word "Hello." When the Submit Query button is clicked, the request is submitted with the parameter name. The JSP page accesses this parameter and uses an EL statement to print the greeting. You'll look at how the request variable is accessed later, in the "Expression-Language Implicit Objects" section. For now, try entering different values within the text box and clicking Submit Query.

## Reserved Words

As with any other language, the JSP EL has many words that are reserved. A reserved word (also known as a keyword) is one that has a special meaning within the language. This means that you cannot use the reserved word to represent anything else, such as a variable identifier. The following are reserved words in the JSP EL:

and

eq

gt

true

instanceof

or

ne

lt

false

empty

not

if

ge

null

div

mod

It's worth noting that not all of these words are currently in the language, but they may be in the future, and developers should avoid using them. You'll see examples of using the majority of the reserved words during the course of this chapter.

## Disabling Scriptlets

As we've mentioned, the EL is intended to replace the use of Java scriptlets in developing JSP-based web applications. To this end, it's possible to disable the evaluation of scriptlets through configuration parameters. This allows a developer to ensure that no one inadvertently uses scriptlets instead of the EL. This can allow best practices to be more easily enforced.

You can disable scriptlets within a page using the web.xml deployment descriptor by choosing to disable evaluation for a single page, a set of pages, or for the entire application.

The tags that you need to add to the deployment descriptor are within the <jsp-config> element. The following example disables scriptlets for all JSP pages within an application:

```
<jsp-config>
  <jsp-property-group>
    <url-pattern>*.jsp</url-pattern>
    <scripting-invalid>true</scripting-invalid>
  </jsp-property-group>
</jsp-config>
```

The <url-pattern> element can represent a single page, for example:

```
<jsp-config>
  <jsp-property-group>
    <url-pattern>/test.jsp</url-pattern>
    <scripting-invalid>true</scripting-invalid>
  </jsp-property-group>
</jsp-config>
```

It can also represent a set of pages, for example:

```
<jsp-config>
  <jsp-property-group>
    <url-pattern>/noscriptlets/</url-pattern>
    <scripting-invalid>true</scripting-invalid>
  </jsp-property-group>
</jsp-config>
```

## Disabling the Expression Language

Just as you can disable scriptlets within a page, you can also disable the evaluation of the EL. In previous versions of JSP, the characters ${ had no special meaning; therefore, it's possible that people have used them in their JSP pages. If you were to try to deploy these pages on a JSP 2.0– or JSP 2.1–compliant web container, you would get errors. Figure 3-2 shows the kind of error that you could expect to see.

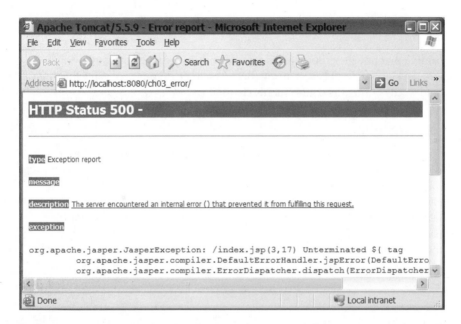

**Figure 3-2.** *A page implemented under an earlier JSP specification may use the characters ${, resulting in an error when the same page is used in a JSP 2.0 or later container.*

It's worth noting that if a web application is deployed by using a Servlet 2.3 deployment descriptor (that is, one that conforms to the 2.3 Document Type Definition, http://java.sun.com/dtd/web-app_2_3.dtd), then the evaluation of the EL is automatically deactivated. This is to reduce the chance that an error will occur when a web container is upgraded. Conversely, if a web application is deployed with a Servlet 2.4 or Servlet 2.5 deployment descriptor (that is, the web application conforms to the 2.4 XML Schema, http://java.sun.com/xml/ns/j2ee/web-app_2_4.xsd, or to the 2.5 XML Schema, http://java.sun.com/xml/ns/javaee/web-app_2_5.xsd), then the EL is enabled by default.

You can disable EL evaluation in two ways:

- Individually on each page by using the page directive

- Within the web.xml file by using a JSP configuration element

To disable the EL for a single page, it's simplest to use the isELIgnored attribute of the page directive in the header of the page:

```
<%@ page isELIgnored="true" %>
```

If you choose to disable evaluation within the web.xml file, you can disable for a single page, a set of pages, or the entire application. The following XML example shows how you might disable the EL for an entire application:

```
<jsp-property-group>
  <url-pattern>*.jsp</url-pattern>
  <el-ignored>true</el-ignored>
</jsp-property-group>
```

To disable the evaluation of the EL for a single page within the deployment descriptor, you can use an XML fragment similar to the following:

```
<jsp-property-group>
  <url-pattern>noel.jsp</url-pattern>
  <el-ignored>true</el-ignored>
</jsp-property-group>
```

To disable the evaluation of the EL for a set of pages within the deployment descriptor, you can use an XML fragment similar to the following:

```
<jsp-property-group>
  <url-pattern>/noel/</url-pattern>
  <el-ignored>true</el-ignored>
</jsp-property-group>
```

If you try to use the EL after you've disabled it, you won't see any errors and the ${expr} expression within the JSP page will appear unaltered in the final output.

# Arithmetic Evaluation Using the Expression Language

Now that you've examined the basic syntax of the EL and where it can be used, you'll look at some specific uses of the language. The first of these is using the EL to evaluate arithmetic operations. There are many cases within web-application development where you need to perform some mathematics on a page. This might be to show a number within the text of a page or to pass a number to a custom tag. In either case, the concepts are exactly the same.

Arithmetic operators are provided to act on both integer and floating-point values. There are six operators that you can use and combine to achieve the vast majority of mathematical calculations with ease:

- Addition: +

- Subtraction: -

- Multiplication: *

- Exponents: E

- Division: / or div

- Modulus: % or mod

The last two operators are presented with two alternative syntaxes (both will produce exactly the same result). This is so that the EL is consistent with both the XPath and ECMAScript syntaxes. You can use all the operators in a binary fashion (that is, with two arguments, such as 2 + 3) and the subtraction operator to represent the unary minus (that is, -4 + -2).

As you would expect, each operator has a precedence that determines the order of evaluation of an expression. This precedence is as follows:

- ()

- - (unary)

- * / div mod %

- + - (binary)

You'll update this list when you look at the comparison operators in the next section. You can, of course, use parentheses to change the order of evaluation, as these take the highest precedence.

With operators of equal precedence, the expression is evaluated from left to right, for example:

```
2 * 5 mod 3
```

is equivalent to (2 * 5) mod 3, which evaluates to 1—rather than 2 * (5 mod 3), which evaluates to 4.

Listing 3-3 is a JSP page that shows an example of all the operators in action.

**Listing 3-3.** *arithmetic.jsp*

```
<html>
<head>
  <title>Arithmetic</title>
  <style>
    body, td {font-family:verdana;font-size:10pt;}
  </style>
</head>
<body>
  <h2>EL Arithmetic</h2>
  <table border="1">
    <tr>
      <td><b>Concept</b></td>
      <td><b>EL Expression</b></td>
      <td><b>Result</b></td>
    </tr>
    <tr>
      <td>Literal</td>
      <td>${'${'}10</td>
      <td>${10}</td>
    </tr>
    <tr>
      <td>Addition</td>
```

```
    <td>${'${'}10 + 10 }</td>
    <td>${10 + 10}</td>
  </tr>
  <tr>
    <td>Subtraction</td>
    <td>${'${'}10 - 10 }</td>
    <td>${10 - 10}</td>
  </tr>
  <tr>
    <td>Multiplication</td>
    <td>${'${'}10 * 10 }</td>
    <td>${10 * 10}</td>
  </tr>
  <tr>
    <td>Division / </td>
    <td>${'${'}10 / 3 }</td>
    <td>${10 / 3}</td>
  </tr>
  <tr>
    <td>Division DIV</td>
    <td>${'${'}10 div 3 }</td>
    <td>${10 div 3}</td>
  </tr>
  <tr>
    <td>Modulus</td>
    <td>${'${'}10 % 3 }</td>
    <td>${10 % 3}</td>
  </tr>
  <tr>
    <td>Modulus</td>
    <td>${'${'}10 mod 3 }</td>
    <td>${10 mod 3}</td>
  </tr>
  <tr>
    <td>Precedence</td>
    <td>${'${'}2 * 5 mod 3 }</td>
    <td>${2 * 5 mod 3}</td>
  </tr>
  <tr>
    <td>Precedence with parens</td>
    <td>${'${'}2 * (5 mod 3) }</td>
    <td>${2 * (5 mod 3)}</td>
  </tr>
  <tr>
    <td>Division by Zero</td>
    <td>${'${'}10 / 0 }</td>
    <td>${10 / 0}</td>
  </tr>
```

```
    <tr>
      <td>Exponential</td>
      <td>${'${'}2E2}</td>
      <td>${2E2}</td>
    </tr>
    <tr>
      <td>Unary Minus</td>
      <td>${'${'}-10}</td>
      <td>${-10}</td>
    </tr>
  </table>
</body>
</html>
```

To run this example, you need to deploy it into a JSP 2.0– or JSP 2.1–compliant web container just as you did earlier:

1. Copy the JSP page in Listing 3-3 to the %TOMCAT_HOME%\webapps\expressionLanguage directory.

2. Start Tomcat, if needed, open your web browser, and go to http://localhost:8080/expressionLanguage/arithmetic.jsp.

Figure 3-3 shows the output of the JSP page.

| Concept | EL Expression | Result |
| --- | --- | --- |
| Literal | ${10} | 10 |
| Addition | ${10 + 10 } | 20 |
| Subtraction | ${10 - 10 } | 0 |
| Multiplication | ${10 * 10 } | 100 |
| Division / | ${10 / 3 } | 3.3333333333333335 |
| Division DIV | ${10 div 3 } | 3.3333333333333335 |
| Modulus | ${10 % 3 } | 1 |
| Modulus | ${10 mod 3 } | 1 |
| Precedence | ${2 * 5 mod 3 } | 1 |
| Precedence with parens | ${2 * (5 mod 3) } | 4 |
| Division by Zero | ${10 / 0 } | Infinity |
| Exponential | ${2E2} | 200.0 |
| Unary Minus | ${-10} | -10 |

**Figure 3-3.** *The arithemetic operators allow you to perform many basic math operations in a JSP page.*

All that this JSP page does is print out the result of the expression next to the expression itself. It also demonstrates an interesting technique: that of displaying the ${ characters on a JSP page. This is easily achieved by embedding the literal '${' in an EL statement. For example, to show the string ${2+3} on a JSP page, you can use the following expression:

```
${'${'}2 + 3 }
```

You may be thinking that the operators that are provided are not powerful enough. For example, where is the square-root operator? Advanced operators are deliberately not provided to the JSP developer because advanced calculations should not be done in a page. They should either be done in the controller layer of the application, or by using view-helper components such as custom tags or EL functions (see the "Expression-Language Functions" section later in this chapter).

# Comparisons in the Expression Language

Another useful feature of the EL is the ability to perform comparisons, either between numbers or objects. This feature is used primarily for the values of custom tag attributes, but can equally be used to write out the result of a comparison (true or false) to the JSP page. The EL provides the following comparison operators:

- == or eq
- != or ne
- < or lt
- > or gt
- <= or le
- >= or ge

The second version of each operator exists to avoid having to use entity references in JSP XML syntax; however, the behavior of the operators is the same.

In the JSP page in Listing 3-4, you can see the comparison operators in use.

**Listing 3-4.** *conditions.jsp*

```
<html>
<head>
  <title>EL Conditions</title>
  <style>
    body, td {font-family:verdana;font-size:10pt;}
  </style>
</head>
<body>
  <h2>EL Conditions</h2>
  <table border="1">
    <tr>
      <td><b>Concept</b></td>
```

```
        <td><b>EL Condition</b></td>
        <td><b>Result</b></td>
      </tr>
      <tr>
        <td>Numeric less than</td>
        <td>${'${'}1 &lt; 2}</td>
        <td>${1 < 2}</td>
      </tr>
      <tr>
        <td>Numeric greater than</td>
        <td>${'${'}1 &gt; 2}</td>
        <td>${1 > 2}</td>
      </tr>
      <tr>
        <td>Numeric less than</td>
        <td>${'${'}1 lt 2}</td>
        <td>${1 lt 2}</td>
      </tr>
      <tr>
        <td>Numeric greater than</td>
        <td>${'${'}1 gt 2}</td>
        <td>${1 gt 2}</td>
      </tr>
      <tr>
        <td>Numeric Greater than or equal</td>
        <td>${'${'}1 &gt;= 1}</td>
        <td>${1 >= 1}</td>
      </tr>
      <tr>
        <td>Numeric Less than or equal</td>
        <td>${'${'}1 &lt;= 1}</td>
        <td>${1 <= 1}</td>
      </tr>
      <tr>
        <td>Numeric less than or equal</td>
        <td>${'${'}1 le 1}</td>
        <td>${1 le 1}</td>
      </tr>
      <tr>
        <td>Numeric greater than or equal</td>
        <td>${'${'}1 ge 1}</td>
        <td>${1 ge 1}</td>
      </tr>
      <tr>
        <td>Numeric equal to</td>
```

```
      <td>${'${'}1 == 1}</td>
      <td>${1 == 1}</td>
    </tr>
    <tr>
      <td>Numeric equal to</td>
      <td>${'${'}1 eq 1}</td>
      <td>${1 eq 1}</td>
    </tr>
    <tr>
      <td>Numeric not equal to</td>
      <td>${'${'}1 != 2}</td>
      <td>${1 != 2}</td>
    </tr>
    <tr>
      <td>Numeric not equal to</td>
      <td>${'${'}1 ne 2}</td>
      <td>${1 ne 2}</td>
    </tr>
    <tr>
      <td>Alphabetic less than</td>
      <td>${'${'}'abe' &lt; 'ade'}</td>
      <td>${'abe' < 'ade'}</td>
    </tr>
    <tr>
      <td>Alphabetic greater than</td>
      <td>${'${'}'abe' &gt; 'ade'}</td>
      <td>${'abe' > 'ade'}</td>
    </tr>
    <tr>
      <td>Alphabetic equal to</td>
      <td>${'${'}'abe' eq 'abe'}</td>
      <td>${'abe' eq 'abe'}</td>
    </tr>
    <tr>
      <td>Alphabetic not equal to</td>
      <td>${'${'}'abe' ne 'ade'}</td>
      <td>${'abe' ne 'ade'}</td>
    </tr>
  </table>
  </body>
</html>
```

Again, you'll deploy the JSP page into a JSP 2.0– or JSP 2.1–compliant web container. Here is the list of steps to create, deploy, and run the JSP page:

1. Enter the JSP code in Listing 3-4 into a file called conditions.jsp and save it to the expressionLanguage folder.

**2.** Start Tomcat, open your web browser, and go to `http://localhost:8080/` `expressionLanguage/conditions.jsp`.

Figure 3-4 shows the web page generated by this JSP page.

**Figure 3-4.** *Conditional operators can be used to compare operators in a JSP page.*

You are now in a position to update your precedence table from the previous section with the comparison operators. Again, parentheses can be used to alter the order of evaluation, and identical precedence operators are evaluated from left to right as follows:

- ()

- - (unary)

- * / div mod %

- + - (binary)

- < > <= >= lt gt le ge

- == != eq ne

# Logical Operators in the Expression Language

The EL also enables you to perform logical operations on Boolean arguments. The logical operators are as follows:

- && or and

- || or or

- ! or not

Once again, there are alternatives for each of the operators.

If either of the arguments is not Boolean, an attempt will be made to convert them to Boolean; if this is not possible, an error will occur.

Listing 3-5 shows some examples of the logical operators in action.

**Listing 3-5.** *logic.jsp*

```
<html>
<head>
  <title>EL Logic</title>
  <style>
    body, td {font-family:verdana;font-size:10pt;}
  </style>
</head>
<body>
  <h2>EL Logic</h2>
  <table border="1">
    <tr>
      <td><b>Concept</b></td>
      <td><b>EL Expression</b></td>
      <td><b>Result</b></td>
    </tr>
    <tr>
      <td>And</td>
      <td>${'${'}true and true}</td>
      <td>${true and true}</td>
    </tr>
    <tr>
      <td>And</td>
      <td>${'${'}true && false}</td>
      <td>${true && false}</td>
    </tr>
    <tr>
      <td>Or</td>
      <td>${'${'}true or true}</td>
      <td>${true or false}</td>
    </tr>
```

```
        <tr>
          <td>Or</td>
          <td>${'${'}true || false}</td>
          <td>${true || false}</td>
        </tr>
        <tr>
          <td>Not</td>
          <td>${'${'}not true}</td>
          <td>${not true}</td>
        </tr>
        <tr>
          <td>Not</td>
          <td>${'${'}!false}</td>
          <td>${!false}</td>
        </tr>
      </table>
  </body>
</html>
```

Once again, you'll run this example by deploying it in a web container:

1. Enter the JSP code in Listing 3-5 into a file called logic.jsp and save it to the expressionLanguage folder.

2. Start Tomcat and go to http://localhost:8080/expressionLanguage/logic.jsp.

Figure 3-5 shows the web page generated by this JSP page.

**Figure 3-5.** *Logical operators can be used with Boolean arguments in a JSP page.*

# Other Operators

Besides the arithmetic, comparison, and logical operators that you've seen so far, several other operators are available to developers using the EL. These operators are mainly related to objects. A property or method of an object can be accessed by using either the . (dot) or [ ] (bracket) operator, which is deliberate in order to align the language with ECMAScript. For example, obj.property is equivalent to obj["property"].

This syntax is also used to access the items within maps, lists, or arrays. For example, to access the item in a map with the key "sam", you could use myMap["sam"] or myMap.sam.

The final operator that you'll look at is the empty operator. The empty operator is a prefix operator that can be used to determine if a value is null or empty. To evaluate the expression empty A, the EL implementation code first checks whether A is null. If A is null, the expression evaluates to true. If A is an empty string, array, map, or an empty list, then the expression also evaluates to true. If A is not null or empty, the expression evaluates to false.

Now that you've seen all the available operators, you can again update your precedence table to include these new operators:

- [ ]

- ( )

- - (unary) not ! empty

- * / div % mod

- + - (binary)

- < > <= >= lt gt le ge

- == != eq ne

- && and

- || or

You'll see much more about these operators in our discussion of using the EL with JavaBeans in the next section.

# JavaBeans and the Expression Language

So far you've looked at the syntax of the EL. This in itself is not very useful when creating web applications. In this section, you'll focus on how to use the EL to read values from JavaBeans to display within a JSP page. In previous incarnations of the JSP specification, you would have had to use code such as the following to read values from a JavaBean:

```
<jsp:getProperty name="myBean" property="name" />
```

An alternative (and more common) method is to use a scriptlet such as the following:

```
<%= myBean.getName()%>
```

As we've discussed, the use of scriptlets does not represent good practice in JSP development. This may make you ask the question, "If I can use the `<getProperty>` standard action, why does anyone use scriptlets?" The answer to this question is simple: We developers are lazy! The scriptlet option represents less code and is a lot quicker to type!

To get around this problem, the EL provides a nice way to access the properties of a JavaBean that is in scope within a page, request, session, or application. To achieve the same as the previous code sample, you can use the following expression:

`${myBean.name}`

This is a nice neat way to access properties; there are no nasty brackets or any other Java-like syntax present. This brings us to another core feature of the EL: the concept of named variables. The EL provides a generalized mechanism for resolving variable names into objects. This mechanism has the same behavior as the `pageContext.findAttribute()` method of the `PageContext` object. Take the following, for example:

`${product}`

This expression will look for the attribute named `product` by searching the page, request, session, and application scopes, in that order, and will print its value. This works regardless of how the object was placed into the particular scope. That is, one JSP page could put an attribute into request, session, or application scope, and another JSP page could access the attribute simply by using an EL statement that uses the name of the attribute. If the attribute is not found, `null` will be returned. This method is also used to resolve the implicit objects that we'll talk about in the next section.

Listing 3-6 is a JSP page that uses EL to access JavaBeans.

**Listing 3-6.** *simpleBean.jsp*

```
<jsp:useBean id="person" class="com.apress.projsp.Person" scope="request">
  <jsp:setProperty name="person" property="*"/>
</jsp:useBean>
<html>
  <head>
    <title>EL and Simple JavaBeans</title>
    <style>
      body, td {font-family:verdana;font-size:10pt;}
    </style>
  <head>
  <body>
    <h2>EL and Simple JavaBeans</h2>
    <table border="1">
      <tr>
        <td>${person.name}</td>
        <td>${person.age}</td>
        <td> </td>
      </tr>
      <tr>
        <form action="simpleBean.jsp" method="post">
```

```
        <td><input type="text" name="name"></td>
        <td><input type="text" name="age"></td>
        <td><input type="submit"></td>
      </form>
    <tr>
  </table>
 </body>
</html>
```

The JSP page in Listing 3-6 uses a JavaBean of type `com.apress.projsp.Person`. That JavaBean is shown in Listing 3-7.

**Listing 3-7.** *Person.java*

```
package com.apress.projsp;
public class Person {
    private String name;
    private int age;
    public Person() {
        setName("A N Other");
        setAge(21);
    }
    public void setName(String name) {
        this.name = name;
    }
    public String getName() {
        return name;
    }
    public void setAge(int age) {
        this.age = age;
    }
    public int getAge() {
        return age;
    }
}
```

Use the following steps to deploy the JSP page and JavaBean into a web container:

1. Create a file called `simpleBean.jsp` in the `expressionLanguage` folder, and enter the code from Listing 3-6 into it.

2. Inside the `expressionLanguage\WEB-INF` directory, create a directory called `classes`.

3. Create a `com\apress\projsp` subdirectory within the `WEB-INF\classes` directory.

4. Create a file called `Person.java` within the `WEB-INF\classes\com\apress\projsp` directory with the contents shown in Listing 3-7, and compile it.

5. Start Tomcat and your web browser and go to `http://localhost:8080/expressionLanguage/simpleBean.jsp`.

You should see something similar to the page shown in Figure 3-6.

**Figure 3-6.** *EL can be used to access JavaBeans and the properties of JavaBeans.*

The JSP page in Listing 3-6 creates a JavaBean of type `com.apress.projsp.Person` with an id of `person`, and sets its properties to the values of parameters in the HTTP request with the same name as the properties. This is achieved with the following code:

```
<jsp:useBean id="person" class="com.apress.projsp.Person" scope="request">
  <jsp:setProperty name="person" property="*"/>
</jsp:useBean>
```

The `<jsp:setProperty>` tag has various syntaxes. When you use `property="*"`, that tells the page implementation class to find each request parameter with the same name as a JavaBean property, and to set the JavaBean property with the value of the request parameter.

The JSP page accesses the object via the `id` given to it in the previous `<useBean>` tag, in this case, `person`. The page then displays the values of the properties of the `Person` JavaBean in a table; this is achieved by the following code:

```
<tr>
  <td>${person.name}<td>
  <td>${person.age}</td>
  <td> </td>
</tr>
```

The `id` is used to access the JavaBean that you declared with the previous `<useBean>` tag. In this example, the object was created and accessed within the same page. However, as we noted earlier, the object could have been created from any page, and still accessed in the `simpleBean.jsp` page.

It's worth noting that you could have used the following code to access the properties of our JavaBean:

```
<tr>
  <td>${person["name"]}</td>
```

```
<td>${person["age"]}</td>
<td> </td>
</tr>
```

Try changing the values in the form and clicking Submit Query. You should see your new values in the table. Now that you've seen a very simple use of JavaBeans and the EL, you'll look at a more complex use of the two technologies.

## Nested Properties of a JavaBean

The EL provides you with a simple mechanism to access nested properties of a JavaBean. For example, Listing 3-8 shows a JavaBean, which has a nested property of type Address (Listing 3-9).

**Listing 3-8.** *Person.java*

```java
package com.apress.projsp;

public class Person {
  private String name;
  private int age;
  private Address address;

  public Person() {
    setName("A N Other");
    setAge(21);

    this.address = new Address();
  }
  public void setName(String name) {
    this.name = name;
  }
  public String getName() {
    return name;
  }
  public void setAge(int age) {
    this.age = age;
  }
  public int getAge() {
    return age;
  }
  public void setAddress(Address address) {
    this.address = address;
  }
  public Address getAddress() {
    return address;
  }
}
```

As you can see, this JavaBean has a property that is in fact another JavaBean—the Address JavaBean (Address.java). Listing 3-9 shows the Address JavaBean.

**Listing 3-9.** *Address.java*

```java
package com.apress.projsp;
import java.util.Collection;
public class Address {
  private String line1;
  private String town;
  private String county;
  private String postcode;
  private Collection phoneNumbers;
  public Address() {
    this.line1 = "line1";
    this.town = "a town2";
    this.county = "a county";
    this.postcode = "postcode";
  }
  public void setLine1(String line1) {
    this.line1 = line1;
  }

  public String getLine1() {
    return line1;
  }
  public void setTown(String town) {
    this.town = town;
  }
  public String getTown() {
    return town;
  }
  public void setCounty(String county) {
    this.county = county;
  }
  public String getCounty() {
    return county;
  }
  public void setPostcode(String postcode) {
    this.postcode = postcode;
  }
  public String getPostcode() {
    return postcode;
  }
  public Collection getPhoneNumbers() {
    return phoneNumbers;
```

```
  }
  public void setPhoneNumbers(Collection phoneNumbers) {
    this.phoneNumbers = phoneNumbers;
  }
}
```

It's simple to access these nested properties by using the EL. With the EL, you can chain the various objects and properties in an EL statement. The following JSP snippet shows how you could use chaining to access the line1 property of the address property of the person JavaBean.

```
${person.address.line1}
```

The Address JavaBean contains a collection of other JavaBeans as one of its properties. Although you can't see it in Listing 3-9, this collection is a collection of JavaBeans—PhoneNumber JavaBeans. This JavaBean is shown in Listing 3-10.

**Listing 3-10.** *PhoneNumber.java*

```
package com.apress.projsp;
public class PhoneNumber {
  private String std;
  private String number;

  public String getNumber() {
    return number;
  }
  public String getStd() {
    return std;
  }
  public void setNumber(String number) {
    this.number = number;
  }
  public void setStd(String std) {
    this.std = std;
  }
}
```

The EL also provides a simple mechanism for accessing such collections and the properties of their enclosed JavaBeans. The following JSP snippet would access the first phone number for a person's address:

```
${person.address.phoneNumbers[1].number}
```

As this snippet shows, you can freely mix both dot and bracket notation as needed to access JavaBean properties.

We can bring this whole discussion together by way of the following example. Listing 3-11 shows a JSP page that displays all the details relating to a person and that person's address. Note how the JSP page uses alternative syntaxes for object property access.

**Listing 3-11.** *complexBean.jsp*

```
<html>
<head>
  <title>EL and Complex JavaBeans</title>
  <style>
    body, td {font-family:verdana;font-size:10pt;}
  </style>
</head>
<body>
  <h2>EL and Complex JavaBeans</h2>
  <table border="1">
    <tr>
      <td>${person.name}</td>
      <td>${person.age}</td>
      <td>${person["address"].line1}</td>
      <td>${person["address"].town}</td>
      <td>${person.address.phoneNumbers[0].std}
          ${person.address.phoneNumbers[0].number}</td>
      <td>${person.address.phoneNumbers[1].std}
          ${person.address.phoneNumbers[1].number}</td>
    </tr>
  </table>
</body>
</html>
```

Unlike previous examples where you loaded the JSP page directly, this example uses a simple Java servlet (Listing 3-12) to set up the information within the JavaBeans. The servlet then adds the object to the request by using the name "person." The JSP page, as mentioned earlier, searches the various scopes to find the JavaBean with the name used in the EL statement.

Listing 3-12, PopulateServlet.java, is the servlet that initializes the various JavaBeans and then uses a RequestDispatcher to forward the request to complexBean.jsp. To compile this class, you'll need to include a servlet library in the CLASSPATH. If you are using Tomcat 5, you can find the library, servlet-api.jar, in the common\lib directory. If you are using some other web container, check your container documentation for the correct servlet library to include.

**Listing 3-12.** *PopulateServlet.java*

```
package com.apress.projsp;
import java.io.IOException;
import java.util.ArrayList;
import javax.servlet.RequestDispatcher;
import javax.servlet.ServletException;
import javax.servlet.http.HttpServlet;
import javax.servlet.http.HttpServletRequest;
import javax.servlet.http.HttpServletResponse;
public class PopulateServlet extends HttpServlet {
```

```
protected void doGet(HttpServletRequest req, HttpServletResponse res)
  throws ServletException, IOException
{

  Person p = new Person();
  p.setName("Sam Dalton");
  p.setAge(26);
  Address a = new Address();
  a.setLine1("221b Baker Street");
  a.setTown("London");
  a.setCounty("Greater London");
  a.setPostcode("NW1 1AA");
  ArrayList al = new ArrayList();
  PhoneNumber ph = new PhoneNumber();
  ph.setStd("01895");
  ph.setStd("678901");
  al.add(ph);

  ph = new PhoneNumber();
  ph.setStd("0208");
  ph.setStd("8654789");
  al.add(ph);
  a.setPhoneNumbers(al);
  p.setAddress(a);
  req.setAttribute("person", p);
  RequestDispatcher rd = req.getRequestDispatcher("complexBean.jsp");
  rd.forward(req, res);
  }
}
```

This servlet class should be placed within the WEB-INF\classes\com\apress\projsp folder. You'll also need to modify the WEB-INF\web.xml file to contain the additional tags in Listing 3-13.

**Listing 3-13.** *web.xml*

```
<?xml version="1.0" encoding="ISO-8859-1"?>
<web-app xmlns="http://java.sun.com/xml/ns/javaee"
         xmlns:xsi="http://www.w3.org/2001/XMLSchema-instance"
         xsi:schemaLocation= ➥
"http://java.sun.com/xml/ns/javaee/web-app_2_5.xsd"
         version="2.5">

  <servlet>
      <servlet-name>BeanTestServlet</servlet-name>
      <servlet-class>com.apress.projsp.PopulateServlet</servlet-class>
  </servlet>
  <servlet-mapping>
      <servlet-name>BeanTestServlet</servlet-name>
```

```
        <url-pattern>/BeanTest</url-pattern>
    </servlet-mapping>
</web-app>
```

Compile all the Java classes and deploy the files to a web container in the manner described for previous examples. The request for this application is `http://localhost:8080/expressionLanguage/BeanTest`. The request is passed to the `BeanTestServlet`. The servlet creates and initializes the various JavaBeans and forwards the request to `complexBean.jsp`. Figure 3-7 shows the web page you would see in your browser.

**Figure 3-7.** *The expression language can easily handle nested properties of JavaBeans.*

This example shows how an object or attribute can be created in one part of the web application and accessed from some other part of the application. The JSP page searches the various scopes until it locates the named object.

# Expression-Language Implicit Objects

Within JSP scriptlets you have many implicit objects available to you. These objects allow you to access things such as the request, session, and page context. The EL also provides you with these implicit objects, and a lot more besides. The objects are always available under well-known names and are resolved to objects in the same way as JavaBeans. Table 3-1 lists the implicit objects, along with brief descriptions of each object.

**Table 3-1.** *JSP Implicit Objects*

| Implicit Object | Description |
| --- | --- |
| applicationScope | This is a Map that contains all application-scoped variables. The Map is keyed on the name of the variable. |
| cookie | This is a Map that maps cookie names to a single Cookie object. If more than one cookie exists for a given name, the first of these cookies is used for that name. |
| header | This is a Map that contains the values of each header name. |

| Implicit Object | Description |
|---|---|
| headerValues | This is a Map that maps a header name to a string array of all the possible values for that header. |
| initParam | This is a Map that maps context initialization parameter names to their string parameter values. |
| pageContext | The PageContext object. |
| pageScope | This is a Map that contains all page-scoped variables. The Map is keyed on the name of the variable. |
| param | This is a Map that contains the names of the parameters to a page. Each parameter name is mapped to a single string value. |
| paramValues | This is a Map that maps a parameter name to a string array of all the values for that parameter. |
| requestScope | This is a Map that contains all request-scoped variables. The Map is keyed on the name of the variable. |
| sessionScope | This is a Map that contains all session-scoped variables. The Map is keyed on the name of the variable. |

Listing 3-14 shows an example JSP page that uses some of these implicit objects.

**Listing 3-14.** *implicit.jsp*

```
<jsp:useBean id="sessionperson" class="com.apress.projsp.Person"
             scope="session" />
<jsp:useBean id="requestperson" class="com.apress.projsp.Person"
             scope="request" />
<html>
  <head>
    <title>Implicit Variables</title>
    <style>
      body, td {font-family:verdana;font-size:10pt;}
    </style>
  </head>
  <body>
    <h2>Implicit Variables</h2>
    <table>
      <tr>
        <td>Concept</td>
        <td>Code</td>
        <td>Output</td>
      </tr>
      <tr>
        <td>PageContext</td>
        <td>${'${'}pageContext.request.requestURI}</td>
        <td>${pageContext.request.requestURI}</td>
      </tr>
      <tr>
        <td>sessionScope</td>
```

```
      <td>${'${'}sessionScope.sessionperson.name}</td>
      <td>${sessionScope.sessionperson.name}</td>
    </tr>
    <tr>
      <td>requestScope</td>
      <td>${'${'}requestScope.requestperson.name}</td>
      <td>${requestScope.requestperson.name}</td>
    </tr>
    <tr>
      <td>param</td>
      <td>${'${'}param["name"]}</td>
      <td>${param["name"]}</td>
    </tr>
    <tr>
      <td>paramValues</td>
      <td>${'${'}paramValues.multi[1]}</td>
      <td>${paramValues.multi[1]}</td>
    </tr>
  </table>
 </body>
</html>
```

This example shows how to use the request- and session-scope maps, the request parameter map, and the request parameter values map as well as the pageContext object. All the other objects are used in exactly the same manner and are not shown here.

If you deploy this example to a web container (as described in the previous sections) and request the page with a URL similar to http://localhost:8080/expressionLanguage/implicit.jsp?name=sam&multi=number1&multi=number2, you'll see a page similar to that shown in Figure 3-8.

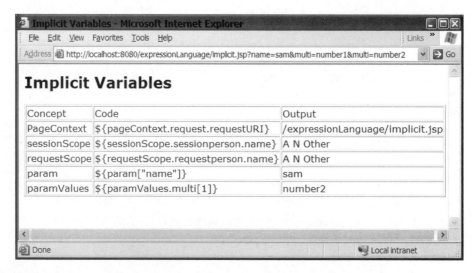

**Figure 3-8.** *Using implicit variables, you can access various objects that provide information about the application, the page, the request, the session, and so on.*

# Expression-Language Functions

This final section discusses perhaps the most interesting part of the JSP EL: functions. An EL function is mapped to a static method of a Java class. This mapping is specified within a tag library descriptor (TLD), as you'll see later.

As with the rest of the EL, a function can appear either in template text or in the attributes of a custom tag.

A function in EL can take any number of parameters, and these are again declared in a deployment descriptor. Functions are assigned a namespace that is used to access a function similar to package specifications in Java classes; for example, the following JSP code invokes an EL function:

```
${MyFunctions:function("param")}
```

The namespace in this example is MyFunctions, which is declared by using this taglib directive:

```
<%@ taglib uri="/WEB-IF/taglib.tld" prefix="MyFunctions" %>
```

You'll see this directive used in other places in this book to declare namespaces for custom tags; in this chapter you'll use it to declare namespaces for EL functions. Functions must always have a namespace, with one exception: if a function is used within the attribute of a custom tag, the function call may omit the namespace as long as the function is declared within the same TLD as the custom tag.

A TLD is an XML file that declares a tag library. The TLD contains information relating to the tags in the library and the classes that implement them. The TLD also contains the declarations and mappings of EL functions. Each TLD can describe zero or more static functions. Each function is given a name and a specific method in a Java class that will implement the function. The method must be a public static method on a public class. If this is not the case, translation-time error will occur. Within a TLD, function names must be unique, and if two functions have the same name, a translation-time error will occur. Here is an example of the TLD entries used to declare a function:

```
<taglib>
...
  <function>
    <name>nickname</name>
    <function-class>com.apress.projsp.Functions</function-class>
    <function-signature>
      java.lang.String nickname(java.lang.String)
    </function-signature>
  </function>
</taglib>
```

This TLD fragment declares a function called nickname, which is intended to return the nickname for a particular user. If you look at the tags, you can see that we declared the name of the function that will be used by the EL by using the <name> element, the class that implements the function by using the <function-class> element, and the signature of the function by using the <function-signature> element. It's this last element that is the most interesting and also the most complex.

The syntax of the `<function-signature>` element is as follows:

```
return_type static_function_name(parameter_1_type,..,parameter_n_type)
```

It's important to note that the parameter and return types must be the fully qualified Java class names. If the declared signature of the function does not match that of the function in the Java class, a translation-time error will occur.

For more information about the content of TLDs, especially those that relate to custom tags, see Chapters 6 through 8.

## A Simple Function

You are now ready to look at some example functions. The first of these examples outputs a greeting to the user. This greeting is customized depending on the time of day. So, for example, if called before midday the greeting will be Good Morning; if called after midday but before 6 p.m., the greeting will be Good Afternoon; and finally, if called after 6 p.m. but before midnight, the greeting will be Good Evening. Listing 3-15, Functions.java, is the Java class that implements this function.

**Listing 3-15.** *Functions.java*

```java
package com.apress.projsp;
import java.util.Calendar;
public class Functions {
  public static String sayHello() {
    Calendar rightNow = Calendar.getInstance();
    int hour = rightNow.get(Calendar.HOUR);
    int AmPm = rightNow.get(Calendar.AM_PM);

    if (AmPm == Calendar.AM) {
      return "Good Morning";
    } else if (AmPm == Calendar.PM && hour < 6) {
      return "Good Afternoon";
    } else {
      return "Good Evening";
    }
  }
}
```

The TLD for this function is very simple, because the function has no parameters. Listing 3-16 shows the TLD, which is named taglib.tld and is located in the tags folder under the WEB-INF folder.

**Listing 3-16.** *taglib.tld*

```xml
<?xml version="1.0" encoding="ISO-8859-1" ?>
<taglib xmlns="http://java.sun.com/xml/ns/javaee"
        xmlns:xsi="http://www.w3.org/2001/XMLSchema-instance"
        xsi:schemaLocation= ➥
```

```
"http://java.sun.com/xml/ns/javaee/web-jsptaglibrary_2_1.xsd"
        version="2.1">

  <tlib-version>1.0</tlib-version>
  <jsp-version>2.1</jsp-version>
  <short-name>projsp</short-name>
  <uri>/projsp</uri>
  <description>
  </description>
  <function>
    <name>greet</name>
    <function-class>com.apress.projsp.Functions</function-class>
    <function-signature>java.lang.String sayHello()</function-signature>
  </function>
</taglib>
```

This TLD declares our function to have the name greet and to return a string and take no parameters. You can use this function in a JSP page, as shown in Listing 3-17. Notice how you declare the namespace for your tag library as projsp in the first line, and that the function name is prefixed with projsp. The function is called by using the name provided by the TLD, rather than by the actual function name in the Java class file.

**Listing 3-17.** *greet.jsp*

```
<%@ taglib prefix="projsp" uri="/WEB-INF/tags/taglib.tld"%>
<html>
  <head>
    <title>Greet</title>
  </head>
  <body>
    <pre>${projsp:greet()}</pre>
  </body>
</html>
```

With this example, we need to make an addition to the deployment descriptor. Listing 3-18 shows the addition to make:

**Listing 3-18.** *tag-lib (Addition to web.xml)*

```
    <taglib>
        <taglib-uri>
            /chapter3
        </taglib-uri>
        <taglib-location>
            /WEB-INF/tags/taglib.tld
        </taglib-location>
    </taglib>
```

To deploy this example, perform the following steps:

1. Add the code shown in Listing 3-18 to `web.xml`.

2. Create and compile the source code for `Functions.java`, shown in Listing 3-15, and save it to the `WEB-INF\classes\com\apress\projsp` directory.

3. Create the JSP page `greet.jsp` (Listing 3-17) and save it to the `expressionLanguage` folder.

4. Create a folder within the `WEB-INF` directory called `tags`, and a file called `taglib.tld` within this folder. The contents of `taglib.tld` are shown in Listing 3-16.

5. Start Tomcat, open your web browser, and go to `http://localhost:8080/expressionLanguage/greet.jsp`.

You should see a page similar to that shown in Figure 3-9. As expected, the output of this JSP page when viewed after 6 p.m but before midnight contains the greeting "Good Evening." If you view the page at different times of the day, you will see different greetings.

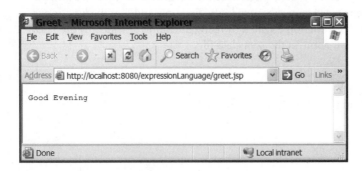

**Figure 3-9.** *The EL can be used to call static functions of Java classes in the web application.*

## A More Complex Function

Having looked at a very simple function that takes no parameters, you are now in a position to look at a more complex function. This function allows you to view the untranslated source of a JSP page presented in HTML format. To do this, the function will accept two parameters. Add the method shown in Listing 3-19 to the `Functions.java` source file that was first presented in Listing 3-15.

**Listing 3-19.** *source() (Addition to Functions.java)*

```
import java.io.BufferedReader;
import java.io.IOException;
import java.io.InputStream;
import java.io.InputStreamReader;
import javax.servlet.jsp.PageContext;
//...
  public static String source(String filename, PageContext pageContext)
    throws IOException {
```

```
  // use the servlet context to read in the file
  InputStream in;
  BufferedReader br;
  StringBuffer buf = new StringBuffer();

  in = pageContext.getServletContext().getResourceAsStream(filename);
  br = new BufferedReader(new InputStreamReader(in));
  String line = br.readLine();
  while (line != null) {
    // replace opening and closing tags
    line = line.replaceAll("<", "&lt;");
    line = line.replaceAll(">", "&gt;");
    // writing out each line as we go
    buf.append(line + "\n");
    line = br.readLine();
  }
  br.close();
  // return the contents of the file
  return buf.toString();
  }
//...
```

You'll notice that this function uses pageContext to read in the JSP file to be displayed. In addition to importing the package for pageContext, you will need to include the jsp-api.jar library in the CLASSPATH to compile the class. For Tomcat 5, the jsp-api.jar library is in the common\lib directory. If you have some other container, consult your container's documentation to determine the correct library. The pageContext is passed in as a parameter, and as such it must be declared in the function signature. The <function> element for this function in the TLD is shown in Listing 3-20. You need to add this element to the TLD in Listing 3-16.

**Listing 3-20.** *<function> (Addition to taglib.tld)*

```
<function>
  <name>source</name>
  <function-class>com.apress.projsp.Functions</function-class>
  <function-signature>
    java.lang.String source(java.lang.String, javax.servlet.jsp.PageContext)
  </function-signature>
</function>
```

As you can see, we've declared the second parameter to this function to be of type javax.servlet.jsp.PageContext.

Listing 3-21 shows a JSP page that calls the function. Notice that that taglib directive defines the prefix for the tag to be "Source". This is in contrast to the <short-name> element of the TLD (Listing 3-16). The JSP specification says that the <short-name> element is the preferred prefix for tags defined in the TLD. However, the prefix attribute in the taglib directive overrides the TLD. The function is thus called with the prefix (from the taglib directive) and name (from the TLD). Two arguments are passed to the function: the request parameter named name and the pageContext implicit object.

**Listing 3-21.** *source.jsp*

```
<%@ taglib prefix="Source" uri="/WEB-INF/tags/taglib.tld"%>
<html>
  <head>
    <title>Source</title>
  </head>
  <body>
    <pre>${Source:source(param.name, pageContext)}</pre>
  </body>
</html>
```

Add Listing 3-19 to `Functions.java` and compile that file. Also, add Listing 3-20 to `taglib.tld`. If Tomcat is running, you will need to restart Tomcat, or reload the `expressionLanguage` web application so that Tomcat will reload the class file.

Open a web browser and enter `http://localhost:8080/expressionLanguage/source.jsp?templateText.jsp` into the address bar. If you created `templateText.jsp` from Listing 3-1, Figure 3-10 shows an example of the page you might see. Notice that the name of the file to be displayed is passed as a request parameter in the URL. You can use this JSP page to view the source of any resource in the `expressionLanguage` web application, as long as you pass the correct path to the file. You cannot use `source.jsp` to view sources in other web applications, because this page has access only to the files that can be seen in the current `pageContext`.

**Figure 3-10.** *You can pass any objects available in the JSP page to an EL function. In this example, a String and a PageContext object were passed to a function.*

## Functions in Tag Attributes

One of the most powerful uses of functions in the EL is to preprocess the attributes passed to standard and custom tags. In this section, you'll look at such a use of the EL. You'll write a function that will convert a tag's parameter to uppercase; although this is not a particularly complex function, it should suffice. We don't want to get bogged down in the details of the function's implementation.

Let's first take a look at the Java method that provides this function, shown in Listing 3-22.

**Listing 3-22.** *toUpperCase() (Addition to Functions.java)*

```java
public static String toUpperCase(String theString) {
  return theString.toUpperCase();
}
```

This is an extremely simple function that merely converts its parameter to uppercase. The TLD entry for the function is shown in Listing 3-23.

**Listing 3-23.** *<function> (Addition to taglibs.tld)*

```xml
<function>
  <name>upper</name>
  <function-class>com.apress.projsp.Functions</function-class>
  <function-signature>
    java.lang.String toUpperCase(java.lang.String)
  </function-signature>
</function>
```

In this example, you'll create a JavaBean and use the standard tag `<jsp:setProperty>` to set the JavaBean's property. Listing 3-24 shows this simple JavaBean, `SourceBean.java`. To show the use of functions with tag attributes, we'll use a function to preprocess the attribute value.

**Listing 3-24.** *SourceBean.java*

```java
package com.apress.projsp;

public class SourceBean {
  String string;
  public String getString() {
    return string;
  }
  public void setString(String s) {
    string = s;
  }
}
```

Now that you've seen the constituent parts, you'll look at a JSP page in Listing 3-25 that uses a function to preprocess the attribute to the `<jsp:setProperty>` tag.

**Listing 3-25.** *tagFunction.jsp*

```
<%@ taglib prefix="projsp" uri="/WEB-INF/tags/taglib.tld"%>
<html>
  <body>
    <jsp:useBean id="sb" class="com.apress.projsp.SourceBean"/>
    <jsp:setProperty name="sb" property="string"
                     value="${projsp:upper('a string')}" />
    ${sb.string}
  </body>
</html>
```

This JSP page creates a JavaBean, uses a `<jsp:setProperty>` tag to set its property, and then displays the value of the property by using the EL statement `${sb.string}`. In the `<jsp:setProperty>` tag, you can see that we use a function to preprocess the string passed to the value attribute. Functions can be used to preprocess the attributes of all standard tags and custom tags (which you will see in later chapters). To deploy this to a web container, follow the steps for the other examples in this chapter. Figure 3-11 shows the web page generated by the JSP page.

**Figure 3-11.** *The value of the attribute was changed to uppercase before the property of the JavaBean was set. When the property is displayed in a web page, the property is displayed in its processed form.*

We've deliberately made this example simplistic, so that we can focus on the concept of calling a function in a tag attribute by using EL. However, you can use this technique to perform any processing that might be needed.

## Nesting Functions

Another powerful use of functions is to nest them together. For example, you can use the uppercase function from the previous example (Listings 3-22 and 3-25) to render the source of a page produced by our view-source function in uppercase. Listing 3-26, `uppersource.jsp`, shows how you might do this.

**Listing 3-26.** *uppersource.jsp*

```
<%@ taglib prefix="projsp" uri="/WEB-INF/tags/taglib.tld"%>
<html>
  <body>
    <pre>
${projsp:upper(projsp:source(param.name, pageContext))}
    </pre>
  </body>
</html>
```

Deploy this JSP page, and then access it with the URL `http://localhost:8080/` `expressionLanguage/uppersource.jsp?name=uppersource.jsp`. Figure 3-12 shows the page that is generated.

**Figure 3-12.** *EL functions can be nested. This example uses the source() function to access a source file, and then the upper() function to convert the source to uppercase.*

Functions can be nested to an arbitrary degree to perform some interesting and powerful operations. The only restricting factor is your imagination. This nesting encourages small functions that perform specialized jobs, which is a very positive design point.

## Expression-Language Functions vs. Custom Tags

As you'll see in later chapters, the JSP specification provides a powerful custom tag mechanism. You might ask why you would use tags over functions and vice versa. There are several factors that can help you to make the choice:

- Is knowledge of the environment required? If the answer is yes, tags are the way to go. A tag provides easy access to `pageContext` and other variables; functions do not. To access these implicit objects within a function, you must pass them in as a parameter.

- Do you require iterative behavior over a body? If the answer is yes, you should use a tag. Functions do not provide functionality to process a body (they don't have one), whereas tags do.

- Are you trying to provide a small, reusable piece of functionality that acts on one or more arguments? If the answer to this is yes, you should use a function. Overall, functions are much simpler to write than tags; therefore, they provide a great opportunity to write small, self-contained pieces of functionality.

- Would you like to reuse existing Java code in a web context? If the answer is yes, functions are ideal. Because functions are no more than static Java methods, you can easily reuse existing code.

The choice of tags versus functions should be eased by consulting these points, but it's worth noting that the true power of the EL becomes evident when it's combined with custom tags.

# Summary

In this chapter, you've looked at the JSP EL. This EL is largely intended to replace scriptlets and to be used in combination with custom tags.

You've examined the following topics in this chapter:

- The reasons that the EL has come about, including a look at its history

- The syntax and usage of the EL, including reserved words, disabling scriptlets in a page, and disabling the evaluation of the EL on a page or set of pages

- The operators within the EL, including arithmetic operators, comparison operators, logical operators, and other operators

- The use of JavaBeans with the EL

- The implicit objects within the EL

- The declaration and use of functions in the EL, including reasons for using functions over tags and vice versa

In the next chapter, you'll learn about the JSTL and the tags contained within it.

# CHAPTER 4

■■■

# JavaServer Pages Standard Tag Library

**D**espite the popularity of using JSP technology to build the dynamic presentation layers required by today's modern web applications, JSP page authors have repeatedly come up against the same problems.

In all but the simplest of web applications, JSP pages have needed to contain some form of logic to tailor the dynamic content, and until recently this has been done by using JSP scriptlets. Although this solution does produce the required output, using too many scriptlets on a page reduces its readability and therefore its maintainability and generally makes a JSP page look ugly. When using scriptlets, it's all too easy to forget a closing brace or something equally as trivial, and in a large JSP page it can take a significant amount of time to track down the source of the resultant error.

Reduced maintainability isn't the only limitation of a scriptlet-based approach; it also places an assumption on the skill set of the JSP page author developing or maintaining the page. Because scriptlets are written in Java, JSP page authors need to be Java developers or at least have more than a basic understanding of the language. Often the specific design skills of a web designer cannot be controlled, or the designer requires some assistance to fully embrace JSP technology. A perfect example of the skills mismatch is that a web designer may have a pre-ferred HTML editor or IDE that may not support Java scriptlets because editors are generally designed for XML-type languages such as HTML.

More recently, a better approach has been for Java developers to create their own custom actions (often known as custom tags) and make them available to web designers via tag libraries. This solution is far better than the scriptlet-based approach, because the use of a custom tag places no assumptions on the skills of the page author—custom tags are simply XML based. One obvious drawback of custom tags is that they must be coded, packaged, and tested before use, which is a nontrivial task and must be done by a Java developer. This can place time constraints on when web designers can start work, and in some cases Java develop-ers have found themselves writing all manner of custom tags for even the simplest of tasks to ensure that no scriptlets are necessary.

The **JavaServer Pages Standard Tag Library (JSTL)** specification 1.0 was first released in June 2002, and its arrival signified a new phase for JSP page authors. The JSTL specification outlines a number of custom actions that are designed to handle the vast majority of common tasks needed by JSP page authors. Gone are the days of using ugly scriptlets, and thanks to the JSTL, hopefully only more complicated functionality warrants the construction of a custom action.

A few days after the JSTL 1.0 specification was released, the Jakarta Taglibs project from Apache followed up with a reference implementation of the specification ready for use.

The first maintenance release of JSTL (JSTL 1.1) was completed in November 2003. A second maintenance release, JSTL 1.2, was started in June 2004. Because that release has not been finalized, we will be using JSTL 1.1 in this chapter. Because JSTL is a maintenance release, most or all of the topics here should still apply when JSTL 1.2 is released.

Throughout this chapter, you'll take an in-depth look at the actions provided by the JSTL. You'll see how actions may be used via examples that will demonstrate just how much simpler it is to build dynamic JSP-based applications with JSTL that avoid many of the problems associated with scriptlets.

To fully appreciate the actions provided by the JSTL, you should be familiar with the syntax of the new expression language (EL)—the subject of the preceding chapter.

# Installing the JavaServer Pages Standard Tag Library

Before you delve too deeply into the details of the tags that compose the JSTL, it's a good idea to understand what's involved with installing the JSTL into a JSP container that's ready for use. Fortunately, the process isn't too demanding and should take only a few minutes.

To be able to use the JSTL, you must have the following:

- At least a Servlet 2.3– and JSP 1.2–compliant container

- An implementation of the JSTL specification

Although Servlet 2.3 and JSP 1.2 are the minimum, we will be using Tomcat 5.5, which implements Servlet 2.4 and JSP 2.1, and we will use the JSTL 1.1 reference implementation. Any compliant container can be used to develop applications using the JSTL. If you're using an alternative container, consult the appropriate documentation for installation instructions. Note that the JSTL installation on other containers may be similar, so it's worth reading on!

Originally, the reference implementation (RI) of the JSTL was provided by the Apache Jakarta project as part of its Taglibs project. Subsequently, Sun Microsystems included the RI as part of the Java Web Services Developer Pack (JWSDP). So you have a couple of options for obtaining the reference implementation. If you need only the JSTL, you can download it from the Jakarta project website (`http://jakarta.apache.org/taglibs`). Alternately, you can get it by downloading the JWSDP from Sun (`http://java.sun.com/webservices/jwsdp`).

In the future, it's possible that most servlet and JSP containers will come preconfigured with an implementation of the JSTL (possibly with the container vendor's own optimized version!) but for now you must download an implementation and install it into Tomcat manually.

At the time of this writing, the latest version of the JWSDP is version 1.6, but there could be a more recent release by the time you're reading this.

After you've downloaded and installed the JWSDP, you'll have access to all of its contents, which include the following:

- JavaServer Faces (JSF)

- XML and Web Services Security (XWS-Security)

- Java Architecture for XML Binding (JAXB)

- Java API for XML Processing (JAXP)

- Java API for XML Registries (JAXR)

- Java API for XML-based RPC (JAX-RPC)

- SOAP with Attachments API for Java (SAAJ)

- JavaServer Pages Standard Tag Library (JSTL)

- Java WSDP Registry Server

- Ant build tool

- Apache Tomcat

As you can see, the JWSDP contains a whole host of useful tools. For now, we are interested in only the JSTL implementation, which can be found in the jstl directory of the JWSDP installation, as shown in Figure 4-1.

**Figure 4-1.** *The JSTL libraries are located in the jstl\lib directory of the JWSDP installation.*

There are two JAR files that you'll need shortly:

- jstl.jar

- standard.jar

If you download and install the JSTL reference implementation directly from the Jakarta project, you are looking for the same two JAR files. They will be located in the lib subdirectory located in the directory where you install the JSTL RI.

To install the JSTL and ensure it's working correctly, let's create a small web application. In the Tomcat directory, you'll find a folder called webapps. Create a directory inside the webapps directory called jstltest. Figure 4-2 shows the structure of the jstltest directory.

**Figure 4-2.** *The jstltest\WEB-INF directory has subdirectories named classes, lib, and tld.*

In the jstltest directory, create a lib directory and a tld directory. The lib directory is where you place any JAR files that the web application requires, and the tld directory holds the tag library descriptor (TLD) files for the tag libraries. You'll learn more about TLD files in the next few chapters.

The deployment descriptor for this test is shown in Listing 4-1. As in previous examples in the book, save it to the WEB-INF directory.

**Listing 4-1.** *web.xml*

```
<?xml version="1.0"?>
<web-app xmlns="http://java.sun.com/xml/ns/javaee"
         xmlns:xsi="http://www.w3.org/2001/XMLSchema-instance"
xsi:schemaLocation="http://java.sun.com/xml/ns/javaee/web-app_2_5.xsd"
         version="2.5">
  <taglib>
      <taglib-uri>http://java.sun.com/jstl/core</taglib-uri>
      <taglib-location>/WEB-INF/tlds/c.tld</taglib-location>
  </taglib>

  <taglib>
```

```
    <taglib-uri>http://java.sun.com/jstl/fmt</taglib-uri>
    <taglib-location>/WEB-INF/tlds/fmt.tld</taglib-location>
  </taglib>

  <taglib>
    <taglib-uri>http://java.sun.com/jstl/xml</taglib-uri>
    <taglib-location>/WEB-INF/tlds/x.tld</taglib-location>
  </taglib>

  <taglib>
    <taglib-uri>http://java.sun.com/jstl/sql</taglib-uri>
    <taglib-location>/WEB-INF/tlds/sql.tld</taglib-location>
  </taglib>
</web-app>
```

The deployment descriptor contains four `taglib` elements that describe the TLD files available for this test application. The JSTL contains four broad categories of tags identified by the TLDs: `c.tld`, `fmt.tld`, `x.tld`, and `sql.tld`. We will discuss the four sets of tags in more detail later in this chapter.

Now that you have a deployment descriptor for the web application, you can install the required JSTL libraries that you downloaded earlier. In the newly created web application structure, locate the `lib` directory in the `jstltest\WEB-INF` directory. Copy the two JSTL JAR files mentioned earlier into the `WEB-INF\lib` directory (see Figure 4-3).

**Figure 4-3.** *To use the JSTL in a web application, you need to copy the JSTL libraries into the web application's lib directory.*

Now you need to copy the TLD files referenced in the deployment descriptor into the `WEB-INF\tld` directory (see Figure 4-4). If you are using the JSTL RI from the Jakarta project, the TLD files are located in the `tld` directory under the JSTL installation directory. If you are using the JWSDP, these TLD files are located in the `jstl\tld` directory the JWSDP installation.

**Figure 4-4.** *The four tld files (c.tld, fmt.tld, sql.tld, and x.tld) are copied into the WEB-INF\tld directory of the web application.*

---

**■Note** If you have JSTL 1.1 from the Jakarta project, you will notice that the `tld` directory contains a number of other TLDs. For example, the files that have `1_0` as part of the filename are the JSTL 1.0 versions of the TLDs.

---

At this point, you're ready to create a JSP page to test one of the tags provided by the JSTL to see whether the installation has succeeded. Create the JSP page shown in Listing 4-2 and save it beneath the `jstltest` directory, at the same level as the `WEB-INF` directory. For now, don't worry too much about understanding the content of the page; it will all be explained in further detail later.

**Listing 4-2.** *test.jsp*

```
<%@ taglib uri="http://java.sun.com/jstl/core" prefix="c" %>
<c:out value="Congratulations, JSTL is working!"/>
```

You're now ready to test the JSTL installation!

Start Tomcat, if needed, and wait a few seconds for the server to start. After the server has started, open a browser and go to the following URL:

```
http://localhost:8080/jstltest/test.jsp
```

You should refer to the application by requesting its context followed by the requested resource, `test.jsp`. As usual, if you altered the port number or installed Tomcat onto a remote machine, make the appropriate changes to the URL. If all is well and JSTL is successfully installed, you should see a web page similar to Figure 4-5 in your browser.

**Figure 4-5.** *If you have created the web application properly, the web page will display the welcome message. If JSTL has not been installed correctly, an error page will most likely be displayed. Tomcat serves an HTTP 500 error page.*

You may be wondering whether you can install the JSTL implementation libraries into a single location so that they're available to all web applications hosted by the container. Although this is possible by placing the JSTL JAR files into the class path of the container, it's discouraged because different web applications may require different versions or even different implementations of the JSTL that could cause complications.

# Understanding the JavaServer Pages Standard Tag Libraries

The JSTL is often referred to as a single tag library when in fact it's a collection of four tag libraries. Each tag library provides useful actions (or tags) based on the following functional areas:

- Core

- Internationalization (I18n) and formatting

- Relational database access

- XML processing

One of the primary goals of the JSTL is to simplify the lives of JSP page authors. Providing a collection of tag libraries reinforces this goal by further separating simple, reusable logic from the page's presentation, thus making the page easier to read and maintain.

Having four tag libraries provides a handy namespace for each available tag, which ultimately makes it easier to identify which functional area a tag belongs to and gives the JSP page author some indication of the intended use for the tag.

Before diving headfirst into an explanation of the tags provided by each of the four libraries, take a step back for a moment to understand the general functionality provided by each.

## The Core Tag Library

As its name suggests, this library contains a whole host of core, general-purpose actions that provide simple but effective solutions to everyday problems experienced in almost every JSP-based web application. Simple tasks such as displaying content based on runtime conditions or iterating over a collection of items, as well as a host of URL-manipulation features, can all be achieved via the actions provided by the Core library. Gone are the days of repeatedly embedding lots of ugly scriptlet code in your JSP pages!

## The Internationalization and Formatting Tag Library

The huge popularity of the Internet has led to more and more organizations employing web-based technology to enable their applications to reach a wider client base. This trend has brought about an important need to interact with clients from around the world by using their own language and formatting conventions.

The process of constructing an application so that it's able to adapt to various languages and regions without any additional engineering effort is known as internationalization, or I18n for short ("internationalization" is a 20-character word that begins with "i," ends with "n," and has 18 letters in between). The Internationalization and Formatting tag library provides a series of actions to aid in the use of the three key components associated with internationalization: locales, resource bundles, and base names.

## The SQL Tag Library

The vast majority of enterprise web applications rely on a relational database to store their enterprise information. Although it's generally preferable to use Model-View-Controller (MVC) architecture to separate the business logic and database access from the presentation tier, sometimes you may need to access a database from JSP pages.

The JSTL provides an assortment of actions via the SQL tag library to facilitate the basic interaction with a relational database by using SQL commands such as SELECT, INSERT, UPDATE, and DELETE.

## The XML Processing Tag Library

The use of XML to represent and exchange enterprise data is rapidly becoming the industry standard. XML is therefore becoming more and more important to the JSP page author, and it should be of little or no surprise to find that the JSTL provides a separate tag library to deal with XML processing. The XML actions provided cater to the basic XML needs a page author is likely to require as well as more complex actions for XML flow control and XML transformations.

---

### TWIN TAG LIBRARIES

We mentioned in an earlier note that the JSTL 1.1 reference implementation from Jakarta includes the JSTL 1.0 TLDs. You also may have noticed that there are two versions of each JSTL 1.0 TLD.

Because JSTL 1.0 was released prior to JSP 2.0, there was a requirement to ensure that the JSTL was fully supported by JSP 1.2-compliant containers. To be able to support both the scripting (rtexprvalues) and the EL (elexprvalues) worlds, it was decided to create a set of twin tag libraries, one to support the new EL and the second to support request-time expressions. Because there are two tag libraries for each functional area, there are two URIs to identify each tag library. The following list shows the URIs for each functional area and each version of the TLD:

- Core expression language TLD: `http://java.sun.com/jstl/core`

- Core runtime values TLD: `http://java.sun.com/jstl/core_rt`

- XML expression language TLD: `http://java.sun.com/jstl/xml`

- XML runtime values TLD: `http://java.sun.com/jstl/xml_rt`

- Formatting expression language TLD: `http://java.sun.com/jstl/fmt`

- Formatting runtime values TLD: `http://java.sun.com/jstl/fmt_rt`

- SQL expression language TLD: `http://java.sun.com/jstl/sql`

- SQL runtime values TLD: `http://java.sun.com/jstl/sql_rt`

If, for whatever reason, you are using the JSTL 1.0 implementation, it's possible to mix the use of the runtime and EL actions. To do so, you just include a `taglib` directive for each library you are using, and use the correct standard tag. For example, in the following code snippet, there is a `taglib` directive for both the EL format library and runtime format library. Within the snippet, you can see the use of the `<fmt:param>` tag used with an EL expression; alternately, in the line that uses a JSP scriptlet, the `<fmt_rt:param>` tag is used.

```
<%@ taglib uri="http://java.sun.com/jstl/fmt" prefix="fmt" %>
<%@ taglib uri="http://java.sun.com/jstl/fmt_rt" prefix="fmt_rt" %>
<fmt:message key="stockPrice">
    <fmt:param value="${closePrice}">
    <fmt_rt:param value="<%=quoteBean.getOpenPrice()%>"/>
</fmt:message>
```

# Using the JavaServer Pages Standard Tag Libraries

Now that you understand the general composition of the JSTL, in this section you'll learn about the tags provided by each of its four libraries.

## The Core Tag Library

As mentioned previously, the Core tag library provides JSP page authors with a set of reusable actions to cater to the simple "core" requirements that almost every JSP application has in some shape or form, such as object manipulation, looping, and so on.

Until now, such common functionality has been implemented via two alternative methods: Java scriptlets and custom actions. As we've discussed, scriptlets are the least favorable approach, because they not only require the JSP page author to understand Java syntax but also add clutter to JSP pages, thus reducing readability. A better alternative has been to encapsulate such functionality into a custom action, but of course it's up to the JSP page author to code such a component, which the author may or may not have the skills to do. Although a custom action has until now been the best solution because it enables a high level of reuse, why should all JSP page authors be forced to write their own libraries of such simple core functionality?

Thankfully, the JSTL provides such a library, thus making it easier for JSP page authors to concentrate on what they do best—building attractive, functional presentation layers—without the burden of having to worry about the intricacies of the Java programming language. The JSTL core library can be split further to expose its main functional areas:

- Scoped variable manipulation

- Conditionals

- Looping and iteration

- URL manipulation

Let's take a closer look at each of the actions.

## Scoped Variable Manipulation

This first group of actions provides the means to work with scoped variables (JSP-scoped attributes) as well as cope with errors.

### The <c:out> Action

As the name suggests, the `<c:out>` action evaluates an expression and outputs it to the current JspWriter. It's equivalent to the JSP syntax `<%= expression %>`.

Here is an example of this simple but useful action:

```
<%@ taglib uri="http://java.sun.com/jstl/core" prefix="c" %>
<c:out value="Good Afternoon!" />
<c:out value="${book.author.name}" default="Unknown"/>
```

The expression to be evaluated is supplied via the `value` attribute, and the result is converted into a string before being returned as part of the response. Notice that an optional default value can be supplied that is returned if the expression evaluates to `null`. Should a Null expression be evaluated and no default value is supplied, an empty string is returned instead.

The `<c:out>` action also has a second form that enables the `default` attribute to be specified as part of the action's body content, which the JSP container will evaluate and trim on your behalf should the default value be required. Therefore, you can rewrite the example as follows:

```
<%@ taglib uri="http://java.sun.com/jstl/core" prefix="c" %>
<c:out value="${book.author.name}">
  Unknown
</c:out>
```

## The <c:set> Action

You can use the <c:set> action to set a variable in a particular web application scope (page, request, session, or application), and it's often used in conjunction with the <c:out> action.

Let's look at an example. Listing 4-3 shows a JSP page that stores the value of the User-Agent request header in session scope, and then accesses the value in another tag.

**Listing 4-3.** *core_set.jsp*

```
<%@ taglib uri="http://java.sun.com/jstl/core" prefix="c" %>
<c:set var="browser" value="${header['User-Agent']}" scope="session" />
Your Browser User Agent is : <c:out value="${browser}"/>
```

The var attribute sets the name by which the variable may be referenced in the given scope. In a similar manner to the <c:out> action, the value of the variable can be specified in two possible ways: first, by simply using the value attribute, or second, by supplying the tag with some body content that is automatically evaluated and trimmed by the JSP container.

In this case, the <c:set> action is being used to store a session-scoped variable called browser, which stores the value of the User-Agent request header that indicates the type of browser that initiated the request. The <c:out> action is then used to output the value stored inside the attribute. Figure 4-6 shows one example of the page generated by the JSP example code in Listing 4-3.

**Figure 4-6.** *One capability of the core actions is to set a variable so that it can be used later in the page. In this example, the value of the User-Agent header was stored and then later printed as part of the page display.*

Note that should a null value be specified for the value attribute, then the scoped variable defined by var and scope is removed (in other words, setting the var to null has the effect of removing the object referred to by var). If a scope is supplied, the behavior is determined by the action of PageContext.removeAttribute(var, scope); if no scope is supplied, the behavior is determined by PageContext.removeAttribute(var). It is these methods that provide the internal implementation.

Another use of the `<c:set>` action is to set a property of a scoped object. To do this, you use attributes named `target` and `property`, as shown in this snippet:

```
<c:set target="person" property="firstName" value="Sondra" />
```

When `target` is an object, the action sets the value of the given `property` with the `value` attribute. If `target` is a `Map`, then `value` is stored in the `Map` using `property` as the key. When `value` is `null`, the `property` is set to `null` when `target` is an object, or the entry given by `property` is removed when `target` is a `Map`.

### The <c:remove> Action

You probably won't be surprised to learn that the `<c:remove>` action removes a variable from a specific application scope. Now, we've never needed to remove a variable's value from a web application, but in case you need that capability, you've got it.

We think that it would most likely be used for variables with session or application scope. Suppose you had a web application that is customized for beginners and expert users. If you used a session variable to track whether the user was a beginner, you would want to remove that variable when the user decided to use expert level. Listing 4-4 shows a JSP page that does this.

**Listing 4-4.** *core_remove.jsp*

```
<%@ taglib uri="http://java.sun.com/jstl/core" prefix="c" %>
<c:if test="${param.expert != null}">
  <c:remove var="level" scope="session"/>
</c:if>
<html>
  <body>
    Your level is <c:out value="${level}" default="Expert"/>
    <c:choose>
      <c:when test="${level != null}">
      <p/>Here are the things you need to do...
      </c:when>
      <c:otherwise>
      <p/>You're the expert, you figure it out...
      </c:otherwise>
    </c:choose>
  </body>
</html>
```

In Listing 4-4, we assume that somewhere else in the application, the user was assigned a level of beginner. At some point, the user decides he can handle expert mode, and a request is sent to this page with the request parameter `expert` set to a non-null value. Because `level` is a session-scoped variable, it needs to be removed in only one place. Now any other page that uses the variable `level` will see that it has been removed. When this JSP page is accessed in expert mode, as shown in Figure 4-7, the page displays expert-mode information.

**Figure 4-7.** *When the variable is removed from the application, that variable is no longer accessible from other tags. Because the variable level is no longer set, this page displays expert-level information.*

---

■**Note**  Okay, we'll be the first to admit that the example in Listing 4-4 is simplistic and could be accomplished in other ways. But frankly, we've never had the need to remove a variable, and any other example we thought of was equally simplistic. If you ever need to remove a variable from a JSP page, you've got the means.

---

As you can see, this is one of the simplest actions provided by the JSTL because it simply accepts a var attribute that indicates the named attribute to remove as well as an optional scope attribute, which indicates the scope from which to remove the attribute.

Again, if an attribute scope is specified, the behavior is specified by the PageContext.removeAttribute(var, scope) method because this is the underlying method that is called; otherwise, the PageContext.removeAttribute(var) method is used when no scope is specified.

### The <c:catch> Action

The <c:catch> action provides a simple mechanism for catching any java.lang.Throwable exceptions that are thrown by any nested actions.

This simple action has a single var attribute that holds a reference to any java.lang.Throwable exceptions that occur during execution of any of the nested actions forming the body content of the action. The JSP container processes each nested action in the standard way, and any output is returned to the current JspWriter.

This action provides JSP developers with granular error handling, thereby allowing errors from multiple actions to be handled in a uniform way in a single place, which makes your applications more robust. It should be noted, however, that this action should not be used to provide error handling to actions that are of central importance to the page. Instead, exceptions from such actions should propagate to predefined error pages in the standard manner. Actions of secondary importance, however, may be enclosed inside the `<c:catch>` action:

```
<%@ taglib uri="http://java.sun.com/jstl/core" prefix="c" %>
<%@ taglib uri="http://java.sun.com/jstl/fmt" prefix="fmt" %>
<c:catch var="exception">
    <fmt:parseDate var="dob" value="${param.birthDate}"
                   pattern="yyyy-MM-dd" />
</c:catch>
<c:if test="${exception != null}">
    <jsp:useBean id="dob" class="java.util.Date" />
</c:if>
```

You can see from this example how the `<c:catch>` action can come in handy for dealing with errors that don't warrant informing the user and forwarding to a separate error page. In this example, the `<fmt:parseDate>` action from the Internationalization and Formatting tag library throws an exception if an invalid date is entered and if it does, the exception is stored in the exception variable. Should an exception be thrown during execution, it can be caught and tested for, and a default value will be used instead without informing the user of the internal error.

Note that the scope of the var attribute will always be page, and should a java.lang. Throwable exception not be thrown by a nested action, then the var variable won't exist. If a value for the var variable isn't supplied, the java.lang.Throwable won't be stored.

## Conditionals

The content delivered by dynamic JSP-based web applications is often dynamic in nature because its generated content is dependent on the values of ever-changing application data. Until the release of the JSTL, JSP page authors were forced to provide such functionality via Java scriptlets containing if statements, which isn't just ugly, but prone to errors as well. The conditional tags provided by the JSTL core tag library are far better suited for this purpose.

### The <c:if> Action

The first and simplest of the conditional actions is `<c:if>`, which decides to evaluate its body content depending on the value of an evaluated Boolean attribute. If the result of the attribute expression evaluates to true, the action's body content will be processed in the standard way by the JSP container and any output will be returned to the current JspWriter.

Let's use a really simple example to produce some dynamic content based on the current hour of the day. Listing 4-5 shows a JSP page that displays a different message based on the hour of the day.

**Listing 4-5.** *core_if.jsp*

```
<%@ taglib uri="http://java.sun.com/jstl/core" prefix="c" %>
<%@ page import="com.apress.projsp.CalendarBean"%>
<jsp:useBean id="cal" class="com.apress.projsp.CalendarBean"/>

The time is currently : <BR><BR>
```

```
<c:out value="${cal.time}"/>,
<c:set var="hour" value="${cal.hour}" scope="request" />
<b>
<c:if test="${hour >= 0 && hour <=11}">
    Good Morning!
</c:if>
<c:if test="${hour >= 12 && hour <=17}">
    Good Afternoon!
</c:if>
<c:if test="${hour >= 18 && hour <=23}">
    Good Evening!
</c:if>
</b>
```

As you can see, this JSP page uses an instance of a simple JavaBean component called CalendarBean (a simple wrapper around the java.util.Calendar class). The page also sets a variable called hour using the <c:set> action introduced earlier. After informing the user of the current time, the page then dynamically provides the user with a greeting depending on whether it's morning, afternoon, or evening. Notice how it takes three separate <c:if> actions to accomplish this task.

Note that the reason for using the CalendarBean class as a wrapper is that the standard java.util.Calendar class isn't a standard JavaBean component and hence cannot be instantiated by the <jsp:useBean> action or manipulated by the EL. An alternative would be to use scriptlet code to provide access to a Calendar object, but as mentioned elsewhere this makes your JSP pages cluttered and harder to maintain.

Figure 4-8 shows the output of the web page generated by core_if.jsp.

**Figure 4-8.** *The <c:if> action can be used to provide conditional output.*

Additionally, the <c:if> action accepts an optional var attribute that represents a scoped variable that can be used to store the result of evaluating the Boolean test expression. The optional variable can be set to either a specific scope or the default page scope. You may be surprised to learn that there is no explicit <c:else> action, but you'll soon see why as we introduce the <c:choose>, <c:when>, and <c:otherwise> actions.

### The <c:choose>, <c:when>, and <c:otherwise> Actions

You've now seen how the <c:if> action can be used to provide content based on a specific condition. The <c:choose> action takes this step a little further and enables you to provide handling for a set of mutually exclusive conditions, instead of just one.

The syntax for the <c:choose> action is as follows:

```
<c:choose>
    body content (<c:when> and <c:otherwise> subtags)
</c:choose>
```

As you can see, the <c:choose> action has two possible nested actions that form its body content: <c:when> and <c:otherwise>. The syntax for each is as follows:

```
<c:when test="testCondition">
    body content
</c:when>
<c:otherwise>
    conditional block
</c:otherwise>
```

The <c:when> action exists simply to provide handling for a specific condition, tested for via its test attribute. Unlimited <c:when> actions may exist within a <c:choose> action to provide handling for a wide range of conditions. The <c:otherwise> action may appear only once because it covers all remaining alternatives and must therefore appear after all <c:when> actions. Because it represents the last possible option, there's no need for it to evaluate a Boolean expression.

Combined, the <c:choose>, <c:when>, and <c:otherwise> actions provide efficient handling for a range of alternative conditions in a similar manner to if, else if, else blocks or case/switch statements in modern programming languages.

When the JSP container first encounters a <c:choose> tag, it evaluates the body of the first <c:when> action whose test condition evaluates to true and returns any output to the current JspWriter without evaluating or processing any further <c:when> or <c:otherwise> actions. Should the test condition of every <c:when> evaluate to false, then and only then does the body of the <c:otherwise> action get processed. If no <c:when> condition evaluates to true and there's no <c:otherwise> action specified, the <c:choose> action will simply do nothing!

Let's revisit the example JSP page that we created for the <c:if> action example, which prints an appropriate welcome based on the time of day:

```
<c:if test="${hour >= 0 && hour <=11}">
    Good Morning!
</c:if>
<c:if test="${hour >= 12 && hour <=17}">
    Good Afternoon!
</c:if>
<c:if test="${hour >= 18 && hour <=23}">
    Good Evening!
</c:if>
```

There are three possible conditions that determine the welcome message returned to the user. This logic would be far better implemented using a `<c:choose>` action instead. Let's make the appropriate changes:

```
<c:choose>
    <c:when test="${hour >= 0 && hour <=11}">
        Good Morning!
    </c:when>
    <c:when test="${hour >= 12 && hour <=17}">
        Good Afternoon!
    </c:when>
    <c:otherwise>
        Good Evening!
    </c:otherwise>
</c:choose>
```

The new implementation of the welcome message logic is superior to the logic from the `<c:if>` example for three reasons. First, the code is more self-describing and readable to a nonprogrammer. Second, the code is more efficient. As soon as the JSP engine has found the first nested action whose test condition evaluates to true, it doesn't need to continue checking the test conditions of any other actions. Compare this to the `<c:if>` example, where every action was tested regardless. Last, because the nested actions of the `<c:choose>` action are mutually exclusive, it's impossible to execute the body of more than one of the conditions. A simple bug in the logic of the `<c:if>` example could easily cause the body of more than one `<c:if>` action to be processed, thereby causing a very strange welcome message!

## Looping and Iteration

Another facility often required by JSP page authors is the ability to generate large amounts of presentation code (usually HTML tables or lists) by looping or iterating around the same JSP code. This functionality has until now usually been implemented via scriptlets that contain either while or for Java statements. Embedding such blocks of code into JSP pages makes it difficult for JSP developers who are not familiar with Java to do their job effectively, and scriptlets have a nasty habit of introducing silly, hard-to-detect bugs as well as reducing the readability of JSP pages. The best JSP pages will contain little, if any, scriptlet code at all!

Thankfully, JSTL offers two useful actions for such purposes: `<c:forEach>` for general data and `<c:forTokens>` for string tokenizing.

### The <c:forEach> Action

The `<c:forEach>` action is probably one of the most useful actions provided by the JSTL that enables its body content to be processed a number of times. The `<c:forEach>` action repeatedly processes its body content over a collection of objects or until a set number of iterations has been achieved.

There are two alternate syntaxes for the `<c:forEach>` action. If you want to iterate over a collection of objects, you would use this syntax (syntax 1):

```
<c:forEach[var="varName"] items="collection" [varStatus="varStatusName"]
    body content
</c:forEach>
```

If you want to iterate a set number of times, you would use this syntax (syntax 2):

```
<c:forEach [var="varName"] [varStatus="varStatusName"]
begin="begin" end="end" [step="step"]>
    body content
</c:forEach>
```

If iterating over a collection (syntax 1), the only required parameter is the collection itself, specified via the items attribute. The object referenced by the items variable can be any one of the following data types:

- An array

- An implementation of java.util.Collection

- An implementation of java.util.Iterator

- An implementation of java.util.Enumeration

- An implementation of java.util.Map

- A string of comma-separated values

Whichever data type items references, the type of the exposed var variable will be that of the object in the underlying collection. The only exceptions to this are arrays of primitives and java.util.Maps that are represented by the object wrapper class of the primitive type and Map.Entry, respectively.

As mentioned earlier, syntax 2 can be used when a fixed number of iterations are required. Using this particular syntax, the type of the exposed var variable will be Integer and will be incremented by 1 or step at the end of each iteration. The body content will be processed repeatedly until the var variable is greater than or equal to the end variable. This option is usually used when iterating over a finite (and known) collection.

Due to the flexibility provided by the <c:forEach> action, it's inevitable that this action will be slightly more complex than some of the others seen so far. For this reason, the complete attribute list for the action is shown in Table 4-1.

**Table 4-1.** *Attributes for the <c:forEach> Tag*

| Attribute | Required | Default | Description |
| --- | --- | --- | --- |
| items | No | None | Collection of items to iterate over. If null, no iteration takes place. |
| begin | No | 0 | If specified, must be >=0. *If* items *specified:* Iteration begins at the item located at the specified value. *If* items *not specified:* Iteration starts from specified value. |
| end | No | Last object in the collection | If specified, must be >=begin. *If* items *specified:* Iteration stops at the item at the specified index (inclusive). *If* items *not specified:* Iteration stops when index reaches specified value. |

| Attribute | Required | Default | Description |
|---|---|---|---|
| step | No | 1 (process all objects) | If specified, must be >=1. Iteration processes every step item in the collection. |
| var | No | None | Name of the scoped variable that represents the current item of the iteration. |
| varStatus | No | None | Name of the scoped variable that represents the status of the iteration. Object is of type javax.servlet. jsp.jstl.core.LoopStatus. |

As an example, imagine that as part of serving a client request, a controlling servlet has caused some business logic to query a database and retrieve a result set. The data retrieved is then used to populate a collection of objects, let's say Book objects, which are placed into the user's session before control is forwarded to a JSP page in the presentation tier to display the results.

The <c:forEach> action is extremely useful for this purpose and is commonly used to retrieve the collection from the user's session and iterate over its contents to build an HTML table. Here is an example of some code to do just that:

```
<c:forEach var="book" items="${sessionScope.books}">
  <tr>
    <td align="right" bgcolor="#ffffff">
    <c:out value="${book.title}"/>
    </td>
  </tr>
</c:forEach>
```

The collection of books (which presumably was stored in the session scope by the name of books) is retrieved from the session, and the action iterates over the collection of Book objects. The action then creates the data for a single row of an HTML table, populated by the title of each book.

## The <c:forTokens> Action

The second iterating action provided by the JSTL is <c:forTokens>, which iterates over a string of tokens separated by a set of delimiters, much in the same way as the functionality provided by the java.util.StringTokenizer class that you may be familiar with.

The syntax for the action is as follows:

```
<c:forTokens items="stringOfTokens" delims="delimiters"
                [var="varName"] [varStatus="varStatusName"]
                [begin="begin"] [end="end"] [step="step"]>
    body content
</c:forTokens>
```

As you can see in Table 4-2, the attribute list is somewhat similar to the <c:forEach> action.

**Table 4-2.** *Attributes for the <c:forTokens> Tag*

| Attribute | Required | Default | Description |
|---|---|---|---|
| items | Yes | None | The string to tokenize. |
| delims | Yes | None | The delimiter characters that separate the tokens of the string. |
| begin | No | 0 | If specified, must be >=0. The token to start with. |
| end | No | Last token in the string to be tokenized. | If specified, must be >=begin. The token to end with. |
| step | No | 1 (process all objects) | If specified, must be >=1. Iteration processes every step item in the collection. |
| var | No | None | Name of the scoped variable that represents the current item of the iteration. |
| varStatus | No | None | Name of the scoped variable that represents the status of the iteration. Object is of type javax.servlet.jsp.jstl.core.LoopStatus. |

Instead of iterating over a collection of objects or between set values like the <c:forEach> tag, the <c:forTokens> tag works with a string of characters separated by designated delimiter characters. Data is often structured in this way, with probably the most common example being the Comma Separated Value (CSV) file often used with spreadsheet and database applications. As the name suggests, a CSV file contains "rows" of data with each "column" or piece of data separated by a comma.

Let's look at a simple example of the <c:forTokens> tag in action. Imagine that you have some comma-separated data, perhaps the contents of a customer marketing CSV spreadsheet that has the following structure:

FirstName,LastName,Sex,Occupation,Location

The previous data is concerned with customer data. You want to present this information in a more readable format such as an HTML table. Because the data is structured with a consistent delimiter character separating the "tokens" of data, this task is easy with the <c:forTokens> tag, as you can see in Listing 4-6.

**Listing 4-6.** *core_tokens.jsp*

```
<%@ taglib uri="http://java.sun.com/jstl/core" prefix="c" %>
<c:set var="queryResult" value="Dan,Jepp,Male,26,Java Developer,London"
        scope="request" />
<html>
<body>
<table border="1">
  <tr>
    <th>First Name</th>
```

```
      <th>Last Name</th>
      <th>Sex</th>
      <th>Age</th>
      <th>Occupation</th>
      <th>Location</th>
   </tr>
   <tr>
   <c:forTokens items="${queryResult}" delims="," var="token">
      <td><c:out value="${token}"/></td>
   </c:forTokens>
   </tr>
</table>
</body>
</html>
```

This simple example has only a single string of data from which it has to build an HTML table with a single row. The main structure of the HTML table is constructed with the `<c:forTokens>` tag; this tag iterates through the string of data held in the `queryResult` variable, extracting each token separated by the comma delimiter (as noted by the `delims` parameter). Notice how each token is accessed from inside the body of the tag via the token variable, which is declared as an attribute of the `<c:forTokens>` tag itself.

The output of the example JSP page in Listing 4-6 is shown in Figure 4-9.

**Figure 4-9.** *The <c:forTokens> tag can be used to split a delimited string into tokens.*

Without the `<c:forTokens>` tag, this simple problem wouldn't have been as easy to overcome and may well have required some ugly JSP scriptlet code and an instance of a `java.util.StringTokenizer` class. You can see that this is a far more readable and maintainable solution!

A slightly more realistic example may combine the use of the `<c:forEach>` tag to store multiple strings of delimited data, which is perhaps the result of a database search for files. As the `<c:forEach>` tag iterates through each delimited string, the `<c:forTokens>` tag can produce the necessary HTML table row.

## URL-Related Actions

Obviously the ability to import, link, and redirect is fundamental in any JSP-based web application. The JSTL provides several useful URL-related actions to simplify these requirements.

### The <c:import> Action

This action imports the content of a URL-based resource and provides a simple, generic way to access URL-based resources that can be either included or processed within the JSP page.

You can see a good example of the <c:import> action as it works with some of the actions from the XML library, which, of course, require an XML document to work with. The <c:import> action is the simplest way to retrieve a file containing XML or XSLT, which is then used by subsequent XML actions for processing. For example:

```
<%@ taglib uri="http://java.sun.com/jstl/core" prefix="c" %>
<%@ taglib uri="http://java.sun.com/jstl/xml" prefix="x" %>
<c:import url="http://mybookstore.com/book.xml" var="url" />
<x:parse xml="${url}" var="book" scope="session" />
```

Here you can see how the <c:import> action is used to retrieve a file called book.xml from a remote location; the file is then utilized by the <x:parse> action from the XML tag library. Note that in this case, because of the presence of the var parameter, the actual contents of the file aren't written to the current JspWriter but are instead stored in the named parameter.

The <c:import> action can also be used to specify absolute, relative, foreign, context-relative, and FTP URL resources to provide a lot more functionality than the standard <jsp:include> action you're so used to having.

### The <c:url> Action

The <c:url> action provides a handy way of constructing correctly formatted URLs that have the correct URL-rewriting rules applied.

As you're no doubt aware, without session tracking, or the ability to recognize a number of requests from the same user, the majority of complex web-based applications wouldn't be functionally possible due to the statelessness of the HTTP protocol. Generally, browsers provide the session-tracking mechanism by storing cookies (small text files stored on the client machine), which are sent back with each request the client makes during a "session." Because most modern browsers enable the user to disable cookies (usually for security reasons), it's important to ensure that any URLs that your web applications use are URL-rewritten so that that their session-tracking capabilities are maintained if cookies are disabled.

A rewritten URL looks something like this:

```
http://www.myserver.com/shop/checkout.jsp;jsessionid=42eab543dc2
```

The actual rewriting of a URL simply involves appending a special value (the session ID) to the end of the query string, which is used to track requests that originate from the same user. These requests are therefore part of the same session.

Previously, JSP scriptlets were typically used to ensure that all URLs were rewritten by calling the encodeURL() method provided by the HttpServletResponse interface.

The `<c:url>` action takes care of all the URL rewriting on your behalf without the need for any scriptlet code! For example, to encode the URL, all that's required is the following:

```
<c:url value="http://www.myserver.com/shop/checkout.jsp" />
```

### The <c:redirect> Action

As the name suggests, the `<c:redirect>` action sends an HTTP redirect to a client.

For example, to redirect a user to an updated site or a moved application, the action is used as follows:

```
<c:redirect url="http://www.myNewUrl.com" />
```

It's as simple as that! The action does also support the use of another optional attribute called `context`, which can be used to identify the name of a context when redirecting to a relative URL that belongs to a foreign context. In simpler terms, this means that you can actually forward the request to another web application hosted inside the same container!

### The <c:param> Action

The `<c:import>`, `<c:url>`, and `<c:redirect>` actions all deal with URLs and as you're probably aware it's pretty common to pass request parameters as part of URLs by appending them to the query string.

The `<c:param>` action is designed solely for this purpose and may be used as a nested tag in the body content of either the `<c:import>`, `<c:url>`, or `<c:redirect>` actions. The `<c:param>` action takes two simple attributes, `name` and `value`, which represent the name of the request parameter along with its value, respectively. Note also that the value of the `name` and `value` attributes are URL encoded by default.

For example:

```
<c:url value="http://www.myBookshop.com/books/catalogue.jsp" >
  <c:param name="isbn" value="123456" />
</c:url>
```

Like many of the JSTL actions, the `<c:param>` action can be used in two forms, first as shown previously, and second, whereby the value for the parameter is given inside the body content of the action itself. Let's take a look at the previous example using the alternative format:

```
<c:url value="http://www.myBookshop.com/books/catalogue.jsp" >
  <c:param name="isbn">123456</c:param>
</c:url>
```

# The Internationalization and Formatting Tag Library

Preparing an application so it's ready for the global marketplace is known as internationalization (or I18n for short). A related term, localization (or l10n), refers to the process of customizing an application for a particular language or region.

The popularity of the Internet has enabled organizations to vastly increase their exposure and client base by providing their services via dynamic web applications. Ensuring that clients from around the world can interact with such applications by using their native language and conventions has never been more important.

The Internationalization and Formatting tag library provided by the JSTL provides a set of simple actions to aid this process and uses three key components associated with internationalization: locales, resource bundles, and base names.

## Setting the Locale

The Internationalization and Formatting tag library provides actions that allow you to control the locale settings for your JSP pages.

### The <fmt:setLocale> Action

As the name suggests, this action can be used to override the client-specified locale for the processing of a JSP page. Any I18n formatting actions such as <fmt:message> that are found on the page will use this specified locale instead of the one sent by the client browser.

The chosen locale is stored in a variable called javax.servlet.jsp.jstl.fmt.locale and can be stored in any chosen scope.

This JSP code first sets the default locale for the page followed by the session:

```
<fmt:setLocale value ="en_US" />
<fmt:setLocale value ="fr_FR" scope="session" />
```

The value attribute accepts either a string representing the locale (a two-letter, lowercase language code followed a two-letter, optional uppercase country code), or a reference to a java.util.Locale object.

---

■**Tip** Locale codes are created by specifying a language code, an underbar, and an optional country code. Language codes are defined by the ISO 639 standard (http://www.loc.gov/standards/iso639-2/langhome.html). Country codes are defined by the ISO 3166 standard (http://www.iso.org/iso/en/prods-services/iso3166ma/02iso-3166-code-lists/index.html).

---

Note that it's also possible to set a default locale for use via the JSTL by using the following configuration setting in the web application's deployment descriptor (web.xml):

```
<context-param>
  <param-name>javax.servlet.jsp.jstl.fmt.locale</param-name>
  <param-value>en</param-value>
</context-param>
```

This configuration uses the locale code for English to set the default locale for the application.

■**Caution** The <fmt:setLocale> action overrides the browser-based locale setting. Therefore, if you use this action, make sure it's placed at the beginning of a JSP page before any I18n formatting actions.

## Messaging Actions

After the locale has been defined for a client request, either by the client's browser settings or by use of the <fmt:setLocale> action, the JSTL messaging actions can be used to display content to the browser in its own language as identified by its locale.

To take advantage of localized messages, it's necessary as a developer to provide a collection of resources (usually strings) for each locale that you intend to support. Each collection of resources is known as a resource bundle and is implemented via a standard key=value properties file. For more information, take a look at the Java 2 Platform, Standard Edition (J2SE) Javadocs for the java.util.ResourceBundle class.

### The <fmt:bundle> and <fmt:setBundle> Actions

To enable the use of localized messages, you need to specify the required resource bundle that provides the localized messages.

Either the <fmt:bundle> or <fmt:setBundle> actions can be used to specify a resource bundle, and they're identified by the basename to be used in the JSP page. Once successfully declared, the resource bundle can then be used to provide localized messages via the <fmt:message> action, which you'll see shortly.

Although similar, the <fmt:bundle> and <fmt:setBundle> actions are used in different ways to produce localized messages in JSP pages.

The <fmt:bundle> action is used to declare an I18n localization context for use by I18n-aware tags within its body content:

```
<fmt:bundle basename="Labels">
    <fmt:message key="labels.firstName"/>
    <fmt:message key="labels.lastName"/>
</fmt:bundle>
```

Here, a resource bundle with the name Labels is declared to provide the localized resources for any nested <fmt:message> actions. The resource bundle contains at least two name-value pairs given by the keys labels.firstName and labels.lastName.

Because the <fmt:bundle> action is designed to work so closely with nested <fmt:message> actions, a handy optional attribute can also be used as follows:

```
<fmt:bundle basename="Labels" prefix="labels">
    <fmt:message key="firstName"/>
    <fmt:message key="lastName"/>
</fmt:bundle>
```

The optional prefix attribute enables the setting of a predefined prefix that is prepended to the key attribute of any nested <fmt:message> actions, which makes their use so much simpler.

The `<fmt:setBundle>` action also provides similar functionality to those you just saw, but with a subtle difference. Instead of having to nest any `<fmt:message>` actions as body content, the `<fmt:setBundle>` action enables a resource bundle to be stored in the configuration variable `javax.servlet.jsp.jstl.fmt.localizationContext`, so any `<fmt:message>` actions that appear elsewhere in the JSP page can access the bundle without having to continually declare it as follows:

```
<fmt:setBundle basename="Labels" />
<fmt:message prefix="labels.firstName" />
```

The `<fmt:setBundle>` action also enables you to declare the exported variable that stores the bundle along with its scope. This flexibility makes it simple to use multiple bundles within the same JSP page interchangeably.

Note that the JSTL does provide a mechanism to set a default resource bundle for a web application via the following configuration setting in the application's deployment descriptor (web.xml):

```
<context-param>
  <param-name>
    javax.servlet.jsp.jstl.fmt.localizationContext
  </param-name>
  <param-value>messages.MyMessages</param-value>
</context-param>
```

### The <fmt:message> Action

As mentioned earlier, localized messages are retrieved from a resource bundle by using the `<fmt:message>` action, which uses a key parameter to extract the message from the resource bundle and print it to the current JspWriter.

You've also seen that the `<fmt:message>` action can be used by itself on a page or as body content to the `<fmt:bundle>` action. Should you wish to use the action by itself, you can specify via the optional bundle attribute the resource bundle to use. This can be the default configured bundle or a localization content that has been configured and stored in a separate variable by the `<fmt:setBundle>` action.

Another optional parameter, var, enables the localized message to be stored in a parameter instead of being printed to the JspWriter. As with most of the JSTL tags, the scope of this variable can be set by using the scope attribute.

Let's build a simple working example to demonstrate the `<fmt:setLocale>`, `<fmt:setBundle>`, and `<fmt:message>` tags working together to create a localized JSP page.

Your first task is to set up the locale-specific resources, and in this case you're simply going to localize some simple strings by utilizing a resource bundle. There are several ways to create a resource bundle, but the simplest is to build a list of name-value pairs representing the locale-specific resources that you wish to externalize from the application code. Let's localize some simple strings and provide implementations in both English and Spanish. Start by creating the properties file shown in Listing 4-7.

**Listing 4-7.** *labels_en.properties*

```
nameQuestion=What is your name?
ageQuestion=How old are you?
locationQuestion=Where do you live?
submit=Send
```

The properties file in Listing 4-7 will be stored on the class path (under the WEB-INF\ classes directory, for example) in a file called labels_en.properties. This file will be the English resource bundle for the localization-aware JSP page. Next, create another resource bundle, this time in Spanish, as shown in Listing 4-8.

**Listing 4-8.** *labels_es.properties*

```
nameQuestion=¿Cómo te llamas?
ageQuestion= ¿Cuántos años tiene?
locationQuestion= ¿Dónde vives?
submit=Mande
```

The names stay the same, but this time the values are in Spanish! This bundle must be placed in a file called labels_es.properties.

Now that you have the resource bundles in place, you can code the localized JSP page shown in Listing 4-9.

**Listing 4-9.** *locale.jsp*

```
<%@ taglib uri="http://java.sun.com/jstl/core" prefix="c"%>
<%@ taglib uri="http://java.sun.com/jstl/fmt" prefix="fmt" %>
<fmt:setLocale value="en_GB" scope="request"/>
<fmt:setBundle basename="labels"/>
<h2>Survey</h2>
<form action="">
<table>
  <tr>
    <td><fmt:message key="nameQuestion"/></td>
    <td><input type="text" size="16"></td>
  </tr>
  <tr>
    <td><fmt:message key="ageQuestion"/></td>
    <td><input type="text" size="16"></td>
  </tr>
  <tr>
    <td><fmt:message key="locationQuestion"/></td>
    <td><input type="text" size="16"></td>
  </tr>
  <tr>
    <td><input type="submit" value='<fmt:message key="submit"/>'></td>
  </tr>
</table>
</form>
```

This JSP page sets the locale to be en_GB and configures the resource bundle by using the <fmt:setBundle> action along with the bundle basename called labels. The rest of the JSP builds a small HTML form that asks the user to input some information about herself. Notice how you have localized the labels for the form input fields by using the <fmt:message> action.

Not surprisingly, when you run this code, the locale is set to en_GB and the appropriate resource bundle is loaded. Because the system cannot find a resource bundle named labels_en_GB.properties, the resource bundle that matches is the next more general file that matches, labels_en.properties. With the help of the <fmt:message> actions, the page shown in Figure 4-10 is built and displayed.

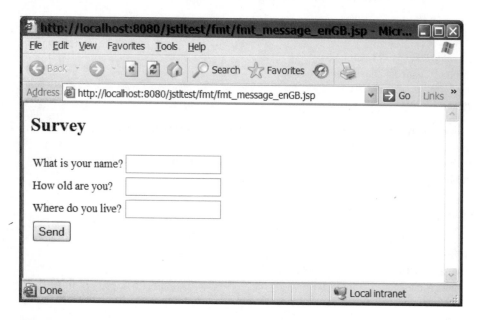

**Figure 4-10.** *With the locale set to en_GB, the page displays the English values for each message key.*

To demonstrate that the page is supported in English-speaking countries as well as Spanish-speaking countries, you simply have to change the following line of code:

```
<fmt:setLocale value="es_ES" scope="request"/>
```

Of course, in the real world, the locale is usually retrieved from a special header that is sent by the client's browser during the initial request. The only reason we explicitly set the locale here is to demonstrate how the JSP page would work in a Spanish-speaking country. The output is shown in Figure 4-11.

**Figure 4-11.** *When the local is set to es_ES, the page displays the Spanish values for the message keys.*

You may be wondering what occurs if the client's browser sends a locale value for which there is no corresponding resource bundle. The answer to this question is left as an exercise to the reader. (Hint: check the spec.)

## Formatting Actions

Ensuring that your clients view your JSP pages in their own language is just the tip of the iceberg with regard to building a fully internationalized and localized application. In addition to language, users from different locales have different standards regarding the following:

- Date and time formats

- Number formats

- Currency formats

- Colors

- Page layouts

- Address standards (zip codes)

Fortunately, to make your job easier, the formatting tag library provided by the JSTL enables various data elements in a JSP page, such as numbers, dates, and times, to be formatted and parsed in a locale-sensitive or customized manner.

### The <fmt:timeZone> and <fmt:setTimeZone> Actions

Date-and-time information on a JSP page can be displayed in a manner consistent with the preferred time zone of a client. This is enormously useful if your server that hosts the page and the client reside in different time zones. The JSTL provides two actions to enable any I18n-aware date-and-time actions to format or parse their date-and-time information in an appropriate manner.

The `<fmt:timeZone>` and `<fmt:setTimeZone>` actions complement each other in a similar fashion as the `<fmt:bundle>` and `<fmt:setBundle>` actions introduced earlier. The `<fmt:timeZone>` action is used to specify a time zone for any nested I18n-aware actions that appear inside its body content, whereas `<fmt:setTimeZone>` can be used to store a reference to a time zone in an exportable variable for use anywhere on a JSP page.

The `<fmt:timeZone>` action is used as follows:

```
<fmt:timeZone value="GMT">
    //...date/time actions go here
</fmt:timeZone>
```

A single attribute called `value` is used to specify the time zone, which can either be a `java.util.TimeZone` object or a string that represents one of the time zone IDs supported by the Java platform (such as "America/Los Angeles" or a custom time zone such as "GMT-8").

The `<fmt:setTimeZone>` action is used as follows:

```
<fmt:setTimeZone value="GMT" var="myTimeZone" scope="request" />
```

This action enables a `java.util.TimeZone` object to be stored in a scoped variable that can be utilized by any I18n-aware actions such as the `<fmt:formatDate>` and `<fmt:parseDate>` actions, which you'll see next.

### The <fmt:formatDate> and <fmt:parseDate> Actions

The two I18n-aware date actions provided by the JSTL are `<fmt:formatDate>` and `<fmt:parseDate>`. Both actions may be used in conjunction with the time-zone actions mentioned earlier.

The `<fmt:formatDate>` action provides flexible, time zone–aware formatting of `java.util.Date` objects so that the date and time may be displayed correctly depending on the client's time zone. In its simplest form, the `<fmt:formatDate>` action applies the default formats of the current time zone and outputs them to the current `JspWriter` as follows:

```
<jsp:useBean id="now"  class="java.util.Date />">
<fmt:formatDate value="${now}"/>
```

As mentioned, the `<fmt:formatDate>` action is highly flexible and provides the ability to display dates and times in predefined or custom formats by using the conventions as set out by the `java.text.DateFormat` class. The ability to store the formatted date in a scoped string variable is also provided.

Listing 4-10 shows just some of the formatting options provided by the `<fmt:formatDate>` action. Notice how the standard `<jsp:useBean>` action is used here to create an instance of the `java.util.Date` class, which is used by the JSTL actions.

**Listing 4-10.** *fmt_formatDate.jsp*

```
<%@ taglib uri="http://java.sun.com/jstl/fmt" prefix="fmt"%>
<jsp:useBean id="now" class="java.util.Date" />
<h1>Examples of Date & Time Formatting</h1>
<hr>
<h2>Default Time Zone</H2>
Default format : <fmt:formatDate value="${now}"/><br>
A Date only in a Custom dd/MM/yyyy format :
 <fmt:formatDate value="${now}" type="DATE" pattern="dd/MM/yyyy"/><br>
A Time only in MEDIUM format :
 <fmt:formatDate value="${now}" type="TIME" dateStyle="MEDIUM"/><br>
A Date and Time in FULL format :
 <fmt:formatDate value="${now}" type="BOTH" dateStyle="FULL"
                 timeStyle="FULL"/><br>
<hr>
<h2>America/Los_Angeles Time Zone</h2>
<fmt:timeZone value="America/Los_Angeles">
Default format : <fmt:formatDate value="${now}"/><br>
A Date only in a Custom MM-dd-yyyy format :
  <fmt:formatDate value="${now}" type="DATE" pattern="MM-dd-yyyy"/><br>
A Time only in MEDIUM format :
  <fmt:formatDate value="${now}" type="TIME" dateStyle="MEDIUM"/><br>
A Date and Time in FULL format :
  <fmt:formatDate value="${now}" type="BOTH" dateStyle="FULL"
                 timeStyle="FULL"/><br>
</fmt:timeZone>
```

Notice that in the first set of examples a time zone isn't specified, so the default time zone is used instead (MDT in this case). There are several examples that demonstrate the predefined date-and-time formats as well as a custom date format of dd/MM/yyyy.

The second set of examples explicitly sets the time zone to America/Los_Angeles by using the `<fmt:timeZone>` action. Notice how the times have been automatically altered to their new time zone—clever, eh! Also notice that you're using a different custom format of MM-dd-yyyy instead this time.

---

**Tip** Valid values for the `value` attribute of the `<fmt:timeZone>` action can be found in the Javadoc for the `java.util.TimeZone` class.

---

Figure 4-12 shows the results of all this formatting.

**Figure 4-12.** *Dates and times can be formatted for specific time zones by using tags in the formatting functional area.*

The `<fmt:parseDate>` action provides complementary functionality to the `<fmt:formatDate>` action by parsing and converting the string representation of dates and times that were formatted in a locale-sensitive or customized manner into `java.util.Date` objects. This action is particularly useful if you need to enable clients from around the world to enter date-and-time information in their own local format and have it correctly parsed into the correct object at the server.

```
<fmt:parseDate type="date" pattern="dd/MM/yyyy" var="parsedDate">
    22/12/2005
</fmt:parseDate>
```

Note that the string representing the date to be parsed can be passed in either via the `value` attribute or in the actions body content as seen earlier. Here a custom date format is used to parse the string `22/12/2005` into a `java.util.Date` object and store a reference to it in the variable called `parsedDate`.

### The <fmt:formatNumber> and <fmt:parseNumber> Actions

As mentioned earlier, there are many forms of data that are represented differently based on the time zone or locale. You've seen the JSTL actions to support date-and-time localization, so it should come as no real surprise that support is also provided for the formatting and parsing of numbers.

The `<fmt:formatNumber>` action is also flexible and capable of formatting a numeric value in a locale-sensitive or custom format as a number, currency, or percentage. For example, the following action ensures that the given number has at least three decimal places:

```
<fmt:formatNumber value="123.4" type="NUMBER" minFractionDigits="3" />
```

The result of this action will be to format the number 123.4 into the value 123.400. To demonstrate the I18n capabilities of the `<fmt:formatNumber>` action, you can also automatically extract the correct currency symbol from the locale when working with monetary values:

```
<%@page contentType="text/html;charset=ISO-8859-15" %>
<c:set var="salary" value="125000" />
<fmt:setLocale value="en_GB"/>
<fmt:formatNumber type="CURRENCY" value="${salary}" /><BR>
<fmt:setLocale value="fr_CH"/>
<fmt:formatNumber type="CURRENCY" value="${salary}" /><BR>
<fmt:setLocale value="fr_FR"/>
<fmt:formatNumber type="CURRENCY" value="${salary}" /><BR>
<fmt:setLocale value="it_IT"/>
<fmt:formatNumber type="CURRENCY" value="${salary}" />
```

The previous example sets the local currency to be first English, then Swiss, then French, and finally Italian. It formats a currency in each case (notice the `type="CURRENCY"` attribute) with the value of 125000 in the current locale. The results of the formatting actions are as follows:

- English locale = £125,000.00
- Swish locale = SFr. 125'000.00
- French locale = 125 000.00 €
- Italian locale = € 125.000,00

Notice how the change in locale and the usage of the page directive content-type attribute radically affects the way the value is interpreted. Depending on the locale, either the British pound, Swiss franc, or Euro symbol is displayed. In addition, notice the usage of various formatting styles for the digits themselves.

As with the `<fmt:parseDate>` action, the `<fmt:parseNumber>` action is the reverse formatting tag, used to convert a formatted string representing either a number, currency, or percentage into an appropriate `java.lang.Number`.

## The SQL Tag Library

The use of SQL or any form of direct-data access from inside the presentation tier is highly discouraged in production or large-scale applications in favor of a three-tier architecture. The benefits of such an architecture are that it encourages the presentation of your data (your JSP pages) to be cleanly separated from your business logic and data access, thereby making your application far more adaptable and maintainable. Embedding SQL into your presentation tier is also a bad idea because of the implications it has on security.

However, as mentioned earlier, the JSTL specification was developed as part of the Java Community Process (JCP), and because enough developers requested a library of actions to access relational databases, their wish was granted. These actions form part of the JSTL specification.

Love them or loathe them, the SQL access actions exist. Their intended use is recommended for Rapid Application Development (RAD) prototyping or very small-scale applications only. Let's take a brief look at the functionality provided by the SQL tag library.

### The <sql:setDataSource> Action

All the actions provided in the SQL tag library operate on a data source defined by the `java.sql.DataSource` class. The primary job of the `<sql:setDataSource>` action is therefore to configure a data source that represents an underlying physical data store and expose it as either a scoped variable or the data source configuration object `javax.servlet.jsp.jstl.sql.DataSource`.

The configured data source is used by the remaining actions in the SQL library to source database connections so they may perform queries and updates, and so on.

A data source can be configured as follows:

```
<sql:setDataSource var="dataSource" driver="org.acme.sql.driver"
                   url="jdbc:msql://localhost/tempDB" user="Dan" password="pwd"/>
```

The `var` attribute sets a label by which the data source can be accessed. The `driver` attribute is the fully qualified class name of the JDBC driver class that is used to communicate with the data source. The `url` attribute is the JDBC URL used to connect to the data source. The `user` and `password` attributes are the username and password used to log in to the data source. More information on JDBC can be found at `http://java.sun.com/products/jdbc`.

Note that it's also possible to supply a relative path to a Java Naming and Directory Interface (JNDI) resource via the optional `dataSource` attribute. If you have a JNDI name for the `dataSource`, then providing it in the `dataSource` attribute will cause the JSP page to perform a JNDI lookup for the data source. In this case, you do not need to provide any of the other attributes because they are provided as part of the resource accessed through JNDI.

### The <sql:query> Action

Simple database query functionality is provided by the `<sql:query>` action:

```
<sql:query var="users" dataSource="${dataSource}" >
  SELECT * FROM User WHERE UserName='Dan'
</sql:query>
```

The dataSource attribute is used to reference a DataSource that was configured by using the <sql:setDataSource> action. The mandatory var parameter is used to store the result of the query and is of type javax.servlet.jsp.jstl.sql.Result. It's possible to pass the string of SQL as either body content or by using the sql attribute.

It's most familiar to see the <sql:query> and <c:forEach> actions working together to display the results of the query in an HTML table as follows:

```
<sql:query var="users" dataSource="myDataSource" >
  SELECT * FROM User WHERE UserName='Dan'
</sql:query>
<table>
<c:forEach var="row" items="${users.row}">
  <tr>
   <td><c:out value="${row.firstName}" /></td>
   <td><c:out value="${row.lastName}" /></td>
   <td><c:out value="${row.phoneNumber}" /></td>
  </tr>
</c:forEach>
</table>
```

---

■**Caution**  If the dataSource attribute is present, the <sql:query> action must not be nested inside a <sql:transaction> action. The <sql:transaction> action is covered later in this chapter.

---

### The <sql:update> Action

To complement the <sql:query> action, the <sql:update> action enables SQL Data Manipulation Language INSERT, UPDATE, and DELETE statements to be executed. It is also used to execute SQL Data Definition Language statements, such as a table creation or alteration statements.

The syntax of this action is similar to that of the <sql:query> action. Again, a var attribute is available to store the result of the <sql:update> action except this time it's not mandatory. The type of the var parameter is java.lang.Integer.

```
<sql:update var="count" dataSource="myDataSource">
  DELETE FROM Users WHERE UserName <> 'Dan'
</sql:update>
```

### The <sql:param> and <sql:dateParam> Actions

Both the <sql:query> and <sql:update> actions provide support for nested <sql:param> and <sql:dateParam> actions that are used to pass parameters into a parameterized string of SQL.

Both actions are incredibly simple and exist only to hold a simple object via its value attribute:

```
<sql:param value="${userName}"/>
```

To see how these tags could be used as part of a parameterized SQL statement, revisit the example you saw in the <sql:update> example:

```
<sql:update var="count" dataSource="myDataSource">
  DELETE FROM Users WHERE UserName <> ? AND Status = ?
  <sql:param value="${userName}"/>
  <sql:param value="${status}"/>
</sql:update>
```

The values held by each nested <sql:param> action are substituted for each parameter marker ("?") in the SQL. The order in which the <sql:param> actions occur determines which parameter is substituted.

### The <sql:transaction> Action

The final action provided by the SQL tag library is the <sql:transaction> action, which enables a series of SQL actions to be grouped together to provide transactional behavior. Transactions enable a series of database actions (such as queries, insertions, deletions, and so on) to be treated as a single atomic action. The transaction is committed permanently to the database only when all the database actions within it complete successfully; otherwise, the transaction is rolled back and any actions are reversed.

Any <sql:query> or <sql:update> actions that wish to be included as part of the transaction are nested inside the <sql:transaction> action itself. For example, let's add the previous examples to demonstrate the <sql:query> and <sql:update> actions inside a transaction:

```
<sql:transaction dataSource="myDataSource" isolation="read_committed">
  <sql:query var="users">
    SELECT * FROM User WHERE UserName='Dan'
  </sql:query>
  <sql:update var="count">
    DELETE FROM Users WHERE UserName <> ? AND Status = ?
    <sql:param value="${userName}"/>
    <sql:param value="${status}"/>
  </sql:update>
</sql:transaction>
```

As you can see, it's simplicity itself! If both the <sql:query> and <sql:update> actions complete successfully, the transaction will automatically be committed! If either the SELECT command or the DELETE command fails, the entire transaction is rolled back.

The only points to be aware of are that any nested SQL tags must not supply their own dataSource attributes because the DataSource is declared by the <sql:transaction> action itself. An optional isolation attribute can also be supplied to set the isolation level of the transaction. This attribute must be one of the following values:

- read_committed

- read_uncommitted

- repeatable_read

- serializable

If not supplied, the isolation level is taken from the data source configuration itself.

# The XML Processing Tag Library

XML has become the de facto standard for representing and exchanging data between enterprise applications. Data represented by XML isn't only "self-describing" and easy to validate, but it's also text based, which has further increased its popularity, especially with the recent rise of web services technologies.

Increasingly, XML is also being used internally by web applications to represent data retrieved from the business or database layer, which is then rendered into an appropriate format (HTML, WML, and so on) by the presentation layer. Therefore, more and more JSP page authors have to manipulate XML in order to generate some content. Until now, using XML data has been a nontrivial task, often requiring specific programming skills of the page author. To address this problem, the JSTL provides an XML processing tag library that is designed to solve many of the common tasks met by page authors using XML data.

The XML processing tag library can be split into the following functional areas concerned with XML data:

- XML core actions

- XML flow control actions

- XML transformation actions

The first two functional areas are very similar in nature to the core and flow control actions provided by the Core tag library, except that they are designed to work with XML data. The XML transformation actions enable XML data to be transformed into other content by using XSL Transformations (XSLT) stylesheets.

Naturally, one of the key requirements when dealing with XML documents is to be able to easily manipulate their content. The actions from the XML processing tag library are no different and are all based around XPath (a W3C recommendation since 1999) to select and specify individual parts of an XML document by a simple XPath expression.

---

■**Note**  To use XPath with the examples in this section, you will need the Xalan libraries. If you downloaded the JWSDP as described in the beginning of this chapter, you can find the Xalan libraries in the `jaxp\lib\endorsed` directory. Alternately, you can download Xalan from Apache. We downloaded the Xalan libraries from `http://xml.apache.org/xalan-j/` and then copied the JAR files to the `lib` directory of the application.

---

The actions provided by the XML processing tag library support the use of only XPath expressions, which are evaluated by an appropriate XPath engine, via the `select` attribute. All other expressions are evaluated in the standard manner by the global EL in use.

In addition to the standard XPath syntax, the XPath engine provided by the JSTL also supports the following "scopes," which may be used in XPath expressions to access data stored in the various web applications' scopes.

```
$param:
$header:
$cookie:
$initParam:
$pageScope:
$requestScope:
$sessionScope:
$applicationScope:
```

You should be familiar with these scopes as they are defined in the same manner as those used in the JSTL EL. Consider the following XPath expression:

```
$sessionScope:user
```

This expression could be used in a similar manner to the standard JSTL EL to reference an attribute called user stored inside the session scope.

## XML Core Actions

As the name suggests, the XML core actions provide fundamental tasks required to interact with an XML document such as parsing and accessing the XML content.

### The <x:parse>, <x:out>, and <x:set> Actions

The <x:parse> action simply parses a named XML document and saves it inside a scoped variable for use by other tags from the XML tag library. For example, let's imagine you're working with the XML file in Listing 4-11 that describes a book:

**Listing 4-11.** *book.xml*

```
<book>
    <title>Professional JSP</title>
    <author>Brown et. al</author>
    <isbn>1-59059-513-0</isbn>
    <published>September 2005</published>
    <publisher>Apress</publisher>
    <url>www.apress.com/book/bookDisplay.html?bID=464</url>
</book>
```

Assuming this file is stored in a file called book.xml, you can parse this file and store the resulting object as follows:

```
<%@ taglib uri="http://java.sun.com/jstl/core" prefix="c" %>
<%@ taglib uri="http://java.sun.com/jstl/xml" prefix="x" %>
<c:import url="book.xml" var="url" />
<x:parse xml="${url}" var="book" scope="session" />
```

Hopefully you'll be comfortable with the `<c:import>` action from the Core library, which is used to generate the appropriate URL to the `book.xml` file (which is stored in the same directory as the JSP page). The `<x:parse>` action parses the XML file and stores it in the session-scoped variable `book`.

In the earlier example, the `var` parameter was used to indicate the name of a scoped variable to hold the object created as a result of the parse. The JSTL specification doesn't define the type for this object and leaves it up to the container to specify the most appropriate type. However, if the parameter `varDom` were used instead, the JSTL specification would insist that the type of the resulting object must be `org.w3c.dom.Document`.

If you're familiar with the JSTL Core tag library introduced earlier, you should be able to guess what the `<x:out>` and `<x:set>` actions do because they're like similarly named tags from the Core tag library. These similarities aren't by chance; the `<x:out>` and `<x:set>` actions from the XML tag library are functionally identical to the `<c:out>` and `<c:set>` actions from the Core tag library except that they're designed to work with XML documents.

The `<x:out>` action evaluates an XPath expression (reference to somewhere in the XML document) and outputs the result of the evaluation to the current `JspWriter`. Let's build on the earlier example to demonstrate the use of the `<x:out>` action. Listing 4-12 shows a JSP page that uses various actions including the `<c:import>`, the `<x:parse>`, and the `<x:out>` actions.

**Listing 4-12.** *xml_out.jsp*

```
<%@ taglib uri="http://java.sun.com/jstl/core" prefix="c" %>
<%@ taglib uri="http://java.sun.com/jstl/xml" prefix="x" %>
<c:import url="book.xml" var="url" />
<x:parse xml="${url}" var="book" scope="session" />
<b><x:out select="$book/book/title"/></b><br>
<x:out select="$book/book/author"/><br>
<x:out select="$book/book/url"/><br>
```

You still parse the XML file in the same way, but this time some `<x:out>` actions have been added that can be used to extract the values of the `title`, `author`, and `url` nodes from beneath the parent `book` node (take a look at the earlier `book.xml` in Listing 4-11 if you're confused). The document is parsed and interrogated by the `<x:out>` actions that use XPath expressions to retrieve the required data. Figure 4-13 shows the output of the JSP page in Listing 4-12.

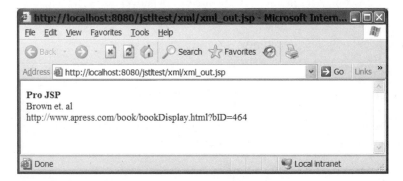

**Figure 4-13.** *XML tags can be used to parse and output values from XML formatted data.*

As mentioned earlier, the <x:set> action is also very close to the <c:set> action from the Core tag library. Instead of evaluating an XPath expression and returning it to the current JspWriter, the <x:set> actions simply store the values inside scoped variables.

Just to demonstrate all three tags working together, let's see how the <x:set> action can be used in the previous example:

```
<%@ taglib uri="http://java.sun.com/jstl/core" prefix="c" %>
<%@ taglib uri="http://java.sun.com/jstl/xml" prefix="x" %>
<c:import url="book.xml" var="url" />
<x:parse xml="${url}" var="book" scope="session" />
<x:set select="$book/book/title" var="title" scope="session"/>
<x:set select="$book/book/author" var="author" scope="session"/>
<x:set select="$book/book/url" var="bookUrl" scope="session"/>
<b><x:out select="$title" /></b><br>
<x:out select="$author" /><br>
<x:out select="$bookUrl" /><br>
```

Instead of using the <x:out> action to retrieve the values from the XML directly, you use the <x:set> action to store the values to scoped variables first and then output them via the <x:out> action.

## XML Flow Control Actions

Now that you've seen how you can parse, store, and retrieve XML data, you can take a look at the XML flow control actions that conditionally process JSP code based on the result of an XPath expression and iterate over elements inside an XML document.

Again, the XML flow control actions bear a striking resemblance to the flow control actions from the Core tag library. The only difference is—yes, you've guessed it—they work with XML documents!

### The <x:if> Action

Like the <c:if> action from the Core tag library, the <x:if> action conditionally processes some JSP code based on a Boolean expression. The only difference is that the <x:if> action uses an XPath expression that is evaluated and converted into a Boolean according to the semantics of the XPath boolean() function:

- A number is true if and only if it's neither zero (positive or negative) nor NaN (Not A Number).

- A nodeset is true if and only if it's nonempty.

- A string is true if and only if its length is nonzero.

The <x:if> action processes its body content only if the Boolean condition evaluates to true.

Let's use the book.xml example again to work on the marketing tactics for new Apress titles! Listing 4-13 shows a JSP page that uses the <x:if> action.

**Listing 4-13.** *xml_if.jsp*

```
<%@ taglib uri="http://java.sun.com/jstl/core" prefix="c" %>
<%@ taglib uri="http://java.sun.com/jstl/xml" prefix="x" %>
<c:import url="book.xml" var="url" />
<x:parse xml="${url}" var="book" scope="session" />
<x:if select="$book/book/publisher='Apress'">
  Another great title from Apress!
  <p>
  <b><x:out select="$book/book/title"/></b><br>
  <x:out select="$book/book/author"/><br>
  <x:out select="$book/book/url"/><br>
</x:if>
```

You can see that the `<x:if>` action enables you to control whether to output any information based on the content of the XML. In this case, if the value of the book's `Publisher` attribute is `Apress`, you'll happily publicize the book and generate some content. If the Boolean condition is `false` and a different publisher has been used, you won't generate any information about the book—sneaky, eh!

According to the `book.xml` you used earlier, the book has indeed been published by Apress and so the body of the previous `<x:if>` action may be processed. Figure 4-14 shows the result.

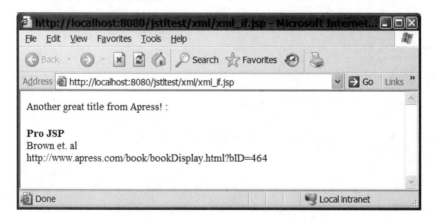

**Figure 4-14.** *The <x:if> action can produce conditional output.*

### The <x:choose>, <x:when>, and <x:otherwise> Actions

To complement the `<x:if>` action mentioned earlier, there are also a set of actions to provide mutually exclusive, XML-dependent conditional behavior in exactly the same way as the actions in the Core tag library.

The following JSP page builds on the earlier example and provides you with the ability to market books from different publishers with different content:

```
<%@ taglib uri="http://java.sun.com/jstl/core" prefix="c" %>
<%@ taglib uri="http://java.sun.com/jstl/xml" prefix="x" %>
```

```
<c:import url="book.xml" var="url" />
<x:parse xml="${url}" var="book" scope="session" />
<x:choose>
  <x:when select="$book/book/publisher='Apress'">
    Another great title from Apress!
  </x:when>

  <x:when select="$book/book/publisher='Bloggs Publisher'">
    A reasonable title from Bloggs Publisher!
  </x:when>

  <x:otherwise>
    A title from an unknown publisher
  </x:otherwise>
</x:choose>
<p>
<b><x:out select="$book/book/title"/></b><br>
<x:out select="$book/book/author"/><br>
<x:out select="$book/book/url"/><br>
```

By using the `<x:choose>` action, you can provide different content depending on the value of an XPath expression, or the value of the `<Publisher>` element in this case. If the value is Apress, you provide the flagship introduction but provide books by Bloggs Publisher with a separate but toned-down introduction. Any titles by other publishers are handled by the `<x:otherwise>` action to give a low-key introduction.

### The <x:forEach> Action

Of course, XML documents in the real world are likely to be far more complicated than the simple book.xml example you've been using. For one, the file contains the description of only a single book. Let's complicate matters slightly by changing the format of the XML to cope with multiple books, as shown in Listing 4-14.

**Listing 4-14.** *books.xml*

```
<books>
  <book>
    <title>Professional JSP</title>
    <author>Brown et. al</author>
    <isbn>1-59059-513-9</isbn>
    <published>September 2005</published>
    <publisher>Apress</publisher>
    <url>www.apress.com/book/bookDisplay.html?bID=200</url>
  </book>
  <book>
    <title>Macbeth</title>
    <author>William Shakespeare</author>
```

```
      <isbn>1123456789</isbn>
      <published>A long time ago</published>
      <publisher>Bloggs Publisher</publisher>
      <url>http://booksrus.co.uk/titles/1123456789.html</url>
   </book>
   <book>
       <title>Fly Fishing</title>
       <author>JR Hartley</author>
       <isbn>987654321</isbn>
       <published>May 1947</published>
       <publisher>ABC Printers Press</publisher>
       <url>http://books.com/books.jsp?id=987654321</url>
   </book>
</books>
```

It should be quite obvious that the existing solution for marketing the books as described by the XML won't work with multiple titles. You've changed the XML structure as well so that the <books> element now contains several <book> elements. You need another solution.

Thankfully, the JSTL XML library provides an iterating action <x:forEach> that is especially designed for such a purpose and works in a similar way to the <c:forEach> action from the Core tag library.

To iterate over the <book> elements, the <x:forEach> action accepts an XPath expression that points to the <book> element and stores it in a scoped variable as follows:

```
<x:forEach select="$book/books/book" var="currentBook">
   ...
</x:forEach>
```

The first <book> element will be stored in the variable currentBook and may be accessed by XML actions such as <x:out>, <x:set>, and so on, inside the body of the action. All you need to do, really, is wrap the existing code from the previous example inside of an <x:forEach> action and the iteration will be handled automatically; then hopefully all the books in books.xml will be publicized!

Listing 4-15 demonstrates this simple functionality. Note that the only other changes that have occurred are some minor HTML changes to make the generated page look a little more professional. For now, just concentrate on spotting how the <x:forEach> action encapsulates all the previous example code you've seen so far.

### Listing 4-15. *xml_forEach.jsp*

```
<%@ taglib uri="http://java.sun.com/jstl/core" prefix="c" %>
<%@ taglib uri="http://java.sun.com/jstl/xml" prefix="x" %>
<c:import url="books.xml" var="url" />
<x:parse xml="${url}" var="book" scope="session" />
<x:forEach select="$book/books/book" var="currentBook">
  <x:choose>
    <x:when select="$currentBook/publisher='Apress'">
```

```
      <font color="red">
        <h1>Another great title from Apress!</h1>
      </font>
    </x:when>

    <x:when select="$currentBook/publisher='Bloggs Publisher'">
      <font color="red">
        <h2>A reasonable title from Bloggs Publisher!</h2>
      </font>
    </x:when>

    <x:otherwise>
      <font color="red">
        <h3>A title from an unknown publisher</h3>
      </font>
    </x:otherwise>
  </x:choose>
  <table border="0">
    <tr>
      <td colspan="2"><b><x:out select="$currentBook/title"/><b></td>
    </tr>
    <tr>
      <td><i>Author :</i></td>
      <td><x:out select="$currentBook/author"/></td>
    </tr>
    <tr>
      <td><i>ISBN :</i></td>
      <td><x:out select="$currentBook/isbn"/></td>
    </tr>
    <tr>
      <td><i>Published :</i></td>
      <td><x:out select="$currentBook/published"/></td>
    </tr>
    <tr>
      <td><i>URL :</i></td>
      <td><a href='<x:out select="$currentBook/url"/>'>
                  <x:out select="$currentBook/title"/></a></td>
    </tr>
  </table>
  <hr>
</x:forEach>
```

To give you an idea of what the finished article looks like, take a look at Figure 4-15. You'll agree that before the JSTL existed, loading, parsing, and building such a page would have been a nontrivial task, but now it's really simple!

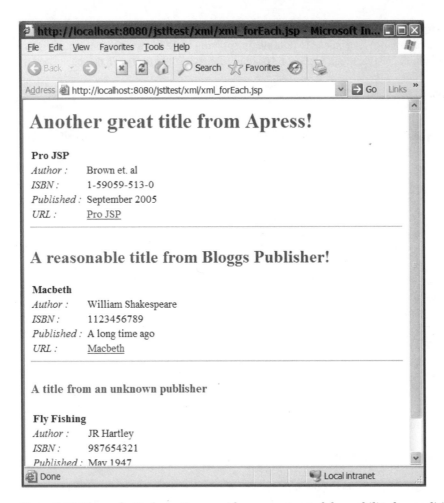

**Figure 4-15.** *The <x:forEach> action provides a more powerful capability for conditional formatting than the <x:if> action.*

## XML Transformation Actions

The XML standard tag library also includes tags that allow you to transform XML data into other formats such as HTML or WML.

### The <x:transform> Action

Quite simply, the XML transformation actions provided by the JSTL are designed to apply an XSLT stylesheet to an XML document. Usually, the result of the XSLT transformation is returned as output, but it's also possible to store the result inside a scoped variable instead so that it may be accessed by some of the other XML actions that you've already seen.

To demonstrate the capabilities of the `<x:transform>` actions, let's transform the `books.xml` file that you saw earlier into a simple HTML table by applying an XSLT transformation. The first step is to create the XSLT stylesheet; Listing 4-16 shows the stylesheet that we'll call `books.xsl`.

**Listing 4-16.** *books.xsl*

```xml
<?xml version="1.0"?>
<xsl:stylesheet version="1.0" xmlns:xsl="http://www.w3.org/1999/XSL/Transform">
<xsl:template match="/">


<html>
<body>
<h2>Our Current Book List</h2>
<table border="2">
  <tr>
    <!-- the header -->
    <td>title</td>
    <td>author</td>
    <td>isbn</td>
    <td>published</td>
    <td>publisher</td>
    <td>url</td>
  </tr>

  <xsl:for-each select="books/book">
    <tr>
      <td><b><xsl:value-of select="title"/></b></td>
      <td><xsl:value-of select="author"/></td>
      <td><xsl:value-of select="isbn"/></td>
      <td><xsl:value-of select="published"/></td>
      <td><i><xsl:value-of select="publisher"/></i></td>
      <td><xsl:value-of select="url"/></td>
    </tr>
  </xsl:for-each>
</table>
</body>
</html>
</xsl:template>
</xsl:stylesheet>
```

Although this chapter isn't intended to be a guide to XSLT transformations, hopefully you can follow this code. In a nutshell, the `<xsl:for-each select="books/book">` expression is a simple way of iterating over a series of elements as defined by the XPath expression `books/book` (all the `<book>` elements beneath the root `<books>` element). The code inside the `<xsl:for-each>` expression creates the data for a single row of the HTML table by extracting the required elements (that is, `<xsl:value-of select="title"/>` extracts the value of the `<title>` element).

To apply this stylesheet (books.xsl) to the XML file (books.xml), you can import the XML and XSL files and use the <x:transform> action as shown in Listing 4-17.

**Listing 4-17.** *xml_transform.jsp*

```
<%@ taglib uri="http://java.sun.com/jstl/core" prefix="c" %>
<%@ taglib uri="http://java.sun.com/jstl/xml" prefix="x" %>
<c:import url="books.xml" var="books" />
<c:import url="books.xsl" var="xslt" />
<x:transform xml="${books}" xslt="${xslt}"/>
```

You must agree that this is a very simple page, but thanks to the JSTL actions you now have a powerful mechanism for producing content from XML files. JSP page authors need not have any Java skills whatsoever in order to produce rich content. Just consider how much more difficult (and cluttered, less maintainable, ugly, and so on) this would have been with a scriptlet-based approach. Thankfully, those days are behind you!

Figure 4-16 shows the outcome of the JSTL-based XSLT transformation.

**Figure 4-16.** *Using the <x:transform> action, XML-formatted data can be transformed into other formats, such as HTML or WML.*

**The <x:param> Action**

It's also possible to pass parameters into XSL transformations by nesting <x:param> actions inside the <x:transform> action. This facility is similar to the <sql:param> and <sql:dateParam> actions from the SQL tag library, which are used to pass SQL parameters to the various actions in the SQL library.

The `<x:param>` action is simple and has only two attributes:

```
<x:transform xml="${books}" xslt="${xslt}">
  <x:param name="myParam" value="myValue"/>
</x:transform>
```

As with the SQL parameters, the value of the `<x:param>` action can be passed either as an attribute or as the body content of the action itself, as follows:

```
<x:transform xml="${books}" xslt="${xslt}">
  <x:param name="myParam">MyValue</x:param>
</x:transform>
```

# Summary

In this chapter, you've learned about the reasons for the creation of the JSTL and about its dependencies on the Java Servlet and JSP specifications. You've taken an in-depth look at the actions provided by the individual tag libraries that collectively form the JSTL.

Here's a quick recap of the topics covered:

- The Servlet/JSP dependencies

- Installation of the JSTL into Tomcat 5

- The JSP 2.1 EL support

- The four tag libraries that are encompassed by the JSTL

After reading this chapter, you should be able to appreciate some of the drawbacks that developers came across before the release of the JSP 2.1 specification. Cluttering JSP pages with too much scriptlet code makes them hard to read and less maintainable. Because one of the primary goals of JSP 2.1 is to make JSP pages easier to write, the JSTL perfectly embodies this ideology and can be used to provide reusable, easy-to-maintain functionality for many simple, everyday tasks that JSP page authors are faced with.

After reading this chapter, you should immediately be able to see how you can install and use the actions provided by the JSTL in your web applications, thereby making them a lot cleaner, easier to read, and ultimately, of a higher quality.

# CHAPTER 5

■ ■ ■

# JavaServer Faces

**J**avaServer Faces (JSF), a relatively new technology in the Java EE world, is designed to further simplify web-application development. JSF makes it easy to build user-interface components and pages, and to connect those components to business objects. It also automates the process of JavaBean usage and page navigation.

JSF is not the first technology to attempt to create a GUI framework for web applications. Other GUI frameworks include Apache's Tapestry project (`http://jakarta.apache.org/tapestry`), Enhydra's Barracuda project (`http://www.barracudamvc.org/Barracuda`), the Sun Java System Application Framework (`http://developers.sun.com/sw/tech/appserver/framework/`), and the Oracle Application Development Framework (ADF) User Interface in XML (UIX) (`http://www.oracle.com/technology/products/jdev/collateral/papers/10g/ADFFAQ`). One of the goals of JSF, as stated in the specification proposal, was to create a standard for Java server application GUIs and to identify synergies in existing frameworks that JSF could take advantage of. The expert group included some of the same organizations that had been working on other GUI frameworks. Version 1.0 of the specification was finalized in March 2004. At the time of this writing, version 1.2 of the specification is in Proposed Final Draft stage.

JSF builds on the experience gained from JSP, Servlet, and the various other web-application GUI frameworks. In particular, JSF builds on the Apache Struts project. This is not surprising considering that the creator of Struts is the lead specification engineer for JSF. (If you're a Struts enthusiast, you might want to know that you can even use JSF with Struts. For more information on Struts, see Chapter 15 and `http://struts.apache.org`).

You might be wondering why we are focusing on JSF in a book about JSP. Simply put, JSF complements JSP. In fact, the JSF specification requires that all JSF implementations support JSP and provide custom actions for JSP corresponding to JSF user-interface components.

In this chapter, you will learn the following:

- Why JSF was developed and how it helps you to create dynamic user interfaces

- How to install JSF

- How to use custom tags for JSF components in JSP pages

- How to use managed JavaBeans with JSF components

- How to control page navigation

- How to convert data and validate input

- How to handle value change events in your JSF application

# Introduction to JSF

The JSF specification lists the following ways that JSF helps web-application developers to create user interfaces (UIs):

- Makes it easy to construct a UI from a set of reusable UI components

- Simplifies migration of application data to and from the UI

- Helps manage UI state across server requests

- Provides a simple model for wiring client-generated events to server-side application code

- Allows custom UI components to be easily built and reused

UI development is easier because UI components are provided as reusable objects. A number of classes, corresponding to UI components, are part of the JSF specification and implementation. Rather than have to worry about the syntax of page layout, you simply drop the UI components into your application. A custom render kit and rendering process convert the components into appropriate page-layout code. The JSF implementation comes with a default render kit for HTML, but the same JSF code can be rendered by other render kits for other client systems. This means that you can use the same JSF code for a variety of client systems, and use different render kits to customize the UI for each client system.

Moving application data to and from the UI is simplified by letting the JSF implementation handle the mechanics of data transfer. You simply specify which data goes where, and the JSF implementation handles the process of moving the data from UI objects to business objects and vice versa. The JSF implementation automatically manages state across user requests, so you do not need to manage or implement any session handling.

Just as it simplifies data handling, JSF provides an easy way to manage event handling. You specify the events of interest and the business objects or classes to handle the events, and the JSF implementation takes care of calling the appropriate methods to handle any events that are generated. The JSF event-handling model is similar to those used in other UI frameworks, such as Java Swing. Specifically, this means that multiple event listeners can respond to a single event.

Finally, because JSF is based on reusable components, it provides a design that allows you to easily create and integrate your own components or third-party components into your JSF-enabled applications. If you are a vendor, JSF allows you to create custom components that can be marketed to developers and page designers.

As with all the enterprise Java technologies, detailed information about the technology can be found in the JSF specification, which can be found at `http://java.sun.com/j2ee/javaserverfaces`.

## The Relationship Between JSF and Other Java EE Technologies

Within the Java Platform, Enterprise Edition 5 (Java EE 5), technologies such as JSP and Servlet are stand-alone technologies. You could, if you wanted to, create an application using only servlets or only JSP pages. JSF is different because it is a *supporting* technology. You use it in conjunction with JSP pages, servlets, or other presentation technologies.

The primary design pattern of JSF is the Model-View-Controller (MVC) pattern. As you saw in Chapter 1, MVC separates an application architecture into three categories of components: model, view, and controller. The model is the abstraction of all the domain data in the system. It is the bank account in a banking application, or a shopping cart in an e-commerce system. The view is the visualization of the model. In a web application, the view consists of the HTML pages and the components that create the HTML pages sent to web browsers, the Wireless Application Protocol (WAP) pages sent to mobile devices, or the UI components sent to a dedicated client. The controller is the set of components that manage the communications between model and view.

As you've learned in the previous chapters, you can create user interfaces with JSP. In fact, as you saw, JSP was designed to make the view component of a web application easy to create and manage. It is also possible, although not as easy, to create UIs with servlets. However, combining JSF with JSP or Servlet technology makes UI creation—and integration of the model, view, and controller—easier by far. JSF brings a component-based model to web-application development that is similar to the model that has been used in stand-alone GUI applications for years.

To use JSF with servlets, you use the components that make up JSF directly; that is, within your servlet, you explicitly create and use instances of UI component classes. However, because this is a book about JSP, we will focus exclusively on using JSF with JSP. The JSF implementation includes a tag library of custom tags, similar to the JSTL (see Chapter 4), that you can use with JSP to easily create JSF-enabled applications.

## Request-Processing Life Cycle

Regardless of whether you are using JSF with JSP pages, servlets, or some other web technology, each request/response flow that involves JSF follows a certain life cycle. Several kinds of request/response cycles can occur in a JSF-enabled application. You can have a request that comes from a previously rendered JSF page (a JSF request) and a request that comes from a non-JSF page (a non-JSF request). Likewise, you can have a JSF response or a non-JSF response. We are concerned with these three request/response pairs:

- Non-JSF request generates JSF response

- JSF request generates JSF response

- JSF request generates non-JSF response

Of course, you can also have a non-JSF request that generates a non-JSF response. Because this does not involve JSF in any way, the JSF life cycle does not apply.

Recall that JSP pages have a relatively simple life cycle. A JSP page source is compiled into a page implementation class. When a web server receives a request, that request is passed to the container, which passes the request to the page class. The page class processes the request and then writes the response back to the client. When other pages are included or the request is forwarded, or when an exception occurs, the process includes a few more components or pages, but basically, a small set of classes processes a request and sends back a response.

When using JSF, the life cycle is more complicated. This is because the core of JSF is the MVC pattern, which has several implications. User actions in JSF-generated views take place in a client that does not have a permanent connection to the server. The delivery of user actions or page events is delayed until a new connection is established. The JSF life cycle must handle this delay between event and event processing. Also, the JSF life cycle must ensure that the view is correct before rendering the view. To ensure that the business state is never invalid, the JSF system includes a phase for validating inputs and another for updating the model only after all inputs pass validation.

In MVC, the presentation of data (the *view*) is separate from its representation in the system (the *model*). When the model is updated, the controller sends a message to the view, telling the view to update its presentation. When the user takes some action with the presentation, the controller sends a message to the model, telling the model to update its data. In JSF, the model is composed of business objects that are usually implemented as JavaBeans, the controller is the JSF implementation, and the UI components are the view.

The JSF life cycle has six phases as defined by the JSF specification:

- **Restore View:** In this phase, the JSF implementation restores the objects and data structures that represent the view of the request. Of course, if this is the client's first visit to a page, the JSF implementation must create the view. When a JSF implementation creates and renders a JSF-enabled page, it creates UI objects for each view component. The components are stored in a component tree, and the state of the UI view is saved for subsequent requests. If this is a subsequent request, the previously saved UI view is retrieved for the processing of the current request.

- **Apply Request Values:** Any data that was sent as part of the request is passed to the appropriate UI objects that compose the view. Those objects update their state with the data values. Data can come from input fields in a web form, from cookies sent as part of the request, or from request headers. Data for some components, such as components that create HTML input fields, is validated at this time. Note that this does not yet update the business objects that compose the model. It updates only the UI components with the new data.

- **Process Validations:** The data that was submitted with the form is validated (if it was not validated in the previous phase). As with the previous phase, this does not yet update the business objects in the application. This is because if the JSF implementation began to update the business objects as data was validated, and a piece of data failed validation, the model would be partially updated and in an invalid state.

- **Update Model Values:** After all validations are complete, the business objects that make up the application are updated with the validated data from the request. In addition, if any of the data needs to be converted to a different format to update the model (for example, converting a String to a Date object), the conversion occurs in this phase. Conversion is needed when the data type of a property is not a String or a Java primitive.

- **Invoke Application:** During this phase, the action method of any command button or link that was activated is called. In addition, any events that were generated during previous phases and that have not yet been handled are passed to the web application so that it can complete any other processing of the request that is required.

- **Render Response:** The response UI components are rendered, and the response is sent to the client. The state of the UI components is saved so that the component tree can be restored when the client sends another request.

For a JSF-enabled application, the thread of execution for a request/response cycle can flow through each phase, in the order listed here and as shown in Figure 5-1. However, depending on the request, and what happens during the processing and response, not every request will flow through all six phases.

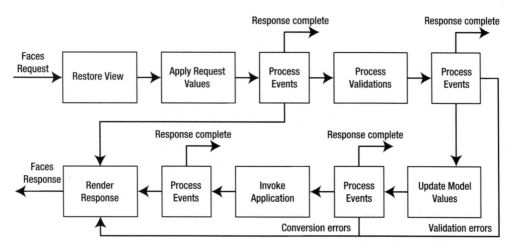

**Figure 5-1.** *When a request is sent to a JSF-enabled application, the request can potentially encompass all six phases of the JSF life cycle.*

In Figure 5-1, you can see a number of optional paths through the life cycle. For example, if errors occur during any of the phases, the flow of execution transfers immediately to the Render Response phase, skipping any remaining phases. One way this might occur is if input data is incorrect or invalid. If data fails validation in either the Apply Request Values or Process Validations phase, information about the error is saved and processing proceeds directly to the Render Response phase. Also, if at any point in the life cycle the request processing is complete and a non-JSF response is to be sent to the client, the flow of execution can exit the life cycle without completing further phases.

# Installing JSF

To run the examples in this chapter, you will need to obtain and install a JSF implementation, and the JSP Standard Tag Library (JSTL) reference implementation. For this chapter, we will use the JSF reference implementation from Sun. If you have an implementation from some other vendor, consult the documentation for that implementation for installation instructions.

If you are running Tomcat 5.0 or 5.5, you can download JSF from http://java.sun.com/ j2ee/javaserverfaces/download.html. Instructions on downloading the JSTL were presented in Chapter 4. For now, simply unpack each distribution as needed into a directory of your choice, remembering where that directory is.

There are two ways that you can make the JSF and JSTL libraries available to your web application running in Tomcat. Both require putting the following eight JAR files, which are located in the lib directory of each distribution, into a location that can be accessed by the server or the web application:

- **Six JSF JARs:** commons-beanutils.jar, commons-collections.jar, commons-digester.jar, commons-logging.jar, jsf-api.jar, and jsf-impl.jar

- **Two JSTL JARs:** jstl.jar and standard.jar

As you saw in Chapter 4, one way to make API libraries available to a web application is to place them into the WEB-INF\lib directory of the web application. Then only that application will have access to those libraries. If you have another JSF application, that application would also need access to those files in its own WEB-INF\lib directory.

Alternatively, if you have several JSF applications, you can put the JAR files into a common location. For Tomcat, that location is %TOMCAT_HOME%\common\lib. When the JAR files are located in the common directory, then every application in the application server has access to them. Note that if you copy the JAR files into the common directory while the server is running, you may need to restart the Tomcat server so the new JAR files can be loaded.

# Using JSF with JSP Pages

Now that you've had an introduction to JSF, let's jump right into creating and deploying a simple JSF application that shows how to use JSF with JSP. Because JSP pages are easy to implement and deploy, this example will clearly demonstrate how to use JSF in a web application. The JSP page holds the template text for the page, and custom tags are used to create the JSF components for the page. The JSF components generate the dynamic content.

The JSF implementation from Sun comes with two libraries of custom actions that you can use with JSP pages: HTML custom actions and core custom actions. The HTML custom actions are for components that vary based on the render kit used. These custom actions are used to create HTML elements. As shown in Table 5-1, the HTML custom actions fall into five categories: input, output, selection, commands, and miscellaneous.

**Table 5-1.** *The HTML Custom Actions*

| Category | Elements | Purpose |
|---|---|---|
| Input | <h:inputHidden>, <h:inputSecret>, <h:inputText>, <h:inputTextarea> | Create various kinds of input elements |
| Output | <h:message>, <h:messages>, <h:outputFormat>, <h:outputLabel>, <h:outputLink>, <h:outputText> | Create various kinds of output elements |
| Selection | <h:selectBooleanCheckbox>, <h:selectManyCheckbox>, <h:selectManyListbox>, <h:selectManyMenu>, <h:selectOneListbox>, <h:selectOneMenu>, <h:selectOneRadio> | Create drop-down menus, list boxes, radio buttons, and check boxes |

| Category | Elements | Purpose |
|---|---|---|
| Commands | `<h:commandButton>`, `<h:commandLink>` | Create buttons or links that cause form submission |
| Miscellaneous | `<h:dataTable>`, `<h:form>`, `<h:graphicImage>`, `<h:panelGrid>`, `<h:panelGroup>`, `<h:column>` | Create various HTML elements such as tables, forms, and panels |

The core custom actions create UI elements that are independent of the render kit. These actions are usually used with the HTML actions listed in Table 5-1 to modify the behavior of those actions. Table 5-2 shows all the core custom actions, listed by category.

**Table 5-2.** *The Core Custom Actions*

| Category | Elements | Purpose |
|---|---|---|
| Converters | `<f:convertDateTime>`, `<f:convertNumber>`, `<f:converter>` | Standard converters |
| Listeners | `<f:actionListener>`, `<f:valueChangeListener>` | Specify a listener for a component |
| Miscellaneous | `<f:attribute>`, `<f:loadBundle>`, `<f:param>`, `<f:verbatim>` | Add attributes or parameters, load a resource bundle, and output verbatim HTML template text |
| Selection | `<f:selectItem>`, `<f:selectItems>` | Specify selection items for HTML selection elements |
| Validators | `<f:validateDoubleRange>`, `<f:validateLength>`, `<f:validateLongRange>`, `<f:validator>` | Standard validators |
| View | `<f:facet>`, `<f:subview>`, `<f:view>` | Create a JSF view or subview |

---

■**Tip**  If you unpack the JSF implementation to your hard drive, a directory of documentation for the custom actions will be saved to the hard drive in `jsf_home\tlddocs\index.html`. This documentation is similar to the Javadoc documentation created with Java source files. For full details on using custom actions, refer to this TLD documentation.

---

In this section, you will see a number of these custom tags in action. We will discuss these tags as we go along.

## Creating a Simple JSF Application

Our example simulates a flight reservation system. Figure 5-2 shows the directory structure of the sample application.

```
Jsf_Ex01
  WEB-INF
    classes
      com
        apress
          projsp
            FlightSearch.class
            FlightSearch.java
    lib
    faces-config.xml
    web.xml
  index.html
  searchForm.jsp
  searchResults.jsp
```

**Figure 5-2.** *The directory structure of the Jsf_Ex01 example*

## Implementing a JavaBean

We'll start this example by showing the JavaBean class that represents the business layer of the web application. This JavaBean will be connected to the presentation layer by the JSF system. The FlightSearch class, shown in Listing 5-1, stores the search parameters entered by the user. Although various parameters can be used when searching for a flight, for this first example we have chosen to include the following: origination airport, destination airport, departure date and time, and arrival date and time.

**Listing 5-1.** *FlightSearch.java*

```java
package com.apress.projsp;

public class FlightSearch {
  String origination;
  String destination;
  String departDate;
  String departTime;
  String returnDate;
  String returnTime;

  public String getDepartDate() {
    return departDate;
  }

  public void setDepartDate(String departDate) {
    this.departDate = departDate;
  }

  public String getDepartTime() {
    return departTime;
  }
}
```

```java
  public void setDepartTime(String departTime) {
    this.departTime = departTime;
  }

  public String getDestination() {
    return destination;
  }

  public void setDestination(String destination) {
    this.destination = destination;
  }

  public String getOrigination() {
    return origination;
  }

  public void setOrigination(String origination) {
    this.origination = origination;
  }

  public String getReturnDate() {
    return returnDate;
  }

  public void setReturnDate(String returnDate) {
    this.returnDate = returnDate;
  }

  public String getReturnTime() {
    return returnTime;
  }

  public void setReturnTime(String returnTime) {
    this.returnTime = returnTime;
  }
}
```

Looking at the class, you can see that it is a standard JavaBean. There is no explicit con-structor, so the compiler provides a default no-argument constructor. There are fields for all the parameters we want to store, and methods for getting and setting each of the fields. This means that all the properties of the class are exposed as read-write properties to the web application. This will allow one part of the application to set the properties and a different part to read the properties. We'll discuss the role of JavaBeans in JSF implementations in more detail later in this chapter, in the "Using Managed Beans" section.

Before deploying this example, you will need to compile the FlightSearch.java source into a class file. Because this source file uses classes from only the java.lang package and does not use any special APIs or classes, you should be able to compile it without needing to reset your CLASSPATH in any way. Use your IDE, your favorite build system, or use `javac` from the command line to compile the class.

## Implementing the View Components

The next part of our example is a web page to accept the user's inputs for searching for a flight. This will be a JSP page with input fields for the origination, destination, departure date and time, and return date and time. Listing 5-2 shows the initial page in our application, `searchForm.jsp`. If you created any of the examples in Chapter 3, you will recall that those examples also used input fields in an HTML page generated by using the expression language (EL) in a JSP page. The `searchForm.jsp` page also uses input fields, but as you will see, they are slightly different from the HTML input fields we used in Chapter 3.

**Listing 5-2.** *searchForm.jsp*

```
<html>
  <%@ taglib uri="http://java.sun.com/jsf/core" prefix="f" %>
  <%@ taglib uri="http://java.sun.com/jsf/html" prefix="h" %>

  <f:view>
  <head>
    <title>Freedom Airlines Online Flight Reservation System</title>
  </head>
  <body>
    <h:form>
      <h2>Search Flights</h2>
      <table>
        <tr><td colspan="4">Where and when do you want to travel?</td></tr>
        <tr>
          <td colspan="2">Leaving from:</td>
          <td colspan="2">Going to:</td>
        </tr>
        <tr>
          <td colspan="2">
            <h:inputText value="#{flight.origination}" size="35"/>
          </td>
          <td colspan="2">
            <h:inputText value="#{flight.destination}" size="35"/>
          </td>
        </tr>
        <tr>
          <td colspan="2">Departing:</td>
          <td colspan="2">Returning:</td>
        </tr>
        <tr>
          <td>
            <h:inputText value="#{flight.departDate}"/>
          </td>
```

```
      <td>
        <h:inputText value="#{flight.departTime}"/>
      </td>
      <td>
        <h:inputText value="#{flight.returnDate}"/>
      </td>
      <td>
        <h:inputText value="#{flight.returnTime}"/>
      </td>
    </tr>
  </table>
  <p>
  <h:commandButton value="Search" action="submit"/>
  </p>
 </h:form>
 </body>
 </f:view>
</html>
```

Throughout Chapters 3 and 4, we talked about ways to remove Java code from JSP pages. And as we stated at the beginning of this chapter, JSF provides another way to do this. Looking at Listing 5-2, you can see there is not a single declaration or scriptlet within the page. There are only two taglib directives, some standard HTML tags, and some tags that look like tags for custom actions. The tags that begin with f: or h: come from the tag libraries defined in the taglib directives.

As you might guess from the taglib directive, the tags that use the prefix f: provide the core JSF functionality for the page, and tags that use the prefix h: provide HTML elements for the page. There is one JSF core tag in the page: the <view> tag. Any page that includes JSF elements must have the <view> tag as the outermost JSF tag. The rest of the JSF tags in the page create HTML elements in the page. The <form> tag creates an HTML form. The <input> tags create input text fields in the form. The <commandButton> tag creates a button in the form.

If you are familiar with HTML forms, you know that every HTML form requires an action attribute and can include an optional method attribute. The action attribute tells the web browser where to submit the form data. The method attribute tells the browser whether to submit a GET request or a POST request. The JSF tag does not use either of these attributes. The JSF specification requires that all JSF forms post to the same URL from which they were served. (If form data is submitted to the same page, how then does the application process the data and move between pages in the application? This question will be answered in Listing 5-4 and in detail in the "Controlling Page Navigation" section later in this chapter.) The specification also requires that all JSF forms use the POST method for submitting form data to web applications. Because both the method and action have mandatory values that the programmer cannot change, they do not need to be specified in the JSF tag.

Also note that the <input> tags have a different syntax than standard HTML for the value attribute. If you read the coverage of the EL in Chapter 3, you will recognize the #{} syntax as EL syntax. With EL, an expression such as #{flight.origination} is used when the JSP page wants to access a property of an object in the page. In Listing 5-1, you can see a property named origination with associated set and get methods. When this JavaBean is made available to a

JSP page, that page can read or write the property when we use the #{flight.origination} expression in the page. The searchForm.jsp page uses the expression with input fields. When we submit this page to the application, the values entered into the fields will be used to set the property in the JavaBean.

In a real web application that provided an online flight reservation system, the system would search for and display flights after the user submits a request. In this example, however, we will start by simply echoing the search parameters back to the user. This is accomplished in the searchResults.jsp page, shown in Listing 5-3.

**Listing 5-3.** *searchResults.jsp*

```
<html>
    <%@ taglib uri="http://java.sun.com/jsf/core" prefix="f" %>
    <%@ taglib uri="http://java.sun.com/jsf/html" prefix="h" %>

    <f:view>
        <head>
            <title>Freedom Airlines Online Flight Reservation System</title>
        </head>
        <body>
          <h3>You entered these search parameters</h3>
          <p>Origination: <h:outputText value="#{flight.origination}"/>
          <p>Depart date: <h:outputText value="#{flight.departDate}"/>
          <p>Depart time: <h:outputText value="#{flight.departTime}"/>
          <p>Destination: <h:outputText value="#{flight.destination}"/>
          <p>Return date: <h:outputText value="#{flight.returnDate}"/>
          <p>Return time: <h:outputText value="#{flight.returnTime}"/>
          <p>Trip type  : <h:outputText value="#{flight.tripType}"/>
        </body>
    </f:view>
</html>
```

As with searchForm.jsp, the outermost JSF tag is the <f:view> tag. Within the view, the page uses <h:outputText> tags. The <outputText> tags are obviously used to output text to the page. As with the <inputText> tags, they use the #{object.property} syntax to access a property of an object in the page. In this case, the object is a JavaBean identified by the name flight. This is the same object used in searchForm.jsp. Notice that the EL expression used to access the object's properties is the same in both the searchForm.jsp and searchResults.jsp. In other words, the syntax of the value expression is the same regardless of whether the page is reading or writing a property. In the searchResults.jsp page, the <outputText> tag reads the property from the object and displays it in the web page generated by this JSP page.

So, now you've seen the three main parts of the web application: an input page, an output page, and a JavaBean to hold the business data. In terms of the MVC pattern, FlightSearch is the model, and searchForm.jsp and searchResults.jsp are the view. What we haven't shown yet is the controller. We also haven't explained how the controller knows where to find the model or the view, and how the controller knows the logic flow through the web application. In the listings presented here, you can see that searchForm.jsp and searchResults.jsp do not have any information that indicates how control is transferred from page to page. Now let's see how this control is managed.

## Directing Traffic in the JSF Application

Information about the view components in the web application and information about how control flows through the application is contained in a special configuration file named `faces-config.xml`, shown in Listing 5-4. Although `faces-config.xml` can contain a lot of information about a web application, for this example we need it to do only two things: identify the flow of control from `searchForm.jsp` to `searchResults.jsp`, and identify the JavaBean used by the application.

**Listing 5-4.** *faces-config.xml*

```xml
<?xml version="1.0"?>

<faces-config xmlns="http://java.sun.com/xml/ns/javaee"
              xmlns:xsi="http://www.w3.org/2001/XMLSchema-instance"
              xsi:schemaLocation= ➥
"http://java.sun.com/xml/ns/javaee/web-facesconfig_1_2.xsd"
              version="1.2">
   <navigation-rule>
       <from-view-id>/searchForm.jsp</from-view-id>
       <navigation-case>
          <from-outcome>submit</from-outcome>
          <to-view-id>/searchResults.jsp</to-view-id>
          <redirect/>
       </navigation-case>
   </navigation-rule>

   <managed-bean>
       <managed-bean-name>flight</managed-bean-name>
       <managed-bean-class>com.apress.projsp.FlightSearch</managed-bean-class>
       <managed-bean-scope>session</managed-bean-scope>
   </managed-bean>
</faces-config>
```

The `faces-config.xml` file identifies the JavaBeans used by the web application in the `<managed-bean>` element. You will have a `<managed-bean>` element for every JavaBean used by your web application. The `<managed-bean>` element in Listing 5-4 contains three subelements:

- The first subelement is the name used to identify the JavaBean in a JSP page. In Listing 5-4 the name is given as `flight`; this is why both `searchForm.jsp` and `searchResults.jsp` can access an instance of the JavaBean by using the expression `#{flight...}`.

- The second element is the fully qualified class name of the JavaBean class. This name tells the JSP container which class to load and instantiate to create an instance of the JavaBean.

- The third element identifies the scope of the object. Session scope means that the object exists for the entire interaction between the user and the application. The container must persist the object across multiple request/response cycles, until the user's session is terminated. We will discuss this in more detail in the "Using Managed Beans" section later in this chapter.

The `faces-config.xml` file is also used to tell the controller how to navigate through the application. Navigation flow is specified in `<navigation-rule>` elements. Our example needs only one element. In general, a `<navigation-rule>` element identifies the start page, a condition, and the page to navigate to when the condition occurs.

In our example, the start page is `searchForm.jsp`. If the page request is submitted with an outcome of `submit`, control is transferred to `searchResults.jsp`. Looking at Listing 5-2, you can see that the `<commandButton>` element has an action of `submit`; when the button is clicked and the form is submitted, this action matches the `<from-outcome>` of the `<navigation-rule>`.

The `<navigation-rule>` element also includes an empty `<redirect>` element. With this element, the response is created by causing the browser to redirect to the `searchResults.jsp` page, which also updates the address bar in the browser. Without this element, the response is still created correctly and sent to the browser, but the address bar of the browser will not be updated and will still display the address for the originating page. We will look at navigation in more detail in the "Controlling Page Navigation" section later in this chapter.

We need just one final piece for our web application. In many of the examples in Chapters 3 and 4, we identified a default page to be served to users when they first access the web application. In this example, our default page will be a standard HTML page that redirects to the correct URL for a JSF application. Listing 5-5 shows `index.html`.

**Listing 5-5.** *index.html*

```
<html>
   <head>
      <meta http-equiv="Refresh" content= "0; URL=searchForm.faces"/>
   </head>
</html>
```

You can see that that the redirect URL is `searchForm.faces`. However, there is no component in our application named `searchForm.faces`. How then does the web application know which page to serve? All requests that are JSF requests are directed to the controller for the application, which is a servlet supplied as part of the JSF reference implementation. As you will see when we deploy this example, we will specify that all URLs of the form `*.faces` should be sent to the controller servlet. This servlet then converts the `searchForm.faces` request to `searchForm.jsp`, processes the JSP page, and sends the response to the browser.

## Deploying the Application to the Tomcat Server

To deploy the application to the Tomcat server, start by creating an application structure like that shown in Figure 5-2. You will also need to write the `web.xml` deployment descriptor, shown in Listing 5-6.

**Listing 5-6.** *web.xml*

```xml
<?xml version="1.0"?>

<web-app xmlns="http://java.sun.com/xml/ns/javaee"
         xmlns:xsi="http://www.w3.org/2001/XMLSchema-instance"
         xsi:schemaLocation= ➥
"http://java.sun.com/xml/ns/javaee/web-app_2_5.xsd"
         version="2.5">

  <display-name>Jsf_Ex01 - Simple JSF Application</display-name>

  <servlet>
    <servlet-name>Faces Servlet</servlet-name>
    <servlet-class>javax.faces.webapp.FacesServlet</servlet-class>
    <load-on-startup>1</load-on-startup>
  </servlet>

  <servlet-mapping>
    <servlet-name>Faces Servlet</servlet-name>
    <url-pattern>*.faces</url-pattern>
  </servlet-mapping>

  <welcome-file-list>
    <welcome-file>index.html</welcome-file>
  </welcome-file-list>
</web-app>
```

The deployment descriptor identifies the controller servlet (Faces Servlet) for the application, specifies a servlet mapping indicating which requests should be sent to the controller servlet, and designates the welcome file for the application.

As explained in the "Installing JSF" section earlier in this chapter, you need to copy the JSF and JSTL JAR files into the application's WEB-INF\lib directory or into the Tomcat common\lib directory. Copy the entire application directory into the Tomcat webapps directory, and deployment is complete.

Alternatively, after creating the directory structure, you can package all the application files into a WAR file by using the Java jar command. After the WAR file has been created, copy it into the Tomcat webapps directory. Tomcat will automatically unpack the WAR file and start the application.

## Running the Application

After you have successfully deployed the application to the server, open a web browser to the address http://localhost:8080/Jsf_Ex01. (As always, replace localhost and 8080 with the correct values for your installation, and replace Jsf_Ex01 with the correct application context name, if you created and deployed your JSF application with a different context name.)

The application starts by loading the index.html page, which immediately redirects to searchForm.faces. Because of the servlet mapping in web.xml, this request is directed to the Faces Servlet controller. The controller knows that searchForm.faces is a request for the searchForm.jsp component. If this is the first request for searchForm.jsp, it is compiled by the server and then sent to the browser, as shown in Figure 5-3.

**Figure 5-3.** *The searchForm.jsp as sent to the browser*

If you examine the source for the page, you can see that the JSF <form> tag has been translated to an HTML <form> tag. As mentioned earlier, the method for the form is POST and the action is the URL for searchForm.jsp. Even though it appears that the form submits to the same JSP page, the controller servlet will use the navigation rules in the faces-config.xml file to ensure page navigation occurs correctly. Also, each JSF input tag has been translated into an HTML input tag. Here is an extract from the HTML source showing these points:

```
<form id="_id0" method="post" action="/Jsf_Ex01/searchForm.faces"
      enctype="application/x-www-form-urlencoded">

  <h2>Search Flights</h2>
  <table>
    <tr><td colspan="4">Where and when do you want to travel?
    </td></tr>
    <tr>
      <td colspan="2">Leaving from:</td>
      <td colspan="2">Going to:</td>
    </tr>
    <tr>
      <td colspan="2">
        <input type="text" name="_id0:_id1" size="35" />
```

Try out the search form by entering values for each of the input fields. Because each property of the FlightSearch JavaBean is of the String type, you can enter anything you want into each text field. After you have finished entering values, click the Search button. The request is passed to the server, and the response generated by searchResults.jsp is sent back to the browser, as shown in Figure 5-4.

**Figure 5-4.** *The searchResults.jsp response from submitting the form in searchForm.jsp*

## Reviewing the JSF Life Cycle for the Sample Application

The JSF_Ex01 application (Listings 5-1 through 5-6) provides examples of two different request/response processes. First, index.html causes a non-JSF request to generate a JSF response when searchForm.jsp is displayed. Then, when searchForm.jsp is submitted, this causes a JSF request to generate a JSF response.

The first request from the browser comes from a standard HTML page and does not contain any data. In the Restore View phase, rather than restoring an existing view, a new component tree is created with the components from the view. This will consist of objects that represent the form and each of the input fields. These objects are stored in the component tree. Because no other processing is required, control passes to the Render Response phase. The UI components are rendered into HTML, and the response is sent to the client.

The life cycle of the request and response from searchForm.jsp to searchResults.jsp follows the phases illustrated in Figure 5-1. The request from searchForm.jsp causes the component tree to be restored in the Restore View phase. Next, the data passed in the form is used to update the state of the view components in the Apply Request Values phase. The Process Validations phase is next, but because the values are all String types, no conversion is needed, and no validation occurs. Next, the JavaBean is updated with the values from the view in the Update Model Values phase. Nothing occurs in the Invoke Application phase. Finally, in the

Render Response phase, the view components from `searchResults.jsp` are translated into HTML, using the data from the JavaBean model, and the response is returned to the client.

# Using Managed Beans

As noted earlier in this chapter, the primary design pattern of JSF is the MVC pattern. As you saw in the previous example, JSF custom actions and JSP pages form the view in the MVC architecture. The `Faces Servlet` provided by a JSF implementation is the controller. However, JSF by itself is not enough to create a working application, because you need the third leg of MVC: the model. JavaBeans provide that part of the MVC pattern. In the example, `FlightSearch` was the model.

JavaBeans are Java components that can be dropped into Java applications. They are simply Java classes that conform to a certain coding style (documented in the JavaBeans specification at `http://java.sun.com/products/javabeans/`). For our purposes, there are two aspects of the JavaBeans specification that are important:

- The JavaBean used in the web application must have a no-argument constructor. This allows the container to construct an instance of the JavaBean.

- Any property to be exposed must have a `get` or `set` method. If only a `get` method is present, the property is read-only. If only a `set` method is used, the property is write-only. If both are present, the property is read-write. The format of the `set` method name is the word `set` followed by the name of the property, with the first letter of the property name capitalized. The `get` method format is the word `get` followed by the name of the property, again with the first letter of the property name capitalized. For Boolean properties, the method is the word `is` followed by the name of the property.

Because JavaBeans follow a particular design, they can be used programmatically, without a developer needing to explicitly write code that uses the JavaBeans. As you saw in the previous example, by simply identifying the JavaBean to the JSF application in the JSP pages and in the configuration file, the JSF implementation was able to use the JavaBean, setting and reading its properties—you didn't need to write any explicit code.

Within the JSF implementation, JavaBean instances that are used by a JSF-enabled application are referred to as **managed beans**, because the JSF implementation manages the creation and use of JavaBean objects.

Within a JSF-enabled application, managed beans appear in two contexts:

- The information needed to create and initialize the managed bean is identified within the configuration files of the application.

- The properties and methods of managed beans are referenced in JSP pages by using value-binding expressions or method-binding expressions.

## Configuring Managed Beans

You saw one method for identifying the managed bean parameters to the application in Listing 5-4, where we used a file named `faces-config.xml` located in the `WEB-INF` directory of the application. However, the JSF specification identifies several other files that can contain managed bean configuration information. The specification states that configuration files will be searched for as follows:

- The JSF implementation looks for and processes files named `META-INF\faces-config.xml`. This is primarily for JSF components packaged as JAR files that are part of the application.

- The JSF implementation checks the `web.xml` deployment descriptor for a context parameter named `javax.faces.CONFIG_FILES`. If the parameter exists, the value of the parameter must be a comma-delimited list of filenames that will be processed as JSF configuration files. The filenames must be relative paths from the application root to the file, such as `WEB-INF\my-config.xml`.

- Finally, the JSF implementation processes the file `WEB-INF\faces-config.xml`, if it exists.

The configuration files are used to identify the managed beans, provide initialization parameters for the beans, and identify the navigation rules for the application (as described in the "Controlling Page Navigation" section later in this chapter). This information can be placed in a single file, as in Listing 5-4, or it can be split among multiple files. For example, you could put all the JavaBean information into one configuration file and all the navigation information into another configuration file. These multiple files would then be listed in the `web.xml` deployment descriptor.

## Identifying Managed Beans

A configuration file provides managed bean information to the application in the element named `<managed-bean>` of the configuration file. The `<managed-bean>` element declares a JavaBean that is created and populated by the JSF implementation. When an expression in a JSP page attempts to use a JavaBean, by accessing one of its properties for example, the JSF implementation attempts to find the object in request, session, and then application scope, in that order. If an object with the given `<managed-bean-name>` (see the first bulleted item that follows) is found, then the JSF implementation uses that object. If an object with the given name is not found in one of the three scopes, an instance of the JavaBean is created and stored in the appropriate scope (see the third bulleted item).

The `<managed-bean>` element has three required subelements:

- **`<managed-bean-name>`:** The string used to identify the bean instance in any JSF component. For example, in Listing 5-4, the bean name was given as `flight`. In Listings 5-2 and 5-3, we referenced the bean instance by using this name.

- **`<managed-bean-class>`:** The fully qualified class name of the class that provides the implementation for the bean.

- **`<managed-bean-scope>`:** The scope of the bean instance. We will discuss scope in more depth in the "Identifying Bean Scopes" section a little later in this chapter.

The `<managed-bean>` element has a number of optional elements, including `<description>`, `<display-name>`, `<icon>`, and `<managed-property>`. The usage of the first three should be relatively obvious, so we will just look at `<managed-property>`, which is used to initialize the properties of a managed bean.

## Initializing Bean Properties

Like `<managed-bean>`, `<managed-property>` can have an optional `<description>`, `<display-name>`, and `<icon>`. It must have a nested `<property-name>` element that identifies the name of an instance variable (property) of the class with a `set` and `get` method. It can have an optional `<property-class>` element that provides the fully qualified class name of the data type of the property. If the data type is not provided, the JSF implementation will attempt to infer the type from the bean class. Finally, it must have one of several elements that initialize the value of the property: `<value>`, `<null-value>`, `<list-entries>`, or `<map-entries>`. For example, if the property of the bean is a Java primitive or a `String`, you can use the `<value>` element like this:

```
<property-name>myProperty</property-name>
<value>3</value>
```

If the type of the property is a Java object and not a primitive, you can also set the value to null, using this form:

```
<property-name>myProperty</property-name>
<null-value/>
```

If the type of the property is some other managed bean, you can initialize the property by referencing the other bean by the name of the bean instance. So, for example, if you have a managed bean of type `Flight`, and you create an instance with the name `flight1`, you can initialize a property of type `Flight` by using a value-binding expression that is the name of the bean:

```
<managed-bean>
   <managed-bean-name>flight</managed-bean-name>
   <managed-bean-class>com.apress.projsp.FlightSearch</managed-bean-class>
   <managed-bean-scope>session</managed-bean-scope>
   <managed-property>
    <property-name>matchingFlight</property-name>
      <value-class>com.apress.projsp.Flight</value-class>
      <value>#{flight1}</value>
   </managed-property>
</managed-bean>
<managed-bean>
  <managed-bean-name>flight1</managed-bean-name>
  <managed-bean-class>com.apress.projsp.Flight</managed-bean-class>
  <managed-bean-scope>none</managed-bean-scope>
</managed-bean>
```

In this snippet, the bean `flight` has a property named `matchingFlight`. The type of `matchingFlight` is `com.apress.projsp.Flight`. The value of `matchingFlight` is initialized by referencing the name of the `Flight` object in the value-binding expression `#{flight1}`. (We'll discuss value-binding expressions in more detail in the "Using Value-Binding Expressions in JSP Pages" section a little later in this chapter.) You can see that an object with this name is specified in the second `<managed-bean>` element.

Finally, if the type of the property is `List` or a subtype of `List`, or `Map` or a subtype of `Map`, you can initialize the `List` or `Map` in the configuration file. For example, in Listing 5-1, suppose we wanted to restrict the departTime and arriveTime properties to the values Morning, Afternoon, or Evening. We could create an additional property, like this:

```
public class FlightSearch {
  List times;
  //...
}
```

We could then initialize the list, like this:

```
<managed-bean>
  <managed-bean-name>flight</managed-bean-name>
  <managed-bean-class>com.apress.projsp.FlightSearch</managed-bean-class>
  <managed-bean-scope>session</managed-bean-scope>
  <managed-property>
    <property-name>times</property-name>
      <list-entries>
      <value>Morning</value>
      <value>Afternoon</value>
      <value>Evening</value>
    </list-entries>
  </managed-property>
</managed-bean>
```

The <list-entries> element can have an optional <value-class> element that provides the fully qualified class name of the objects stored in the list. If used, it appears before the <value> elements. When <value-class> is used, the JSF implementation will attempt to create objects of that type, initialize those objects with the given values, and store them in the List. You can also use the <null-value> element to store null values in the list.

Initializing a Map is similar. Given a property of type Map:

```
public class FlightSearch {
  Map airportNames;
  //...
}
```

you initialize the Map like this:

```
<managed-bean>
  <managed-bean-name>flight</managed-bean-name>
  <managed-bean-class>com.apress.projsp.FlightSearch</managed-bean-class>
  <managed-bean-scope>session</managed-bean-scope>
  <managed-property>
    <property-name>airportNames</property-name>
    <map-entries>
      <key-class>java.lang.String</key-class>
      <value-class>java.lang.String</value-class>
        <map-entry>
        <key>BOS</key>
        <value>Logan International Airport</value>
```

```
      </map-entry>
      <!-- and so on -->
    </map-entries>
  </managed-property>
</managed-bean>
```

In the element, both `<key-class>` and `<value-class>` are optional. The JSF implementation will choose appropriate classes if you do not provide either element. There can be zero or more `<map-entry>` elements, and each `<map-entry>` that appears must have a `<key>` and either a `<value>` or `<null-value>`.

## Identifying Bean Scopes

When you configure a JavaBean to be used in a JSF page, you can configure it with one of four scopes:

- **None:** Objects with this scope are not visible in any JSF page. When used in the configuration file, they indicate managed beans that are used by other managed beans in the application. Objects with none scope can use other objects with none scope.

- **Request:** Objects with this scope are visible from the start of the request until the end of the request. Request scope starts at the beginning of a request and ends when the response has been sent to the client. If the request is forwarded, the objects are visible in the forwarded page, because that page is still part of the same request/response cycle. Objects with request scope can use other objects with none, request, session, or application scope.

- **Session:** An object with session scope is visible for any request/response cycle that belongs to a session. Objects with this scope have their state persisted between requests and last until the object or the session is invalidated. Objects with session scope can use other objects with none, session, or application scope.

- **Application:** An object with application scope is visible in all request/response cycles for all clients using the application, for as long as the application is active. Objects with application scope can use other objects with none or application scope.

You may recall from Chapter 1 that when you use the `<useBean>` standard action, you can specify similar scopes for the JavaBean. The difference is that JSP scope includes an additional scope named page. Because JSF requests often involve navigation between pages, objects with page scope have no value in a JSF application. For example, in the initial example in this chapter, the properties of a JavaBean were set in one JSP page, and those values were displayed in another page. If the `FlightSearch` JavaBean had been given page scope, the `searchResults.jsp` page would not have access to the `FlightSearch` JavaBean, and so would not have been able to display the data stored in the JavaBean.

Most often, you will define your managed beans to have session scope. However, in some cases, you may have a managed bean that encapsulates global data. For example, you may have a managed bean that holds information common to every page in the application; in that case, you would define the managed bean to have application scope. Managed beans that you use only within a single request/response will have request scope.

# Using Value-Binding Expressions in JSP Pages

When using JSF custom actions in your JSP pages, the JSF implementation can set or get the value of JavaBean properties, based on the tag usage. For example, Listing 5-2 includes this tag:

```
<h:inputText value="#{flight.origination}" size="35"/>
```

---

■**Tip**  The syntax in the preceding example is sufficient for Java primitive and `String` values. However, if the property is some other data type, you will probably need to supply a converter as well. See the "Converting Data" section later in this chapter for details.

---

This is also referred to as a **value-binding expression** because it binds the value of some bean property (using an EL statement in the form #{object.property}) to an attribute or property of some JSF element. The expression to the left of the dot is some object accessible to the page, and the expression to the right of the dot is some property of the object. You can also chain expressions, like this:

```
object1.object2.object3.property
```

Each expression in the chain, reading from left to right, is evaluated as an object reference, and the final expression is a property of the last object.

Another syntax you can use to write a value-binding expression uses brackets to denote the property. We refer to this syntax as **bracket notation**:

```
flight["origination"]
flight['origination']
```

You would use the form with double quotes when using single quotes to delimit attribute values, and use single quotes when double quotes are used to delimit the attribute values. So, the preceding inputText element could be written in either of these ways:

```
<h:inputText value="#{flight['origination']}" size="35"/>
<h:inputText value='#{flight["origination"]}' size="35"/>
```

When creating chained expressions, you can freely mix dot and bracket notation. In fact, as you will see shortly, when creating an expression to access a List or Map, mixed notation can be used to create dynamic expressions.

## Getting and Setting Bean Properties

When the searchForm.jsp page is rendered, the JSP page implementation class calls the get method for the origination property of the FlightSearch class to get the value of the property. This value is then included in the rendering of the page. The JSP page class does this for all the properties that are referenced in the page. When the page is first loaded, the properties of the FlightSearch object have no values, so the page is rendered with empty text fields.

During the processing of the request from searchForm.jsp, the values entered into the form are saved by the UI components that correspond to the UI widgets on the page. After these values are converted as necessary and validated, the JSF implementation updates the model (the FlightSearch object) by calling the set method for the property.

After the model is updated, the life cycle advances to the render phase, and the searchResults.jsp page (Listing 5-3) is rendered. At this point, the FlightSearch object has some data, and so when the page is rendered, the JSF implementation calls the get methods for the properties that the page displays, and these values are used in the rendering and display of the page.

Notice that by using the same simple #{flight.origination} syntax, the JSF implementation calls different code depending on the current phase of the JSF life cycle. Note also that the action does not depend on the tag type. The action taken for the <h:inputText> tag can be either a get or set method of the property, regardless of the fact that the <h:inputText> tag renders as an HTML <input> tag.

### Accessing List, Array, and Map Property Types

You can also easily access bean properties that are of type List, array, and Map. You can access an element of the List or array by using a value-binding expression. For example, earlier we presented a possible List property added to FlightSearch:

```
public class FlightSearch {
  List times;
  //...
}
```

After the bean is initialized, we could access the first value in the list by using any of the following expressions:

```
#{flight.times["1"]}
#{flight.times['1']}
#{flight.times[1]}
#{flight.times["var"]}
#{flight.times.var}
#{flight.times[var]}
```

---

■**Note**  For a complete list of valid expression forms, see Section 5.1.2 of the JSF specification.

---

As mentioned earlier, you can chain expressions together to create a value-binding expression. The last expression following the dot, or inside the brackets, must evaluate to an integer or must be convertible to an integer. When updating the model, the JSF implementation will attempt to set the element at the given index. If the given index does not exist, a PropertyNotFoundException will occur. When reading from the model, the implementation will call the get method to get the element at the given index. Again, if the index does not exist, a PropertyNotFoundException will occur.

One difference between value-binding expressions for List and Map objects is that you can use bracket notation to create dynamic value-binding expressions. Suppose you had an object with some intProperty that evaluates to an integer and you tried this syntax:

```
flight.times.object.intProperty
```

The expression would cause an evaluation error. The JSF implementation expects `object` to be a property of `times`, which is not the case. However, you can use a mixed form with both dot and bracket notation:

```
flight.times[object.intProperty]
```

When this expression is evaluated, the `object.intProperty` expression evaluates to an integer, which is then used to access the value stored in the `List` at that index. The same syntax can be used when accessing `Map` entries.

Given the `Map` property of `FlightSearch`:

```
public class FlightSearch {
  Map airportNames;
  //...
}
```

any of the following expressions will cause the `Map` methods `get(key)` or `set(key, value)` to be called, depending on which life-cycle phase is currently being processed:

```
flight.airportNames.key
flight.airportNames[key]
flight.airportNames["key"]
```

## Using Method-Binding Expressions in JSP Pages

Just as you can bind managed bean properties to expressions in the JSP page, you can also bind managed bean methods to expressions. You use method binding when setting the attribute values for actions, validators, action listeners, and value change listeners.

The syntax for method-binding expressions is the same as the syntax for value-binding expressions. You can use either dot or bracket notation. As with value-binding expressions, every expression in the chain, except the last expression, is evaluated as an object reference. The last expression in the chain must be a method name of a method. The method signature must follow a specific pattern, which depends on whether the method binding is used for an action, a validator, an action listener, or a value change listener.

You will see how to use method-binding expressions for actions in the "Controlling Page Navigation" section later in this chapter. You will also look at using method-binding expressions for validators in the "Validating Input" section. Value change listeners and action listeners are covered in the "Event Handling" section later in the chapter.

## Expanding the JSF Sample Application

Let's update the first example in this chapter (Listings 5-1 through 5-6) to demonstrate some of the concepts we just discussed. For this version, we'll change the search form so that a user is required to select either a one-way trip or a round-trip. We'll also constrain the departure time and return time to be Morning, Afternoon, or Evening, as shown in Figure 5-5.

**Figure 5-5.** *The search form now has radio buttons for one-way or round-trip and drop-down boxes for departure and return times.*

When the user enters the search parameters, the search results page will still echo the search parameters, but will also list two matching flights (imaginary flights, since we will hard-code them into the application).

The directory structure for the `Jsf_Ex02` example, shown in Figure 5-6, is similar to the one we used for the first example. The new files are `FlightTypes.java`, `FlightTimes.java`, and `Flight.java`.

```
Jsf_Ex02
    WEB-INF
        classes
            com
                apress
                    projsp
                        Flight.class
                        Flight.java
                        FlightSearch.class
                        FlightSearch.java
                        FlightTimes.class
                        FlightTimes.java
                        FlightTypes.class
                        FlightTypes.java
        lib
        faces-config.xml
        web.xml
    index.html
    searchForm.jsp
    searchResults.jsp
```

**Figure 5-6.** *The directory structure for Jsf_Ex02*

Listing 5-7 shows `FlightTypes.java`. This class is basically a data holder class with no operations. It holds the two values `Roundtrip` and `One Way` in an array of type `javax.faces.SelectItem`. This data type is used as part of the list-creation capability of JSF, which you will explore later when you look at the new `searchForm.jsp` (Listing 5-12). You will need to add `jsf-api.jar` to your CLASSPATH to compile this file.

**Listing 5-7.** *FlightTypes.java*

```java
package com.apress.projsp;

import javax.faces.model.SelectItem;

public class FlightTypes {
  static SelectItem[] tripTypes = new SelectItem[] {
      new SelectItem("Roundtrip", "Roundtrip"),
      new SelectItem("One way", "One way") };

  public SelectItem[] getTripTypes() {
    return tripTypes;
  }
  public void setTripTypes(SelectItem[] tripTypes) {
    FlightTypes.tripTypes = tripTypes;
  }
}
```

Listing 5-8 shows `FlightTimes.java`. It is also a data holder class, this time for the departure and return time values. This source file also requires `jsf-api.jar` to be compiled.

**Listing 5-8.** *FlightTimes.java*

```java
package com.apress.projsp;

import javax.faces.model.SelectItem;

public class FlightTimes {
  static SelectItem[] times = new SelectItem[] {
      new SelectItem("Anytime", "Anytime"),
      new SelectItem("Morning", "Morning"),
      new SelectItem("Afternoon", "Afternoon"),
      new SelectItem("Evening", "Evening") };

  public SelectItem[] getTimes() {
    return times;
  }
  public void setTimes(SelectItem[] times) {
    FlightTimes.times = times;
  }
}
```

Listing 5-9 shows a new version of `FlightSearch.java` (Listing 5-1). This new class has two additional fields: one for trip type and one for matching flights (flights that supposedly match the search parameters). In the process of creating the `FlightSearch` managed bean, the `matchingFlights` field will be filled with two `Flight` objects. We will do this in the `faces-config.xml` file. Because we are not going to actually search for flights, each `set` method in this class will also update the appropriate fields in the `Flight` objects.

**Listing 5-9.** *FlightSearch.java*

```java
package com.apress.projsp;

import java.util.List;
import java.util.ArrayList;

public class FlightSearch {
  String origination;
  String destination;
  String departDate;
  String departTime;
  String returnDate;
  String returnTime;
  String tripType;
  ArrayList matchingFlights = new ArrayList();

  public String getDepartDate() {
    return departDate;
  }
  public void setDepartDate(String departDate) {
    this.departDate = departDate;
    ((Flight) matchingFlights.get(0)).setDepartDate(departDate);
    ((Flight) matchingFlights.get(1)).setDepartDate(departDate);
  }
  public String getDepartTime() {
    return departTime;
  }
  public void setDepartTime(String departTime) {
    this.departTime = departTime;
    ((Flight) matchingFlights.get(0)).setDepartTime(departTime);
    ((Flight) matchingFlights.get(1)).setDepartTime(departTime);
  }
  public String getDestination() {
    return destination;
  }
  public void setDestination(String destination) {
    this.destination = destination;
    ((Flight) matchingFlights.get(0)).setDestination(destination);
    ((Flight) matchingFlights.get(1)).setDestination(destination);
```

```
      ((Flight) matchingFlights.get(0)).setFlightNum("133");
      ((Flight) matchingFlights.get(1)).setFlightNum("233");
    }
    public String getOrigination() {
      return origination;
    }
    public void setOrigination(String origination) {
      this.origination = origination;
      ((Flight) matchingFlights.get(0)).setOrigination(origination);
      ((Flight) matchingFlights.get(1)).setOrigination(origination);
    }
    public String getReturnDate() {
      return returnDate;
    }
    public void setReturnDate(String returnDate) {
      this.returnDate = returnDate;
      ((Flight) matchingFlights.get(0)).setReturnDate(returnDate);
      ((Flight) matchingFlights.get(1)).setReturnDate(returnDate);
    }
    public String getReturnTime() {
      return returnTime;
    }
    public void setReturnTime(String returnTime) {
      this.returnTime = returnTime;
      ((Flight) matchingFlights.get(0)).setReturnTime(returnTime);
      ((Flight) matchingFlights.get(1)).setReturnTime(returnTime);
    }
    public String getTripType() {
      return tripType;
    }
    public void setTripType(String tripType) {
      this.tripType = tripType;
    }
    public List getMatchingFlights() {
      return matchingFlights;
    }
    public void setMatchingFlights(List matchingFlights) {
      this.matchingFlights.addAll(matchingFlights);
    }
}
```

Listing 5-10 shows the Flight.java code. If you inspect the code in Listing 5-10, you will notice that many of the properties of the Flight class are identical to the fields of the FlightSearch class. Again, for this example, Flight is simply a data holder class with no significant behavior. It does, however, have a toString() method. This method is called by the JSF implementation when the matching flights are displayed in the search results page.

**Listing 5-10.** *Flight.java*

```java
package com.apress.projsp;

public class Flight {
  String flightNum;
  String origination;
  String destination;
  String departDate;
  String departTime;
  String returnDate;
  String returnTime;

  public String getFlightNum() {
    return flightNum;
  }
  public void setFlightNum(String flightNum) {
    this.flightNum = flightNum;
  }
  public String getDepartDate() {
    return departDate;
  }
  public void setDepartDate(String departDate) {
    this.departDate = departDate;
  }
  public String getDepartTime() {
    return departTime;
  }
  public void setDepartTime(String departTime) {
    this.departTime = departTime;
  }
  public String getDestination() {
    return destination;
  }
  public void setDestination(String destination) {
    this.destination = destination;
  }
  public String getOrigination() {
    return origination;
  }
  public void setOrigination(String origination) {
    this.origination = origination;
  }
  public String getReturnDate() {
    return returnDate;
  }
  public void setReturnDate(String returnDate) {
```

```
    this.returnDate = returnDate;
  }
  public String getReturnTime() {
    return returnTime;
  }
  public void setReturnTime(String returnTime) {
    this.returnTime = returnTime;
  }
  public String toString() {
    return "Flight " + flightNum + " departing " + origination + " at "
        + departTime + " arriving " + destination + " 2 hours later";
  }
}
```

The index.html welcome page and web.xml deployment descriptor remain essentially unchanged for this example, so you can reuse Listing 5-5 and Listing 5-6 (if needed) for these two files. You may, however, want to change the <display-name> element in the deployment descriptor so that it is correct for this example.

Let's next look at the faces-config.xml file, shown in Listing 5-11. The navigation rule is unchanged. When the user clicks the Search button, the application will navigate to the search results form. The first significant change is in the <managed-bean> entry for the FlightSearch bean. The configuration file now includes an initializer for the new matchingFlight property of the FlightSearch bean. The matchingFlight list is initialized with two objects, given by the names flight1 and flight2. Note that the beans flight1 and flight2 are created farther down in the configuration file, with a scope of none. The none scope is appropriate because these two beans are not referenced directly in any page of the application. The configuration file also initializes instances of FlightTypes and FlightTimes.

**Listing 5-11.** *faces-config.xml*

```
<?xml version="1.0"?>

<faces-config xmlns="http://java.sun.com/xml/ns/javaee"
              xmlns:xsi="http://www.w3.org/2001/XMLSchema-instance"
              xsi:schemaLocation= ➥
"http://java.sun.com/xml/ns/javaee/web-facesconfig_1_2.xsd"
              version="1.2">
  <navigation-rule>
    <from-view-id>/searchForm.jsp</from-view-id>
    <navigation-case>
      <from-outcome>submit</from-outcome>
      <to-view-id>/searchResults.jsp</to-view-id>
      <redirect/>
    </navigation-case>
  </navigation-rule>

  <managed-bean>
    <managed-bean-name>flight</managed-bean-name>
```

```
            <managed-bean-class>com.apress.projsp.FlightSearch</managed-bean-class>
            <managed-bean-scope>session</managed-bean-scope>
            <managed-property>
             <property-name>matchingFlights</property-name>
             <list-entries>
               <value-class>com.apress.projsp.Flight</value-class>
               <value>#{flight1}</value>
               <value>#{flight2}</value>
             </list-entries>
            </managed-property>
        </managed-bean>
        <managed-bean>
            <managed-bean-name>times</managed-bean-name>
            <managed-bean-class>com.apress.projsp.FlightTimes</managed-bean-class>
            <managed-bean-scope>session</managed-bean-scope>
        </managed-bean>
        <managed-bean>
            <managed-bean-name>types</managed-bean-name>
            <managed-bean-class>com.apress.projsp.FlightTypes</managed-bean-class>
            <managed-bean-scope>session</managed-bean-scope>
        </managed-bean>
      <managed-bean>
        <managed-bean-name>flight1</managed-bean-name>
        <managed-bean-class>com.apress.projsp.Flight</managed-bean-class>
        <managed-bean-scope>none</managed-bean-scope>
      </managed-bean>
      <managed-bean>
        <managed-bean-name>flight2</managed-bean-name>
        <managed-bean-class>com.apress.projsp.Flight</managed-bean-class>
        <managed-bean-scope>none</managed-bean-scope>
      </managed-bean>
</faces-config>
```

Listing 5-12 shows the searchForm.jsp page. This page includes some new features. Instead of using just text fields for input, the form includes elements for creating radio buttons and drop-down menu lists: <h:selectOneRadio> and <h:selectOneMenu>. There are two ways to identify the items in these two elements. First, you can explicitly code a <selectItem> element for each element in the list. The code for that would look like this:

```
<h:selectOneRadio value="#{foo.bar}">
  <f:selectItem itemValue="Item 1"/>
  <f:selectItem itemValue="item 2"/>
</h:selectOneRadio>
```

In this code snippet, the JSF implementation creates a set of radio buttons, with one radio button for each <f:selectItem> element. The value of the itemValue attribute of the selected radio button is used to set the value attribute of the <h:selectOneRadio> element.

The second way to create a set of selection elements is to use a `<selectItems>` element. This is the technique we use in Listing 5-12. The `<selectItems>` element has an attribute named `value`, which is set by a value-binding expression that returns an array of `SelectItems`. For example, in the value-binding expression `#{types.tripTypes}`, the name `types` refers to a bean of type `FlightTypes` (see Listing 5-7). This object has a property named `tripTypes` of type `SelectItem[]`. When the page is rendered, the array of `SelectItems` is converted into a selection element, with one element for each item in the array. The same occurs for the two `selectOneMenu` elements.

**Listing 5-12.** *searchForm.jsp*

```html
<html>
  <%@ taglib uri="http://java.sun.com/jsf/core" prefix="f" %>
  <%@ taglib uri="http://java.sun.com/jsf/html" prefix="h" %>

  <f:view>
  <head>
    <title>Freedom Airlines Online Flight Reservation System</title>
  </head>
  <body>
    <h:form>
      <h2>Search Flights</h2>
      What type of flight do you need?
      <h:selectOneRadio layout="lineDirection"
                        value="#{flight.tripType}">
        <f:selectItems value="#{types.tripTypes}"/>
      </h:selectOneRadio>
      <p/>
      <table>
        <tr><td colspan="4">Where and when do you want to travel?</td></tr>
        <tr>
          <td colspan="2">Leaving from:</td>
          <td colspan="2">Going to:</td>
        </tr>
        <tr>
          <td colspan="2">
            <h:inputText value="#{flight.origination}" size="35"/>
          </td>
          <td colspan="2">
            <h:inputText value="#{flight.destination}" size="35"/>
          </td>
        </tr>
        <tr>
          <td colspan="2">Departing:</td>
          <td colspan="2">Returning:</td>
        </tr>
        <tr>
```

```
        <td>
          <h:inputText value="#{flight.departDate}"/>
        </td>
        <td>
          <h:selectOneMenu value="#{flight.departTime}">
            <f:selectItems value="#{times.times}"/>
          </h:selectOneMenu>
        </td>
        <td>
          <h:inputText value="#{flight.returnDate}"/>
        </td>
        <td>
          <h:selectOneMenu value="#{flight.returnTime}">
            <f:selectItems value="#{times.times}"/>
          </h:selectOneMenu>
        </td>
      </tr>
    </table>
    <p>
    <h:commandButton value="Search" action="submit"/>
    </p>
  </h:form>
  </body>
  </f:view>
</html>
```

Finally, Listing 5-13 shows an updated search results page. The only additions to this file are the new <outputText> element for trip type and the <outputText> elements for the matching flights. Note that the matching flights are displayed using the two variations of bracket notation for value-binding expressions.

**Listing 5-13.** *searchResults.jsp*

```
<html>
  <%@ taglib uri="http://java.sun.com/jsf/core" prefix="f" %>
  <%@ taglib uri="http://java.sun.com/jsf/html" prefix="h" %>

  <f:view>
    <head>
      <title>Freedom Airlines Online Flight Reservation System</title>
    </head>
    <body>
        <h3>You entered these search parameters</h3>
        <br/>Trip Type  : <h:outputText value="#{flight.tripType}"/>
        <br/>Origination: <h:outputText value="#{flight.origination}"/>
        <br/>Depart date: <h:outputText value="#{flight.departDate}"/>
        <br/>Depart time: <h:outputText value="#{flight.departTime}"/>
```

```
            <br/>Destination: <h:outputText value="#{flight.destination}"/>
            <br/>Return date: <h:outputText value="#{flight.returnDate}"/>
            <br/>Return time: <h:outputText value="#{flight.returnTime}"/>
            <p/>Matching Flights
            <p/><h:outputText value="#{flight.matchingFlights[0]}"/>
            <p/><h:outputText value="#{flight.matchingFlights['1']}"/>
        </body>
    </f:view>
</html>
```

After entering all the code and compiling the Java files into classes, deploy the application to your web container. When you load the search form page (see Figure 5-5), you should see the new radio buttons and drop-down menu boxes. After entering some data and clicking the Search button, you should see a results page similar to Figure 5-7.

**Figure 5-7.** *The search results page now shows two "matching" flights.*

# Controlling Page Navigation

As you saw in Listing 5-11, page navigation in your JSF application is handled by providing navigation rules in a configuration file. The navigation can specify which web component initiates the request, which web component handles the response, and which value causes navigation to follow the flow. So far, you have seen only navigation based on the hard-coded string value of an action attribute. You can also control navigation by using value-binding expressions and method-binding expressions. Navigation then depends on the value of the expression.

## Static and Dynamic Navigation

When you control navigation through string values of the action attribute, the path of navigation is known when the application is deployed. We call this **static navigation**, because the flow is statically determined and does not change. It is the same for every request.

When using static navigation, you explicitly code a value into the action attribute of a JSF custom tag. You then define navigation rules in a configuration file. The rule specifies navigation flow when the `<from-outcome>` of a page matches the value of the action attribute. When that occurs, navigation flows to the specified `<to-view-id>`. These elements are part of a navigation rule element in a configuration file, such as faces-config.xml (see Listing 5-11).

When you control navigation through value-binding expressions or method-binding expressions, the path of navigation is not known when the application is deployed. In fact, navigation flow can vary from request to request depending on the value of the expression. We call this **dynamic navigation**.

For dynamic navigation, you use a value-binding expression or method-binding expression as the value of the action attribute. With value-binding expressions, the value of the property must be of type String. With method-binding expressions, the method must take no parameters and return a value of type String:

```
public String search();
```

The String value returned by the method is compared to the value specified in the navigation rule to determine where control flow should go.

## Navigation Rules

Two JSF custom tags are used to control page navigation in conjunction with navigation rules: `<commandButton>` and `<commandLink>`.

You specify navigation rules in a configuration file. In this chapter, we have done this in the faces-config.xml file. However, navigation rules can be in their own configuration file, which is then identified in the deployment descriptor web.xml.

The general syntax of navigation rules is as follows:

```
<navigation-rule>
  <from-view-id>/searchForm.jsp</from-view-id>
  <navigation-case>
    <from-outcome>search</from-outcome>
    <to-view-id>/searchResults.jsp</to-view-id>
  </navigation-case>
</navigation-rule>
```

The `<from-view-id>` element is optional; it contains the path to the page from which navigation starts. In the configuration file, you use the correct name of the file, searchForm.jsp, as we do in Listing 5-11, rather than searchForm.faces. Note also that the path to the resource begins with a leading forward slash (/) and is the full path to the resource. So, if searchResults.jsp were in the WEB-INF\pages\results directory, you would use the path /WEB-INF/pages/results/searchForm.jsp. The <from-outcome> element is the string value that is compared to the value of the action attribute.

You need to specify the <from-view-id> only one time. This allows you to define multiple <navigation-case> elements that apply to one page. You use this when a page has multiple command buttons or command links.

If you have an action that applies to every page in the application, you can use a <navigation-rule> element without a <from-view-id>. For example, suppose every page in your application had a link to your privacy policy. Because the following navigation rule does not have a <from-view-id>, it applies to every page in the application:

```
<navigation-rule>
  <navigation-case>
    <from-outcome>privacy-policy</from-outcome>
    <to-view-id>/WEB-INF/privacy.jsp</to-view-id>
  </navigation-case>
</navigation-rule>
```

In some cases, you may have a rule that applies to some pages, but not all pages, in your application. If the pages are in a common location, you can use a wildcard to select the <from-view-id>:

```
<navigation-rule>
  <from-view-id>/products/*</from-view-id>
  <navigation-case>

    .  .  .

  </navigation-case>
</navigation-rule>
```

In this rule, the navigation case applies to every page that is served from the products directory.

There are a number of optional elements you can use with <navigation-case>. Three of them, <description>, <display-name>, and <icon>, we will not cover here. The three optional elements we will look at are <from-outcome>, <from-action>, and <redirect>.

The <from-outcome> element is used to match an outcome string. The outcome string can be a literal string specified in the action attribute of a command element (see the <h:commandButton> element in Listing 5-12, for example). The outcome string can also be returned from the execution of an application action method. Action methods are called when a tag specifies a JavaBean method in its action attribute by using a method-binding expression. If <from-outcome> is used, the navigation case will be followed only if the outcome string matches the element's value. If not used, this case will be followed no matter what the outcome value is.

The <from-action> element is used in the <navigation-case> element. If you have a single page with multiple command actions or command links, and the command actions or links have the same value (the same <from-outcome>) for the action attribute, you use the

`<from-action>` element to distinguish between the actions. Suppose we give the `FlightSearch` bean two methods named `search()` and `save()`. Both methods will return the value `success` when used in a method-binding expression. Because each returns the value `success`, we need some way to distinguish between a `success` from `search()` and a `success` from `save()`. You do this with the `<from-action>` element:

```
<navigation-rule>
  <from-view-id>/searchForm.jsp</from-view-id>
  <navigation-case>
    <from-action>#{flight.search}</from-action>
    <from-outcome>success</from-outcome>
    <to-view-id>/searchResults.jsp</to-view-id>
  </navigation-case>
  <navigation-case>
    <from-action>#{flight.save}</from-action>
    <from-outcome>success</from-outcome>
    <to-view-id>/searchForm.jsp</to-view-id>
  </navigation-case>
</navigation-rule>
```

Because the outcome values are the same, the case that is matched is the one with the matching action reference. If `<from-action>` is not used, the case will be matched no matter which action reference was executed (or if no action reference was executed).

The final optional element is `<redirect>`. When you submit a request from a JSF form, the request is sent to the originating page. When you do not use `<redirect>`, the origination page forwards the request to the response page during the Render Response phase, so when your browser receives the response, it displays the URL of the originating page. When you use `<redirect>`, the originating page sends a redirect to the browser, which causes the browser to make a request for the response page, and updates the browser's address bar to the address of the responding page. With the `<redirect>` in place, both of the earlier examples show `searchResults.jsp` in the address bar when the response is received; without `<redirect>`, the address bar would continue to display `searchForm.jsp`.

## Adding Dynamic Navigation to the Sample JSF Application

We can now modify the Flight Search example we have been building in this chapter to use dynamic navigation. The directory structure for this example, `Jsf_Ex03`, is shown in Figure 5-8. We will modify the example to simulate searching for flights that match the search criteria. In the example, the matching flights will actually be hard-coded into a JavaBean.

Figure 5-9 shows the search results page for this example. Notice that the page no longer echoes the search parameters. Instead, it lists flights that match the search parameters and has links for selecting each flight.

When a link is clicked, the response page shows which flight was selected, as shown in Figure 5-10.

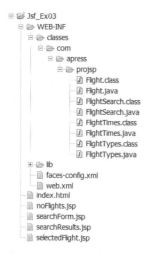

**Figure 5-8.** *Directory structure for Jsf_Ex03*

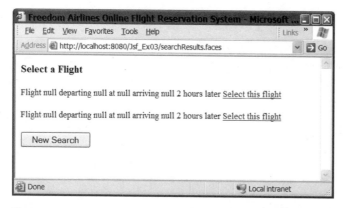

**Figure 5-9.** *The search results page for Jsf_Ex03 has a link to select a matching flight.*

**Figure 5-10.** *The flight selection page shows which flight was selected.*

In this example, the files index.html (Listing 5-5), web.xml (Listing 5-6), FlightTypes.java (Listing 5-7), FlightTimes.java (Listing 5-8), and Flight.java (Listing 5-10) remain unchanged from the Jsf_Ex02 example, so we will not repeat that code here.

You need to make only a single change to searchForm.jsp. Listing 5-14 shows the one line that is changed in the JSP page. In the <commandButton> element, we change the action attribute to refer to the method-binding expression #{flight.search}. This method does not exist yet; we will add it to the FlightSearch class (Listing 5-19) shortly.

**Listing 5-14.** *searchForm.jsp*

```
...
    <h:commandButton value="Search" action="#{flight.search}"/>
...
```

The rest of the searchForm.jsp page remains the same as in Listing 5-12. When you click the Search button on the searchForm.jsp page, it will submit the search parameters to the searchResults.jsp page shown in Listing 5-15.

**Listing 5-15.** *searchResults.jsp*

```
<html>
    <%@ taglib uri="http://java.sun.com/jsf/core" prefix="f" %>
    <%@ taglib uri="http://java.sun.com/jsf/html" prefix="h" %>

    <f:view>
        <head>
            <title>Freedom Airlines Online Flight Reservation System</title>
        </head>
        <body>
            <h3>Select a Flight</h3>
            <h:form>
            <p/><h:outputText value="#{flight.matchingFlights[0]}"/>
            <h:commandLink action="#{flight.select}"
                           value="Select this flight">
              <f:param name="flightNum"
                 value="#{flight.matchingFlights[0].flightNum}" />
            </h:commandLink>
            <p/><h:outputText value="#{flight.matchingFlights[1]}"/>
            <h:commandLink action="#{flight.select}"
                           value="Select this flight">
              <f:param name="flightNum"
                 value="#{flight.matchingFlights[1].flightNum}" />
            </h:commandLink>
            <p/>
            <h:commandButton value="New Search" action="#{flight.reset}"/>
            </h:form>
        </body>
    </f:view>
</html>
```

In this new search results page, we have removed the lines that echo the search parameters. Instead, there are two similar blocks of code that print out a line of text and a link. The <outputText> elements use a value-binding expression to print out an element of the matchingFlights List property of the FlightSearch object. Following the outputText element is a <commandLink> element. When the link created by the <commandLink> element is clicked, the JSF implementation calls the select() method of the FlightSearch class, which is specified by the method-binding expression #{flight.select}. Like the search() method, select() is a new method. Nested within the <commandLink> element is a <param> element. It creates a name-value pair that is passed as a request parameter when the link is clicked. When you look at the select() method of the FlightSearch class, you will see how a class in the application is able to read the request parameter. Also notice in Listing 5-15 how the value-binding expression to access the flightNum property of the Flight object (#{flight.matchingFlights[0].flightNum}) is a chained expression. As mentioned earlier in this chapter, you can use both dot notation and bracket notation to create chained value-binding expressions.

In this example, we need a page that will display which flight was selected by the user on the search result page. This page is selectedFlight.jsp, shown in Listing 5-16.

**Listing 5-16.** *selectedFlight.jsp*

```
<html>
  <%@ taglib uri="http://java.sun.com/jsf/core" prefix="f" %>
  <%@ taglib uri="http://java.sun.com/jsf/html" prefix="h" %>

  <f:view>
  <head>
    <title>Freedom Airlines Online Flight Reservation System</title>
  </head>
  <body>
    <h3>Flight Reservation</h3>
    <h:form>
      <p/>You selected this flight:
      <p/><h:outputText value="#{flight.matchingFlight}"/>
      <p/><h:commandButton value="New Search" action="#{flight.reset}"/>
    </h:form>
  </body>
  </f:view>
</html>
```

The last page we need to implement is the page that tells the user that no flights were found that match the search parameters. This is the noFlights.jsp page, shown in Listing 5-17.

**Listing 5-17.** *noFlights.jsp*

```
<html>
  <%@ taglib uri="http://java.sun.com/jsf/core" prefix="f" %>
  <%@ taglib uri="http://java.sun.com/jsf/html" prefix="h" %>

  <f:view>
```

```
    <head>
        <title>Freedom Airlines Online Flight Reservation System</title>
    </head>
    <body>
        <h3>Search Results</h3>
        <h:form>
        <p/>No flights that match your search parameters were found.
        <p/><h:commandButton value="New Search" action="#{flight.reset}"/>
        </h:form>
    </body>
  </f:view>
</html>
```

Each of these pages, except for the first search form page, has a New Search button, which allows the user to reset the search parameters and go back to the search form page. We need to update the faces-config.xml file to specify this navigation rule and the rules for moving from the search form to the other pages. Listing 5-18 shows the necessary additions and changes. Note that the managed bean entries in the file are the same as in Listing 5-11, so we do not show them here.

**Listing 5-18.** *faces-config.xml*

```
<?xml version="1.0"?>

<faces-config xmlns="http://java.sun.com/xml/ns/javaee"
              xmlns:xsi="http://www.w3.org/2001/XMLSchema-instance"
              xsi:schemaLocation= ➥
"http://java.sun.com/xml/ns/javaee/web-facesconfig_1_2.xsd"
              version="1.2">
  <navigation-rule>
    <from-view-id>/searchForm.jsp</from-view-id>
    <navigation-case>
      <from-outcome>success</from-outcome>
      <to-view-id>/searchResults.jsp</to-view-id>
      <redirect/>
    </navigation-case>
    <navigation-case>
      <from-outcome>no flights</from-outcome>
      <to-view-id>/noFlights.jsp</to-view-id>
      <redirect/>
    </navigation-case>
  </navigation-rule>

  <navigation-rule>
    <from-view-id>/searchResults.jsp</from-view-id>
    <navigation-case>
      <from-outcome>select</from-outcome>
```

```
      <to-view-id>/selectedFlight.jsp</to-view-id>
      <redirect/>
    </navigation-case>
  </navigation-rule>

  <navigation-rule>
    <navigation-case>
      <from-action>#{flight.reset}</from-action>
      <from-outcome>success</from-outcome>
      <to-view-id>/searchForm.jsp</to-view-id>
      <redirect/>
    </navigation-case>
  </navigation-rule>

<!-- managed beans are the same as in Listing 5-11 and are not shown -->

</faces-config>
```

The navigation rule for searchForm.jsp now has an additional element: the Search button on the page calls the FlightSearch search() method. This returns two possible values: success or no flights. The rule specifies which page sends the response for each return value. There is a new rule for the search results page. When a link on that page is clicked, its action value causes the navigation to transfer to selectedFlight.jsp. Finally, there is a rule that applies to all pages, because it has no <from-view-id> element. This applies anytime the New Search button is clicked.

The final piece, presented in Listing 5-19, is FlightSearch.java. Much of this class is the same as in Listing 5-9, so we show only the new properties and methods.

**Listing 5-19.** *FlightSearch.java*

```java
package com.apress.projsp;

import java.util.List;
import java.util.ArrayList;
import java.util.Map;
import javax.faces.context.FacesContext;

public class FlightSearch {
  //properties:
  //origination, destination, departDate, departTime same as Listing 5-9
  //returnDate, returnTime, tripType, matchingFlights same as Listing 5-9
  String flightNum;
  Flight matchingFlight;

  //methods from Listing 5-9 not shown here

  //new methods are reset(), search(), and
  //get and set methods for flightNum and matchingFlight
```

```java
public String reset() {
  this.setDepartDate("");
  this.setDepartTime("");
  this.setDestination("");
  this.setOrigination("");
  this.setReturnDate("");
  this.setReturnTime("");
  this.setTripType("");
  return "success";
}
public String search() {
  if (origination.equals("BOS") && destination.equals("ORD")) {
    return "success";
  } else {
    return "no flights";
  }
}
public Flight getMatchingFlight() {
  for (int i = 0; i < matchingFlights.size(); i++) {
    matchingFlight = (Flight) matchingFlights.get(i);
    if (matchingFlight.flightNum.equals(flightNum)) {
      break;
    }
    matchingFlight = null;
  }
  return matchingFlight;
}
public void setMatchingFlight(Flight flight) {
  matchingFlight = flight;
}
public String getFlightNum() {
  return flightNum;
}
public void setFlightNum(String string) {
  flightNum = string;
}
public String select() {
  FacesContext context = FacesContext.getCurrentInstance();
  Map requestParams =
    context.getExternalContext().getRequestParameterMap();
  flightNum = (String) requestParams.get("flightNum");
  return "select";
}
}
```

The reset() method simply resets all the properties to be empty strings and returns the value success. The matchingFlights List contains entries for two flights that both originate in Boston (BOS) and fly to Chicago (ORD). If the origination and destination match these values, the search() method returns success; otherwise, it returns no flights.

The <commandLink> element on the searchResults.jsp page causes the select() method to be called. Within this method, the code gets a reference to the context for the application, and then uses the context to get a reference to the map that holds all the request parameters. From this Map, the code accesses the request parameter with the name flightNum. Referring back to Listing 5-15, you can see that the page created a request parameter with that name. The code sets the flightNum property of the instance and returns the value select. The flightNum property becomes important for the getMatchingFlight() method.

Although most of the get methods simply return the current value of a property, the getMatchingFlight() method iterates through the matchingFlights list to find the flight with the same flight number as the flightNum property. In other words, get and set are not constrained to simply access or modify the value of properties, but can perform processing when they are called. The matchingFlight property is set to this object, and is also the return value from this method. This method is called because of the value-binding expression #{flight.matchingFlight} in the selectedFlight.jsp page.

Compile the classes and deploy the application to your server. When you load the welcome page at http://localhost:8080/Jsf_Ex03 (replacing the host, port, or name as necessary), the search form page will load, as shown earlier in Figure 5-5. If you enter BOS in the Leaving From text field and ORD in the Going To text field, and then click the Search button, the search results page will display as shown in Figure 5-9. On the search results page, clicking either link will display the selectedFlight.jsp page (see Figure 5-10). If you enter any other data in either the Leaving From field or Going To field and click the Search button, you should see the noFlights.jsp page, as shown in Figure 5-11.

**Figure 5-11.** *The noFlights.jsp page is served when no flights are found.*

# Accessing Context Data in Beans

Although JSF makes it easy for you to connect the view with the model without writing any code, at times you may need direct access to the request data or other data of your web application. We saw such a situation in Listing 5-19. In that listing, a request parameter had been set in the JSF page, and the FlightSearch JavaBean needed to access that request parameter.

JSF provides access to the request data and other data through the FacesContext object. As the Javadoc states, "FacesContext contains all of the per-request state information related to the processing of a single JavaServer Faces request, and the rendering of the corresponding response . . . . A FacesContext instance is associated with a particular request at the beginning of request processing." Because a FacesContext instance, and the objects it contains, are associated with the thread processing a particular request, any references to the FacesContext instance or its contained objects must not be passed to another thread or stored for subsequent requests.

As you saw in Listing 5-19, you access the FacesContext object like this:

```
FacesContext context = FacesContext.getCurrentInstance();
```

After you have a reference to the FacesContext for the request, you can access all the request and application data through the ExternalContext object. The reference to the ExternalContext object is obtained through the call to the getExternalContext() method.

Table 5-3 shows the methods of ExternalContext that return collections of request and application data. You can use these methods to access request data, session data, request header data, cookie data, and other sets of data in the application.

**Table 5-3.** *Request and Application Data Available Through ExternalContext*

| Method | Description |
|--------|-------------|
| Map getApplicationMap() | Returns a mutable Map representing the application scope attributes for the current application |
| String getInitParameter (java.lang.String name) | Returns the value of the specified application initialization parameter (if any) |
| Map getInitParameterMap() | Returns an immutable Map whose keys are the set of application initialization parameter names configured for this application, and whose values are the corresponding parameter values |
| String getRemoteUser() | Returns the login name of the user making the current request if any; otherwise, returns null |
| Map getRequestCookieMap() | Returns an immutable Map whose keys are the set of cookie names included in the current request, and whose values (of type javax.servlet.http.Cookie) are the first (or only) cookie for each cookie name returned by the underlying request |
| Map getRequestHeaderMap() | Returns an immutable Map whose keys are the set of request header names included in the current request, and whose values (of type String) are the first (or only) value for each header name returned by the underlying request |

| Method | Description |
|--------|-------------|
| Map getRequestHeaderValuesMap() | Returns an immutable Map whose keys are the set of request header names included in the current request, and whose values (of type String[]) are all of the value for each header name returned by the underlying request |
| Map getRequestMap() | Returns a mutable Map representing the request scope attributes for the current application |
| Map getRequestParameterMap() | Returns an immutable Map whose keys are the set of request parameter names included in the current request, and whose values (of type String) are the first (or only) value for each parameter name returned by the underlying request |
| Iterator getRequestParameterNames() | Returns an Iterator over the names of all request parameters included in the current request |
| Map getRequestParameterValuesMap() | Returns an immutable Map whose keys are the set of request parameter names included in the current request, and whose values (of type String[]) are all of the values for each parameter name returned by the underlying request |
| Map getSessionMap() | Returns a mutable Map representing the session scope attributes for the current application |

Most likely, if you are accessing request or application data in a managed bean, you will be accessing request data or session data. As you can see in Table 5-3, you access request data through the getRequestParameterMap() or getRequestParameterValuesMap() method. You can access session data through the getSessionMap() method.

# Converting Data

Looking at the FlightSearch and Flight objects, we notice that it would probably make more sense for the departDate and returnDate fields to be actual Date objects rather than String objects. (To be honest, we noticed this much earlier, but did not want to address that issue until this point in the chapter.)

Modify the FlightSearch and Flight objects so that the departDate and returnDate fields are java.util.Date objects and redeploy the application. Now, bring up the search page, enter data into the fields, and click the Search button. If the application works correctly, you should see the search page again.

At this point, you should be wondering why the search page was redisplayed, especially if you entered valid data into all the input fields. The redisplay of the search page indicates that there was an error in the data.

When an error occurs in a JSF page, the JSF implementation redisplays the originating page. In this case, the problem is that the JSF implementation does not know how to convert a string into a Date object, which is what is required for the FlightSearch object. Unfortunately, with the sample JSP pages we have deployed so far, we did not include any code to inform you of what the error is. Let's take care of that now.

Modify the searchResults.jsp page by adding an id attribute to the inputText elements and a message element following each inputText element. These changes are shown here:

```
<h:inputText id="departDate" value="#{flight.departDate}"/>
<h:message for="departDate"/>
 . . .
<h:inputText id="returnDate" value="#{flight.returnDate}"/>
<h:message for="returnDate"/>
```

The id attribute allows you to use the value of the attribute to refer to the JSF custom tag from other tags. The <message> element obtains a message from the component identified by the for attribute. If that component does not have a message, the <message> element keeps an empty string as its value. If the message component has a nonempty string value, that string is displayed when the page is rendered.

Deploy the search page with the new source, enter some data, and click the Search button again. This time, the search page is redisplayed with a message indicating the error. For example, if you enter 11/30/2005 for the depart or return date, you get the message "Conversion Error setting value '11/30/2005' for 'null Converter'," as shown in Figure 5-12.

**Figure 5-12.** *The message element displays an error message when a UI component has an error.*

In cases where the bean property is a Java primitive (int, float, boolean, and so on), a Java BigInteger, a Java BigDecimal, or a Java String, the JSF implementation will automatically convert the input data to the correct type. This is done with standard converters. When the bean property is a Java Date, there is a standard converter, but you need to explicitly tell the

JSF implementation to perform the conversion. When the bean property is some other data type, you need to provide a converter for the data.

## Using Standard Converters

The JSF implementation comes with two standard converters, one for numbers and one for dates and times:

- **<convertNumber>:** Converts strings to numbers, and vice versa. You can include optional attributes to format the numbers in various ways including as currency, as integers, and as floating-point numbers.

- **<convertDateTime>:** Converts strings to dates or times, and vice versa. You can include optional attributes to format by using various styles and time zones.

To use one of these converters, you nest the converter tag inside the <inputText> tag. In general, you can nest a converter inside any of the input or output custom tags. The converter will be called by the JSF implementation in the Update Model Values and Render Response phases of the JSF life cycle. If the conversion succeeds, the life cycle continues. If the conversion fails, the life cycle transitions to the Render Response phase, where the originating page is rendered, and the error message displayed (if the page contains message tags).

---

■**Note**  You do not need to use a converter if the type of the property is a primitive type (int, double, and so on), a Boolean, a BigInteger, a BigDecimal, or a String. You do need to use a converter if the type of the property is any other object, including Date.

---

The JSF implementation will automatically convert input values to numbers when the bean property is some primitive numeric type. If automatic conversion will not convert the number properly, you can explicitly control conversion through the standard <convertNumber> converter tag. For example, the <convertNumber> tag has attributes that allow you to convert the input value to a currency value.

The other standard converter is the <convertDateTime> tag. By using various attributes of this tag, you can convert dates or times, in various formats, to Date or Time properties in the managed bean. Let's modify the searchForm.jsp page to use the <convertDateTime> tag. The new <inputText> tags look like this:

```
<h:inputText id="departDate" value="#{flight.departDate}">
  <f:convertDateTime pattern="MM/dd/yy"/>
</h:inputText>
<h:message for="departDate"/>
  . . .
<h:inputText id="returnDate" value="#{flight.returnDate}">
  <f:convertDateTime pattern="MM/dd/yy"/>
</h:inputText>
<h:message for="returnDate"/>
```

The <convertDateTime> tag is nested in the <inputText> tag. The <convertDateTime> tag has several attributes that control the date conversion. We've used the pattern attribute to identify the pattern of the date string that will be converted. The symbols that you can use in pattern strings are the same symbols recognized by the java.text.SimpleDateFormat class. (Can you guess what the JSF implementation uses to do the conversion?) We've identified that the input value will consist of the two-digit month, followed by the two-digit day, followed by the two-digit year, with forward slashes delimiting each value. Now when you click the Search button, the JSF implementation will convert the date (assuming it follows the *MM/dd/yy* format), and the search results page will be sent to the browser.

## Using Custom Converters

If you could use only the <convertNumber> and <convertDateTime> tags, your ability to create feature-rich web applications would be limited. Fortunately, as you might guess from the title of this section, you can create and use custom converters in your JSF applications.

To create a custom converter, you write a class that implements the javax.faces.convert. Converter interface. This interface has two methods:

```
Object getAsObject(javax.faces.context.FacesContext context,
    javax.faces.component.UIComponent component, java.lang.String value)
String getAsString(javax.faces.context.FacesContext context,
    javax.faces.component.UIComponent component, java.lang.Object value)
```

The getAsObject() method converts the String value (which can be null) to an instance of the supported type and returns the new instance. This method throws a ConverterException if the conversion fails. The getAsString() method converts the provided value of the supported type (which can again be null) to a String instance and returns the new instance. This method also throws a ConverterException if the conversion fails.

If you check the JSF Javadoc, you will see that the JSF implementation includes a number of implementations of the javax.faces.convert.Converter interface. These are the standard converters that handle converting input and output values to the primitive types.

Let's create an Airport object that will be used as the data type for the origination and destination fields of the FlightSearch class. We will write a converter that converts between String and Airport objects.

Listing 5-20 shows the Airport object. It is a simple object that holds an airport code and the name of the airport.

**Listing 5-20.** *Airport.java*

```
package com.apress.projsp;

public class Airport {
  String code;
  String name;
  public Airport(String code, String name) {
    this.code = code;
    this.name = name;
  }
```

```
  public String toString() {
    return code;
  }
}
```

The converter, shown in Listing 5-21, will create an `Airport` object when given a string with the airport code.

**Listing 5-21.** *AirportConverter.java*

```java
package com.apress.projsp;

import javax.faces.application.FacesMessage;
import javax.faces.component.UIComponent;
import javax.faces.context.FacesContext;
import javax.faces.convert.Converter;
import javax.faces.convert.ConverterException;

public class AirportConverter implements Converter {
  public Object getAsObject(FacesContext ctxt, UIComponent comp,
    String value) {
    Airport airport = null;
    if ("BOS".equalsIgnoreCase(value)) {
      airport = new Airport("BOS", "Logan International Airport");
    }
    if ("ORD".equalsIgnoreCase(value)) {
      airport = new Airport("ORD", "O'Hare International Airport");
    }
    if (airport == null) {
      FacesMessage message =
        new FacesMessage(
          FacesMessage.SEVERITY_ERROR,
          "UnrecognizedAirportCode",
          "Airport code " + value + " is not recognized");
      throw new ConverterException(message);
    }
    return airport;
  }
  public String getAsString(FacesContext ctxt, UIComponent comp,
    Object obj) {
    if (obj != null) return obj.toString();
    return "";
  }
}
```

This converter is very simple. When converting from a string to an object (the `getAsObject()` method), the code looks for a value that matches either the string "BOS" or

"ORD". If either of those values is found, an `Airport` object is created. (In a real-world application, we would obviously use a more robust lookup such as a database search, which would recognize all possible airport codes.) If neither string is found, the converter throws a `ConverterException` that holds a `FacesMessage` object. The `FacesMessage` object holds a summary string and a detail string, which is displayed by the `<message>` tag when an error occurs.

To convert an object to a `String`, the `getAsString()` method simply calls the `toString()` method of the object passed to the method. Since this object should be an instance of `Airport`, the `toString()` method of `Airport` will be called, and that will return the airport code string.

If more involved processing is needed, each method has access to the `FacesContext` of the application and the `UIComponent` of the component instance in the page that the object or string is associated with. As you saw earlier, the `FacesContext` instance can be used to access various maps that hold parameters from the page and request being processed.

We will add these two classes to the Flight Search application. Figure 5-13 shows the directory structure for this example. We will add the classes to the `WEB-INF` directory. After adding the classes, we need to tell the JSF implementation when to call the converter.

```
Jsf_Ex04
  WEB-INF
    classes
      com
        apress
          projsp
            Airport.class
            Airport.java
            AirportConverter.class
            AirportConverter.java
            Flight.class
            Flight.java
            FlightSearch.class
            FlightSearch.java
            FlightTimes.class
            FlightTimes.java
            FlightTypes.class
            FlightTypes.java
    lib
    faces-config.xml
    web.xml
  index.html
  noFlights.jsp
  searchForm.jsp
  searchResults.jsp
  selectedFlight.jsp
```

**Figure 5-13.** *Directory structure for Jsf_Ex04*

One way to identify a converter to the JSF implementation is to specify a unique `converter-id` for the converter in a configuration file, and then use that ID in the JSP page. To do this, we would add this `<converter>` element to the `faces-config.xml` file:

```
<converter>
  <converter-id>airport.converter</converter-id>
  <converter-class>com.apress.projsp.AirportConverter</converter-class>
</converter>
```

Then, in the JSP page, we would use the ID in a `<converter>` tag, like this:

```
<h:inputText value="#{flight.origination}">
  <f:converter converterId="airport.converter"/>
</h:inputText>
```

or this:

```
<h:inputText value="#{flight.origination}" converter="airport.converter"/>
```

Another way to identify a converter is to define a default converter for all properties of type Airport. This `<converter>` element in the `faces-config.xml` file does that:

```
<converter>
  <converter-for-class>com.apress.projsp.Airport</converter-for-class>
  <converter-class>com.apress.projsp.AirportConverter</converter-class>
</converter>
```

With this entry, every time you use an input or output tag that references a property of type Airport, like this:

```
<h:inputText value="#{flight.origination}"/>
```

the JSF implementation detects that `origination` is of type Airport and calls the `AirportConverter` for this element. If you use the technique of defining a default converter, you must be sure that the converter works for all possible input strings. This is the technique we will use. Add the preceding `<converter>` element to the `faces-config.xml` file for this example, `Jsf_Ex04`.

---

■**Note** A third way to identify the converter involves creating an object known as a "backing bean." Interested readers should check the JSF specification for details on using backing beans.

---

If you have not yet done so, enter the `Airport.java` and `AirportConverter.java` source code (Listings 5-20 and 5-21) and save them in the correct directory.

In the `Flight.java` source file, change the data type of origination and destination to Airport, and change the set and get methods appropriately.

In the `FlightSearch.java` file, change the data type of origination and destination to Airport, and change the set and get methods appropriately. Change the `reset()` method to set the origination and destination to null. Also, change the `search()` method:

```
public String search() {
  if (origination.code.equals("BOS") &&
      destination.code.equals("ORD")) {
    return "success";
  } else {
    return "no flights";
  }
}
```

Finally, make this change to the inputText fields for origination and destination in the searchForm.jsp page:

```
<h:inputText id="origination"
    value="#{flight.origination}" size="35"/>
<h:message for="origination"/>
</td>
<td colspan="2">
<h:inputText id="destination"
    value="#{flight.destination}" size="35"/>
<h:message for="destination"/>
```

All the other files in the example remain the same as in the previous example, Jsf_Ex03. Compile the classes and deploy the application to the server. Unlike the previous addition of the date converter, this addition to the application will change the application's behavior. If you enter any airport code other than BOS or ORD in the Origination or Destination fields in the search form, the application responds with a conversion error and displays the detail string from the message generated by the converter. If you enter BOS as the origination and ORD as the destination, the application will find the matching flights. If you enter ORD as the origination and BOS as the destination, the application will return the noFlights.jsp page. Previously, you could enter any airport codes, and the application returned noFlights.jsp if the codes did not match BOS and ORD. Now, the only way to see the noFlights.jsp page is to enter ORD as the origination and BOS or ORD as the destination.

# Validating Input

If you've worked with web applications before, you know that a lot of effort is involved in ensuring that the data entered by the user of your application is correct. JSF provides a means to simplify data validation, through the use of standard and custom validators.

## Using Standard Validators

JSF provides three standard validators as part of the JSF implementation through the following custom tags:

- **<validateDoubleRange>:** Validates that a value is a double. You can include the optional attributes minimum and maximum to set minimum and maximum values.

- **<validateLongRange>:** Validates that a value is a long. You can include the optional attributes minimum and maximum to set minimum and maximum values.

- **<validateLength>:** Validates a string value for length. You can include the optional attributes minimum and maximum to set minimum and maximum values.

With all three validators, both of the attributes are optional. This means you could add a validator tag without either a minimum or maximum attribute. In that case, no validation will be performed. When you provide only a minimum, the validator checks that the value is greater than or equal to the minimum. When you provide only a maximum, the validator checks that the value is less than or equal to the maximum. When you provide both a minimum and a maximum, the validator checks that the value is greater than or equal to the minimum and less than or equal to the maximum.

One other validation you can perform in your JSF application is to require a value. The <input> and <output> tags include an optional attribute: required. For example, the following tag would require that you enter a value in the text field:

```
<h:inputText id="origination"
   value="#{flight.origination}" size="35" required="true"/>
```

If you do not enter a value, the JSF implementation will return the originating page with a message that you did not enter a required value (assuming there is a <message> tag for the id origination).

## Using Custom Validators

You create a custom validator by creating a class that implements the javax.faces.validator. Validator interface. All validators must implement this interface. The Validator interface has a single method that your class must implement:

```
void validate(javax.faces.context.FacesContext context,
  javax.faces.component.UIComponent component, java.lang.Object value)
```

In the validate() method, if the value argument passes the validation check, you can simply return from the method. This signals to the JSF implementation that the value passed the validation check. If it does not pass the validation check, you throw a javax.faces.validator. ValidatorException. The ValidatorException instance includes a FacesMessage instance with summary and detail messages describing the validation error.

If you check the JSF Javadoc, you will see that the JSF implementation includes a number of implementations of the javax.faces.validator.Validator interface. These are the standard validators that handle validating doubles, longs, and string lengths.

Suppose we wanted to create a date validator to ensure that dates entered by the user of our Flight Search application are greater than or equal to the day after the current date, and less than one year from the current date. Listing 5-22 shows the code for this validator.

**Listing 5-22.** *DateValidator.java*

```
package com.apress.projsp;

import java.util.Calendar;
import java.util.Date;
import javax.faces.application.FacesMessage;
import javax.faces.component.UIComponent;
import javax.faces.context.FacesContext;
import javax.faces.validator.Validator;
import javax.faces.validator.ValidatorException;
```

```
public class DateValidator implements Validator {
  public void validate(FacesContext arg0, UIComponent arg1, Object arg2)
    throws ValidatorException {
    Calendar date = Calendar.getInstance();
    date.setTime((Date) arg2);

    Calendar tomorrow = Calendar.getInstance();
    tomorrow.set(Calendar.HOUR, 0);
    tomorrow.set(Calendar.MINUTE, 0);
    tomorrow.set(Calendar.SECOND, 0);

    Calendar oneYear = Calendar.getInstance();
    oneYear.set(Calendar.HOUR, 0);
    oneYear.set(Calendar.MINUTE, 0);
    oneYear.set(Calendar.SECOND, 0);
    oneYear.add(Calendar.YEAR, 1);

    if (date.before(tomorrow) || date.after(oneYear)) {
      FacesMessage message =
        new FacesMessage(
          FacesMessage.SEVERITY_ERROR,
          "Date Error",
          "Date must be between tomorrow and one year from today");
      throw new ValidatorException(message);
    }
  }
}
```

The code in the validate() method creates two Calendar objects: tomorrow corresponds to the day after the current date, and oneYear corresponds to one year from the current date. Then the code compares the argument passed to the validate() method to see if it is between the dates represented by those two Calendar objects. If the argument is not between those two Calendar objects, a ValidatorException is thrown; if it is between those two dates, the method simply returns.

The validator is registered with the JSF implementation with the <validator> element in a configuration file. The <validator> element has two required subelements:

- **<validator-id>:** Used to create an ID string that you can use in the <validator> tag to specify a validator instance. This ID must be unique within the application.

- **<validator-class>:** The fully qualified class name of the validator class.

Here is an example of the element you could place in the faces-config.xml configuration file for this validator:

```
<validator>
  <validator-id>date.validator</validator-id>
  <validator-class>com.apress.projsp.DateValidator</validator-class>
</validator>
```

And in the searchForm.jsp, you could nest this <validator> tag in an inputText tag:

```
<h:inputText id="departDate" value="#{flight.departDate}">
  <f:convertDateTime pattern="MM/dd/yy"/>
  <f:validator validatorId="date.validator"/>
</h:inputText>
```

Notice that the value of the validatorId in the <f:validator> tag is the same string used in the <validator-id> element.

To use this validator with the application, enter and compile Listing 5-22 and save it with the web application. Then make the changes to faces-config.xml and searchForm.jsp shown in the preceding code. Now, the application will accept only dates that occur between the day after the current day and one year from the current day. If you enter an invalid date, you should see the page shown in Figure 5-14.

**Figure 5-14.** *When an entered date does not pass validation, an error message is displayed by the application.*

## Bypassing Validation

Validation is an important aspect of your web application, because it ensures that all input values are valid before the model is updated, thereby enforcing model integrity. However, at times you will not want validation to occur.

For example, various pages of the Flight Search application have a New Search button. If this button occurred on a page that also specified validators for any fields, we could have a problem. In the normal JSF life cycle, the validators would be executed before the New Search button was processed. Validators are executed during the Process Validations phase, whereas command buttons are processed after the Invoke Application phase, which occurs after the Process Validations phase. By providing a New Search button, we are acknowledging that the user might want to throw away whatever values are in the page and start a new search. Thus, we would not want validations to occur when the user clicks the New Search button.

We can tell the JSF implementation to process the event from the button click after the Apply Request Values phase (before the Process Validations phase) by adding an attribute named immediate to the <action> tag. So, for example, if we wanted the New Search button to bypass validations in a page, the tag would look like this:

```
<h:commandButton value="New Search" action="#{flight.reset}"
                 immediate="true"/>
```

# Event Handling

There's one final improvement we want to make to the Flight Search application. You may have noticed that when you select either Roundtrip or One Way as the trip type, no change is made to the display. In other words, when the user selects One Way, the search form still displays labels and fields for the return trip. In a real web application, the presentation would likely change in response to picking a one-way trip. There's no sense in displaying fields for return trip date and time if the user doesn't want a return ticket.

There are many ways we could deal with this situation. However, since we still need to discuss event handling in a JSF application, we will deal with it by creating an event handler. There are two basic types of event handlers in JSF: value change listeners and action listeners.

## Value Change Listeners

Value change listeners are attached to input elements such as text fields, radio buttons and check boxes, and menus. When you want your application to respond to a value change event, you attach a value change listener to the input element:

```
<h:selectOneRadio layout="lineDirection"
                  value="#{flight.tripType}"
                  valueChangeListener="#{flight.typeChanged}"
                  onclick="submit()"
                  immediate="true">
    <f:selectItems value="#{flight.tripTypes}"/>
</h:selectOneRadio>
```

The preceding code snippet shows the <selectOneRadio> element from the searchForm.jsp page. As you can see, you use the valueChangeListener attribute with a method-binding expression to specify which method should be called when a value change event occurs. The FlightSearch class does not yet have a typeChanged() method; you will look at it later in this section. Additionally, input elements do not cause a form submission on their own, so you need to include an onclick event handler as well. Finally, because we do not want to validate inputs when the user changes flight types, the code uses the immediate attribute.

Listing 5-23 shows the typeChanged() method of the FlightSearch class. In Listing 5-23, we show only the new method, and the import needed for the class to compile. Because you tell the JSF implementation which method to call by using a method-binding expression, the value changed method can have any name you want to give it. The only requirements for the method signature are that the method must be public, must return void, and must accept a ValueChangeEvent as the only parameter.

**Listing 5-23.** *typeChanged() method of Flight Search.java*

```
...
import javax.faces.event.ValueChangeEvent;
...
public class FlightSearch {
...
  public FlightSearch() {
    setTripType("Roundtrip");
  }
...
  public void typeChanged(ValueChangeEvent event) {
    if ("Roundtrip".equals(event.getNewValue().toString())) {
      setTripType("Roundtrip");
    } else {
      setTripType("One Way");
    }
    FacesContext.getCurrentInstance().renderResponse();
  }
}
```

Within the method, you can perform any processing you need to handle the event. In the typeChanged() method in Listing 5-23, we set the trip type property of the bean. However, you can do whatever is needed to handle the event. The last thing that the method does is call the renderResponse() method. If the typeChanged() method did not do this, the JSF implementation would proceed through the normal JSF life cycle. However, we do not want this to happen. If you have selected a trip type before entering any other search parameters, proceeding through the normal life cycle would cause a validation error. Calling renderResponse() transitions the JSF processing directly to the Render Response stage, bypassing validation. If you want to validate the form data normally, your code would not call renderResponse().

So now that the FlightSearch class changes state in response to the user selecting Roundtrip or One Way, what can we do with this information? Well, as we mentioned, we would like the presentation of the search form to change so that return trip information is not displayed to the user. Listing 5-24 shows the new searchForm.jsp. Notice that we have used the JSTL <c:if> action to control whether the input fields for the return trip are displayed. When the test for the <c:if> action is true, HTML comment markers are included as part of the template text, causing some the fields between the markers to be hidden. When the test is false, the comment markers are not rendered, so the fields are displayed.

**Listing 5-24.** *searchForm.jsp*

```jsp
<%@ taglib uri="http://java.sun.com/jsf/core" prefix="f" %>
<%@ taglib uri="http://java.sun.com/jsf/html" prefix="h" %>
<%@ taglib uri="http://java.sun.com/jsp/jstl/core" prefix="c" %>

<html>
  <f:view>
  <head>
    <title>Freedom Airlines Online Flight Reservation System</title>
  </head>
  <body>
    <h:form>
      <h2>Search Flights</h2>
      <h:outputText value="What type of flight do you need?"/>
      <h:selectOneRadio layout="lineDirection"
                        value="#{flight.tripType}"
                        valueChangeListener="#{flight.typeChanged}"
                        onclick="submit()"
                        immediate="true">
        <f:selectItems value="#{types.tripTypes}"/>
      </h:selectOneRadio>
      <p/>
      <table>
        <tr><td colspan="4">Where and when do you want to travel?</td></tr>
        <tr>
          <td colspan="2">Leaving from:</td>
          <td colspan="2">Going to:</td>
        </tr>
        <tr>
          <td colspan="2">
            <h:inputText id="origination"
              value="#{flight.origination}" size="35"/>
            <h:message for="origination"/>
          </td>
          <td colspan="2">
            <h:inputText id="destination"
              value="#{flight.destination}" size="35"/>
            <h:message for="destination"/>
          </td>
        </tr>
        <tr>
          <td colspan="2">Departing:</td>
          <td colspan="2">
            <c:if test="${flight.tripType == 'One Way'}">
              <!--
            </c:if>
```

```
            <h:outputText value="Returning:"/>
          <c:if test="${flight.tripType == 'One Way'}">
            -->
          </c:if>
        </td>
    </tr>
    <tr>
      <td>
        <h:inputText id="departDate" value="#{flight.departDate}">
          <f:convertDateTime pattern="MM/dd/yy"/>
          <f:validator validatorId="date.validator"/>
        </h:inputText>
        <h:message for="departDate"/>
      </td>
      <td>
        <h:selectOneMenu value="#{flight.departTime}" id="departTimes">
          <f:selectItems value="#{times.times}"/>
        </h:selectOneMenu>
      </td>
      <td>
        <c:if test="${flight.tripType == 'One Way'}">
          <!--
        </c:if>
        <h:inputText id="returnDate" value="#{flight.returnDate}">
          <f:convertDateTime pattern="MM/dd/yy"/>
          <f:validator validatorId="date.validator"/>
        </h:inputText>
        <h:message for="returnDate"/>
      </td>
        <c:if test="${flight.tripType == 'One Way'}">
          -->
        </c:if>

      <td>
        <c:if test="${flight.tripType == 'One Way'}">
          <!--
        </c:if>
        <h:selectOneMenu value="#{flight.returnTime}" id="returnTimes">
          <f:selectItems value="#{times.times}"/>
        </h:selectOneMenu>
        <c:if test="${flight.tripType == 'One Way'}">
          -->
        </c:if>
      </td>
    </tr>
</table>
<p>
```

```
      <h:commandButton value="Search"
                       action="#{flight.search}"/>
      </p>
   </h:form>
   </body>
   </f:view>
</html>
```

All of the other parts of the application remain unchanged. When you first access the search page of the application, you will see the same page as in previous versions of the application. However, if you click the One Way radio button, the page is submitted, the value change event is handled, and the page is redisplayed without the return trip date and time fields, as shown in Figure 5-15.

**Figure 5-15.** *When the One Way radio button is selected, the page displays without the return trip date and time fields.*

## Action Listeners

Action listeners are provided by JSF to make it easier to handle action events. JSF already provides some event handling. For example, in Listing 5-24, clicking a button on the search page (an event) causes the search() method of the FlightSearch class to be called. However, that event handler is limited in what it can do, because it has no access to the state of the user interface. Action listeners do receive information about the user interface, and thus can be used for more robust event handling.

Action listeners are attached to the two JSF command elements: command buttons and command links. Action events are handled in a manner very similar to value change events. You attach a listener to a command element with the actionListener attribute. For example, the searchForm.jsp page has a command button. You can attach an action listener to it by using this syntax:

```
<h:commandButton value="Search"
                 actionListener="#{flight.confirm}"
                 action="#{flight.search}"/>
```

When the button is clicked, the JSF implementation calls the action listener during the Invoke Application phase. The action listener method then has a chance to perform any processing related to the command element selected by the user. You can perform any processing you need to inside the method. The method can have any name, must be public, return void, and accept an ActionEvent as its only parameter.

After the action listener method is called, the method bound by the action attribute will be called, and the JSF implementation will determine where to navigate next.

Because the action listener method is called before the action method, the action listener method is able to modify the response that the action method returns. For example, the Flight Search application could have some links that direct the user to searches for lodging, transportation, or other services. Without action listeners, you would need to write a different action method for each link, because the action method cannot have parameters and thus does not know what part of the user interface was clicked. As the number of links increased, so would the number of action methods. However, the action listener does have access to the user interface through the ActionEvent, and could determine which link was clicked. It could store that information as a bean property that the action method could access. With this technique, a single action listener method and a single action method could handle any number of links.

## Calling Multiple Listeners

There may be situations in which you want multiple value change listeners or multiple action listeners to respond to an event. In that case, you need a slightly different syntax to attach the listeners to the JSF element.

In the preceding examples, we attached a value change listener or an action listener to a JSF element by using the valueChangeListener or actionListener attributes. When using the attribute syntax, you use a method-binding expression to bind a method as a listener. However, this works only when attaching a single listener.

When you need to attach multiple listeners, there is a JSF tag for value change listeners and one for action listeners that can be used to attach one or more listeners to an element. When using the tag syntax, you will be specifying a class that implements a listener interface.

For value change listeners, the tag is <f:valueChangeListener>, with an attribute named type that is the class name of the listener. The interface that the listener must implement is javax.faces.event.ValueChangeListener. It has a single method that must be implemented:

```
void processValueChangeEvent(ValueChangeEvent);
```

So, if we assume that the FlightSearch and FlightTypes classes both implement ValueChangeListener, we could attach both of them to an element like this:

```
<h:selectOneRadio layout="lineDirection"
                  value="#{flight.tripType}"
                  onclick="submit()"
                  immediate="true">
```

```
    <f:valueChangeListener type="com.apress.projsp.FlightSearch"/>
    <f:valueChangeListener type="com.apress.projsp.FlightTypes"/>
    <f:selectItems value="#{types.tripTypes}"/>
</h:selectOneRadio>
```

For action listeners, the tag is `<f:actionListener>`, with an attribute named `type` that is the class name of the listener. The interface that the listener must implement is `javax.faces.event.ActionListener`. It has a single method that must be implemented:

```
void processAction(ActionEvent);
```

If we assume that the `FlightSearch` and `FlightTypes` classes both implement `ActionListener`, we could attach both of them to an element, like this:

```
<h:commandButton value="Search"
                 action="#{flight.search}">
  <f:actionListener type="com.apress.projsp.FlightSearch"/>
  <f:actionListener type="com.apress.projsp.FlightTypes"/>
</h:commandButton>
```

In either of the two preceding examples, both listeners will be called at the appropriate time to respond to the event. If any listeners are attached by using attribute syntax, they will be called first. Then any listeners attached by using tag syntax will be called, in order of declaration.

# Using Message Bundles

With the global nature of the Web, many web applications must be internationalized. JSF provides a facility to make it easy to internationalize your web application. The features of JSF that are used for internationalization build on the internationalization capability provided in the Java core libraries.

To provide an internationalized version of your web application, all the text strings used in your application must be collected into a properties file that your application can load and use. Listing 5-25 shows a properties file of messages that you could use with the `searchForm.jsp` page we have developed in this chapter as part of the Flight Search application. This file holds the English language strings for the application.

**Listing 5-25.** *messages.properties*

```
title=Freedom Airlines Online Flight Reservation System
head=Search Flights
type=What type of flight do you need?
searchLabel=Where and when do you want to travel?
departAirport=Depart:
arriveAirport=Arrive:
departLabel=Depart Date:
returnLabel=Return Date:
searchButton=Search
```

Save this file somewhere in the CLASSPATH for your application. In the Flight Search example, we could save it in the `com\apress\projsp` directory. When we cause the properties file to be loaded, we will reference it by a name that includes the CLASSPATH.

The properties file is included in a JSP page with the `<loadBundle>` custom action:

```
<f:loadBundle basename="com.apress.projsp.messages" var="msgs"/>
```

The `<loadBundle>` custom action has two required attributes: `basename` and `var`. The basename attribute is the CLASSPATH qualified base name of the properties file. We reference the `messages.properties` file by using the same package qualified name as if it were a Java class file. Notice that we do not need to provide the `.properties` extension of the file. When combined with locale information, the basename is the initial part of the name of the file to be loaded. A locale code is appended with an underscore, followed by the `.properties` extension, to create the full filename. With no locale information, the basename shown in the preceding example tells the JSF implementation to look for the file `messages.properties` in the directory `com\apress\projsp` of the application. The var attribute is the name that you will use in the JSP page to access the messages stored in the `messages.properties` file.

You can use these strings in your application by using a value-binding expression. For example, to add the page header to the `searchForm.jsp` page, you would replace the original page header element:

```
<h2>Search Flights</h2>
```

with the following `<outputText>` element:

```
<h2><h:outputText value="#{msgs.head}"/></h2>
```

In elements such as `<commandButton>`, you can use the value-binding expression directly in the value attribute of the `<commandButton>` element:

```
<h:commandButton value="#{msgs.searchButton}" action="#{flight.search}"/>
```

This provides two big advantages. First, if you want to change the text used in the web application, you need to change only the `messages.properties` message bundle. Second, and the big reason for message bundles, is that you can easily internationalize your application by providing additional message bundles for other languages. For example, you can create a second message bundle named `messages_es.properties`, as shown in Listing 5-26. This file holds the Spanish versions of all the strings.

**Listing 5-26.** *messages_es.properties*

```
title=Freedom Airlines Online Flight Reservation System
head=Busque los Vuelos
type=¿Qué tipo del vuelo necesita usted?
searchLabel=¿Dónde y cuándo usted quiere viajar?
departAirport=Salida:
arriveAirport=Llegada:
departLabel= Fecha de salida:
returnLabel= Fecha de regreso:
searchButton=Buscar
```

---

**■Tip** If you want to include Unicode characters with an ASCII code greater than 127, you need to encode them as escape sequences in the form \uxxxx. This provides the ability to support non-Western languages. And you don't need to type in these sequences by hand. The Java utility `native2ascii` can convert native characters to escape sequences for you.

---

You add an entry to the `faces-config.xml` file that identifies which languages your application supports. For our Flight Search application, you would add this entry to the `faces-config.xml` file:

```
<application>
  <locale-config>
    <default-locale>en</default-locale>
    <supported-locale>es</supported-locale>
  </locale-config>
</application>
```

You need to add a `<supported-locale>` element with a locale code for every language that your application supports. The two-letter and three-letter locale codes are listed at `http://www.loc.gov/standards/iso639-2/englangn.html`.

When a user accesses your application, and the user's browser is set to accept Spanish as the default language, your application will access strings from the `messages_es.properties` file, as shown in Figure 5-16. Note that you do not need to change the `<loadBundle>` tag in your JSP pages. The browser sends a header parameter that it accepts Spanish as its default language. The JSF implementation uses that parameter to determine the locale code, and then combines the `basename` attribute with the locale code `es` to determine which message bundle to load.

**Figure 5-16.** *The search form page with Spanish text*

Adding this language bundle to the Flight Search example is left as an exercise for the reader. To see the Flight Search application with other languages, you will also need to set the language preferences of your browser. For Microsoft Internet Explorer, click Tools ➤ Internet Options, and then click the Languages button. If you have a different browser, you should be able to set the language preference in a similar fashion.

---

**■Tip** Although we left this as the last topic for the chapter, in the real world you would not want to leave the message bundle setup for last. Initially writing your web application with internationalization is much easier than attempting to retrofit your application with internationalization. This does not mean that you must write message bundles for every possible language up front. You should write a default message bundle and then add other languages as needed.

---

# Summary

After completing this chapter, you should know the following:

- JSF was developed to make it easier to create customizable UIs for web applications using a component-based system. JSF provides a set of UI components that can easily be added to web applications and connected to business objects. The components are converted into user interfaces through the use of a render kit.

- The JSF implementation comes with a set of custom actions in two tag libraries that allow you to easily integrate JSF with JSP pages. All JSF implementations must support JSP pages.

- JavaBeans are the business objects in your JSF application. JSF makes it easy to connect JavaBeans with UI components. The JSF implementation handles all the work of moving data from the UI into the bean, and moving data from the bean to the UI.

- Page navigation in a JSF application is handled by adding navigation rules to a configuration file. Navigation can be controlled through value-binding expressions or method-binding expressions.

- Data conversion and validation is handled by converters and validators. The JSF implementation provides two standard converters: one for numbers and one for dates. The JSF implementation provides three standard validators for validating the ranges of doubles or longs and validating the length of strings.

- You can implement your own converters or validators to perform custom conversion and validation.

- JSF applications can be designed to respond to events and actions by using value change listeners and action listeners.

- Message bundles provide an easy facility for internationalizing and customizing the pages in your web application.

# CHAPTER 6

■ ■ ■

# Tag Files and Simple Tags

**P**rior to this chapter, we showed how to write JSP pages by using several mechanisms that allow dynamic content to be created.

First, we presented scriptlets in the page, which provide an easy way to get started with JSP, particularly because they allow existing Java code to be easily migrated into a JSP-based environment. We also showed how JavaBeans could be integrated with JSP, making it easier to maintain and manipulate information residing within these reusable components. Chapter 3 covered the JSP expression language (EL), which provides a way to create dynamic content through scripting expressions.

In Chapter 4, we presented the JSP Standard Tag Library (JSTL), which contains useful, prebuilt tags that achieve tasks such as iterating over collections. In addition to helping you perform these common tasks easily, the tags contained within the JSTL are extremely valuable for improving the readability and maintainability of the page. In Chapter 5, we showed how to create dynamic user interfaces with JavaServer Faces (JSF). The JSF reference implementation includes a set of custom tags that encapsulate the JSF API and make it available to use within JSP pages.

JSP also provides the capability for you to encapsulate reusable functionality into your own custom tags. Custom tags, also known as tag extensions, were first introduced in JSP 1.1 and carried forward into JSP 1.2. These custom tags are known as classic tags. Classic tags get their behavior from a Java class known as a tag handler. When a JSP page is translated, the custom tag in the page is translated into a call to the tag handler class.

JSP 2.0 introduced two major additions to the tag extension mechanism: tag files and simple tags. Tag files are custom tags written entirely as JSP pages. Simple tags are similar to classic tags because they get their behavior from a tag handler class. However, as you will see when you get to Chapter 7, simple tags are simpler to implement.

This chapter covers tag files and simple tags. You'll also look at the differences between tag files, simple tags, and classic tags. Specifically you'll be looking at the following:

- What custom tags are and why they are useful

- Tag terminology

- The differences between simple tags and classic tags

- How to create and use tag files

- How to create and use simple tags

In Chapter 7, we will cover the topic of classic tags. Then in Chapter 8, we will finish the discussion of custom tags by looking at some advanced topics, such as writing cooperating tags, validating tag usage, and deploying tag libraries.

# Understanding JSP Custom Tags

Custom tags, also known as JSP tag extensions (because they extend the set of built-in JSP tags), provide a way of encapsulating reusable functionality on JSP pages. One of the major drawbacks of scripting environments such as JSP is that it's easy to quickly put together an application without thinking about how it will be maintained and grown in the future. For example, the ability to generate dynamic content by using Java code embedded in the page is a very powerful feature of the JSP specification. Custom tags allow such functionality to be encapsulated into reusable components. As you've already seen with the JSTL, custom tags provide a great way for the logic behind common and recurring tasks to be wrapped up in an easy-to-use package. However, one question still remains: why should you go to all the trouble and effort of building custom tags when you can simply write code inside the JSP pages?

In this section, you'll learn why and how custom tags are used. You'll also learn about the differences between JavaBeans and custom tags, and the differences between simple and classic tags.

## The Need for Custom Tags

Among the best practices that have been established around JSP, one of the most important suggests that there should be as little Java code embedded inside a JSP page as possible. Experience has shown us that three key factors benefit from this practice:

- Reusability

- Readability

- Maintainability

We covered these in detail in Chapter 1, so we'll just review them here.

### Reusability

Reuse is a common goal associated with any programming language. Because you can embed Java code inside JSP pages, you may be tempted to reuse code on a source-code level between JSP pages. This kind of reuse brings with it a dramatic decrease in maintainability as changes and bugs slowly creep in and around the system. Ideally, you're looking for reusability at the class or component level.

The way that JSP allows you to reuse code is through custom tags and tag libraries. A **tag library** is simply a collection of one or more custom tags. A tag library can be reused on a single page, on several pages in an application, or across different applications. Obviously, the best option is to reuse tag libraries across applications.

## Readability

Custom tags improve readability by encapsulating Java code away from the page. As you may have noticed while developing JSP pages, the more you intermix scriptlets with template text, the harder it is to read the page. Encapsulating the Java code in a custom tag removes this code from the page, making the page cleaner, shorter, and more readable. Choosing appropriate names for your custom tags can also make a page easier for page designers to read.

## Maintainability

An important concept in maintainability is removing duplication from your code. If you have 50 copies of the same method scattered throughout a Java application, you have 50 places to make corrections when an error is found. If, however, you extract that method and have 50 calls to that one method, the bug needs to be fixed in only one place. The same is true of JSP pages. If you can encapsulate some bit of functionality in a custom tag, changes or fixes to that functionality are made only to the custom tag, and then every JSP page that uses the tag automatically gets the fix.

There are several signs that help identify whether a system will be easy or difficult to maintain. Good use of custom tags is one of those signs for a JSP application.

# Tag Terminology and Concepts

Now that you know why using custom tags is a good idea, let's quickly look at some of key tag concepts and the principles behind how tags work.

## Tags and Tag Libraries

A tag library (commonly known as a taglib) is a collection of individual **custom tags** that are typically related to each other. For example, the JSTL Core tag library contains all of those tags that help you solve some of the common problems that you encounter when building JSP pages, such as iterating over collections and performing simple conditional logic on the page. Another example, again from JSTL, is the Internationalization and Formatting tag library that contains tags related to the formatting of information on the page. As you'll see throughout this chapter, and as you've already seen in preceding chapters, there are several ways that tags can be built and deployed.

## Importing and Using Tags

A defined and deployed tag library must be made available to a JSP page if it's to be used. As you saw when using the JSTL and JSF tag libraries, this is done by importing the tag library through the JSP `taglib` directive, and by giving that tag library a namespace (or prefix) on the page to differentiate it from other tag libraries—in the same way that you place classes inside packages. After the tag library has been imported, the tags within that library can be used with XML syntax. For example, if the tag library contained a tag called `copyright`, you simply use the tag as follows:

```
<tags:copyright></tags:copyright>
```

Here, you simply use the tag as an XML tag on the page, with the start and end tags being explicitly stated. In this example, there is no content between the start and end tags, although this is possible, too, and is written as follows:

```
<tags:copyright>2005</tags:copyright>
```

Alternatively, if an XML tag has nothing between its start and end tags, that tag can be used in its shortened format as follows:

```
<tags:copyright/>
```

Semantically, this shortened usage is identical to using the tag in its longer, more verbose syntax.

## Body Content

Body content is defined as anything that falls between the start and end tags. When first introduced, three types of body content were defined: empty, tagdependent, and JSP. JSP 2.1 supports the same three categories of body content, and an additional category named scriptless (introduced in JSP 2.0). Table 6-1 defines the four categories. As you'll see later in this chapter, these options enable you to define the type of content that you'll permit within your tags.

**Table 6-1.** *Valid Body-Content Values for Tag Extensions*

| Category | Definition |
| --- | --- |
| empty | As you've seen, a tag has empty body content when there is nothing between the start and end tags. If start and end tags are used (as opposed to shortened format) then nothing at all, not even whitespace, can appear between the tags when the body content is empty. |
| JSP | JSP body content is defined as anything that can usually appear within JSP pages. This includes content such as HTML, Java scriptlets, other custom tags, and so on:<br>`<prefix:myTag>Here is some <b>HTML content</b></prefix:myTag>` |
| scriptless | This body content is effectively the same as JSP body content with the restriction that it cannot contain any Java code wrapped up as scriptlets. As you've seen, moving Java code off the page and into reusable components is one of the best practices associated with JSP development, and using a body content of scriptless provides a way to enforce this. At translation time, the JSP container looks at the body content and will throw a fatal translation error if scriptlets are found. For new developments, a body content type of scriptless is recommended over JSP. |
| tagdependent | With tagdependent body content, the custom tag has complete control over how its body content is included or evaluated in the page. Essentially, the body content is treated as plain text, meaning that JSP constructs and expressions simply aren't evaluated. Although seemingly useless at first glance, there are a few good uses of this type of body content, including, for example, a tag that interprets its body content as another language. A custom tag could be written and used as a container for another language such as ColdFusion or another scripting language. The tag could then take its body content and pass it on to a parser that would execute the code. |

### Attributes

The final key concept related to how custom tags are used on the page is that of attributes. As you'll see later in the chapter, custom tags can be customized through the use of attributes in the same way that methods can be customized through the use of parameters. If you are familiar with HTML or XML tags, you will immediately recognize that custom tag attributes are the same concept as HTML or XML tag attributes. Attributes are written as name=value pairs within the tag itself, as shown here:

```
<prefix:myTag attributeName="attribute value"/>
```

In this example, the tag has a single attribute called attributeName, with a value of attribute value. A tag may have one or more attributes, and as you'll see later, you have full control over some of the attribute characteristics such as the type and whether it's required.

## JavaBeans vs. Custom Tags

Now that you understand the purpose of custom tags and how they are used, you need to know when to use tags as opposed to JavaBeans for wrapping up reusable functionality. After all, JavaBeans are reusable components and the JSP specification provides a built-in mechanism for integrating and utilizing the features provided by JavaBeans. Although both technologies can be used to achieve the same goal, that of encapsulating and abstracting data away from the JSP page, there are significant differences between the two.

JavaBeans are good general-purpose objects that encapsulate state in a portable "bucket." We will continue to use these in our examples because they make great business objects.

Tags are a web-specific technology. Tags are primarily for generating presentation elements, and as such they primarily encapsulate behavior. In addition, custom tags are aware of the environment in which they are running. For example, custom tags have access to the same implicit objects as the ones available when developing JSP pages: pageContext, request, response, session, and so on. JavaBeans, however, are components that can be reused within any Java environment; hence, they don't know about such JSP specifics. Therefore, custom tags are a much better choice for encapsulating reusable functionality that will be used on JSP pages. You'll look more closely at this in the discussion of custom tag best practices in Chapter 8, but for the moment, keep in mind the following rules:

- Use JavaBeans for representing and storing information and state. An example is building JavaBeans to represent the business objects in your application.

- Use custom tags to represent and implement actions that occur on those JavaBeans, as well as logic related to the presentation of information. An example from JSTL is iterating over a collection of objects or conditional logic.

## Differences Between Simple and Classic Tags

From a tag developer's perspective, there are several important differences between simple and classic tags.

To build classic tags, you write the functionality provided by the custom tag as a Java class that implements the javax.servlet.jsp.tagext.Tag interface. This class containing the functionality provided by the tag is called the tag handler. One of the biggest problems with building tags in this way is that the Tag interface, the tag life cycle, and the semantics of its usage in the container are rather complex.

Through feedback and the Java Community Process (JCP, http://www.jcp.org), two new ways for building custom tags have been introduced: **tag files** and **simple tags**. Both are the subject of this chapter and as you'll see shortly, tag files and simple tags allow the functionality of custom tags to be implemented by using JSP fragments and Java code, respectively. Although they use different paradigms, they both greatly simplify the way in which custom tags can be built and have changed the way that JSP-based web applications are built.

Other changes to custom tags introduced in JSP 2.0 include the ability of a custom tag to take any number of undefined (dynamic) attributes, and the ability to use the JSP EL with custom tags. Although these changes were introduced in JSP 2.0, both changes affect classic tags and simple tags. We'll see examples using EL statements in the examples in this chapter. We will look at dynamic attributes in Chapter 7.

# Using Tag Files

Tag files provide a very simple way for content and functionality to be abstracted away from JSP pages and into reusable components. So, what is a tag file?

In short, a tag file is simply a JSP fragment containing some content or JSP code that you would like to use over and over again. This fragment is accessed by using a custom tag. In the past, you've typically achieved the same thing by taking JSP code out of a JSP page, placing it in a separate JSP file, and including it wherever necessary. So why do you need tag files? Let's answer this question with an example showing how you can reuse content between JSP pages.

## Reusing Content

On many websites, small pieces of content are abstracted away from the main pages and into smaller JSP pages that are included wherever necessary. Typical examples include header pages that contain references to cascading style sheets (CSS) and common JavaScript functions, or alternatively, footer pages that may include a brief copyright and usage notice about the website. We'll recap how this is done with the JSP include directive, and then we'll look at how to accomplish the same result with tag files.

### Reusing Content with Included JSP Files

If you take an example where footer information is abstracted away from the main page, the following sample could be placed into a separate JSP file:

```
Copyright 2005, Apress
```

As you can see, there isn't a great deal of content within this JSP file. Although it seems trivial, the copyright text is a good example of the kind of information that you would want to abstract out of a JSP page. It is common to most or all of the pages in a website. Abstracting common information into reusable custom tags increases the maintainability of the web application. If you need to add to or change the copyright notice, moving it into a separate file means that you have to change the content in only a single place.

There are a couple of ways to include such pages, although with static content the `include` directive is generally used:

```
<%@ include file="copyright.jsp" %>
```

At translation time, the text contained within the referenced file simply gets inlined into the resulting JSP page. This is a common technique for including static content, so why do you need tag files and how can you reuse content with them?

## Reusing Content with Tag Files

One of the real problems with including files is that with many `include` directives on the page, the content of each included file can sometimes be cryptic. The content of `copyright.jsp` may seem clear, but other included files may not be as obvious. In addition, there is no standard method for distributing included files for reuse in other web applications. Tag files can help address both of these drawbacks.

### Defining Content in a Tag File

Building a tag file is almost the same as building the included JSP file—you simply copy out the content that you would like to reuse and place it in a file ending with a `.tag` extension, as shown in Listing 6-1.

**Listing 6-1.** *copyright.tag*

```
Copyright 2005, Apress
```

As this example shows, there is, in fact, no difference between the content of this tag file and the content of the included JSP page. There is a minor difference in the name of the file. The key difference is in how tag files are deployed and used.

To promote the use of custom tags to page authors and people who might not understand the Java programming side of JSP, the expert group behind JSP provided a very simple approach to defining tag files. Through a convention defined in the specification, tag files should be saved with a `.tag` file extension in a directory called `tags` (or a subdirectory of this) underneath the `WEB-INF` directory of your web application.

### Using the Tag File

Tag files are used from within a JSP page as a custom tag in the same way that you've seen the custom tags in the JSTL used. Before using tag files on the page, you have to indicate that the tag file is a tag and import the tag library containing that tag.

For this example, let's say that the tag file that we just defined is saved in our web application as `WEB-INF\tags\copyright.tag` along with any other tag files that may be defined in that directory. Because the individual tags are being placed within the `tags` directory, it could be said that the `tags` directory represents a collection of tags, or a tag library. For this reason, and to use the tags, you can import the tag library that corresponds to this directory by using a `taglib` directive. Listing 6-2 shows a JSP page that uses the tag file in Listing 6-1.

**Listing 6-2.** *tagfile.jsp*

```
<%@ taglib prefix="tags" tagdir="/WEB-INF/tags" %>
<tags:copyright/>
```

Behind the scenes, the container looks for all files that have a .tag extension in the directory specified by the tagdir attribute and makes them available to the page as custom tags with the specified prefix. The mechanics behind how each tag file is made available as a custom tag is up to the container, but the convention is that the name of the file is used as the name of the tag. For example, the copyright.tag file will become known as a custom tag called copyright. The process of importing the tag library by using the taglib directive makes the tag files within that directory available to use on the page, meaning that the <copyright> tag can be used just like standard actions or JSTL tags.

As this example shows, the <copyright> tag is used in the same way as any other tag—by specifying the prefix and the name of the tag. Compared to the original included JSP file, the actual usage of this tag isn't all that different. What is important here is that we now have a standard way to reuse this content. In addition, as you'll see in Chapter 8, using tag files provides a standard way to deploy and distribute the tag file to other project members, project teams, and organizations.

This, of course, is just a simple example to introduce the concept of tag files. To really appreciate the power and flexibility that they can provide page authors, let's look at a more complicated example that uses templating—again, it's something that often crops up in real-world projects.

## Customizing Templates by Using Attributes

Many e-commerce websites have blocks on their home pages that stand out and inform potential customers of new products that have recently become available, or of special offers that are currently running (see Figure 6-1).

**Figure 6-1.** *Tag files can be used to create custom user interfaces for your web application. This page shows text blocks created by using tag files.*

As Figure 6-1 illustrates, often there will be more than one of these blocks, each of which may have the same look and feel with only the content changing between them. One way to implement this is to write the HTML code for the first block and simply copy it, modifying the content as necessary. For static websites this is very common. However, when building such a page by using JSP, there are several other options available, all of which increase the reusability of common code, and therefore the readability, quality, and maintainability.

## Templating with Included JSP Files

One option is to take the common code (in this case HTML code) and place it in its own JSP file. Because we want to parameterize each usage of the template, this rules out using the static include directive that you saw in the previous example. Instead, you have to use the <jsp:include> tag so that you can dynamically include this JSP file at runtime, substituting the content as appropriate.

## Defining a Template

Listing 6-3 shows how you could write a JSP page to represent the template to be dynamically included. The tag file in Listing 6-3 is used to create the blocks in the web page in Figure 6-1.

**Listing 6-3.** *box.jsp*

```
<table width="320" bordercolor="${param.color}" border="1" cellpadding="4"
      cellspacing="0">
  <tr bgcolor="${param.color}" color="#ffffff">
    <td class="boxHeader" nowrap>
      ${param.title}
    </td>
  </tr>
  <tr>
    <td valign="top" class="boxText">
      ${param.body}
    </td>
  </tr>
</table>
```

This example contains three factors that we would like page authors to customize: the title of the box, the content displayed within the box, and the color of the box. We have enabled these to be specified at runtime by using parameters, the values of which are simply inserted into the appropriate place in the template by using JSP EL expressions.

---

**■Note**  You may notice that Listing 6-3 (and other listings in this chapter and the book) has elements that include an attribute named class (for example, <td class="boxHeader" nowrap>). The class attribute references elements from a cascading style sheet. Because these tag files are meant to be included in another JSP page, the stylesheet reference exists in the enclosing JSP (for example, the index.jsp shown in Figure 6-1). The stylesheet is not listed in this chapter but is available with the code download for the book, at the Source Code area of the Apress website (http://www.apress.com/book/download.html).

---

### Using a Template

With the JSP page in Listing 6-3 saved as part of a web application, it can be used with the `<jsp:include>` tag as follows:

```
<jsp:include page="box.jsp">
  <jsp:param name="color" value="#314289"/>
  <jsp:param name="title" value="Professional JSP 2.1"/>
  <jsp:param name="body" value=" Professional JSP 2.1 is now out. It covers all
    of the new features of the JSP 2.1 specification, backed up by real-world
    examples that you can take and adapt to your own projects.
    <br><br>
    [
      <a href=\"projsp21.html\">More information...</a>
    ]"/>
</jsp:include>
```

Note that the value of the `page` attribute is the appropriate absolute or relative path to the included file. In the preceding snippet, the page that included `box.jsp` is located in the same directory as `box.jsp`. If `box.jsp` is not located in the same directory as the JSP page that includes it, you would need to change the path so that `box.jsp` could be located.

As this sample shows, templating is a great way to separate content and the presentation of that content. However, from a page author's perspective, using a fairly low-level construct can look a little raw. Another point to note is that as you're passing the customized content as parameters to the included JSP, you have to ensure that you properly escape any special characters such as double quotes. Although this has worked in the past and will continue to work in the future, there is now a better way to achieve the same outcome. That better way is a feature called tag files.

## Templating with Tag Files

As you've seen, tag files are small snippets of content that have been abstracted out of the main page and wrapped up for reuse. In addition, tag files can be customized by attributes at runtime. We will first look at how to create tag files, and then later in the chapter we will look at various ways to use attributes.

### Defining a Customizable Template

Using Listing 6-3 as a starting point, Listing 6-4 shows how to implement a tag file to represent the same template.

**Listing 6-4.** *box.tag*

```
<%@ attribute name="color" required="true" rtexprvalue="false" %>
<%@ attribute name="title" required="true" rtexprvalue="false" %>
<table width="320" bordercolor="${color}" border="1" cellpadding="4"
      cellspacing="0">
  <tr bgcolor="${color}" color="#ffffff">
```

```
    <td class="boxHeader" nowrap>
      ${title}
    </td>
  </tr>
  <tr>
    <td valign="top" class="boxText">
      <jsp:doBody/>
    </td>
  </tr>
</table>
```

Although the actual content and intent of the tag file is the same as that of box.jsp, there are three subtle differences.

The first is the way that attributes are defined. Rather than obtaining values through the normal request implicit object, the attributes for a tag file are declared at the top of the file by using the attribute directive, a directive that is valid only in tag files. Using this directive in a tag file indicates to the JSP container that the custom tag used to access the tag file can accept an attribute with the specified name:

```
<%@ attribute name="color" required="true" rtexprvalue="false" %>
<%@ attribute name="title" required="true" rtexprvalue="false" %>
```

There are some other directives that are valid only within tag files. Like the JSP page directive, these directives allow aspects of the tag file to be configured. For more information about these directives, see Chapter 1.

In this example, we've declared two required attributes—one for the color of the box, and one for the title. Because we want the user to specify the values of the attributes when writing the page, we prevent the use of request-time expressions by setting the value of rtexprvalue to false. This means that the values for the color and title attributes can be only static strings, such as #000000 and My title, respectively, rather than JSP expressions.

The second difference is in the way that the attributes are accessed within the tag file. To access an attribute in a tag file, all that is needed is a simple EL expression. For example, to access the value of the color attribute, we use the expression ${color}, with the result being that the value of the color attribute is substituted at runtime. Notice that we don't need to look up the value as a parameter with the ${param.color} syntax as we did in Listing 6-3:

```
<tr bgcolor="${color}" color="#ffffff">
```

The final difference is that you no longer have to declare an attribute for actual content that is to be displayed in the box. Instead, you'll use the body content of the custom tag to single out this content, which is specified between the start and end tags. To access the content, you use the new <jsp:doBody> tag that is again only valid in tag files:

```
<td valign="top" class="boxText">
  <jsp:doBody/>
</td>
```

All that the <jsp:doBody> tag does is ask the JSP container to invoke (or evaluate) the body content that was passed to the tag and in this case write it out to the page. An additional benefit of passing the text as the body of the tag is that you can write the body content as is, without having to escape characters  as we did in the code snippet in the "Using a Template" section earlier.

## Using a Customizable Template

With the template defined, you can now use the tag file in the same way that you saw previously. That is, you import the tag library corresponding to the directory in which you saved the tag file. For this example, enter and save Listing 6-4 as box.tag in the WEB-INF\tags directory. You then import the tag library that corresponds to this directory by using the following taglib directive:

```
<%@ taglib prefix="tags" tagdir="/WEB-INF/tags" %>
```

As previously discussed, the container looks for all files that have a .tag extension in the specified tagdir directory and makes them available to the page as custom tags with the specified prefix. Once imported through the taglib directive, the tag can be used as follows:

```
<tags:box>
  <jsp:attribute name="color">#314289</jsp:attribute>
  <jsp:attribute name="title">Professional JSP 2.1</jsp:attribute>
  <jsp:body>
    Professional JSP 2.1 is now out. It covers all of the new features of the JSP
    2.1 specification, backed up by real-world examples that you can take and
    adapt to your own projects.
    <br><br>
    [
      <a href="projsp21.html">More information...</a>
    ]
  </jsp:body>
</tags:box>
```

As this example shows, the <box> tag is used in the same way as any other tag—by specifying the prefix and the name of the tag. In a similar way to how the parameters were passed to the included JSP page, the attributes for this tag are passed using the <jsp:attribute> tags, nested within the start and end <box> tags. As for the content that is being displayed within the box, it's passed as a section of JSP code and wrapped inside the <jsp:body> tags, which are again nested between the start and end <box> tags. At runtime, these attributes and the body content are passed to the tag and substituted into the template, as you would expect.

Compared to the original included JSP fragment (Listing 6-3), the actual usage of this tag isn't all that different. After all, you have the same structure, with attributes being passed in a rather verbose way. You could certainly use include directives or actions to create the same view, but using tag files provides a much better way to create dynamic presentations.

A minor example of the difference between using an <include> action and a tag file is that tag files can use attributes to pass data to the tag code:

```
<tags:box color="#314289" title="Professional JSP 2.1">
  Professional JSP 2.1 is now out. It covers all of the new features of the JSP
  2.1 specification, backed up by real-world examples that you can take and adapt
  to your own projects.
```

```
  <br><br>
  [
    <a href="projsp21.html">More information...</a>
  ]
</tags:box>
```

In this example, the attributes are passed through as true attributes of the XML tag rather than as nested elements. This usage is cleaner and more concise, which makes it easier to understand what is happening on the page. Also, because the attributes are being passed in this way, the content to be displayed no longer needs to be wrapped inside a `<jsp:body>` tag; the content is now truly the body of the tag.

Both methods of passing attributes are permitted by the JSP specification, although some syntax rules exist. If the attributes are passed by using the `<jsp:attribute>` tag, any body content must be wrapped inside a `<jsp:body>` tag. The reason behind this is that with the extra `<jsp:attribute>` tags, the JSP container can't guess what you want the body content of the tag to be, and therefore you have to explicitly demarcate it. If, on the other hand, you specify all attributes as attributes of the XML tag, the body content of the tag is implicitly taken to be anything that falls between the start and end tags.

# Attributes

As earlier examples of the JSTL tags have demonstrated, it's possible to customize the use of the custom tag by using attributes. Without this ability, you would have to build a separate JSP file, or a separate tag for every different piece of content that you wanted to put in the template.

Prior to the JSP 2.0 specification, there was only a single way to specify attributes: inside the opening tag as a normal tag attribute. In JSP 2.1, however, you can specify attributes by using nested tags.

## Specifying Attributes Within the Tag

This is the traditional way of specifying attributes for custom tags, and as you've seen in the JSTL examples, it means that those attributes are written in the same way that attributes for other XML tags are written, for example:

```
<tags:box title="My Title"/>
```

Here, an attribute called `title` has been provided for the tag as a name and value pair and is written inside the tag itself. As with XML attributes in general, the value of an attribute must be wrapped inside quotation characters. This example uses double quotes, but there's nothing stopping you from using single quotes instead. This flexibility is particularly useful if the value of the attribute contains characters that need to be escaped, such as double quote characters.

## Specifying Attributes as Nested Tags

The other mechanism for specifying attributes is the `<jsp:attribute>` tag. Using the same example, this can now be written in one of the following ways:

```
<tags:box>
  <jsp:attribute name="title" value="My Title"/>
</tags:box>
```

or

```
<tags:box>
  <jsp:attribute name="title">My Title</jsp:attribute>
</tags:box>
```

One of the biggest problems with passing attributes to XML tags is that often attributes with large values make the tag awkward to read. Therefore, the new syntax can be used instead. Both syntaxes are equivalent, and although the traditional syntax is certainly the most concise, the newer syntax improves the readability with particularly long attribute values.

### Required or Optional

The core elements of any attribute are its name and its value. However, when using custom tags, various characteristics can be configured. The first is to define whether an attribute is required or optional. In other words, this allows you to state whether an attribute and its value must be specified for any given custom tag. This is useful in many situations because it forces you to specify values for attributes.

Looking at the template example, you may decide that all boxes should have a title. This isn't something that you can achieve easily with dynamically included JSP files, but with custom tags it's trivial. When an attribute is marked as required and is omitted, a fatal translation error will occur, indicating that the attribute hasn't been specified. By using custom tags, you can force users to specify a title in this example.

### Static or Dynamic (Request-Time Expressions)

Another characteristic that is commonly defined for attributes is whether their values can be the result of a request-time expression. In the JSTL examples, the value of many of the attributes was simply a static string passed to the tag. For example, looking at the JSTL <forEach> tag that provides iteration over a collection, you can see that the name of the variable with which you'll access each item in the collection (myVar) is supplied to the tag as a static string through the var attribute:

```
<c:forEach var="myVar" items="${myItems}">
  <c:out value="${myVar.name}"/>
</c:forEach>
```

This is known as a static attribute because its value is statically defined in the JSP page. A dynamic attribute, or a request-time expression as it's formally known, is written using one of the following methods:

- The JSP EL, such as ${myItems}

- Java code, such as <%= pageContext.findAttribute("myItems") %>

In either case, if an attribute is marked as supporting request-time expressions, it means that expressions can be used to specify the value of the attribute. In the previous JSTL example, the actual collection over which the tag should iterate is being passed to the tag at request-time (runtime) by using an EL expression.

Now let's look at how you can build a tag file equivalent to the dynamically included JSP file you saw earlier.

## Why Use Tag Files?

As these examples have demonstrated, it's possible to wrap up content and reuse it elsewhere. Because this has always been possible with included JSP files, you might be asking why tag files have been introduced into the JSP specification and what their benefits are.

First of all, there are the technical aspects. Tag files provide a much cleaner way to build and subsequently use templates on JSP pages. However, there are some other, softer, benefits that arise from using tag files over JSP include directives. Essentially, using custom tags gives you the ability to provide a natural interface to the content and functionality that you would like people to use and reuse. Having a custom tag called box, with the appropriate attributes, is much more understandable than having a generic JSP include. Also, naming custom tags appropriately provides page authors and developers maintaining the page with a much better idea of a tag's intent, which in turn makes it easier to use, read, understand, and maintain.

Using tag files to build templates is a great way to separate the content from the presentation of that content, and this makes it a natural progression from simply mixing the two together in JSP pages. However, there will be times when you want to encapsulate more than just pure presentation into a custom tag. Perhaps you have some Java code that you would like to wrap up and make reusable. Generally, any code that can appear in a JSP page can appear in a tag file. However, the best practices about keeping Java code out of JSP pages are also applicable to tag files. To wrap up logic that contains more code than content, simple tags are the answer.

# Using Simple Tags

Previous versions of the JSP specification have supported the notion of building custom tags with Java code for some time. The JSP 2.1 specification simplifies this process greatly through the use of **simple tags**. When using tag files, the content and logic that you would like to reuse is defined using normal JSP syntax, thereby providing an easy way to wrap up reusable functionality and make the process of building tags available to those people who may not necessarily know how to program in Java. However, with simple tags, the reusable functionality is encapsulated within a Java class that implements a specific interface. As we said earlier, this class is called the tag handler.

The characteristics of the tag, such as its name and a list of any attributes that it takes, are then defined in a tag library descriptor (TLD) file. When the tag is finally used on the page, an instance of the tag handler class is created and its methods are called to execute the reusable functionality.

Ultimately, this method of writing tags is more complex than building tag files, but it does provide a much greater level of flexibility and control over the functionality that a tag file can provide. Before you look at how to build a simple tag, take a look at the interface that a simple tag handler must implement.

## The SimpleTag Interface

The SimpleTag interface defines the basic contract between simple tags and the JSP page on which they are used. The interface itself serves two purposes:

- It provides the simple tag with information about its execution environment.

- It provides a method for executing the functionality encapsulated by the simple tag handler.

Listing 6-5 shows the SimpleTag interface.

**Listing 6-5.** *SimpleTag.java*

```
package javax.servlet.jsp.tagext;
public interface SimpleTag extends JspTag {
  public void doTag() throws JspException, IOException;
  public JspTag getParent();
  public void setJspBody(JspFragment jspBody);
  public void setJspContext(JspContext jspContext);
  public void setParent(JspTag parent);
}
```

## The Basic Tag Life Cycle

Although the SimpleTag interface supplies the contract that a simple tag must provide, interfaces in Java cannot specify the order in which operations are called. This information is instead specified within the JSP specification. Figure 6-2 shows the order in which the tag methods are called when a tag is evaluated.

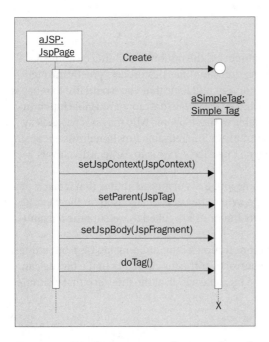

**Figure 6-2.** *This UML sequence diagram shows how a page implementation class calls the methods of a tag handler class.*

With classic tags, one of the most complex pieces of the tag life cycle is how tag handler instances can be pooled by the container and reused. Although this tends to increase performance and reduce the number of object instantiations that occur, the semantics for reusing tag handlers often causes confusion and hence side effects from misunderstanding the tag life cycle. Therefore, simple tags are used once and only once before the tag handler reference is discarded. In other words, each simple tag invocation causes the creation of a new tag handler instance, therefore greatly simplifying the programming model.

### Creating a Tag Handler Instance

When a custom tag is used on a JSP page, the first thing that the JSP container must do is create a new instance of the tag handler class. Later you'll see just how the JSP container locates the correct tag handler class for any given custom tag, but for now you should assume that this has been found and an instance is created.

### Setting the Context

Next, the tag handler instance is made aware of the environment in which it's running through the setJspContext() method. This just involves passing a reference to the current JspContext into the tag handler.

One of the useful classes available to JSP developers is PageContext from the javax. servlet.jsp package. This is available from a JSP page as an implicit object called pageContext. It's effectively provided as a convenient way to access various objects that are used during JSP development. For example, the PageContext class provides an easy way to access attributes that are bound to any of the available scopes (request, page, session, and application). It can also get a reference to the current output JspWriter and programmatically include and forward requests. Although these features are available through the standard JSP actions or the JSP EL, the power behind the PageContext class is that it can be used within custom tags.

One of the changes to the JSP API that occurred with JSP 2.0 is that some of the functionality previously provided by the PageContext class has been abstracted away into a new class called JspContext, which PageContext now extends. This new base class provides all the functionality that is not directly related to the Java Servlet API, including the methods that allow you to retrieve and set scoped attributes and obtain a reference to the current JspWriter. From a tag developer perspective, having access to this sort of information and the execution environment means that you can write tags utilizing values from the request, page, session, or application and write output from the tags directly back to the JSP page. You'll see some examples of how to use the JspContext and PageContext classes throughout this and the following chapters.

### Setting the Parent

During our discussion of body content types, you saw that it's possible for the body content of custom tags to contain regular JSP syntax between the start and end tags. This body content can include custom tags, which means that custom tags can be nested. The following block of code shows an example of nesting custom tags with JSTL. Here, the outer <forEach> tag iterates over each item in the specified collection, while the inner <out> tag outputs the name of each item:

```
<c:forEach var="myVar" items="${myItems}">
  <c:out value="${myVar.name}"/>
</c:forEach>
```

As you'll see in Chapter 8, it's possible for custom tag handlers to cooperate and communicate with one another. Therefore, part of the information about a tag's execution environment includes a reference to the closest enclosing tag handler, which is set by calling the setParent() method. That reference is of type JspTag (the superinterface for all tag handlers), but can be null if the tag isn't nested within another tag.

### Setting the Body Content

After the context has been set, an object representing the body content of the tag is passed to it. At runtime, the JSP container wraps up the body content between the start and end tags, creates a JspFragment object to represent it, and passes this JspFragment instance to the tag by calling the setJspBody() method. If there is no body content between the start and end tags, a null reference is passed to this method instead.

As you'll see later in this chapter, having a reference to the body content opens up a whole new way that custom tags can be implemented.

### Executing the Functionality

Finally, with the context and body content set, the only thing left to do is execute the functionality that the tag handler embodies. This is achieved by calling the doTag() method, and it's this method that contains the Java code responsible for the actions performed by the tag.

## The SimpleTagSupport Class

Although implementing the SimpleTag interface is not a complex task, for convenience, the JSP specification provides the javax.servlet.jsp.tagext.SimpleTagSupport class, which provides default implementations for all the methods previously described. This class can be used as a starting point for building your own simple tags if you extend it and override the doTag() method. This, as you'll see throughout this chapter, is the most common way to build simple tags.

Now that you understand the mechanics behind simple tags, you are now in a position to write one.

## A Simple Example

As an example of the type of functionality that might be encapsulated within a custom tag, let's display the current date and time on the page. You could use Java code written inside a scriptlet or an EL function. Instead, you'll use a custom tag because it provides flexibility when you later need to add functionality.

## Writing the Tag Handler

Now that you've decided that you're going to build a custom tag, the first step is to write the tag handler, which is the Java class that will embody the functionality that the custom tag will provide. Listing 6-6 shows the tag handler DateTimeTag.java, which extends the SimpleTagSupport class. Because we want to focus on the syntax of creating simple tag handlers, and not the semantics or use of tag handlers, we've deliberately chosen a simplistic example for our first tag handler.

**Listing 6-6.** *DateTimeTag.java*

```
package com.apress.projsp;
import java.io.IOException;
import java.text.DateFormat;
import java.util.Date;
import javax.servlet.jsp.JspException;
import javax.servlet.jsp.tagext.SimpleTagSupport;
public class DateTimeTag extends SimpleTagSupport {
  public void doTag() throws JspException, IOException {
    DateFormat df = DateFormat.getDateTimeInstance(
        DateFormat.MEDIUM, DateFormat.MEDIUM);
    // now write out the formatted date to the page
    getJspContext().getOut().write(df.format(new Date()));
  }
}
```

As you can see, the actual code for the tag handler is pretty straightforward. The SimpleTag interface provides the doTag() method, and as defined by the simple tag life cycle, this method is called to execute the functionality encapsulated within the tag. In this example, a DateFormat object is created and used to format the current date. This string is then output back to the page by using the JspContext object. The getOut() method on the JspContext object returns a reference to the JspWriter instance that is being used to render the JSP page. This is one of the reasons why a tag needs to know about the environment in which it's running. If it didn't, the tag would never be able to output content directly back to the page.

At this point, you may be saying to yourself, "Why would I want to write a 14-line Java class file (and a 21-line descriptor in the upcoming Listing 6-7) to do the same work that can be accomplished in a 2-line JSP scriptlet?" There are several reasons, which we've touched on in other parts of the book, and which we'll repeat here.

First, page developers are often not Java developers. By abstracting Java code out of the page, page developers can focus on what they do best. You may find it trivial to write a 2-line scriptlet that uses DateFormat and Date objects, but the page developer may not find it so trivial.

Second, by encapsulating this behavior in a tag, you can guarantee that every use of the tag will produce the same presentation, something you can't guarantee with cut-and-paste reuse of scriptlets.

Third, you increase the maintainability of your JSPs. If a change or fix is made, you have to edit only the tag handler class, and every page automatically is changed. With scriptlets, someone would need to locate and fix every scriptlet.

Finally, this simplistic example hides the true power of tag handlers. Because tag handlers are Java classes, they can use all the features of Java to provide extremely rich and powerful behavior. For example, the tag handler could connect to a database and retrieve some data, then use that data to access a web service, and then use the results of the web service to perform some other action. This same behavior implemented as scriptlets would result in a JSP page that had scriptlet code mixed with template text in a source file that would be hard to read and hard to maintain.

## Compiling the Tag Handler

Compiling tag handlers is a straightforward task and requires that the JSP API JAR file is present in your CLASSPATH. The JSP library you need is `jsp-api.jar`, which contains classes that make up the core JSP and tag APIs, including classes and interfaces such as `SimpleTag`, `SimpleTagSupport`, and `JspContext`. In Tomcat 5, this JAR file can be found in the `TOMCAT_HOME\common\lib` directory.

---

**■Tip**  If you are using a different container, check your container documentation to find the JAR file that contains the JSP API classes.

---

## Writing the Tag Library Descriptor File

With the tag handler written and compiled, the next step is to write the TLD file, which is an XML file that describes the tag, how it will be used on the page, the type of body content, whether the tag accepts any attributes, and so on. Listing 6-7 shows the TLD file for this example.

**Listing 6-7.** *ch06.tld*

```
<?xml version="1.0" encoding="UTF-8" ?>
<taglib xmlns="http://java.sun.com/xml/ns/javaee"
  xmlns:xsi="http://www.w3.org/2001/XMLSchema-instance"
  xsi:schemaLocation="http://java.sun.com/xml/ns/javaee/web-jsptaglibrary_2_1.xsd"
  version="2.1">
  <description>
    Tag library for Professional JSP 2.1, Chapter 6.
  </description>
  <jsp-version>2.1</jsp-version>
  <tlib-version>1.0</tlib-version>
  <short-name>ch06</short-name>
  <uri>http://www.apress.com/projsp/ch06</uri>
  <tag>
    <name>datetime</name>
    <tag-class>com.apress.projsp.DateTimeTag</tag-class>
    <body-content>empty</body-content>
```

```
    <description>
      Outputs the current date and time to the page.
    </description>
  </tag>
</taglib>
```

At first glance this file looks fairly complicated, but in fact only a small portion of it is applicable to the custom tag that you're building. The first thing you notice is the standard XML header that indicates which version of XML you're using:

```
<?xml version="1.0" encoding="UTF-8" ?>
```

Next is the root element, along with the details of the XML schema to which this document must conform:

```
<taglib xmlns="http://java.sun.com/xml/ns/javaee"
  xmlns:xsi="http://www.w3.org/2001/XMLSchema-instance"
  xsi:schemaLocation="http://java.sun.com/xml/ns/javaee/web-jsptaglibrary_2_1.xsd"
  version="2.1">
  ... body of XML document ...
</taglib>
```

---

■**Note**  For backward compatibility, JSP containers must still support the DTD-based (Document Type Definition) TLDs that were a part of the earlier JSP 1.1 and JSP 1.2 specifications. This means that TLDs can still be defined using these older mechanisms. This is particularly useful for tag library developers who are targeting older versions of the specification, or for those developers who want to reach the widest audience.

---

The next set of elements within the TLD file, nested between the start and end `<taglib>` elements, describes the tag library. Rather than bundle custom tags individually, all tags must be part of a tag library. Implementing this requires grouping the tags and defining them within the same TLD file. Using those tags requires importing the tag library with the `taglib` directive.

For this example, you'll bundle all the tags that you've built in this chapter into their own tag library, the definition of which is as follows:

```
  <description>
    Tag library for Professional JSP 2.1, Chapter 6.
  </description>
  <jsp-version>2.1</jsp-version>
  <tlib-version>1.0</tlib-version>
  <short-name>ch06</short-name>
  <uri>http://www.apress.com/projsp/ch06</uri>
```

First is a short textual description of the tag library, followed by the `jsp-version` and `tlib-version` elements, which allow you to define the required JSP and tag library versions, respectively.

Next is a short name for the tag library, used for identification purposes in JSP authoring or web-application management tools. For example, it could be used in a menu that lists the tag libraries available to the user.

Finally, you have the `uri` element. This causes the most confusion when writing tag libraries. Although the value of this element should be a valid URI, this simply represents a unique identifier for the tag library. The example uses the absolute URI `http://www.apress.com/projsp/ch06`, even though there's nothing to stop a relative URI such as `/ch06` or even `/myTaglibs/chapter06` from being used instead. What is important here is that the URI is unique among the tag libraries that you'll be using. The URI doesn't have to exist in the real world; if you go to `http://www.apress.com/projsp/ch06` you'll find nothing there—it's simply a unique, symbolic identifier.

The final part of the TLD file has the tag description itself:

```
<tag>
  <name>datetime</name>
  <tag-class>com.apress.projsp.DateTimeTag</tag-class>
  <body-content>empty</body-content>
  <description>
    Outputs the current date and time to the page.
  </description>
</tag>
```

A definition of a custom tag falls between the start and end `<tag>` tags and in this example has four characteristics that are being defined. First is the name of the tag. This doesn't have to reflect the actual class name of the tag handler, but rather the name that you would like to use for the tag on the page. Following this is the fully qualified class name of the tag handler.

---

■**Caution**  One of the common pitfalls encountered when building custom tags is that the tag handler classes are often placed in the default package—that is, the `package` statement is omitted from the source code. Because of the way that JSP pages are translated into Java servlets, attempting to use unpackaged tag handler classes almost always results in exceptions, such as `ClassNotFoundException`, when the tag is used on the page. To ensure that this doesn't happen, you should always place your tag handler classes within a package.

---

Next, you have a definition of the type of body content for the tag. Earlier in this chapter, you looked at the various types of body content that a custom tag can have, and it's here that this is defined for a custom tag. For the `<datetime>` tag, the body content is stated to be `empty`, meaning that no content is required or permitted between the start and end tags. Because the `<datetime>` tag simply outputs the current date and time to the page, it's not necessary for this tag to have any body content. The `<body-content>` element was optional prior to JSP 2.0. It is now required when writing TLD files.

Finally, there's a short description about the tag itself. Again, this is optional but it's useful for anybody reading the TLD file, whether it's somebody on your own team using the tag on your project, or somebody on the other side of the world who is reusing your tag library on their own project.

With the tag handler class and TLD file written, the next step is to deploy the tag. There are a couple of ways that tag libraries can be deployed and used—one in which the tag library is unpackaged and one in which it's packaged and ready to be reused easily. The former method is typically how many developers deploy their tag libraries in a development environment, so let's take a look at that one and leave the other until Chapter 8, where you'll examine deployment in more depth.

### Deploying the Tag Library

The first step is to ensure that the class files for the tag handlers in the tag library have been compiled and are available within the class path of your web application. In other words, you should ensure that your class files reside in either the `WEB-INF\classes` directory of your web application, or within a JAR file that has been copied into the `WEB-INF\lib` directory of your web application. If your tag handlers reference any other classes that you or a third party has written, don't forget that these must also be made available in one of these two ways.

With the classes residing within the web-application directory structure, the next step is to place the TLD file within the web-application directory structure too. By convention, the JSP specification suggests that all TLD files be placed within the `WEB-INF\tlds` directory. Although this isn't mandatory, placing all TLD files here provides a central place for people to find them at a later date. For this example, we will place the TLD named `ch06.tld` in the `WEB-INF\tlds` directory. With these steps complete, you can now use the tag library.

As you saw with the JSTL examples in Chapter 4 and the tag file example in this chapter, using a tag library requires that the tag library be imported via the `taglib` directive. This allows you to specify the prefix that references the tags within that tag library. With the TLD file for our example located at `WEB-INF\tlds\ch06.tld`, you can directly import this on a JSP page by using the following directive:

```
<%@ taglib uri="/WEB-INF/tlds/ch06.tld" prefix="ch06" %>
```

Here, you're using the `uri` attribute of the `taglib` directive to explicitly specify the location of the TLD that represents the tag library that you would like to use. The `prefix` attribute allows you to specify the prefix of the tags in the tag library. Figure 6-3 shows the output you might see when the `<datetime>` tag is used on a page as follows:

```
The current date and time is <ch06:datetime/>
```

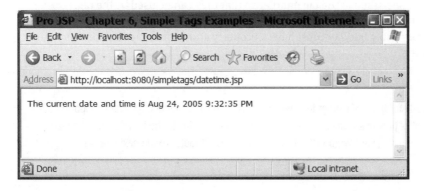

**Figure 6-3.** *Simple tags can provide powerful functionality for customizing JSP pages.*

Of the many ways to deploy and use custom tags, this method is one of the most common. This is primarily because it allows you to save the TLD file straight into the web-application directory structure (that is, underneath the WEB-INF directory) and to explicitly specify the tag library that you would like to import. This, therefore, makes it easy to quickly create and deploy a tag library in a development environment where the build and deploy and test cycles generally tend to be shorter than usual.

However, although it works, this method doesn't really take into account the ability that tag libraries have to be reusable. After all, tag libraries can be reused over the pages in a single project, over the pages of multiple projects, and within multiple organizations. Adopting this method for all of those projects means copying the tag handler classes and the TLD files into every web application. Therefore, the JSP specification provides an alternative mechanism for packaging and then using and reusing tag libraries (see Chapter 8).

As this example illustrates, simple tags enable you to wrap up reusable functionality that is typically written using Java code. This is different from the template examples that you saw earlier in the chapter; whereas they were about parameterizing and reusing content, these are about reusing functionality. Of course, reusing the same functionality again and again is useful only up to a certain point. Fortunately, functionality—like content—can be parameterized and customized through the use of attributes.

# Customizing Functionality with Attributes

Now that you understand the basics behind developing simple tags such as the tag handler class and the TLD file, you are now in a position to look at some of the more advanced features. Like tag files, simple tags can also be customized by using attributes. The difference is in how the attributes are implemented. With simple tags, attributes are implemented on the tag handler class.

As you saw in the tag file examples, attributes are defined within the tag file by using the attribute directive, and it's here where you can specify the name and whether the attribute is required. When using simple tags, this information is defined within the TLD file.

## The Tag Life Cycle with Attributes

Introducing attributes into a custom tag does change the tag life cycle slightly because before the functionality of the tag can be executed (the doTag() method in the case of simple tags), the attributes must be passed to the tag handler so that they can be used by the tag.

The way that the JSP specification allows this is through properties and **setter methods** of the tag handler class. A tag handler must have a property and a setter method for every attribute that it supports.

---

■**Note** The necessity for the tag handler to have a property and setter method for every supported attribute is a requirement of previous versions of the JSP specification. But with the introduction of dynamic attributes, this is not strictly true anymore. You'll look at dynamic attributes in the next chapter.

---

These setter methods must conform to the standard JavaBeans naming convention, meaning that to support an attribute called name of type String, the tag handler must declare a setter method with the following signature:

```
public void setName(String s)
```

In this example, at request time, the value of the name attribute will be passed to the setName() method. With this in mind, you can now see how supporting attributes alters the tag life cycle. As an example, consider the following custom tag usage:

```
<prefix:myTag attribute1="abc" attributeN="def"/>
```

Here, the tag has two attributes that are being specified. By looking at the tag life cycle in Figure 6-4, you can see what happens behind the scenes.

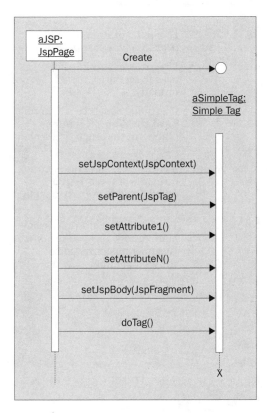

**Figure 6-4.** *The life cycle of a simple tag with parameters*

As this diagram shows, the setter methods for the attributes are called before the doTag() method is executed, and in the same order that the attributes appear within the usage of the tag, from left to right. When it comes to implementing attributes in tag handler classes, attribute setter methods typically store a copy of the attribute away in an instance variable, ready for the doTag() method to use.

## Attribute Types

The examples you've seen so far have used static strings to represent the values of attributes. However, these values can be Boolean values, numbers, and characters through an automatic conversion mechanism provided by the JSP container. In fact, even objects can be the values of tag attributes. The JSP implementation will automatically convert the string attribute in the page to the required type based on the signature of the corresponding setter method. Table 6-2 shows the conversions that are possible. Note that for each method signature shown in Table 6-2, the substring PropertyName in setPropertyName() would be replaced by the actual property name, for example setPath or setSuffix for properties named path and suffix.

**Table 6-2.** *Automatic Conversions of String Attributes to Built-In Java Types*

| Java Type | Method Signature | Notes |
|-----------|------------------|-------|
| String | public void setPropertyName(String s) | |
| char | public void setPropertyName(char s) | First letter of string attribute is used to set the char property. |
| Character | public void setPropertyName(Character c) | First letter of string attribute is used to set the Character property. |
| boolean | public void setPropertyName(boolean b) | If attribute equals true (ignoring case), the property is true; otherwise, the property is set to false. |
| Boolean | public void setPropertyName(Boolean b) | If attribute equals true (ignoring case), the property is true; otherwise, the property is set to false. |
| byte | public void setPropertyName(byte b) | The conversion of strings to any numeric type follows the normal Java rules for conversion of strings to numbers. |
| Byte | public void setPropertyName(Byte b) | |
| short | public void setPropertyName(short s) | |
| Short | public void setPropertyName(Short s) | |
| int | public void setPropertyName(int i) | |
| Integer | public void setPropertyName(Integer i) | |
| long | public void setPropertyName(long l) | |
| Long | public void setPropertyName(Long l) | |
| float | public void setPropertyName(float f) | |
| Float | public void setPropertyName(Float f) | |
| double | public void setPropertyName(double d) | |
| Double | public void setPropertyName(Double d) | |

## Object Attributes

We've said that the JSP container can automatically convert the string values supplied to attributes into a specific type such as a primitive int. However, because the JSP page is written (behind the scenes) as a Java class, and the tag handlers are also Java classes, there is nothing to stop objects from being passed as the values of attributes.

To achieve this, a reference to an object needs to be specified as the value of the attribute, and this is typically done by using a request-time expression or an EL expression as follows:

```
<prefix:myTag x="${myObject}"/>
<prefix:myTag x="<%= myObject %>"/>
```

Assuming that myObject is of type MyObjectType, then the corresponding setter method would be as follows:

```
public void setPropertyName(MyObjectType o)
```

When called, the JSP implementation class would set the property of the tag handler to the value of the object reference used in the JSP page. In the tag handler, the setter method for the attribute can be defined to take any arbitrary object type, regardless of whether it's a part of the Java APIs or a user-defined type. You'll see examples of this in the next chapter.

## JspFragment Attributes

One type of object that gets special support in JSP is JspFragment. A JspFragment object is essentially a class that wraps up a particular section (or fragment) of JSP code. At runtime, JspFragment objects can be invoked, meaning that the JSP code that they wrap up is translated and executed as if it were included in a regular JSP page.

If an attribute is defined as taking a JspFragment, this means that scriptless content can be passed as a JSP fragment into the tag handler. The only caveat here is in the way that the value of such an attribute can be specified: it can be passed only by using the body content of the <jsp:attribute> tag:

```
<prefix:myTag>
  <jsp:attribute name="x">Hello ${name}</jsp:attribute>
</prefix:myTag>
```

At runtime, the JSP container wraps up the value of the attribute and passes it as a JspFragment instance to the tag handler. During the execution of that tag, the tag handler can invoke and evaluate the fragment to have the results included whenever necessary.

Now you'll see an example of how to use attributes.

# Displaying Thumbnails with a Tag

Imagine that you've been asked to write a JSP page presenting a list of thumbnail images to the user. There are several ways to do this. First, you could statically code the page, writing the appropriate HTML tags to present a thumbnail of all images in a particular directory. The downside to this approach is that when the images change, your page will also have to change. Therefore, instead of taking this approach you'll perform this dynamically, and rather than write a whole load of Java code into the JSP, you'll build a custom tag that you could reuse elsewhere.

The functionality provided by the custom tag will, given a directory name, look in that directory and generate the appropriate HTML to display the thumbnails. Figure 6-5 shows an example of how the finished page might look.

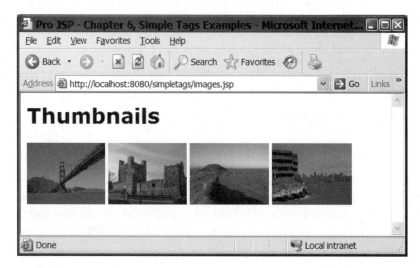

**Figure 6-5.** *In this web page, a simple tag generates HTML based on input parameters.*

For the custom tag that is used to help generate this page, rather than hard-coding the directory in which the tag handler should look for images, you'll pass this as an attribute. In doing so, the ability to customize this tag opens it up for reuse elsewhere. In addition, you'll want to be able to specify the types of files that are displayed and do it by filtering only those files with a specific file extension. For example, you might want to display only .jpg files.

## Building the Thumbnail Tag Handler

From an implementation perspective, the code for the tag is fairly straightforward, as you can once again use the SimpleTagSupport class as a starting point. Listing 6-8 shows the class, ThumbnailTag.java, which has two properties that allow it to create a customized thumbnail web page.

**Listing 6-8.** *ThumbnailTag.java*

```
package com.apress.projsp;
import java.io.IOException;
import java.util.*;
import javax.servlet.jsp.JspException;
import javax.servlet.jsp.PageContext;
import javax.servlet.jsp.tagext.SimpleTagSupport;
public class ThumbnailTag extends SimpleTagSupport {
  private String path;
  private String suffix;
  public void setPath(String s) {
```

```java
    this.path = s;
  }
  public void setSuffix(String s) {
    this.suffix = s;
  }
  public void doTag() throws JspException, IOException {
    // first of all, find the names of the files
    Collection files = findFiles();
    if (files != null && !files.isEmpty()) {
      String filename;
      // now that the names have been found, iterate over each of them
      // and generate the appropriate HTML
      Iterator it = files.iterator();
      while (it.hasNext()) {
        filename = (String)it.next();
        getJspContext().getOut().write("<img src=\".");
        getJspContext().getOut().write(filename);
        getJspContext().getOut().write("\" width=\"128\" height=\"96\"> ");
      }
    }
  }
  private Collection findFiles() {
    PageContext pageContext = (PageContext)getJspContext();
    Collection resources =
      pageContext.getServletContext().getResourcePaths(path);
    List filteredResources = new ArrayList();
    if (resources == null || resources.isEmpty()) {
      return filteredResources;
    }
    Iterator it = resources.iterator();
    String uri;
    String testSuffix;
    if (this.suffix != null) {
      testSuffix = this.suffix;
    } else {
      testSuffix = ".jpg";
    }
    // now filter out those files that don't end in the suffix
    while (it.hasNext()) {
        uri = (String)it.next();
        if (uri.endsWith(testSuffix)) {
            filteredResources.add(uri);
        }
    }
    return filteredResources;
  }
}
```

The two properties that store the values of your two attributes are suffix and path. The class includes the setter methods for those attributes.

Finally, the class has the doTag() method, which contains the functionality that your tag provides. For simplicity, a private helper method has been created to locate the files in a specific directory, while the doTag() method is responsible for outputting the information.

Although there's a fair amount of code, all this tag does is look for all the files within a specified directory, and then filter these to include only those that end with the specified suffix or file extension. With this list, the doTag() method then iterates over each in turn and generates an HTML <img> tag to display the image on the page.

However, to list all the files in a directory, the class needs access to the PageContext object, which is a servlet resource. To access the PageContext object, the class performs a widening conversion on the JspContext object. One of the aims in keeping simple tags simple to use is that they, unlike classic tags, don't rely directly on features provided by the servlet API. A benefit of this is that simple tags can be used within other technologies in the future. The price of this, however, is that you must now explicitly cast the JspContext to PageContext in order to access any of the servlet-specific features such as the current servlet context.

## Describing the Thumbnail Tag

With the tag handler class written, the next step is to write the TLD file describing the tag and its characteristics. For this example, you'll use the same TLD file as before, shown in Listing 6-9. For brevity, the descriptions of the tag library and the <datetime> tag have been omitted.

**Listing 6-9.** *ch06.tld*

```
<?xml version="1.0" encoding="UTF-8" ?>
<taglib xmlns="http://java.sun.com/xml/ns/javaee"
    xmlns:xsi="http://www.w3.org/2001/XMLSchema-instance"
    xsi:schemaLocation="http://java.sun.com/xml/ns/javaee/web-jsptaglibrary_2_1.xsd"
    version="2.1">

  ... the description of the tag library ...
  ... the description of the <datetime> tag ...
  <tag>
    <name>thumbnail</name>
    <tag-class>com.apress.projsp.ThumbnailTag</tag-class>
    <body-content>empty</body-content>
    <description>
      Given a path, this tag generates HTML to display thumbnail images.
    </description>
    <attribute>
      <name>path</name>
      <required>true</required>
      <rtexprvalue>true</rtexprvalue>
    </attribute>
    <attribute>
      <name>suffix</name>
```

```
      <required>false</required>
      <rtexprvalue>false</rtexprvalue>
    </attribute>
  </tag>
</taglib>
```

As before, the content between the `<tag>` elements describes the `<thumbnail>` tag, with the `<name>`, `<tag-class>`, `<body-content>`, and `<description>` elements you've seen before. What's new here is that the TLD file defines the attributes that this tag supports. Attributes are defined within the body of the `<tag>` element, and the characteristics of each attribute are defined between the `<attribute>` tags.

In this example, you have two attributes—one named `path` that is marked as required and one called `suffix` that is optional (not required). To make it easier for page authors to use the tag, you shouldn't force them to specify the `suffix` attribute; this is why it's marked as optional. For this to work properly, you should always ensure that tag handlers work correctly regardless of whether a value is specified for optional attributes. Therefore, the code inside the tag handler checks whether the suffix has been specified and defaults to `.jpg` if it hasn't.

---

**Tip** As in all programming situations where supplying a value is optional, you should always have a sensible default value to fall back on if an optional attribute is not supplied. In doing so, you not only make your tag easier to use, but you make it usable regardless of whether the value has been specified.

---

Finally, the `path` attribute allows request-time expressions, and you'll see how this can be put to good use shortly.

### Using the Thumbnail Tag

After the tag handler has been written, compiled, and deployed, you're ready to start using the tag. Because you're using the same tag library from the previous examples, you can use the same import statement:

```
<%@ taglib uri="/WEB-INF/tlds/ch06.tld" prefix="ch06" %>
```

You can now use the tag in either of the following ways because the `suffix` attribute is optional:

```
<ch06:thumbnail path="/ch06/photos"/>
<ch06:thumbnail path="/ch06/photos" suffix=".jpg"/>
```

In these examples, both usages will look in the ch06\photos directory for any `.jpg` files and generate the HTML that displays them as thumbnails.

Alternatively, you could use request-time expressions written using the EL to specify the path. For example, if you specified the path as a parameter to the JSP page on which the tag is being used (by appending `?path=/ch06/photos` to the URL), you could pass this information to the tag with a short EL expression:

```
<ch06:thumbnail path="${param.path}"/>
```

In this instance, the expression is evaluated automatically by the JSP container and the result is passed in as the value of the attribute.

---

■ **Tip**  Earlier versions of the JSP specification supported only request-time expressions using Java code. For example, the equivalent of ${param.path} would be <%= request.getParameter("path") %>. Although this is still supported, JSP 2.0 and JSP 2.1 promote the use of the EL for request-time expressions. Not only is the EL more concise, but it removes Java code  from the page—something that helps improve the readability of JSP pages.

---

This example shows how easy it is to parameterize the functionality encapsulated within a custom tag. By allowing attributes to be used to specify the location and types of files, you've built a fairly generic custom tag that can be used in many other places. However, in this example you have hard-coded the presentation within the tag handler class. The HTML might be dynamically generated, but the actual presentation of the list of files is locked away and wrapped up inside Java code. From a reusability perspective this is poor because it somewhat restricts how the tag can be used by other people. Also, maintaining the content means modifying the class file, recompiling it, and redeploying the tag library.

To wrap up this chapter on building simple tags, let's take a look at how you can combine templating and customization to build a truly reusable component: a tag that evaluates its own body content.

## Evaluating Body Content

In the previous sections on tags, we defined some templated content within a tag file. Essentially this is just regular JSP code that has been abstracted out of the page so it can easily be reused.

With the <thumbnail> tag, the functionality of finding the list of files was wrapped up alongside the presentation of that list. Although we've made the presentation as simple as possible, we can imagine a scenario where every usage of the tag requires a slightly different HTML to be generated. Perhaps the list of thumbnails should be a bulleted list, or perhaps it should be enclosed within an HTML table. To achieve this goal, ideally you need to break out the content (the files) from the presentation (generating the HTML). This is something that is easy to implement by using JSP fragments, or tag body content.

Essentially, the objective is to leave the content on the page where it belongs and to have the custom tag look up and locate the files. After the tag has this list, in a similar way to the JSTL <forEach> tag, it should then evaluate its body content repeatedly for every file that is found. Consider the following JSP code:

```
<ch06:list path="/photos" suffix=".jpg">
  <img src=".${filename}" width="128" height="96">
</ch06:list>
<ch06:list path="/photos" suffix=".jpg">
  <td align="center">
```

```
    <img src=".${filename}" alt="${filename}" width="128" height="96">
  </td>
</ch06:list>
```

By splitting the content (what is being displayed) from the presentation (how it's being displayed), you're introducing a separation between the list of files and its presentation in HTML. In addition to enabling this tag to be reused more often, this separation promotes easy maintenance and modification of the presentation. In other words, should you need to modify the way that the list of files is presented, you can do this by editing the JSP page rather than the tag handler code.

# Separating Content from Presentation

With the previous example in mind, let's build a tag that is capable of generating a list of any type of file. The tag won't generate a list of HTML <img> tags, but rather it will implement a generic mechanism enabling you to generate whatever HTML you like.

## Building the Directory List Tag

Listing 6-10 shows DirectoryListTag.java, the tag handler for the list tag. As a simple tag, it extends the SimpleTagSupport class.

**Listing 6-10.** *DirectoryListTag.java*

```java
package com.apress.projsp;
import java.io.IOException;
import java.util.*;
import javax.servlet.jsp.JspException;
import javax.servlet.jsp.PageContext;
import javax.servlet.jsp.tagext.JspFragment;
import javax.servlet.jsp.tagext.SimpleTagSupport;
public class DirectoryListTag extends SimpleTagSupport {
  private String path;
  private String suffix;
  public void setPath(String s) {
    this.path = s;
  }
  public void setSuffix(String s) {
    this.suffix = s;
  }
  private Collection findFiles() {
    PageContext pageContext = (PageContext)getJspContext();
    Collection resources =
        pageContext.getServletContext().getResourcePaths(path);
    List filteredResources = new ArrayList();
    if (resources == null || resources.isEmpty()) {
      return filteredResources;
    }
```

```java
      Iterator it = resources.iterator();
      String uri;
      String testSuffix;
      if (this.suffix != null) {
        testSuffix = this.suffix;
      } else {
        testSuffix = ".jpg";
      }
      // now filter out those files that don't end in the suffix
      while (it.hasNext()) {
        uri = (String)it.next();
        if (uri.endsWith(testSuffix)) {
          filteredResources.add(uri);
        }
      }
      return filteredResources;
    }
  public void doTag() throws JspException, IOException  {
      // first of all, find the names of the files
      Collection files = findFiles();
      if (files != null && !files.isEmpty()) {
        String filename;
        // now that the names have been found, iterate over each of them
        // and invoke the body content (JspFragment)
        Iterator it = files.iterator();
        while (it.hasNext()) {
          filename = (String)it.next();
          JspFragment jspBody = getJspBody();
          if (jspBody != null) {
            getJspContext().setAttribute("filename", filename);
            jspBody.invoke(getJspContext().getOut());
          }
        }
      }
    }
}
```

This class, in the same way as before, has two instance variables and setter methods to support the attributes for the tag.

The code also includes the same findFiles() helper method as ThumbnailTag.java, Listing 6-8.

The key difference between this and the previous <thumbnail> tag is in the way that the doTag() method behaves. Whereas the <thumbnail> tag generated HTML that was output back to the page, this time you just want to invoke (or evaluate) the body content of the custom tag for each file in the resulting list.

If you think back to the tag life cycle, part of the tag creation and initialization process involves a reference to a JspFragment object, which represents the tag's body content, being passed to the tag via the setJspBody() method. The JspFragment has one method that is of interest here: invoke(). Calling this method effectively asks the JSP container to evaluate and process the body content and send it back to the page. This seemingly simple process provides a great deal of flexibility in building custom tags.

For example, it allows you to programmatically evaluate and include the body content, perhaps including the body content only if a certain condition is met. In this example, you're invoking the body content object only if there are files that were found, and for each file found, you invoke the body content and therefore generate some more content.

In addition to programmatically evaluating the body content, you can also evaluate the body content multiple times. Again, in this example, if files are found, you're invoking the body content of the tag once for each of them.

## Describing the Directory List Tag

Listing 6-11 shows the TLD for this tag. Again, you'll use the same TLD as before; the listing omits the previous tags for brevity.

**Listing 6-11.** *ch06.tld*

```xml
<?xml version="1.0" encoding="UTF-8" ?>
<taglib xmlns="http://java.sun.com/xml/ns/javaee"
    xmlns:xsi="http://www.w3.org/2001/XMLSchema-instance"
    xsi:schemaLocation="http://java.sun.com/xml/ns/javaee/web-jsptaglibrary_2_1.xsd"
    version="2.1">

  ... the description of the tag library ...
  ... the description of the <datetime> tag ...
  ... the description of the <thumbnail> tag ...
    <tag>
      <name>list</name>
      <tag-class>com.apress.projsp.DirectoryListTag</tag-class>
      <body-content>scriptless</body-content>
      <description>
        Given a path, this tag provides a list of the files in that path.
      </description>
        <attribute>
            <name>path</name>
            <required>true</required>
            <rtexprvalue>true</rtexprvalue>
        </attribute>
        <attribute>
            <name>suffix</name>
            <required>false</required>
            <rtexprvalue>false</rtexprvalue>
        </attribute>
    </tag>
</taglib>
```

Describing this tag is pretty much the same as before, with the `<list>` tag having a required `path` attribute and an optional `suffix` attribute. Once again, the `path` attribute can accept an expression.

### Using the Directory List Tag

As before, you first import the tag library and then use it in the way that we outlined previously—with the body content of the tag representing the presentation and formatting:

```
<%@ taglib uri="/WEB-INF/tlds/ch06.tld" prefix="ch06" %>
<table width="100%">
  <tr>
    <ch06:list path="/photos" suffix=".jpg">
      <td align="center">
        <img src=".${filename}" alt="${filename}" width="128" height="96">
      </td>
    </ch06:list>
  </tr>
</table>
```

As this example shows, it's possible to fuse together the concepts of templating and wrapping up reusable functionality to form a custom tag that is not only flexible, but reusable too. With the previous implementation, the tag generated the HTML code and the information was presented in a limited way. However, by using this tag you can locate a list of files in a specific directory and then, by customizing the body content, display a list of names, a list of hyperlinks, a set of thumbnails, and so on. The possibilities are vast.

# Summary

This chapter has introduced the concepts of encapsulating your own content and functionality as reusable software components known as JSP tag extensions or, informally, as custom tags. These tags provide a great way to promote several of the factors associated with JSP development, including the reusability, readability, and maintainability of JSP pages. Removing common Java code, content, and presentation from the page provides a way to clean up JSP pages, by speeding up development, increasing quality, and permitting a quicker time to market through reuse.

Traditionally, common content such as that found in headers and footers has been abstracted away from JSP pages and included wherever necessary. Although this promotes maintainability and reuse, using the raw JSP constructs can often seem awkward to those who are not familiar with the technology and are more focused on the look and feel of a web application rather than the mechanics of how it works. Tag files help solve these problems by providing an easy-to-use mechanism for wrapping up and reusing common content. Next, you also learned how such content can be templated with tag files and parameterized with attributes. In addition to solving some technical problems, tag files provide a more natural interface for anybody using the tags.

Simple tags were added in the JSP 2.0 specification. Previous versions of JSP technology featured a way to wrap up common and recurring functionality as reusable custom tags, although the life cycle and semantics behind these techniques were often seen as too complicated by many developers. To address this, the SimpleTag interface was introduced to provide an effortless way to wrap up common functionality that is generally implemented in Java code as opposed to JSP code. As a convenience, the SimpleTagSupport class is also provided by the JSP specification to serve as a starting point for your tags.

While looking at this interface, you saw the development of a fairly trivial tag, followed by a look at how attributes can be used to customize the functionality. This led to a further discussion on how custom tags can best be used, which culminated in the assertion that content and presentation should ideally be separated if the best degree of reuse is to be achieved. Backing this up was a modified example of the <thumbnail> tag that allowed page authors to be flexible in the way that they used the tag as well as the content that they subsequently generated.

Tag files and the SimpleTag interface are great ways to wrap up reusable content and functionality for use by page authors in the pages of one or more web applications. For backward compatibility, JSP 2.1-compliant containers still need to support the classic method for building custom tags. This is particularly useful when reaching a wide audience is desired, or when you are looking for more control of the functionality that tags provide. Therefore, you'll look at classic tags in the next chapter.

■ ■ ■

# CHAPTER 7

# Classic Tags

In the previous chapter, you looked at tag files and simple tags, both of which are mechanisms for writing custom tags introduced as a part of the JSP 2.0 specification. As the examples in Chapter 6 demonstrated, these new mechanisms remove some of the complexity that was typically associated with building custom tags in the past. Rather than abandon the existing method of writing custom tags, JSP 2.1 supports full backward compatibility with it.

In this chapter, you'll take a look at the facilities provided by former versions of the JSP specification for writing custom tags. As you'll see throughout the chapter, these previous methods, now called **classic tags**, provide more flexibility than current methods and therefore are still useful in some scenarios. You'll also see how classic tags can take advantage of some of the new features that are now a part of the JSP specification, including how custom tags can support dynamic attributes.

As this chapter presents classic tags, you'll learn how to use them in web applications. Specifically you'll be looking at the following:

- What classic tags are and why they are useful

- The differences between classic tags and simple tags

- How to customize functionality by using attributes

- How to use dynamic attributes

- How to use classic tags for iteration

- How to use classic tags to evaluate body content

## Classic Tags Overview

There are now three mechanisms for building custom tags outlined in the JSP 2.1 specification: tag files, simple tags, and classic tags.

As you saw in the previous chapter, tag files provide an easy way to abstract common behavior away from JSP pages and into reusable components. Because tag files allow this content to be written by using regular JSP constructs, wrapping up content is fairly straightforward for JSP developers who might not necessarily know the Java programming language.

The next step up, in terms of complexity, is simple tags. These custom tags encapsulate reusable functionality in a Java class called a tag handler. Although this process does require familiarity with the Java programming language, it allows complex behavior to be wrapped up and used by page authors in a straightforward way. As you saw in the previous chapter, simple tags offer a great deal of flexibility in the way that the functionality is encapsulated and, through body content and JSP fragments, they allow separation between content and content presentation.

Classic tags are the original tag development methodology introduced in version 1.1 of the JSP specification. JSP 1.2 then added new functionality and simplified the programming model slightly, but essentially the model was the same, and it remains the same in the JSP 2.1 specification. As with simple tags, classic tags use the concept of a tag handler class that is written by using Java code. This is then described with a tag library descriptor file in the same way it is with simple tags, and the resulting custom tags are again used in the same way.

So, what differentiates classic tags from simple tags? You'll learn about the differences in this section. You'll also take a look at the classic tag interface, tag life cycle, and `TagSupport` class, and will build a small classic tag.

# The Differences Between Simple and Classic Tags

There are several key differences between simple and classic tags. Let's take a quick look at each in turn and evaluate what it means to you as a tag developer.

## The Tag Handler Interface

The fundamental difference between simple and classic tags is the way in which the tag handler class is implemented. When you're using simple tags, any tag handlers you build must implement the `javax.servlet.jsp.tagext.SimpleTag` interface. When you're using classic tags, however, the tag handlers must implement the `javax.servlet.jsp.tagext.Tag` interface or, as you'll see in this chapter, one of its subinterfaces.

For you as a developer, this means you need to learn a slightly different programming model. For example, when using simple tags, all of the functionality to be encapsulated within the tag is defined within the `doTag()` method. When using classic tags, there are two methods you must implement: `doStartTag()` and `doEndTag()`.

Feedback from tag developers over the past couple of years has been mixed, and many people find the concepts employed by classic tag handlers confusing. Therefore, the interface has been simplified and simple tags are the result of this process.

## The Tag Life Cycle

Another key, though often neglected, difference relates to the tag life cycle.

With simple tags, an instance of the tag handler class is created when needed and that instance is used to serve only a single invocation of a custom tag. In other words, a unique tag handler instance is created for each usage of a simple tag on a page.

With classic tags, this may or may not be the case because the JSP specification enables container vendors to optionally improve classic tag performance by pooling and reusing tag handler instances. This means that, for example, a single tag handler instance could be created and reused to service all invocations of that custom tag per page. The rules around reuse are fairly complicated, and to make matters worse, JSP container vendors don't always choose to implement this optional piece of the specification. Therefore, if you're using classic tags, you must be aware of whether your container pools and reuses tag handler instances.

The problems that arise between different JSP containers is another reason simple tags were introduced, and it's another area in which the complexity associated with developing them has been reduced. The downside is that there may be times when you'd like tag instances pooled and reused. For example, your tag might acquire some expensive resource when it is created. In this example, it makes sense to take advantage of any performance benefits that the container may provide. In many scenarios, however, this just isn't an issue and simple tags are more than adequate.

With this brief overview of the differences between simple and classic tags over, let's take a look at the interface that classic tag handlers must implement.

## The Tag Interface

The Tag interface, like the SimpleTag interface, provides the basic contract that must be upheld between the JSP page and the tag. Listing 7-1 shows the Tag interface.

**Listing 7-1.** *Tag.java*

```
package javax.servlet.jsp.tagext;
import javax.servlet.jsp.JspException;
public interface Tag {
  public final static int SKIP_BODY = 0;
  public final static int EVAL_BODY_INCLUDE = 1;
  public final static int SKIP_PAGE = 5;
  public final static int EVAL_PAGE = 6;
  void setPageContext(PageContext pc);
  void setParent(Tag t);
  int doStartTag() throws JspException;
  int doEndTag() throws JspException;
  void release();
}
```

## The Tag Life Cycle

As you learned in Chapter 6, the life cycle of simple tags consists of the tag handler being created, contextual and environmental information being passed to it, and finally, the doTag() method being executed. As Figure 7-1 shows, classic tags are not too different in this respect.

### Creating a Tag Handler Instance

As with simple tags, when a classic tag is used on a JSP page, the first thing that the JSP container must do is create a new instance of the tag handler class. Again, this is performed by invoking the default, no-arguments constructor.

**Figure 7-1.** *This UML diagram shows the life cycle of a classic tag in terms of the calling sequence of the class tag methods.*

## Setting the Context

The next step in the tag life cycle is to make the tag handler instance aware of the environment in which it is running. This involves passing the tag handler a reference to the current PageContext through the setPageContext() method. Like JspContext, this method provides an easy way to access other objects such as the current output writer and scoped attributes. Notice here that it's a PageContext instance that gets passed to the tag and not a JspContext instance, as happens with simple tags. This moves simple tags away from being dependent on services and features provided by the Java Servlet API; PageContext uses such features, whereas JspContext doesn't. However, for consistency and backward compatibility with earlier versions of the JSP specification, PageContext actually extends JspContext.

## Setting the Parent

Like simple tags, classic tags can be nested, and as you'll see in Chapter 8, it's possible for custom tag handlers to cooperate and communicate with one another. As an example, a child (nested) tag may ask for information from its parent tag. For this reason, the setParent() method is called and passes a reference to the closest enclosing tag handler, or null if the tag isn't nested.

For simple tags, this reference is of type JspTag (the superinterface for all tag handlers), but again for classic tags this reference is of type Tag (a subinterface of JspTag) for backward compatibility.

## Executing the Functionality

With the context set, the next thing to do is execute the functionality provided by the tag. With classic tags, this means calling the doStartTag() and doEndTag() methods.

When you looked at how custom tags can be used on the page, you saw that they can be written in a long or shortened form as follows:

```
<prefix:myTag></prefix:myTag>
<prefix:myTag/>
```

In the long format you explicitly write the start (opening) and end (closing) tags, and in the shortened format you combine them. Regardless of how you write them, both the doStartTag() method and the doEndTag() method are called on a tag handler instance. Figure 7-2 shows the tag life cycle from a slightly different viewpoint and illustrates how the doStartTag() and doEndTag() methods can also affect the tag life cycle by the values that are returned by them.

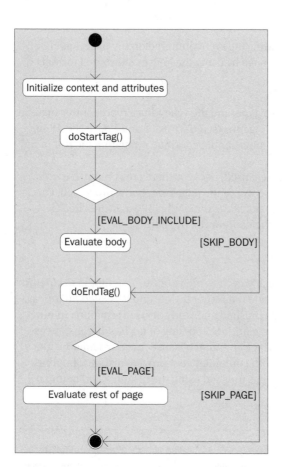

**Figure 7-2.** *This UML digram shows how the doStartTag() and doEndTag() methods are called to evaluate a tag.*

### The Start Tag

The doStartTag() method is called when the starting tag is encountered on the page:

```
int doStartTag() throws JspException;
```

The method signature from the Tag interface states that a primitive int value is to be returned. This signals to the JSP page what do to next. Two values can be returned from tags implementing this interface, SKIP_BODY and EVAL_BODY_INCLUDE, which are defined as constants within the Tag interface.

Returning SKIP_BODY signals to the JSP page that after the doStartTag() method has been called, any body content for the tag should be ignored. For example, any body content such as JSP code, Java code, or content that would normally be output to the page is simply dropped. Following this, processing proceeds to the doEndTag() method.

On the other hand, returning EVAL_BODY_INCLUDE from the doStartTag() method signals that any body content should be evaluated and output to the page.

### The End Tag

The doEndTag() method is called when the ending tag is encountered on the page, again, regardless of whether the tag is written on the page by using the long or shortened format:

```
int doEndTag() throws JspException;
```

This method also specifies an integer return type, and the valid return types for this method are the other two constants defined within the Tag interface, SKIP_PAGE and EVAL_PAGE. Here, these return values signal whether the JSP container should continue evaluating the rest of the JSP page.

In reality, the SKIP_PAGE return value is rarely used, because there aren't many circumstances in which you'll want to actually stop the rest of the page from being processed. One such example might be a security tag that appears at the top of the JSP page and checks whether the current user is authorized to see the contents of the page.

## Releasing State

The final method to be called as part of the tag life cycle is the release() method. This method is called to ask the tag handler to release any state it may be storing, and it's called on the tag handler only when that tag handler instance is finished and won't be used anymore. In other words, with JSP containers that don't support the optional pooling of tag handler instances, the release() method is called after the doEndTag() method because that particular instance will never be used again. On the other hand, with containers that provide instance pooling, this method is called only when the container has finished using the instance and before it gets garbage collected.

---

■**Caution** It's a common misconception that release() is always called directly after the doEndTag() method and hence is used to clear the values of instance variables. This is not the case, and relying on this behavior means that your tags might not work as expected in all vendors' JSP containers. The next chapter looks at some of the best practices for using and taking advantage of the tag life cycle.

---

# The TagSupport Class

Although the `Tag` interface contains more methods than the `SimpleTag` interface, providing an implementation is trivial. However, for convenience and in the same way that the `SimpleTagSupport` class provides a default implementation of the `SimpleTag` interface, the JSP specification provides the `TagSupport` class that you can use as a starting point for your own tag handlers. Here, the default implementations of the `doStartTag()` and `doEndTag()` methods return `SKIP_BODY` and `EVAL_PAGE`, respectively. We use this in many of this chapter's examples.

# A Simple Example

You're now ready to build a small classic tag. To help provide a direct comparison with simple tags, you'll rebuild the `<datetime>` tag example from the previous chapter.

### Building the <datetime> Tag Handler

The first step is, of course, to build the tag handler class. You'll extend the `TagSupport` class as shown in Listing 7-2.

**Listing 7-2.** *DateTimeTag*

```
package com.apress.projsp;
import java.io.IOException;
import java.text.DateFormat;
import java.util.Date;
import javax.servlet.jsp.JspException;
import javax.servlet.jsp.JspTagException;
import javax.servlet.jsp.tagext.TagSupport;

public class DateTimeTag extends TagSupport {

  public int doStartTag() throws JspException {
    DateFormat df = DateFormat.getDateTimeInstance(
                            DateFormat.MEDIUM, DateFormat.MEDIUM);
    try {
      pageContext.getOut().write(df.format(new Date()));
    } catch (IOException ioe) {
      throw new JspTagException(ioe.getMessage());
    }
    return SKIP_BODY;
  }
}
```

The functionality provided by the tag is implemented within the `doStartTag()` method. In situations when it doesn't matter whether a custom tag will be used in the long or shortened form on the page (in other words, when the tag has no body), the functionality associated with the tag can be implemented within either the `doStartTag()` or the `doEndTag()` method.

As you can see, the code that provides the functionality of the tag is pretty much the same as that you used with the simple tag example in the previous chapter. The only real difference is in the way that this code is packaged within the tag handler. One point to note is that unlike the doTag() method on the SimpleTag interface, the doStartTag() and doEndTag() methods don't declare that they throw IOException; therefore, you must catch and handle this exception.

In this example, you're throwing a JspTagException (a subclass of JspException) to tell the JSP page that something went wrong. Throwing a JspTagException instead of a more generic JspException is a useful way to specify that the problem may be related to a custom tag rather than the page itself, during development and debugging.

Finally, because you're not interested in the body content of this tag, the doStartTag() method returns SKIP_BODY. Note that the tag handler does not supply an implementation of the doEndTag() method. Because we are not providing any special behavior for the closing tag, we can simply let the default implementation in TagSupport handle the closing tag. Alternatively, we could have implemented the needed behavior in doEndTag() and let the default doStartTag() handle the opening tag.

## Describing the <datetime> Tag

With the tag handler written, the next step is to describe the tag. As with simple tags, you do this by using the tag library descriptor (TLD) file. Listing 7-3 shows the TLD for this example.

**Listing 7-3.** *ch07.tld*

```xml
<?xml version="1.0" encoding="UTF-8" ?>
<taglib xmlns="http://java.sun.com/xml/ns/javaee"
        xmlns:xsi="http://www.w3.org/2001/XMLSchema-instance"
        xsi:schemaLocation=➡
"http://java.sun.com/xml/ns/javaee/web-jsptaglibrary_2_1.xsd"
        version="2.1">

  <description>
    Tag library for Professional JSP 2.1, Chapter 7.
  </description>
  <jsp-version>2.1</jsp-version>
  <tlib-version>1.0</tlib-version>
  <short-name>ch07</short-name>
  <uri>http://www.apress.com/projsp</uri>
  <tag>
    <name>datetime</name>
    <tag-class>com.apress.projsp.DateTimeTag</tag-class>
    <body-content>empty</body-content>
    <description>
      Outputs the current date and time to the page.
    </description>
  </tag>
</taglib>
```

As this code illustrates, describing a tag with a TLD file is the same regardless of whether that tag is a simple tag or a classic tag.

The way that custom tags are used on the page provides a nice abstraction for those tags and the way they're built. It's perfectly acceptable to mix simple and classic tags together in the same TLD file, and page authors will never know how the tags are actually implemented. In fact, as you'll see in the next chapter, you can also describe tag files in the TLD, which makes it possible to wrap up any type of tag for easy reuse.

## Using the <datetime> Tag

If you assume that the TLD file has been saved at the location `WEB-INF\tlds\ch07.tld`, then importing and using the tag library is the same as before:

```
<%@ taglib uri="/WEB-INF/tlds/ch07.tld" prefix="ch07" %>
The current date and time is <ch07:datetime/>
```

Not surprisingly, the results of using the tag are also the same as before, as you can see in Figure 7-3. As this example shows, building trivial classic tags isn't much different from building the simple tags you saw in the previous chapter, and essentially it's just a matter of using the `Tag` interface and implementing your functionality within the `doStartTag()` or `doEndTag()` method.

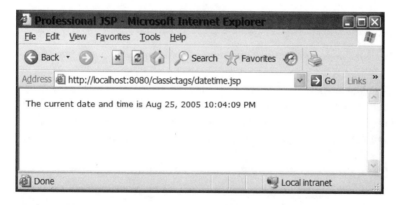

**Figure 7-3.** *Classic tags can be used to encapsulate simple functionality, as shown in this tag that prints the current date and time.*

Let's now continue this tour of classic tags by seeing how they, like other custom tags, can be customized by using attributes.

# Customizing Functionality by Using Attributes

In the previous chapter, you learned how you can customize tag files and simple tags by using attributes. With tag files this meant that you could parameterize content as templates, and with simple tags it meant that you could parameterize functionality.

Classic tags provide just another way to wrap up functionality, and therefore the same principle applies: you can use attributes to configure that functionality. In fact, the way that attributes are implemented with classic tags is exactly the same as with simple tags. An example of this follows.

## Building Lists in HTML Forms

A common feature of many websites and HTML forms is a drop-down control that allows users to select an item from a list. Figure 7-4 shows a user registration form enabling users to select the country they live in from a list.

**Figure 7-4.** *Drop-down boxes allow you to limit the choices a user can make on a web page form.*

If the items in the list were available as a collection of JavaBeans (for example, a `java.util.List` containing `Country` beans), it would be possible to dynamically generate such a list with features provided by the JSP expression language and the JSTL. One option is to use the JSTL `<forEach>` tag to iterate over the collection and generate the appropriate HTML for each item in the collection.

To hold each country's information, consisting of an ID and a name, a simple `Country` JavaBean might look like the class in Listing 7-4.

**Listing 7-4.** *Country.java*

```java
package com.apress.projsp.domain;
public class Country {
  private int id;
  private String name;
  public Country() {
  }
  public Country(int id, String name) {
    this.id = id;
    this.name = name;
  }
  public int getId() {
```

```
    return this.id;
  }
  public void setId(int i) {
    this.id = i;
  }
  public String getName() {
    return this.name;
  }
  public void setName(String s) {
    this.name = s;
  }
}
```

With a collection of Country objects available as a page-scoped attribute (for example), the following JSP code snippet shows how the JSTL can be used to help build the list:

```
<%@ taglib uri="http://java.sun.com/jstl/core_rt" prefix="c" %>
  Countries :
  <select name="country">
    <c:forEach var="country" items="${countries}">
      <option value="${country.id}">${country.name}</option>
    </c:forEach>
  </select>
```

Here, you're using the JSTL to iterate over the collection. Short JSP EL expressions within the JSTL tags extract the ID and name from the Country JavaBeans within that collection. Although this works, the logic related to building the list is embedded within the JSP page, meaning that it's not easily reusable. Also, the code itself is a little raw and unreadable, particularly because the HTML for the select control is mixed in with JSTL and EL expressions. A better way to implement this is to use a custom tag that generates the content for you.

## Identifying the Attributes

Before building the tag handler, let's look at what you might want to allow users to customize when they use the tag. In the previous example, there are four things that you can customize:

- The name property of the HTML select control

- The value that is being displayed in the list (the label)

- The value behind the scenes that acts as a key for each item (the value)

- The collection of items to be displayed

Looking at what can be customized is an important step in figuring out what attributes a custom tag might need. This review also allows the custom tag itself to be as generic as possible. After all, if you can specify all of the preceding information by using attributes, it means that you can build a generic HTML <select> tag rather than one that displays just country names.

## Building the <select> Tag Handler

Keeping in mind the attributes you can customize, let's look at how to implement the tag handler. Listing 7-5 shows the tag handler for a <select> tag. As before, the tag handler class will extend the TagSupport class.

**Listing 7-5.** *SelectTag.java*

```java
package com.apress.projsp;
import java.beans.PropertyDescriptor;
import java.util.Collection;
import java.util.Iterator;
import javax.servlet.jsp.*;
import javax.servlet.jsp.tagext.TagSupport;
public class SelectTag extends TagSupport {
  private String name;
  private String label;
  private String value;
  private Collection items;
  public void setName(String s) {
    this.name = s;
  }
  public void setLabel(String s) {
    this.label = s;
  }
  public void setValue(String s) {
    this.value = s;
  }
  public void setItems(Collection coll) {
    this.items = coll;
  }
  public int doStartTag() throws JspException {
    Iterator iterator = items.iterator();
    try {
      JspWriter out = pageContext.getOut();
      out.print("<select name=\"");
      out.print(name);
      out.print("\">");
      while (iterator.hasNext()) {
        // get the next JavaBean from the collection
        Object o = iterator.next();
        // and use it to create a description of the property used
        // to represent the displayable label
        PropertyDescriptor labelPD =
          new PropertyDescriptor(label, o.getClass());
        // and the property used to represent the hidden value
```

```
      PropertyDescriptor valuePD =
        new PropertyDescriptor(value, o.getClass());
      // and now generate the HTML
      out.print("<option value=\"");
      // call the accessor method for the value property
      // (this is the same as calling get<PropertyName>() on
      // the JavaBean instance)
      out.print(
        valuePD.getReadMethod().invoke(o, new Object[] {}).toString());
      out.print("\">");
      // and do the same for the label property
      out.print(
        labelPD.getReadMethod().invoke(o, new Object[] {}).toString());
      out.print("</option>");
    }
    out.print("</select>");
  } catch (Exception e) {
    throw new JspTagException(e.getMessage());
  }
  // and skip the body
  return SKIP_BODY;
  }
}
```

The class has fields that correspond to the various attributes for the tag. These are implemented in exactly the same way as with simple tags, by having an instance variable and **setter method** for each attribute.

As in this book's previous examples, three of the four attributes here are simple string values. First, you have the name of the select control on the page. Then you have label and value, both of which are strings representing the name of the JavaBean property containing the information you'd like to extract from each JavaBean. For example, with the Country JavaBean, these attributes would be set to name and id, respectively.

The fourth and final instance variable is of type java.util.Collection. When we covered attributes in the previous chapter, we mentioned that they can be more than just simple strings—they can be Boolean values, numeric values, and even objects. For this example, and in the same way as the items attribute in the JSTL <forEach> tag, you want to pass your tag handler a reference to a fully populated java.util.Collection instance containing the items that are to be displayed in the list. Therefore, the instance variable and setter method are defined to take Collection rather than String, and at request time the setter method will be called with a Collection of Country objects.

The only other part of the tag handler that you must define is the functionality provided by the tag. As in the previous example, this functionality is implemented within the doStartTag() method, although the doEndTag() method can also be used. However, don't implement the same functionality in the doStartTag() and doEndTag() methods, because they both get called.

First, the doStartTag() method sets up an Iterator instance that will operate over the collection. Next, it generates and writes the opening <select> tag back to the page. Then, for each item in the collection, it generates the appropriate HTML. To do this, it uses a feature of the Java reflection mechanism to extract the values of the specified JavaBean properties:

```
PropertyDescriptor labelPD =
    new PropertyDescriptor(label, o.getClass());
// and the property used to represent the hidden value
PropertyDescriptor valuePD =
    new PropertyDescriptor(value, o.getClass());
```

---

**Tip** Using `PropertyDescriptor` objects provides an easy way to find the getter and setter methods associated with a JavaBean property and saves you from writing the code to determine the method names.

---

Finally, with the HTML generated for every item in the collection, the `doStartTag()` method generates and outputs the closing `</select>` tag and returns `SKIP_BODY`, because the tag is not interested in the body content of this custom tag.

This technique does have at least one drawback, however. It is not possible to pass customized attributes to the HTML element created by the tag. That is, there are many other attributes that can be added to the `<select>` element, such as event handlers (`onclick`, `onchange`) or CSS attributes. There is no way to dynamically pass these to the tag handler in Listing 7-5, unless you are willing to create properties in the tag handler for every possible attribute. You will look at a way around this drawback in the "Dynamic Attributes" section later in this chapter.

## Describing the <select> Tag

Once again, you must next describe the custom tag by using the TLD file. Listing 7-6 shows the TLD for this custom action. Some of the information in the TLD file is omitted for brevity.

**Listing 7-6.** *ch07.tld*

```
<?xml version="1.0" encoding="UTF-8" ?>
<taglib xmlns="http://java.sun.com/xml/ns/javaee"
        xmlns:xsi="http://www.w3.org/2001/XMLSchema-instance"
        xsi:schemaLocation=➧
"http://java.sun.com/xml/ns/javaee/web-jsptaglibrary_2_1.xsd"
        version="2.1">

  ... the description of the tag library ...
  ... the description of the datetime tag ...
    <tag>
      <name>select</name>
      <tag-class>com.apress.projsp.SelectTag</tag-class>
      <body-content>empty</body-content>
      <description>
        Creates an HTML select control based upon a collection of objects.
```

```
      </description>
      <attribute>
        <name>name</name>
        <required>true</required>
        <rtexprvalue>false</rtexprvalue>
      </attribute>
      <attribute>
        <name>label</name>
        <required>true</required>
        <rtexprvalue>false</rtexprvalue>
      </attribute>
      <attribute>
        <name>value</name>
        <required>true</required>
        <rtexprvalue>false</rtexprvalue>
      </attribute>
      <attribute>
        <name>items</name>
        <required>true</required>
        <rtexprvalue>true</rtexprvalue>
      </attribute>
    </tag>
</taglib>
```

There's nothing really new in concept here except that in addition to having three required attributes (name, label, and value), you have the items attribute that is required and allows request-time expressions. The only way to pass object attributes into tag handlers is to ensure that they support request-time expressions. This is made possible by setting the value of the rtexprvalue element to true in the TLD file for the attribute.

## Using the <select> Tag

To use the tag, you just import the tag library the same way you did before. Assuming that a collection of Country JavaBeans is accessible with the EL expression ${countries}, you can use the tag in the following way:

```
<%@ taglib uri="/WEB-INF/tlds/ch07.tld" prefix="ch07" %>
Countries :

<ch07:select name="country" label="name" value="id"
             items="${countries}"/>
```

Of course, you can also use the traditional request-time expressions in the page as follows:

```
<ch07:select name="country" label="name" value="id"
      items="<%= (java.util.Collection)
             pageContext.findAttribute("countries") %>"
/>
```

In doing this, you introduce a lot of Java code into the page, and this is where things start to become unreadable—something that the JSP EL aims to fix, which is a very good reason to adopt the EL. However, even using the tag in this manner is better than writing the code to generate the HTML select control within the JSP page, because you've now encapsulated the logic to generate the appropriate HTML and made it reusable. By looking at the source code for the page, you can see that the generated HTML is as follows:

```
Countries : <select name="country"><option value="1">England</option>➥
<option value="2">Wales</option><option value="3">Scotland</option></select>
```

Admittedly, the generated HTML isn't as neat, tidy, and well laid out as if you had written it yourself, but the important point is that you have a component that you can reuse to generate HTML select lists on other pages and within other web applications. There is, however, an inherent problem with the tag: this custom tag cannot be used to customize the HTML select control.

One of the most common uses for custom tags since their inception has been to write custom tag versions of the standard HTML form controls such as text fields, lists, and buttons. However, this use has always been contentious because it provides advantages at the cost of introducing limitations.

On the plus side, custom tags provide a great way to automate the creation of HTML form controls. For example, you can automatically set default values for text fields, automatically set the current selection in a list, and so on. A great way to implement this is through Jakarta Struts. Struts provide a complete framework for handling requests and linking up JavaBean instances with HTML form controls so that the information contained within the JavaBean is automatically populated into the form. For further information about Struts, please see Chapters 14 and 15.

On the negative side, building a set of tags to mimic the standard HTML form controls means that page authors are no longer using standard HTML tags and are therefore limited in the tools that they can use to help build the page. Many page authors use visual editors such as Macromedia Dreamweaver to help them lay out and configure the HTML tags, but generally these types of editors are not able to use these custom tags.

Probably the most important issue, though, is that unless HTML tags are properly implemented, the ability to customize the generated HTML is reduced. Each HTML form control tag has many, many attributes that can be used to customize how it looks and behaves on the page. For example, there are attributes that can be used to specify the CSS style to be used, and others that can be used to specify JavaScript event handlers that fire when actions occur to the controls. To customize all the possible attributes through a mimicked tag such as that in Listing 7-5 would mean providing fields for every attribute, and methods to set and get the fields in the tag handler class. Struts achieves this, but it's no small task.

So, coming back to the <select> tag that you've just built, the inherent problem is that you've effectively stopped people from customizing the HTML that's being generated. What would happen if you wanted to change the drop-down list, which displays a single item when not selected, into a list box that displays multiple items? Well, if you were writing the HTML, it would be as simple as specifying an attribute called size when you used the HTML <select> tag. Previously for your custom tag implementation, this would have meant going back to the tag handler, adding a new instance variable and setter method, amending the TLD file, and then redeploying the tag. Fortunately,  the JSP specification provides a great new feature to help you solve just this problem: dynamic attributes.

# Dynamic Attributes

All the attributes that you've seen up to this point have been static. In other words, a tag's attributes have all been defined up front within the TLD file, and support for those attributes has been specifically implemented within the tag handler class. The JSP 2.0 specification introduced the concept of **dynamic attributes**, in which the attributes for any tag don't have to be determined and defined in the TLD file. The benefit of dynamic attributes is increased flexibility, particularly when the full set of attributes is either very large or unknown at the time of development. Let's see how your own tag handlers can take advantage of this functionality.

## The DynamicAttributes Interface

The ability to support dynamic attributes is provided through an interface called DynamicAttributes within the javax.servlet.jsp.tagext package. The interface shown in Listing 7-7 is fairly straightforward and provides a single method through which a dynamic attribute can be set.

**Listing 7-7.** *DynamicAttributes.java*

```
package javax.servlet.jsp.tagext;
import javax.servlet.jsp.JspException;
public interface DynamicAttributes {
  public void setDynamicAttribute(
    String uri, String localName, Object value) throws JspException
}
```

You can have a mixture of static and dynamic attributes for any specific tag. When that tag is used on the page, the JSP container looks at the attributes that have been (statically) defined in the TLD file. If an attribute is statically defined, the regular setter method is called in the same way that you've seen before. However, if the attribute isn't defined, the setDynamicAttribute() method on the tag handler is called instead.

The parameters of the setDynamicAttribute() method provide information about the namespace, name, and value of the attribute. The name and value of an attribute are self-explanatory, and the namespace simply provides a way to prevent attributes with the same name from clashing. For example, dynamic attributes could be used to customize some underlying content that's generated by the tag, or perhaps passed through to another JavaBean or component in order to configure it. In this situation, the same attribute name might be used more than once. To prevent attributes from clashing, a namespace can be applied to the attribute. The final point to note about this method is that it can throw a JspException, and this can be used to indicate to the JSP container that the tag doesn't support the specified attribute. If this is the case, no more methods on the tag handler will be called, effectively stopping invocation of the tag. To illustrate how dynamic attributes work in practice, let's look at an example.

> **Note** Although you didn't see this in the previous chapter, providing support for dynamic attributes in simple tag handlers is achieved in exactly the same way as in classic tags, and the concepts that you'll see in the next example are all applicable to simple tags, too.

# Further Customization with Dynamic Attributes

Taking the <select> tag as a basis, let's modify it to support dynamic attributes. This way, you'll be able to customize the generated HTML without resorting to explicitly supporting all of the attributes that the true HTML <select> tag can support.

### Building the <selectWithDynamicAttributes> Tag Handler

Listing 7-8 shows the <selectWithDynamicAttributes> tag handler. As before, you'll use TagSupport as a starting point, although the tag will also implement the DynamicAttributes interface.

**Listing 7-8.** *SelectTagWithDynamicAttributes.java*

```
package com.apress.projsp;

import java.beans.PropertyDescriptor;
import java.util.*;
import javax.servlet.jsp.*;
import javax.servlet.jsp.tagext.DynamicAttributes;
import javax.servlet.jsp.tagext.TagSupport;

public class SelectTagWithDynamicAttributes
            extends TagSupport implements DynamicAttributes {
  private String name;
  private String label;
  private String value;
  private Collection items;
  private Map dynamicAttributes = new HashMap();
  public void setName(String s) {
    this.name = s;
  }
  public void setLabel(String s) {
    this.label = s;
  }
  public void setValue(String s) {
    this.value = s;
  }
```

```java
public void setItems(Collection coll) {
  this.items = coll;
}

public void setDynamicAttribute(String uri, String name, Object value)
    throws JspException {
  dynamicAttributes.put(name, value);
}

public int doStartTag() throws JspException {
  Iterator iterator = items.iterator();
  try {
    JspWriter out = pageContext.getOut();
    // write the starting tag of the select control
    out.print("<select name=\"");
    out.print(name);
    out.print("\"");
    // insert the dynamic attributes
    Iterator it = dynamicAttributes.keySet().iterator();
    while (it.hasNext()) {
      String key = (String)it.next();
      out.print(" ");
      out.print(key);
      out.print("=\"");
      out.print(dynamicAttributes.get(key));
      out.print("\" ");
    }
    out.print(">");

    while (iterator.hasNext()) {
      // get the next JavaBean from the collection
      Object o = iterator.next();
      // and use it to create a description of the property used
      // to represent the displayable label
      PropertyDescriptor labelPD =
        new PropertyDescriptor(label, o.getClass());
      // and the property used to represent the hidden value
      PropertyDescriptor valuePD =
        new PropertyDescriptor(value, o.getClass());
      // and now generate the HTML
      out.print("<option value=\"");
      // call the accessor method for the value property
      // (this is the same as calling get<PropertyName>() on
      // the JavaBean instance)
```

```
      out.print(
        valuePD.getReadMethod().invoke(o, new Object[] {}).toString());
      out.print("\">");
      // and do the same for the label property
      out.print(
        labelPD.getReadMethod().invoke(o, new Object[] {}).toString());
      out.print("</option>");
    }
    // write the ending tag of the select control
    out.print("</select>");
  } catch (Exception e) {
    throw new JspTagException(e.getMessage());
  }
   // and skip the body
  return SKIP_BODY;
  }
}
```

The class has instance variables for the static attributes and setter methods for each variable. One of the limitations of using dynamic attributes is that you can't specify which of them, if any, are required. By keeping the core attributes of your custom tags as statically defined, you have the best of both worlds: flexibility through dynamic attributes and the ability to ensure that people use your tag in the correct manner.

The class needs some way to store and retrieve dynamic attributes so they can be used during the actual processing of the tag. For this reason, and because you don't know the names of the dynamic attributes, the class uses a HashMap to store the dynamic attribute names and values. The class also has an implementation of the DynamicAttributes interface's setDynamicAttribute() method. This implementation is fairly straightforward and involves inserting the dynamic attributes as key-value pairs into the map. Because we're not worried about the names of attributes clashing, the method does not use the namespace URI that's a part of the method signature.

Finally, the class has an implementation of the doStartTag() method. The core functionality provided by this method hasn't changed too much, although the HTML select control is being generated to include any dynamic attributes that have been specified.

### Describing the <selectWithDynamicAttributes> Tag

Although the tag handler implements the DynamicAttributes interface, in the TLD file (see Listing 7-9) you also have to define that the tag supports dynamic attributes. Using the dynamic-attributes element as follows does this.

**Listing 7-9.** *ch07.tld*

```
<?xml version="1.0" encoding="UTF-8" ?>
<taglib xmlns="http://java.sun.com/xml/ns/javaee"
        xmlns:xsi="http://www.w3.org/2001/XMLSchema-instance"
```

```
        xsi:schemaLocation=➡
"http://java.sun.com/xml/ns/javaee/web-jsptaglibrary_2_1.xsd"
        version="2.1">


... the description of the tag library ...
... the description of the datetime tag ...
  <tag>
    <name>selectWithDynamicAttributes</name>
    <tag-class>
      com.apress.projsp.SelectTagWithDynamicAttributes
    </tag-class>
    <body-content>empty</body-content>
    <description>
      Creates an HTML select control based upon a collection of objects.
    </description>
    <attribute>
      <name>name</name>
      <required>true</required>
      <rtexprvalue>false</rtexprvalue>
    </attribute>
    <attribute>
      <name>label</name>
      <required>true</required>
      <rtexprvalue>false</rtexprvalue>
    </attribute>
    <attribute>
      <name>value</name>
      <required>true</required>
      <rtexprvalue>false</rtexprvalue>
    </attribute>
    <attribute>
      <name>items</name>
      <required>true</required>
      <rtexprvalue>true</rtexprvalue>
    </attribute>
    <dynamic-attributes>true</dynamic-attributes>
  </tag>
</taglib>
```

Essentially, this is all that's required to indicate to the JSP container that a tag supports dynamic attributes. If this element isn't specified, the default value is assumed to be `false`.

---

■**Caution** Neglecting to implement the `DynamicAttributes` interface and indicate a tag's ability to support dynamic attributes in the TLD file will result in your tag not working as expected.

---

## Using the &lt;selectWithDynamicAttributes&gt; Tag

Using the new version of the tag is the same as before, but remember that you can now specify more than just four attributes:

```
<%@ taglib uri="/WEB-INF/tlds/ch07.tld" prefix="ch07" %>
Countries :
<ch07:selectWithDynamicAttributes name="country" label="name"
        value="id" items="${countries}" size="3"/>
```

In this example, we're also specifying a `size` attribute to effectively transform the original drop-down control into an HTML list control. Figure 7-5 shows how this affects the HTML generated by the JSP.

**Figure 7-5.** *Using dynamic attributes allows your custom tags to accept any number of attributes. It increases the flexibility of your custom tags when using custom tags to generate HTML controls.*

Again, the generated HTML shows you what really happens and how the additional `size` attribute has been used:

```
Countries :
<select name="country" size="3">
  <option value="1">England</option>
  <option value="2">Wales</option>
  <option value="3">Scotland</option>
</select>
```

As this example demonstrates, using dynamic attributes is a great way to increase the flexibility of custom tags, allowing page authors to further customize content and/or functionality. As you saw in the previous chapter, mixing too much content and presentation logic eventually leads to limitations in the way that the content can be presented. Therefore, it's best to use dynamic attributes only where fairly fine-grained customizations are required, such as this example that allows additional, optional attributes for underlying HTML controls. For more advanced customization, taking the approach outlined in the previous chapter (in which content was templated within the body content of the custom tag) is a much better option and is made possible by returning EVAL_BODY_INCLUDE from the doStartTag() method to signal to the JSP container that it should include/evaluate the body content.

# Iteration Tags

Now that you're familiar with the Tag life cycle, you're in a good position to compare its functionality to that offered by the newer SimpleTag interface. For instance, both allow you to wrap up reusable functionality, generate content, and customize the tag through the use of static and dynamic attributes. Also, you can write a classic custom tag that evaluates or ignores its body content, achieving the same result as simple tags invoking or not invoking their body content via the supplied JspFragment reference that represents the tag's body content.

One difference between a classic tag and a simple tag is that a simple tag can invoke its body content multiple times by repeatedly calling the invoke() method of the JspFragment. With the Tag interface, this isn't possible; the return value from the doStartTag() method determines whether the body content should be evaluated once or not evaluated at all. In terms of evaluating body content more than once, to implement similar functionality to that provided by the simple tag, you must use another classic tag interface called IterationTag.

## The IterationTag Interface

The IterationTag interface (see Listing 7-10) was introduced as a part of the JSP 1.2 specification in an attempt to simplify the procedure for evaluating and reevaluating body content multiple times. This was previously possible with the JSP 1.1 BodyTag interface (we cover this interface later in the chapter), although the implementation details were complex.

**Listing 7-10.** *IterationTag.java*

```
package javax.servlet.jsp.tagext;
import javax.servlet.jsp.JspException;
public interface IterationTag extends Tag {
  public final static int EVAL_BODY_AGAIN = 2;
  int doAfterBody() throws JspException;
}
```

The interface itself is fairly small, and this is because it extends the Tag interface. Effectively, a single method has been added to the tag life cycle called doAfterBody(), and it's this method that provides you with the ability to ask that a tag's body content is evaluated more than once. Let's see how this affects the tag life cycle.

## The Iteration Tag Life Cycle

Figure 7-6 illustrates the iteration tag life cycle and shows where the new doAfterBody() method fits in with the life cycle of a custom tag.

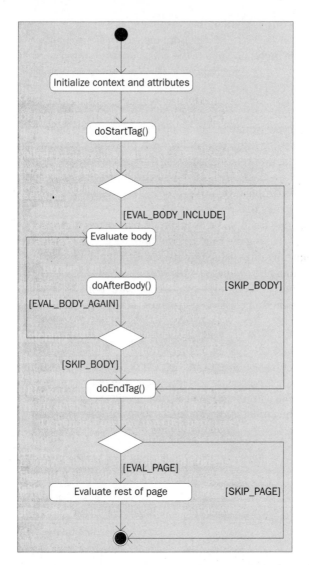

**Figure 7-6.** *To support iteration, the doAfterBody() method is called after doStartTag(). The return value of doAfterBody() indicates whether the tag body is evaluated again or processing continues to the doEndTag() method.*

### Setting the Context

As before, the first thing that happens is that the contextual information (the `PageContext` and parent `Tag`) is passed to the tag handler instance.

### The Start Tag

After the context has been set, the `doStartTag()` method is called and one of two things can happen. First, the `doStartTag()` method can return `SKIP_BODY`, meaning that the body content is ignored and processing proceeds to the doEndTag() method as before. Alternatively, a value of EVAL_BODY_INCLUDE can be returned from the doStartTag() method, signaling to the JSP container that the body content should be evaluated and included in the page. Again, this is the same as with the Tag interface, although it's after the body content has been evaluated that things start to change.

### After the Body

After the body content has been evaluated, the new doAfterBody() method is called, the primary purpose of which is to determine whether the body content should be reevaluated. If this is the case, the method should return the EVAL_BODY_AGAIN constant defined within the IterationTag interface. On the other hand, and when no more evaluations of the body content should happen, the SKIP_BODY value should be returned.

### The End Tag

Finally, regardless of whether or not the body was evaluated and reevaluated multiple times, the doEndTag() method is called in the same way as the other tags that you've seen in this chapter. Again, possible return values are EVAL_PAGE and SKIP_PAGE.

## The TagSupport Class Revisited

You've already seen how the TagSupport class provides a convenient starting place for you to build classic tags, and we said that it provides a default implementation of the Tag interface. This is only half of the truth, as the TagSupport class actually provides a default implementation of the IterationTag interface, meaning that it can be used as a starting point for building iteration tags too. The default implementations of the doStartTag() and doEndTag() methods return SKIP_BODY and EVAL_PAGE, respectively (as you've seen before), and default implementation of the doAfterBody() method returns SKIP_BODY. Let's look at an example.

## Evaluating Body Content Multiple Times

As you learned in Chapter 4, the JSTL provides a standard <forEach> tag that enables you to perform iteration over a set of items by using simple JSP code. Although the JSTL is a standard, at times you still might want to build your own tag that performs iteration. For example, perhaps you have a graph of objects that can't easily be iterated over without some preprocessing, or perhaps you're unable to use JSTL for reasons beyond your control. Either way, let's see how you can build a tag that evaluates its body content more than once, in the same way as the JSTL <forEach> tag and the <list> tag that you saw in the previous chapter.

### Building the Iteration Tag Handler

Listing 7-11 shows the IteratorTag class, which extends the TagSupport class.

**Listing 7-11.** *IteratorTag.java*

```
package com.apress.projsp;
import java.util.Collection;
import java.util.Iterator;
```

```
import javax.servlet.jsp.JspException;
import javax.servlet.jsp.tagext.TagSupport;

public class IteratorTag extends TagSupport {
  private String var;
  private Collection items;
  private Iterator iterator;

  public void setVar(String s) {
    this.var = s;
  }
  public void setItems(Collection coll) {
    this.items = coll;
  }

  public int doStartTag() throws JspException {
    // set up the iterator to be used
    iterator = items.iterator();
    if (iterator.hasNext()) {
      // if there are elements, put the first one into page
      // scope under the name provided by the "var" attribute
      pageContext.setAttribute(var, iterator.next());
      // and include the body
      return EVAL_BODY_INCLUDE;
    } else {
      // there are no elements so skip the body
      return SKIP_BODY;
    }
  }
  public int doAfterBody() throws JspException {
    if (iterator.hasNext()) {
      // if there are more elements, put the next one into page
      // scope under the name provided by the "var" attribute
      pageContext.setAttribute(var, iterator.next());
      // and instruct the JSP engine to reevaluate the body of this tag
      return EVAL_BODY_AGAIN;
    } else {
      // there are no more elements so skip the body
      return SKIP_BODY;
    }
  }
}
```

The class has instance variables and setter methods to support any attributes that the tag will take. In this case, the class has two—one for the name of the attribute that will represent each item in the iteration (var) and one for the collection to be specified (items).

Next, the class has a `java.util.Iterator` instance. Because it will be iterating over the collection, it needs some way to keep track of where it is in that collection. When you looked at the simple `<list>` tag example in the previous chapter, the iteration over the entire collection of items was performed within the `doTag()` method. However, here you must perform the iteration over several methods; hence you use an instance variable to maintain your position.

Now you get to the functionality provided by the tag in the `doStartTag()` method. The first thing to do is check whether there are items to be iterated over and, if so, get a reference to the first one in the collection. With this reference obtained, the method sets a page-scoped attribute under the name specified by `var` to point to this first item. It then asks the JSP container to evaluate the body content of the tag. An EL statement inside the tag body can be used to access the page-scoped attribute.

Alternatively, if there are no items, the `doStartTag()` method simply ignores any body content and proceeds straight to the `doEndTag()`method, a default version of which is implemented by the `TagSupport` class.

As you may recall from the iteration tag life cycle, after the body content has been evaluated, the `doAfterBody()` method is called on the tag handler. The purpose of the `doStartTag()` method is to find the first item in the collection, put it into the page scope, and evaluate the body content. If there are more items in the collection, the method repeats the action again.

Here, `doAfterBody()` checks for more items, and if it finds them, it gets the next one, puts it into page scope, and asks the JSP container to evaluate the body content again. After the body content has again been evaluated, the `doAfterBody()` method is called. This cycle of calling `doAfterBody()` and evaluating the body content continues until there are no more items in the collection. At this time, the method returns `SKIP_BODY`, indicating that no more body content evaluations are required.

---

**■Tip** Don't forget to eventually return `SKIP_BODY` from the `doAfterBody()` method; otherwise, you'll run into an infinite loop by continuously evaluating the body content.

---

## Describing the Iteration Tag

After the tag handler is built, you must, of course, describes the iteration tag with the TLD file. Listing 7-12 shows the additional entries in the `ch07.tld` file that describe the iteration tag.

**Listing 7-12.** *ch07.tld*

```
<?xml version="1.0" encoding="UTF-8" ?>
<taglib xmlns="http://java.sun.com/xml/ns/javaee"
        xmlns:xsi="http://www.w3.org/2001/XMLSchema-instance"
        xsi:schemaLocation= ➥
"http://java.sun.com/xml/ns/javaee/web-jsptaglibrary_2_1.xsd"
        version="2.1">

    ... the description of the tag library ...
    ... the description of the datetime tag ...
    ... the description of the select tag ...
```

```
  <tag>
    <name>iterate</name>
    <tag-class>com.apress.projsp.IteratorTag</tag-class>
    <body-content>scriptless</body-content>
    <description>
      Iterates over a specified java.util.Collection instance.
    </description>
    <attribute>
      <name>var</name>
      <required>true</required>
      <rtexprvalue>false</rtexprvalue>
    </attribute>
    <attribute>
      <name>items</name>
      <required>true</required>
      <rtexprvalue>true</rtexprvalue>
    </attribute>
  </tag>
</taglib>
```

Once again, the concepts here are the same as you've seen before, with the <iterate> tag having two required attributes: var and items.

## Using the Iteration Tag

Using the iteration tag is also straightforward, with the same usage pattern as the JSTL <forEach> tag:

```
<%@ taglib uri="/WEB-INF/tlds/ch07.tld" prefix="ch07" %>
Countries :
<ul>
<ch07:iterate var="country" collection="${countries}">
  <li>${country.name}
</ch07:iterate>
</ul>
```

The tag handler places each object in the collection into page scope (under the name supplied by the var attribute); the JSP page uses a simple EL expression to access that object on the page.

Before the introduction of JSTL, this was the only way that iteration functionality could be implemented without resorting to Java code on the page. Consequently, fewer and fewer developers will need to use the functionality provided by the IterationTag interface, although for completeness we've included it here. Most of the time, you will probably be able to use the JSTL iterator to accomplish what you need. However, at times you may need the additional flexibility that building your own tag can provide. With this in mind, don't forget that it's easier to achieve the same functionality with the SimpleTag interface. You saw an example of this with the <list> tag in the previous chapter, in which the doTag() method repeatedly invoked the body content in the same way as you've just seen with the <iterate> tag. Additionally, this technique is useful if, for some reason, you can't work with a container that supports JSP 2.0 or greater.

The final topic that you will look at in this chapter is body tags, a concept that takes iteration tags one step further by allowing precise control over what actually gets written back to the page.

# Body Tags

So far, you've seen that classic tags can evaluate their body content zero, or one or more, times. This is particularly useful when the content to be evaluated is trivial or, in other words, when no transformation or manipulation of the content is required before it's output to the page. If such transformation is required prior to the content being written to the page, you must turn to the BodyTag interface.

## The BodyTag Interface

The BodyTag interface (see Listing 7-13) further extends the IterationTag interface to add even more flexibility and capability.

**Listing 7-13.** *BodyTag.java*

```
package javax.servlet.jsp.tagext;
import javax.servlet.jsp.JspException;
public interface BodyTag extends IterationTag {
  public final static int EVAL_BODY_BUFFERED = 2;
  void setBodyContent(BodyContent b);
  void doInitBody() throws JspException;
}
```

Once again, this interface adds another new constant and two methods that are related to the body content of the tag in question. As you might expect, this means a slightly different life cycle for body tags.

## The Body Tag Life Cycle

Figure 7-7 summarizes the tag life cycle.

### Setting the Context

As with all of the other classic tags, first the contextual information (the PageContext and parent Tag) is passed to the tag handler instance.

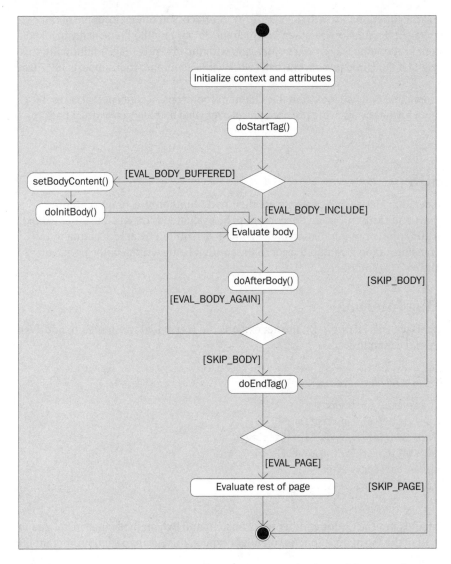

**Figure 7-7.** *The life cycle of a tag handler that implements the BodyTag interface*

## The Start Tag

After the context has been set, the doStartTag() method is called, and with the BodyTag inter-face there are three different return values.

As before, the doStartTag() method can return SKIP_BODY, meaning that the body content is ignored and processing proceeds to the doEndTag() method, or it can return EVAL_BODY_INCLUDE, signaling that the body content should be evaluated and included in the page.

The difference is that the doStartTag() method can now return the EVAL_BODY_BUFFERED constant defined in the BodyTag interface. Returning this value indicates to the JSP container that you want to use the features provided by the BodyTag interface—specifically, that the tag handler will manipulate the body content.

### Setting the Body Content

Assuming that you return EVAL_BODY_BUFFERED from the doStartTag() method to indicate that you want to manipulate the body content, the setBodyContent() method is called on the tag handler so that the tag can hold on to the BodyContent reference and use it later. As you may remember from the previous chapter, simple tags have a similar method called setJspBody() that passes a JspFragment instance representing the actual body of the tag. With the BodyTag interface, this process is slightly different. Instead of being passed a JspFragment representing the body content that can subsequently be invoked, the tag handler is passed an object of type BodyContent.

Throughout our look at classic tags, generating content was simply a matter of finding the JspWriter instance associated with the page and outputting the content. The BodyContent class is a subclass of JspWriter and can be thought of as a temporary scratch-pad area to which content can be written. Behind the scenes, when the JSP container calls the setBodyContent() method, the regular output stream (the JspWriter) is swapped out for a BodyContent object—the same one that gets passed to the tag. This means that any content output from this point onward (until the end tag is reached) is actually written into this temporary scratch pad and not to the page.

The JSP container then calls the doInitBody() method, which can be used to set up any state before the body content is eventually evaluated. The effect of replacing the original JspWriter is that when evaluated, any content between the start and end tags is also written into the BodyContent object, providing you with a way to access the generated content and manipulate it later.

### After the Body

As with the IterationTag interface, the doAfterBody() method is called after the body content has been evaluated. There are no changes here; the method should return EVAL_BODY_AGAIN or SKIP_BODY to signal whether more evaluations of the body content are required.

### The End Tag

Finally, regardless of whether or not the body was evaluated and reevaluated multiple times, the doEndTag() method is called in the same way as the other tags you've seen in this chapter. Again, possible return values are EVAL_PAGE and SKIP_PAGE.

At this point in the life cycle, all of the body content has been evaluated and output into the BodyContent object (the temporary scratch pad). With this in mind, you can now take this content and manipulate/transform it. When you're done, you can then write the final result to the original JspWriter instance.

## The BodyTagSupport Class

Because the functionality associated with the BodyTag interface is slightly different from that provided by the other classic tag interfaces, another convenient base class, BodyTagSupport, has been provided for you to use as a starting point when building body tags. Talking about the BodyTag interface makes it sound fairly complex, so let's see it in action.

# Filtering Content

Imagine that you're building a web-based mailing list or forum, a great example of which can be found at http://saloon.javaranch.com. One of the features that many of these types of forums offer is the ability to hide e-mail addresses from users so that potential spammers can't obtain this information. This facility, a piece of presentation logic, is undoubtedly useful not only for this project, but also perhaps for other web applications that you may build in the future. Therefore, let's wrap it up as a custom tag.

## Building the Filter Tag Handler

Listing 7-14 shows the EmailAddressFilterTag, which extends the BodyTagSupport class.

**Listing 7-14.** *EmailAddressFilterTag.java*

```java
package com.apress.projsp;

import java.io.IOException;
import java.util.regex.Matcher;
import java.util.regex.Pattern;
import javax.servlet.jsp.JspException;
import javax.servlet.jsp.JspTagException;
import javax.servlet.jsp.tagext.BodyTagSupport;

public class EmailAddressFilterTag extends BodyTagSupport {
  public int doEndTag() throws JspException {
    if (bodyContent != null) {
      try {
        String content = bodyContent.getString();
        content = filter(content);
        // now clear the original body content and write back
        // the filtered content
        bodyContent.clearBody();
        bodyContent.print(content);
        // finally, write the contents of the BodyContent object back to the
        // original JspWriter (out) instance
        bodyContent.writeOut(getPreviousOut());
      } catch (IOException ioe) {
        throw new JspTagException(ioe.getMessage());
      }
    }
    return EVAL_PAGE;
  }

  private String filter(String s) {
```

```
    Pattern p = Pattern.compile("@[A-Za-z0-9_.]+\\.[A-Za-z]{2,}");
    Matcher m = p.matcher(s);
    return m.replaceAll("@...");
  }
}
```

Because you want to filter the body content of the tag, it makes sense to wait until that body content has been evaluated before you look at it. Therefore, you'll leave the processing until the doEndTag() method is called. This way, the JSP container will have already evaluated the tag's body content.

The doEndTag() method checks that the body content object isn't null. This is an important step because using this tag with an empty body content will cause the container to skip the call to setBodyContent().

Next, the method uses the BodyContent object to get a copy of its contents as a string. After it obtains the body content as a string, it then calls a private helper method to filter out all the e-mail addresses.

With the content filtered, the method deletes (clears) the original body content and puts the filtered copy in its place.

To ensure that the filtered copy actually gets output to the page, you must not forget to write out the contents of the BodyContent object (the temporary scratch-pad area) back to the page. This is possible because when the BodyContent instance is created, it's provided with a reference to the original (enclosing) JspWriter.

---

■**Caution** Neglecting to write the contents of the BodyContent object back to the enclosing writer will result in it being lost as soon as the object goes out of scope.

---

You can see that the doEndTag() method uses a method named getPreviousOut(). The getPreviousOut() method is just a convenience method supplied by the BodyTagSupport class for getBodyContent().getEnclosingWriter().

As far as the filter() method is concerned, you're just using the new regular expressions functionality that is a part of version 1.4 of the JDK. The Pattern class is used to represent a compiled regular expression, and the Matcher class is used to perform searches and replacements for that pattern on a particular string.

## Describing the Filter Tag

Once again, although you've learned some new tag handler concepts from this example, the actual description of the tag is pretty much same as before. Listing 7-15 shows the new entries in the ch07.tld file for this tag. In fact, because this tag has no attributes, its definition is fairly short.

**Listing 7-15.** *ch07.tld*

```
<?xml version="1.0" encoding="UTF-8" ?>
<taglib xmlns="http://java.sun.com/xml/ns/javaee"
        xmlns:xsi="http://www.w3.org/2001/XMLSchema-instance"
```

```
          xsi:schemaLocation=➡
"http://java.sun.com/xml/ns/javaee/web-jsptaglibrary_2_1.xsd"
          version="2.1">

... the description of the tag library ...
... the description of the datetime tag ...
... the description of the select tag ...
... the description of the iterate tag ...

<tag>
  <name>emailAddressFilter</name>
  <tag-class>
    com.apress.projsp.EmailAddressFilterTag
  </tag-class>
  <body-content>scriptless</body-content>
  <description>
    Filters out the domain from e-mail addresses.
  </description>
</tag>
</taglib>
```

## Using the Filter Tag

Using the tag is straightforward, and because the body content of the tag is defined to be scriptless, it provides a great deal of flexibility in the way that it can be used. For example, you can include EL expressions to generate content, which in turn are filtered by the tag. The following code snippet shows how you would use the filter tag in a JSP page to hide users' real e-mail addresses and help prevent spammers from obtaining such information:

```
<%@ taglib uri="/WEB-INF/tlds/ch07.tld" prefix="ch07" %>
<table>
<ch07:emailAddressFilter>
  <tr>
    <td><h1>${subject}</h1></td>
  </tr>
  <tr>
    <td><b>From : </b>${name} (${emailAddress})</td>
  </tr>
  <tr>
    <td>${message}</td>
  </tr>
  <tr>
    <td><br><br><input type="submit" value="Reply"></td>
  </tr>
</ch07:emailAddressFilter>
<table>
```

Assuming that the relevant information is accessible through the preceding EL expressions, the result of requesting the page would be similar to that shown in Figure 7-8. As is, the filter tag is useful for filtering only e-mail addresses of the form name@domain. Note that you could probably make this tag more generic. If you found that you were developing other filters for other kinds of patterns, you might consider passing the filter pattern as an attribute to the tag handler.

**Figure 7-8.** *Tag handlers that implement the BodyTag interface can be used to process the body of a custom tag.*

As you can see from the HTML code, the e-mail address has been completely filtered by the tag:

```
<table>
  <tr>
    <td><h1>Help with custom tags needed</h1></td>
  </tr>
  <tr>
    <td><b>From : </b>Simon Brown (simon@...)</td>
  </tr>
  <tr>
    <td>
      This is my first message to the mailing list - can anybody
      help me understand how custom tags work, please?
    </td>
  </tr>
  <tr>
    <td><br><br><input type="submit" value="Reply"></td>
  </tr>
  <table>
```

The BodyTag interface provides a powerful way to transform and manipulate body content before it is finally sent to the JSP page and ultimately the user. In this example, you specified a body content of scriptless for the tag, meaning that the content was evaluated in the typical way by the container.

## Tag-Dependent Body Content

The other body content type supported by the JSP 2.1 specification is called tagdependent. Here, any content between the start and end tags is completely ignored (that is, it isn't processed) by the JSP container, and it's up to the custom tag to do something with it. For example, changing the body content of your <emailAddressFilter> tag to tagdependent yields the result shown in Figure 7-9.

**Figure 7-9.** *When the body content of the tag is tagdependent, processing of the body must be performed by the tag handler, not by the JSP implementation page.*

The JSP container simply doesn't process any expressions, custom tags, or Java code, leaving the body content exactly as is. So why is tagdependent body content useful?

One possible use of a custom tag that uses tagdependent body content is a tag that provides a way to emulate another programming language. Using tagdependent body content, you could write code in this other programming language between the start and end tags, and then use the BodyTag interface to extract it and execute it in some way. When the code has been run (perhaps through an external interpreter), the body content could be cleared of the code and the results inserted instead.

# Summary

After covering simple tags in the previous chapter, we moved on to discuss the traditional methods for building custom tags, now called classic tags, in this chapter. The key differences between classic and simple tags are the interface that tag handlers must implement and the life cycle requirements around tag handler pooling and reuse. The complexity associated with these two differences is the primary reason simple tags were introduced into the JSP specification.

We started our tour of classic tags by examining the Tag interface and the associated tag life cycle, and we presented a simple example to provide a direct comparison between a classic tag and a simple tag. Next, we covered how to customize classic tags with attributes by implementing a <select> tag that generated an HTML select control from a list of items. Then we showed the inherent problems in building such tags and introduced the DynamicAttributes interface as a way to help solve such problems. In essence, the DynamicAttributes interface allows fine-grained customizations to be made to tags in which the set of attributes is not fully known at development time.

The next topic was the IterationTag interface, which provides a way to evaluate and reevaluate body content repeatedly. This functionality is easily achievable with simple tags, although at times slightly more flexibility may be required—for example, when iterating over a tree-like structure.

Finally, we discussed one of the most powerful features of custom tags: the BodyTag interface. This interface allows the body content of a tag to be evaluated and then subsequently modified, transformed, and manipulated. You put these concepts into practice in the <emailAddressFilter> tag example, which illustrated how you can achieve postprocessing of body content.

The previous chapter and this chapter have provided a fairly comprehensive look at the facilities provided by the JSP specification for building custom tags, and you should now be able to build many of the tags that you might need for your own web applications. To wrap up our coverage of custom tags, the next chapter presents some of the more advanced features and best practices that will help make your tags even more powerful.

# CHAPTER 8

■■■

# Custom Tag Advanced Features and Best Practices

**N**ow that you understand the basics of building custom tags, it's time to wrap up your understanding by looking at more-advanced features and best practices.

As some of the examples in the previous chapters have shown, it's possible for custom tags to place objects into the various scopes so that those objects can be used elsewhere in the page with an EL expression. Before the introduction of the EL, such functionality was achieved by tags introducing JSP scripting variables into the page, and this is the first topic that we'll cover in this chapter. Although developers no longer see introducing JSP scripting variables into the page as the best way, this method is still possible—and often useful—if you need to use Java code on the page, perhaps to integrate with some existing components or for maintenance reasons.

We'll then move on to show how both simple and classic tags can cooperate on the page. This is an important use of custom tags and one that allows tags to be more flexible in the way that they're used on the page. As you'll see, this use of tags can increase page readability.

Next, we'll introduce validation, specifically how to implement the logic to validate that a tag's attributes are being used correctly. This is an often-overlooked topic, but it's important for anybody who is building tags that will be reused on many other web applications.

After this, we'll show how exceptions can be handled with custom tags. Again, this is a topic that is often overlooked but provides a way to build much more reliable and resilient tags.

Having covered how to build tags, we'll then turn our focus to deployment and how tag libraries can be packaged for reuse. In particular, we'll show how to package a tag library and all of its constituent components as a single JAR file that can be easily distributed and reused by others. Then we'll discuss why it's important to test custom tags, and we'll cover the new tools available to help automate this process.

To wrap up our custom tag coverage, we'll discuss some of the softer aspects around building custom tags. We'll examine what makes a good tag, some guidelines on naming tags, and some common usage patterns.

## Introducing Scripting Variables into the Page

In the previous examples, you've seen that it's possible for custom tags to place objects into one of the various scopes (`request`, `page`, `session`, or `application`) so that those objects can subsequently be used elsewhere in the page or within the tag's body content. For example, in the `<list>` tag from Chapter 6, we placed the name of each file into the page scope so that the filename could be used with an EL expression within the body content of the tag. Here is the line of code from Chapter 6 that performed that task:

```
getJspContext().setAttribute("filename", filename);
```

The `PageContext` class has always been available to custom tags, so this mechanism of placing information into one of the available scopes was available in previous versions of the JSP specification. However, before the introduction of the JSP EL, one of the biggest problems associated with using these objects was that you had to access them with Java code on the page. Taking the same example again, instead of an EL expression such as `${filename}`, the name of the file would have traditionally been accessed with a request-time expression such as the following:

```
<%= pageContext.findAttribute("filename") %>.
```

To provide a simpler way of accessing information from within a JSP page, it's possible for custom tags to introduce scripting variables back into the page, meaning that the variable can be accessed directly rather than through the `PageContext` class. For example, if the `<list>` tag introduced a scripting variable into the page to represent the filename, that value could be accessed by using a simple expression such as `<%= filename %>`. Invoking the custom tag would lead to the creation of a Java scripting variable on the page.

This is a tried and tested method for allowing custom tags to introduce information (in this case, Java objects) into the JSP page, but it brings with it some consequences. The first consequence is that the information is most easily accessible on the page by using Java scriptlets and expressions, and a downside to this is that it can make the page difficult to read, particularly because of the verbose syntax. In addition, having Java scripting variables ready to use on the page tends to encourage people to use more and more Java code on their JSP pages. As we've mentioned before, this is now seen as a bad practice because it not only reduces the maintainability of the page, but also tends to encourage copy-and-paste–style reuse.

To support backward compatibility with older versions of the JSP specification, this method of introducing scripting variables into the page is still possible. Therefore, for completeness, let's take a quick look at how to do this. Also, this technique is useful if you find yourself working on previous versions of the JSP specification or if you need to integrate with other pages/components that require Java variables to be available on the page.

There are two methods for placing scripting variables into the JSP page. The first is to provide the definitions of those variables within the TLD file (declaratively). The second is achieved by using a `TagExtraInfo` class (programmatically).

## Defining Variables in the TLD File

Behind the scenes, the process of introducing scripting variables into the JSP page is fairly straightforward. All you need to do is place an object in one of the available scopes (`request`, `page`, `session`, or `application`) and then indicate to the JSP container that you'd like to be able to access this as a scripting variable. Then, when the tag is invoked, the JSP container finds your object and automatically declares a scripting variable for you.

So how do you indicate to the JSP container that it should create a variable? Well, the easiest way is to place this information in the TLD file. Let's look at an example.

## Building the Cookie Tag Handler

In this section, you'll build a custom tag that looks up a named cookie and makes it available as a scripting variable. Let's look first at the tag handler, which is shown in Listing 8-1. In this case, you'll extend the classic TagSupport class because this makes it easier to gain access to some of the HTTP-specific classes that you need to access cookies.

---

**■Note** Remember, the Tag interface relies on features provided by the Java Servlet API, unlike the SimpleTag interface, which relies only on the JSP API.

---

**Listing 8-1.** *CookieTag.java*

```java
package com.apress.projsp;

import javax.servlet.http.Cookie;
import javax.servlet.http.HttpServletRequest;
import javax.servlet.jsp.JspException;
import javax.servlet.jsp.tagext.TagSupport;

public class CookieTag extends TagSupport {
  private String name;
  public void setName(String s) {
    this.name = s;
  }
  public int doStartTag() throws JspException {
    // find the current cookies
    HttpServletRequest request;
    request = (HttpServletRequest)pageContext.getRequest();
    Cookie cookies[] = request.getCookies();
    // now try to find the named cookie
    Cookie cookie = getCookie(cookies, name);
    if (cookie != null) {
      // the cookie was found so evaluate the body content
      pageContext.setAttribute(id, cookie);
      return EVAL_BODY_INCLUDE;
    } else {
      // the cookie wasn't found so skip the body content
      return SKIP_BODY;
    }
  }
  private Cookie getCookie(Cookie cookies[], String name) {
    if (cookies != null) {
      for (int i = 0; i < cookies.length; i++) {
        if (cookies[i].getName().equals(name)) {
          return cookies[i];
```

```
        }
      }
    }
    // we got this far so the specified cookie wasn't found
    return null;
  }
}
```

This tag will have two attributes: id and name. You use the id attribute to specify the name of the scripting variable on the page, and you use the name attribute to specify the name of the cookie that you'd like to look up. Another benefit of using the TagSupport class in this example rather than the SimpleTagSupport class is that the instance variable and setter method for the id attribute are already provided. Traditionally, the id attribute has been used to specify the name of scripting variables on the page and, because it used to be such a common requirement, the id attribute has been implemented for us in the TagSupport class.

Next, you have the processing associated with this tag. Essentially, all this does is look up the named cookie with a private helper method. If the cookie is found, the Cookie object is placed into page scope under the name supplied by the id attribute. The body content of the tag is then evaluated. If the cookie isn't found, the body content is simply skipped. This is yet another example of how tags can programmatically evaluate their body content.

Note that you don't mention anything about scripting variables—the object that you'd like to access as a scripting variable is just placed into page scope.

## Describing the Cookie Tag

Now you must describe the tag in the TLD file. The TLD file in Listing 8-2 indicates to the JSP container that you'd like a scripting variable with which to access your object.

**Listing 8-2.** *ch08.tld*

```xml
<?xml version="1.0" encoding="UTF-8" ?>
<taglib xmlns="http://java.sun.com/xml/ns/javaee"
        xmlns:xsi="http://www.w3.org/2001/XMLSchema-instance"
        xsi:schemaLocation= ➡
          "http://java.sun.com/xml/ns/javaee/web-jsptaglibrary_2_1.xsd"
        version="2.1">
  <description>
    Tag library for Professional JSP 2.1, chapter 8.
  </description>
  <jsp-version>2.1</jsp-version>
  <tlib-version>1.0</tlib-version>
  <short-name>ch08</short-name>
  <uri>http://www.apress.com/projsp</uri>
  <tag>
    <name>cookie</name>
    <tag-class>com.apress.projsp.CookieTag</tag-class>
    <body-content>JSP</body-content>
    <description>
```

```
      Looks up a named cookie and makes it
      available as a scripting variable.
    </description>
    <variable>
      <name-from-attribute>id</name-from-attribute>
      <variable-class>javax.servlet.http.Cookie</variable-class>
      <declare>true</declare>
      <scope>NESTED</scope>
    </variable>
    <attribute>
      <name>id</name>
      <required>true</required>
      <rtexprvalue>false</rtexprvalue>
    </attribute>
    <attribute>
      <name>name</name>
      <required>true</required>
      <rtexprvalue>false</rtexprvalue>
    </attribute>
  </tag>
</taglib>
```

There are two points to note about this otherwise normal tag description. First, the body content of the tag has been set to JSP. This means that any JSP content (tags, scriptlets, and so on) can appear within the body content of the tag. If scriptless were used instead, a page-translation error would occur if you attempted to use Java scriptlets or expressions.

The second difference is that you've added a new variable element to the tag description, and this is where the scripting variable is defined. In a similar way to defining attributes, this section allows you to define the name and type of the variable, along with some other information.

When you're defining the name of a scripting variable in a TLD file, you can use two tags. The first of these is <name-given>, which allows you to statically define the name of the scripting variable. As a result, the scripting variable will be accessible through the same name on every page where that tag is used. The drawback to this approach is that the name you statically define may clash with existing variables on the page, causing a page-translation error to occur. The other option you have is to use the <name-from-attribute> tag, as shown in this example. Instead of statically defining the name of the variable, you tell the JSP container to use the value of the named attribute. In this example, you're telling the JSP container that the scripting variable should be given the name provided by the id attribute.

Next is the <variable-class> element. This is just the fully qualified class name of the scripting variable. Because you're introducing a cookie into the page, the class name is javax.servlet.http.Cookie, a class from the Servlet API.

Finally, you have two elements that are related to how the variable is used on the page. You can decide whether a new variable should be declared on the page with the <declare> element. If you specify true (the default value), a new variable is automatically created. If you choose false, the JSP container assumes that a variable has already been declared for it to use. Subsequently, if that variable hasn't been previously declared on the page, a compilation error will occur when the JSP page is translated into a Java servlet.

Following this is the `<scope>` element, which can have one of the following values:

- AT_BEGIN
- NESTED (the default value)
- AT_END

The `<scope>` element allows you to define where on the page the scripting variable will be accessible. The three possible values mean from the start tag until the end of the page, between the start and end tags, and anywhere from the end tag until the end of the page, respectively. For this example, you want the variable accessible only between the start and end tags, so you choose NESTED.

### Using the Cookie Tag

As with the other examples, using the tag is then just a matter of importing the tag library and using the correct prefix:

```
<%@ taglib uri="/WEB-INF/tlds/ch08.tld" prefix="ch08" %>
<ch08:cookie id="myCookie" name="lastVisited">
  You last visited this website on <%= myCookie.getValue() %>
</ch08:cookie>
```

At request time, this JSP snippet looks for a cookie called lastVisited. If it finds lastVisited, the Cookie object is made available as a scripting variable called myCookie within the body content of the tag, and the body content is then evaluated. If the cookie can't be found, the body content is skipped. As this example demonstrates, this type of functionality is useful for providing customized pages to the users of your web application, and it's another way that custom tags can help you build JSP-based web applications.

## Defining Variables in a TagExtraInfo Class

The other method for declaring scripting variables in the page is programmatically, by using a TagExtraInfo class. This was the original JSP 1.1 method by which variables were introduced into the page, and it allows for an additional level of flexibility in the way that variables are defined. Although the `<variable>` element in the TLD file allows you to be flexible in the name you give to the scripting variable, it doesn't provide a way to specify the type of that variable to be defined at page creation time; instead, it allows you only to statically define the type within the TLD file.

Consider the `<iterate>` tag example from Chapter 7. You might like a scripting variable available to access each element of the collection over which you're iterating, as shown in the following JSP snippet:

```
<%@ taglib uri="/WEB-INF/tlds/ch08.tld" prefix="ch08" %>
Countries :
<ul>
<ch08:iterate id="country" type="com.apress.projsp.domain.Country"
  items="${countries}">
  <li><%= country.getName() %>
</ch08:iterate>
</ul>
```

There are several differences between this code and the code for the <iterate> tag that you built in the previous chapter, and the way in which that tag was used on the page. First, you now have an id attribute through which to specify the name of the scripting variable. Second, you have a new attribute called type that is used to specify the fully qualified class name of the objects within the collection. Within the body content, you can then access each item in the collection through Java code, perhaps with an expression or inside a scriptlet. So, how do you implement this type of functionality, where the variable type is declared on the page instead of within the TLD file?

## Building the Iterate Tag

As before, you have the tag handler class (see Listing 8-3) that extends the TagSupport class. In fact, this is almost identical to the version you saw in the previous chapter, except that you have id and type attributes.

**Listing 8-3.** *IteratorTag.java*

```java
package com.apress.projsp;
import java.util.Collection;
import java.util.Iterator;
import javax.servlet.jsp.JspException;
import javax.servlet.jsp.tagext.TagSupport;
public class IteratorTag extends TagSupport {
  private String type;
  private Collection items;
  private Iterator iterator;

  public void setType(String s) {
    this.type = s;
  }
  public void setItems(Collection coll) {
    this.items = coll;
  }
  public int doStartTag() throws JspException {
    // set up the iterator to be used
    iterator = items.iterator();
    if (iterator.hasNext()) {
      // if there are elements, put the first one into page
      // scope under the name provided by the "id" attribute
      pageContext.setAttribute(id, iterator.next());
      // and include the body
      return EVAL_BODY_INCLUDE;
    } else {
      // there are no elements so skip the body
      return SKIP_BODY;
    }
  }
  public int doAfterBody() throws JspException {
```

```
      if (iterator.hasNext()) {
        // if there are more elements, put the next one into page
        // scope under the name provided by the "id" attribute
        pageContext.setAttribute(id, iterator.next());
        // and instruct the JSP engine to reevaluate the body of this tag
        return EVAL_BODY_AGAIN;
      } else {
        // there are no more elements so skip the body
        return SKIP_BODY;
      }
    }
  }
}
```

## Building the Iterate TagExtraInfo Class

This is where things are slightly different from the <iterate> tag in the previous chapter. You need to additionally write a class that extends the TagExtraInfo class. This class, shown in Listing 8-4, will provide information about the variable being exposed to the JSP page.

**Listing 8-4.** *IteratorTagExtraInfo.java*

```
package com.apress.projsp;
import javax.servlet.jsp.tagext.TagData;
import javax.servlet.jsp.tagext.TagExtraInfo;
import javax.servlet.jsp.tagext.VariableInfo;
public class IteratorTagExtraInfo extends TagExtraInfo {

  public VariableInfo[] getVariableInfo(TagData data) {
    return new VariableInfo[] {
      new VariableInfo(
        data.getId(),
        data.getAttributeString("type"),
        true,
        VariableInfo.NESTED)
    };
  }
}
```

Here you're implementing a single method called getVariableInfo(), which is called by the JSP container to obtain information about the variables that your tag wishes to make accessible. A TagData object is passed to this method, and this is just a translation-time view of the tag's usage on the page, specifically including information about its attributes.

To signal to the JSP container that you'd like a scripting variable accessible on the page, you return an array of VariableInfo objects containing one VariableInfo object for each scripting variable that you'd like. The API provided by the TagData class provides you with a method to look up the values of a tag's attributes and, using this method, you can easily find out the name and type of the scripting variable that you want to introduce into the page.

The VariableInfo class constructor takes four parameters. These parameters map to the subelements of the <variable> element within the TLD file: name (name-given or name-from-attribute), variable-class, declare, and scope. In this example, the name is being set as the value of the id attribute (available through the convenient getId() method on the TagData class), the variable class is being set as the value of the type attribute, and the other properties are being statically defined as before.

## Describing the Tag

Whereas in the previous example you defined the variables within the TLD file, all you need to do here is tell the JSP container that you wish to use a TagExtraInfo (TEI) class. This is specified in a similar way to the tag handler class, as shown in Listing 8-5.

**Listing 8-5.** *ch08.tld*

```xml
<?xml version="1.0" encoding="UTF-8" ?>
<taglib xmlns="http://java.sun.com/xml/ns/javaee"
        xmlns:xsi="http://www.w3.org/2001/XMLSchema-instance"
        xsi:schemaLocation= ➥
          "http://java.sun.com/xml/ns/javaee/web-jsptaglibrary_2_1.xsd"
        version="2.1">

    ... the description of the tag library ...
    ... the description of the cookie tag ...
    <tag>
      <name>iterate</name>
      <tag-class>com.apress.projsp.IteratorTag</tag-class>
      <tei-class>
        com.apress.projsp.IteratorTagExtraInfo
      </tei-class>
      <body-content>JSP</body-content>
      <description>
        Iterates over a specified java.util.Collection instance.
      </description>
      <attribute>
        <name>id</name>
        <required>true</required>
        <rtexprvalue>false</rtexprvalue>
      </attribute>
      <attribute>
        <name>type</name>
        <required>true</required>
        <rtexprvalue>false</rtexprvalue>
      </attribute>
      <attribute>
        <name>items</name>
        <required>true</required>
```

```
          <rtexprvalue>true</rtexprvalue>
        </attribute>
      </tag>
</taglib>
```

### Using the Iterate Tag

As you've seen already, using the tag is then a matter of setting the values for the id and type attributes before you can use the new scripting variable within the body content of the tag:

```
<%@ taglib uri="/WEB-INF/tlds/ch08.tld" prefix="ch08" %>
Countries :
<ul>
<ch08:iterate id="country" type="com.apress.projsp.domain.Country"
  items="${countries}">
  <li><%= country.getName() %>
</ch08:iterate>
</ul>
```

Both implementation techniques shown here for introducing scripting variables into the page are useful for previous versions of the JSP specification and for when you really do need to have a scripting variable declared in the page. However, as you've seen in previous chapters, it's much better to use a simple EL expression and not introduce scripting variables into the page. After all, allowing people to use Java code in one page tends to encourage them to use it elsewhere, and before you know it you have a mass of unmaintainable Java code sitting inside your JSP pages.

---

**Tip** We recommend you use the JSP EL when you can or, failing that, the JSTL with its expression language.

---

# Cooperating Tags

Until now, the examples we've presented have all been tags that work on their own to achieve a specific goal. However, custom tags don't have to work in isolation—they can cooperate with one another, either by sharing information or by directly accessing methods/fields on other tag handlers that are being used on the page. These are useful techniques and, as you'll see, they allow you to make your tags more generic and therefore more reusable.

## Cooperating by Sharing Information

The most common way that custom tags cooperate is by sharing information, which is typically implemented by using one of the available scopes (request, page, session, or application) as a shared resource in which information can be placed and retrieved later. There are generally two ways that this can happen.

In the first method, a tag places an object in one of the available scopes, and then the name of that object is passed to another tag as an attribute. A good example of this in practice is the `<jsp:useBean>` tags that you saw in Chapter 1. To demonstrate this, you'll use a simple JavaBean called `Forum` that has `id` and `name` properties:

```
<jsp:useBean id="forum"
  class="com.apress.projsp.domain.Forum" scope="page">
  <jsp:setProperty name="forum" property="id" value="1"/>
  <jsp:setProperty name="forum" property="name" value="Servlets"/>
</jsp:useBean>
```

Here, the `<jsp:useBean>` tag is setting up a page-scoped variable called `forum`, and the name of this object is being passed to the `<jsp:setProperty>` tags so that they can find the object for themselves. To achieve this type of functionality within your own tags, you need to use the `setAttribute()` and `getAttribute()` methods on the `JspContext` and `PageContext` classes for simple tags and classic tags, respectively. Essentially, information is being shared in a specific scope, under a name that is well known to both tags.

With the introduction of the JSP EL, the second way that tags commonly share information is through EL expressions. Let's again look at an example, this time from the JSTL:

```
<c:forEach var="forum" items="${forums}">
  <c:out value="${forum.name}"/>
</c:forEach>
```

Here, assuming that a collection of `Forum` JavaBeans is accessible with the EL expression `${forums}`, this small snippet provides iteration over that collection and displays the name of each forum. You're using the `<c:out>` tag to actually write out the information, and this information is being specified by another EL expression. Although behind the scenes a `Forum` bean is being placed into page scope upon each iteration, instead of simply passing the name of the object, you're now using an EL expression to pass the actual information that the tag needs to perform its processing. In this case, the processing is to output the specified information.

Although these two techniques differ slightly, they're very useful and commonly used in sharing information between custom tags, therefore allowing them to cooperate to achieve a common goal. However, sometimes a little more flexibility is required in that the child (nested) tags should pass information on to their parents. In this situation, you can use a tag's ability to directly access its parent tag or tags.

## Cooperating by Accessing Other Tag Handlers

Something that happens early in the tag life cycle is that a tag is passed a reference to its closest enclosing parent via the `setParent()` method on the tag handler class. Using this reference to a `JspTag` or a `Tag` on a simple or classic tag, respectively, you can directly access the parent tag handler instance and directly call methods on it. So, why is this useful?

In the previous example of how tags can cooperate on the page, you saw that it's easy for a parent tag to pass an object to its child tags, effectively using one of the available scopes as a shared area. However, a side effect of this technique is that unless the information is removed from the scope when it's finished, that information is readily available to other tags on the page. Although this generally isn't a problem, having all this information lying around could interfere with other parts of the page—or worse, the application—making debugging more difficult.

Another situation in which sharing information isn't appropriate is when you'd like to use nested tags to configure the characteristics of the enclosing parent tag. If you look back to the

<select> tag example in Chapter 7, you can see that you were able to configure it through the use of dynamic attributes, meaning you could customize the HTML select control that was eventually generated. One of the ways that you can customize the select control is to add a JavaScript event handler that forwards the user to another page when an item in the list is selected—this is something that is done on websites, such as JavaRanch, that allow users to easily navigate between the many forums. Because these event handlers are implemented as attributes on the generated HTML tag, forwarding the user to another page is fairly easy to achieve with the dynamic attributes version of the <select> tag from the previous chapter:

```
<ch07:selectWithDynamicAttributes
  name="forum" label="name" value="id" items="${forums}">
  <jsp:attribute name="onChange">
    window.location=('view-forum.jsp&forumId='
                     + this.options[this.selectedIndex].value)
  </jsp:attribute>
</ch07:selectWithDynamicAttributes>
```

Remembering that attributes can be specified by using the <jsp:attribute> tag, in essence all you're doing is specifying an attribute called onChange, the value of which is the JavaScript code that you'd like executed when an item in the list is selected. Although this works, imagine that you'd like to build a custom tag to explicitly specify this information instead, the usage of which would be as follows:

```
<ch08:select name="forum" label="name" value="id" items="${forums}">
  <ch08:eventHandler name="onChange">
    window.location=('view-forum.jsp&forumId='
                     + this.options[this.selectedIndex].value)
  </ch08:eventHandler>
</ch08:select>
```

The benefit of adopting this sort of approach is twofold. First, it provides a standard and natural way to add event handlers to the generated HTML tag. Having a specific <eventHandler> tag is more readable than having a generic <jsp:attribute> tag. Second, it provides a way to ensure that the JavaScript code doesn't get interpreted in any way by the JSP compiler; you can specify the body content of the <eventHandler> tag as tagdependent. For this to work, the <eventHandler> tag will take the body content (the JavaScript code) and pass it directly to the enclosing <select> tag. The <select> tag can then use this information when generating the underlying HTML.

## Building the Tag Handlers

The first step is to build the tag handlers, and you'll start with the <select> tag. This time you'll implement the <select> tag as a simple tag and the <eventHandler> tag as a classic tag. The reason for this is so that you can see how to perform cooperation between a simple and a classic tag.

Starting with the <select> tag (Listing 8-6), the implementation is pretty much the same as before in that you have four instance variables and their setter methods to support the four attributes you need.

**Listing 8-6.** *SelectTag.java*

```java
package com.apress.projsp;

import java.beans.PropertyDescriptor;
import java.io.IOException;
import java.util.*;
import javax.servlet.jsp.*;
import javax.servlet.jsp.tagext.SimpleTagSupport;

public class SelectTag extends SimpleTagSupport {
  private String name;
  private String label;
  private String value;
  private Collection items;
  private HashMap eventHandlers;

  public SelectTag() {
    this.eventHandlers = new HashMap();
  }
  public void setName(String s) {
    this.name = s;
  }
  public void setLabel(String s) {
    this.label = s;
  }
  public void setValue(String s) {
    this.value = s;
  }
  public void setItems(Collection coll) {
    this.items= coll;
  }
  public void doTag() throws JspException, IOException {
    try {
      // first of all we must evaluate the body content
      if (getJspBody() != null) {
          getJspBody().invoke(getJspContext().getOut());
      }
      JspWriter out = getJspContext().getOut();
      // write the starting tag of the select control
      out.print("<select name=\"");
      out.print(name);
      out.print("\"");
      // and now write out any event handlers
      Iterator it = eventHandlers.keySet().iterator();
      String eventHandlerName;
      while (it.hasNext()) {
```

```java
        eventHandlerName = (String)it.next();
        out.print(" ");
        out.print(eventHandlerName);
        out.print("=\"");
        out.print(eventHandlers.get(eventHandlerName));
        out.print("\"");
      }
      out.print(">");
      it = items.iterator();
      while (it.hasNext()) {
        // get the next JavaBean from the collection
        Object o = it.next();

        // and use it to create a description of the property used
        // to represent the displayable label
        PropertyDescriptor labelPD =
          new PropertyDescriptor(label, o.getClass());
        // and the property used to represent the hidden value
        PropertyDescriptor valuePD =
          new PropertyDescriptor(value, o.getClass());
        // and now generate the HTML
        out.print("<option value=\"");
        // call the accessor method for the value property
        // (this is the same as calling get<PropertyName>() on
        // the JavaBean instance)
        out.print(
          valuePD.getReadMethod().invoke(o, new Object[] {}).toString());
        out.print("\">");
        // and do the same for the label property
        out.print(
          labelPD.getReadMethod().invoke(o, new Object[] {}).toString());
        out.print("</option>");
      }
      // write the ending tag of the select control
      out.print("</select>");
    } catch (Exception e) {
      e.printStackTrace();
      throw new JspTagException(e.getMessage());
    }
  }
  public void addEventHandler(String name, String code) {
    eventHandlers.put(name, code);
  }
}
```

The class has a HashMap to contain the event handlers for the generated tag. The HashMap is initialized within the public no-arguments constructor, which is called when the tag handler instance is created. Because event handlers on HTML controls are just name=value pairs, you can store the event handler information easily in a map.

The processing associated with the tag occurs in the doTag() method. All that additionally happens in this version is that before any processing occurs, the body content of the tag is invoked. This is necessary because it allows the child tags to be processed, and these child tags provide the invoked tag with the information on any event handlers that should be included in the generated HTML. After this has been done, the class generates the HTML as before, including the list of event handlers.

So, how do child tags actually pass information about event handlers to this tag? The class implements a public method that they can call, named addEventHandler(String, String), which places the information into the HashMap the tag handler maintains.

With the code for the <select> tag written, it's time to turn to the <eventHandler> tag (Listing 8-7). Because you'd like the body content for this tag to be tagdependent, you'll use the BodyTagSupport class as a starting point. Having tagdependent body content is possible with simple tags, although getting hold of the content is easier to achieve with body tags.

**Listing 8-7.** *EventHandlerTag.java*

```
package com.apress.projsp;
import javax.servlet.jsp.JspException;
import javax.servlet.jsp.tagext.BodyTagSupport;
import javax.servlet.jsp.tagext.TagAdapter;
public class EventHandlerTag extends BodyTagSupport {
  private String name;
  public void setName(String s) {
    this.name = s;
  }
  public int doEndTag() throws JspException {
    if (bodyContent != null) {
      // get the body content (the JavaScript code)
      String content = bodyContent.getString();
      // now find the parent tag
      SelectTag tag = (SelectTag)((TagAdapter)getParent()).getAdaptee();
      // and add the event handler to the select tag
      if (tag != null) {
        tag.addEventHandler(name, content);
      }
    }
    return EVAL_PAGE;
  }
}
```

With this tag you have a single attribute called name, and this attribute is used to represent the name of the event handler.

As with the other body tags that you've seen, the processing associated with this tag takes place in the doEndTag() method, because this allows you to gain access to the body content. Here, with the body content representing the JavaScript code for the event handler, all that you need to do is get that body content, find the parent tag, and pass the information by using the public method that you defined in the SelectTag class.

One of the reasons for choosing to show cooperation between simple and classic tags is that it's not as straightforward as cooperation between tags of the same type. If you're solely using simple tags, the getParent() method will return an object of type JspTag—the superclass of all tag interfaces. However, with classic tags, historically the getParent() method returns an object of type Tag, and this has been maintained for backward compatibility. In this example, the outer tag is a simple tag (of type SimpleTag), and the inner tag is a classic tag (of type BodyTag).

An object implementing the SimpleTag interface can't be cast to the Tag interface, and therefore the JSP container provides an adapter class called TagAdapter that wraps up a SimpleTag and makes it look like a Tag. Behind the scenes, it's this object that's passed to the setParent() method on your EventHandlerTag, which is why you need to do some additional processing to extract a reference to the enclosing tag handler instance. Basically, it all comes down to providing backward compatibility for existing classic tags while making them fully interoperable with the newer simple tags.

An alternative way to find a specific parent tag is with the findAncestorWithClass() method provided by the SimpleTagSupport and TagSupport classes. This method provides a way to automatically search through all of the parent tag handler instances until it finds an instance that implements a specific interface.  For example, you could use the following line of code to locate the parent SelectTag class:

```
SelectTag tag = (SelectTag)findAncestorWithClass(this, SelectTag.class);
```

This line says, "Starting from this tag handler, look at each parent in the tree in turn until you find one that is of type SelectTag." This will even work if you're mixing tag types and the actual tag handler is wrapped up inside the TagAdapter class behind the scenes.

Another benefit is that you can search for parent tags that implement a specific Java interface, making it possible to allow the implementation of cooperating tags to be substituted, provided that they implement the same interface. A good example is that the SelectTag class could implement an interface that allows event handlers to be added. The <eventHandler> tag can then look for a parent implementing this interface, which gives you the flexibility to use the <eventHandler> tag nested inside other event-handler–capable tags and to substitute the implementation of the <select> tag if necessary.

## Describing the Tags

Next, you must describe both tags in a TLD file (Listing 8-8). The <select> tag is the same as before—it has scriptless body content and the four required attributes. The <eventHandler> tag, on the other hand, has tagdependent body content and a single, required attribute called name.

**Listing 8-8.** *ch08.tld*

```
<?xml version="1.0" encoding="UTF-8" ?>
<taglib xmlns="http://java.sun.com/xml/ns/javaee"
        xmlns:xsi="http://www.w3.org/2001/XMLSchema-instance"
        xsi:schemaLocation= ➡
          "http://java.sun.com/xml/ns/javaee/web-jsptaglibrary_2_1.xsd"
```

```
      version="2.1">

... the description of the tag library ...
... the description of the <cookie> tag ...
... the description of the <iterate> tag ...
  <tag>
    <name>select</name>
    <tag-class>com.apress.projsp.SelectTag</tag-class>
    <body-content>scriptless</body-content>
    <description>
      Creates an HTML select control
      based upon a collection of objects.
    </description>
    <attribute>
      <name>name</name>
      <required>true</required>
      <rtexprvalue>false</rtexprvalue>
    </attribute>
    <attribute>
      <name>label</name>
      <required>true</required>
      <rtexprvalue>false</rtexprvalue>
    </attribute>
    <attribute>
      <name>value</name>
      <required>true</required>
      <rtexprvalue>false</rtexprvalue>
    </attribute>
    <attribute>
      <name>items</name>
      <required>true</required>
      <rtexprvalue>true</rtexprvalue>
    </attribute>
  </tag>
<tag>
  <name>eventHandler</name>
  <tag-class>com.apress.projsp.EventHandlerTag</tag-class>
  <body-content>tagdependent</body-content>
  <description>
    Used to represent a JavaScript event handler.
  </description>
  <attribute>
    <name>name</name>
    <required>true</required>
    <rtexprvalue>false</rtexprvalue>
  </attribute>
</tag>
</taglib>
```

### Using the Tags

As you've already seen, using the tags is simply a matter of nesting one inside the other:

```
<%@ taglib uri="/WEB-INF/tlds/ch08.tld" prefix="ch08" %>
Forums :
<ch08:select name="forum" label="name" value="id" items="${forums}">
  <ch08:eventHandler name="onChange">
    window.location=('view-forum.jsp&forumId='
                     + this.options[this.selectedIndex].value)
  </ch08:eventHandler>
</ch08:select>
```

If you then look at the generated HTML, you can see how the event handler has been implemented on the control:

```
<select name="forum" onChange="window.location=('view-forum.jsp& ➥
forumId='+this.options[this.selectedIndex].value)"><option value="1"> ➥
Servlets</option><option value="2">JSP</option><option value="3"> ➥
EJB</option><option value="4">JMS</option></select>
```

As we mentioned at the start of this example, having a dedicated tag with which to specify event handlers can help make the JSP page more readable and provide you with a way to ensure that the JavaScript code doesn't get mistaken for JSP code. However, you might be wondering whether the additional development overhead of this example provides any substantial, tangible benefit over using the dynamic attributes version that you built in the previous chapter. To answer this question, let's look at how you can put some validation around the use of tag attributes.

# Tag Validation

Having built custom tags, you're now probably aware that the JSP container does, in fact, perform some rudimentary validation of the way that custom tags are used on the page. For example, it checks that you've specified the start and end tags correctly, that the body content matches up with that defined in the TLD file, and that you've specified any required attributes for your tags. The failure of any of these checks results in a page-translation error.

This is useful in ensuring that, at a basic level, the tags are used properly on the page, but it would be nice if you could go a step further and check the actual values of attributes. This way, you could detect problems up front if attributes were being misused, perhaps because a value was out of your desired range. Thankfully, the JSP specification provides two mechanisms to perform validation: the TagLibraryValidator and TagExtraInfo classes.

## Validation with a TagLibraryValidator Class

The TagLibraryValidator (TLV) class was introduced in version 1.2 of the JSP specification. It provides an extremely flexible method to perform validation. Behind the scenes, when a JSP page is being translated into a servlet, an intermediate version of the page is generated that is represented as a pure XML document. This document is useful because it provides a standard way for JSP containers to parse, process, and validate the JSP page. In essence, in the XML view of the page, all the elements of the JSP page (content, directives, actions, scriptlets, and so on) are converted and represented as XML tags. When using the TLV class, it's possible to get a reference to this document and validate anything on the page. This could include anything from checking that the values of tag attributes are acceptable to looking at the structure of the page and determining whether your tags have been used correctly (perhaps checking that they've been nested in the right way).

Unfortunately, this flexibility comes at a price in that TLV classes are fairly complicated to build because they require a fair amount of XML knowledge. Therefore, they aren't often used, and the TagExtraInfo class is favored.

# Validation with a TagExtraInfo Class

TagExtraInfo (TEI) classes are inherently much simpler to use than TLV classes, but of course they don't offer anywhere near as much flexibility, with the main function of TEI classes being to validate tag attributes. However, for those developers who need to implement such validation logic, a TEI class is usually sufficient.

Implementing a TEI class is fairly straightforward, although the process has changed slightly from previous versions of the JSP specification. Before JSP 2.0, the validation logic would be implemented within a method called isValid(), returning true if valid and false otherwise. Although this was simple to implement, it couldn't provide anybody with information should a particular tag not be valid. Of course, a System.out.println() statement can be used to output error details to the console, but this is hardly a desirable solution.

For this reason, JSP 2.0 introduced similar functionality to that provided by the much more complex TagLibraryValidator class with a method called validate(). Instead of returning true or false, JSP 2.0 and JSP 2.1 allow an array of ValidationMessage instances to be returned to the JSP container that details exactly what the problem is. Let's put this into practice with an example.

## Building the TagExtraInfo Class

For this example, imagine that you'd like to add some validation to the <eventHandler> tag to check that the value of the name attribute (the name of the JavaScript event handler) is valid. To do this, you can define a list of the permitted names and compare the value of the name attribute to this list. Listing 8-9 shows a class that does this and then can be used to validate the <eventHandler> tag.

**Listing 8-9.** *EventHandlerTagExtraInfo.java*

```
package com.apress.projsp;
import java.util.ArrayList;
import java.util.List;
import javax.servlet.jsp.tagext.*;
public class EventHandlerTagExtraInfo extends TagExtraInfo {
  private static List EVENT_HANDLERS = new ArrayList();
  static {
    // here is a list of the valid event handlers for the select tag
    EVENT_HANDLERS.add("onblur");
    EVENT_HANDLERS.add("onchange");
```

```
      EVENT_HANDLERS.add("onclick");
      EVENT_HANDLERS.add("ondblclick");
      EVENT_HANDLERS.add("onfocus");
      EVENT_HANDLERS.add("onkeydown");
      EVENT_HANDLERS.add("onkeypress");

      EVENT_HANDLERS.add("onkeyup");
      EVENT_HANDLERS.add("onmousedown");
      EVENT_HANDLERS.add("onmousemove");
      EVENT_HANDLERS.add("onmouseout");
      EVENT_HANDLERS.add("onmouseover");
      EVENT_HANDLERS.add("onmouseup");
    }
  public ValidationMessage[] validate(TagData data) {
    String name = data.getAttributeString("name");
    // validate that the name is valid
    if (!EVENT_HANDLERS.contains(name.toLowerCase())) {
      return new ValidationMessage[]{
        new ValidationMessage(null, "Event handler called " +
                              name + " not valid")
      };
    } else {
      return null;
    }
  }
}
```

Now all the validate() method has to do is find the value of the name attribute through the API provided by the TagData class and compare it with the list of valid values. The TagData class itself is just a translation-time view onto the way the tag has been used on the page; this view allows the values of a tag's attributes to be obtained.

---

■Note  Because TagData is a view of the tag's attributes at page-translation time, it isn't possible to get the values of those attributes that are request-time expressions because the page hasn't yet been requested—it's still in the process of being translated into a Java servlet.

---

If the value of the name attribute is in the list of permitted values, we chose to return a null value from the validate() method, indicating that the attributes are valid. The specification also allows a zero length array to be returned if the attributes are valid. The TEI class is used by the JSP container, so the choice of whether to return a null or a zero-length array is mostly a matter of personal preference. There is no inherent advantage in one choice over the other. An array containing a ValidationMessage instance is returned to indicate that something is wrong.

## Describing the Tag

Now that you've built the TEI class, you must tell the JSP container that you want to use it. To do this, you define the TEI class within the description of the tag in the TLD file (see Listing 8-10).

**Listing 8-10.** *ch08.tld*

```xml
<?xml version="1.0" encoding="UTF-8" ?>
<taglib xmlns="http://java.sun.com/xml/ns/javaee"
        xmlns:xsi="http://www.w3.org/2001/XMLSchema-instance"
        xsi:schemaLocation= ➥
          "http://java.sun.com/xml/ns/javaee/web-jsptaglibrary_2_1.xsd"
        version="2.1">

  ... the description of the tag library ...
  ... the description of the <cookie> tag ...
  ... the description of the <iterate> tag ...
  ... the description of the <select> tag ...
  <tag>
    <name>eventHandler</name>
    <tag-class>com.apress.projsp.EventHandlerTag</tag-class>
    <tei-class>
      com.apress.projsp.EventHandlerTagExtraInfo
    </tei-class>
    <body-content>tagdependent</body-content>
    <description>
      Used to represent a JavaScript event handler.
    </description>
    <attribute>
      <name>name</name>
      <required>true</required>
      <rtexprvalue>false</rtexprvalue>
    </attribute>
  </tag>
</taglib>
```

As with the name of the tag handler class, the name of the TEI class must be a fully qualified class name.

## Using the Tags

With the TEI class in place, you can use the tags in the same way as before. At page-translation time, the information about a tag's attributes is passed to the TEI class so that the validation can happen. The way in which JSP containers present error messages varies among vendors, but with Tomcat 5, the error in Figure 8-1 is shown if you try to set the value of the name attribute of the <eventHandler> tag to onDoubleClick.

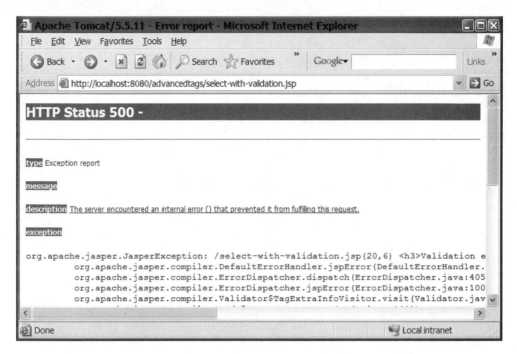

**Figure 8-1.** *This error page is returned by Tomcat when the container detects a validation error with the use of the EventHandlerTag. The full error message is "org.apache.jasper.JasperException: /select-with-validation.jsp(20,6) <h3>Validation error messages from TagExtraInfo for ch08:eventHandlerValidate</h3><p>Event handler called onDoubleClick not valid</p>".*

As this example shows, validating the values of attributes is a useful way to ensure that your tags are used correctly. More important, validating the values helps guarantee that the generated HTML is error-free. After all, picking up these sorts of errors is easier to do up front during the JSP translation process at deployment rather than at request time, when users start to complain that the pages of your application don't seem to work correctly.

With the usage of the tags now more resilient, let's see how you can make the tags themselves more robust in the way that they handle exceptions.

# Handling Exceptions

Because custom tags have full access to the rich set of APIs provided by Java, it's possible that something could go wrong. For example, a network connection might be unexpectedly terminated, or perhaps a file read could fail. Typically, you'd just wrap functionality that may potentially fail inside a `try-catch` block, and with simple tags this isn't much of a problem because all the processing associated with the tag is wrapped up within the `doTag()` method. However, when you're using classic tags, this logic can potentially be split across the `doStartTag()`

method, the tag's body content, and the doEndTag() method. Therefore, it's not possible to place a try-catch block around all of this logic. The JSP specification addresses this issue through the TryCatchFinally interface that classic tag handlers can implement.

# The TryCatchFinally Interface

The TryCatchFinally interface was introduced in the JSP 1.2 specification. This interface provides a way to gracefully handle exceptions that may occur during the processing of classic tags, regardless of whether the tag implements the Tag, IterationTag, or BodyTag interface (see Listing 8-11).

**Listing 8-11.** *TryCatchFinally.java*

```
package javax.servlet.jsp.tagext;
import javax.servlet.jsp.*;
public interface TryCatchFinally {
  void doCatch(Throwable t) throws Throwable;
  void doFinally();
}
```

The TryCatchFinally interface has two methods, doCatch() and doFinally(), in which you can place functionality that might typically be written into catch and finally blocks. For example, in the doCatch() method, you might choose to roll back a transaction, and in the doFinally() method, you might choose to close a file or a connection to a remote resource. In essence, tags should implement this interface if you want them to have more control over exception handling. Figure 8-2 shows a UML diagram of the tag life cycle for a tag that implements the TryCatchFinally interface. Next, we'll cover each of the methods in turn.

## The doCatch() Method

The JSP specification guarantees that the doCatch() method will be called if an exception is thrown in the doStartTag() method, the tag's body content, or the doEndTag() method. Additionally, if the tag handler implements the IterationTag or BodyTag interface, the doCatch() method will be executed if an exception is thrown within the doAfterBody() and doInitBody() methods, respectively.

Something to notice is that the doCatch() method won't be called if an exception is thrown before the execution of the doStartTag() method—perhaps when the context or attributes are being set. Therefore, it's best not to put any logic into attribute setter methods that may cause an exception to be thrown.

If the exception should be propagated further up the calling stack, perhaps by a JSP error page, the doCatch() method can handle the exception as required and then subsequently rethrow the same or a new exception. This is useful because there's no way to tell the tag handler class to catch only specific subclasses of Exception in the same way you would when writing try-catch blocks in your code. Instead, the doCatch() method handles all exceptions, and it's up to us as tag developers to decide which to handle and which to rethrow.

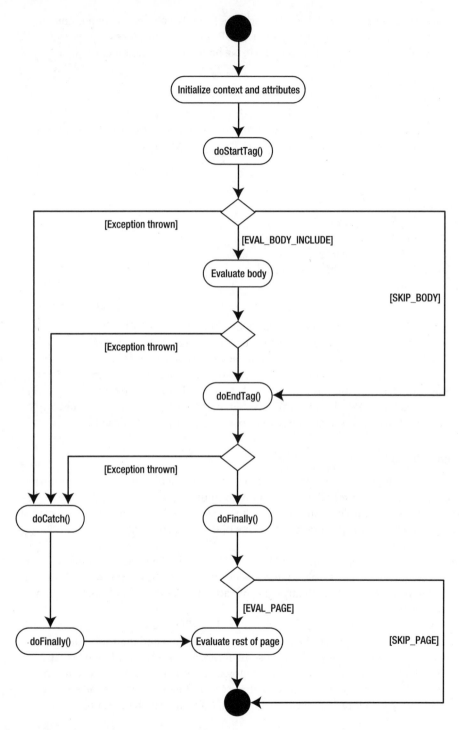

**Figure 8-2.** *During the tag life cycle, there are several opportunities where doCatch() or doFinally() might be called to handle an exception.*

### The doFinally() Method

When you write `try-catch-finally` blocks in regular Java code, the `finally` block always gets called, regardless of whether an exception was thrown. Similarly, the `doFinally()` method on the tag handler will always get called.

Although tag handlers are generally small components, there is still much that can go wrong, especially when you're dealing with databases and remote objects such as Enterprise JavaBeans. Implementing the `TryCatchFinally` interface is a way to build tags that are better equipped to deal with such problems; it will make your tag libraries more robust and resilient to failure. With this in mind, let's now take a look at how you can deploy these resilient tags and make them available for use in the easiest possible way.

# Tag Library Deployment

Tag libraries can be deployed and used within web applications in several ways. The examples that you've seen until this point have all used one of these methods that focuses on deploying tag libraries within a development environment. There is, however, a much better way of deploying tag libraries that allows you to package all of your tag resources into a single JAR file. Before we cover how to do this packaging, we'll briefly recap the former method of deployment.

## Deploying a Tag Library for Development

Assuming that the tag handler classes have been written and compiled, the first step is to ensure that the class files for the tag handlers in the tag library are in the CLASSPATH of your web application. In other words, the class files should reside in the `WEB-INF\classes` directory of your web application or, if you've placed your class files within a JAR file, this JAR file has been copied into the `WEB-INF\lib` directory of your web application. If your tag handlers reference any other classes that you or a third party has written, don't forget that these classes must also be present in one of these two places.

As you've seen in the previous examples, the next step is to place the TLD file within the web-application directory structure. By convention, the JSP specification suggests that all TLD files be placed within the `WEB-INF\tlds` directory, and although this isn't mandatory, placing all TLD files there provides a central place for people to find them at a later date.

Importing the tag library is then simply a matter of using the `taglib` directive. This allows you to specify the tag library that you want to import and the prefix with which to reference the tags within that tag library. As an example, you used the following directive in Chapter 6 to import the tags within the tag library that you built:

```
<%@ taglib uri="/WEB-INF/tlds/ch06.tld" prefix="ch06" %>
```

The `uri` attribute of the `taglib` directive explicitly specifies the location of the TLD representing the tag library that you'd like to use, and the prefix dictates how that tag library will be used and identified on the page.

As we've said before, this method of deploying tag libraries is mainly used when deploying custom tags within a development environment. This approach allows you to save the TLD file straight into the web-application directory structure, underneath the `WEB-INF` directory, and to explicitly specify the tag library from within the JSP page. In an agile development environment, the build-deploy-test cycles are generally very short, and this is one reason this mechanism for deploying tags is often adopted—it's very quick and lightweight.

However, a drawback to this method is that it makes tag libraries harder to reuse. You have to copy all the tag handler and dependent classes along with the TLD file into a new web-application structure and place them in the correct directories. Although this procedure isn't complicated, individual files could easily get lost. What happens when new versions of the tags are available? Also, you haven't considered reusing tag files that simply reside underneath the WEB-INF\tags directory.

Thankfully, the JSP specification addresses these issues by providing an alternative mechanism for packaging and deploying tag libraries containing all types of tags.

## Deploying a Tag Library for Reuse

The key to achieving reuse with tag libraries, as with many other Java technologies, is the JAR file. Packaging a tag library for reuse requires creating a JAR file that contains the following items:

- The (compiled) tag handler classes, along with any dependent classes you've created

- The TLD file that describes the tag library

As with other JAR files, the classes must be stored within the JAR file, with the directory structure mirroring the package structure maintained. As for the TLD file, this must reside inside the JAR file in a directory called META-INF. The only requirement here is that the TLD file must have a file extension of .tld so the JSP container can find it.

---

■**Note** A requirement of previous versions of the JSP specification was that the TLD file would have to be called taglib.tld. This requirement has since been lifted. In fact, it's possible to place more than one TLD file in the META-INF directory for distributing more than one tag library in the same JAR file.

---

### Creating the JAR File

Creating the JAR file is a fairly simple process that can be achieved with the regular jar command-line tool or via a build tool such as Jakarta Ant. To learn how you might create such a JAR file to contain a tag library, you'll take the examples from Chapter 6 and package them.

First, create an empty directory. In this directory, place the class files that are required for the tag library, and don't forget to maintain the directory structure representing the packages to which these classes belong. Next, create a META-INF directory and place the TLD file inside it. Figure 8-3 shows the directory structure for the tags from Chapter 6.

**Figure 8-3.** *The directory structure of a tag distribution*

At a command prompt, change to the directory that you created to contain the classes and TLD file and run the `jar` command as follows:

```
jar cvf ch06.jar .
```

Using the current location as a starting point, this creates a JAR file that includes everything in the appropriate structure. To check that this was successful, run the following command to list the contents of the JAR file:

```
jar tf ch06.jar
```

Figure 8-4 shows the output of this command. This screen shot shows that the tag handler class files are located within the appropriate directory structure and that the TLD file resides in the META-INF directory.

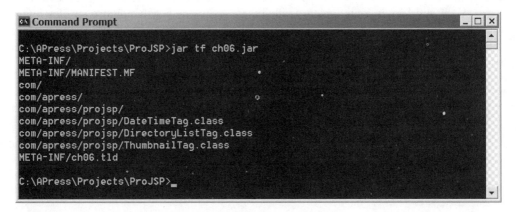

**Figure 8-4.** *One method to check the contents of a Java ARchive is to use the jar command with the t option. This lists the contents to the screen.*

## Deploying the Tag Library

With the JAR file built, the final step in deploying the tag library contained within is to copy the JAR file into the WEB-INF\lib directory of your web application.

## Using the Tag Library

Use of the tag library is made possible with the `taglib` directive. However, rather than explicitly specifying the location of the TLD file representing the tag library, specify the URI (the unique identifier for the tag library) that you defined in the TLD. In this example, the tag library can be used on the page with the following `taglib` directive:

```
<%@ taglib uri="http://www.apress.com/projsp/ch06" prefix="ch06" %>
```

Notice that the URI you're using is the same as the one you defined for the tag library in the TLD file. From a usage perspective, because you've specified the same prefix, the tags within the imported tag library can be used in the same way as before.

---

■**Tip** Remember, the URI is just a unique identifier for the tag library—it doesn't have to represent a valid resource on the Internet.

---

## Packaging Tag Files

This method works because the custom tags in the tag library are described by using a tag library descriptor file, something that you don't have to do for tag files. However, the packaging mechanism does allow for tag files to be deployed alongside simple and classic tags by providing a way for them to be described in the TLD too.

To do this, the first step is to ensure that the tag files will be included in the correct place within the JAR file structure. The JSP specification states that tag files must reside underneath the `META-INF` directory, in a subdirectory called `tags`. In Chapter 6, you built two tag files: one to generate a copyright statement and another to generate a template for an HTML box that can be used to highlight areas of importance on the page. Figure 8-5 shows the directory structure of the JAR file with the tag file directories.

**Figure 8-5.** *When packaging tag files as part of tag library, the tag files must be located in the META-INF\tags directory.*

Next, you must define the tag files within the TLD file. This is made possible by using the `<tag-file>` element. Listing 8-12 shows a `<tag-file>` element for the tag files from Chapter 6.

**Listing 8-12.** *ch06.tld*

```xml
<?xml version="1.0" encoding="UTF-8" ?>
<taglib xmlns="http://java.sun.com/xml/ns/javaee"
        xmlns:xsi="http://www.w3.org/2001/XMLSchema-instance"
        xsi:schemaLocation= ➥
          "http://java.sun.com/xml/ns/javaee/web-jsptaglibrary_2_1.xsd"
        version="2.1">

  ... the description of the tag library ...
  ... the description of the <datetime> tag ...
  ... the description of the <thumbnail> tag ...
  ... the description of the <list> tag ...
  <tag-file>
    <name>box</name>
    <path>/META-INF/tags/box.tag</path>
  </tag-file>
  <tag-file>
    <name>copyright</name>
    <path>/META-INF/tags/copyright.tag</path>
  </tag-file>
</taglib>
```

Two subelements to the `<tag-file>` element, `name` and `path`, represent the name of the tag as it will be used on the page and the path to the corresponding tag file in the JAR file, respectively. After the JAR file has been generated and deployed, the tag library can be used in the same way as before—just import the tag library and use the tags within it.

There are many benefits to adopting this approach to deploying tag libraries, but the primary benefit is that it makes deployment and reuse of tag libraries easy. Another benefit relates to technology independence. With the ability to define a mixture of tag files, simple tags, and classic tags within a tag library, the end users of that tag library will never know how those tags are actually implemented. This means that should you need to reimplement a tag by using a different technology in the future, this is no problem. Essentially, custom tags provide a nice abstraction to reusable Java components.

# Best Practices

To wrap up this chapter's look at custom tags, we'll briefly cover some of the best practices that have emerged over the past few years.

## Common Usage Patterns and Granularity

Custom tags have access to the full range of APIs that are provided by the Java Standard Edition and Java Enterprise Edition platforms. This means that they can pretty much wrap and provide any functionality for use on JSP pages, from generating content and providing iteration to reading files and accessing remote data sources. However, just because you can provide this type of functionality doesn't necessarily mean that you should. One of the key things to remember when you design custom tags is your audience. Who will be using the tags? Generally, there are two user extremes, although most people tend to fit somewhere in between.

At one extreme are web designers (or page authors). These people are responsible for the look and feel of a web application. As part of their role, they're much more concerned with the creative aspects of the JSP pages than the mechanics behind how the pages work. At the other extreme are developers, who are more focused on providing functionality than on how the web application looks. This split of responsibility may not be as clear-cut on many of your own projects, but the principles are worth bearing in mind.

Typically, the skill sets of these two types of people will be dramatically different. One has expert knowledge in web design and markup, and the other has expert knowledge of how a web application works from a technical perspective. This is why it's important to consider your audience when you design custom tags and to work with that audience to ensure that your custom tags meet the audience's needs.

When programming, we as developers are typically used to building up high-level functionality from a series of low-level constructs. For example, to iterate over a collection we might choose to use a `for` loop. Within the `for` loop, we might use the `counter` variable to find a specific item in the collection. Although this may seem basic to us, it won't to web designers; therefore, they won't want to see such logic on JSP pages. The point is that custom tags should be fairly granular in nature. In other words, to achieve a specific goal you shouldn't have to use many custom tags in cooperation with one another. A good example is providing iteration over an array. Before the introduction of the JSTL, many people would build two custom tags to implement iteration functionality—one tag to loop and one tag to get the next item in the collection, as follows:

```
<prefix:for from="0" to="10">
  <prefix:getBean id="myBean" array="${myBeans}"/>
  ... content to be displayed on each iteration ...
</prefix:for>
```

From a developer's perspective this makes sense, but from a page author's perspective it doesn't. In summary, keep the tags as simple as possible and don't try to simply replicate programming constructs.

## Naming

On a related note, the name you give to a tag or its attributes can also affect how that tag is perceived by others. Using overly technical language for naming these items can cause confusion. For example, the tag that provides iteration in the JSTL is called `<forEach>`, and the list of items that it iterates over is called `items` instead of collection, list, or array. Once again, keep your audience in mind when describing your tags—if you're wrapping up technology-focused functionality such as accessing databases or using XML, then generally these tags are going to be used only by technologists anyway. Giving tags simple, appropriate names is a great way to make JSP pages readable and maintainable.

Another point related to naming is giving cooperating tags an appropriate name that reflects their intent. For example, you built a specific <eventHandler> tag to specify event handlers for the <select> tag. Although passing this information to the <select> tag is possible with dynamic attributes, a side effect is that the readability of the page suffers. The key is to make tags and using those tags seem natural, and you can help by providing good names for tags and making them easy to use together, in cooperation.

## What Makes a Good Tag Library?

Finally, let's address the question of what makes a good tag library. A useful comparison to make is between tags and other development disciplines such as object orientation (OO) and component-based development (CBD). A common goal in these disciplines is reuse. With OO, you aim to get reuse at the class level, and with CBD, you aim to get reuse at the component level. Mapping this back to custom tags, you can see that you'd like to get reuse at the tag level. With OO and CBD, a good class or component is one that has high cohesion and low coupling. In other words, the class contains highly related functionality and doesn't depend too much on other classes/components.

You can go one step further and look for reuse at the package level or, with custom tags, at the tag library level. Ideally, you'd like to be able to take a tag library and reuse it as-is on other web applications in the future.

So, coming back to the question of what makes a good tag library, essentially it's the same aspects of achieving reuse at the package level with OO and CBD. The tags within a tag library should form a highly cohesive collection of functionality that's loosely coupled to other tag libraries. You'd like to take a tag library and reuse it elsewhere without having dependencies on other libraries. In this way, your initial goals to increase the readability, reusability, and maintainability of JSP development are all achieved.

# Summary

In this final chapter on custom tags, you looked at some of the more advanced custom tag features. First, you learned how custom tags can introduce scripting variables into the page. This is something that has always been possible in previous versions of the JSP specification, and in essence nothing has changed. However, with the introduction of the JSP EL, you should see scripting variables being used within JSP pages less and less, meaning that these techniques should also be used less frequently by people writing new tags. After all, the JSP EL provides a much better, cleaner way to access information from within a JSP page.

Next, you examined how tags can cooperate with one another on the page. You learned that this is possible through a couple of methods: one in which information is shared between the tags, and one in which child (nested) tags look up their parent and directly access the corresponding tag handler instance. Both methods are widely implemented and allow custom tags to be more flexible in the way that they're used on the page. Also, these methods provide a way for more-generic tags to be created that can be used in cooperation with different tags to achieve different goals.

Then you looked at how more-resilient tags can be built by using techniques that allow a tag's attributes to be validated. This is an often-overlooked part of tag development, although it provides an easy way to ensure that your tags are used in the way that is expected and therefore work in the way that is expected. After this, you took a brief look at the TryCatchFinally interface, which allows you to make your tags more resilient to failure. This is particularly important if you're working with files and network connections, for example.

With our look at developing tags over, we then focused on how tag libraries can be deployed in both development environments and specifically for reuse. We described how it's possible to mix tag files, simple tags, and classic tags into a single tag library that is distributable and deployable as a single JAR file. Also, we covered the importance of testing custom tags and the options available to automate this process.

Finally, we discussed some of the important best practices relating to developing custom tags, particularly with respect to how tags are used on the page and how the audience can make a difference in how your tags are perceived. To wrap up, we showed what makes a good tag library and how this can help you achieve the original goals we outlined when we started presenting custom tags as a technology—that is, increased readability, reusability, and maintainability.

■ ■ ■

# Data Access Options for Web Applications

**N**ow that you have a full understanding of web applications, JSP, and servlets, it's time to start discussing how these technologies fit together in a JSP application. No matter what type of JSP application you're writing, you'll need to either store the data that is created by your application or use data from an external source in your application. You need **data access**. There are many options for data access from a JSP application including file storage, object-oriented databases, XML databases, and relational databases. In almost all cases, a relational database is the best choice.

For simple applications intended for small-scale use on a single-instance application server, you might choose to store your data in files. However, if you want to scale your application up to meet the needs of a large number of users, then you'll need to distribute application processing across multiple servers. All Java EE application servers make this easy and transparent to you, the application programmer, but you need to store your data in a location that is accessible to all of your servers. Unfortunately, file system storage isn't the best way to do this.

For more complex larger-scale applications, you should use a database, but what type of database should you choose? Although object-oriented and XML databases might be appealing to some developers, most IT managers prefer to use tried-and-true relational database technology. Relational database technology is preferred because it's ubiquitous, well understood, standardized, and supported by a tremendous number of tools and applications.

In this chapter, we'll discuss five Java database access options, several JSP database access architectures, and an example of a JSP database application. By the end of this chapter you should have enough knowledge to evaluate and select a database access technology, design database access architecture, and implement database access for your JSP application.

This chapter assumes that you have knowledge of Java, JavaBeans, JSP, JDBC, SQL, and relational database technology.

## Data Access Technologies

Database access has been part of Java since Sun Microsystems added the JDBC API as an add-on to Java 1.0. Since then, Sun has also added Enterprise JavaBeans (EJBs) and most recently Java Data Objects (JDO) to Java. That isn't all; Sun is only one of the many organizations supporting database access from Java. Numerous vendors have sprung up over the years to provide JDBC implementations and Object-Relational Mapping (O/R) frameworks for Java.

The good news is that there are a lot of choices for data access. That's also the bad news. In this section, we'll sort out the choices by dividing them into five categories starting with the simplest and ending with the most sophisticated. The five data access technologies, from simplest to most sophisticated, are as follows:

- JSP tags for SQL

- JDBC

- O/R frameworks

- JDO

- EJB entity beans

When you choose a data access technology, you should consider both the nature of the web application that you're developing and the skills of your development and support teams. Generally speaking, if you have simple requirements and a less experienced team, you should favor the simple end of the spectrum. If you have more complex requirements and a more experienced team, you should favor the sophisticated side. Here are some questions to consider:

- Does your application have fairly simple database access requirements? Perhaps you need only to display a couple of reports based on information in a database. For simple applications, you might want to avoid the learning curve, complexity, and overhead of a more sophisticated data access technology.

- Will your application have a complex Java object model that must be persisted to a database? If so, you might find that you really cannot do without the sophisticated automated object-relational mapping capabilities of an O/R framework or of EJB container-managed persistence (CMP).

- Is your application one that is highly transactional, requires high availability, and is likely to support a large number of concurrent users? If so, you might need the declarative transaction support, fault tolerance, and load balancing provided by EJB servers.

- Which Java data access technologies do your developers know? What level of database knowledge do your developers have? Will you need training? If your team has previous experience with database access, that might influence your selection of a database access technology.

With these types of questions in mind, let's discuss the pros and cons of each of the five data access options, starting with the most simple.

## JavaServer Pages Tags for SQL

The JSTL, which is covered in Chapter 4, includes a set of JSP tags that allow you to access a database via SQL directly from your JSP pages.

The obvious advantage of the JSP tags for SQL is simplicity. It's easy to query the database and to throw the results up on a web page. This is great for simple applications that need only to display database data on a web page and make simple database table updates—JSP tags for SQL work well. The `<sql:query>` tag executes an SQL query and returns a result set object that you can iterate over and display with other JSTL tags. You can also perform database table updates. The `<sql:update>` tag executes an SQL update.

For larger projects, there are a couple of disadvantages to keep in mind. One disadvantage is that you must embed SQL queries with table and field names into your JSP pages. If database table and field names change, you'll have to make the corresponding changes in your JSP files. For a small project, this might not be a big problem, but larger projects should consider other data access options. Other data access options, such as O/R frameworks and EJB, can provide some level of indirection so that changes to the database schema do not have as much of an effect on your application code.

Another disadvantage is updates. The JSP tags for SQL allow you to perform updates on a database, but you have to build the SQL update string yourself. Again, for small projects with simple updating needs, this might not be a problem, but larger projects should consider other data access options. Other data access options can provide infrastructure to make updates much easier to program.

## JavaServer Pages Tags for SQL Example

Listing 9-1 is an example of JSP tags for SQL. This example illustrates how to execute a query, iterate through the results, and display the results in an HTML table.

**Listing 9-1.** *jstl-example.jsp*

```
<%@ page language="java" %>
<%@ taglib uri="/WEB-INF/c.tld" prefix="c"%>
<%@ taglib uri="/WEB-INF/sql.tld" prefix="sql"%>
<!DOCTYPE HTML PUBLIC "-//w3c//dtd html 4.0 transitional//en">
<html><head><title>jstl-example</title></head>
<body bgcolor="#ffffff">
<sql:query var="items"
  dataSource="jdbc:hsqldb:hsql://localhost,org.hsqldb.jdbcDriver,sa">
  SELECT TITLE,TIME FROM ITEM ORDER BY TIME
</sql:query>

<h1>News Items</h1>

<table border="1">
  <th>Title</th><th>Time</th>

  <c:forEach var="row" items="${items.rows}">
    <tr>
      <td><c:out value="${row.TITLE}"/></td>
      <td><c:out value="${row.TIME}"/></td>
    </tr>
  </c:forEach>
</table>
</body>
</html>
```

Figure 9-1 shows a screen shot of the page generated by the JSP page.

**Figure 9-1.** *The JSP page has accessed a database table and displayed two columns from the table.*

Let's examine the code more closely. At the top of the page, you see the two `taglib` directives:

```
<%@ taglib uri="/WEB-INF/c.tld" prefix="c"%>
<%@ taglib uri="/WEB-INF/sql.tld" prefix="sql"%>
```

The first directive declares that this example uses JSTL Core tags and the second directive declares use of the JSTL SQL tags. The corresponding TLD files, `c.tld` and `sql.tld`, must be in the example web application's `WEB-INF` directory.

The next interesting block of code is the actual query itself, shown here, and expressed using the JSTL `<sql:query>` tag:

```
<sql:query var="items"
  dataSource="jdbc:hsqldb:hsql://localhost,org.hsqldb.jdbcDriver,sa">
  SELECT TITLE,TIME FROM ITEM ORDER BY TIME
</sql:query>
```

The tag has two attributes: `var` and `dataSource`. The `var` attribute specifies the name of an object (of type `javax.servlet.jsp.jstl.sql.Result`) that will be created by the query to hold the results of the query.

The `dataSource` attribute specifies the database connection string. This is a comma-separated string with the format connection URL, the JDBC driver class name, the username, and password. In the example, the password is an empty string and can be omitted from the connection string. The `<sql:query>` tag will use these parameters to obtain a connection from the JDBC driver manager. Within the body of the `<sql:query>` tag is the SQL query string to be executed: `SELECT TITLE,TIME FROM ITEM ORDER BY TIME`.

After the query has been executed and the results are available in the `items` object, you display the HTML table by using the JSTL `<c:forEach>` tag to iterate through the rows that are contained in the `items` object:

```
<table border="1">
  <th>Title</th><th>Time</th>
  <c:forEach var="row" items="${items.rows}">
    <tr>
      <td><c:out value="${row.TITLE}"/></td>
      <td><c:out value="${row.TIME}"/></td>
    </tr>
  </c:forEach>
</table>
```

For each row of data, you use the `<c:out>` tag to display each column of data.

We presented a summary of the JSTL SQL tags in Chapter 4, and Listing 9-1 gives a brief example of how to use a few of the tags. If you want to learn more about the JSTL, you can find more information at Sun's JSTL web page (`http://java.sun.com/products/jsp/jstl/`). The Sun Web Services tutorial (`http://java.sun.com/webservices/docs/1.0/tutorial/index.html`) also covers JSTL and includes a section on the JSTL SQL tags.

## Java Database Connectivity

JDBC is a standard part of Java and provides a uniform API that can be used to access any relational database. The low-level JDBC API is the foundation for the other database access technologies discussed in this chapter, but many programmers use the JDBC API directly. If your application has fairly limited database access needs, JDBC might be all you need.

The advantages of JDBC are simplicity and flexibility. There are only about 25 classes and interfaces in JDBC, and for the most part, to use them you need to know only the basics of SQL. It's simple. You execute queries and updates written in standard SQL, and each query returns a `ResultSet` object containing the resulting rows and columns of data. The JDBC API is simple, but it still provides the flexibility to do just about anything you'll need to do with a database.

The simplicity of JDBC is also a disadvantage. If you have a lot of queries and updates to do, using JDBC can be a lot of work. You'll find yourself writing a lot of repetitive boilerplate code to build up query and update strings, iterate through the `ResultSet` objects returned by your queries, and map Java object fields to and from database table fields. In the next section, we'll discuss how using an O/R persistence framework can eliminate the repetitive boilerplate coding required by JDBC.

JDBC gives you cross-database portability, which is wonderful, but that portability isn't perfect. You still have to watch for SQL incompatibilities, data-type differences, and other problems. You still have to write a database creation script for each type of database you intend to support.

JDBC is a relatively small and easy-to-use API, but complete coverage of JDBC is really beyond the scope of this book. Several resources with information on JDBC are available; here are three:

- *Beginning Java Databases* by Kevin Mukhar, Todd Lauinger, and John Carnell (2001, Wrox Press)

- JDBC home page: http://java.sun.com/products/jdbc/

- JDBC tutorial: http://java.sun.com/docs/books/tutorial/jdbc/basics

## Obtaining a JDBC Connection in a Web Application

All of the database access technologies that are discussed in this chapter are built on the foundation laid by JDBC. So, before you can use any of them you need to understand how to configure a JDBC database connection. Let's discuss the two database connection mechanisms provided by JDBC: the java.sql.DriverManager and the javax.sql.DataSource.

### Using the java.sql.DriverManager

The java.sql.DriverManager is a standard part of JDBC and a standard part of Java available to stand-alone Java programs, JSP applications, and application server-hosted Java EE applications in general.

If you're going to use the DriverManager to obtain a database connection or if you're configuring a software package that does, you'll need to provide the following database connection parameters:

- The name of the JDBC driver class to be used

- The JDBC connection URL for your database

- Your database username-password combination

Using the DriverManager to obtain a database connection is a two-step process. First you must load your JDBC driver class by name, which causes it to become registered with the DriverManager. Second, you call the static DriverManager.getConnection() method, passing in your database connection parameters, and receiving in return a Connection ready for use. For example, the following code shows how to obtain a connection to MySQL by using the JDBC driver class org.gjt.mm.mysql.Driver:

```
Class.forName("org.gjt.mm.mysql.Driver");
Connection con = DriverManager.getConnection(
    "jdbc:mysql://localhost/ag","username","password");
```

Note that if you explicitly load the class by using Class.forName(), you need to call the forName() method only once in your program. After the driver is loaded by the JVM, it is available to any code within the JVM.

Alternately, you can provide the driver class name as a system parameter to the JVM. The system parameter name is jdbc.drivers. Thus, to tell the JVM to load the MySQL driver, you would use a command line similar to the following:

```
java -Djdbc.drivers=org.gjt.mm.mysql.Driver MyProgram
```

If you need to load multiple drivers, they can be separated by using a colon as the delimiter. When you are using this technique, your code no longer needs to call `Class.forName()`. The JVM will automatically load the driver class for you (assuming that the class is on the CLASSPATH).

However, those connection parameters are a problem. If you use the `DriverManager`, you'll have to manage those connection parameters. You know you cannot hard-code them in your Java classes or JSP pages and you cannot store them in the database, so you'll probably end up storing them in a property file. When your application is installed, somebody will have to edit that property file.

### Using a javax.sql.DataSource

The `javax.sql.DataSource` interface was introduced as part of the JDBC 2.0 Standard Extension to provide Java applications with a standard way to tap into the database connection management and connection-pooling functionality provided by Java application servers.

If you use the `javax.sql.DataSource` approach, you no longer have to manage database connection parameters in your code. Instead, you declare the names of the data sources required by your application and you expect the administrator who installs your application to set up those data sources for you in the deployment environment. Within the container, the administrator configures a data source and binds it to a name.

In your application you need to declare this data source by adding a resource reference to the application's `web.xml` file, as shown here:

```
<resource-ref>
  <res-ref-name>jdbc/agdb</res-ref-name>
  <res-type>javax.sql.DataSource</res-type>
  <res-auth>Container</res-auth>
</resource-ref>
```

After this is done, you can use the following code to look up this data source via JNDI and to obtain a database connection:

```
javax.naming.InitialContext ctx = new javax.naming.InitialContext();
javax.sql.DataSource ds =
        (javax.sql.DataSource) ctx.lookup("java:comp/env/jdbc/agdb");
Connection con = ds.getConnection();
```

Note that the lookup name is the name `jdbc/agdb` with an added prefix of `java:comp/env/`. This prefix indicates to the container that the resource is an internal resource.

### Setting Up a javax.sql.DataSource

So, how do you set up one of these data sources? That depends on your application server, and every application server is a little different. Some application servers include a web interface that allows you to set up new data sources and to administer the connection pools associated with those data sources. Other application servers require you to edit configuration files.

For example, on the Tomcat servlet container, you can use either technique. You can configure a global or application-specific data source by using Tomcat's web-based administration tool. Figure 9-2 shows the page for configuring an application-specific data source. On this web page, you enter the parameters for the JDBC driver class name, the connection URL, the JNDI name, the database URL, and the username and password for the database. After this is done, you can access the data source as shown in the preceding code snippets.

**Figure 9-2.** *Using Tomcat's web-based administration tool, you can create an application-specific data source.*

You can also create a global data source in a similar manner. Figure 9-3 shows the web page for configuring a global data source. You enter the same parameters as for an application-specific data source.

**Figure 9-3.** *Using Tomcat's web-based administration tool, you can create a global data source.*

After creating a global data source, you must configure a link from the application to the global data source. Figure 9-4 shows how to do this by using the Resource Links web page for the application. On this page, you enter the name used by your application to access the data source, and the JNDI name of the global resource. This maps the application name to the global name and allows different applications to use different names to access the global resource.

**Figure 9-4.** *Before an application can access a global data source, you must create a link to the data source for the application.*

Alternately, you can manually configure your application's data source. The configuration is stored in a file named context.xml in the application's META-INF directory. The following is the Tomcat 5.0 context entry for this chapter's example application (see "Implementing the RSS Newsreader Example" later in this chapter):

```
<Context path="/ch09" docBase="ch09" debug="0">
  <Resource name="jdbc/agdb" auth="Container" type="javax.sql.DataSource" />
  <ResourceParams name="jdbc/agdb">
    <parameter>
      <name>factory</name>
      <value>org.apache.commons.dbcp.BasicDataSourceFactory</value>
    </parameter>
    <parameter><name>username</name><value>sa</value></parameter>
    <parameter><name>password</name><value></value></parameter>
    <parameter>
      <name>driverClassName</name>
      <value>org.hsqldb.jdbcDriver</value>
    </parameter>
```

```
    <parameter>
      <name>url</name>
      <value>jdbc:hsqldb:hsql://localhost</value>
    </parameter>
  </ResourceParams>
</Context>
```

---

■**Note**  Your application server may store the database configuration files in a different location and under a different name. Check your container's documentation for information on how to configure database resources.

---

Within the `Context` element, you declare the data source as a resource named `jdbc/agdb`, and then you declare the parameters for the data source. As you can see, you specify the same parameters that you had hard-coded before into the JSP code. These include the JDBC driver class name, the database connection URL, the database username, and the corresponding password. If you need to change any of these values, you no longer have to modify the code of your application as you would when using the JDBC driver manager.

Note that before you can use JDBC, you need to ensure that your JDBC driver JAR file is in the right CLASSPATH. If you're using the JDBC driver manager to obtain your connections, you can put your JDBC driver JAR in your application's `WEB-INF\lib` directory. However, if you're using a JDBC data source, you'll need to ensure that your JDBC driver JAR is in your server's CLASSPATH. On Tomcat, this means putting your JDBC driver JAR into the `%TOMCAT_HOME%\common\lib` directory.

You can also find information on configuring data sources in Tomcat at the Apache Jakarta Tomcat websites:

- Apache Jakarta Tomcat website: `http://jakarta.apache.org/tomcat`

- Apache Jakarta Tomcat 5.5 JNDI DataSource How-To: `http://jakarta.apache.org/tomcat/tomcat-5.5-doc/jndi-datasource-examples-howto.html`

## Object/Relational Persistence Frameworks

O/R persistence frameworks make it easy to store and retrieve Java objects in a relational database. O/R frameworks come in a variety of shapes and sizes, but generally speaking, an O/R framework is a class library and a small set of development tools that support the storage and retrieval of Java objects in a relational database. The following are the main advantages of using an O/R framework over JDBC:

- **Easier to program**: With an O/R framework, you can easily store and retrieve your Java objects without writing a lot of repetitive boilerplate code to map fields to and from SQL queries.

- **Better cross-database support**: O/R frameworks make it easier for you to support different vendors' databases because the framework handles query creation and data-type mapping. Some frameworks will even generate database creation (DDL) scripts for different databases.

- **Better performance**: O/R frameworks often include database connection pooling, object caching, and other performance-enhancing features.

There are a number of ways to use an O/R framework. The authors of the open-source Hibernate O/R framework wrote about four approaches to O/R persistence. Table 9-1 describes each approach. Most of the O/R frameworks support these four approaches, so let's take a look at each one.

**Table 9-1.** *Approaches to Object-Relational Persistence in the Hibernate Framework*

| Name | Description |
|------|-------------|
| Top-down | Starting with an existing set of Java objects, you develop a mapping-specification file that describes your objects and their relationships, use tools provided by the O/R framework to generate a DDL script to create database tables to store your objects, and use the O/R frameworks API to store and retrieve your objects in the database. |
| Bottom-up | Starting with an existing database schema, you develop a mapping-specification file that describes your tables and their relationships, use tools provided by the O/R framework to generate your Java objects, and use the O/R frameworks API to store and retrieve your objects in the database. |
| Middle-out | In this approach you start by writing a mapping specification that describes your objects and their relationships, use tools provided by the O/R framework to generate both your Java objects and your DDL script, and use the O/R frameworks API to store and retrieve your objects in the database. |
| Meet-in-the-middle | Take this approach if you already have an existing set of Java objects and an existing database schema. All you have to do is write a mapping specification that maps your Java objects to your database tables, and then you're ready to use the O/R frameworks API to store and retrieve your objects in the database. |

O/R persistence frameworks are popular among Java web-application developers, and there are many choices, both commercial and open source. Popular commercial O/R frameworks include TopLink, now owned by Oracle, and CocoBase, developed by Thought Inc. Some open-source O/R frameworks are Castor, Hibernate, and Jakarta OJB.

Later in this chapter, you'll use the open-source Hibernate framework because it's well supported and well documented. This chapter will give you enough information to evaluate the strengths and weaknesses of the various other O/R frameworks for yourself.

The following are links to the websites of the O/R frameworks previously mentioned:

- Castor (open source): http://www.castor.org/

- CocoBase (Thought, Inc.): http://www.thoughtinc.com

- Hibernate (open source): http://www.hibernate.org/

- Jakarta OJB (open source): http://db.apache.org/ojb/

- TopLink (Oracle): http://www.oracle.com/technology/products/ias/toplink/index.html

## Java Data Objects

Each of the O/R frameworks previously mentioned has its own unique API and its own unique way to specify the mapping of Java objects to database tables. This is a problem because it means that Java programmers may have to learn multiple persistence APIs and mapping techniques as they move through their careers, and because the Java programs written by those programmers will each be locked into one persistence API. Wouldn't it be better if there were only one standard persistence API? Sun thinks so, and that is why Sun worked closely with the Java community to create the Java Data Objects (JDO) API specification.

JDO is a relatively new Java API specification designed to provide a standard API to enable the persistent storage of Java data in relational databases, object databases, and other enterprise information systems. The JDO specification (http://www.jcp.org/en/jsr/detail?id=12) was finalized in March 2002; a maintenance release of the specification occurred in 2003, and maintenance review was completed at the end of 2004. In addition, at the time of this writing, public review of the next major update to JDO, JDO 2.0 (http://www.jcp.org/en/jsr/detail?id=243), has been completed and the expert committee is working on a final draft specification. Since the initial specification release, a number of commercial and open source implementations have been released. Commercial JDO implementations include small-name vendors such as Signsoft and SolarMetric. Open-source implementations include Jakarta OJB and TriActive JDO (TJDO).

The advantages of using JDO are that it provides the same benefits as using an O/R framework and that it does so through a standardized API and mapping technique. As a Java standard, JDO is likely to be very well supported and very well known among Java developers. The disadvantage of using JDO is that it's new and, some would say, untested. The big-name Java vendors, IBM, BEA Systems, and Oracle, haven't committed to JDO, and the open-source JDO implementations aren't yet ready for production use.

It's important to note that JDO is very different from Microsoft's ActiveX Data Objects (ADO) API, despite the similar names. ADO is a lower-level API, similar to JDBC, that allows you to execute SQL queries and retrieve data as RecordSet objects of tabular data. JDO, on the other hand, allows you to save and retrieve any arbitrary Java object to and from a database. JDO includes an object query language (OQL) and when you execute an OQL query, you receive a collection of objects instead of tabular data as you would with ADO or JDBC.

Like JDBC, JDO is a fairly small API, but complete coverage is well beyond the scope of this book. For more information, refer to Sun's JDO home page, the JDO central website, and the various vendors that are supporting JDO. The following are links to these resources:

- Sun's JDO home page: http://java.sun.com/products/jdo

- JDO central: http://www.jdocentral.com

- IntelliBO JDO (Signsoft): http://www.intellibo.com/

- Kodo JDO (SolarMetric): http://www.solarmetric.com/Software/Kodo_JDO

- Jakarta OJB (open source): http://jakarta.apache.org/ojb/

- TJDO (open source): http://tjdo.sourceforge.net/

# EJB Entity Beans

EJB is a Java API specification that provides a component architecture for the development and deployment of distributed business objects, but many Java programmers use EJB only for its database access and Java object-persistence capabilities. If your application is highly transactional, requires high availability, and is likely to have many concurrent users, you might want to consider using EJB.

EJB is a standard part of the Java EE and is therefore supported by all Java EE–compliant application servers. Application servers that support EJB do so by providing an EJB container that hosts EJB components, just as a servlet container hosts servlets and JSPs. And just as servlet containers may be clustered to provide load balancing and fault tolerance for servlets, EJB containers can be clustered to provide the same functionality for distributed business objects.

An EJB container can support three types of components: entity beans, session beans, and message beans. We won't discuss session and message beans because they aren't persistent. We'll focus on entity beans, which can be persisted to a data store by using one of the following two mechanisms:

- **Container-managed persistence (CMP)**: You provide a mapping that specifies how to map fields from your entity bean objects to fields in a database, and the EJB container manages the persistence of your entity beans in the database.

- **Bean-managed persistence (BMP)**: You implement the persistence of your objects by using JDBC, an O/R framework, JDO, or some other technology. The EJB container will notify your code when it's time to store or retrieve an object to or from the database.

The benefits provided by using EJB for persistence are many; here are some of the most significant:

- **Built-in O/R framework**: If you use EJB CMP, you get all the benefits of using an O/R framework plus the added benefits of EJB. However, the O/R mapping capabilities of CMP don't address some of the harder tasks in O/R mapping such as optimistic locking, batch updates, and so on.

- **Scalability and high availability**: EJB containers can be clustered to allow your application to scale up to meet the needs of more and more users. If an EJB container fails, the objects that were running in that container will automatically and transparently failover to continue execution in another EJB container.

- **Declarative transaction support**: EJB allows you to declare the transactional characteristics of your business objects. Instead of writing the code to begin and end transactions, you simply declare the transactional requirements of each of your object's methods and let the EJB container do the rest. If you have a complex and highly transactional system, this is an important benefit.

- **Declarative method-level security**: EJB allows you to declare the security characteristics of your business objects. Instead of writing code to ensure that only certain users working in certain roles can use your objects, you simply declare the security constraints of each of your object's methods and let the EJB container handle the security.

- **Distributed object support**: EJB is designed to support the development and deployment of distributed business objects that are callable via Java Remote Method Invocation (RMI) or CORBA Internet Inter-ORB Protocol (IIOP).

One disadvantage of EJB is complexity. The technology is complex, and the learning curve is steep. To learn EJB development, you need to learn the EJB philosophy, the EJB API, recommended EJB patterns, EJB development tools, and the EJB deployment descriptors. To learn EJB deployment, you need to learn how to use the administration and deployment tools provided by the various Java EE application servers that you intend to support, each of which can vary quite significantly.

Another disadvantage of EJB is development overhead. When EJBs were first introduced, you needed to create at least three (often four) files for a single EJB. Tools such as XDoclet made the process easier, but until recently there was a lot of complexity in developing even simple beans. EJB 3.0, part of the latest Java Platform, Enterprise Edition 5 specification, has made steps to make the writing process easier, but there are still many issues to understand and consider. There is also considerable runtime overhead associated with using entity beans as the container interposes a variety of services for your beans.

EJB does a lot for you, but with increased complexity and significant development overhead. Make sure that you really need the benefits provided by EJB before you commit to using it in your application.

## Comparing the Choices

Now that you've learned about the five data access options, JSTL, JDBC, O/R, JDO, and entity beans, Table 9-2 reviews the pros and cons of each.

**Table 9-2.** *Comparison of Various Data Access Options*

| Option | Pros | Cons |
|--------|------|------|
| JSTL | Simple and easy to use with JSP | Useful only for displaying query results and performing simple updates |
| JDBC | Simple and easy to use. Also very flexible and powerful | Can require repetitive, tedious, and error-prone boilerplate coding |
| O/R | Makes it easy to persist objects to DB Eliminates much repetitive boilerplate coding Good tool support Better support for portability Many open- and closed-source implementations | Each O/R framework has its own nonstandard API and query language |
| JDO | The official standard Java persistence API with growing momentum among developers Easy to persist objects to DB Easy to use API and OQL Most of the same benefits as O/R frameworks | Currently, supported only by small vendors |
| EJB | Widely supported, well-known, well-documented, and standard Java API EJB CMP provides a built-in O/R framework Scalability and high-availability features Declarative transactions and security Distributed object support | Complex solution, lots to learn High development overhead Poor performance if used improperly |

# Data Access Architectures

We have discussed several data access technologies and now we'll discuss how data access fits into the architecture of a web application. Of course, there isn't one true web-application architecture. Every application is different, and different applications often need different architectures.

According to UML gurus Grady Booch, James Rumbaugh, and Ivar Jacobson in *The Unified Modeling Language User Guide* (Addison-Wesley, 2005), one definition of architecture is the "set of significant decisions about the organization of a software system." When you come up with a new architecture, you're deciding how to divide your software into different parts and you're deciding how these parts will work together. These decisions will affect your application's performance, maintainability, reusability, ease of development, and resilience to change.

Architectural decisions often require trade-offs that can be made only by somebody who knows the unique requirements of the software being developed. In this section, we'll discuss architectures at three increasing levels of complexity. You'll learn the advantages and disadvantages of each type of architecture, so that you can decide for yourself which architecture is best for each of your web applications.

## Example: RSS Newsreader

Before we discuss the three types of architectures, we should introduce the example application that we'll use to illustrate these architectures. This chapter's example is a JSP-based Rich Site Summary (RSS) newsreader.

RSS is a simple XML-based format for representing the current news stories available on a website. A website that supports RSS may provide several RSS news feeds, each covering one topic and each available at a different URL. An RSS news feed is represented by an RSS file, which is dynamically generated and updated on a regular schedule. An RSS file contains a `<channel>` element that describes the contents of the file, and that channel element contains a series of `<item>` elements with each representing one news story. Each news item has a title, description, publication time, and link that points to the full story on the website that is associated with the news feed. Here's one `<item>` element from an RSS that was recently available from a common news site:

```
<item>
  <title>iPod Owners Make Friends And Influence People (TechWeb)</title>
  <link>http://us.rd.yahoo.com/dailynews/rss/digitalmusic/ ➥
*http://news.yahoo.com/s/cmp/20051026/tc_cmp/172900215</link>
  <guid isPermaLink="false">cmp/20051026/172900215</guid>
  <pubDate>Tue, 25 Oct 2005 18:00:00 GMT</pubDate>
  <description>TechWeb - Owners of Apple Computer's iPods are among ➥
the Internet's most influential users, a study says.</description>
</item>
```

An RSS newsreader allows a user to subscribe to one or more RSS news feeds, and then to view the news stories from those news feeds within a single interface such as a desktop application or a web page. RSS newsreaders are often referred to as aggregators because they typically read news stories from multiple sites and aggregate them together for display.

In this chapter, you'll develop a simple JSP-based RSS newsreader. If you would like to see a more full-featured web-based RSS newsreader, take a look at O'Reilly's Meerkat, (http://www.oreillynet.com/meerkat/), which can aggregate and filter news stories from numerous professional sources. An alternative is Atlassian's JavaBlogs.com, which aggregates numerous Java-oriented weblogs (http://www.javablogs.com).

---

**Note**  Because of the large amount of code in this example, only a few code listings from the example are included in this chapter. The complete source code for the example is available as part of the code download for the book, at the Source Code area of the Apress website (http//:www.apress.com/book/download.html).

---

Now that you know a little bit about RSS and RSS newsreaders, you're equipped to understand the examples that follow. Now, let's move on to the architectures.

## One-Layer Architecture

In the simplest JSP data access architecture, an application accesses data directly from the presentation layer. You might be tempted to use this type of architecture because it seems like the easy route. After all, you don't have to design and implement a business layer or a data layer. Figure 9-5 illustrates the single-layer architecture. As you can see, the presentation layer not only depends on the Servlet API, but also has a direct dependence on the data access technology, which might be JDBC, JDO, or some other persistence framework.

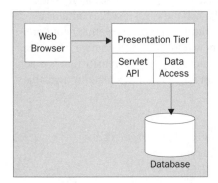

**Figure 9-5.** *In a single-layer architecture, the presentation logic, business logic, and data access logic all reside within the same application code.*

With single-layer architecture, you're sacrificing maintainability, reusability, and resilience to change in order to make development a little easier. This might be acceptable for a smaller application, but for a larger application this type of architecture will make your code have the following characteristics:

- **Difficult to maintain:** Presentation, business, and persistence logic are all mixed together and cannot be considered or changed separately.

- **Difficult to reuse:** The business logic cannot easily be separated from the presentation logic. If you need to create a new application or a web service that uses your business logic, you're out of luck because your business logic is mixed in with your JSP and servlet-based presentation code.

- **Not resilient to change:** If you need to switch to a new data access technology, you'll have to make sweeping changes in your code. You cannot change the persistence logic without putting the business logic and presentation logic at risk.

## Two-Layer Architecture

Splitting your application into a presentation layer and a business layer can solve the one-layer problems previously mentioned. This is a more difficult task because it requires designing business objects to model the business concepts and entities in your application. It also requires creating an interface or a set of interfaces through which your presentation layer can invoke business operations and access business objects.

Figure 9-6 illustrates the two-layer architecture. As you can see, the presentation layer depends on the Servlet API but it calls upon the business layer to perform business operations and data access. The business layer depends on data access technology, which again can be JDBC, JDO, or some other persistence framework. Looking at Figure 9-6, you can see that the business layer is now an independent and reusable software entity. You could take that business layer and place it in a desktop application or you could take it and build a SOAP-accessible web service around it.

**Figure 9-6.** *In a two-layer architecture, the presentation logic is separated from the business logic and data access logic.*

You're probably wondering what is going on inside the business layer box in Figure 9-6. The best way to understand the concepts of business interfaces and business objects is by example. So, let's take a look at the business objects and business interface of the RSS newsreader that was mentioned earlier.

An RSS newsreader allows a user to subscribe to a number of news feeds and then to read the news items retrieved from those news feeds. By looking at the nouns in that sentence, you can see what objects are going to be involved in this application. You'll need objects to model users, subscriptions, news feeds, and news items. Figure 9-7 is a UML diagram that shows these objects, their attributes, and their relationships.

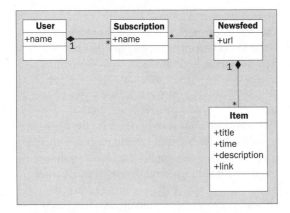

**Figure 9-7.** *A User has one or more Subscriptions. A Subscription consists of Newsfeeds, which consists of Items.*

The diagram, which uses UML notation, shows that the users have a one-to-many relationship with subscriptions, subscriptions have a many-to-many relationship with news feeds, and news feeds have a one-to-many relationship with items. In this example, you'll have a one-to-one correspondence between classes and database tables. So you'll have User, Subscription, Newsfeed, and Item objects as well as corresponding user, subscription, newsfeed, and item tables.

Now that you've designed the objects needed for your application, you'll need to design the business-layer interface. This interface will be used by the presentation layer to invoke newsreader operations and to access the newsreader objects that were discussed earlier.

To implement the presentation layer, you need to be able to add subscriptions, remove subscriptions, access users, and run the news feed aggregation operation. Listing 9-2 shows an interface that fulfills all of these requirements.

**Listing 9-2.** *Aggregator.java*

```java
package com.apress.projsp;
  /**
    * Business interface for Newsfeed aggregation.
    */
  public interface Aggregator {
    /** Gets user by name, create new user if necessary. */
    public User getUser(String userName) throws Exception;

    /** Add new subscription and associate with a newsfeed. */
    public Subscription addSubscription(
        User user, String name, String url) throws Exception;

    /** Remove subscription by id. */
    public void removeSubscription(String id) throws Exception;
```

```
/** Run the aggregator and fetch items from all Newsfeeds. */
public void aggregate() throws Exception;
}
```

The Aggregator interface distills the interface between the presentation layer and the business layer down to only four methods. The interface is so simple because the getUser() method does a lot of work. It returns a User object that has a collection of Subscription objects. Each Subscription has a Newsfeed object, and each Newsfeed has a collection of Item objects, the most recent news stories retrieved from the Newsfeed's website.

The addSubscription() and removeSubscription() methods allow you to manage subscription in the presentation layer. Finally, the aggregate() method allows you to launch the aggregate operation, which visits each of the news feeds represented by subscriptions in the database, parses the RSS from the news feed into Item objects, and stores those objects in the database.

With the simple Aggregator interface previously discussed, you can totally separate the presentation layer of the RSS newsreader from the business layer. The presentation layer doesn't need to know anything about what is going on behind that interface. It doesn't need to know what type of RSS parser is being used to parse the incoming news feeds. It doesn't need to know what type of data access technology is being used to persist business objects.

A two-layer architecture is usually sufficient, but in some cases you may wish to take the architecture one step further and use a three-layer architecture.

## Three-Layer Architecture

The two-layer architecture works well. It allows you to separate presentation logic from business logic, and that is good. However, you didn't separate the business logic from the data access logic. Business logic and data access logic seem to go together. Business rules are often built right into database schemas in the form of database constraints, and business logic is often coded into databases in stored procedures and triggers.

But if two is good, three must be better. Figure 9-8 shows an illustration of a three-layer architecture. In the three-layer architecture, business logic is further separated from data access logic.

**Figure 9-8.** *In a three-tier architecture, presentation, business, and data are separated into different components, making it easier to change components in a tier without affecting the other tiers.*

Why would anybody want to introduce yet another layer into an application? After all, each additional layer adds another layer of complexity, and all these layers cannot be good for performance. You have to think carefully before you decide to add another layer to your application, but there are at least two reasons that you might want to do so. These reasons to consider separate business and data layers come right off the list of trade-offs that we discussed when we introduced the topic of architecture:

- **Reusability:** Someday you may want to turn your business layer into a stand-alone desktop application that doesn't require a database. If your data access logic is mixed in with your business logic, this task is going to be difficult and error-prone.

- **Resilience to change:** Changes in the persistence logic will be less likely to affect the business logic, and changes in the business logic will be less likely to affect the persistence logic. For example: Someday you might find that the O/R persistence framework you chose has a fatal flaw or is no longer going to be supported. You might need to replace your chosen O/R framework with something else, and separation of business logic and data access logic will make this task easier.

Reusability and resilience to change are forms of flexibility, and most developers consider flexibility to be a good thing. However, it's important to realize that flexibility comes at the price of added complexity, and complexity makes software more difficult to develop and to maintain. You don't want to do a lot of extra work now for some event that may possibly occur at some point in the future, especially if that extra work is going to make your application more difficult to maintain. The following are a couple of other reasons *not* to use separate business and data layers:

- Developing an abstract interface to data access isn't an easy task. It requires some knowledge of each of the various data access technologies that you may wish to use behind that interface.

- Hiding your data access technology behind an abstract interface may make it difficult to use some of that technology's advanced features.

## The Data Access Object Pattern

If you decide that you do want to implement a three-layer architecture and you do want to separate out your data access logic into a data layer, then you should consider using the **Data Access Object (DAO) pattern**. As you may already know, a pattern is a general design for a recurring problem. The DAO pattern is a general design for encapsulating data access. The DAO pattern is a popular pattern and is documented as part of the Sun J2EE Patterns Catalog (http://java.sun.com/blueprints/corej2eepatterns/).

Here is how the DAO pattern works. Instead of calling the JDBC or some other persistence API directly from all of your Java classes that need to access data, you encapsulate all of your data access code in one or more data access objects, or DAOs. Typically a DAO will include methods for creating, retrieving, updating, and deleting objects from the database as well as methods for querying the database to retrieve collections of objects. Depending on how you implement the DAO pattern, you could have a DAO for each class of object in your application or you could have a single DAO that is responsible for creating, retrieving, updating, and deleting all of your objects.

In your RSS newsreader application example, there is a single DAO called `AggregatorDAO`, which is shown in Listing 9-3. The `AggregatorDAO` contains methods for creating, retrieving, updating, and deleting all the different types of objects that are part of the application. These objects are `User`, `Subscription`, `Newsfeed`, and `Item`.

**Listing 9-3.** *AggregatorDAO.java*

```java
package com.apress.projsp.persist;

import com.apress.projsp.Item;
import com.apress.projsp.Newsfeed;
import com.apress.projsp.Subscription;
import com.apress.projsp.User;
import java.util.List;

  /** Aggregator Data Access Object (DAO) interface. */
  public interface AggregatorDAO {
    /** Gets user by name, create new user if necessary. */
    public User getUser(String userName) throws DAOException;
    /** Add new subscription and associate with a newsfeed */
    public Subscription addSubscription(
      User user, String name, String url) throws DAOException;

    /** Retrieve subscription by ID */
    public Subscription retrieveSubscription(String id) throws DAOException;
    /** Remove subscription but not associated Newsfeed. */
    public void removeSubscription(Subscription sub) throws DAOException;

    /** Get all newsfeeds. */
    public List getAllNewsfeeds() throws DAOException;

    /** Remove newsfeed and associated subscriptions. */
    public void removeNewsfeed(Newsfeed feed) throws DAOException;

    /** Store newsfeed. */
    public void storeNewsfeed(Newsfeed feed) throws DAOException;
    /** Add item to newsfeed. */
    public void addItem(Newsfeed feed, Item item) throws DAOException;

    /** Add a newsfeed (for testing only). */
    public Newsfeed addNewsfeed(String url) throws DAOException;
    /** Get all items (for testing only). */
    public List getAllItems() throws DAOException;
  }
```

`AggregatorDAO` is an interface that you could implement by using just about any data access technology. For example, you could write a `JdbcAggregatorDAO` class that implements data access with JDBC or you could write an `XmlAggregatorDAO` that stores `User`, `Subscription`,

Newsfeed, and Item objects in an XML file. In the next section, you'll learn the steps involved in implementing the AggregatorDAO interface when using the Hibernate O/R persistence framework.

# Implementing the RSS Newsreader Example

The RSS newsreader example that we have been discussing in this chapter is developed by using a three-layer architecture as described in the previous section. The application includes a presentation layer, a business layer, and a data layer. In this section, we'll first discuss the package organization of the RSS newsreader and then we'll cover each of the steps that were taken in the development of the application.

## Package Organization

Before talking about the steps involved in building this application, let's talk a little more about how the pieces fit together. Figure 9-9 shows the three layers of the application, the Java packages that exist within each layer, and the dependencies that exist between these packages indicated by arrows.

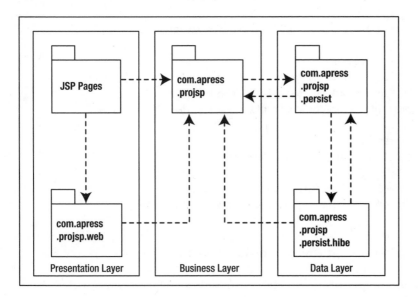

**Figure 9-9.** *The RSS application has three layers (or tiers). Each component in the application is part of a single layer. The components work together to provide the functionality of the application.*

The business layer is made up of the business objects and the AggregatorImpl class, which implements the Aggregator business interface that was discussed earlier in the section on two-layer architectures. The business layer depends only on the data layer, and the sole interface to the data layer is the AggregatorDAO interface.

The presentation layer is implemented with JSP pages, JSTL tags, and Java classes in the package `com.apress.projsp.web`, which are responsible for parsing request parameters and calling the business layer. The presentation layer depends only on the business layer. The sole interface to the business layer is the `Aggregator` business interface.

The data layer exists under the `com.apress.projsp.persist` package and is made up of the `AggregatorDAO` interface, the `DAOException` class, and the DAO implementation class `HibeAggregatorDAO`. The DAO implementation uses the Hibernate O/R persistence framework.

## Step 1: Implementing the Object Model

You've already learned the first steps in the RSS newsreader development process. These steps were the design of the object model, the design of the business interface, and the design of the DAO interface that will encapsulate data access.

The next step in the process is to implement the object model. This is easy because there are only four business objects, and these business objects are simple JavaBeans with each having only a small number of properties. Listing 9-4 is an example of one of the business objects, the `Item` class.

**Listing 9-4.** *Item.java*

```java
package com.apress.projsp;
import java.util.Date;
import java.util.Set;
/**
 * Represents a single news item retrieved from a newsfeed.
 */
public class Item {
  private String mId;
  private String mLink;
  private String mDescription;
  private String mContent;
  private String mTitle;
  private Date mTime;
  private Newsfeed mNewsfeed;
  private Item mItem;

  /**
   * Construct Item using all field values.
   * @param title  Title of this news item.
   * @param time  Time of publication.
   * @param link  Link article on originating website.
   * @param desc  Description of article (or full text of article).
   * @param content (Optional) full text of article.
   */
  public Item( String title, Date time, String link,
    String description, String content ) {
```

```java
    mTitle = title;
    mTime = time;
    mLink = link;
    mDescription = description;
    mContent = content;
  }
  /** Default constructor */
  public Item() {
  }
  public String getId() {
    return mId;
  }
  public void setId(String id) {
    mId = id;
  }
  public Newsfeed getNewsfeed() {
    return mNewsfeed;
  }
  public void setNewsfeed(Newsfeed newsfeed) {
    mNewsfeed = newsfeed;
  }
  public String getTitle() {
    return mTitle;
  }

  public void setTitle(String title) {
    mTitle = title;
  }
  public String getContent() {
    return mContent;
  }
  public void setContent(String content) {
    mContent = content;
  }
  public String getDescription() {
    return mDescription;
  }
  public void setDescription(String description) {
    mDescription = description;
  }
  public String getLink() {
    return mLink;
  }
  public void setLink(String link) {
    mLink = link;
  }
  public Date getTime() {
```

```
    return mTime;
  }
  public void setTime(Date time) {
    mTime = time;
  }
}
```

Similar JavaBeans exist for User, Subscription, and Newsfeed.

# Step 2: Creating an Object-Relational Mapping

The next step in the development of the RSS newsreader is the development of the data layer to store and retrieve the business objects developed in step 1.

This step is a little more difficult because you must learn the ins and outs of your persistence choice—in our case the Hibernate O/R persistence framework. Luckily, the Hibernate documentation is very good and Hibernate is fairly easy to use.

Before you can use Hibernate to store Java objects in a relational database, you have to create an object-relational mapping for each object to be stored. A mapping specification is an XML file that describes how to map one or more Java classes to tables in a database. For example, the mapping for the com.apress.projsp.Newsfeed class, from the file Newsfeed.hbm.xml, is shown in Listing 9-5.

**Listing 9-5.** *Newsfeed.hbm.xml*

```xml
<?xml version="1.0"?>
<!DOCTYPE hibernate-mapping PUBLIC
    "-//Hibernate/Hibernate Mapping DTD 2.0//EN"
    "http://hibernate.sourceforge.net/hibernate-mapping-2.0.dtd">

<hibernate-mapping>
   <!-- ag.Newsfeed root -->
   <class name="com.apress.projsp.Newsfeed" table="newsfeed">
      <id column="id" name="id" >
         <generator class="uuid.hex"/>
      </id>
      <property name="url" column="url" type="string"
                not-null="true" unique="true" />
      <set name="items" table="item" cascade="delete" >
         <key column="newsfeed_id" />
         <one-to-many class="com.apress.projsp.Item" />
      </set>
      <set name="subscriptions" table="subscription" cascade="delete">
         <key column="newsfeed_id" />
         <one-to-many class="com.apress.projsp.Subscription" />
      </set>
   </class>
</hibernate-mapping>
```

Let's analyze the contents of the Hibernate mapping.

After the standard XML declaration and the DOCTYPE tags, you find the root element of a Hibernate mapping file, the `<hibernate-mapping>` element. Within the root element, you'll find one or more `<class>` tags. The `<class>` tag maps one class to a database table, so the tag has two attributes. The `name` attribute specifies the name of the Java class, and the `table` attribute specifies the name of the table that the Java class is to be mapped to:

```
<hibernate-mapping>
  <class name="com.apress.projsp.Newsfeed" table="newsfeed">
```

The first element within the class mapping is the `<id>` element. This element specifies which JavaBean property and which database table column are to be used as a primary key for the class. Within the `<id>` tag is the `<generator>` tag, which specifies which method should be used to generate primary keys for new objects:

```
<id column="id" name="id" >
  <generator class="uuid.hex" />
</id>
```

Hibernate supports 10 primary-key generation methods. The `class="uuid.hex"` method results in a 32-character key that is generated by using the IP address of the machine upon which Hibernate is running. It's also possible to tell Hibernate to allow the database to generate the key by using `class="sequence"` or to allow the application to assign the key by using `class="assigned"`.

The `<property>` tag maps a simple `java.lang.String` property named `url` to a database column called `url`. The property isn't allowed to be null and is required to be unique.

```
<property name="url" column="url" type="string"
          not-null="true" unique="true" />
```

The next two elements are interesting. The `<set>` tag indicates that you're mapping a `java.util.Set` collection to the database. Each `Newsfeed` is associated with a collection of `Item` objects and a collection of `Subscription` objects. This is a classic one-to-many relationship. The `com.apress.projsp.Newsfeed` objects are stored in the `newsfeed` table, the `com.apress.projsp.Item` objects are stored in the `item` table, and the two tables are related by a `newsfeed_id` column in the `item` table:

```
<set role="items" table="item" cascade="delete">
  <key column="newsfeed_id" />
  <one-to-many class="com.apress.projsp.Item" />
</set>
<set role="subscriptions" table="subscription" cascade="delete">
  <key column="newsfeed_id" />
  <one-to-many class="com.apress.projsp.Subscription" />
</set>
```

If you're having a hard time visualizing these relationships, refer to Figure 9-7 in the "Two-Layer Architecture" section, which shows the relationships between `User`, `Subscription`, `Newsfeed`, and `Item` objects.

It's possible to map more than one class within a single `<hibernate-mapping>` element, but it's a recommended practice to map only one class per mapping file. At runtime, the `Newsfeed.hbm.xml` file should be placed in the same package as the `Newsfeed.class` so that Hibernate can find it.

The Hibernate mapping file may look complicated, but it's complicated for a reason. The mapping is designed to accommodate all the different data and relationship types that you might use in a Java application and in a relational database schema. If you have problems coming up with the right mappings, consult your friendly database administrator. Ask for help on the Hibernate mailing list.

## Step 3: Creating the Database Tables

Creating the object-relational mappings for the RSS newsreader classes is relatively difficult, but once you have those mappings Hibernate starts to earn its keep.

Hibernate includes a command-line tool that reads mapping files and can then either generate a database creation script or connect to your database and create the tables for you. This tool is called SchemaExport and it can handle 16 database dialects including Oracle, Sybase, Microsoft SQL Server, MySQL, and PostgreSQL.

SchemaExport is just a command-line Java program, so it may be easily run from an Ant build script. For example, the following Ant build script excerpt is used to run SchemaExport and create the tables for the RSS newsreader example:

```
<target name="create-tables">
    <java classname="net.sf.hibernate.tool.hbm2ddl.SchemaExport"
          fork="true" dir="./build/5130ch09/WEB-INF/classes">
        <arg value="--quiet"/>
        <arg value="--output=../ag.ddl"/>
        <arg value="--properties=hibernate.properties"/>
        <arg value="./com/apress/projsp/Subscription.hbm.xml"/>
        <arg value="./com/apress/projsp/Newsfeed.hbm.xml"/>
        <arg value="./com/apress/projsp/Item.hbm.xml"/>
        <arg value="./com/apress/projsp/User.hbm.xml"/>
        <classpath>
            <path refid="jdbcdriver.path"/>
            <path refid="hibernate.path"/>
            <pathelement
            path="./build/5130ch09/WEBINF/classes/com/apress/projsp/"/>
        </classpath>
    </java>
</target>
```

The `<java>` element runs the class `cirrus.hibernate.tools.SchemaExport` within the `build` directory so that it can find the mapping files. The `-output` argument tells the Schema-Export to generate a database creation script named `rss.ddl`. The `-properties` argument tells SchemaExport where to find the Hibernate properties file, which contains the database connection parameters needed to connect to the target database. The rest of the arguments indicate which mappings are to be processed.

The `create-tables` target in the previous example code comes from an Ant build script. This Ant build script compiles the example Java classes, builds the example WAR file, and creates the example's database tables by using the `create-tables` target. You can find the build script with the code download for this book (`http://www.apress.com/book/download.html`).

## Step 4: Implementing the AggregatorDAO

The next step in RSS newsreader development is to write the Hibernate implementation of the `AggregatorDAO` interface. This implementation is in the package `com.apress.projsp.persist.hibe` and is named `HibeAggregatorDAO`.

This task requires some knowledge of the Hibernate API, but the excellent Hibernate Reference Document (available at `http://www.hibernate.org/hib_docs/v3/reference/en/html/`) and Javadocs really shortens the learning curve. Obviously, we don't want to discuss every line of code in the implementation. Looking at the code for the constructor and the logic for persisting one object should give you a good understanding of the implementation.

Listing 9-6 is the source code for the `HibeAggregatorDAO` class. We have split this code listing into parts, so that we can more easily discuss the various methods of the class. The constructor creates a Hibernate `Datastore`, loads the mappings for the classes that will be persisted, and creates a `SessionFactory` for use during the rest of the lifetime of the DAO object. The `SessionFactory` represents a database connection pool and is responsible for creating `Session` objects. The `Session` interface is the main Hibernate interface used by a Java program; a `Session` object holds a database connection.

**Listing 9-6.** *HibeAggregatorDAO.java (Package, Imports, and Constructor)*

```
package com.apress.projsp.persist.hibe;
import com.apress.projsp.*;
import com.apress.projsp.persist.*;
import net.sf.hibernate.*;
import net.sf.hibernate.cfg.*;
import java.util.List;
/** Hibernate implementation of Ag DAO. */
public class HibeAggregatorDAO implements AggregatorDAO {
    private static SessionFactory sessionFactory;
    public HibeAggregatorDAO() throws DAOException {
        try {
            Configuration config = new Configuration();
            config.addClass(Newsfeed.class);
            config.addClass(Subscription.class);
            config.addClass(User.class);
            config.addClass(Item.class);
            sessionFactory = config.buildSessionFactory();
        }
        catch (MappingException e) {
            throw new DAOException(e);
        }
```

```
    catch (HibernateException e) {
        throw new DAOException(e);
    }
}
```

The storeNewsfeed() and storeObject() methods, as shown next, illustrate the code necessary to add a new object into the data store. The first step in the method is to open a session, which begins a database transaction. Next, you'll save the object database. To finalize the operation, you commit the transaction. If an exception occurs, roll back the transaction and throw a DAOException so that the business layer can handle the error condition. The finally block ensures that, no matter what happens, the session is closed and therefore the database connection that was used by the connection is released back to the database connection pool.

**Listing 9-6.** *HibeAggregatorDAO.java (storeNewsfeed() and storeObject() Methods)*

```
public void storeNewsfeed(Newsfeed feed) throws DAOException {
    storeObject(feed);
}
private void storeObject(Object obj) throws DAOException {
    Session ses = null;
    try {

        ses = sessionFactory.openSession();
        ses.saveOrUpdate(obj);
        ses.flush();
        ses.connection().commit();
    } catch (Exception e) {
        try { ses.connection().rollback(); }
        catch (Exception ex) { e.printStackTrace(); };
        throw new DAOException(e);

    } finally {
        try { ses.close(); }
        catch (Exception ex) { ex.printStackTrace(); };
    }
}
```

The retrieveNewsfeed() method and retrieveObject() methods in the following continuation of Listing 9-6 show the code necessary to retrieve an object from the database by using the object's primary key. The steps are simple. You open a session, load the object, close the session, and return the object.

**Listing 9-6.** *HibeAggregatorDAO.java (retrieveNewsfeed() and retrieveObject() Methods)*

```
public Newsfeed retrieveNewsfeed(String id) throws DAOException {
    return (Newsfeed)retrieveObject(Newsfeed.class, id);
}
```

```java
private Object retrieveObject(Class clazz, String id) throws DAOException {
  Object obj = null;
  Session ses = null;
  try {
    ses = sessionFactory.openSession();
    obj = ses.load( clazz, id );

  } catch (Exception e) {
    throw new DAOException(e);

  } finally {
    try { ses.close(); }
    catch (Exception ex) { ex.printStackTrace(); };
  }
  return obj;
}
```

The getAllNewsfeeds() method, shown in the following excerpt, illustrates the code necessary to fetch a collection of objects from the database by using a query. This is also a simple operation. You open a session and run a query to get all news feeds by using the ses.find() method. The query is expressed by using Hibernate's own OQL, which is similar to but not quite the same as SQL.

**Listing 9-6.** *HibeAggregatorDAO.java (getAllNewsfeeds() Method)*

```java
public List getAllNewsfeeds() throws DAOException {
  List feeds = null;
  Session ses = null;
  try {

    ses = sessionFactory.openSession();
    feeds = ses.find("from newsfeed in class " +
                     "com.apress.projsp.Newsfeed");
  } catch (Exception e) {
    throw new DAOException(e);
  } finally {
    try { ses.close(); }
    catch (Exception ex) { ex.printStackTrace(); };
  }
  return feeds;
}
```

The removeNewsfeed() and removeObject() methods show the code necessary to remove an object from the database. The steps here are very similar to the steps involved in the storeNewsfeed() method, except that we call ses.delete() to delete the object. Note that, because you specified the cascade="true" attribute in the mapping for the associated Item

CHAPTER 9 ■ DATA ACCESS OPTIONS FOR WEB APPLICATIONS

and Subscription collections, any items and subscriptions associated with the Newsfeed object will also be removed from the database.

You might be wondering why you have to call ses.load() on the object before you can delete it. That call is necessary because objects have associations, and associations will not be handled properly at delete-time if the object and its associations aren't created within the same session as the ses.delete() call.

**Listing 9-6.** *HibeAggregatorDAO.java (removeNewsfeed() and removeObject() Methods)*

```
public void removeNewsfeed(Newsfeed feed) throws DAOException {
  removeObject(Newsfeed.class, feed.getId(), feed);
}
private void removeObject(Class clazz, String id, Object obj)
     throws DAOException {
  Session ses = null;
  try {
    ses = sessionFactory.openSession();
    obj = ses.load(clazz,id);
    ses.delete(obj);
    ses.flush();
    ses.connection().commit();
  } catch (Exception e) {
    try { ses.connection().rollback(); }
    catch (Exception ex) { e.printStackTrace(); };
    throw new DAOException(e);
  } finally {
    try { ses.close(); }
    catch (Exception ex) { ex.printStackTrace(); };
  }
}
```

# Step 5: Implementing the Business Layer Interface

The next step after implementing the AggregatorDAO interface is to implement the business-layer interface. The business-layer interface is the Java interface Aggregator and the implementation is the Java class AggregatorImpl.

The Aggregator interface is a very small interface and most of its methods correspond directly to methods in the AggregatorDAO interface, so they are easy to implement.

The only real application logic that exists in this sample application is the Aggregator. aggregate() method. This method is responsible for walking the list of news feeds in the database, fetching the RSS data for each news feed, parsing the RSS data, and saving the news items found in each news feed to the database.

The code for the aggregate() method is shown in Listing 9-7. The method uses an RSS parsing API from an open-source product known as Flock.

Listing 9-7 shows a class that implements the Aggregator interface. First, you create a FlockFeedFactory to help you to parse the RSS XML. Next, you get an iterator so that you may iterate over all the news feeds in the database. You call upon Flock to parse each news feed into articles. Each article is then stored into the database by using the AggregatorDAO.addItem() method.

**Listing 9-7.** *AggregatorImpl.java*

```java
package com.apress.projsp;
import net.sourceforge.flock.FlockArticleI;
import net.sourceforge.flock.FlockFeedI;
import net.sourceforge.flock.parser.FlockFeedFactory;
import java.net.URL;
import java.util.Iterator;
import com.apress.projsp.persist.*;
public class AggregatorImpl implements Aggregator {
  private AggregatorDAO dao;

  public AggregatorImpl(AggregatorDAO dao) {
    this.dao = dao;
  }
  /** Run aggregation, collection items, store them in database */
  public void aggregate() throws Exception {
    FlockFeedFactory factory = new FlockFeedFactory();

    Iterator feedIter = dao.getAllNewsfeeds().iterator();
    while ( feedIter.hasNext() ) {
      Newsfeed feed = (Newsfeed)feedIter.next();
      String url = feed.getUrl();


      try {
        FlockFeedI flockFeed = factory.createFeed(new URL(url));
        Iterator articleIter = flockFeed.getArticles().iterator();

        while ( articleIter.hasNext() ) {
          FlockArticleI article = (FlockArticleI)articleIter.next();
          Item item = new Item(
            article.getTitle(),
            article.getCreationTime(),
            article.getLink().toString(),
            article.getDescription(),
            "");
          dao.addItem(feed,item);
        }
      } catch (Exception e) {
        e.printStackTrace();
```

```
      }
    }
  }
  /** Gets user by name, create new user if necessary. */
  public User getUser( String userName ) throws Exception {
    return dao.getUser(userName);
  }

  /**
   * Add new subscription and associate with a newsfeed, creating
   * a new newsfeed only if necessary.
   */
  public Subscription addSubscription(
    User user, String name, String url) throws Exception {
    return dao.addSubscription(user,name,url);
  }

  /**
   * Remove subscription but not associated Newsfeed.
   */
  public void removeSubscription(String id) throws Exception {
    Subscription sub = dao.retrieveSubscription(id);
    dao.removeSubscription(sub);
  }
}
```

For more information on the Flock RSS news aggregator and parser, check out the Flock website: http://flock.sourceforge.net/.

## Step 6: Implementing the Web User Interface

The final step in the development of the RSS newsreader is the creation of the presentation layer. The presentation layer is made up of a simple controller servlet, three action classes, and three JSP pages that correspond to those three action classes. The controller servlet and the action classes constitute a very simple Struts-like Model-View-Controller (MVC) framework. All requests are handled initially by the controller servlet, com.apress.projsp.web.Controller. The controller determines which action to call and does so. All of the action classes implement the com.apress.projsp.web.Action interface. Each action class follows the same pattern:

1. Perform an action.

2. Load some objects (the model) into scope.

3. Forward the request to a JSP page (this is the view).

Table 9-3 summarizes the three web pages and lists the JSP page and action class for each page.

**Table 9-3.** *Action Classes and JSP Pages in the RSS Application*

| Name | Action Class | JSP Page | Description |
|------|-------------|----------|-------------|
| Login or Change User | com.apress.projsp.web.<br>LoginAction | login.jsp | Allows user to log in by entering a username. If username doesn't exist in database, new user will be created. |
| Manage Subscriptions | com.apress.projsp.web.<br>SubscriptionAction | subs.jsp | Allows user to add new subscriptions and to remove existing subscriptions. |
| Read News | com.apress.projsp.web.<br>AggregationAction | news.jsp | Allows user to view news items that have been previously aggregated and to request aggregation of new news items. |

### The SubscriptionAction Class

Before you dive into Java code, let's take a look at how the Manage Subscriptions page looks in a web browser. Figure 9-10 shows a screen shot of the page generated by the presentation layer just after a new subscription was added.

**Figure 9-10.** *The Manage Subscriptions page of the RSS application allows a user to add or remove subscriptions.*

The page starts out with a title, Manage Subscriptions, and a menu that allows the user to access the Read News page and the Change User page. After that there is a status message area and one status message that indicates the result of the last action performed. In this case, the last action performed was the addition of a new subscription named Yahoo Personal Tech. Under the status message is the Add a New Subscription form. The form includes a subscription name field, a subscription URL field, and a button to submit the form. Finally, under the Subscriptions heading, there is a list of the user's current subscriptions.

How does the page work? Let's start from the beginning. As you can see in the screen shot, the URL is http://localhost:8080/5130ch09/ag/subs. The /ag part of the URL maps the incoming request to the controller servlet. The controller servlet uses the path-info part of the URL (in this case subs is the path-info) to determine which action is to be called. Then it calls the action object's doGet(request, response) method to process the request. In this example, the path-info subs maps to an action object of class com.apress.projsp.web.SubscriptionAction.

SubscriptionAction is responsible for responding to posts from the Add a New Subscription form, for removing subscriptions, for adding to scope the objects required for displaying the Manage Subscriptions page, and, finally, for forwarding the request to the subs.jsp page for display. Let's take a closer look at SubscriptionAction.java. Listing 9-8 shows the code for the SubscriptionAction class, interspersed with comments.

**Listing 9-8.** *SubscriptionAction.java*

```java
package com.apress.projsp.web;
import com.apress.projsp.User;
import java.util.Collection;
import javax.servlet.ServletContext;
import javax.servlet.http.HttpServletRequest;
import javax.servlet.http.HttpServletResponse;
/** Action for subscription management. */
public class SubscriptionAction extends BaseAction {
  public SubscriptionAction(ServletContext mContext) throws Exception {
    super(mContext);
  }
}
```

The previous code shows the class declaration and the constructor. The class implements the Action interface, but like the other action classes, it does so by extending the BaseAction class.

**Listing 9-8.** *SubscriptionAction.java (continued)*

```java
/** Process subscription action. */
public void doGet(HttpServletRequest req, HttpServletResponse res) {
  try {
    String verb = req.getParameter("verb");
    String name = req.getParameter("name");
    String url = req.getParameter("url");
    String remove = req.getParameter("remove");
```

```
      // Perform action specified by request attribute 'verb'
      if ((verb != null) && verb.equals("Add")) {
        User user = (User) req.getSession().getAttribute("ag.user");
        mAggregator.addSubscription(user, name, url);
        req.setAttribute("processMessage", "Added subscription [" + name + "]");
      } else if ((remove != null) && verb != null && verb.equals("Remove")) {
        mAggregator.removeSubscription(remove);
        req.setAttribute("processMessage", "Removed subscription ["
                          + remove + "]");
      }
```

The first half of the doGet() method looks for a request parameter called verb. If that parameter equals add, the action attempts to add a subscription. If it equals remove, the action attempts to remove a subscription. If either of these actions succeeds, a status message is put into the request as a request attribute using the name processMessage. If there is an exception, an error message is put into the request using the name processError.

**Listing 9-8.** *SubscriptionAction.java (continued)*

```
      // Load model into context for page
      User user = (User) req.getSession().getAttribute("ag.user");
      user = mAggregator.getUser(user.getName());
      req.setAttribute("user", user);
      Collection subs = user.getSubscriptions();

      req.setAttribute("subs", subs);
      // Forward to view
      req.getRequestDispatcher("subs.jsp").forward(req, res);
    } catch (Exception e) {
      String msg = "ERROR Processing form action [" +
                   e.getCause().getMessage() + "]";
      req.setAttribute("processError", msg);
      mContext.log(msg, e);
    }
  }
}
```

The second half of the doGet() method places the objects required by the Manage Subscriptions page into the appropriate scope. In this case the appropriate scope is request scope. Finally, it uses the request dispatcher to forward the request to the subs.jsp page for display.

## The subs.jsp Page

Now let's take a close look at the subs.jsp code. The code is shown in Listing 9-9 in its entirety, interspersed with comments.

**Listing 9-9.** *subs.jsp*

```
<%@ page language="java" %>
<%@ taglib uri="/WEB-INF/c.tld" prefix="c"%>
```

You start the page by including the Core JSTL taglib from the file WEB-INF\c.tld. After the familiar <html> and <body> tags, you emit a menu consisting of links to the other actions in the application news and login.

**Listing 9-9.** *subs.jsp (continued)*

```
<!DOCTYPE HTML PUBLIC "-//w3c//dtd html 4.0 transitional//en">
<html>
<head>
    <style type="text/css"><jsp:include page="/ag.jsp" /></style>
    <title>Ag - Manage Subscriptions</title>
</head>
<body bgcolor="#FFFFFF">
<h1>Ag - Manage subscriptions</h1><hr />
<p>
   <b>Manage Subscriptions</b> |
   <a href="news">Read News</a> |
   <a href="login">Change User <c:out value="[${user.name}]" /></a>
</p>
```

To display status information, you start using some of the objects that were put into the request by the action object. The user object is a business layer object of type com.apress. projsp.User. The processMessage and processError objects are strings that, if they exist, contain status or error information.

**Listing 9-9.** *subs.jsp (continued)*

```
<c:if test="${ processMessage != '' }">
  <p><font color="green"><c:out value="${processMessage}" /></font></p>
</c:if>
<c:if test="${ processError != '' }">
  <p><font color="red"><c:out value="${processError}" /></font></p>
</c:if>
```

Next, you have the Add a new subscription form. This form has two fields, called name and url. As you can see, this form posts to the subs action.

**Listing 9-9.** *subs.jsp (continued)*

```
<h2>Add a new subscription</h2>
<form action="subs" method="POST">
      Name <input type="text" name="name" />
      Newsfeed URL <input type="text" name="url" size="40"/>
      <input type="submit" name="verb" value="Add"/>
</form>
```

Finally, there is the Subscriptions list. Here, you use a JSTL <c:forEach> tag to loop through the subs collection that was placed into the request by the SubscriptionAction object. For each com.apress.projsp.Subscription object in the collection, you use the JSTL <c:url> tag to construct a remove link. The remove link is just a link back to the subs action, but with a request parameter named remove whose value is the ID of the subscription to be removed.

**Listing 9-9.** *subs.jsp (continued)*

```
<h2>Subscriptions</h2>
<p>You are currently subscribed to these newsfeeds:</p>
<c:forEach var="sub" items="${subs}">
    [<c:url value="subs" var="url">
         <c:param name="verb" value="Remove"/>
         <c:param name="remove" value="${sub.id}"/>
     </c:url>
    <a href="<c:out value='${url}'/>">  Remove </a> ]
    <b>Name:</b> <c:out value="${sub.name}"/>
    <b>URL:</b> <c:out value="${sub.newsfeed.url}"/> <br/>
</c:forEach>
</body>
</html>
```

## Castor: An Alternative to Hibernate

Castor is an open-source persistence framework like Hibernate. Although Castor has been around longer than Hibernate and may be more widely accepted, Hibernate was chosen for this chapter because it has better documentation. However, the RSS newsreader example program can be configured to use either Hibernate or Castor.

If you look at the example source code, you'll find a class in the package ag.persist.castor named CastorAggregatorDAO. This class is an implementation of the AggregregatorDAO interface that uses Castor instead of Hibernate. If you would like to compare the Castor and Hibernate APIs, compare the methods in HibeAggregatorDAO class to the methods in the CastorAggregatorDAO class. You'll find that, in some cases, the APIs are very similar. If you would like to configure the RSS newsreader example to use Castor instead of Hibernate, refer to the example readme.txt file for instructions on how to make the switch.

# Summary

In this chapter, you've learned the basics of using JDBC in a simple JSP application, the advantages of using an object-relational persistence framework, and how to design a sophisticated data access architecture.

With your new knowledge of basic JDBC concepts, you should be able to add data access to simple JSP applications by using JDBC code in JSP pages or by using the JSTL SQL tags. You should be able to access any sort of database as long as it has a JDBC driver. In addition, you should also be able to configure a JDBC driver by using either the old data manager approach or the newer JNDI data source technique.

With your new knowledge of the concepts behind O/R persistence frameworks, you should be able to work with any of the frameworks available from commercial software vendors and from open-source projects. Your knowledge of one-, two-, and three-layer architectures as well as your understanding of the flexibility-complexity trade-off will help you choose the appropriate architecture for your next JSP application.

You've also taken a close look at a complete example JSP application, the RSS newsreader, which illustrates how to use an O/R persistence framework within a modular three-layer architecture. You can use the RSS newsreader example as a starting point for your own projects. The example relies only on open-source components that are free of charge and free for you to distribute with your own applications.

You should now have enough knowledge to evaluate database access technologies and to design and implement database access within your JSP applications.

# CHAPTER 10

■■■

# Introduction to Filtering

**F**iltering is a standard feature of all Servlet 2.5–compliant containers. Since its introduction in the Servlet 2.3 specification, filters have found widespread use among Java EE developers. Some popular uses for filters include authentication, auditing, compression, encryption, and on-the-fly format transformation, to name but a few. For the very first time, an application-level programmer can tap into the request-processing pipeline of the container—in a portable, nonserver-specific manner. Servlet 2.5 further enhances container support of filters by providing filtering for dispatched requests—a feature that you'll be looking at in detail over this chapter and the next.

The unique positioning of filters in the processing pipeline, the relative ease with which they can be written and designed, and the versatile way these filters can be configured make them ideal design choices for a wide range of web-application features that were formerly impossible, difficult, or awkward to implement.

In this chapter, you'll learn the following:

- What a filter is, what it can do, and why it's needed

- How filters fit in with the rest of the servlets and JSP machinery

- What life cycle is followed by container-managed filters

- The power of filter mapping

- What the importance of filter chaining is

- How `RequestDispatcher` interacts with the action of filters and filter chains

- How to develop filters by using three complete code samples

- How filters differ from interceptors and valves

- What some best practices for filter design and coding are

The material covered in this chapter will provide a basic understanding of what Servlet 2.5 filtering is all about. You'll dive into the important concepts and illustrate them with easy-to-understand code wherever necessary. We have purposely deferred advanced concepts in filtering, together with detailed design issues for more complex filters, to the next chapter.

This chapter is concept-heavy and code-light, while the next one will be both concept- and code-heavy as we provide insight into the design and coding of many typical filters. Chapter 11 focuses on the techniques used in programming filters and serves as a "cookbook" for the practicing JSP programmer, letting you incorporate filters into your favorite application recipes.

# Common Filter Applications

Before you take a technical look at what a filter really is, let's start with a quick look at some applications of filters in the real world. Here is a short list of common filter applications, together with a description of the specific feature that makes the filter appropriate for the application:

- Filters can **intercept request header information before it reaches the resource** in the processing pipeline and can therefore be used to create customized authentication schemes. For example, a filter can be written to authenticate a user against an external legacy system before allowing access to a resource. Having "wide open" exposure to all the request headers, filters can be written to perform sophisticated logging and auditing. Combining the use of filters with URL pattern–based filter mapping, you can have fine-grained control on the set of resources to protect or audit.

- Filters are also useful in **data transformation**. For example, you can use filters to present an XML document as HTML via an XSLT transformation filter on the fly. Another form of data transformation filter might perform encryption or compression. For example, a filter can first detect whether a user agent (browser) supports compressed data streams. If the browser can handle the compression, the filter can then compress the response from a resource on the fly.

- Filters can **preempt the serving of a particular resource** altogether and generate their own response. One example could be a time-sensitive filter that blocks access to certain resources (such as an Internet proxy server) outside certain set hours. Yet another interesting application in this category is customized caching. A filter can maintain a cache of most frequently requested (static) resources based on prespecified criteria, and serve a cached copy instead of accessing the real resource whenever possible.

By strategically combining the request dispatcher and filters, web-application frameworks designers can create specialized filters that perform a service such as form validation, data pre-fetch, and other functions. In these cases, filters can become fully fledged, bona fide resource processors in the request-processing pipeline.

# The Big Picture of Filtering

The middle-tier component of the Java EE architecture consists of an application server often fronted by a web server. These servers serve up web content and execute servlets and JSP pages in response to incoming client requests. Figure 10-1 illustrates how client requests flow through a stand-alone application server such as Tomcat:

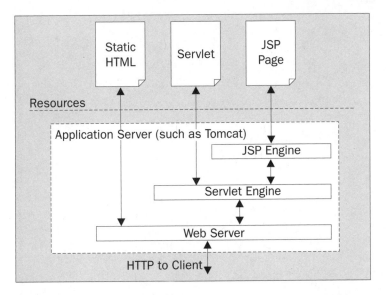

**Figure 10-1.** *A client can request various types of resources from a web server. The web server routes the request and returns the appropriate resource to the client.*

One way of looking at this diagram is to view it as a server for resource requests. In this view, you don't differentiate between static and dynamically generated resources. Therefore, the middle-tier server becomes a server that serves one of three types of resources based on incoming requests:

- Static content (HTML, images, and so on)

- A servlet

- A JSP page (which may be considered a specialized case of a servlet)

---

■**Note** This chapter and the next continually refer to this resource-based view of request processing. This is the way a filter designer looks at the container. Note that servlets and JSP pages are sometimes called "processing resources" because they can actively perform processing on a request.

---

Figure 10-2 illustrates this simplified view of the middle-tier server, emphasizing the request and response flow and showing where filters fit into the picture.

You can see that the filters are positioned in the **processing pipeline**, between the application server and the client. A filter provides application-level access in the request-handling pipeline of the container.

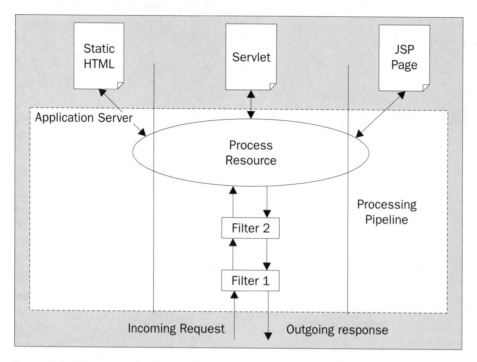

**Figure 10-2.** *Filters are called by the application server both prior to and subsequent to the resource processing of a request.*

Before the advent of filters, there was no way for web applications to participate in the processing being performed along the request-handling path. A web application could only supply and define the resources that were being served. If an application required access to the processing pipeline, you had to resort to nonportable server-level extensions (interceptors, valves, and the like which you'll look at later).

Due to their strategic position in the request-processing pipeline, filters can easily handle the pre- and postprocessing of requests for resources (such as HTML pages, JSP pages, and servlets). The specialized construction of filters, as you'll discover later, will actually allow them to participate in the processing of the request or response throughout the processing path.

You also have the option of chaining several filters together dynamically to process each incoming request. This allows the filter deployer to combine the action of two or more filters at deployment time. At runtime, the container uses filter mappings to determine the filter or filters that each request and response will pass through.

## Filtering the Pipeline

Filters enable a developer to tap into the pipeline of request and response processing. A filter can do its work just before the resource is fetched (or executed in the case of dynamic output), and immediately after the resource is fetched and executed. It's even possible to inject custom behavior *while* the request is being processed by the resource.

More specifically, when you apply this notion to the HTTP-based request and response that is serviced by the middle-tier servers, filters can be used to do the following:

- Inspect the request header and data before it reaches the resource

- Inspect the response header and data after it has been sent by the resource

- Provide a modified version of the request to the resource being processed by the container

- Access and modify the response from the resource before returning it

- Stop a request from reaching a resource altogether

This behavior is depicted in Figure 10-3.

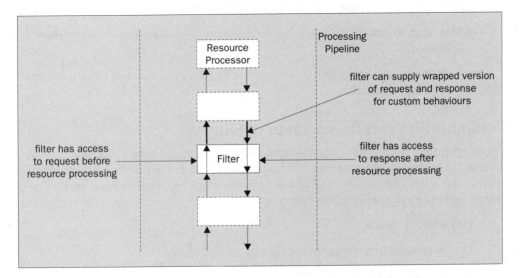

**Figure 10-3.** *Filters can act on the request before it reaches the resource, and on the response after the resource has been accessed.*

You'll examine filter implementations that perform each of these actions in this chapter and the next. You should note that code implemented in filters can have the same power, if not more, as code implemented in resources (in other words, servlets and JSP pages) when it comes to request processing. In some ways, you can view the servlet engine and the JSP engine simply as end-point filters in this processing pipeline.

# Filters in Depth

You'll now take a more concrete, technical look at what filters really are. First, you'll become intimately acquainted with the single interface that defines a filter: the `Filter` interface.

## The Filter Interface

A filter is simply a class that implements the `javax.servlet.Filter` interface. Similar to the `javax.servlet.Servlet` interface, there are three life-cycle methods that a filter must implement:

- **`public void init(FilterConfig config)throws ServletException:`** The container is responsible for setting the `FilterConfig` object before the `doFilter()` method (described next) is called for the first time. The `FilterConfig` object provides the initialization parameters for the filter and also allows access to the associated `ServletContext`.

- **`public void doFilter(ServletRequest req, ServletResponse res, FilterChain chain) throws IOException, ServletException:`** The `doFilter()` method contains the logic of the filter. It's where almost all of the work of a filter is done. The container will call this method each time an applicable request is being handled. You'll see how to associate filters with types of requests in the next section.

- **`public void destroy():`** The container calls `destroy()` when the filter is being taken out of service.

Any class that implements this interface is officially a filter and can then be included as a component of a web application.

## Configuration and Deployment of Filters

In the deployment phase, filters are an integral part of a web application, at the same level as servlets, JSP pages, or static resources. Filters are typically created by developers and delivered as bytecode classes within a web application. Typically, a web application's filters are configured at deployment by specifying the following:

- Which filter(s) to use

- Any initialization parameters to the filter

- Where to apply the filter

- The order in which multiple filters are chained together (if applicable)

All of the previous items are specified within the standard Java EE web-application deployment descriptor (`web.xml`).

In this way, filters are configured and deployed in a similar fashion as servlets in a web application. The servlet container supporting filters will parse the following two types of filter-related declarations present within this file:

- **Filter definition:** Tells the container the textual name associated with the filter

- **Filter mapping:** Tells the container which resources the filter will be applied to

You'll cover these in more detail shortly when you examine filter definition and configuration.

Now that you know what a filter is, you need to take a look at the interactions that occur between a container and the filter and specifically the life cycle of a filter.

# The Life Cycle of a Filter

Just like servlets and JSP pages, the container manages the life cycle of a filter. You'll learn the following in this section:

- When the container instantiates a filter

- How initialization parameters are passed into a filter

- How the container determines how many instances of the filter to create

- When the doFilter() method is called

- How filters can clean up on application shutdown

Figure 10-4 illustrates the life cycle of a filter by using a block diagram to represent states that the filter can be in. As you can see, the filter life cycle is almost identical to that of the servlet life cycle. The four stages of the filter life cycle (instantiation, initialization, filter execution, and destruction) are analogous to the servlet life cycle (instantiation, initialization, request execution, and destruction). Of the four stages, there are only two explicit states: initialization and filter execution. In the other two stages, the filter instance does not exist; it is either being created or being destroyed.

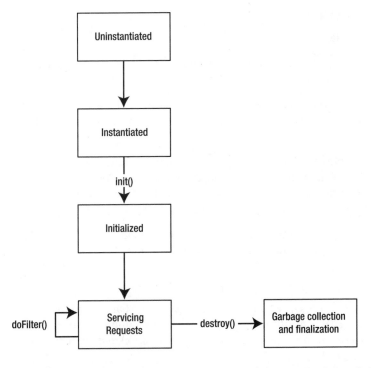

**Figure 10-4.** *The life cycle of a filter is similar to the life cycle of a servlet. The filter is created and initialized, it processes requests, and it is destroyed when no longer needed.*

For each filter definition in the web application (as specified in web.xml), the container will create and initialize a filter instance.

Every filter must implement the javax.servlet.Filter interface. This interface defines three methods: init(), doFilter(), and destroy(). These three methods, and the constructor, correspond to the four stages of the filter life cycle. The constructor is called during the instantiation phase. The init() method is called for initialization. The doFilter() method, which contains all the filter-processing logic, handles the filter execution phase. Finally, the destroy() method is used in the destruction phase.

That single filter instance, with its initial parameters, will service all requests that correspond to its filter mapping specified within the deployment descriptor. The only exception to this occurs when the engine consists of multiple Java Virtual Machine (VM) servicing requests. In this case, the container mechanism will create one instance in each VM, thereby allowing all participating VMs to service filtered resources equally. The container will call destroy() when the web application is shut down.

The initialization must occur before the first request is mapped through the filter instance. During initialization, the container passes a FilterConfig object via the init() method of the javax.servlet.Filter interface.

The FilterConfig can be used by the filter to obtain initialization parameters of the filter, the textual name of the filter, or the ServletContext that the application is running under.

## The FilterConfig Interface

The FilterConfig interface declares four methods:

- **public String getFilterName():** You can use this method to obtain the textual name of the filter, as defined in the web.xml deployment descriptor.

- **public String getInitParameter(String paramName):** The getInitParameter() method obtains the string value of a specific initialization parameter by name. Returns null if not found.

- **public Enumeration getInitParameterNames():** This method obtains a java.util. Enumeration consisting of all the names of the initialization parameters for this instance. These parameters are specified in the web.xml deployment descriptor within the <filter> definitions. Returns an empty enumeration if no parameter is set.

- **public ServletContext getServletContext():** This method obtains the ServletContext that the filter is executing within. This context is typically specified in the server.xml file of the server.

In all cases, after a filter is instantiated and initialized, the container will send all requests that the filter maps to through the filter's doFilter() method. For most static pages, JSP pages, and servlet resources, this means that many threads of execution may be executing the doFilter() method at the same time. Therefore, you must take care to write filters that are thread-safe.

The filter instance will be kept alive to process a request until the container (or a VM in the container) shuts down or the associated web application is undeployed. Before this happens, the container calls destroy() to give the filter a chance to perform any cleanup work that may be necessary.

## Filter Definitions

Filters can be defined for each web application. Filter definitions appear in the web.xml deployment descriptor inside the <filter> element. Each <filter> element must have a <filter-name> child element, a <filter-class> child element, and optionally one or more <init-param> child elements. Here is a brief description of each:

- **<filter-name>:** Textual name to associate with the filter. Used in filter mapping. This is a mandatory element.

- **<filter-class>:** The actual class that implements a filter. Should be a fully qualified class name with a package prefix. This is a mandatory element.

- **<init-param>:** Specifies the initial parameters to supply to this instance of the filter. Contains <param-name> and <param-value> subelements, specifying the name and value of the parameter, respectively. Note that <init-param> is an optional child element of <filter>, which can also appear multiple times—once for each initialization parameter for the filter.

As an example, consider an audit filter that logs all access to certain specified resources. The AuditFilter class would be set up in the application's web.xml file as follows:

```
<filter>
  <filter-name>Audit Filter</filter-name>
  <filter-class>filters.AuditFilter</filter-class>
</filter>
```

The previous segment associates the name Audit Filter with the filter implementation in AuditFilter.class.

You'll examine the details of the initial parameters of filters after you've looked at how filters are mapped to resources.

## Filter Mapping

You've seen how to define a filter in the web.xml deployment descriptor file. Now let's move on to look at how to map a filter. Filter mapping allows you to specify resources that the filter will be applied to within your application on a by-request basis. Applying a filter to a resource literally means adding the filter to the processing pipeline when accessing that resource.

Filter mappings are XML-based entries, specified per web application within the web.xml file. The "mapping" that is performed is between the filter's textual name and one or more resources that the filter will be applied to. Because the filter mapping uses the filter's textual name, the corresponding <filter> element must precede a <filter-mapping> element within the web.xml file.

This is what the filter mapping for our audit filter might look like:

```
<filter-mapping>
  <filter-name>Visual Audit Filter</filter-name>
  <servlet-name>mylocate</servlet-name>
</filter-mapping>
```

Here, the mapping specifies that the filter declared as `Visual Audit Filter` (in a previous `<filter>` declaration) will be applied only when a request is received for the servlet resource called `mylocate`. It's assumed, of course, that the servlet name is defined within the same `web.xml` file, like this:

```
<servlet>
  <servlet-name>mylocate</servlet-name>
  <servlet-class>FindProd</servlet-class>
</servlet>
```

To map a filter to more than one resource, you need to either create multiple mapping entries or create a filter mapping that uses a URL pattern. Now let's take a look at how to use URL patterns.

## Matching URL Patterns

The real power of filter mapping becomes evident when you use URL pattern matching. URL patterns allow users to apply a filter to a group of resources with some commonality in its URL. You can also use wildcard characters (such as *) within the URL to match multiple URLs. This is similar to the handling of the `<servlet-mapping>` element.

Depending on how the URL pattern is specified, you can apply a filter to a set of homogeneous resources (for instance, just servlets) or a set of heterogeneous resources (a mix of static HTML files, servlets, and JSP pages). Table 10-1 lists some sample URL patterns.

**Table 10-1.** *Example Filter Mapping Patterns*

| URL Pattern | Matches |
| --- | --- |
| /* | Everything that is served by this web application, including static pages, servlets, and JSP pages |
| /servlet/* | All servlets (assuming all servlets are mapped under the /servlet path) |
| /jsp/*.jsp | All JSP pages located on the /jsp path |
| /dept/accounting/* | All resources in the accounting department branch of the web application |

The following is an example of filter mapping that uses a URL pattern:

```
<filter-mapping>
  <filter-name>Audit Filter</filter-name>
  <url-pattern>/*</url-pattern>
</filter-mapping>
```

This declaration applies the `Audit Filter` filter to all resources served by the application. Here's another example:

```
<filter-mapping>
  <filter-name>Stop Games Filter</filter-name>
  <url-pattern>/servlet/*</url-pattern>
</filter-mapping>
```

Assuming that servlets in this web application are mapped under the `/servlet` path, this filter mapping would apply the `Stop Games Filter` to all servlets in the application.

# Insertion of Filters into the Request Flow

Prior to Servlet 2.4, filters could operate only on requests as they originated from the client. However, many modern web applications and frameworks make extensive use of the ability to dispatch requests from one processing resource to another (servlet to servlet, servlet to JSP, JSP to servlet, JSP to JSP, and so on). The inability of filters to work in the processing pipeline between dispatch points handicapped earlier versions of servlet containers. This was changed with the Servlet 2.4 specification, and containers such as Tomcat 5.5 have full flexibility to insert filters into the request flow—even in-between programmatically dispatched points.

### Filters and the Request Dispatcher

To better understand how the request dispatcher interacts with filters, we'll present a series of figures depicting the request flow in a servlet container. First, we'll show the action of Servlet 2.3–compliant containers. These containers support filters but don't support interactions with the request dispatcher.

### Servlet 2.3–Compliant Container Filtering

Consider a filter mapping similar to the following:

```
<filter-mapping>
  <filter-name>F1</filter-name>
  <url-pattern>/*</url-pattern>
</filter-mapping>
<filter-mapping>
  <filter-name>F2</filter-name>
  <url-pattern>/*</url-pattern>
</filter-mapping>
<filter-mapping>
  <filter-name>F3</filter-name>
  <url-pattern>/*</url-pattern>
</filter-mapping>
```

Figure 10-5 illustrates the filtering that will be performed.

**Figure 10-5.** *An incoming request is processed by zero or more filters, and the response from the web resource can be processed by the same set of filters.*

The previous figure is the conventional request flow. The incoming request is optionally passed through a mapped filter chain before being sent to the final processing resource— typically a servlet or JSP page. This is the typical filtered request data flow for older Servlet 2.3–compliant containers.

Figure 10-6 reveals what happens when you use the same filter mapping with two resources that are included by the main web resource (via `RequestDispatcher.include()` in a servlet or an `include` directive in JSP) when using Servlet 2.3–compliant containers.

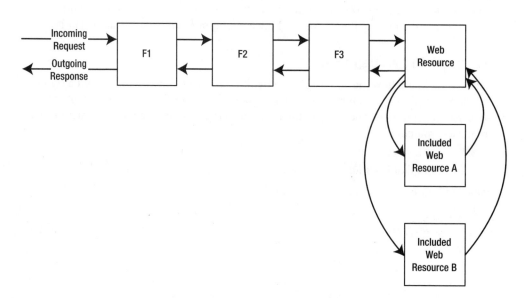

**Figure 10-6.** *When a resource in a Servlet 2.3 container includes other resources, these resources do not get processed by the filters.*

In other words, under Servlet 2.3–compliant container control, when the primary web resource uses the request dispatcher to include other processing resources, the included processing resource cannot be filtered. The same thing happens when the web resource uses the request dispatcher to forward the request to other processing resources (via the `RequestDispatcher.forward()` method in a servlet or the `<jsp:forward>` tag in JSP). Figure 10-7 illustrates this situation.

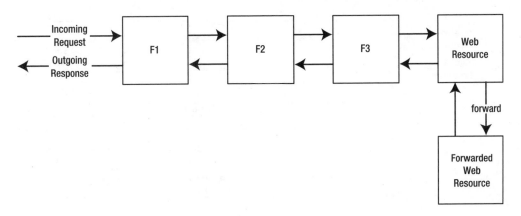

**Figure 10-7.** *In Servlet 2.3 containers, filters are not applied to the request or the response between the original resource and the forwarded resource. Filters are only applied between the client and the request resource.*

## Servlet 2.5–Compliant Container Filtering

A container, such as Tomcat 5.5, allows filtering to occur with both the include and forward action of the request dispatcher. Consider the following filter mapping:

```
<filter-mapping>
  <filter-name>F1</filter-name>
  <url-pattern>/*</url-pattern>
  <dispatcher>REQUEST</dispatcer>
  <dispatcher>INCLUDE</dispatcher>
</filter-mapping>
<filter-mapping>
  <filter-name>F2</filter-name>
  <url-pattern>/*</url-pattern>
  <dispatcher>REQUEST</dispatcer>
  <dispatcher>INCLUDE</dispatcher>
</filter-mapping>
<filter-mapping>
  <filter-name>F3</filter-name>
  <url-pattern>/*</url-pattern>
  <dispatcher>REQUEST</dispatcer>
  <dispatcher>INCLUDE</dispatcher>
</filter-mapping>
```

The <dispatcher> subelement of a filter mapping allows you to specify that filtering is to be performed during regular request dispatch as well as when the request dispatcher is called to include additional web resources. Figure 10-8 illustrates the action of this filter mapping on the included web resource.

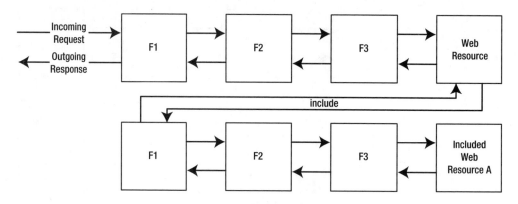

**Figure 10-8.** *When a resource in a Servlet 2.4 or 2.5 container includes another resource, zero or more filters can be applied as part of the include action.*

Now filters can be applied in-between the first processing resource and any included resources. For example, if the first JSP page included the output from multiple JSP pages or servlets, filters could be applied to each included resource.

Next, you'll look at the case when the request dispatcher forwards processing to a web resource. Consider the following filter mapping:

```
<filter-mapping>
    <filter-name>F1</filter-name>
    <url-pattern>/*</url-pattern>
    <dispatcher>REQUEST</dispatcher>
    <dispatcher>FORWARD</dispatcher>
</filter-mapping>
<filter-mapping>
    <filter-name>F2</filter-name>
    <url-pattern>/*</url-pattern>
    <dispatcher>REQUEST</dispatcher>
    <dispatcher>FORWARD</dispatcher>
</filter-mapping>
<filter-mapping>
    <filter-name>F3</filter-name>
    <url-pattern>/*</url-pattern>
    <dispatcher>REQUEST</dispatcher>
    <dispatcher>FORWARD</dispatcher>
</filter-mapping>
```

In this case, the filter chain will operate on both the standard request processing and the forwarded web-resource processing, as shown in Figure 10-9.

This time the first web resource uses the request dispatcher's forwarding capability. The resource that the request is forwarded to is responsible for generating the actual output for the client. Here, the filter is applied before the primary web resource, and before the resource being forwarded to.

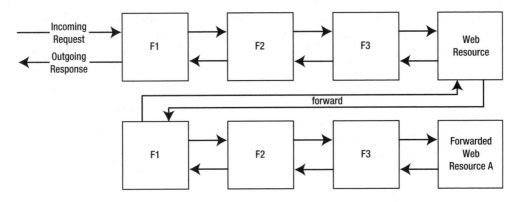

**Figure 10-9.** *Zero or more filters can be applied to the request and response when a resource forwards a request to another resource.*

Filter interactions with the dispatcher are controlled by the `<dispatcher>` subelement of `<filter-mapping>`, as you saw earlier. Let's take a more detailed look at this new subelement.

### The <dispatcher> Element

The `<dispatcher>` subelement in `<filter-mapping>` is optional. If omitted, the `<filter-mapping>` declaration is backward compatible with Servlet 2.3 containers. In this case, the mapped filter will work only on the request level, and not when the request is dispatched via a request dispatcher. This compatibility mode is entirely equivalent to specifying the following `<filter-mapping>` segment:

```
<filter-mapping>
  <filter-name>F1</filter-name>
  <url-pattern>/*</url-pattern>
  <dispatcher>REQUEST</dispatcher>
</filter-mapping>
```

### REQUEST, FORWARD, INCLUDE, or ERROR <dispatcher> Values

Table 10-2 shows the allowed values inside a `<dispatcher>` element.

**Table 10-2.** *Valid Subelements of the <dispatcher> Tag*

| Value | Description |
|---|---|
| REQUEST | Enables filter mapping for incoming requests |
| FORWARD | Enables filter mapping for forwarded requests by using the request dispatcher |
| INCLUDE | Enables filter mapping when the request dispatcher is used to include the output of multiple processing resources |
| ERROR | Enables filter mapping when the request is forwarded to an error-handling resource |

For any single filter mapping, you can specify one or more of these values, thereby allowing fine-grained control over filter action. Using these values enables you to apply some filters under all circumstances and selectively apply others.

### Error Filters

Using ERROR as the value of the <dispatcher> element will cause the filter to be called whenever a request is forwarded to an error-handling resource. This use of the <dispatcher> element enables specific filters to be configured to work with the error-handling resource—the filters will be applied before the request reaches the actual error-handling resource.

# Filter Chaining

**Chaining** is the action of passing a request through multiple filters in sequence before accessing the resource requested. For example, you may want an authentication filter on an XML-based resource that is also processed by an XSLT transformation filter. The good news is that all filters are inherently chainable. Unlike most other chaining mechanisms, however, filter chaining also means passing the response from the resource back through the chains of filters in the reverse order. This is an important concept and is an essential component in the versatility of filters.

### The FilterChain Interface

The container and the filter implementation work together to ensure that every filter is chainable. This is done through a filter chain object that implements the javax.servlet.FilterChain interface. This filter chain object is passed into the core doFilter() method of a filter by the container. This object allows the filter to directly call the next filter in the chain after its own processing. The interface contains this doFilter() method:

```
public void doFilter(ServletRequest req, ServletResponse res)
    throws IOException, ServletException
```

Calling this method invokes the doFilter() method of the next filter in the chain. If the filter is the very last filter in the chain, the actual resource processing will occur. This method doesn't return until all downstream filters have returned from their doFilter() calls. Also note that from the point of view of the filter, all of the nonfilter logic request processing is "folded" into the call to the doFilter() method of FilterChain. This allows us to do something that is typically very difficult to perform in other request/response intercepting mechanisms. Because all the processing of the request and response occurs in the same doFilter() method and in the same thread, we can easily share variables between the preprocessing and the postprocessing logic.

### All Filters Are Chainable

Compatibility with filter chaining is an integral requirement of every filter. Filter chaining is provided by a series of interactions between the container and the filter. Figure 10-10 is a UML diagram of the interactions.

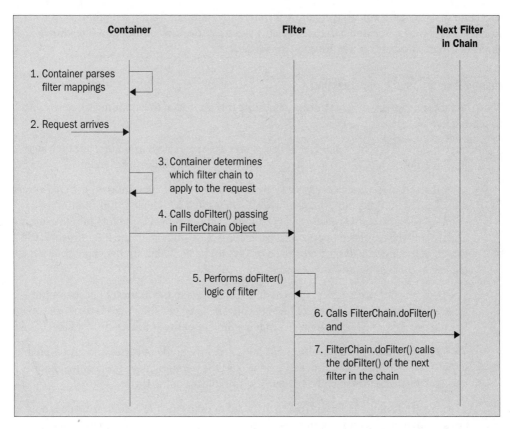

**Figure 10-10.** *The design of the Filter API provides an inherent chaining capability. The container works with each filter to filter and process the request as specified in the deployment descriptor.*

Here is an explanation of what happens:

1. The container parses the filter mappings defined in the web.xml file of the application.

2. A request arrives, accessing a resource in the application.

3. The container determines the filter chain that will be applied to this request.

4. The container invokes the doFilter() method of the first filter in the chain, passing in the request, a response (holder), and a FilterChain object reference. The container loads the filter chain information into the FilterChain object that is passed in.

5. The filter performs its doFilter() logic.

6. The filter completes its filter logic and calls the doFilter() method of the FilterChain object reference, passing in the request and response. All filters are required to do this, because all filters are intrinsically chainable.

7. Logic in the doFilter() method of the FilterChain object calls the doFilter() method of the next filter chain to be called. Steps from step 4 are repeated until the last filter in the chain has completed its work. The FilterChain.doFilter() call on the last filter in the chain will cause the access of the resource to occur.

Note that the mechanism of chaining is inherently different from most other conventional filtering or server extension mechanisms (such as Apache modules and Microsoft's Internet Information Server and Internet Server API).

## Unique Properties of Filter Chaining

Note the following interesting properties regarding this approach to extending server functionality:

- Each of the `FilterChain.doFilter()` method calls are stacked upon one another, so program flow is blocked in a nested fashion across all the filters involved.

- After the actual resource access, the `FilterChain.doFilter()` method on the chain's last filter returns. At this point, the response object is filled with header information and content from the actual resource access. This last filter now has the freedom to examine and modify the response header and body content at will. When the filter finishes, the thread of execution will return from `doFilter()`. The next filter up the chain then gets a chance to process the response, and so on.

- The logic in a filter's `doFilter()` method has full access to the request in its incoming flow, prior to the `FilterChain.doFilter()` call. The logic in a filter's `doFilter()` method has full access to the response in its outgoing flow, after the `FilterChain.doFilter()` call.

- The local variables declared within the `doFilter()` method are consistent and available to both the incoming flow-processing logic and the outgoing flow-processing logic because the same thread will be executing both pieces of the logic.

These properties of the chaining mechanism are perhaps the hardest filtering concepts to understand. In essence, filter chaining is not a "call and forget" mechanism provided by container intervention, but rather a "nested call" mechanism assisted by the container.

Of course, you must realize that even though filter chaining is built into every filter, the processing logic within the filter is not obliged to chain to the next filter. In fact, this is one major application area for filters—blocking access to the actual resource. For example, an authorization filter can determine that the client isn't allowed to access a resource and can generate a refusal response all on its own without further chaining.

## A Fly in the Filtering Ointment

The avid reader (and indeed experienced JSP and servlet programmer) will realize that not all containers buffer their resource response in the response object after the resource completes processing. JSP pages and servlets may write and flush their output stream as the response is generated. This places dubious value on the processing window that each filter gets during a response's return trip through the filter chain. Although this processing window is perfect for resources and containers that do encapsulate the entire output in the response object, you must also deal with the reality of those that don't.

The way that filters deal with processing resources that generate output on the fly is via a customized wrapped-response object. That is, the filter will pass a specialized version of the response object to the `FilterChain.doFilter()` method instead of the one that it received as its invocation parameter.

This wrapped-response object can then provide its own version of `OutputStream` and `PrintWriter` for downstream filters or resources to work on. You'll delve into these wrapped-response and wrapped-request mechanisms in the next chapter.

When working with dispatched requests, note that wrapped-response and wrapped-request objects will be passed down the processing chain—except in the case of an error dispatch. In this case, it's the original container-generated request and response that will be passed to the error-processing resource (and any filters that may be associated with it). This is necessary because of the asynchronous nature of the error-handling mechanism.

---

■**Tip**  Custom wrapped-response and wrapped-request classes can be used to provide downstream processors with enhanced functionality (through special extended APIs) not available with the default response or request classes. In these cases, the filter and processing resources must cooperate with one another.

---

## Mapping Requests Through a Filter Chain

The order of `<filter-mapping>` elements in the `web.xml` file is significant. This is the order in which the container will build filter chains. Therefore, filter declarations within `web.xml` must be in the order that you want them to be applied to a resource. Applying filter A and then filter B to a request will not necessarily result in the same outcome as applying filter B followed by filter A.

When the order of chaining for the same set of filters is changed, the final result can be completely different. This typically happens when a downstream filter depends on the result of an upstream filter for proper operations. For example, imagine a filter that transforms XML data from a resource to HTML by using XSL Transformations (XSLT), and another filter that translates the HTML document via cascading style sheets, level 1 (CSS1, another stylesheet language, typically for HTML). As shown in Figure 10-11, if you place the XSLT filter first in the chain, the XML resource will be translated to HTML and subsequently formatted by the CSS1 filter. If you place the CSS1 filter first, however, it won't work on the XML data (see Figure 10-11). As a result, only the XSLT transformation will be applied in this chain.

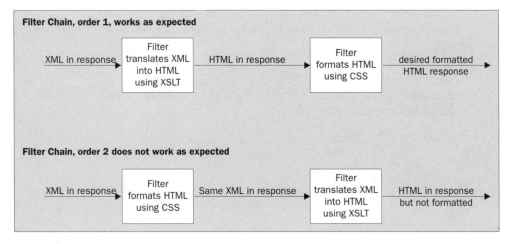

**Figure 10-11.** *In some cases, the order in which filters are applied can make a difference in whether the request is correctly processed.*

The filter application order has been determined by the order that the `<filter-mapping>` elements occur in the `web.xml` file. For example, consider the following set of filter mappings:

```
<filter-mapping>
  <filter-name>Audit Filter</filter-name>
  <url-pattern>/*</url-pattern>
</filter-mapping>
<filter-mapping>
  <filter-name>Authentication Filter</filter-name>
  <url-pattern>/*</url-pattern>
</filter-mapping>
```

In this case, both `Audit Filter` and `Authentication Filter` are mapped to all resources served by this server—both filters will be applied to all resources. The order of application will be `Audit Filter` followed by `Authentication Filter`. Remember that the order of chained filter execution on the incoming request is **down** the filter stack, whereas the order of chained filter execution on the outgoing path is **up** the filter stack.

Given an incoming request, the container will go through the list of filter mappings to determine which filter to apply on a per-request basis. For example, say you have the following filter mappings defined in order:

```
<filter-mapping>
  <filter-name>Audit Filter</filter-name>
  <url-pattern>/*</url-pattern>
</filter-mapping>
<filter-mapping>
  <filter-name>Authentication Filter</filter-name>
  <url-pattern>/servlet/*</url-pattern>
</filter-mapping>
<filter-mapping>
  <filter-name>Visual Audit Filter</filter-name>
  <servlet-name>mylocate</servlet-name>
</filter-mapping>
```

An incoming request for `http://tomcathost/myapp/index.html` will have the following filter applied:

- `Audit Filter`

In contrast, an incoming request for `http://tomcathost/myapp/servlet/listprod` will have the following filters applied in order:

- `Audit Filter`

- `Authentication Filter`

Finally, an incoming request for `http://tomcathost/myapp/servlet/mylocate` will have the following filters applied in order:

- Audit Filter

- Authentication Filter

- Visual Audit Filter

# Initial Parameters for Filters

You can specify `<init-param>` as a child element of `<filter>` to provide initial parameters for the filter instance, as in the following snippet. This `web.xml` file segment controls the hours that the `Stop Games Filter` may operate (this filter blocks game playing):

```
<filter>
  <filter-name>Stop Games Filter</filter-name>
  <filter-class>filters.StopGamesFilter</filter-class>
  <init-param>
    <param-name>starthour</param-name>
    <param-value>10</param-value>
  </init-param>
  <init-param>
    <param-name>stophour</param-name>
    <param-value>11</param-value>
  </init-param>
</filter>
```

The container will associate the textual name `Stop Games Filter` with the `StopGamesFilter` filter class. The parameters are accessed within the filter and instruct the filter to restrict gaming activities between 10 and 11 a.m. by default. The `starthour` and `stophour` will be accessible within the filter via a call to the `FilterConfig` object:

```
String startHour = filterConfig.getInitParameter("starthour");
String stopHour = filterConfig.getInitParameter("stophour");
```

## Initialization for Multiple Instances of Same Filter

Note that a container will create an instance of a filter for each `<filter>` definition encountered within the application. You can therefore define two instances of the same filter within the same web application—each with different initialization parameters. Of course, the two instances should have different textual names. For example, you may want to set up an instance of a `StopGamesFilter` to block access from 8 a.m. to 10 p.m. for the Administration department, and another instance to block access from 8 a.m. to 9 a.m. for the Engineering department, (because if you don't block access, the engineers will play games right through breakfast):

```
<filter>
  <filter-name>Stop Games Filter For Administration Department</filter-name>
```

```
  <filter-class>filters.StopGamesFilter</filter-class>
  <init-param>
    <param-name>starthour</param-name>
    <param-value>8</param-value>
  </init-param>
  <init-param>
    <param-name>stophour</param-name>
    <param-value>22</param-value>
  </init-param>
</filter>
<filter>
  <filter-name>Stop Games Filter For Engineering Department</filter-name>
  <filter-class>filters.StopGamesFilter</filter-class>
  <init-param>
    <param-name>starthour</param-name>
    <param-value>8</param-value>
  </init-param>
  <init-param>
    <param-name>stophour</param-name>
    <param-value>9</param-value>
  </init-param>
</filter>
```

### Interaction with the Filter Life Cycle

When working with filter initial parameters, it's important to bear in mind that these parameters are set only once per filter instance: when the filter instance is first instantiated and before the arrival of the first filtered request. Subsequently, all new requests will be processed through the same filter instance—potentially concurrently via multithreading. In containers that use multiple Java VMs, there will be one instance of a declared filter per container Java VM. You can use `filterConfig.getInitParameter()` to obtain the initial parameters' values from inside the `doFilter()` method when you need them. The handling of these initial parameters is very similar to servlets' parameter handling. If a filter instance is removed from service by the container (say, due to server system load), the container is responsible for ensuring that a new instance is created and initialized to process any future requests. Such removals and reinstantiations should be completely transparent to the filter creator.

This concludes the initial conceptual coverage of filters. It's time to get your hands on some code and implement your very own filter.

# Hands-On Filter Development

In this section, you'll discover how to set up a development and testing environment for filters. You'll also code, configure, and test some simple filters in this environment.

The very first version of Tomcat to support the Servlet 2.5 specification is Tomcat 5. While the 4.x series of Tomcat supports filters, the Servlet 2.4 functionality (namely support for filtering the request dispatcher pipeline) will be available only in the 5.x versions.

# Our First Filter—SimpleFilter

Before coding your first filter, let's take a quick look at one additional interface that you'll be using within the filters sample.

## The ServletContext Interface

Using the getServletContext() method on the javax.servlet.FilterConfig object, the filter can obtain a reference to the current ServletContext that it's executing under. There is a ServletContext for each running web application. Because of this single-instance nature, the ServletContext is frequently used for sharing information globally.

Using this reference, the filter can utilize the context's logger service. It can also use this interface to attach arbitrary attributes to the context during runtime. An attribute can be an arbitrary object associated with a String name. Attaching attributes to ServletContext is a popular way to pass information between processing agents during runtime. For example, state information can be passed between filter instances by using these attributes. Here are several of the most frequently used methods by filter writers, and you'll see them used in the sample filters later:

- **Object getAttribute(String name):** Obtains the value of a named attribute

- **void setAttribute(String name, Object object):** Attaches a named attribute to the ServletContext

- **void removeAttribute(String name):** Removes a previously attached attribute

- **Enumeration getAttributeNames():** Returns a java.util.Enumeration consisting of the names of all the currently attached attributes

You'll need to write to the log file in your filters, using the following methods of the ServletContext object:

- **void log(string msg):** Writes a string to the currently active logging facility associated with the context

- **void log(String msg, Throwable throw):** Writes a string and a stack trace to the log

## Coding the Filter

Your first filter is called SimpleFilter. Listing 10-1 shows the source code for SimpleFilter, which implements the Filter interface. To compile this class, you'll need to include the appropriate library JAR for the servlet API. This JAR is named servlet-api.jar and is located in the Tomcat common\lib directory. This simple filter won't do anything useful for now. It will simply make a log entry before calling FilterChain.doFilter() and another one right after it.

**Listing 10-1.** *SimpleFilter.java*

```java
package com.apress.projsp.filters;

import java.io.*;
import javax.servlet.*;

public final class SimpleFilter implements Filter {
  private FilterConfig filterConfig = null;

  public void doFilter(ServletRequest request, ServletResponse response,
      FilterChain chain) throws IOException, ServletException {

    filterConfig.getServletContext().log("in SimpleFilter");
    chain.doFilter(request, response);
    filterConfig.getServletContext().log("Getting out of SimpleFilter");
  }

  public void init(FilterConfig filterConfig) {
    this.filterConfig = filterConfig;
  }

  public void destroy() {}
}
```

As mentioned before, all filters must implement the `javax.servlet.Filter` interface, and the `SimpleFilter` is no exception. The filter does its work in the `doFilter()` method. Note the parameters: a `request`, `response`, and a `FilterChain` object.

However, before the container calls `doFilter()`, it will pass a `FilterConfig` object to the filter through the `init()` method. If the filter needs to access any resources from the `FilterConfig` object, the class must save a reference to that object.

To write to the log, you access the `ServletContext` from `FilterConfig` as provided by the container. The `log()` method will write a line by using the logger set up earlier for this context.

The rest of the methods are standard trivial implementations required for the `Filter` interface.

## Declaring the Filter and Configuring Filter Mapping

Now, you need to add a `<filter>` element to the `web.xml` file, the deployment descriptor for your web application. Listing 10-2 shows the `web.xml` file for this example.

**Listing 10-2.** *web.xml*

```xml
<?xml version="1.0" encoding="UTF-8"?>
<web-app xmlns="http://java.sun.com/xml/ns/javaee"
         xmlns:xsi="http://www.w3.org/2001/XMLSchema-instance"
         xsi:schemaLocation= ➥
"http://java.sun.com/xml/ns/javaee/web-app_2_5.xsd"
         version="2.5">
```

```
<display-name>ProJSP Example Filters</display-name>
<distributable />
<filter>
  <filter-name>Simple Filter</filter-name>
  <filter-class>com.apress.projsp.filters.SimpleFilter</filter-class>
</filter>
<filter-mapping>
  <filter-name>Simple Filter</filter-name>
  <url-pattern>/*</url-pattern>
</filter-mapping>
</web-app>
```

■**Note** If you're working with the source-code distribution downloaded from the book's website, these filter definitions and mappings are included but commented out. You should uncomment each set as appropriate as you progress through the example.

All that's left to do now is to create a resource to access. Listing 10-3 shows a simple JSP page. Because we're more interested in the filter processing than the JSP processing, this JSP page does no processing; it is just a convenient resource we can access to demonstrate filter processing.

**Listing 10-3.** *index.jsp*

```
<html>
  <head></head>
  <body>
    <h1>Welcome to Filtering Demo Application!</h1>
  </body>
</html>
```

## Testing the Filter

You're now ready to test the filter. Assuming that Tomcat isn't currently running, perform the following steps:

1. Go to Tomcat's logs subdirectory and delete all files.

2. Create a web application with the filter and index.jsp and deploy it.

3. Start Tomcat 5.

4. Start a browser and navigate to http://localhost:8080/filters1/index.jsp.

5. After the web page has loaded in the browser, shut down Tomcat.

Now to check that the filter has actually worked for this simple static page, let's read the application log file found lurking in the Tomcat logs directory. The log file will be named after the current date, something like localhost_log.2005-08-04.txt.

Inside, you should find the two log entries written by the filter, one entry created by the log() method prior to the doFilter() method call, and one created by the log() method after the doFilter() method call. On our test system, here are the two log entries:

```
2005-07-27 10:09:58 StandardContext[/filters1]in SimpleFilter
2005-07-27 10:09:59 StandardContext[/filters1]Getting out of SimpleFilter
```

## Experimentation with Filter Chaining

Now you'll create a second filter called SimpleFilter2 (see Listing 10-4). Like SimpleFilter, it just logs each request in the log file. Chaining these filters together will give us some insight into the action of filter chaining under Tomcat 5.

**Listing 10-4.** *SimpleFilter2.java*

```java
package com.apress.projsp.filters;

import java.io.IOException;
import javax.servlet.*;

public final class SimpleFilter2 implements Filter {
  private FilterConfig filterConfig = null;

  public void doFilter(ServletRequest request, ServletResponse response,
      FilterChain chain) throws IOException, ServletException {

    filterConfig.getServletContext().log("in SimpleFilter2");
    chain.doFilter(request, response);
    filterConfig.getServletContext().log("leaving SimpleFilter2");
  }

  public void init(FilterConfig filterConfig) {
    this.filterConfig = filterConfig;
  }

  public void destroy() {}
}
```

### Additions to web.xml

You can now add SimpleFilter2 to the chain. Listing 10-5 shows the updated web.xml, with a new entry for SimpleFilter2, and an updated sequence of <filter-mapping> elements. Ensure the ordering of <filter-mapping> entries is followed exactly.

**Listing 10-5.** *web.xml*

```xml
<?xml version="1.0" encoding="UTF-8"?>

<web-app xmlns="http://java.sun.com/xml/ns/javaee"
         xmlns:xsi="http://www.w3.org/2001/XMLSchema-instance"
         xsi:schemaLocation= ➡
"http://java.sun.com/xml/ns/javaee/web-app_2_5.xsd"
         version="2.5">

  <display-name>ProJSP Example Filters</display-name>
  <distributable />

  <filter>
    <filter-name>Simple Filter</filter-name>
    <filter-class>com.apress.projsp.filters.SimpleFilter</filter-class>
  </filter>

  <filter>
    <filter-name>Simple Filter 2</filter-name>
    <filter-class>com.apress.projsp.filters.SimpleFilter2</filter-class>
  </filter>

  <filter-mapping>
    <filter-name>Simple Filter</filter-name>
    <url-pattern>/*</url-pattern>
  </filter-mapping>

  <filter-mapping>
    <filter-name>Simple Filter 2</filter-name>
    <url-pattern>/*</url-pattern>
  </filter-mapping>

</web-app>
```

This mapping now maps both SimpleFilter and SimpleFilter2 to all resources being accessed. This effectively chains them for all resources.

Deploy the new web application to Tomcat. Clear the log files, start Tomcat, access the URL http://localhost:8080/filters1/ again, and then shut down Tomcat. Now, open the log file again and you should see something similar to the following:

```
2005-07-27 10:21:52 StandardContext[/filters1]in SimpleFilter
2005-07-27 10:21:52 StandardContext[/filters1]in SimpleFilter2
2005-07-27 10:21:53 StandardContext[/filters1]leaving SimpleFilter2
2005-07-27 10:21:53 StandardContext[/filters1]Getting out of SimpleFilter
```

Notice the nesting of the log entries, which clearly show that the filter-chaining mechanism consists of a series of nested doFilter() calls on the two participating filters. The chaining order is the order of `<filter-mapping>` declaration within the `web.xml` file, as expected.

## Creating an AuditFilter

Both `SimpleFilter` and `SimpleFilter2` just write to the log, so now let's create the first filter that delivers a little extra. It will audit resource access by logging the time of access, the IP address of the client, the resource being accessed, and the time spent fulfilling the request.

For brevity, we'll show the code for only the `doFilter()` method from the `AuditFilter` class here (see Listing 10-6); the rest of the code is no different from the previous filters. This filter takes advantage of the request object to obtain the required information. It also times the access to the resource by storing the system time before the `FilterChain.doFilter()` call. After the resource processing, it creates the log entry containing all the information.

**Listing 10-6.** *AuditFilter.java (doFilter() Method)*

```
public void doFilter(ServletRequest request, ServletResponse response,
    FilterChain chain) throws IOException, ServletException
{
  long startTime = System.currentTimeMillis();
  String remoteAddress = request.getRemoteAddr();
  String remoteHost = request.getRemoteHost();
  HttpServletRequest myReq = (HttpServletRequest) request;
  String reqURI = myReq.getRequestURI();
  chain.doFilter(request, response);
  filterConfig.getServletContext().log(
      "User at IP " + remoteAddress + "(" + remoteHost
          + ") accessed resource " + reqURI + " and used "
          + (System.currentTimeMillis() - startTime) + " ms");
}
```

Note the ease with which this summary information is maintained and written, using local variables in the `doFilter()` method itself. Thanks to the nested-call nature of filters, maintaining states across the two processing windows before and after resource access is simple.

Edit the `web.xml` file by adding the following declarations to the file and changing the `<filter-mapping>` entries for `SimpleFilter` and `SimpleFilter2` from the previous example:

```
<filter>
  <filter-name>Audit Filter</filter-name>
  <filter-class>com.apress.projsp.filters.AuditFilter</filter-class>
</filter>
<filter-mapping>
  <filter-name>Audit Filter</filter-name>
  <url-pattern>/*</url-pattern>
</filter-mapping>
<filter-mapping>
  <filter-name>Simple Filter</filter-name>
  <url-pattern>/index.jsp</url-pattern>
</filter-mapping>
```

```
<filter-mapping>
  <filter-name>Simple Filter 2</filter-name>
  <url-pattern>/index.jsp</url-pattern>
</filter-mapping>
```

This new mapping tells the container to apply the audit filter to all resources, and the simple filters only to requests for index.jsp. To make things more interesting, we'll use a different JSP resource to do this test.

## The FindProd.jsp

Listing 10-7 shows the JSP page that will be accessed to test the audit filter. Again, this JSP page is very straightforward. It uses an expression language statement to display the DEPT request parameter value on screen.

**Listing 10-7.** *FindProd.jsp*

```
<html>
  <head></head>
  <body>
    <h1>You have submitted as ${param.DEPT} department!</h1>
  </body>
</html>
```

Deploy the FindProd JSP, AuditFilter, and web.xml. Now we're ready to test. Follow these steps:

1. Clear out the Tomcat logs directory.

2. Start Tomcat.

3. Navigate to http://localhost:8080/filters1/FindProd.jsp?DEPT=Engineering.

4. Next, go to http://localhost:8080/filters1/FindProd.jsp?DEPT=Accounting.

5. Open http://localhost:8080/filters1/.

6. Shut down Tomcat.

Now, if you examine the log file, you'll see the audit trail left by AuditFilter:

```
2005-07-27 12:46:24 StandardContext[/filters1]User at IP 127.0.0.1 ➥
(127.0.0.1) accessed resource /filters1/FindProd.jsp and used 1578 ms
2005-07-27 12:46:30 StandardContext[/filters1]User at IP 127.0.0.1 ➥
(127.0.0.1) accessed resource /filters1/FindProd.jsp and used 15 ms
2005-07-27 12:46:36 StandardContext[/filters1]in SimpleFilter
2005-07-27 12:46:36 StandardContext[/filters1]in SimpleFilter2
2005-07-27 12:46:37 StandardContext[/filters1]leaving SimpleFilter2
2005-07-27 12:46:37 StandardContext[/filters1]Getting out of SimpleFilter
2005-07-27 12:46:37 StandardContext[/filters1]User at IP 127.0.0.1 ➥
(127.0.0.1) accessed resource /filters1/ and used 563 ms
```

You can glean some interesting data from this. The initial compiling and loading of the JSP page took 1578 milliseconds to complete, whereas subsequent access required negligible time. Also, you can see that the requests for `FindProd.jsp` were processed by only the audit filter. In contrast, the last request for `http://localhost:8080/filters1/` was processed by all three filters. Notice that because the audit filter did not log anything during the request portion of the processing, its only entry to the log appears after the return from `SimpleFilter2` and `SimpleFilter1`.

Writing this potentially useful auditing filter has been quite painless. You'll find in general that, after you're familiar with the model of operation of the Servlet 2.5 filter, writing highly functional filters can be quite straightforward.

# Other Filter-Like Technologies

Prior to Servlet 2.4 filters, there had been many server extension mechanisms based on similar concepts to filtering. In fact, **interceptors** form a key server-extension mechanism that is used quite heavily in many Tomcat 3.x-based containers. Tomcat 4.x uses a technology called valves to perform filter-like processing. However, there are fundamental differences between filters and these mechanisms: they aren't the same. This section briefly describes the essential differences between the technologies.

## Filters Aren't Tomcat 3.x Interceptors

Interceptors are a server-level extension mechanism for servers that support them. Interceptors are not an application-level technology. Being a server-extension technology, it's specific to Tomcat. Furthermore, effects of interceptors are typically global to the server—filter effects are local to the web application that the filters belong to.

The general architectures of interceptors and filters are completely different. Interceptors are "hooked in" modules that are called at specified points in the processing pipeline by the container. There are different types of interceptors for different access points. Filters, however, rely on nested chain calling (and custom wrapping of the request or response) to get their work done. There is only one "type" of filter. All filters implement the same `javax.servlet.Filter` interface.

## Filters Aren't Valves

Valves are a system-level mechanism used extensively within the design of Tomcat 4.x and 5.x. On an architectural level, they're almost identical to filters. But that's where the similarity ends.

Valves are Tomcat-specific and typically aren't portable to other Servlet 2.5–compatible servers. On the other hand, filters are portable. Valves are also internal to the Tomcat server and have privileged access to many structures and resources that application-level filters cannot access.

# Filter Design Best Practices

There are a few rules of thumb that you should consider when designing and writing filters. Some of these may give you novel ideas on how you can use filters in your own applications, while others may save you significant debugging time during the development cycle. This section presents an encapsulation of six such guidelines. You'll see several more in the next chapter when you explore the design and coding of more complex filters.

## Make Code Thread-Safe

Making code thread-safe cannot be stressed enough. Remember that there is typically only one instance of a filter per Java VM (unless the same filter is declared multiple times with different names or initial parameters). This makes it inevitable that the doFilter() method will be entered by many threads simultaneously, so your filter code must be thread-safe. This means the following:

- Local variables in doFilter() may be used freely (except for complex objects that may hold references to instance variables, in which case the next bullet applies).

- Instance variables in the filter class scope should be read-only, or the scope's access must be synchronized.

- Beware of calling methods that may modify instance variables indirectly or outside of synchronization.

Figure 10-12 provides a spatial representation of this approach.

**Figure 10-12.** *One of the first steps to writing thread-safe filters is to make instance variables read-only, or access protected. Local variables are generally thread-safe and can be used to store request-specific information.*

## Handle State Carefully

State information can be readily maintained via local variables in doFilter(). The prerequest and postresponse processing window within the doFilter() method has full access to this state information. To pass state information between filters on the same chain, you can associate attributes with the ServletContext, returned by the FilterConfig.getServletContext() method. The reason why ServletContext attributes rather than request attributes can be used will be clear when you examine request and response wrapping in the next chapter.

You should note that, in general, filters should not maintain state across multiple requests because the very same instance of a filter can service a large number of requests in a given period. Logic requiring this degree of state maintenance is best served by servlets or JSP pages. In other words, the filter should depend on little or no session information to process a request or response.

## Think of Filters As In-Series Resource Processors

When designing web applications that follow the well-documented Model-View-Controller (MVC) design pattern or Model 2 JSP architecture, consider the use of filters as in-series resource processors in conjunction with the request dispatcher.

For example, in a push-model web application, a filter may perform part of the controller's responsibility by fetching data from the model and attaching it to the request in the form of attributes for the view component to display.

Another interesting example is form processing. When a form is submitted and before the controller component is called, a filter can be used to perform data validation on the incoming form data.

## Reusing a Filter via Chaining

Break up your filter-processing work into reusable, independent, chainable filters whenever possible. This will enhance the reuse potential of the filters and also allow users to use your filters in new and innovative ways. Also design your filters to be easily configurable at deployment time. Often a filter can be reused through the careful planning and use of initialization parameters.

## Avoid Duplicating System Features

Many problems addressed by filters can be solved instead via configuration of standard server features. This is especially true with Tomcat 5, which has logging, authentication, authorization, and fine-grained access control support built-in. Encrypted sessions via Transport Layer Security (TLS), more commonly known as secure sockets (HTTPS), are also supported natively.

You should avoid duplicating system features in your filter design. Investigate all the server features first, looking to see whether your filter application can be accomplished by simple server configuration. Write your filter only after you have determined that it's the only appropriate solution, given project requirements and constraints.

## Avoid Unnecessary Filter Mappings

When mapping filters, always use the most restrictive mapping possible—use `<servlet-name>` instead of `<url-pattern>` if possible. The overhead of filter operations can be significantly increased if the filter is consistently applied to web resources that don't need it.

# Summary

In this chapter, you've been introduced to the filtering feature of Servlet 2.5 containers (such as Tomcat 5). You've discovered the following:

- Filters enable web-application programmers to tap into the request-processing pipeline of the container.

- Filters are packaged code components in a web application, at the same level as servlets and JSP pages.

- Filters are deployed in the same way as servlets and JSP pages, through the deployment descriptor for the application.

- The filter has access to incoming requests before they reach the final resource and to the outgoing response immediately after the resource processing.

- Filters can also substitute their own version of the request and response (typically wrapped) for consumption of the resource.

- Symbiotic, well-defined interactions between the request dispatcher and filters enable you to create filters that act as in-series processors for request-switching web applications and application frameworks such as Apache's Struts and Turbine.

You've explored the life cycle of a filter, as managed by the container. You've seen how to define filters in deployment descriptors, how to supply initialization data to a filter instance, how to specify its interaction with the request dispatcher, and how to define filter mappings. You've noted how Servlet 2.3 is unable to filter dispatched requests and learned how Servlet 2.4 has remedied the situation.

Next, we discussed the very important concept of filter chaining. You learned that Servlet 2.5 filter chaining uses a nested call mechanism, unlike most other filtering schemes. One major advantage of this approach is the preservation of thread state throughout the filter invocation.

Working with code, you've created two simple filters and practiced deploying them. You've experimented with filter chaining and observed its effect by using log files. You've also created a useful audit filter and learned how easily it can be constructed.

Finally, we provided some guidelines for you to follow when programming filters and contrasted two other filterlike mechanisms (valves and interceptors)—noting the differences in approach and level of abstraction to that of filters.

This chapter has hopefully provided a sound foundation for proceeding to the next chapter, which will be code-intensive as you explore a variety of filter designs. Along the way, you'll create wrapped requests and responses to offer customized dynamic behavior throughout the request-processing pipeline.

■ ■ ■

# CHAPTER 11

# Advanced Filtering Techniques

In the previous chapter, we discussed Servlet filtering. Filtering offers the ability to intercept and process requests and responses before and after processing by the underlying resource. Filters can add great value to many Java EE web applications by transforming the behavior of existing servlets, JSP pages, or even static pages.

Chaining multiple filters together combines their transformations, offering the application developer or deployer great flexibility when configuring the final behavior of a web application. Now that you've built and configured some simple filters in the preceding chapter to experiment with the basic concepts, you'll turn your attention to the more advanced techniques used in applied filter programming.

This chapter is a cookbook for the application of filters. Our goal is to deliver sample code that covers a broad spectrum of the most frequently applied areas for filters. We've designed each sample to illustrate several subtleties or important points to consider when you program each type of filter.

## Filters for Five Problem Domains

You'll build, test, and deploy five filters in this chapter. These five filters, as shown in Table 11-1, cover five problem domains that you might encounter while developing web applications. These are not the only domains where filters might be useful. However, looking at these five filters will give you the tools to develop filters for many other possible uses.

**Table 11-1.** *The Five Filters Developed in This Chapter*

| Application Domain | Filter Sample |
| --- | --- |
| Auditing | A visual auditing filter that includes audit information inline with every resource that it services |
| Authorization | A filter that disallows access to the server during certain hours of the day |
| Adapter (legacy) | An adapter filter that allows newly formatted queries to work with a legacy set of resources |
| Authentication | An ad hoc authentication filter that can add simple login protection to any (group of) resources |
| Pipeline processing | A data-processing filter that takes advantage of the request flow along the processing pipeline |

First we'll present the functionality and design considerations for each filter. Then we'll provide the actual code, annotated with detailed comments highlighting the design issues addressed. Finally, we'll give detailed deployment, configuration, and testing information for each filter.

Many filter applications fall into one or more of the five problem domains, so the code we'll present serves as a base for your own filter development. Furthermore, during the development of several of this chapter's filters, we'll pause to cover the main techniques used in filter programming. These are the very same "filter application patterns" that you'll see again and again when designing filters—they're an encapsulation of the type of work that a filter can perform, on a conceptual level. An understanding of these patterns can prove helpful in your own experimentation and application of filters.

Table 11-2 lists the techniques used in the various filter examples of this chapter.

**Table 11-2.** *Techniques and Filters Covered in This Chapter*

| Technique Illustrated | Filter |
| --- | --- |
| Transforming incoming request headers | Adapter filter |
| Stopping downstream request flow | Authorization filter<br>Authentication filter |
| Generating response | Authorization filter<br>Authentication filter |
| Transforming outgoing response content | Auditing filter |
| Dynamically adapting filter behavior based on incoming requests | Authentication filter |
| Wrapping request objects | Adapter filter |
| Wrapping response objects | Auditing filter |
| Adding to or modifying the attributes of a request in a processing pipeline | Pipeline processing filter<br>Authentication filter |
| Interacting with the request dispatcher's include() and forward() actions | Pipeline processing filter |

Be warned that this chapter is extremely code intensive. By the end of the chapter, you'll be fluent in filter concepts, design, and programming. To boot, you'll have an extensive code framework and library to start your filter projects immediately.

# Setting Up the Development Environment

If you download the code for this book, you will find that most of the code for the filters in this chapter is in a package called com.apress.projsp. The classes are located under the filters2\WEB-INF\classes directory.

In this chapter, several resources will be used to show the results of filter processing. As with Chapter 10, for the most part we won't care about the actual resource, so the processing done by the JSP or other resource will be minimal.

# The FindProd JSP Page

Let's start with a simple JSP page. Listing 11-1 shows FindProd.jsp, which you may recall from the previous chapter. This trivial JSP page is used to test the handling of JSP resources.

**Listing 11-1.** *FindProd.jsp*

```
<html>
  <head></head>
  <body>
    <h1>You have submitted as the ${param.DEPT} department!</h1>
  </body>
</html>
```

This JSP page prints out a message containing the department name by using EL and expects the client to supply the DEPT parameter. In a new web application, we would control the client that calls FindProd.jsp to ensure that it does supply the required parameter. (In Chapter 10, we did that by specifying the URL to be entered to access the resource.)

# The FindProd Servlet

Now we'll simulate a legacy resource. Listing 11-2 shows a servlet named FindProd. This servlet simulates a legacy resource being accessed by a user. It's hard-coded to display the DEPT parameter (department information). We're going to assume that we've had the opportunity to update the servlet to process this department information. However, we're also going to assume that the legacy clients are out of our control, so they can't be updated to provide the department information. Later, we'll create a filter that automatically provides this parameter even though the client system accessing the legacy resource doesn't know how to supply it. Save this code in the WEB-INF\classes directory. To compile the servlet, you'll need to add Tomcat's servlet-api.jar file to your CLASSPATH.

**Listing 11-2.** *FindProd.java*

```java
package com.apress.projsp;

import javax.servlet.http.*;
import java.io.*;

public class FindProd extends HttpServlet {
  public void doGet(HttpServletRequest req, HttpServletResponse res)
      throws java.io.IOException {
    res.setContentType("text/html");
    PrintWriter out = res.getWriter();
    out.println("<html><head></head>");
    out.println("<body><h1>You have called from the "
        + req.getParameter("DEPT"));
    out.println(" department!</h1></body></html>");
    out.close();
  }
}
```

# The Deployment Descriptor

Now we need to create a deployment descriptor for this simple web application. Listing 11-3 shows a simple version of web.xml that will get us started. As we proceed through the chapter, we will add more entries to it.

**Listing 11-3.** *web.xml*

```xml
<?xml version="1.0" encoding="UTF-8"?>
<web-app xmlns="http://java.sun.com/xml/ns/javaee"
         xmlns:xsi="http://www.w3.org/2001/XMLSchema-instance"
xsi:schemaLocation="http://java.sun.com/xml/ns/javaee/web-app_2_5.xsd"
         version="2.5">
  <display-name>Pro JSP Example Filters 2</display-name>
  <distributable />
  <servlet>
    <servlet-name>findprod</servlet-name>
    <servlet-class>com.apress.projsp.FindProd</servlet-class>
  </servlet>

  <servlet-mapping>
    <servlet-name>findprod</servlet-name>
    <url-pattern>/findprod</url-pattern>
  </servlet-mapping>
</web-app>
```

# A Brief Word on Terminology

Before you read any further, let's clarify some of the terminology that is used throughout this chapter. Figure 11-1 shows a request from a client as the request flows through a set of filters and is handled by a web resource. Notice that Figure 11-1 shows filter 3 being applied twice to the request/response cycle. Although this is not a common practice, it is technically possible. For example, you could have an adapter filter that modifies a request. Using initialization parameters, you could control how the filter modifies the request. Thus one instance of the filter could modify one aspect of the request, and a second instance of the same filter could modify a different aspect of the request.

The request originates from the client and goes through a **chain of filters** before reaching the final **resource processor** in this figure. First, the request travels from the client, through the first filter, through the second filter, and so on. We call this the **downstream**, or **inbound**, trip. The downstream trip is always toward the final goal: the resource processor. After the resource processor has finished with the request, a response then will travel **upstream**, or **outbound**, back through all the filters and onward to the client. Upstream trips are always away from the resource processor and toward the client.

New to Servlet 2.4 is the ability of filters to participate in the forward and include redirection requests of the request dispatcher. This is a very important advance architecturally. We discuss this new feature in depth in the last section of this chapter.

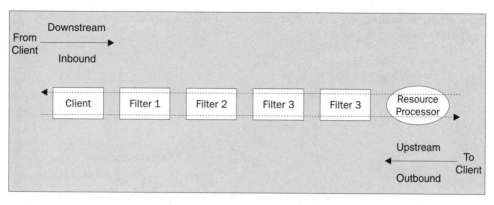

**Figure 11-1.** *A request from a client constitutes the downstream (inbound) trip of a request/response cycle. The response from a web application constitutes the upstream (outbound) trip.*

# Filter 1: A Visual Auditing Filter

The first filter that you'll tackle is similar to the AuditFilter that you developed toward the end of Chapter 10. Like the AuditFilter, it will be deployed by using the following web.xml fragment:

```
<filter>
  <filter-name>VisAudit Filter</filter-name>
  <filter-class>com.apress.projsp.VisAuditFilter</filter-class>
</filter>
<filter-mapping>
  <filter-name>VisAudit Filter</filter-name>
  <url-pattern>/*</url-pattern>
</filter-mapping>
```

Unlike the previous AuditFilter, instead of quietly writing the audit information to the log, this filter will include the auditing information in the output of the resource. Figure 11-5 in the section "Configuring and Testing the Filter" shows an example of this filter being applied to a JSP web page. Note the audit information at the bottom of the page—this information is inserted by the filter, and it changes with every access to the page.

## Wrapping the Response Object for Content Modification

The crucial concept to understand from this example is **custom response wrapping**. This is also one of the most difficult techniques to grasp for novice filter programmers. In custom response wrapping, you provide your own implementation of a custom response object to downstream filters and resources, with the response object that was passed to you wrapped inside. This means that you can modify the response content (inside your custom response wrapper object) after the resource has completed processing the request. Figure 11-2 illustrates the interception.

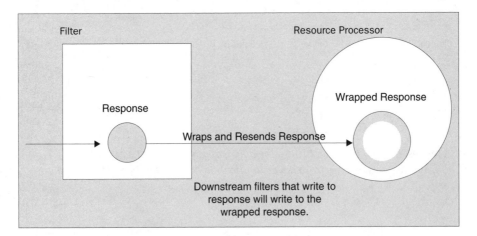

**Figure 11-2.** *To allow upstream processing of a response, the standard response object is contained inside a response wrapper.*

In the VisAuditFilter example, you'll use your own custom OutputStream class (VisAuditOutputStream) and a wrapped response class (VisAuditResponseWrapper). The classes you'll use and their relationships are shown in Figure 11-3.

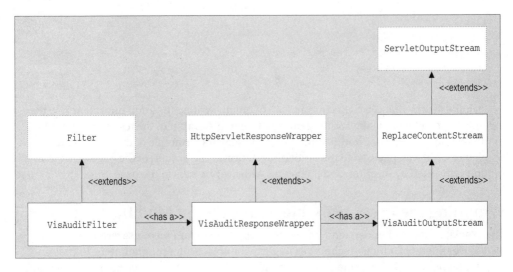

**Figure 11-3.** *This UML class diagram illustrates the classes in the VisAudit Filter example.*

Together, these classes will intercept the output of the web resource added to the auditing information footer. The interaction diagram in Figure 11-4 shows how this interception is carried out.

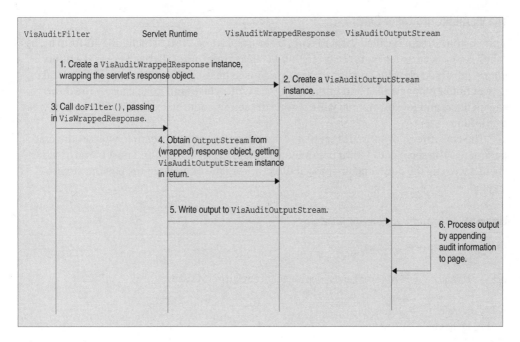

**Figure 11-4.** *This sequence diagram shows how the various VisAudit classes cooperate to filter the response from a web component.*

Note that you must wrap the response with your own custom version during the request's inbound trip, before you call Chain.doFilter(). In fact, the following happens:

1. The filter supplies a custom wrapped version of the response to downstream filters when it calls the Chain.doFilter() method.

2. This custom wrapped response object hands down a custom OutputStream or PrintWriter object that is actually a byte array managed in your own code.

3. When downstream filters, or the resource processor, write to your custom OutputStream or PrintWriter, you're buffering all the output.

4. When downstream filters, or the resource processor, flush or close your custom OutputStream or PrintWriter, you examine the buffered output for the closing </body> tag and insert your auditing information just before it (if found).

Any downstream filters on the inbound trip (including the actual resource processor) are writing their data into your custom stream. Of course, it's possible that some other downstream filters may perform further wrapping of your custom response with one of their own. The filter-chaining mechanism supports this successive nested wrapping of the response (and the request) as a means of multiple layers of content interception. In this case, your custom response wrapper object will add the "Big Brother is watching you" visual audit message to all resources that are accessed through this filter. End users will see this auditing message at the bottom of every resource that they access and won't be able to tell that the output originates from a filter.

Now let's examine the source code for this filter.

## The VisAuditOutStream Class

Your custom stream is called VisAuditOutStream (see Listing 11-4), which inherits from a class called ReplaceContentOutputStream (Listing 11-7). ReplaceContentOutputStream is a utility library (abstract) class for creating custom streams to be used in response wrapping. It takes care of buffer management and intercepting the write, close, and flush calls by the downstream filters and processors. You will examine the source code for ReplaceContentOutputStream a little later.

The constructor of your VisAuditOutStream takes the output stream to wrap as the first parameter. The second and third parameters contain the IP address and host name of the client accessing the page, and are passed directly from the filter when the custom stream is created.

**Listing 11-4.** *VisAuditOutStream.java*

```java
package com.apress.projsp;

class VisAuditOutStream extends ReplaceContentOutputStream
{
  String addr;
  String host;

  public VisAuditOutStream(String inAddr, String inHost) {
    addr = inAddr;
    host = inHost;
  }

  public byte[] replaceContent(byte[] inBytes) {
    StringBuffer sb = new StringBuffer(inBytes.length);
    String result = new String(inBytes);
    String srchString = result.toLowerCase();
    int endBody = srchString.indexOf("</body>");
    if (endBody != -1) {
      sb.append(result.substring(0, endBody));
      sb.append("<br><small><i>Big Brother is watching you. ")
          .append("You have accessed our page from ").append(addr)
          .append(" and on a machine called ").append(host)
          .append("</i></small></br>")
          .append(result.substring(endBody));
    } else {
      sb.append(result);
    }
    return sb.toString().getBytes();
  }
}
```

The single method that a child class must override, because the method is declared abstract in ReplaceContentOutputStream, is the replaceContent() method. This method takes a byte array as input—this is the content written into the buffer by the downstream filters and processors. The return value is another byte array, which is the content that will be written to the client. In this case, the code looks for the </body> closing tag to know where to insert the additional content. If the </body> tag is found, the auditing information is added just before the end of the document.

## The Customized Response Wrapper Class

The next class we'll define is the response wrapper called VisAuditResponseWrapper (Listing 11-5). It conveniently inherits from javax.servlet.http.HttpServletResponseWrapper. By using this wrapper class, we can readily wrap any HttpServletResponse object and override only the methods that we want to customize. The HttpServletResponseWrapper class has provided trivial implementations of all the methods of the HttpServletResponse interface—they all call the corresponding method of the class being wrapped.

**Listing 11-5.** *VisAuditResponseWrapper.java*

```
package com.apress.projsp;

import java.io.PrintWriter;
import javax.servlet.*;
import javax.servlet.http.*;

public class VisAuditResponseWrapper extends HttpServletResponseWrapper
{
  private PrintWriter tpWriter;
  private VisAuditOutStream tpStream;

  public VisAuditResponseWrapper(ServletResponse inResp, String inAddr,
                                 String inHost)
      throws java.io.IOException
  {
    super((HttpServletResponse) inResp);
    tpStream = new VisAuditOutStream(inAddr, inHost);
    tpWriter = new PrintWriter(tpStream);
  }

  public ServletOutputStream getOutputStream()
      throws java.io.IOException
  {
    return tpStream;
  }

  public PrintWriter getWriter() throws java.io.IOException {
    return tpWriter;
  }
}
```

The constructor creates an instance of VisAuditOutStream and passes the IP address and host name of client to the VisAuditOutStream constructor. It also creates a PrintWriter object based on the stream. The VisAuditOutStream will be used by static pages and servlets; the PrintWriter is used by JSP pages.

The two other methods that the class overrides are getOutputStream() and getWriter(). These methods hand out your customized stream instead of the response's actual stream.

## The Filter Logic

Finally, we get to the actual filter class in Listing 11-6, VisAuditFilter. You'll recognize the general organization from the preceding chapter's examples. Focus your attention on the doFilter() method.

**Listing 11-6.** *VisAuditFilter.java*

```java
package com.apress.projsp;

import java.io.*;
import javax.servlet.*;

public final class VisAuditFilter implements Filter
{
  private FilterConfig filterConfig = null;

  public void doFilter(ServletRequest request,
                       ServletResponse response, FilterChain chain)
    throws IOException, ServletException
  {
    String clientAddr = request.getRemoteAddr();
    String clientHost = request.getRemoteHost();
    filterConfig.getServletContext().log("in VisAuditFilter");
    VisAuditResponseWrapper myWrappedResp =
      new VisAuditResponseWrapper(response,
                                  clientAddr,
                                  clientHost);
    chain.doFilter(request, myWrappedResp);

    PrintWriter writer = myWrappedResp.getWriter();
    writer.close();
    response.setContentType(myWrappedResp.getContentType());
    ReplaceContentOutputStream rcos =
      (ReplaceContentOutputStream) myWrappedResp.getOutputStream();
    byte[] result = rcos.getResult();
    response.setContentLength(result.length);
    ServletOutputStream out = response.getOutputStream();
    out.write(result);
```

```
    filterConfig.getServletContext().log(
        "Getting out of VisAuditFilter");
  }

  public void init(FilterConfig filterConfig) {
    this.filterConfig = filterConfig;
  }

  public void destroy() {}
}
```

Code in the doFilter() method, prior to the chain.doFilter() call, is executed on the inbound request. The code retrieves the client's IP address and the host name. This information will be passed down to the custom stream. After a little logging, the class creates a new customized wrapped response, passing in the actual response as well as the IP address and host name. Then the class calls chain.doFilter(), passing the wrapped response downstream to other filters and the resource processor.

Some resource processor and downstream filter combinations don't close the output stream properly, so after chain.doFilter() returns, the code forces a close on the PrintWriter. You'll see shortly that the implementation of the ReplaceContentOutputStream class is guarded against multiple closes, so this is safe even if the stream was closed previously.

The rest of these methods implement the filter interface and are standard implementations that you saw within the samples of Chapter 10.

## The ReplaceContentOutputStream Class

The custom stream, VisAuditOutStream, depends on the ReplaceContentOutputStream class (Listing 11-7) to do a lot of its magic. This class wraps an OutputStream and does the following:

- Supplies its own byte array–based stream for the write() method, called by downstream filters and the resource processor.

- Handles the close() method by calling a child's replaceContent() method to transform the byte array stream.

- Provides the transformed content through the getResult() method. This method is called by the filter when the filter writes the response.

This class can be used for any filter that transforms or replaces the response content.

**Listing 11-7.** *ReplaceContentOutputStream.java*

```
package com.apress.projsp;

import java.io.*;
import javax.servlet.*;

public abstract class ReplaceContentOutputStream
```

```java
    extends ServletOutputStream
{
  byte[] result;
  private ByteArrayOutputStream baStream;
  private boolean closed = false;

  public ReplaceContentOutputStream() {
    baStream = new ByteArrayOutputStream();
  }

  public void write(int i) throws java.io.IOException {
    baStream.write(i);
  }

  public void close() throws java.io.IOException {
    if (!closed) {
      processStream();
      closed = true;
    }
  }

  public abstract byte[] replaceContent(byte[] inBytes)
      throws java.io.IOException;

  public void processStream() throws java.io.IOException {
    result = replaceContent(baStream.toByteArray());
  }

  public byte[] getResult() {
    return result;
  }
}
```

This abstract class extends another abstract class, called ServletOutputStream, which is the base class of the OutputStream returned by getOutputStream() on a response. ServletOutputStream requires the write(int) method to be implemented by its subclass. It implements all the other write() variants based on this method. The ReplaceContentOutputStream requires the replaceContent() method to be implemented by all its subclasses.

Note the use of the flag variable closed: Initially false, this variable is used to ensure that the wrapped stream is closed only once, regardless of how many times the close() method may be called.

The constructor creates the memory-based ByteArrayOutputStream for the downstream processors.

Next, the class implements the required write(int) method, which writes to the in-memory byte array stream called baStream. This ensures that all writes on this stream write to baStream (essentially a buffer).

When `close()` is called for the first time, the class transforms the output in the in-memory stream. After the transformation, the class stores the results so the filter can retrieve them later. Multiple calls to `close()` don't cause a problem in this case.

The `processStream()` method calls the `replaceContent()` method to transform the in-memory stream and write the transformed output to the wrapped output stream. The `replaceContent()` method is abstract. Subclasses of this class will provide an implementation for the method. The intention is for subclasses to transform the input byte array and return the transformed array. As you saw in Listing 11-4, `VisAuditOutStream.java`, that subclass transforms the `inBytes` byte array by adding additional data to the stream.

This is the end of the code analysis for the `ReplaceContentOutputStream` abstract class. You'll rely on this class for two subsequent filters that transform their outgoing response's content.

## Configuring and Testing the Filter

To deploy the filter, add the filter definition and filter mapping in Listing 11-8 to the `web.xml` file.

**Listing 11-8.** *<filter> and< filter-mapping> Elements for web.xml*

```
<filter>
  <filter-name>VisAudit Filter</filter-name>
  <filter-class>com.apress.projsp.VisAuditFilter</filter-class>
</filter>
<filter-mapping>
  <filter-name>VisAudit Filter</filter-name>
  <url-pattern>/*</url-pattern>
</filter-mapping>
```

This mapping will apply the filter to every resource served by the application. Start by loading the JSP page `FindProd.jsp`, as shown in Figure 11-5, using the appropriate test URL for the application you created.

**Figure 11-5.** *The VisAuditFilter can be used to filter JSP pages. It appends an audit message to the end of the response.*

Next, you'll try a servlet resource instead. Open `http://localhost:8080/filters2/servlet/findprod` (note that `findprod` is lowercase). Figure 11-6 shows that the output is once again intercepted and the auditing information is appended.

**Figure 11-6.** *Filters can act upon any web resource including static HTML pages, JSP pages, and, as shown here, servlets.*

If you're creating filters that must work across many types of resources, you must test against each type of resource. This is necessary because each type of resource is passed through a different resource processor, each of which potentially has different assumptions and behavior from the others (servlets are passed to Catalina, JSP pages are passed to Jasper first, and so on).

# Filter 2: An Authorization Filter

A filter can generate its own output and deprive the downstream filters and resource processor of a chance to see the request altogether. Obviously, there's very little application for a filter that does this all the time, but a filter that does this based on some dynamic criterion can be useful. One example is a filter that blocks resource access based on the time of day. You'll create such a filter in this section.

## Generating Your Own Response

The filter you're going to create falls into the authorization filter application domain. More specifically, it allows or disallows an incoming request to reach its destined resource processor depending on the time of day. The application is intended to stop users from accessing game-playing resources during certain hours. Figure 11-7 illustrates the filter action.

If a request arrives during the allotted time window, the user is allowed through to the resource processor to play games. If a request arrives outside of the allotted time window, the filter generates a response of its own, depriving the downstream resource processor of a chance to see the request. This effectively blocks the use of the game resources.

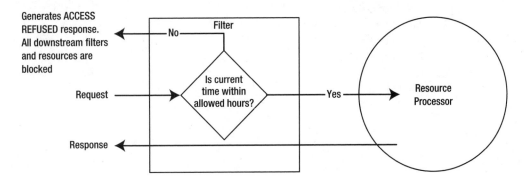

**Figure 11-7.** *When a request is made outside the allowable hours, the filter denies access to the requested resource.*

Listing 11-9 shows the code for StopGamesFilter. The filter is designed to allow you to make the range of allowable hours a configurable parameter, to make the filter flexible enough for use in different environments. It also gives you a chance to see how to access and work with initial parameters in filters.

**Listing 11-9.** *StopGamesFilter.java*

```java
package com.apress.projsp;

import java.io.*;
import javax.servlet.*;
import java.util.Calendar;

public final class StopGamesFilter implements Filter {
  private FilterConfig filterConfig = null;
  private int starthour = 0;
  private int stophour = 24; // default is to allow all the time

  public void doFilter(ServletRequest request,
                       ServletResponse response,
      FilterChain chain) throws IOException, ServletException {
    Calendar myCal = Calendar.getInstance();
    int curhour = myCal.get(Calendar.HOUR_OF_DAY);
    filterConfig.getServletContext().log(
        "in StopGamesFilter cur:" + curhour + ", start: " + starthour
            + ", end: " + stophour);
    if ((curhour >= stophour) || (curhour < starthour)) {
      PrintWriter out = response.getWriter();
```

```
        out.println("<html><head></head><body>");
        out.println("<h1>Sorry, game playing is not " +
                    "allowed at this time!</h1>");
        out.println("</body></html>");
        out.flush();
        filterConfig.getServletContext()
                    .log("Access to game page denied");
        return;
    }
    filterConfig.getServletContext()
                .log("Access to game page granted");
    chain.doFilter(request, response);
    filterConfig.getServletContext()
                .log("Getting out of StopGamesFilter");
    }

  public void init(FilterConfig arg0) throws ServletException {
    this.filterConfig = arg0;
  }

  public void destroy() {}
}
```

The class has two instance variables to hold the default hours of operation, which allows game playing all the time. These parameters are used if the filter is configured without initial parameters, or if the access to the initial parameters failed. It's always a good idea to set some usable default value for the filter.

In the doFilter() method, the class obtains the current hour, which depends on a 24-hour clock to make things simple. The class also assumes that the start and stop hours don't cross the 12 a.m. boundary to keep the logic simple. Next, the class makes a log entry to show the various values, which is useful for auditing or debugging purposes.

If the incoming request arrives outside of the allowed time range, doFilter() simply generates the content of the response. The generated content lets the user know that access to the game resource page is disallowed. If the request arrives within the allowed hours, the filter lets the request through to access the game resource by passing the request and response to chain.doFilter().

## Thread-Safety Considerations

One question that you may have is, "Where do I access the initialization parameters?" The answer is, generally *not* in the doFilter() method. This goes back to our discussion in the previous chapter about thread-safe programming. The starthour and stophour variables are instance-scoped variables. Modifying the value of instance-scoped variables in doFilter() requires careful synchronization, because doFilter() *will* be accessed in multiple threads at the same time. Following the filter life cycle, however, there's a natural place to set the value of your initialization parameters.

After an instance of a filter has been created, and before the very first doFilter() is called, the container calls the init() method to set the FilterConfig object for the filter. This is a natural point at which to perform any initialization required, and it's conceptually equivalent to the init() method of a servlet.

In this case, you'll take advantage of it by setting your instance variables with values from the filter definition. Listing 11-10 shows the init() method for the StopGamesFilter. The container always calls init() in a single thread when it sets up the filter instance. In the init() method, the filterConfig.getInitParameter() method reads the web.xml file for initialization parameters. The init() method in Listing 11-10 replaces the init() method in Listing 11-9.

**Listing 11-10.** *init() (To Be Added to StopGamesFilter.java)*

```
public void init(FilterConfig arg0) throws ServletException {
  String tpString;
  filterConfig = arg0;
  if ((tpString = filterConfig.getInitParameter("starthour")) != null)
    starthour = Integer.parseInt(tpString, 10);
  if ((tpString = filterConfig.getInitParameter("stophour")) != null)
    stophour = Integer.parseInt(tpString, 10);
}
```

## Installing and Configuring the StopGamesFilter

To install and configure the filter, first make sure all other <filter> and <filter-mapping> elements are removed or commented out of the web.xml file. Then add the following entries

```
<filter>
  <filter-name>Stop Games Filter</filter-name>
  <filter-class>com.apress.projsp.StopGamesFilter</filter-class>
  <init-param>
    <param-name>starthour</param-name>
    <param-value>8</param-value>
  </init-param>
  <init-param>
    <param-name>stophour</param-name>
    <param-value>9</param-value>
  </init-param>
</filter>
<filter-mapping>
  <filter-name>Stop Games Filter</filter-name>
  <url-pattern>/games/*</url-pattern>
</filter-mapping>
```

Make sure that you've configured the `starthour` and `stophour` variables to make the current time outside of the allowable range, and create a `games` directory off the `filters2` web-application directory that contains an appropriate `index.html` file. Start Tomcat and try to access the following URL through a browser:

```
http://localhost:8080/filters2/games/index.html
```

You should see an "access denied" message as shown in Figure 11-8.

**Figure 11-8.** *When a request is made outside allowable hours, the filter blocks the request.*

This is the custom-generated response straight from the filter. Now, modify the `<filter>` element in `web.xml` to include the current time within the range. Reload the web application by using Tomcat's management tool, or restart Tomcat, and try to access the same URL. Figure 11-9 shows the page you should now see.

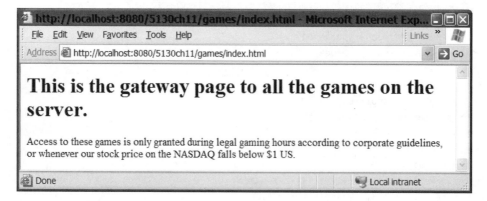

**Figure 11-9.** *When a request is made within allowable hours, the filter passes the request down the chain.*

# Filter 3: A Filter for Adapting to Legacy Resources

The next filter you will examine addresses a common problem in the real world that occurs when two independent systems refer to each other through hyperlinks. Over time, the requirement and access changes because of independent evolution. Imagine that because of the size of the independent projects, or because of political situations, you can't change the links to either one of the systems. To keep them working, you'll create a filter that adapts one system to another, without modifying a single line of code in either system. Figure 11-10 shows the action of just such an "adapter" filter within a typical system.

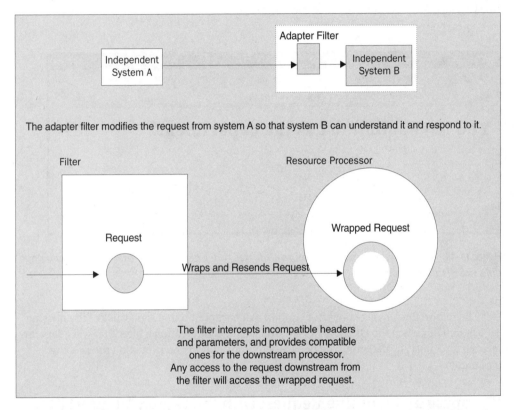

**Figure 11-10.** *Filters can modify requests so that two systems that were not built to work together can be integrated.*

In this example, a JSP page represents the legacy resource. A centralized administrative server that is accessed by multiple departments in a company services this JSP page. This legacy system requires the originating department information to be supplied in the form of a DEPT parameter in order to work properly. Unfortunately, because of political situations in this hypothetical company, the links coming into this server don't and won't contain the originating department information (the DEPT parameter). Therefore, you'll design a filter to adapt the two systems. Figure 11-11 shows the result when the FindProd.jsp page receives a request without the required request parameter.

This filter intercepts the request, examines where it's from, and generates the required DEPT parameter for the JSP resource so that it can function properly. It determines the department of the incoming client by examining its subnet portion of the IP address corresponding to the client (assume you have the subnet IP to department-mapping information). Therefore, this adapter translates an incoming IP address to a required DEPT parameter and allows two incompatible systems to work together.

You can easily imagine many more complex examples from the real world that may require significantly more adaptation code; however, the general structure and technique for creating such adapter filters remains the same.

**Figure 11-11.** *When a request does not contain the necessary department, the resulting web page does not display correctly.*

The reason the message does not contain a department name is because of the missing DEPT parameter when the URL is accessed. You'll fix this by creating a filter that will adapt any incoming requests by detecting the department information and providing the missing parameter.

## Wrapping an Incoming Request with the LegacyAdapterFilter

To perform its work, the filter will add the DEPT parameter to the request before it reaches the underlying JSP resource. In other words, the filter will modify the request. To do this, the filter will use a request wrapper. Listing 11-11 shows the LegacyAdapterRequestWrapper class.

**Listing 11-11.** *LegacyAdapterRequestWrapper.java*

```
package com.apress.projsp;

import java.util.Map;
import javax.servlet.http.HttpServletRequest;
import javax.servlet.http.HttpServletRequestWrapper;
```

```java
public class LegacyAdapterRequestWrapper extends HttpServletRequestWrapper {
  String myDept = null;

  public LegacyAdapterRequestWrapper(HttpServletRequest inReq,
                                     String deptString) {
    super(inReq);
    myDept = deptString;
  }

  public Map getParameterMap() {
    Map tmpMap = super.getParameterMap();
    tmpMap.put("DEPT", myDept);
    return tmpMap;
  }

  public String[] getParameterValues(String paramName) {
    if (paramName.equalsIgnoreCase("DEPT")) {
      String[] tpAry = new String[1];
      tpAry[0] = myDept;
      return tpAry;
    } else {
      return super.getParameterValues(paramName);
    }
  }

  public String getParameter(String paramName) {
    if (paramName.equalsIgnoreCase("DEPT")) {
      return myDept;
    } else {
      return super.getParameter(paramName);
    }
  }
}
```

In this example, the filter wraps the incoming request. Unlike the VisAudit filter (which wrapped the response), this filter will actually be modifying header information associated with the incoming request.

This wrapper class, called LegacyAdapterRequestWrapper, extends the useful HttpServletRequestWrapper class. HttpServletRequestWrapper will take as an argument for its constructor the actual HttpServletRequest to wrap. It implements all of its methods by calling the methods of the wrapped request. By inheriting from this class, we can choose to override only the methods that we're interested in.

Note that the class takes the department as an argument for the constructor, and stores the value in an instance variable.

The methods that the class provides custom implementation for are getParameterMap(), getParameterValues(), and getParameter(). This ensures that the class can work with most of the resources that may access parameters. In fact, for the specific JSP that will be filtered, the class had to override only the getParameter() method because this is the only method the JSP uses. In each of the method overrides, you can see how the DEPT parameter is added. The downstream filter or processor accessing the headers will have no way of knowing that the DEPT parameter was added by your filter and not from the original request. This demonstrates the beauty of filter chaining.

## Writing the LegacyAdapterFilter

The filter will perform several tasks:

- Determine the incoming IP address

- Map the IP address from which the request originates to a department

- Add the DEPT parameter to the request before it reaches the underlying JSP resource

The last task in the list is being handled by the LegacyAdapterRequestWrapper class. Listing 11-12 shows the LegacyAdapterFilter class, which will handle the first two tasks.

**Listing 11-12.** *LegacyAdapterFilter.java*

```java
package com.apress.projsp;

import java.io.IOException;
import javax.servlet.*;
import javax.servlet.http.HttpServletRequest;

public final class LegacyAdapterFilter implements Filter {
  private FilterConfig filterConfig = null;

  public void doFilter(ServletRequest request,
                       ServletResponse response,
                       FilterChain chain)
    throws IOException, ServletException {

    String clientAddr = request.getRemoteAddr();
    System.out.println("the addr is " + clientAddr);
    int idx = clientAddr.indexOf(".");
    clientAddr = clientAddr.substring(idx + 1);
    idx = clientAddr.indexOf(".");
    clientAddr = clientAddr.substring(idx + 1);
    idx = clientAddr.indexOf(".");
    clientAddr = clientAddr.substring(0, idx);
    System.out.println("the subnet is " + clientAddr);
    String dept = null;
    if (clientAddr.equals("0")) {
      dept = "Engineering";
```

```
    } else {
      dept = "Accounting";
    }
    LegacyAdapterRequestWrapper aCustomReq =
      new LegacyAdapterRequestWrapper(
        (HttpServletRequest) request, dept);
    filterConfig.getServletContext().log("in LegacyAdapterFilter");
    chain.doFilter(aCustomReq, response);
    filterConfig.getServletContext()
                .log("leaving LegacyAdapterFilter");
  }

  public void init(FilterConfig filterConfig) {
    this.filterConfig = filterConfig;
  }

  public void destroy() {
  }
}
```

The filter first determines the department that the request is coming from. It does so by mapping the subnet of the IP address to a department. In this case, it examines the subnet—if it's zero, DEPT=Accounting is used; otherwise DEPT=Engineering is used.

Next, it creates a wrapper request, passing in the department and calling downstream filters/processor via filter chaining.

## Installing and Configuring the LegacyAdapterFilter

To install and configure the filter, first make sure all other <filter> and <filter-mapping> definitions are removed or commented out (you want to reduce the side effect of chaining other sample filters). Then add the following entries to the web.xml file:

```
<filter>
  <filter-name>Legacy Adapter Filter</filter-name>
  <filter-class>com.apress.projsp.LegacyAdapterFilter </filter-class>
</filter>
<filter-mapping>
  <filter-name>Legacy Adapter Filter</filter-name>
  <url-pattern>/jsp/FindProd.jsp</url-pattern>
</filter-mapping>
```

This will specifically apply the filter to the FindProd.jsp resource. Deploy and, if needed, reload the application or restart Tomcat. Open the following address:

```
http://localhost:8080/filters2/jsp/FindProd.jsp
```

Figure 11-12 shows the result of the filter.

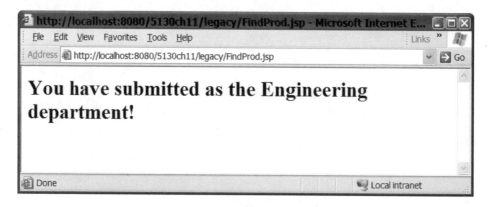

**Figure 11-12.** *The legacy adapter filter determines the department based on the Internet address and adds the appropriate department parameter to the request.*

Note that the message now prints a department name, even though no department name is passed as part of the original request. The JSP page is picking up the DEPT parameter from your wrapped request. If you can do so, you may want to access the JSP page from another subnet to see the automatic department detection at work.

# Filter 4: An Ad Hoc Authentication Filter

Tomcat 5 and almost all Servlet 2.5–compliant containers come with extensive authentication and authorization support, so in theory there should be little need to implement your own authentication filter. In fact, we will cover authorization and authentication in detail in Chapter 12. In practice, however, there's almost always room to apply an ad hoc authentication filter on a selected resource without affecting the rest of the application or requiring the overhead of setting up, say, JDBC realms.

You should always analyze the problem at hand to see whether it would be better solved by the native authentication support of the server. When you need simple, temporary protection of selected resources, the AdHocAuthenticate filter can be the best choice.

The action of this filter is straightforward. It triggers basic authentication on the client browser. Almost all known browsers, including even the earliest versions, support basic authentication. The authentication process works like this:

1. A client attempts to access a protected resource.

2. The server examines the client's request to determine whether there's any authorization data in the "Authorization" header.

3. If authorization data isn't found, the server sends back HTTP status code 401 (unauthorized access) and a header with WWW-authenticate: BASIC realm=<realm>, where realm is a text string that will be displayed to the client.

4. The client browser pops up a login screen in which the user should enter a username and password.

5. When the user enters the username and password, the client encodes the username and password by using simple base64 encoding and sends both to the server.

6. The server examines the client request to determine whether there's any authorization data, decoding the base64-encoded password if necessary. If there's no authorization data, the process goes back to step 3.

7. The server verifies the password and either allows or rejects access.

---

■**Note**  Basic authentication isn't very secure, because base64 encoding can easily be deciphered. However, for applications that just need to protect resources from casual access, it's usually sufficient. For more details on different kinds of authentication, see Chapter 12.

---

## The AdHocAuthenticateFilter Class

The AdHocAuthenticate filter in Listing 11-13 recognizes two passwords: one for "regular" users and one for privileged, "gold member" users. Both passwords are configured as initial parameters for the filter. If a user logs on using the "gold member" password, a Boolean attribute is created and attached to the request. You'll learn later (in the pipeline-processing filters section) how this attribute is used. For now, let's focus on the authentication action of this filter.

**Listing 11-13.** *AdHocAuthenticateFilter*

```
package com.apress.projsp;

import java.io.IOException;
import javax.servlet.*;
import javax.servlet.http.*;
import sun.misc.BASE64Decoder;

public final class AdHocAuthenticateFilter implements Filter {
  private FilterConfig filterConfig = null;
  private String adhocPassword = null;
  private String adhocGoldPassword = null;

  public void doFilter(ServletRequest request,
                       ServletResponse response,
                       FilterChain chain)
    throws IOException, ServletException
  {
    HttpServletRequest myReq = (HttpServletRequest) request;
    HttpServletResponse myResp = (HttpServletResponse) response;
    String authString = myReq.getHeader("Authorization");
```

```java
    if (authString == null) {
      myResp.addHeader("WWW-Authenticate", "BASIC realm=\"PJSP2\"");
      myResp.setStatus(HttpServletResponse.SC_UNAUTHORIZED);
      return;
    } else { // authenticate
      BASE64Decoder decoder = new BASE64Decoder();
      String enString = authString.substring(6);
      String decString = new String(decoder.decodeBuffer(enString));
      int idx = decString.indexOf(":");
      String uid = decString.substring(0, idx);
      String pwd = decString.substring(idx + 1);
      if (externalGoldAuthenticate(uid, pwd)) {
        request.setAttribute("goldmember", new Boolean(true));
      } else {
        if (!externalAuthenticate(uid, pwd)) {
          myResp.addHeader("WWW-Authenticate",
                           "BASIC realm=\"PJSP2\"");
          myResp.setStatus(HttpServletResponse.SC_UNAUTHORIZED);
          return;
        }
      }
    }
    filterConfig.getServletContext().log("in AdHocAuthenticateFilter");
    chain.doFilter(request, response);
    filterConfig.getServletContext().log(
        "Getting out of  " + "AdHocAuthenticateFilter");
  }

  private boolean externalAuthenticate(String user, String password) {
    if (adhocPassword == null)
      return false;

    return adhocPassword.equals(password);
  }

  private boolean externalGoldAuthenticate(String user,
                                                String password) {
    if (adhocGoldPassword == null)
      return false;

    return adhocGoldPassword.equals(password);
  }

  public void destroy() {}

  public void init(FilterConfig filterConfig) {
```

```
  if (adhocPassword == null)
    adhocPassword = filterConfig.getInitParameter("adhocpassword");
  if (adhocGoldPassword == null)
    adhocGoldPassword = filterConfig.getInitParameter("goldpassword");
  this.filterConfig = filterConfig;
  }
}
```

There's no need to wrap the response or request in this filter. Note the instance variables that will be used to hold the two read-only passwords: adhocPassword and adhocGoldPassword. These variables are initialized by the container from the web.xml values via the init() method.

In the doFilter() method, the class casts the request and response to their HTTP servlet versions to access and manipulate the headers associated with them. The class then attempts to get the authorization information from the request header. If no information is found, the filter sends an authorization request to the client.

If the filter finds authorization data, it decodes the username and password. The authorization header begins with the token Basic, so the filter uses substring(6) to skip over the constant string Basic of the authorization header, getting to the beginning of the base64-encoded username and password.

The filter calls the methods externalGoldAuthenticate() and externalAuthenticate() to perform the actual authentication for "gold member" users and "regular" users, respectively. The externalAuthenticate() and externalGoldAuthenticate() methods encapsulate the authentication mechanism. In this case, each authenticates against a single password from the initial parameters. You can modify each to perform any type of authentication you desire, including authentication against some physically external servers. Successful authentication allows access to the protected resource. In addition, "gold member" authentication will result in the, ahem, goldmember Boolean attribute being attached to the request. Failed authentication will cause the login dialog box to pop up again on the client's browser.

If everything has been authenticated properly, access to the resource is allowed, and the filter calls the chain.doFilter() method.

## Installing and Configuring the AdHocAuthenticateFilter

To install and configure the filter, add the following entries to web.xml:

```
<filter>
  <filter-name>AdHoc Authentication Filter</filter-name>
  <filter-class>com.apress.projsp.AdHocAuthenticateFilter</filter-class>
  <init-param>
    <param-name>adhocpassword</param-name>
    <param-value>bestofbreed</param-value>
  </init-param>
   <init-param>
      <param-name>goldpassword</param-name>
      <param-value>viponly</param-value>
    </init-param>
</filter>
<filter-mapping>
```

```
    <filter-name>AdHoc Authentication Filter</filter-name>
    <url-pattern>/jsp/*</url-pattern>
</filter-mapping>
```

Note that if you tried the legacy adapter filter in the previous section, it is now chained with the AdHocAuthenticate filter. The legacy adapter filter supplies the missing originating department information for the JSP page. The authenticate filter protects all JSP access with the passwords bestofbreed and viponly. Deploy the new filter and go to the following URL:

```
http://localhost:8080/filters2/jsp/FindProd.jsp
```

You should be prompted with a login dialog box. Enter the username (any username will do) and an invalid password. You'll see that you're barred from accessing the protected resource until you enter one of the correct passwords.

# Filter 5: A Filter in the Request-Processing Pipeline

Thus far, this chapter's focus has been on filters that either control the flow of a request (stopping it or letting it through) or generate the response to a request. Vast as their fields of application may be, these design styles only partially cover the potential spectrum of filter applications. The fact that these filters are directly responsible for some portion of the response HTML page's final appearance often makes them difficult to compose (that is, to chain them together in a value-added component fashion). This is because, by definition, they're specific to the page output that they directly generate.

The pipeline data-processing model provides a new style of filter that our fifth and final filter exemplifies. The first enabler for this model is the new <dispatcher> child element of the servlet <filter-mapping> definition. The new element enables filters to participate in every stage of the pipeline request-processing model. In this model, filters are themselves bona fide processors for a request traveling through a pipeline.

## Understanding the Pipeline Model

There are many names given to the pipelined data-processing model. It's often identified as the enabling element of **Model-View-Controller** (**MVC**) web-application design, and sometimes it's referred to as the **push model** of application design, in contrast with the more conventional **pull model**.

The idea is simple, but you have to think beyond the conventional web-application wisdom to get the bigger picture. Consider the illustration of the model shown in Figure 11-13.

A request enters the system and is shuttled along a pipeline. As it traverses the pipeline, a sequence of processors has access to the content of the request. Each processor performs some task on the request, and then it either attaches some new attribute or modifies an existing attribute as the result of that work. The request remains intact until it hits the final stage of the pipeline, in which special processors called **renderers** examine all the work being done to the request and produce the final response (renderers are also called the **view component** in the MVC paradigm because they alone are responsible for the final presentation to the user). You can see why this is often called the "push" model; data attributes are fetched by processors, pushed along the pipeline with the request, and rendered only at the final stage.

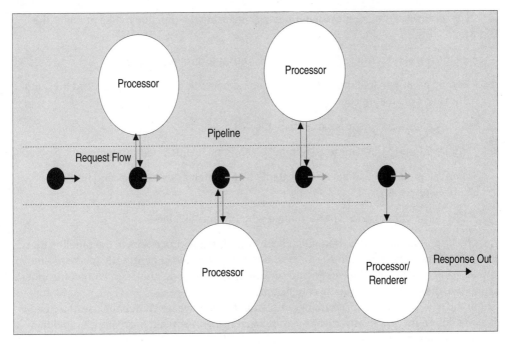

**Figure 11-13.** *In the pipeline model, different processers can act upon a request as it travels through the system.*

Another common analogy for the pipeline model is a conveyer belt or assembly line; each processor mirrors the workers (or robots) along the belt or line.

Some of the highly desirable properties of a pipeline model are as follows:

- The request stays intact as it traverse the pipeline, with work being carried out only on the attached attributes (sometimes called decorators).

- Data management, business logic, and presentation logic can be cleanly separated into different processors and renderers.

- The processors can be designed to be completely composable (that is, chained in any order) or highly specialized (to work only with specific attributes created or modified by other processors).

- Multiple renderers can compose the final output (such as data to XML to HTML via XSLT).

- The state of the request travels with the request through the pipeline. The processors and renderers don't keep track of the request-dependent state at all. This makes it possible to duplicate or shuttle the request and its state between multiple physical servers if necessary.

In general, designing request-handling logic by using the pipeline model provides the following:

- Processors and renderers that are readily reusable as components

- Strong and clear separation between data management, business logic, and presentation logic in an application

- Applications that are more maintainable

- Applications that are more adaptable to changing business requirements

- Robust applications that will be scalable with container technology and hardware advances

- Web applications whose performance is highly optimizable

The last point may not be immediately obvious, but any processors in the pipeline that don't depend on others' outcomes can in principle be executed concurrently (perhaps on two physical processors, for instance) and any grouping of processors that has an outcome independent of others can also execute concurrently.

In the past, limitations in container implementation have prevented the use of a clean pipeline design model. Servlet 2.5 has features that bring the dream of creating a pipelined application closer to reality.

## Inserting Filters into the Pipeline

The `<dispatcher>` subelement enables you to insert filters into the request-processing pipeline. Recall that the `<dispatcher>` element now allows filters to intercept the request dispatcher's `forward()` and `include()` calls. These are additional locations in the processing pipeline previously unavailable with Servlet 2.3 containers, where filters can go to work for you. You learned in Chapter 10 how this mechanism works, so let's see it in action here.

First, you'll revisit the `SimpleFilter` class that you saw in Chapter 10. All it did was write a couple of lines to the log, letting you know that it had been invoked. Now you'll change it to process the request traveling through the pipeline.

Instead of directly generating log output, it will now simply change attached attributes. The modification looks to see whether an attribute named `MsgOut` exists in the request. If it does exist, the code will append `" : SimpleFilter"`; otherwise, `MsgOut` will be set to `"SimpleFilter"` (without the leading colon). The first time the filter (processor) operates on a request, the attached `MsgOut` attribute will be set to `"SimpleFilter"`. After the second time, it will contain `"SimpleFilter : SimpleFilter"`, and after the third time, `"SimpleFilter :SimpleFilter : SimpleFilter"`.

Eventually, the `MsgOut` attribute will be displayed on an HTML page, so you can see the number of times that this filter has operated on the specific request as it traveled through the pipeline. Listing 11-14 shows the code for the `com.apress.projsp.SimpleFilter` class.

**Listing 11-14.** *SimpleFilter.java*

```java
package com.apress.projsp;

import java.io.*;
import javax.servlet.*;

public final class SimpleFilter implements Filter {
  private FilterConfig filterConfig = null;

  public void doFilter(ServletRequest request,
                       ServletResponse response,
                       FilterChain chain)
    throws IOException, ServletException
  {

    filterConfig.getServletContext().log("in SimpleFilter");
    Object curVal = request.getAttribute("MsgOut");
    if (curVal == null) {
      request.setAttribute("MsgOut", new String("SimpleFilter"));
    } else {
      request.setAttribute("MsgOut", (String) curVal +
                           " : SimpleFilter");
    }
    chain.doFilter(request, response);
    filterConfig.getServletContext().log("leaving SimpleFilter");
  }

  public void init(FilterConfig arg0) throws ServletException {
    this.filterConfig = arg0;
  }

  public void destroy() {
  }
}
```

We'll also revamp the FindProd.jsp file (the renderer processor in your pipeline) to display the new attribute. Expression language is great for creating renderers—that is, JSP pages that render HTML from attached attribute values. Listing 11-15 shows the new JSP page, which we've renamed Sub.jsp.

**Listing 11-15.** *Sub.jsp*

```jsp
<html>
  <head></head>
  <body>
```

```
    <h1>You have accessed this page
        from the ${param.DEPT} department!</h1>
    ${param.MsgForwarder}<br/>
    ${requestScope.MsgOut}
  </body>
</html>
```

The MsgOut attribute, attached to the request, is displayed using EL here. Note that a parameter called MsgForwarder is also displayed. You'll see this parameter used later when you work with the forward() action of the request dispatcher.

### Default REQUEST-Only Filtering: Servlet 2.3 Compatibility

To specify that filtering is to be performed only for requests that come directly from outside of the container, you can add the following <dispatcher> element inside the filter's <filter-mapping> element:

```
<dispatcher>REQUEST</dispatcher>
```

For example, you might have the following in web.xml:

```
<filter>
  <filter-name>Simple Push Filter</filter-name>
  <filter-class>com.apress.projsp.SimpleFilter</filter-class>
</filter>
<filter-mapping>
  <filter-name>Simple Push Filter</filter-name>
  <url-pattern>/jsp/*</url-pattern>
  <dispatcher>REQUEST</dispatcher>
</filter-mapping>
```

Now, if you open the following URL:

```
http://localhost:8080/filters2/jsp/Sub.jsp?DEPT=Accounting
```

you'll see a page similar to the one shown in Figure 11-14.

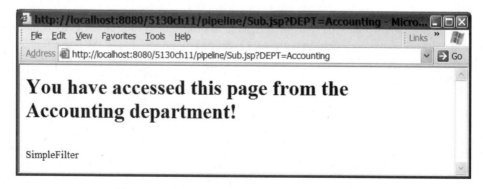

**Figure 11-14.** *The Simple Filter added a parameter to the request, which was then printed to the page when the page was rendered.*

Note the EL rendering of the MsgOut attribute on the page—you know that the filter has been called once. This behavior is all that you have with filter support prior to the Servlet 2.4 standard. It's also the default behavior with Tomcat 5 if you don't specify any <dispatcher> subelement for compatibility reasons.

## INCLUDE-Only Filtering

With Tomcat 5 and Servlet 2.4 or Servlet 2.5, you can specify that your filter work only on included requests. Try this out by changing web.xml to this:

```
<filter-mapping>
  <filter-name>Simple Push Filter</filter-name>
  <url-pattern>/jsp/*</url-pattern>
  <dispatcher>INCLUDE</dispatcher>
</filter-mapping>
```

Reload the application, or restart Tomcat, and try accessing Sub.jsp directly via the following URL:

```
http://localhost:8080/filters2/jsp/Sub.jsp?DEPT=Accounting
```

Notice that the MsgOut attribute isn't present, indicating that the resulting page hasn't passed through SimpleFilter.

By specifying INCLUDE in the <dispatcher> subelement, you're saying that the filter should map only to included requests. To see this in action, Listing 11-16 shows a new JSP, Master.jsp, that will include Sub.jsp.

**Listing 11-16.** *Master.jsp*

```
<html>
  <head></head>
  <body>
    <h1>First Inclusion</h1>
    <jsp:include page="/jsp/Sub.jsp" flush="true">
      <jsp:param name="DEPT" value="Accounting"/>
    </jsp:include>
    <hr/>
    <h1>Second Inclusion</h1>
    <jsp:include page="/jsp/Sub.jsp" flush="true">
      <jsp:param name="DEPT" value="Engineering"/>
    </jsp:include>
  </body>
</html>
```

This JSP file makes two calls to the request dispatcher, each time to include the /jsp/ Sub.jsp that you've been working with. The output from both of these include() actions is merged as the output response. Note that you're also supplying a different DEPT parameter with each inclusion.

Figure 11-15 shows what you should see if you reload the new application and navigate to the following URL:

```
http://localhost:8080/filters2/jsp/Master.jsp
```

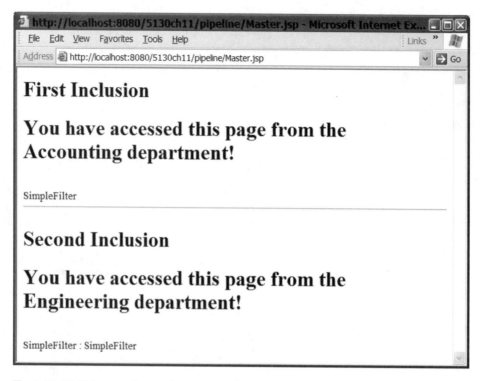

**Figure 11-15.** *This page shows what occurs when a filter acts upon resources that are called with the <jsp:include> standard action.*

Note the MsgOut attribute value—it reflects the action of SimpleFilter. The attribute is "SimpleFilter" after the first inclusion of Sub.jsp and "SimpleFilter : SimpleFilter" after the second inclusion. The request has been operated on by SimpleFilter twice, once for each inclusion in Master.jsp.

### FORWARD-Only Filtering

To make the filter operate only on forwarded requests, modify the web.xml file as follows:

```
<filter-mapping>
  <filter-name>Simple Push Filter</filter-name>
  <url-pattern>/jsp/*</url-pattern>
  <dispatcher>FORWARD</dispatcher>
</filter-mapping>
```

Because FORWARD is specified in the `<dispatcher>` element, only forwarded requests will be passed to the filter. To see this in action, we'll create one last JSP, Forwarder.jsp, shown in Listing 11-17.

**Listing 11-17.** *Forwarder.jsp*

```
<jsp:forward page="/jsp/Sub.jsp">
  <jsp:param name="DEPT" value="Accounting"/>
  <jsp:param name="MsgForwarder" value="Forwarded from forwarder.jsp"/>
</jsp:forward>
```

This JSP page simply forwards the request to Sub.jsp, and sets the DEPT and MsgForwarder parameters. Both parameters are displayed in Sub.jsp by using EL.

Reload the application or restart Tomcat. Now try the following URLs in turn:

```
http://localhost:8080/filters2/jsp/Sub.jsp?DEPT=Accounting
http://localhost:8080/filters2/jsp/Master.jsp
http://localhost:8080/filters2/jsp/Forwarder.jsp
```

For the first two URLs, notice that direct request and included requests are no longer being filtered. The third URL should result in a page similar to Figure 11-16.

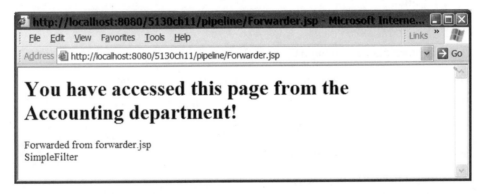

**Figure 11-16.** *This page results when the filter is applied to resources that are called by using the `<jsp:forward>` standard action.*

You can see from this experiment that only the forwarded request is filtered.

## Combining Dispatcher Actions

Of course, you can use more than one `<dispatcher>` element to indicate multiple locations for the filter to apply to. For example:

```
<filter-mapping>
  <filter-name>Simple Push Filter</filter-name>
  <url-pattern>/jsp/*</url-pattern>
  <dispatcher>FORWARD</dispatcher>
```

```
     <dispatcher>INCLUDE</dispatcher>
     <dispatcher>REQUEST</dispatcher>
   </filter-mapping>
```

Now, try the three previous URLs, and you'll observe the following:

- **URL 1:** The filter is active on Sub.jsp when requested alone.

- **URL 2:** The filter is active on Master.jsp *plus* each of the included Sub.jsps.

- **URL 3:** The filter is active on Forwarder.jsp *plus* the forwarded Sub.jsp.

# Summary

In this chapter, we've worked through five complete filter examples covering these application domains:

- Auditing

- Authorization

- Adapting legacy resources

- Authentication

- Request-processing pipeline

Working through the code to these filters, we've discussed the following:

- Generating our own response and blocking downstream processing

- Wrapping a response to transform or replace its content

- Wrapping a response to change its headers

- Wrapping a request to modify headers

- Accessing initialization parameters

- Dynamically altering filter behavior based on the incoming request

- Controlling the interaction of filters and the request dispatcher

- Applying filters in a processing pipeline configuration

You now have five examples that you can use as the basis for your own filter implementation. You also have one versatile class, ReplaceContentOutputStream, that you can use whenever you need to wrap a response to modify its content.

You should now be fluent in filtering technology, and you should be able to apply filters to many challenges that the real world may throw at you.

# CHAPTER 12

# Security in Web Applications

**A** web application lives a hazardous existence in the land of 1s and 0s. The Internet—the virtual environment we all know and love—can be a dark and dangerous place. It's filled with calm, collected programmer types like us, but there are also zealous hackers wandering through the dark alleys, scanning for open ports and passwords to steal. Is your web application safe? Have you protected your resources from the vulnerable, open, and sometimes dangerous information superhighway? In such a treacherous environment, most web applications will have security requirements, such as encrypting passwords or protecting certain pages from unauthorized viewing. Sun Microsystems has come to the rescue and made this easier for Java developers. In the Java Servlet specification, compliant containers are required to have built-in mechanisms to support your security requirements.

In this chapter, we will focus on building several examples that show different methods for authentication and access control. A more common name for these methods is **declarative security**, which basically involves changing an XML file (`web.xml`) to control who can log in and who can do what. This allows you to keep an application's security configuration separate from your servlet and JSP code. Declarative security can be very helpful in making your application more portable across application servers, as well as making it easier for a deployer (versus a developer) to change.

This chapter covers the aspects of security that we've encountered as web developers, particularly with JSP-based web applications. In this chapter, you will look at the following:

- Authentication mechanisms (form, basic, digest, and client certification)

- Secure Sockets Layer (SSL) and security certificates

- Java Authentication and Authorization Service (JAAS)

- Form-based authentication tips and tricks

- Servlet 2.5 changes

## Overview of Application Security

First, we should define "authentication" and "authorization." **Authentication** is the process by which a web application verifies that *you are who you say you are*. For example, when a user logs in to a web page with a username and password, the web application validates the entered credentials against its user data store (for example, file-, database-, or Lightweight

Directory Access Protocol [LDAP]-based) and the login succeeds or fails. **Authorization**, on the other hand, occurs when the application checks to see whether you're *allowed* to do something. For example, to delete a user from the database, you need to be an administrator.

Having security built into servlet containers isn't something new in the Servlet 2.5 specification—it's been around since Servlet 2.2 with the advent of the web.xml deployment descriptor. The security features that all servlet containers provide are as follows:

- **Authentication**: The process of proving your identity to an application

- **Access control for resources**: The means by which interactions with resources are limited to users, roles, or programs for the purpose of enforcing integrity, confidentiality, or availability constraints

- **Data integrity**: The means for proving that a third party hasn't modified information while it was in transit

- **Confidentiality or data privacy**: The means used to ensure that information is made available only to users who are authorized to access it

So far, you've learned how to develop the different components in a web application. Now we'll show you how to use the built-in mechanisms of the servlet and JSP APIs to configure authentication and authorization. It's really quite simple. Container-managed authentication, where you configure or *declare* in your web.xml deployment descriptor file who can access your web application, is one of these built-in mechanisms, and it takes only about 5 minutes to set up when you're using a Java EE–compliant server.

---

■**Note**  When we refer to an "application" in this chapter, we're speaking about a web application unless otherwise specified. When we refer to "application servers" or "servlet containers," we're speaking about Java EE application servers that have a servlet container.

---

In this chapter, we'll concentrate on securing the front end of an application. However, security is important in all tiers of an application, from the presentation layer (JSP pages, HTML, JavaScript) to the underlying hardware and the network that the application uses. You must ask yourself whether your database, network, and operating system are secure. If you leave any of these open to attack, there would be no point in securing the front end of your application.

---

■**Note**  For more information on securing your database, network, or operating system, see http://www.owasp.org and http://online.securityfocus.com.

---

As a web developer, you shouldn't be tasked with the security in these areas, but it's something you should be aware of. You also need to prevent your application from a **denial**

**of service (DoS)** attack, in which your application or site is attacked by an enormous number of hits at the same time. Most good application servers have mechanisms to handle this, but it's a good idea to test for DoS if you're developing a highly visible site or application.

In this chapter, you will see how to build a secure application, complete with user authentication and authorization. Using the security mechanisms in this chapter will further translate into the other layers of your application, particularly if you're using Enterprise JavaBeans (EJBs).

We've worked on projects in the past in which we rolled our own security mechanism. Although it worked well (interfacing with LDAP), it was a real pain to maintain and difficult for new developers to understand. By using container-managed security, your application will be much easier to maintain and comprehend. You can easily add new roles to your application by adding or altering a few lines in your application's deployment descriptors. Using container-managed security also makes it easy to switch from using a file-based user data store (or realm) to a database or LDAP-based realm. If you use what Java EE provides—and a new developer should be familiar with Java EE—then understanding your application's architecture will be a breeze.

In the Servlet 2.5 specification, not much is new regarding security. The specification still recommends that you use the deployment descriptor as your primary vehicle to implement security. This is so the application developer doesn't get bogged down with implementation details, and the application deployer has control over matters such as which roles to allow, which resources to protect, and so on. It's easy to roll your own security mechanism when you fulfill both the application developer and application deployer roles on your development team. However, if you work in a large team or you're developing a product for customers to install, an application with declared security will be much easier to maintain. Read on, and we'll show you how easy it is to develop and maintain container-managed security.

# Using Authentication

One of the most popular JSP/servlet sample applications produced today is the "how to log in" application. This application usually consists of a couple of JSP pages, some Java Database Connectivity (JDBC) code to access a database, and possibly a tag library that rejects or allows users on the basis of their logged-in status. Although these elements make for easy-to-understand applications, they promote an overly difficult method of performing authentication.

Container-managed authentication has existed since the Servlet 2.2 specification, but unfortunately many application server vendors didn't implement it correctly. Tomcat has an awesome implementation of container-managed authentication. All that is needed is some deployment descriptor manipulation, and your resources are protected. The beauty of container-managed authentication is that the level of security is up to the developer or the deployer.

First, we'll define a couple of terms that we use throughout this section. According to the Tomcat documentation (`http://jakarta.apache.org/tomcat/tomcat-5.5-doc/realm-howto.html`), "A **Realm** is a 'database' of usernames and passwords that identify valid users of a web application (or set of web applications), plus an enumeration of the list of roles associated with each valid user. You can think of roles as similar to *groups* in Unix-like operating systems, because access to specific web-application resources is granted to all users possessing a particular role (rather than enumerating the list of associated usernames). A particular user can have any number of roles associated with their username."

All configuration settings (servlet or filter mappings, URL patterns, and so on) in the web.xml file relate to the root directory of your web application. They don't include your application's context path. To prove how easy it is to use container-managed authentication, you can add the following lines to your web.xml file to protect your entire application. The following <security-constraint> and <login-config> elements should be entered toward the bottom of your web.xml file:

```
<security-constraint>
  <web-resource-collection>
    <web-resource-name>My Application</web-resource-name>
    <url-pattern>/*</url-pattern>
  </web-resource-collection>
  <auth-constraint>
    <role-name>*</role-name>
  </auth-constraint>
</security-constraint>
<login-config>
  <auth-method>BASIC</auth-method>
</login-config>
```

The significant elements in the preceding code are <url-pattern>, <role-name>, and <auth-method>:

- The <url-pattern> element defines the characters to look for in a client's request. This value can be a path-based pattern (such as /admin/*) or an extension-based pattern (such as /admin/*.jsp), and it doesn't include the context path. Any resources that match this path will be secured by the container.

- The <role-name> element indicates the roles allowed to view the secured resource(s). There can be one or more role names defined, and an asterisk (*) indicates all roles defined in the realm.

- The <auth-method> defines the type of authentication mechanism to use, such as basic (a simple dialog box with the username/password) or form (a redirect to an HTML-based login page).

Figure 12-1 shows an illustration of the <security-constraint> element adapted from a similar illustration in the Servlet 2.5 specification. As you can see, there are very few required elements. The <security-constraint> element can occur zero or more times within the <web-app> element of the deployment descriptor. If it occurs, then it must have a <web-resource-collection> subelement. The <web-resource-collection> element is required to have <web-resource-name> and <url-pattern> subelements. More details on how to use the <security-constraint> element can be found in the Servlet 2.5 specification.

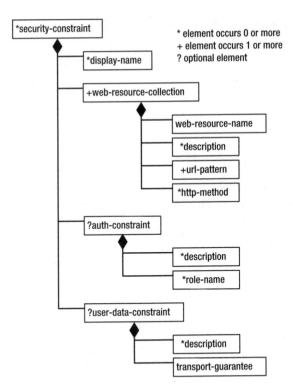

**Figure 12-1.** *The <security-constraint> element of the deployment descriptor is used to provide descriptive security to a web application.*

When you add the `<security-constraint>` element to the deployment descriptor of a web application installed in Tomcat, the application will be protected by Tomcat's default memory realm. The `<security-constraint>` element, through the use of the wildcard for `<role-name>`, allows all roles to access the web application.

There should already be a `tomcat` user in `%TOMCAT_HOME%\conf\tomcat-users.xml` with a role `tomcat` and password `tomcat`. Thus, if you accessed a web application protected by the preceding `<security-constraint>`, you could access it with the username and password `tomcat/tomcat`. The `tomcat-users.xml` file in our release has the following entries by default:

```
<tomcat-users>
  <role rolename="tomcat"/>
  <role rolename="role1"/>
  <role rolename="manager"/>
  <role rolename="admin"/>
  <user username="tomcat" password="tomcat" roles="tomcat"/>
  <user username="both" password="tomcat" roles="tomcat,role1"/>
  <user username="role1" password="tomcat" roles="role1"/>
  <user username="admin" password="hinkar" roles="admin,manager"/>
</tomcat-users>
```

Here, `username` represents the username used for logging in, and the `roles` element is a comma-delimited list of roles for the given user. A role in this list should match the security-role in your web.xml file. To add a new user named projsp with the password test to this file (aka realm), simply create a new line:

```
<tomcat-users>

  <user name="projsp"    password="test"    roles="tomcat" />
</tomcat-users>
```

You will need to restart Tomcat for this change to take effect.

In the <security-constraint> example shown earlier, we used an * to indicate that all roles were allowed to access the web application. Keep in mind this is a simple example of how to protect your entire application and how to allow all roles in your realm. If you do add roles by name in the <auth-constraint> subelement, you'll also need to add the following <security-role> element to the deployment descriptor. For example, if the <role-name> subelement of <auth-constraint> specified the role apress, then the <security-role> element of the deployment descriptor would include the following:

```
<security-role>
    <role-name>apress</role-name>
</security-role>
```

Also, if you want to name your realm so the user sees a friendly name in the login dialog box, you can add a <realm-name> element to <login-config>:

```
<login-config>
    <auth-method>BASIC</auth-method>
    <realm-name>My Test Application</realm-name>
</login-config>
```

When the client displays the login dialog box (see Figure 12-2), the dialog will display the specified realm name.

**Figure 12-2.** *When you provide a realm name in the deployment descriptor, it is used in the login dialog box displayed to the user.*

If you don't define a `realm-name`, the realm's value will be *server:port*, such as `localhost:8080`. This simple example of basic authentication in an application brings us to the authentication options.

## Authentication Options

Using a deployment descriptor, a web client can authenticate to a web server by using one of the mechanisms listed in Table 12-1.

**Table 12-1.** *Authentication Mechanisms for Web Applications*

| Mechanism | Configuration |
|---|---|
| HTTP basic authentication | `<auth-method>BASIC</auth-method>` |
| HTTP digest authentication | `<auth-method>DIGEST</auth-method>` |
| HTTPS client authentication | `<auth-method>CLIENT-CERT</auth-method>` |
| Form-based authentication | `<auth-method>FORM</auth-method>` |

When using HTTP basic authentication, the server will authenticate a user by using a username and password from the client. In a web environment, the client browser uses a pop-up dialog box (see Figure 12-2) to collect the user's username and password. Figure 12-3 shows the sequence of interactions between a client and server when basic authentication is used. The authentication is based on a username and password, and the password is sent by using simple base64 encoding, but it isn't encrypted.

**Figure 12-3.** *When a client requests a protected page, the server returns the HTTP status 401. The client collects username and password data from the user and sends the data to the server. If the user is authorized to view the resource, the server sends the requested resource.*

The target server isn't authenticated; therefore, this isn't a secure mechanism. The client has no proof that the server is who it says it is. For a server to prove its identity, it needs to obtain an SSL certificate from a certificate authority (such as VeriSign). If you need greater security but still wish to use basic authentication, you can combine it with SSL or a virtual private network (VPN).

HTTP digest authentication also authenticates a user on the basis of a username and password. However, the client transmits the password in an encrypted form, such as Secure Hash Algorithm (SHA) or Message Digest 5 (MD5). In the web arena, HTTP 1.1–enabled browsers will support this. According to the Servlet 2.5 specification, HTTP digest authentication isn't currently in widespread use; therefore, servlet containers are encouraged but not required to support it. Tomcat, JBoss, and Resin support this authentication method. When you use HTTP digest authentication, the user is prompted with a username/password dialog box that looks similar to the basic authentication dialog box shown in Figure 12-4. However, the digest authentication dialog box indicates that the user is accessing a secure site.

**Figure 12-4.** *When digest authentication is used, the dialog box indicates that the user is accessing a secure site.*

HTTPS client authentication requires the user to possess a **Public Key Certificate (PKC)** and is based on HTTP over SSL, hence the name HTTPS. To use this, users will have to apply for, receive, and then install into their browser a certificate. This verifies the browser's identity and often prompts the user for a password even if the certificate is present. PKCs are useful in applications with strict security requirements and also for single sign-on from within the browser. Servlet containers that you want to be Java EE compliant are required to support the HTTPS protocol.

Form-based authentication is the final option when using declarative security. It seems to be the most desirable and it's also our favorite. Unlike the others, it allows the developer (or web designer) to customize the look and feel of the login screen. This is what most people expect when using a web application, so it fits into the web paradigm nicely. It also allows for simple instructions on the login screen and usability features such as password hints and help links. All the web applications that we've developed (that required user authentication) have used an HTML-based implementation. For this reason, we show you how to implement form-based authentication along with a few tricks.

## Form-Based Authentication

To understand how form-based authentication works, let's look at the five steps that occur in a successful login. Figure 12-5 shows those steps again, along with numbered keys that will guide the discussion that follows the figure.

**Figure 12-5.** *When a client requests a protected page, the client and server work together to provide the resource only if the client is authenticated and authorized to view the resource.*

Here are the steps in the interaction between a client and server when the client attempts to access a protected resource. Each numbered item in the following list corresponds to a number in Figure 12-5.

1. A user requests a protected resource (defined as protected in web.xml) by clicking a link, selecting a bookmark, or typing in a URL.

2. The login form associated with this protected resource is sent to the client, and the container stores the URL that the client tried to access. This is to say that the container remembers that the client originally requested /do/mainMenu.

---

**■Tip** The current servlet API doesn't allow you to get the URL the user originally tried to access. However, some servlet containers will store this value as a hidden field in the form. View the servlet container documentation to see whether yours does.

---

3. The user populates the form with her username and password and submits it.

4. The container attempts to authenticate the user with the form's information.

5. If authentication succeeds, the client is redirected to the resource by using the stored URL path.

Unfortunately, this authentication mechanism was designed to resemble HTTP basic authentication, meaning that when a user enters an incorrect username or password, the server returns an HTTP status code of 401. HTTP status code 401 means "This resource requires HTTP authentication." Therefore, your deployment descriptor will contain entries for a login form and an error page; the error page is served up when a 401 error is encountered. This process (see Figure 12-6) includes the same steps as those described previously, except the last step changes to the following:

6. If authentication fails, the error page is returned and the status code of the response is set to 401.

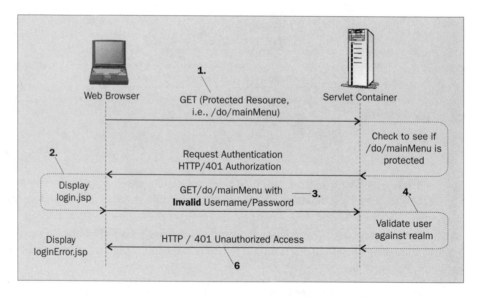

**Figure 12-6.** *When form-based authentication is used, the last step in the process is changed slightly.*

To implement form-based authentication, the first thing you need is a page with a form. The only requirements mandated by the specification are that the form's action is j_security_check, and that the username and password fields are named j_username and j_password, respectively. Listing 12-1 shows an example of how this might be coded in an HTML or JSP page.

**Listing 12-1.** *login.jsp*

```
<html>
<body>
<form id="loginForm" method="post" action="j_security_check">
  <p>
    Username: <input type="text" name="j_username" id="j_username" />
    <br/>
    Password: <input type="password" name="j_password" id="j_password" />
    <br/>
    <button type="submit">login</button>
  </p>
</form>
</body>
</html>
```

The form error page can contain anything, but most likely the page will explain that the user entered an invalid username or password.

To configure form-based authentication in the deployment descriptor, let's build upon the earlier example. The following code snippet is a `<security-constraint>` element where the `<auth-method>` has been changed to `FORM`, and a login page and error page have been defined:

```
<security-constraint>
    <web-resource-collection>
        <url-pattern>/*</url-pattern>
    </web-resource-collection>
    <auth-constraint>
        <role-name>*</role-name>
    </auth-constraint>
</security-constraint>
<login-config>
    <auth-method>FORM</auth-method>
    <form-login-config>
        <form-login-page>/login.jsp</form-login-page>
        <form-error-page>/loginError.jsp</form-error-page>
    </form-login-config>
</login-config>
```

You'll notice we removed the `<realm-name>` from the `<login-config>` block, mainly because it won't be displayed anywhere and is therefore useless. If you've never configured form-based authentication before, we encourage you to try entering these lines in the `web.xml` of one of the example applications from this book. If you decide to try this, don't forget to create `login.jsp` and `loginError.jsp` in the root directory.

Although the preceding `<security-constraint>` element works fine on Tomcat, it may not work on other application servers. This is because the `<security-constraint>` in the preceding code snippet uses `/*` as the `<url-pattern>` to protect all resources. Therefore, you might need to adjust the `<url-pattern>` to protect only certain resources, rather than all of the application's resources.

After a user has successfully logged in, an instance of HttpSession is created for him or matched up with an existing session he created. This session is active for the duration that the <session-timeout> value specifies in the deployment descriptor (web.xml). This value determines how long the server retains a user's session between interactions. Thus, if the user clicks a link or somehow sends a request to the application, the server will recalculate how long it will wait to expire the session. After the session expires or is killed by a reboot of the application server, the user will be required to log in again. If a <session-timeout> value isn't specified, a default of 30 minutes is used. Some application servers have the ability to persist sessions to the file system (or a database), so a session can live through a reboot (provided it hasn't timed out).

It's important to note that it isn't currently possible to configure logout declaratively. Logging out is usually done by using a JSP page or servlet that calls session.invalidate(). When you use session.invalidate(), all objects bound to the session are removed. If the user tries to access a protected resource again, he'll be prompted for a username/password again. In most instances, logging out is accomplished by placing a link on a page that calls logout.jsp or a Logout.java servlet. Other ways that a user can log out are by closing the browser or by exceeding the minutes of inactivity specified by the <session-timeout> parameter.

In an early draft of the Servlet 2.4 specification, a logout() method was proposed for the HttpSession interface. This method would log the client out of the web server and invalidate all sessions associated with this client. However, the method was dropped from the final draft of the specification.

## Tomcat Realms

This section illustrates how to set up different realms in Tomcat. As mentioned previously, a realm is a "database" of usernames, passwords, and user roles. We'll show you how to set up a MemoryRealm, a JDBCRealm, a JNDIRealm, and later in this chapter, a JAASRealm.

### MemoryRealm

If you have a fresh Tomcat installation that you've been using to run these examples, you should be able to log in by using tomcat/tomcat for the username/password. These values are specified in %TOMCAT_HOME%\conf\tomcat-users.xml. This file is considered a MemoryRealm, which stores basic user information. This is the default realm for Tomcat, as specified in its server.xml file (located in the same directory).

In Tomcat 5.0.30, the realm and its database are specified like this (we've deleted irrelevant information from the excerpt):

```
<Server port="8005" shutdown="SHUTDOWN" debug="0">
  <GlobalNamingResources>
    <Resource name="UserDatabase" auth="Container"
              type="org.apache.catalina.UserDatabase"
       description="User database that can be updated and saved">
    </Resource>
    <ResourceParams name="UserDatabase">
      <parameter>
        <name>factory</name>
        <value>org.apache.catalina.users.MemoryUserDatabaseFactory
        </value>
```

```
        </parameter>
        <parameter>
          <name>pathname</name>
          <value>conf/tomcat-users.xml</value>
        </parameter>
      </ResourceParams>
    </GlobalNamingResources>
    <Service name="Catalina">
      <Engine name="Catalina" defaultHost="localhost" debug="0">
        <Realm className="org.apache.catalina.realm.UserDatabaseRealm"
                   debug="0" resourceName="UserDatabase"/>
      </Engine>
    </Service>
  </Server>
```

Note that in the `<ResourceParams>` element, you can configure the location of the user database.

Tomcat 5.5.9 has streamlined the elements:

```
<Server port="8005" shutdown="SHUTDOWN">
  <GlobalNamingResources>
    <Resource name="UserDatabase" auth="Container"
          type="org.apache.catalina.UserDatabase"
          description="User database that can be updated and saved"
          factory="org.apache.catalina.users.MemoryUserDatabaseFactory"
          pathname="conf/tomcat-users.xml" />
  </GlobalNamingResources>
  <Service name="Catalina">
    <Engine name="Catalina" defaultHost="localhost">
      <Realm className="org.apache.catalina.realm.UserDatabaseRealm"
            resourceName="UserDatabase" />
    </Engine>
  </Service>
</Server>
```

Other application servers will likely support a similar file-based mechanism for storing user information, but we doubt you'd ever see this on a production system. One of the main problems with using a file-based mechanism is that most servers require a shutdown and restart to pick up any changes. It's great to use for prototyping, but if you decide to add more user information, you'll likely want to use a database or directory service. Although it's possible to use a file-based realm for usernames and passwords, and a database for the rest of the users' information, the realm will be easier to maintain if everything is kept in the database. For that, Tomcat provides you with the JDBCRealm.

### JDBCRealm

The JDBCRealm allows you to configure *declaratively* the location for storing your users' information. When we say "declaratively," we mean that the location is typed in an XML file, rather than programmed and compiled into a Java class. Tomcat also supports a JNDIRealm for looking up and authenticating users in an LDAP directory server. When using either of these methods, you'll have to create a Context for your application, so you can override the default MemoryRealm. Listing 12-2 shows a file named context.xml, which you can place in the META-INF directory of the web application. It shows an example of using a JDBCRealm to authenticate with a MySQL database named security.

**Listing 12-2.** *context.xml*

```
<Context path="/security" docBase="security" debug="0">
    <Realm className="org.apache.catalina.realm.JDBCRealm" debug="99"
          driverName="com.mysql.jdbc.Driver"
          connectionURL="jdbc:mysql://localhost:3306/security?autoReconnect=true"
          connectionName="test"
          connectionPassword="test"
          userTable="users"
          userNameCol="username"
          userCredCol="password"
          userRoleTable="user_roles"
          roleNameCol="role_name" />
</Context>
```

By placing context.xml in the META-INF directory of the web application, you are protecting only the given application. Tomcat also allows you to place this file in various other locations. See the Tomcat documentation (http://jakarta.apache.org/tomcat/tomcat-5.5-doc/config/context.html) for more information about using context.xml.

Listing 12-2 defines two tables for users and roles. The userTable attribute in Listing 12-2 defines the users table to be a table named users. The users table must contain at least two columns, identified by the userNameCol and userCredCol attributes; the userNameCol is the column that contains usernames, and the userCredCol is the column that contains the user's password. The roles table (user_roles) also has at least two columns. The roles table contains one row for every valid role that is assigned to a particular user. A user can have zero, one, or many roles. The column that contains the role data is identified by the roleNameCol attribute. The username from both the users table and the roles table should match the value a person enters as a username. The role name value will match up to roles specified in the application's web.xml file.

The following example SQL script in Listing 12-3 creates the needed tables. This script has been tested only on MySQL.

**Listing 12-3.** *security.sql*

```
create database if not exists security;
grant all privileges on security.* to test@localhost identified by "test";
grant all privileges on security.* to test@"%" identified by "test";
use security;

create table users (
    username        varchar(50) not null primary key,
    password        varchar(25) not null
```

```
);
create table user_roles (
  username          varchar(50) not null,
  role_name         varchar(20) not null,
  primary key (username, role_name)
);
```

Now you need to add a user to both the users and user_roles tables. You can do this with the following SQL:

```
insert into users (username, password) values ('tomcat', 'jdbc');
insert into user_roles (username, role_name) values ('tomcat', 'developer');
```

---

■**Tip** A script to create the security database and a default user is located with the code download for this book, at the Source Code area of the Apress website (http://www.apress.com/book/download.html).

---

The next step is to place a copy of the JDBC driver you'll be using inside the %TOMCAT_HOME%\common\lib directory. You can download the latest MySQL JDBC driver JAR file at www.mysql.org.

Next, create Listing 12-4. This will be a test page that we will try to access.

**Listing 12-4.** *index.jsp*

```
<html>
<body>
Congratulations, you've authenticated successfully!
</body>
</html>
```

As with all web applications, we need a deployment descriptor. Listing 12-5 shows the deployment descriptor for this example. Note that you're allowing all roles to log in to this application.

**Listing 12-5.** *web.xml*

```
<?xml version="1.0" encoding="ISO-8859-1"?>
<web-app xmlns="http://java.sun.com/xml/ns/javaee"
         xmlns:xsi="http://www.w3.org/2001/XMLSchema-instance"
   xsi:schemaLocation="http://java.sun.com/xml/ns/javaee/web-app_2_5.xsd"
         version="2.5">
    <display-name>Security Example</display-name>
    <description>Web Application Security Example</description>
    <security-constraint>
        <web-resource-collection>
            <web-resource-name>My Application</web-resource-name>
            <url-pattern>/*</url-pattern>
        </web-resource-collection>
```

```
        <auth-constraint>
            <role-name>*</role-name>
        </auth-constraint>
    </security-constraint>
    <login-config>
        <auth-method>BASIC</auth-method>
        <realm-name>My Test Application</realm-name>
    </login-config>
</web-app>
```

To demonstrate that this code works, perform the following steps:

1. Create a `security` directory in the `webapps` directory, and copy the `index.jsp` file shown in Listing 12-4 to this directory.

2. If you are using Tomcat 5.5, enter Listing 12-2 into a file named `context.xml` and save it to the `%TOMCAT_HOME%\webapps\security\META-INF` directory. If you are using Tomcat 5.0, take the `<Realm>` element from Listing 12-2 and add it to `server.xml`.

3. Create a `WEB-INF` directory in the `security` directory, and add the deployment descriptor from Listing 12-5.

4. Ensure that a JDBC driver library for the database has been copied into the `common\lib` directory. We used `mysql-connector-java-3.1.10-bin.jar` for this example.

5. Start Tomcat and navigate to `http://localhost:8080/security`. You should be prompted with a dialog box that looks like Figure 12-7.

6. After you enter a username of `tomcat` and a password of `jdbc`, you should see a screen like that in Figure 12-8.

**Figure 12-7.** *The login dialog box for the security web application*

**Figure 12-8.** *When you successfully log in to the security application, you should see this JSP page.*

You can also use JDBC to protect all the applications of a Tomcat server. To do this, you take the <Realm> element from Listing 12-2 and put it into Tomcat's conf\server.xml file in place of the existing <Realm> element. Note that if you do this, you need to ensure the database contains the admin and manager users and roles to keep using the existing Tomcat applications.

If you'd rather authenticate with an LDAP server, you can configure a JNDIRealm in Tomcat. On most large projects we've worked on, an LDAP server was involved in storing user information.

### JNDIRealm

Configuring a JNDIRealm is similar to configuring a JDBCRealm; however, the realms' attributes are slightly different. For this example, we installed OpenLDAP version 2.2.19 on a Microsoft Windows XP Pro machine.

We installed the OpenLDAP server according to the quick start guide at http://www.openldap.org/doc/admin/quickstart.html. Then we edited the slapd.conf file. At the top of the file, we had to include two additional schema entries. By default, only core.schema was included; we added cosine.schema and inetorgperson.schema:

```
include        C:/openldap/etc/schema/core.schema
include        C:/openldap/etc/schema/cosine.schema
include        C:/openldap/etc/schema/inetorgperson.schema
```

Obviously, you may need to adjust the paths based on your system. Regardless of whether you are trying this example on a Windows system or a Unix-based system, the include directives in the slapd.conf file must be the correct paths to the files being included.

In the same file, at the bottom, we changed the settings as follows:

```
database bdb
suffix "dc=raibledesigns,dc=com"
rootdn "cn=Manager,dc=raibledesigns,dc=com"
rootpw secret
directory C:/openldap/var/openldap-data
```

You would, of course, modify the settings as needed for your system. For example, you might have a different directory location for the openldap-data file, or the root password may not be secret, or your domain may be different from raibledesigns.com.

Then we created an **LDAP Data Interchange Format (LDIF)** file to create our top-level organization entry, the organization units for groups and people and, finally, the tomcat user with a password of jndi and the developer role (see Listing 12-6).

**Listing 12-6.** *entries.ldif*

```
# Define top-level entry
dn: dc=raibledesigns,dc=com
objectClass: dcObject
objectClass: organization
o: Raible Designs, Inc.
dc: raibledesigns

# Define Manager Role to authenticate with
dn: cn=Manager,dc=raibledesigns,dc=com
objectclass: organizationalRole
cn: Manager
description: Directory Manager

# Define an entry to contain people
# searches for users are based on this entry
dn: ou=people,dc=raibledesigns,dc=com
objectClass: organizationalUnit
ou: people

# Define a user entry for Tomcat User
dn: uid=tomcat,ou=people,dc=raibledesigns,dc=com
objectClass: inetOrgPerson
uid: tomcat
sn: user
cn: tomcat user
mail: tomcat@raibledesigns.com
userPassword: jndi

# Define an entry to contain LDAP groups
# searches for roles are based on this entry
dn: ou=groups,dc=raibledesigns,dc=com
objectClass: organizationalUnit
ou: groups

# Define an entry for the "developer" role
dn: cn=developer,ou=groups,dc=raibledesigns,dc=com
objectClass: groupOfUniqueNames
cn: developer
uniqueMember: uid=tomcat,ou=people,dc=raibledesigns,dc=com
```

We named this file `entries.ldif`, placed it in the `root` user's home directory, and imported it by using the `ldapadd` command:

```
ldapadd -x -D "cn=Manager,dc=raibledesigns,dc=com" -W -f ~/entries.ldif
```

Following this procedure should result in a number of `adding new entry` lines displayed in your console window, as shown in Figure 12-9.

**Figure 12-9.** *As the LDAP server processes each entry in the LDIF file, it will display a message to the console.*

If you get any errors, we found that it was easy to start over by stopping LDAP (using the `kill` command) and removing the contents of the `usr\local\var\openldap-data` directory.

The `slapd.conf` and `entries.ldif` files used for this example can be found with the code download for the book; the files are located with the code for this chapter in the directory `jndi`. To enable use of the `JNDIRealm` (instead of the `JDBCRealm`), replace the previous realm configuration with the following:

```
<Realm className="org.apache.catalina.realm.JNDIRealm" debug="99"
        connectionName="cn=Developer,dc=raibledesigns,dc=com"
        connectionPassword="secret"
        connectionURL="ldap://localhost:389"
        userPassword="userPassword"
        userPattern="uid={0},ou=people,dc=raibledesigns,dc=com"
        roleBase="ou=groups,dc=raibledesigns,dc=com"
        roleName="cn"
        roleSearch="(uniqueMember={0})"
/>
```

You'll need the JNDI drivers for LDAP in your CLASSPATH for this to work. You can download the latest LDAP Service Provider (version 1.2.4) from `http://java.sun.com/products/ jndi/downloads/index.html`. After you've downloaded it, extract `ldap.jar` into `%TOMCAT_HOME%\ common\lib`.

As with the JDBC realm, you can protect a single application by nesting the `<Realm>` element in a `<Context>` element in the file `context.xml` in the `META-INF` directory of the application. Optionally, you can set the default realm for your entire server to be a JNDI realm. To do this, edit Tomcat's `server.xml` file (in `%TOMCAT_HOME%\conf`), and replace the default realm (shown next) with your desired realm's information. Note that if you still want to use the Tomcat Manager or Admin applications, your LDAP server will need appropriate user and role entries to allow this.

If everything has been installed and configured correctly, then when you try to access a protected web page, you will see the same login dialog or form (depending on whether you have specified basic or form authentication). After you enter a username and password, Tomcat will make a JNDI call to the LDAP server to authenticate the username.

### JAASRealm

Tomcat has support for a `JAASRealm` as well. We show you how to configure a `JAASRealm` in the "Java Authentication and Authorization Service" section later in this chapter. For the purposes of this chapter and its associated example application, we will generally use a `JDBCRealm`.

## Using Secure Sockets Layer

So far, we've discussed setting up a form-based login and configuring it to talk to a realm. One problem with the example so far is that the communication between the browser and server isn't secure. If someone were listening with a password sniffer, your security would be compromised. Furthermore, these sniffers are easy to come by—try searching Google for "password sniffer."

According to "The Guide to Building Secure Web Applications, Version 1.1.1" from the Open Web Application Security Project (`http://www.owasp.org`), "The most common method of securing the HTTP protocol is to use SSL. The **Secure Sockets Layer** protocol, or **SSL**, was designed by Netscape and was introduced in the Netscape Communicator browser in 1994. It's most likely the widest-spoken security protocol in the world, and is built into all commercial web browsers and web servers. The current version is version 2. Since the original version of SSL is technically a proprietary protocol, the **Internet Engineering Task Force (IETF)** took over responsibilities for upgrading SSL, and have now renamed it **Transport Layer Security (TLS)**. The first version of TLS is version 3.1, and has only minor changes from the original specification."

SSL is a technology that allows web browsers and web servers to communicate over a secure channel. In SSL, data is encrypted at the browser (before transmission) and then decrypted at the server before reading the data. This same process takes place when the server returns data to the client. This process is known as the **SSL handshake**. There currently are three levels of encryption supported by this protocol: 40-bit, 56-bit, and 128-bit. The more security you need, the more bits you should use. For more on the SSL handshake, visit `http://medialab.di.unipi.it/doc/JNetSec/jns_ch11.htm`.

The best way to gain a good understanding of SSL is to implement it. The first step to setting up SSL on your web server (in this case, Tomcat) is to generate a certificate. Keep in mind that if you are proxying your JSP/servlet requests through a traditional web server (such as Apache or IIS), you'll need to set up SSL on those servers. The documentation for setting up Tomcat's SSL support is excellent, but we'll go over it here so it's familiar to you.

## Secure Sockets Layer on Tomcat

If you're using Java 1.4, or Java 5 Standard Edition, Java Secure Socket Extension (JSSE) has been integrated into its core, so no additional download is needed.

---

**Note** More information about JSSE can be found at `http://java.sun.com/products/jsse/`.

---

Create a certificate keystore by executing the following command:

```
$JAVA_HOME/bin/keytool -genkey -alias tomcat -keyalg RSA
```

Specify a password value of changeit. This process should resemble the session shown in Figure 12-10.

```
C:\Program Files\Java\jdk1.5.0_03\bin>keytool -delete -alias tomcat
Enter keystore password:  changeit

C:\Program Files\Java\jdk1.5.0_03\bin>keytool -genkey -alias tomcat -keyalg RSA
Enter keystore password:  changeit
What is your first and last name?
  [Unknown]:  localhost
What is the name of your organizational unit?
  [Unknown]:
What is the name of your organization?
  [Unknown]:
What is the name of your City or Locality?
  [Unknown]:
What is the name of your State or Province?
  [Unknown]:
What is the two-letter country code for this unit?
  [Unknown]:
Is CN=localhost, OU=Unknown, O=Unknown, L=Unknown, ST=Unknown, C=Unknown correct
?
  [no]:  yes

Enter key password for <tomcat>
        (RETURN if same as keystore password):

C:\Program Files\Java\jdk1.5.0_03\bin>
```

**Figure 12-10.** *The output of the keytool program when creating a certificate keystore for Tomcat*

The keytool application will prompt you for information such as first and last name, city, state, and so on. We've used **localhost** as the first and last name values, because this is the value matched by your browser when verifying authenticity of the certificate. It actually shows up as the *certification path* in the resulting certificate. For testing purposes, you can accept the default values for most of the other prompts. When the tool prompts you to verify the data, type **yes** and press Enter. Finally, press Enter to accept the keystore password as the user password.

This is still not a valid certificate because you're generating it yourself. To get a valid certificate, you must purchase one from a **certificate authority (CA)** such as VeriSign. In this example, using localhost will result in one less warning in the user's browser.

Now, edit %TOMCAT_HOME%/conf/server.xml and remove the comments around the SSL HTTP/1.1 Connector entry. After you've set this up, you should be able to access Tomcat by using https://localhost:8443. Don't forget the s after http. The port has to be specified because it isn't the default port for HTTPS (port 443).

Tomcat expects the .keystore file that was created by the keystore tool to be in a particular location (the user's home directory). If you are having trouble accessing Tomcat over SSL (particularly if the error log has messages about not being able to access the .keystore file), you can tell Tomcat where the .keystore file is by adding this attribute to the SSL <Connector> element of servler.xml:

```
keystoreFile="path_to_keystore\.keystore"
```

If you don't want to specify your port numbers on your URLs when using Tomcat, you can easily change them in the server.xml file. When accessing Tomcat for the first time on its SSL port, you should be prompted with a security alert (see Figure 12-11).

**Figure 12-11.** *When accessing a secure site over SSL by using a certificate that was created by someone other than a CA, the browser will display a security alert informing you of that fact.*

If you use your real name rather than localhost when generating this certificate, the security alert will warn you that the certificate's name doesn't match the name of the page you're trying to view (see Figure 12-12).

**Figure 12-12.** *If the name on the certificate has a problem, the security alert will also display that information.*

---

■**Caution** We've encountered problems when running Tomcat on 80/443 and IIS on a Windows machine at the same time. Shutting down IIS allowed us to run Tomcat on 443. The strange part is that IIS was running on port 81 and we had no secure port running. When you see Tomcat start and then immediately shut down, a port conflict is often the cause of the problem.

---

One thing you'll probably notice after setting this up is that your browser warns you about the certificate. This is because the issuer of the certificate is unknown (you) and the browser doesn't recognize you as a CA. CAs, such as VeriSign (http://www.verisign.com), Thawte (http://thawte.com), and TC TrustCenter (http://www.trustcenter.de/set_en.htm), are trusted organizations that verify and certify that a server is who it says it is. Also, you can obtain client certificates if you want to set up both client and server certificates. This may be necessary in highly secure, top-secret, *X Files*–flavored applications, but it's not necessary for most web applications.

One drawback to using SSL in a web application is that it tends to significantly decrease the throughput of the server. This is mainly due to the encryption and decryption process on each end of the connection. Therefore, we recommend that you use SSL only for the parts of your application that really need it—for instance, when a user logs in or when a user submits a credit card number.

---

■**Note** You can find more information on performance degradation with SSL at http://www.computerworld.com/securitytopics/security/story/0,10801,58978,00.html. This article also contains links to other articles and options for SSL acceleration.

---

Later in this chapter, we'll show you how to do SSL switching upon user login and also before the user logs in.

# Java Authentication and Authorization Service

You might be wondering how **Java Authentication and Authorization Service (JAAS)** fits into all of this. JAAS provides a framework and standard programming interface for authenticating users and for assigning privileges. Together with Java 2, an application can provide code-centric access control, user-centric access control, or a combination of the two. JAAS was invented to make login services independent of authentication technologies and allow **Pluggable Authentication Modules (PAM)**. Most modern application servers use JAAS under the covers to configure container-managed security—you're using it without even knowing that you are!

JAAS can be helpful when you need to use complex authentication schemas or when you grant resource-specific privileges to users (for example, inserting a row in the database or assigning write permissions to a file). At its core, JAAS is essentially a security mechanism that allows you to specify authentication and authorization via policy files. It became an integral part of Java starting with J2SE 1.4. When you run your application server with a security manager, a policy file is checked, and then the user is allowed to run your application or is prompted for credentials. As we mentioned, JAAS does allow for complex login schemas, such as a Windows NT domain or smart cards (for example, RSA SecurID).

---

**Note** You can find more information on the login schemas supported at `http://java.sun.com/j2se/1.4/docs/guide/security/jaas/JAASRefGuide.html#AppendixB`.

---

To set up your application server to use JAAS specifically for your application, rather than its own authentication mechanism, you usually have to select a JAAS custom realm and then perform a few additional steps. The following steps set up a `JAASRealm` on Tomcat 5 (on a Windows machine) to authenticate with an NT domain.

The easiest way to do this is to download Andy Armstrong's JAAS login modules from `http://free.tagish.net/jaas/`. These modules were written specifically for authenticating with a Windows NT domain and are similar to the helper classes that make the `JDBCRealm` work behind the scenes. After you've downloaded the ZIP file, extract the contents of the downloaded file to a `jaas-modules` directory. At the time of this writing, version 1.0.3 was the latest available download.

After you've downloaded the login modules, copy the file `NTSystem.dll` file to the Tomcat `bin` directory. Copy the `tagishauth.jar` to the Tomcat `common\lib` directory.

In the `Samples` config folder of the Tagish JAAS distribution, you'll find a `tagish.login` file and a `java.security.sample` file. Copy the last few lines from `java.security.sample` and put it at the end of the `java.security` file (located in `$JAVA_HOME\jre\lib\security`). This line looks as follows:

```
# Login configs
login.config.url.1=file:${java.home}/lib/security/tagish.login
```

Replace the token ${java.home} with the actual path to Java home on your system. For example, if ${java.home} evaluates to C:\Program Files\Java\jre1.5.0_03\, the entry would be as follows:

```
login.config.url.1=file:C:/Program Files/Java/jre1.5.0_03/lib/security/tagish.login
```

Then move the tagish.login file into the same directory ($JAVA_HOME\jre\lib\security). If your users always log in to the same domain (which is what we've configured here), just set the defaultDomain property in tagish.login as follows:

```
NTLogin
{
    com.tagish.auth.win32.NTSystemLogin required returnNames=true
        returnSIDs=false defaultDomain=NT_DOMAIN_OR_WORKGROUP;
};
```

where NT_DOMAIN_OR_WORKGROUP is the NT domain of your login, or the Windows Workgroup of your login.

---

■**Tip** Make sure to change the defaultDomain value from NT_DOMAIN_OR_WORKGROUP to the domain you want to communicate with.

---

After you've completed these setup steps, you need to change your context to have the following realm configuration:

```
<Realm className="org.apache.catalina.realm.JAASRealm" debug="10"
       appName="NTLogin"
       userClassNames="com.tagish.auth.win32.typed.NTUserPrincipal"
       roleClassNames="com.tagish.auth.win32.typed.NTGroupPrincipal" />
```

Listing 12-7 shows the context.xml file for Tomcat 5.5. If you are using Tomcat 5.0, put the <Realm> element in the server.xml file. If you are using Tomcat 5.5, nest the <Realm> element in a <Context> element in the file META-INF\context.xml.

**Listing 12-7.** *context.xml*

```
<Context path="/5130ch12_jaas" docBase="5130ch12_jaas" debug="99">
  <Realm className="org.apache.catalina.realm.JAASRealm" debug="10"
         appName="NTLogin"
         userClassNames="com.tagish.auth.win32.typed.NTUserPrincipal"
         roleClassNames="com.tagish.auth.win32.typed.NTGroupPrincipal" />
</Context>
```

Next, add the entry in Listing 12-8 to the deployment descriptor.

**Listing 12-8.** *<security-constraint> and <login-config> Elements for web.xml*

```
<security-constraint>
  <web-resource-collection>
    <web-resource-name>Security Example</web-resource-name>
    <url-pattern>/*</url-pattern>
  </web-resource-collection>
  <auth-constraint>
    <role-name>*</role-name>
  </auth-constraint>
</security-constraint>

<login-config>
  <auth-method>FORM</auth-method>
  <form-login-config>
    <form-login-page>/login.jsp</form-login-page>
    <form-error-page>/loginError.jsp</form-error-page>
  </form-login-config>
</login-config>
```

The file login.jsp was shown in Listing 12-1; we've left loginError.jsp for you to write as you please.

---

■**Caution** There appears to be a bug in the Tagish distribution that causes basic authentication to fail. That is why we use form authentication for this example. For more information, see http://blog.cmaeda.com/ ?p=22.

---

We tested this setup and configuration on a Windows XP machine, and everything worked smoothly. We were able to log in using the same username/password combination we used for logging onto Windows XP. Also, we didn't have a domain, just a workgroup, and everything worked flawlessly there as well.

If you don't want to use Andy Armstrong's JAAS login modules, you can create your own file-based JAAS LoginModule by performing the following steps.

First, create a LoginModule class as shown in Listing 12-9 that implements javax.security. auth.login.LoginContext.

**Listing 12-9.** *MyLoginModule.java*

```
package com.apress.projsp;

import java.io.IOException;
import java.security.Principal;
import java.util.Map;
import javax.security.auth.Subject;
```

```java
import javax.security.auth.callback.*;
import javax.security.auth.login.*;
import javax.security.auth.spi.LoginModule;

public class MyLoginModule implements LoginModule
{
  protected CallbackHandler callbackHandler = null;
  protected boolean committed = false;
  protected boolean debug = false;
  protected Map options = null;
  protected Principal principal = null;
  protected Map sharedState = null;
  protected Subject subject = null;

  protected void log(String message) {
    System.out.print("MyLoginModule: ");
    System.out.println(message);
  }

  public boolean abort() throws LoginException {
    log("abort");
    return (true);
  }

  public boolean commit() throws LoginException {
    log("commit phase");
    // If authentication was not successful, just return false
    if (principal == null) {
      log("no principal commit fails");
      return (false);
    }
    if (!subject.getPrincipals().contains(principal))
      subject.getPrincipals().add(principal);
    // add role principals
    subject.getPrincipals().add(new MyRolePrincipal("admin"));
    committed = true;
    log("commit successful");
    return (true);
  }

  public void initialize(Subject subject,
                         CallbackHandler callbackHandler,
                         Map sharedState, Map options)
  {
```

```java
    // Save configuration values
    this.subject = subject;
    this.callbackHandler = callbackHandler;
    this.sharedState = sharedState;
    this.options = options;
  }

  public boolean login() throws LoginException {
    log("login phase");
    // Set up our CallbackHandler requests
    if (callbackHandler == null)
      throw new LoginException("No CallbackHandler specified");
    Callback callbacks[] = new Callback[2];
    callbacks[0] = new NameCallback("Username: ");
    callbacks[1] = new PasswordCallback("Password: ", false);
    // Interact with the user to retrieve the username and password
    String username = null;
    String password = null;
    try {
      callbackHandler.handle(callbacks);
      username = ((NameCallback) callbacks[0]).getName();
      password = new String(((PasswordCallback) callbacks[1])
          .getPassword());
    } catch (IOException e) {
      throw new LoginException(e.toString());
    } catch (UnsupportedCallbackException e) {
      throw new LoginException(e.toString());
    }
    if (!authenticate(username, password))
      return false;
    principal = new MyPrincipal(username);
    return true;
  }

  public boolean logout() throws LoginException {
    subject.getPrincipals().remove(principal);
    committed = false;
    principal = null;
    return (true);
  }

  boolean authenticate(String s, String p) {
    if (s == null || p == null)
      return false;
    return (s.compareTo("jaas") == 0) && (p.compareTo("jaas") == 0);
  }
```

```
  static public void main(String args[]) throws Exception {
    LoginContext ctx = new LoginContext("TomCatAdminApplication");
    ctx.login();
  }
}
```

Note that the valid username and password are hard-coded into the authenticate() method. Obviously, in a real-world application, the class would verify the username and password by using a more robust technique.

Now we need to write a class to represent a user and a user role. Listing 12-10 shows the MyPrincipal class that implements java.security.Principal.

**Listing 12-10.** *MyPrincipal.java*

```
package com.apress.projsp;

public class MyPrincipal implements java.security.Principal
{
  String m_Name = new String("");

  public MyPrincipal(String name) {
    m_Name = name;
  }

  public boolean equals(Object another) {
    try {
      MyPrincipal pm = (MyPrincipal) another;
      return pm.m_Name.equalsIgnoreCase(m_Name);
    } catch (Exception e) {
      return false;
    }
  }

  public String getName() {
    return m_Name;
  }

  public int hashCode() {
    return m_Name.hashCode();
  }

  public String toString() {
    return m_Name;
  }
}
```

Listing 12-11 shows a role class (which extends the MyPrincipal class from Listing 12-10).

**Listing 12-11.** *MyRolePrincipal.java*

```java
package com.apress.projsp;

public class MyRolePrincipal extends MyPrincipal
{
  /** Creates a new instance of MyRolePrincipal */
  public MyRolePrincipal(String s) {
    super(s);
  }
}
```

Compile these three classes and make them accessible to your web application. You can do this by putting them in `WEB-INF\classes`, or by putting them in a JAR file, and copy the JAR file to the application's `WEB-INF\lib` or to Tomcat's `common\lib`. Now you'll need to configure your application's context to use these newly created (and compiled, of course) classes.

```xml
<Realm className="org.apache.catalina.realm.JAASRealm" debug="99"
    appName="ProJSP"
    userClassNames="com.apress.projsp.MyPrincipal"
    roleClassNames="com.apress.projsp.MyRolePrincipal" />
```

If you are using Tomcat 5.0, put the `<Realm>` element in the `server.xml` file. If you are using Tomcat 5.5, nest the `<Realm>` element in a `<Context>` element in the file `META-INF\context.xml`.

Create a login configuration file for the `MyLoginModule`. (See `http://java.sun.com/j2se/ 1.4.2/docs/guide/security/jaas/JAASRefGuide.html` for more information about login configuration files.) The Tagish distribution named its file `tagish.login`; as Listing 12-12 shows, we'll name ours `projsp.login`.

**Listing 12-12.** *projsp.login*

```
ProJSP {
    com.apress.projsp.MyLoginModule required;
};
```

There are a couple of things to note here. First, the `appName` attribute in the `<Realm>` element must match the application name in the login configuration file. Second, the configuration file can list multiple login modules. Just add each additional login module sequentially, using a semicolon to separate each entry.

Finally, we need to tell the JVM where to find this login configuration file. As with the `tagish.login` file, we do this in the `java.security` configuration file, `jre\lib\security\ java.security`:

```
login.config.url.n=file:${path/to/projsp.login}
```

The security configuration file consists of a set of security properties that you can configure. The `n` in the preceding line is replaced with a unique integer so that you can list multiple config URLs. The value of the `login.config.url.n` property is the path to the login configuration file. So, if `JAVA_HOME` is `c:\java`, then the entry in the `java.security` file for `projsp.login` would be as follows:

```
login.config.url.1=file:c:/java/jre/lib/security/projsp.login
```

Finally, edit or create the `<security-constraint>` and `<login-config>` elements of the deployment descriptor.

# Form-Based Authentication Tips and Tricks

Now that we've discussed how to use form-based authentication with your server's realms, we'd like to share some tips and tricks. Many of these have been client requests or usability enhancements, and we think they'll make developing your secure application easier.

## Using the Welcome File

It's important in a web application to configure the opening page that users will see. Adding the following `<welcome-file-list>` element to your `web.xml` file can do this:

```
<welcome-file-list>
    <welcome-file>index.jsp</welcome-file>
</welcome-file-list>
```

In some application servers, the default welcome file is already configured to be `index.html` and `index.jsp`, but it doesn't hurt to specify this and increase your application's portability. Also, note that your welcome file can be named with any arbitrary name; you are not restricted to naming the welcome file `index.jsp` or `index.html`. After you've configured your welcome file, it's easy to add a few simple lines to forward the user to a protected resource:

```
<% response.sendRedirect("/welcome.do"); %>
```

One nice addition to the Servlet 2.4 specification is that you can actually set your welcome file to use a servlet; you were unable to do this in earlier versions. This is to say that the following will work when using a Servlet 2.4– or Servlet 2.5–compliant container:

```
<welcome-file>/welcome.do</welcome-file>
```

When you use form-based authentication and you forward to a protected resource, you're presented with the page specified in your `web.xml` file—in this chapter's example application, it's `login.jsp`. To make this page friendlier than just a login form, we usually do one of the following:

- Include a welcome message on this page

- Include a welcome message from another JSP by using `<jsp:include>`

- Use a templating mechanism such as Tiles or SiteMesh to combine the two pages and the appropriate URL in the redirect's value

---

**■Note** You can find more information on Tiles and SiteMesh at `http://jakarta.apache.org/ struts/userGuide/dev_tiles.html` and `http://www.opensymphony.com/sitemesh/`, respectively.

---

### Allowing Login on an Error Page

With HTTP basic authentication, users may find it frustrating when their login fails. If you enter invalid credentials when using some browsers (Internet Explorer for the Mac, for example), an HTTP status code (401 – Unauthorized) is returned and an error message is displayed on the screen. Mozilla handles this better by prompting you again for valid credentials. This is the ideal situation and is what most usability experts recommend. The default behavior with form-based authentication is similar to the undesirable behavior previously described.

Don't worry, though—a couple of techniques can help solve this problem. The first uses one JSP page to serve up both the login page and the error page. The second uses cookies to capture the requested URL and reuse it.

Using the same page as your `form-login-page` and `form-error-page` is as simple as configuring your `web.xml` to handle this:

```
<form-login-config>
    <form-login-page>/login.jsp</form-login-page>
    <form-error-page>/login.jsp</form-error-page>
</form-login-config>
```

One problem with this approach is that the user will see the same page again—with no error information—if the login fails. So let's add a little indicator to the `form-error-page` to indicate that the login has failed:

```
<form-error-page>/login.jsp?error=true</form-error-page>
```

Now it's possible to grab this parameter in your JSP page and display an error message if authentication fails:

```
<c:if test="${param.error != null}">
    <div class="error">
        Invalid username and/or password, please try again.
    </div>
</c:if>
```

Though this seems easy enough, it has been known to fail on some containers. When this happens, the containers are still complying with the specification. However, you can work a little magic to attempt to log in again from the error page.

In working with iPlanet Application Server 6.x, which required two separate pages in `<login-config>`, we stumbled upon this solution when viewing the source of the `login.jsp` in the browser. The HTML source showed all kinds of good information, in particular the original URL requested as a hidden field. Using this hidden field, we were able to set this value as a cookie and reuse it in our form's action on the `login-error-page`.

---

**■ Note**  You can find the details of this procedure at `http://husted.com/struts/resources/`
`fb-auth.htm`.

---

Unfortunately, there's no portable mechanism to acquire the URL that was originally
requested, and there's no guarantee that this is even possible. All you know is that the container has detected that a protected URL was requested and that there was no user currently
authenticated. One solution might be to use a filter to track all recently requested URLs and
get the last requested URL from it. You'll want to make sure your login form is a `*.jspf` (JSP
fragment) file so you can include it in both the `form-login-page` and `form-error-page`.

## Using Secure Sockets Layer for Login Only

As mentioned earlier, using SSL can slow the performance of your application, so it's wise to
use it only when it's needed. A good use of SSL is when a user logs in. This means that a user
who accesses the login page by using the HTTP protocol (`http://`) will be switched over to
HTTPS (`https://`) when the username and password are sent across the wire. In this example,
you'll use a `Login` servlet to process the initial login request, switch to SSL, and then redirect to
the container's authentication mechanism.

The code download for this book comes with a fully featured application for demonstrat-
ing security techniques. Unfortunately, it is too lengthy to fully list here. We provide extracts
as we explain the application in the following pages. This application, which we refer to as
`security-example.war` for simplicity's sake, is designed to hold all the security mechanisms
described in this chapter. Both source code and binary versions of this application are available for download. You can complete most of these exercises by using the binary version and
tweaking the `security-example.xml` file and the application's `web.xml` file.

### Using a Servlet

The first feature that this application offers is an SSL-based login. To provide this SSL-
based login, the application has a servlet that will intercept login requests. This servlet is
called `LoginServlet`, and it maps to a `<url-pattern>` of `/auth/*`. Then, rather than using
`j_security_check` for the login form's `action` attribute, you'll use `auth/`. Here's what the form
looks like on the login page:

```
<form id="loginForm" method="post" action="auth/">
```

To turn secure login on, you need to edit the `web.xml` file that ships with this application,
setting the `isSecure` init-parameter to `true`:

```
<servlet>
    <servlet-name>login</servlet-name>
    <display-name>Login Servlet</display-name>
    <servlet-class>org.appfuse.webapp.action.LoginServlet</servlet-class>
     <init-param>
        <param-name>authURL</param-name>
        <param-value>j_security_check</param-value>
     </init-param>
```

```
        <init-param>
            <param-name>isSecure</param-name>
            <param-value>true</param-value>
        </init-param>
        <init-param>
            <param-name>encrypt-password</param-name>
            <param-value>false</param-value>
        </init-param>
        <init-param>
            <param-name>algorithm</param-name>
            <param-value>SHA</param-value>
        </init-param>
        <load-on-startup>3</load-on-startup>
    </servlet>
```

If you're building the security-example project from source, the parameters for the login servlet are specified at build time. The default settings are contained in the app-settings.xml file and can be overwritten from the command line by using –Dname=<value> (which would mean –Dsecure.login=true in this case). The secure.login is turned off by default, so you'll need to add secure.login=true to your build.properties file or pass it in on the command line.

Now let's dig into this servlet and see what makes it tick. First, we must confess that we did get some of the magic that makes this work from a *JavaWorld* article by Steve Ditlinger. We're using two classes from this article: SslUtil and RequestUtil.

---

**■Note** You can find Steve Ditlinger's article, titled "Mix Protocols Transparently in Web Applications," online at http://www.javaworld.com/javaworld/jw-02-2002/jw-0215-ssl.html.

---

If your HTTP and HTTPS ports are different from the defaults, 80 and 443, you'll need to change the two context parameters in web.xml for the HTTP and HTTPS ports. In the source distribution, you can edit web.xml in the web\WEB-INF folder. Currently, these values are set as follows:

```
<context-param>
    <param-name>listenPort_http</param-name>
    <param-value>8080</param-value>
</context-param>
<context-param>
    <param-name>listenPort_https</param-name>
    <param-value>8443</param-value>
</context-param>
```

These values, along with the servlet's initialization parameters, are loaded when the servlet starts. We don't provide the code here, because we're guessing you already understand how to retrieve context and initialization parameters. Here's the LoginServlet.init() method, which retrieves these values from web.xml:

```
public void init() throws ServletException
{
    // Get the container authentication URL for form-based Authentication
    // J2EE specification says should be j_security_check
    authURL = getInitParameter(Constants.AUTH_URL);
    // Get the encryption algorithm to use for encrypting passwords before
    // storing in database
    algorithm = getInitParameter(Constants.ENC_ALGORITHM);
    /* This determines if the login uses SSL or not */
    secure = Boolean.valueOf(getInitParameter("isSecure"));
    /* This determines if the password should be encrypted programmatically */
    encrypt = Boolean.valueOf(getInitParameter("encrypt-password"));
    if (log.isDebugEnabled()) {
        log.debug("Authentication URL: " + authURL);
        log.debug("Use SSL for login? " + secure);
        log.debug("Programmatic encryption of password? " + encrypt);
        log.debug("Encryption algorithm: " + algorithm);
    }
    // ensure the authorization url parameter is present
    if (authURL == null) {
        throw new ServletException(
            "No 'authURL' Context Parameter supplied in web.xml");
    }
    initializeSchemePorts(getServletContext());
    getServletContext().setAttribute(Constants.HTTP_PORT, httpPort);
    getServletContext().setAttribute(Constants.HTTPS_PORT, httpsPort);
    getServletContext().setAttribute(Constants.SECURE_LOGIN, secure);
    getServletContext().setAttribute(Constants.ENC_ALGORITHM, algorithm);
    if (log.isDebugEnabled()) {
        log.debug("HTTP Port: " + httpPort);
        log.debug("HTTPS Port: " + httpsPort);
    }
}
```

In this servlet's execute() method—which both doGet() and doPost() call—you have the following code to determine whether the current protocol is correct and, if not, to switch protocols:

```
String redirectString = SslUtil.getRedirectString(request,
    getServletContext(), secure.booleanValue());
if (redirectString != null) {
    // Redirect the page to the desired URL
    response.sendRedirect(response.encodeRedirectURL(redirectString));
```

```
    if (log.isDebugEnabled()) {
        log.debug("switching protocols, redirecting user");
    }
}
```

In the preceding code, secure.booleanValue() is the value set by the isSecure <init-param> of the servlet. After you have the correct protocol (in this case, HTTPS), you execute the servlet again, and this time the redirectString will be null. Therefore, the rest of the code will execute:

```
/* URLEncoder.encode is called to convert any non-allowed characters to
 * their URL Safe equivalent - response.encodeURL only adds the session id
 * The URLEncoder.encode method has changed its signature between J2SE 1.3.1
 * and 1.4, and therefore we use the org.apache.struts.util.RequestUtils class
 * from Struts. This class uses reflection to determine the appropriate
 * encoding.
 */
    String req = authURL + "?j_username=" + RequestUtils.encodeURL(username)
                + "&j_password=" + RequestUtils.encodeURL(encryptedPassword);
    if (redirectString == null) {
        // signifies already correct protocol
        if (log.isDebugEnabled()) {
            log.debug("Authenticating user '" + username + "'");
        }
        response.sendRedirect(response.encodeRedirectURL(req));
    }
```

### Using a Tag Library

If you're running your application on the default HTTP (80) and HTTPS (443) ports, you can use a tag library to force the use of a protocol on that particular page. A nonstandard port for HTTPS causes problems in Internet Explorer and results in a Server Not Found error. The preceding "Using a Servlet" section describes a nice workaround for this problem.

In the example application, we have a Secure.java tag library (written by Jon Lipsky, http://www.javablogs.com/views/ViewBlog.action?id=13055) that can be used to force SSL or non-SSL on a particular JSP. Its syntax is as follows:

```
<security-example:secure mode="secured"/>
```

Here, mode can be secured, unsecured, or either. Also, if you leave out the mode attribute, it will default to secured mode.

Building on the Servlet example, where the variable secureLogin is set in the application scope, you can retrieve it and use it on your login.jsp page to force SSL:

```
<c:if test="${applicationScope.secureLogin == 'true'}">
    <security-example:secure />
</c:if>
```

**Secure Sockets Layer Summary**

Hopefully, this section has given you an idea of how you can control SSL for a specific servlet in your application. If you need to guarantee SSL for your entire application, we recommend setting the `<transport-guarantee>` element in the web.xml file to INTEGRAL or CONFIDENTIAL. This value is used to specify how data should be sent between the client and server. In the example application, this value is set as illustrated here:

```
<user-data-constraint>
    <description>
        Encryption is not required for the application in general.
    </description>
    <transport-guarantee>NONE</transport-guarantee>
</user-data-constraint>
```

Table 12-2 shows how the Servlet specification defines each of these.

**Table 12-2.** *Meaning of <transport-guarantee> Values*

| Value | Description |
|---|---|
| NONE | The application doesn't require any transport guarantee. This is the same as not including the `<user-data-constraint>` element in web.xml. |
| INTEGRAL | The application requires that the data sent between the client and server be sent in such a way that it can't be changed in transit. |
| CONFIDENTIAL | The application requires that the data be transmitted in a fashion that prevents other entities from observing the contents of the transmission. |

Most servlet containers will switch the client to SSL when this value is set to INTEGRAL or CONFIDENTIAL. Although this switch is great for applications that require it, you have to be careful when implementing it. On most servlet containers, if you set this value to either INTEGRAL or CONFIDENTIAL, your application will be available *only* on the SSL port. The slick thing is that the server will automatically redirect you to https://serverName:443 when you try to access your application. However, if you're running your secure server on a port other than 443, you'll get a Server Not Found error in Internet Explorer. This leads into our next trick: using a filter to inspect requests to your protected resources.

## Using a Filter on Protected Resources

When you filter protected resources, it's possible to use the same SSL switch to make your entire application secure on any port and also to retrieve a user's information. After the user has authenticated with your application, you'll probably want to get more information about that user. One limitation of container-managed security is that all you'll know about a user is her username and what roles she belongs to. To solve this, we suggest using a filter that checks for a User object in the session and populates it if it's null. To demonstrate this, you need to create a User object, a database access code, and a database to talk to.

**■Note** In the security project, you can create a populated MySQL database by using a `setup-db` Ant task. The download has a `security-example.sql` file in it that you can use to create and populate the database as well.

Now that you've populated the database, you can get information from it by using your filter. We've created a filter named `ActionFilter.java` that is mapped to the same `<url-pattern>` (`*.do`) as our protected resources. This way, it will get called only after someone has authenticated successfully. We like to use a helper class for calling the persistence layer—this class is named `UserManager.java`, and it uses the **Business Delegate** pattern.

**■Note** You can find more information about the Business Delegate pattern at `http://java.sun.com/blueprints/corej2eepatterns/Patterns/BusinessDelegate.html`.

It's important to hide the implementation details from your filter by using a Business Delegate so that you can switch to a new persistence layer (for example, EJBs) at any given time. We don't go into the details behind the `UserManager` and how it works, so you'll have to trust us when we say that the `UserManager.getUser()` method returns a populated JavaBean of user properties. Take a look at the deployment descriptor for this filter:

```
<filter>
  <filter-name>actionFilter</filter-name>
  <display-name>Action Filter</display-name>
  <filter-class>com.apress.projsp.filter.ActionFilter</filter-class>
  <init-param>
     <!-- Change this value to true if you want
          to secure your entire application. -->
     <param-name>isSecure</param-name>
     <param-value>false</param-value>
  </init-param>
</filter>
...
<filter-mapping>
  <filter-name>actionFilter</filter-name>
  <url-pattern>*.do</url-pattern>
</filter-mapping>
```

In the `doFilter()` method, the following code executes before `chain.doFilter()` is called:

```
UserForm userForm = (UserForm) session.getAttribute(Constants.USER_KEY);
ServletContext ctx = filterConfig.getServletContext();
String username = request.getRemoteUser();
// user authenticated, empty user object
if (username != null && userForm == null) {
```

```
try {
    ses = getSession(); // get persistence session
    UserManager mgr =
        new UserManagerImpl((String) ctx.getAttribute(Constants.DAO_TYPE));
    UserForm user = mgr.getUser(ses, username);
    session.setAttribute(Constants.USER_KEY, user);
} catch (Exception e) {
        log.error("Error getting user's information " + e);
        e.printStackTrace();

        RequestDispatcher dispatcher =
            request.getRequestDispatcher("/error.jsp");
        dispatcher.forward(request, response);

        return;
}}
```

The UserManager retrieves the user's information and hides the dirty work (which is the filter, in this case) from the client. In this example, the getUser(ses, username) method call throws an exception when the user isn't found. The catch block gets a RequestDispatcher and forwards to a JSP page that explains the problem.

It's important to hide the implementation of retrieving the user's details so that you have the ability to switch to LDAP at a later date, or to another type of user database. To use LDAP, all you'd need to do is create a new class that implements UserManager and talks to LDAP, rather than to a database. To make it even better, you can add a context parameter in your web.xml to allow switching between a database and LDAP. The nice thing about using a directory server such as LDAP is that you get encrypted passwords as part of your data store. With file and database realms, you have to either encrypt passwords programmatically or configure your servlet container to do it for you.

## Encrypting Passwords

In Tomcat, it's easy to encrypt passwords by adding the digest attribute to a realm definition. The value must be one of the digest algorithms supported by the java.security.MessageDigest class (SHA, MD2, or MD5). To expand on the earlier example, the XML snippet shown next adds SHA encrypting to a file-based realm:

```
<Realm className="org.apache.catalina.realm.UserDatabaseRealm"
       debug="0" resourceName="UserDatabase" digest="SHA" />
```

To log into the application, you now need to encrypt the password stored in tomcat-users.xml to its encrypted form. You can do this by executing the following command:

```
java org.apache.catalina.realm.RealmBase -a SHA {cleartext-password}
```

where catalina.jar is in the CLASSPATH. Now, copy and paste this new password into the %TOMCAT_HOME%\conf\tomcat-users.xml file.

The problem with this method of password encryption is that it might not be portable. Let's take a look at programmatic encryption. The good news is that you've already created a LoginServlet, so you can use it to encrypt passwords. Because it's off by default, you'll need to add `encrypt.password=true` to the `build.properties` file, pass it in from the command line with ant `–Dencrypt.password=true`, or edit the default setting in `app-settings.xml`. If you're using the binary version (`.war` file) of this application, simply edit the following `<init-param>` of the `LoginServlet` (in the `web.xml` file):

```
<init-param>
  <param-name>encrypt-password</param-name>
  <param-value>true</param-value>
</init-param>
```

Next, you need to actually encrypt the password within your servlet. To do this, create an `encodePassword(String password, String algorithm)` method in a `StringUtil.java` class. This method uses the `MessageDigest` class from JSSE to encrypt a string:

```
import java.security.MessageDigest;
public static String encodePassword(String password, String algorithm) {
    byte[] unencodedPassword = password.getBytes();
    MessageDigest md = null;
    try {
        // first create an instance, given the provider
        md = MessageDigest.getInstance(algorithm);
    } catch (Exception e) {
        log.error("Exception: " + e);
        return password;
    }
    md.reset();
    // call the update method one or more times
    // (useful when you don't know the size of your data, e.g. stream)
    md.update(unencodedPassword);
    // now calculate the hash
    byte[] encodedPassword = md.digest();
    StringBuffer buf = new StringBuffer();
    for (int i = 0; i < encodedPassword.length; i++) {
        if (((int) encodedPassword[i] & 0xff) < 0x10) {
            buf.append("0");
        }
        buf.append(Long.toString((int) encodedPassword[i] & 0xff, 16));
    }
    return buf.toString();
}
```

This method encrypts a string based on the algorithm you pass in. This algorithm is defined in `LoginServlet` and configurable when building via the `${encrypt-algorithm}` variable. The default setting is `SHA`.

---

**Note** More information on these algorithms and how they work is available at `http://theory.lcs.mit.edu/~rivest/crypto-security.html#Algorithms`.

---

If you're using password encryption and also have a `retrieve password` feature, you'll probably want to add a `password_hint` column in your user store. It's hard enough to remember all the passwords you keep, and it's annoying when you have to create a new password, so the "send me a hint" tactic is useful.

## Servlet 2.5 Security Changes

The Servlet 2.5 specification has a whole chapter on security, but not much has changed. The JSP 2.1 specification doesn't contain any security-related information. It simply points out helpful information for programming security via the `HttpServletRequest` interface, giving you the following methods:

- `getRemoteUser()`

- `isUserInRole(String roleName)`

- `getUserPrincipal()`

The `getRemoteUser()` method returns the authenticated user's login name or `null` if no authenticated user exists. The `isUserInRole()` method is helpful in determining a role's authorization to certain resources.

One important thing to remember about roles, if you're coding them into your servlets, is to create links by using the `<security-role-ref>` element in `web.xml`. Here's an example:

```
<security-role-ref>
    <role-name>admin</role-name>
    <role-link>accounting</role-name>
</security-role-ref>
```

This way, you can code your servlets without worrying whether the `admin` role changes from the accounting group to the IT department. All you have to do is configure/code with `admin` and know that your code will be safe from change. Of course, we recommend placing this value in a `Constants.java` file so you can change it easily if the need does ever arise.

The `HttpSession` interface has the `session.invalidate()` method for logging out users. It has worked fine for us. When you call `session.invalidate()`, it invalidates the session and then unbinds any objects bound to it.

## Other Authentication Options and Considerations

There are alternative options to container-managed authentication if you aren't satisfied with its ease of development or you have stricter security requirements. The most common option is to build a custom authentication mechanism. If you decide to go this route, we highly recommend you look into JAAS and try to use its APIs.

### Security Filter

Security Filter (`http://securityfilter.sourceforge.net/`) is an open-source project that mimics container-managed security. It looks exactly like container-managed security, and it supports the programmatic security methods of `HttpServletRequest`. Unfortunately, it doesn't automatically propagate the `Principal` object for a user to EJB calls.

## Secure Sockets Layer Extension for Struts

The SSL Extension for Struts (`http://sslext.sourceforge.net/`) is good for HTTP/HTTPS switching. It is an open-source project that allows you to configure HTTP/HTTPS switching by using modified Struts tag libraries and configuration settings in the Struts configuration file. It was written by Steve Ditlinger, who also authored the previously mentioned SSL switching article.

## Remembering Passwords

You've probably seen the "remember my password" feature on many portal sites (such as Yahoo!). Usually, this is done by storing the user's username and password combination in a cookie. If you have an application that requires a login, and you'd like to add this feature, it would be fairly simple to do, especially with Servlets 2.5. You could use a servlet as your welcome file and check for the cookie's existence. Of course, you could also use a JSP to mimic this same behavior, grab the username and password cookies, and redirect to the `LoginServlet` with these cookies as parameters. The nice thing about most modern browsers is that they offer to remember your passwords, and this is probably more secure than a cookie.

## Remember Me Feature

As an example of how this functionality might be implemented, you'll add a `Remember Me` feature to the example application that comes with the code download. You do this by using cookies to remember the username and password, and looking for these when the user first accesses the application. If the cookies exist, you attempt to authenticate the user. Three cookies are involved in this process; the first two were mentioned previously. The third cookie is used to indicate that the user wants to use the `Remember Me` feature. You then use a filter to detect whether these cookies are present and, if so, attempt to log in the user.

First, add a check box to the `login.jsp` page to allow the user to indicate that he wants the application to remember his password:

```
<input type="checkbox" name="rememberMe" id="rememberMe" /> Remember Me
```

If this box is selected, set a cookie to indicate that the user wants to use this feature. Also, set a cookie to remember the user's username and password. Because you're using `LoginServlet` to forward the login request to `j_security_check`, you add the code to set these cookies in the `execute()` method:

```
if (request.getParameter("rememberMe") != null) {
    response =
        RequestUtil.setCookie(response, "rememberMe", "true", false);
    response =
        RequestUtil.setCookie(response, "password",
                        StringUtil.encodeString(encryptedPassword),
                        false);
}
```

For the password cookie, you use an encodeString() method from the StringUtil.java class. This is a simple method that encrypts the password cookie's value by using the sun.misc.BASE64Encoder():

```
public static String encodeString(String str) throws IOException {
    sun.misc.BASE64Encoder encoder = new sun.misc.BASE64Encoder();
    String encodedStr = new String(encoder.encodeBuffer(str.getBytes()));
    return (encodedStr.trim());
}
```

The base64 encoding works well for this feature because it can be decoded (you'll need this for autologin) and it ensures clients' passwords aren't stored in plain text.

If you're not using a LoginServlet, and you're simply using j_security_check as the action on your form, you can still use this feature. Just use a little JavaScript to set these cookies in the onsubmit() handler of your form. You'll lose the encrypted password functionality, but this feature will still work.

The real meat of this feature resides in the BreadCrumbFilter.java class. This class does the checking and autologin if the required cookies exist. In the doFilter() method for this class, the following code handles this logic:

```
// Get the relevant cookies for the "remember me" feature
Cookie rememberMe = RequestUtil.getCookie(request, "rememberMe");
Cookie passCookie = RequestUtil.getCookie(request, "password");
String password =
    (passCookie != null)
    ? URLDecoder.decode(passCookie.getValue(), "UTF-8") : null;
// Detect if authentication has failed - indicated by the error=true
// parameter from the <form-error-page> in web.xml
// StringUtils.equals is a convenience method from commons-lang that handles
// nulls gracefully.
boolean authFailed =
    StringUtils.equals(request.getParameter("error"), "true");
// Check to see if the user is logging out, if so, remove the
// rememberMe cookie and password cookie.
if ((authFailed ||
        (request.getRequestURL().indexOf("logout") != -1)) &&
        (rememberMe != null)) {
    if (log.isDebugEnabled()) {
        log.debug("deleting rememberMe-related cookies");
    }
    response =
        RequestUtil.deleteCookie(response,
                                 RequestUtil.getCookie(request,
                                                       "rememberMe"));
    response = RequestUtil.deleteCookie(response, passCookie);
}
```

```
// Check to see if the user is logging in. If so, check to see
// if he/she has enabled rememberMe functionality.
// Only attempt to authenticate when "login" is requested
if ((request.getRequestURL().indexOf("login") != -1)) {
    // Check to see if we should automatically log in the user
    // container is routing user to login page, check for remember me cookie
    Cookie userCookie = RequestUtil.getCookie(request, "username");
    String username =
        (passCookie != null)
        ? URLDecoder.decode(userCookie.getValue(), "UTF-8") : null;
    if ((rememberMe != null) && (password != null)) {
        // authenticate user without displaying login page
        String route =
            request.getContextPath() +
            "/auth?j_username=" + username +
            "&j_password=" + StringUtil.decodeString(password);
        if (log.isDebugEnabled()) {
            log.debug("I remember you '" + username +
                    "', attempting authentication...");
        }
        response.sendRedirect(response.encodeRedirectURL(route));
        return;
    }
}
```

That's it! It even handles password changes in the realm by checking for the error parameter—a slick feature that we've added into most of the recent applications we've worked on.

## Authorization

After a user has logged in to the application, you might have requirements for what the user can do or see. This is made much simpler with container-managed security, as you'll have the user's role available to you. Using your own authentication architecture, you could probably get a similar result, but you might not be able to take advantage of the wealth of available plug-ins. By **plug-ins**, we are referring to tag libraries and other Java-related packages that allow for role configuration. For instance, the Struts Logic tag library has a <logic:present> tag that allows you to perform logic based on a user's role. The Tiles templating framework also allows you to configure showing/hiding sections of your template based on roles.

In this section, we'll supply a few recommendations and tricks for controlling *who sees what* within a web application. Most of these techniques are much easier to implement if you're using container-managed authentication, but it's not required.

The first thing you'll want to consider is what choices a user should have after that user has logged in. Usually these choices are in the form of links, but they can be other menu-type systems, such as pick lists or DHTML drop-downs. One simple way to control what links a user might see is to show or hide links on the basis of a user's role. However, this is just hiding the link, and it might still be reachable by typing in the URL.

One recommended practice is to place your JSP files and fragments under the WEB-INF directory when deploying your application. By doing this, you'll prevent browsers from directly accessing JSP pages by using a URL, and it also forces you (as a developer) to follow the MVC pattern. Your JSP pages will be protected, because all resources under WEB-INF are secluded and not accessible from a URL. The Servlet specification mandates that security be provided inside WEB-INF, and it also ensures good separation of controller and view by forcing each request to go through a servlet controller. However, we've seen some containers that don't support this—they either allow access to WEB-INF through the browser or don't allow you to render JSP pages that live under WEB-INF. If your servlet container is Java EE–compliant, it should allow you to do this.

If you're working with a framework that allows configuration of your servlet-to-JSP mappings, this is fairly easy to do. We usually develop JSP pages in a directory alongside directories for stylesheets, JavaScript files, and images. Then when we deploy, we move the directory containing the JSP pages (pages) into a directory under WEB-INF.

By placing your JSP pages under WEB-INF, you ensure that the necessary application logic will be executed before displaying them. After all, users will have to navigate through this logic to get to your JSP.

After securing the locations of your pages, you'll need to secure access to them so that unauthorized users can't execute the logic to get to them. You can do this in a couple of ways. The method built in with servlets is to use a different <security-constraint> for each servlet (or group of servlets) that you want to protect. To do this, you'll have to create servlet mappings for each servlet or group—your web.xml may become quite large if you have many servlets. An easier way is to proxy all requests through an initial servlet that checks permissions and forwards appropriately, or even better, use a filter. We've also seen another alternative in which you put a tag library at the top of every JSP file. This tag library does a check to see whether the user has access to that page.

The problem with programmatically checking for user roles and dispatching accordingly, or displaying an error message in the case of the JSP page, is that it can become a maintenance nightmare. We've been on projects where we used this type of architecture, and maintenance became much easier after we moved to container-managed authentication.

# Summary

We hope we've convinced you that security is pretty easy to add to a web application. It offers many benefits after it's been added: customization based on role, an auditing log, and password encryption. In our experience, using container-managed security has made our development existence more enjoyable. We've done it programmatically by using LDAP and lots of application logic to show or hide links and to allow or deny access to pages. Even though it worked, and it worked well, it took much longer to program initially, and it was quite a nuisance to maintain. On the other hand, if you already have an authentication and authorization framework that offers you all the same benefits, you should, by all means, use it, and if it's portable and works well, share it!

Our biggest issues with container-managed security have been related to the servlet container's implementation of the Servlet specification. We recommend testing your application on Tomcat if you're experiencing problems with configuring security. If your application works on Tomcat, your container might have some problems, and it's time to do some research or write a workaround, or even to move to a different container (if that's an option). Developing on Tomcat can be a great time-saver!

■ ■ ■

# CHAPTER 13

# Improving Web-Application Performance and Scalability

The distributed and multiuser nature of web applications makes performance and scalability an important concern. Web applications are distributed systems. Users access web applications from remote clients distributed across a network, and web applications typically depend on remote systems such as databases, enterprise information systems, and web services. Network connection overhead, slow network connections, and slow remote systems can cause your web application to exhibit poor performance.

Web applications are often called upon to scale up to meet the needs of an increasing number of users. After a web application is put into production, it seems very easy to add more users because there is no client-side software required for access, other than the ubiquitous web browser. Adding more users is easy, but ensuring that your application will perform well with these additional users takes some effort.

In this chapter, you'll look at some of the steps you can take and techniques you can employ to improve the performance and scalability of your web applications. Before you get started, we should clarify the terms used in this chapter:

- **Performance:** Each application will have its own definition of performance. For a web application, a common performance metric is **response time**—the time taken for the application to complete any given request from the end user. So, you might demand of your application a maximum response time of 3 seconds. However, to be complete, any such metric must account for the number of users that are likely to be interacting with the application at any given time. So, a more complete performance statement might read: *The application must support 100 simultaneous users, with a maximum response time of 3 seconds.*

- **Scalability:** With reasonable coding skills and enough hardware, you may find it fairly easy to meet a performance target such as the preceding one. However, suppose that your application is a success and, as a result, is suddenly required to support 200 users. If you double your processing power, in the form of additional Java VMs on each server or additional server computers, will your application be able to support (roughly) double the number of users, while continuing to meet performance requirements? If the answer is yes, then your application is scalable.

So, how do you go about ensuring that your JSP applications meet their performance and scalability requirements? As a software developer, you're probably familiar with the following classic performance quote attributed to Donald Knuth:

*We should forget about small efficiencies, say about 97% of the time: premature optimization is the root of all evil.*

In this chapter we won't focus on small efficiencies and we'll avoid premature optimization; instead, we'll focus on the larger steps that you can take to ensure you meet your JSP application performance goals. We'll start by covering two specific techniques that can definitely enhance the performance and scalability characteristics of JSP applications: **page caching** and **database connection pooling**. We'll move on to discuss more general performance tips and best practices, before finishing with a discussion of how you can actually go about testing the performance and scalability of your application to ensure that you're really meeting your requirements.

## General Principles

The following items apply to the development of high-performance web applications in general and thus are guiding principles for your JSP application design:

- **Don't execute code unnecessarily.** One of the best ways to improve code performance is to simply avoid executing it. Don't execute code unless absolutely necessary. We'll discuss how page caching can help in this regard.

- **Don't create objects unnecessarily.** Creating new objects is an expensive operation, both in terms of the processing time to create them and the memory required to store them. As you write your code, try to minimize the number of objects that you create. Where possible, reuse the objects that you do create. One of the most expensive objects in a JSP application is the database connection object. In this chapter, we'll discuss how to use database connection pooling to avoid repeatedly creating database connection objects.

- **When you must create objects, create them in the right scope.** In a web application, there are three levels of scope: **request**, **session**, and **application**. To scale a web application to meet the needs of a large number of users, carefully consider what is to be stored in the session scopes. We'll discuss this and other ways to ensure that your application is ready to scale.

Now that we've covered the general principles, we'll next discuss the details of how you can apply the concepts of page caching and database connection pooling to JSP applications.

## Page Caching

In a typical JSP application, web pages are dynamically generated by Java code that pulls data from a database and formats that data for display. This processing takes time, causes the creation of Java objects, and uses network resources. If we could find a way to avoid regenerating a page for every incoming page request, we could not only speed up the page response time, but also improve the overall performance and scalability of our JSP application. What we would really like to do is save each dynamically generated page in cache memory. When a request comes in for a page that we've already generated, we could just pull that page out of the cache and send it out to the browser. This technique is called **page caching** and it can dramatically improve the performance of a JSP application.

## When Should You Use Page Caching?

You've probably used caching before, perhaps by writing your own simple cache. If you're using an MVC framework such as Struts, you could use a simple cache for objects that you built from database data and have little need for page caching. When do you need page caching?

Page caching is useful when you can't put all the data needed for a web page into context before the JSP page or servlet that's responsible for emitting the page is called. Also, page caching is useful when your JSP pages are composed of multiple JSP tags or other components that themselves are responsible for expensive operations such as fetching data or rendering complex HTML.

## How Long Should You Cache Data?

To reduce the load on your servers, you'll want to cache pages for as long as possible. How long is that? The answer depends on the nature of your application. Of course, for highly interactive pages, you might not be able to use caching at all, or you may be able to cache only some small, fairly static portions of the pages. You might decide to cache some pages for a very long time but to flush some portion or all of the cache every time your site's database is updated.

To get a better understanding of page caching technology, let's take a closer look at one of the most popular open-source Java caching packages: OSCache.

## OSCache

**OSCache** is an open-source caching library that's available free of charge from the OpenSymphony organization (the downloading and installation instructions can be found at http://www.opensymphony.com/oscache). OSCache includes a set of JSP tags that make it easy to implement page caching in your JSP application, along with a `ServletFilter`-based cache implementation so that you can cache content that's generated by any servlet, not just JSP pages.

OSCache applies the following general page caching concepts:

- **Cache entry**: An object that's stored into a page cache is known as a cache entry. In a JSP application, a cache entry is typically the output of a JSP page, a portion of a JSP page, or a servlet.

- **Cache key:** A page cache is like a hash table. When you save a cache entry in a page cache, you must provide a cache key to identify the entry. In a JSP application, you might combine several request parameters together to form a cache key, or you might use a page's request URI as its cache key.

- **Cache duration:** This is the period of time that a cache entry will remain in a page cache before it expires. When a cache entry expires, it's removed from the cache, and the application that placed it in the cache will be forced to regenerate it. For a JSP page that displays frequently updated data, you should set a short cache duration so that the cache is updated frequently and users aren't presented with stale information. For a JSP page that displays data that's infrequently updated, you can set a longer cache duration.

- **Cache scope:** This is the scope at which the cache is stored. In a JSP application, it makes sense to store cache entries at either the application scope, so that cache entries are shared by all users, or at the session scope, so that cache entries are stored on a per-user basis.

## OSCache JSP Tags

Using the OSCache tags is simple. Assuming you have installed and configured OSCache, all you need to do is place the <os:cache> tag around the sections of your JSP pages that you wish to have cached. The example JSP page in Listing 13-1 indicates how to do this.

**Listing 13-1.** *longop-cached.jsp*

```
<%@ page language="java" %>
<%@ taglib uri="/WEB-INF/oscache.tld" prefix="os" %>
<!DOCTYPE HTML PUBLIC "-//w3c//dtd html 4.0 transitional//en">
<html>
  <head><title>Long operation - cached</title></head>
  <body>
    <h1>Long operation - cached</h1>
    <os:cache time="60">
      <% Thread.sleep(10000); %>
      <p>Woke up at: <%= new java.util.Date().toString() %></p>
    </os:cache>
    <p>
      The reason this JSP page took so long to load is because
      it contains a 10 second sleep.
    </p>
    <p>
      This page uses page cache with a 60 second timeout,
      so if you run this page again in the next 60 seconds
      it will take less than a second to run.
    </p>
  </body>
</html>
```

In the preceding example, you have a JSP page that sleeps for 10 seconds and then displays a wake-up time and some other text. As you can see, the call to the sleep() method and the wake-up time message are enclosed inside <os:cache> tags with a cache time of 60 seconds.

The first time that this page is executed, it takes 10 seconds. However, it caches a copy of the output that was produced inside the `<os:cache>` tags. If you run the page again, within 60 seconds, it will take less than a second to run because it will return the output from the cache instead of executing the code inside the `<os:cache>` tags. If you wait 60 seconds and then run the page again, you'll have to wait for the 10-second sleep to complete because the cache entry will have timed out and the output will have to be regenerated.

In this example, you didn't specify a cache key so, by default, OSCache will use the request URI to key the cache entry. You also didn't specify a cache scope so, by default, application scope will be used.

## OSCache Servlet Filter

You can also use OSCache to cache the output of servlets, using the OSCache servlet filter class, `com.opensymphony.module.oscache.web.filter.CacheFilter`. All you have to do is add this filter to the application's `web.xml` file and add filter mappings for all the URL patterns that you wish to have cached.

For example, the code download for this chapter includes a servlet that takes 10 seconds to run. This `LongOpServlet` produces almost the same output as the `longop.jsp` page that we discussed in the previous section. To cache the output of the `LongOpServlet` in the same way as you cached the JSP page, you need to add the OSCache `CacheFilter` to your web application. Listing 13-2 shows an example deployment descriptor with an entry for the OSCache `CacheFilter`.

**Listing 13-2.** *web.xml*

```xml
<?xml version="1.0" encoding="UTF-8"?>
<web-app xmlns="http://java.sun.com/xml/ns/javaee"
     xmlns:xsi="http://www.w3.org/2001/XMLSchema-instance"
xsi:schemaLocation="http://java.sun.com/xml/ns/javaee/web-app_2_5.xsd"
     version="2.5">
  <context-param>
      <param-name>debug</param-name>
      <param-value>true</param-value>
  </context-param>
  <filter>
      <filter-name>CacheFilter</filter-name>
      <filter-class>
          com.opensymphony.module.oscache.web.filter.CacheFilter
      </filter-class>
      <init-param>
          <param-name>time</param-name>
          <param-value>60</param-value>
      </init-param>
  </filter>
  <filter-mapping>
      <filter-name>CacheFilter</filter-name>
      <url-pattern>/servlets/*</url-pattern>
```

```
    </filter-mapping>

    <servlet>
        <servlet-name>LongOpServlet</servlet-name>
        <servlet-class>
            com.apress.projsp.servlets.LongOpServlet
        </servlet-class>
    </servlet>
    <servlet-mapping>
        <servlet-name>LongOpServlet</servlet-name>
        <url-pattern>/servlets/longop</url-pattern>
    </servlet-mapping>
</web-app>
```

The `<filter>` element configures the `CacheFilter` itself. It specifies the class name for the filter and sets one parameter: the cache time. As with the `longop.jsp` example in the previous section, the cache time is set to 60 seconds. Other parameters, such as the cache key and cache scope, have been omitted, so default values will be used. The `<filter-mapping>` element configures the `CacheFilter` so that it will cache the response output for all request URLs that match the pattern `/servlets/*`. This works well for the `LongOpServlet`, because it's mapped to the URL `/servlets/longop`.

For more information on servlet filters, refer to Chapters 10 and 11. For more information on OSCache, visit the following URLs:

- **OpenSymphony website:** `http://www.opensymphony.com`

- **OSCache website:** `http://www.opensymphony.com/oscache`

- **OSCache WIKI:** `http://www.opensymphony.com:8668/space/OSCache`

# Database Connection Pooling

Page caching can help reduce the frequency of database access in a JSP application, but it can't eliminate database access entirely. Eventually, the application will have to open a database connection to query, create, update, and delete records in the database. Unfortunately, opening a database connection is an expensive operation that consumes processing time, memory, and network resources.

One of the most effective ways to boost JSP application performance is to use a technique called **database connection pooling**. By using this technique, you keep a pool of database connections open at all times. When you need a connection, you take it from the pool, and when you're done with it, you return it to the pool.

Database connection pooling is a very well-known technique that's available in almost every Java EE application server. It's also built into many JDBC drivers and some persistence frameworks. For example, the Hibernate persistence framework discussed in Chapter 9 includes an easy-to-use database connection pool.

There are a lot of database connection pool alternatives, and we won't discuss them all here. Instead, we'll discuss the common database connection pool configuration parameters and then present an example. Most database connection pools allow you to set the following configuration parameters:

- **Maximum active connections:** This is the maximum number of connections that are allowed to be open in the pool. If a request is made for a connection while all connections in the pool are in use, then the call to the getConnection() method will block until a connection is released by another thread or until a configurable maximum wait time is reached.

- **Maximum idle connections:** This is the maximum number of connections that are allowed to be open but not in use in the pool. If you set this parameter to zero, no maximum limit will be set.

- **Maximum wait time:** This is the maximum length of time that a call to getConnection() will block while waiting for a connection to released. If the wait exceeds this time, the getConnection()call will throw an exception, or you can use some other technique to indicate that a connection isn't available.

- **Abandoned connection timeout:** In some cases, an application may fail to properly release a database connection. This is called abandoning a connection and is a serious problem because until a connection is released, it isn't returned to the pool for reuse. Some database connection pools monitor unreleased connections, and if one has been idle for longer than the abandoned connection timeout, it's considered to be abandoned and is automatically released and returned to the pool.

## Jakarta Commons Database Connection Pool

It isn't possible for us to cover all the options for database connection pooling, so instead we'll give you a close look at Jakarta Commons Database Connection Pool (DBCP). DBCP is the database connection pooling technology built into the popular open-source Tomcat servlet engine. Because it's included with Tomcat, you don't need to download or install any files or libraries.

Normally, to deploy an application to the Tomcat servlet engine, you just copy the application's WAR file, or deployment directory, to the Tomcat webapps directory. However, to configure DBCP for your application, you need to do a bit more work: you need to add the application to the Tomcat server configuration file conf/server.xml.

To do this, you need to add a new <Context> entry to the Tomcat server.xml file. Open the server.xml file with your favorite editor and look for the Tomcat Root Context. You need to add the <Context> entry in the correct part of the server.xml file. For example, you can add it after the ROOT context and before the examples context, as in the snippet shown here:

```
<!-- Tomcat Root Context -->
<!--
  <Context path="" docBase="ROOT" debug="0"/>
-->
<Context path="/myapp" docBase="roller" debug="0">
  <Resource name="jdbc/mydb" auth="Container" type="javax.sql.DataSource" />
  <ResourceParams name="jdbc/mydb">
```

```
        <parameter>
          <name>factory</name>
<!-- Use the following value for Tomcat 5.0:
          <value>org.apache.commons.dbcp.BasicDataSourceFactory</value>
-->
<!-- Use this value for Tomcat 5.5: -->
          <value>org.apache.tomcat.dbcp.dbcp.BasicDataSourceFactory</value>

        </parameter>
        <parameter><name>maxActive</name><value>100</value></parameter>
        <parameter><name>maxWait</name><value>100</value></parameter>
        <parameter><name>username</name><value>scott</value></parameter>
        <parameter><name>password</name><value>tiger</value></parameter>
        <parameter>
          <name>driverClassName</name>
          <value>org.gjt.mm.mysql.Driver</value>
        </parameter>
        <parameter>
          <name>url</name>
          <value>jdbc:mysql://localhost:3306/mydb?autoReconnect=true</value>
        </parameter>
      </ResourceParams>
    </Context>
    <!-- Tomcat Examples Context -->
    <Context path="/examples" docBase="examples" debug="0"
        reloadable="true" crossContext="true">
        <Logger className="org.apache.catalina.logger.FileLogger"
            prefix="localhost_examples_log." suffix=".txt" timestamp="true"/>
```

The preceding example shows how to configure DBCP for an application called myapp. The first entry inside the <Context> element is the <Resource> declaration. The <Resource> declaration declares a javax.sql.DataSource and binds it to the JNDI name jdbc/mydb. The <ResourceParams> element and the nested <parameter> elements within specify the DBCP parameters for the application's database connection pool. We've already discussed the maxActive and maxWait parameters. The driverClassName and url parameters are standard JDBC connection parameters. (More information on JDBC is in Chapter 9.)

---

■**Note** The value for the factory parameter will vary based on the Tomcat distribution. Tomcat 5.0 and earlier versions used the Jakarta Commons DBCP library. Starting with Tomcat 5.5, the DBCP library has been changed from the Commons version to a Tomcat-specific library. If you want to double check that the value you use is correct, check the Tomcat JAR files in Tomcat's common\lib directory, find the BasicDataSourceFactory class, and use the fully qualified class name of the class you find.

---

The next code excerpt shows how to obtain a connection from the previous connection pool. First, you use JNDI to look up a `javax.sql.DataSource` interface, and then you ask that interface for a connection. When you've finished with the connection, you close it and return it to the pool for reuse. Closing the connection doesn't actually close the underlying physical connection; it just returns the connection to the pool.

```
javax.naming.InitialContext context = new InitialContext();

// Look up the data source
javax.sql.DataSource dataSource =
  (javax.sql.DataSource)context.lookup ("java:comp/env/jdbc/mydb");
// Get a connection from the pool
java.sql.Connection conn = dataSource.getConnection();
// ...Use the connection...
// Close the connection to return it to the pool
conn.close();
```

For a working example that uses DBCP, see the section "Obtaining a JDBC Connection in a Web Application" in Chapter 9.

# Designing for Scalability

Java application servers are designed to support scalability. By using your application server's administrative console or by editing configuration files, you can increase the amount of memory devoted to each server process, increase the number of request-processing threads within each process, add additional server processes, and configure additional server machines to run server processes.

No matter how you design your application, you'll probably be able to make it run faster and serve more users by running it on a more powerful computer. If your server is a multi-processor machine, you can configure your application server to use more threads to process requests. If your server has lots of memory, you can configure your application server to devote more memory to each server process. Your application server documentation should provide some guidelines to help you decide how to configure these thread and memory settings.

There is a limit to what you can do with one server process running on one server machine. Your Java application server will allow you to scale up beyond a single process running on a single machine, but to take advantage of this, you need to follow some simple guidelines in the development of your JSP applications:

- **Minimize the data that's stored in each session.** In a typical JSP application, a session object of type `javax.servlet.HttpSession` is created for each user. As the amount of data stored per session increases, the number of users that can be supported by each server decreases. This is just simple arithmetic. For example, say the application server is running in a Java VM that's configured for a 100 MB heap. If the application server itself uses 10 MB of memory, and each user session consumes 1 MB of memory, then you can support a maximum of 90 simultaneous users per application server instance.

- **Where possible, avoid creating sessions**. Each session that's created uses some memory so, wherever possible, try to handle requests without creating sessions.

- **Store only serializable objects in the session object.** Java EE application servers support scalability by running JSP applications in parallel across multiple servers. When a session is created, it's assigned to one server. A technique called **load balancing** is used to ensure that sessions are distributed evenly across all participating servers. Some Java EE application servers, such as IBM WebSphere, support a special load-balancing technique called **session migration.** If session migration is enabled and one server becomes overloaded, sessions from that server may be migrated to another, less busy server. Session migration is usually implemented by serialization, so in order for a JSP application to work with session migration you need to make sure that every object stored in the session implements the interface `java.io.Serializable`.

- **Don't write to the file system.** If a JSP application is running across multiple servers, you can't use the file system for storage. Files that you write to one server may not be available on all of the other servers running the application. In this case, use a database rather than the file system for storage.

# Other Performance Tips and Resources

A good source of information for best practices for performance and scalability is the IBM website. A search for "performance" on the WebSphere and developerWorks website (`http://www.ibm.com/developerworks`) reveals a series of white papers and best practices guides for WebSphere development. Most of the information on WebSphere also applies to other Java EE application servers and to JSP applications in general.

The white paper "WebSphere Application Server Development Best Practices for Performance and Scalability" (`http://www-306.ibm.com/software/webservers/appserv/ws_bestpractices.pdf`) is especially useful. Again, most of the best practices in this white paper apply to any Java EE application server. Many of the recommendations apply to EJB applications only, but a good number apply to JSP applications, for example:

- **Avoid thread synchronization and single-threading.** Synchronizing methods and blocks of code can make a JSP application behave as if it is single-threaded, and this results in lower throughput. It's important that JSP pages and servlets are thread-safe, so don't be tempted to use the `isThreadSafe=false` page directive. When you write a servlet, don't be tempted to implement the `javax.servlet.SingleThreadModel` interface. (In fact, as of Servlet 2.4, the `SingleThreadModel` interface is deprecated.)

- **Avoid use of** `System.out.println()`. The seemingly harmless `System.out.println()` method is actually pretty harmful. According to the IBM white paper, "Because `System.out.println()` statements and similar constructs synchronize processing for the duration of disk I/O, they can significantly slow throughput." Instead of using `System.out` and `System.err`, consider using a logging system such as log4j.

- **Avoid string concatenation.** This is widely known, but it bears repeating. Using the + and += operators to concatenate strings is slow and results in the creation of unnecessary temporary objects. Instead, use the `java.lang.StringBuffer` class to concatenate strings.

# Measuring JSP Application Performance

In addition to implementing the best practice design advice that we've been discussing, you need to be able to prove that your application will meet the performance criteria set by your customers. You need to be able to profile your application and root out and fix any code that's taking up undue resources or memory, or is causing contention issues that will reduce scalability.

A wide variety of web-application performance-testing tools and products are available, and any of these can be applied to measuring JSP application performance. Typically, a performance-testing tool will support the following features:

- **Customizable test plans** to simulate what users are doing as they use a particular JSP application

- **Response time statistics** to measure and collect the minimum, maximum, and average response time of each page

- **Load testing** to simulate any number of users accessing a site

- **Error detection** to detect and log when errors occur on any page

One option for performance testing is the open-source **Apache JMeter** product. JMeter allows you to develop test plans for testing HTTP-, FTP-, and JDBC-accessible database servers. JMeter can handle servlet authentication by using cookies and URL rewriting, so it works well for testing JSP applications. The biggest advantage of JMeter is that it's free. You can download it, try it out, learn about performance testing, and if you like it you can keep it. If you find that it's unsatisfactory, you can evaluate one of the other performance-testing tools. At the end of this section is a list of some of the popular performance-testing products.

---

**■Note**  You can download JMeter from the Apache Jakarta website (`http://jakarta.apache.org/jmeter`).

---

Let's take a look at JMeter and use it to test one of the performance recommendations that we discussed earlier in this section. You'll use a very simple JSP page with a 3-second runtime, which is shown in Listing 13-3.

**Listing 13-3.** *threesec.jsp*

```
<%@ page language="java" %>
<!DOCTYPE HTML PUBLIC "-//w3c//dtd html 4.0 transitional//en">
<html>
  <head><title>Three second operation</title></head>
  <body>
    <h1>Three second operation</h1>
    <p>
      The reason this page JSP took 3 seconds to load is because
      it contains a 3 second sleep.
    </p>
    <% Thread.sleep(3000); %>
  </body>
</html>
```

The page takes 3 seconds to run because it includes a 3-second sleep. To test this page in JMeter, you first create a thread group with five threads and a loop count of 100. This will simulate the effects of five browsers, each running through the test plan 100 times. You do this by right-clicking the Test Plan icon in the tree and then choosing the Add ➤ Thread Group menu option to add a thread group. Figure 13-1 shows the Thread Group page of the JMeter tool.

**Figure 13-1.** *The JMeter application lets you create any number of threads that can execute your web application as many times as desired.*

You're going to test only one page, so under the thread group you'll create one HTTP request and configure it to access your threesec.jsp page. Next, add an Aggregate Report so you can view the minimum, maximum, and average response times for running the test page. Figure 13-2 shows the test plan, with the HTTP request editor loaded into the right pane.

**Figure 13-2.** *After configuring the threads, JMeter displays a page that lets you configure which resource will be tested.*

The next step is to run the test plan. Use the JMeter Run ➤ Start menu item to do this. The test should take a couple of minutes to run. As the test runs, you can watch the results in the Aggregate Report window, and when the test completes that window should look like Figure 13-3. Your results will differ depending on your hardware, operating system, and servlet engine.

**Figure 13-3.** *After running a test, you can view the results in JMeter.*

Looking at the Aggregate Report window results, you can see that 500 requests were processed with an average response time of 3024 milliseconds. This makes sense because the page included a 3-second sleep and almost nothing else. You can see that no errors occurred and that you achieved a throughput rate of 1.7 requests per second, or 102 requests per minute.

One of our performance recommendations was to avoid single-threading. There may be an occasion when you feel it's necessary to serialize access to a certain call in a JSP page. However, you should be aware that, if this call is made often, it could have drastic performance consequences. Let's see what happens when you run the same test, but with a single-threaded JSP page. To do this, you need to make a simple modification to your `threesec.jsp` page. You'll add a lock to the class so that all access to the `Thread.sleep()` call is synchronized. Listing 13-4 shows the new `threesec-single.jsp` page.

**Listing 13-4.** *threesec-single.jsp*

```
<%@ page language="java" %>
<!DOCTYPE HTML PUBLIC "-//w3c//dtd html 4.0 transitional//en">
<html>
  <head><title>Three second operation: single-threaded</title></head>
  <body>
    <%! static String lock = new String(); %>
    <h1>Three second operation: single-threaded</h1>
    <p>
      The reason this page JSP took 3 seconds to load is because
      it contains a 3 second sleep.
    </p>
<% synchronized (lock)
  {
    Thread.Sleep(3000);
  }
%>

  </body>
</html>
```

Now run the test again. This time, it takes about 20 minutes rather than 5 minutes. The results are shown in Figure 13-4.

**Figure 13-4.** *Synchronizing the JSP causes its performance to deteriorate significantly.*

As expected, the performance of the single-threaded page is much worse than that of the multithreaded page. The throughput of the single-threaded page is 20.1 requests per minute compared to 102 requests per minute for the thread-safe JSP.

For more information on web-application performance testing, visit the following product sites:

- **Apache JMeter:** `http://jakarta.apache.org/jmeter/`

- **Mercury LoadRunner:** `http://www.mercury.com/us/products/performance-center/loadrunner/`

- **Web Performance Inc.:** `http://www.webperformanceinc.com/`

The Web Performance Inc. site in particular is a good resource. It includes a glossary of performance-testing terms, presentations on performance testing, and a report that compares the performance of Java EE servlet engines including Tomcat, WebSphere, Orion, Jetty, and Resin.

# Testing the Performance Techniques

Now you'll put the techniques we covered in this chapter into practice by applying them to a realistic example program. You'll use an enhanced version of the data access example from Chapter 9 because it's a simple but fairly typical database-driven web application.

As you may remember, the Chapter 9 example is a web-based RSS newsreader program called Ag. Ag allows you to sign in by entering a username, maintain a list of subscriptions to RSS news feeds, fetch the news items for your subscriptions, and view the headlines for each of your news feeds.

For the purposes of this case study, we've added a new front page to Ag. This new front page displays the most recent news feed items from all users and allows visitors to view the items in reverse-chronological order or by the number of hits that each item has received. With this new front page, Ag is a lot like the popular community news feed aggregation websites JavaBlogs.com (`http://javablogs.com`) and Weblogs at ASP.NET (`http://weblogs.asp.net`). Figure 13-5 shows a screen shot of the new front page.

With a small number of users hitting the new Ag front page, performance seems to be fine. The page is displayed in a second or less. However, when you use JMeter to simulate a large number of users hitting the site, the performance drops to an unacceptable level. The page takes 5 to 10 seconds to display, and the load on the server rises to an unacceptable level (see Figure 13-6.).

Each page is taking an average of 4 seconds to run. On top of this, during this test, the CPU meter is at 100%. Ag is dragging the whole server down. Why is Ag performing so poorly? For each incoming request, Ag must obtain a database connection, make a database query, and render the results as HTML. How can you reduce the amount of work per request? Let's start by applying database connection pooling.

**Figure 13-5.** *The front page of the news reader application from Chapter 9*

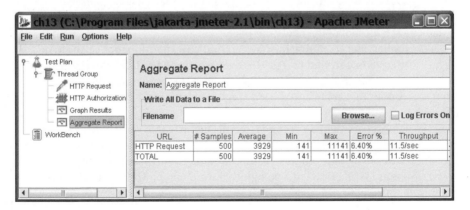

**Figure 13-6.** *JMeter shows the dismal performance of the news reader application under a load.*

# Applying Database Connection Pooling

Database connection pooling should help improve performance because it will eliminate the overhead that surrounds opening and closing database connections. When the application needs a database connection, it will obtain it from a pool of already opened database connections.

So, how do you go about applying database connection pooling to the Ag application? Well, it turns out that because Ag uses Hibernate for all database access, Ag is already using database connection pooling. Hibernate has built-in connection pooling. Hibernate connection pooling is configured in the Hibernate configuration file, `hibernate.properties`, in which you specify your application's database connection parameters. The following is the Hibernate configuration file for the Ag application:

```
hibernate.connection.driver_class=org.hsqldb.jdbcDriver
hibernate.connection.url=jdbc:hsqldb:hsql://localhost
hibernate.connection.username=sa
hibernate.connection.password=
hibernate.connection.pool_size=30
hibernate.statement_cache.size=6
hibernate.dialect=net.sf.hibernate.dialect.HSQLDialect
```

Hibernate's built-in connection pooling is convenient, no doubt, but it isn't always the right answer. Your application server administrator may prefer that you configure your application to use the database connection pooling capabilities of your application server or those of your JDBC driver. How do you do that?

If you're using Hibernate, you specify the name of the JNDI data source, provided by your application server administrator, in the Hibernate configuration file. You'll also have to specify the database dialect. The following example is configured for accessing an Oracle data source that's bound to the JNDI name `java:comp/env/jdbc/oracle`. There's no need to specify a JDBC driver class, connection URL, or anything else because those were specified by your server administrator when he configured the data source. For more information on data source usage and configuration, see the section "Obtaining a JDBC Connection in a Web Application" in Chapter 9.

```
hibernate.connection.datasource=java:comp/env/jdbc/oracle
hibernate.dialect=net.sf.hibernate.dialect.Oracle9Dialect
```

Adding database connection pooling isn't going to do you any good because you're already using it, so let's move on to applying page caching.

# Applying Page Caching

The new Ag front page is rendered by the JSP file `main.jsp`, so that's where you'll add your caching. You'll use OSCache JSP tags that we discussed earlier in this chapter.

You already have the OSCache JAR file in your application's `WEB-INF\lib` directory and the `oscache.properties` file in the `WEB-INF\classes`, so all you need to do is add the OSCache JSP `taglib` declaration to the top of `main.jsp` and the OSCache tags around the part of the page that you wish to cache. Listing 13-5 shows the code for `main.jsp` with the new OSCache additions.

**Listing 13-5.** *main.jsp*

```
<%@ page language="java" %>
<%@ taglib uri="/WEB-INF/c-rt.tld" prefix="c" %>
<%@ taglib uri="/WEB-INF/oscache.tld" prefix="os"%>
<!DOCTYPE HTML PUBLIC "-//w3c//dtd html 4.0 transitional//en"><html>
<head>
  <style type="text/css"><jsp:include page="/ag.jsp" /></style>
  <title>Ag - RSS Newsreader and Aggregator</title>
</head>
<body bgcolor="#FFFFFF">

<h1>Ag - RSS Newsreader and Aggregator</h1>
<hr />
<p>News Items from all users Subscriptions are aggregated below.</p>
<p>You may login to <a href="subs">Manage your Subscriptions</a>.</p>
<os:cache time="3600" key="${param.mode}">
<c:choose>
   <c:when test="${param.mode == 'popular'}" >

      <h2>Most Popular Newsfeed Items</h2>
      View: Popular | <a href="main?mode=recent">Recent</a>

      <c:set var="items" value="${ag.popularItems}" />
   </c:when>
   <c:otherwise>

      <h2>Recent Newsfeed Items</h2>
      View: <a href="main?mode=popular">Popular</a> | Recent

      <c:set var="items" value="${ag.recentItems}" />
   </c:otherwise>
</c:choose>
<c:forEach var="item" items="${items}">
   <c:url var="url" value="/ag/link">
     <c:param name="link" value="${item.link}"/>
   </c:url>

   <h3><a href="${url}">${item.title}</a></h3>
   ${item.description} <br />
   <b>Posted: ${item.time}, Hits: ${item.hits}</b>

</c:forEach>
</os:cache>
<hr />
</body>
</html>
```

The OSCache tags were added around the portion of the page that's responsible for fetching the items to be displayed and for displaying those items. Let's focus on the OSCache tags:

```
<os:cache time="3600" key="${mode.param}">   . . .
</os:cache>
```

The cache time is set to 3600 seconds, or 1 hour. This means that the main page will be refreshed with new data every hour. The cache key is set to use the request parameter mode because the page has two modes of operation. In "popular" mode, the page displays the items with the most hits first. In "recent" mode, the page displays the most recent items first. By using the parameter value as the cache key, you ensure that both versions of the page are cached.

Now that you've applied page caching to your page, you'll rerun the very same JMeter test. The results, shown in Figure 13-7, indicate a dramatic improvement. The page now runs 10 times faster. It runs, on average, in 0.391 seconds rather than 4 seconds. During the test, the server's CPU was running at about 5% instead of 100%.

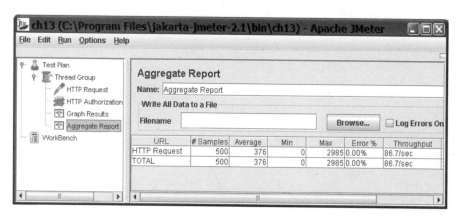

**Figure 13-7.** *By using caching, the news reader application runs much faster.*

# Summary

In this chapter, we covered many techniques for improving the performance of JSP applications. We discussed how to use the OSCache page-caching system to avoid regenerating a page for every incoming page request. Knowing that a database connection is an expensive operation that consumes processing time, memory, and network resources, we discussed the use of connection pooling to minimize the cost of this operation in JSP applications.

Performance and scalability are primary concerns for any JSP application. After a JSP application is deployed on a corporate intranet or on the Internet, it may become more popular than initially envisaged. If you apply the design practices discussed in this chapter, you have a much better chance of meeting your customer's performance requirements and continuing to meet them as your user base expands. We showed you a specific performance-testing tool, Apache JMeter, which you can use during development to prove that performance and scalability requirements are being met.

As you read about JSP application frameworks in the following chapters, keep in mind what you've learned about designing for performance and scalability.

■ ■ ■

# CHAPTER 14

# Web-Application Design and Best Practices

The previous chapters covered a great deal of the functionality provided by the JSP specification. You're now in a good position to take this knowledge and start using it to build Java-based web applications. So then, why should you read this chapter? Well, although knowing the classes and APIs is important in getting the most out of JSP and servlets, there are some other key factors that will really help you to achieve success. This chapter brings together the techniques covered earlier in the book and shows you how to build maintainable, extensible Java-based web applications.

In this chapter, you will look at the importance of good design and how it can help you build high-quality web applications that are easy to maintain and extend in the future. To do this, you'll learn about some of the standard architectures that have been proven to help achieve these goals. Continuing on the theme of good design, you'll then take a lower-level look at how to use design patterns to help implement these architectures. Specifically, we'll show you how some of the best practices for building Java-based web applications have been documented as patterns and explain how you can apply them to your own web applications.

Of course, having a good design is essential, but not if the actual task of implementing the web application is neglected. Therefore, we'll present some of the best practices for development and testing. We'll cover topics ranging from the use of logging and debugging to how to actually test web applications and design them to be testable. Finally, we'll discuss some general guidelines covering topics such as how to enhance the user's experience with your web application. By the end of the chapter, you'll be able to take the knowledge you already have and apply it in a much more structured way, which will help you build better web applications.

## The Importance of Design

When we talk about **design**, regardless of whether it's used within the context of software engineering or some other endeavor, what we're essentially talking about is the thought process that goes into something before it's created. This up-front thinking helps us come up with the best possible way for achieving our end goal. For example, you normally wouldn't just go and build a new kitchen without considering the location of items such as water pipes, electricity outlets, windows, doors, and so on. Although you could just go ahead and build the kitchen, without some up-front thought you probably wouldn't come up with the best solution. This is equally applicable to software. You could just dive straight in, but some forethought is required.

The software industry is often likened to many other forms of industry, although probably the best-known analogy is to the building industry. Although this comparison works on many levels, there are several key differences between making software and creating buildings. Buildings are designed for a specific purpose and must be designed to withstand known tolerances caused by the environment. Software, on the other hand, is much more dynamic. After all, in general, building software isn't currently seen as being as precise as building houses. This isn't to say that it shouldn't be—it's just that it isn't there as an industry yet. When was the last time you saw bug-free software? The other point to pick up on here is that software typically changes throughout its lifetime. Sometimes these changes are simple bug fixes; more often than not, they're major functionality changes/additions. It's this characteristic of the software industry that makes design important. To try to quantify the importance of design, let's look at some of the characteristics that it can directly affect.

## Maintainability

**Maintainability** is the ability to maintain a piece of software. It works at several levels. At its most basic level, maintainability involves the work needed to keep that particular piece of software up and running (cleaning up logs, archiving old data, and so on). At another level, maintaining an application can include fixing bugs as they're reported and making performance enhancements to cope with the increasing demands of the business. Maintainability isn't something that can easily be measured, although it is related to how well the software is designed and implemented. Well-designed software is easier for anybody maintaining the software to understand, and those people can make the small changes required with the knowledge that they aren't about to break unrelated features. The same can't be said for badly designed software.

## Extensibility

The other aspect affected by the design of a system is **extensibility**, the ability to extend and enhance the software. Again, well-designed software will typically have a defined structure so that existing features can be changed and new features can be added easily, without causing side effects to the remainder of the system. Particularly for mission-critical business systems, extensibility is important because it allows the software to keep up with the business processes that it's realizing with a minimum of cost and overhead.

# Web-Application Architectures

Now that you understand that design—even just a little design—is important, let's take a look at two of the common and proven architectures for Java-based web applications.

# Page-Centric (Model 1)

The first common architecture for building web applications is **page-centric**, which is more commonly known within Java web-application circles as the **Model 1 architecture** (see Figure 14-1). We've mentioned this architecture in several places in this book. This architecture provides the easiest way to put a web application together. It involves simply building the application as a set of JSP pages.

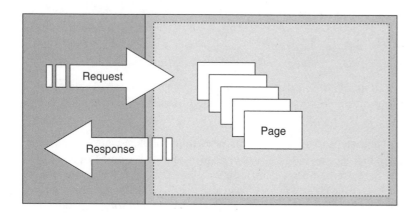

**Figure 14-1.** *In a Model 1 architecture, all requests are handled in a single tier of the application. For example, all the display logic, business logic, and data are contained in JSP pages.*

Of course, applications are generally built to share information (typically from some sort of database) with the users, and in page-centric applications, information is typically represented in a couple of ways.

The first of these is that any information required by a page is accessed directly from the database by using embedded Structured Query Language (SQL) statements. Usually this SQL code is written straight into the page along with the code to make the database connections and retrieve the results. As a twist on this paradigm, the code to deal with the database connections is often pushed into reusable Java classes or custom tags such as those found in the JSTL. Of the various ways to build a web application, this is probably the least maintainable because all the logic to access data is embedded right inside the JSP pages. Any change to the database schema means potentially opening up every page in the application to fix it.

The other mechanism for accessing data within page-centric applications is to use JavaBeans to represent the persistent entities within your system. For example, you might have a JavaBean called Customer to represent the customers within your system. By taking this approach, data-access code is kept off of the individual pages and can be pushed back into reusable Java classes (see Figure 14-2). You instantly attain a greater level of code reuse throughout the application while at the same time you increase the maintainability of the application. For example, when data access is moved to a separate tier, changes to the database schema require changes to a select few Java classes.

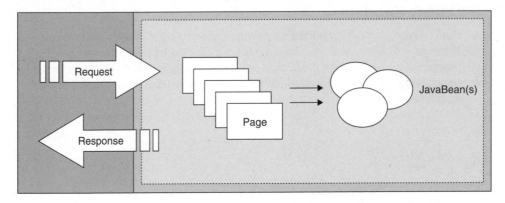

**Figure 14-2.** *Even a simple change to the application, such as moving data access to a separate tier, can improve the reusability and maintainability of an application.*

So, although you can take steps to increase the maintainability of page-centric applications, the real limitation lies within your ability to change or modify the end-to-end functionality provided by the system. In page-centric applications, the pages that the user sees are all implemented as stand-alone JSPs. In fact, you can also use servlets, but the principle is the same: building applications this way has limitations. If you want to add some functionality to every page (such as logging), you have to open up each page and edit it. Want to add a new flow of functionality through the application? Chances are that you'll have to open up a large number of pages to edit links and ensure that the required data is available to the pages. The main problem is that the pages of the application have too much responsibility. They contain the business logic to gather the appropriate information (and make changes to that information) alongside the presentation logic of displaying that information to the user. Ideally, changes to the business logic should be independent of the presentation logic and vice versa.

## Model-View-Controller (Model 2)

The other major architecture used to build web applications is based on the classic **Model-View-Controller (MVC)** architecture and is sometimes also referred to as **Model 2**. In page-centric web applications, a single request is generally serviced by a single page containing the business and presentation logic. MVC, however, uses three major components in the servicing of a request, as summarized in Figure 14-3.

The first of these is the **controller,** the component through which all requests are routed to be serviced. It acts as the gateway to the functionality provided by the web application and is typically implemented as a Java servlet. Having a single point of access for all requests in the system has a couple of benefits. First, it provides a common location for systemwide aspects such as security, logging, and so on. Second, it's the responsibility of the controller to find and execute the business logic that will be used to service the request. This responsibility could range from simply locating information that is to be displayed, to processing an update request and modifying some data residing in a database. The important point to note about the controller is that it doesn't have anything to do with the presentation of information back to the user.

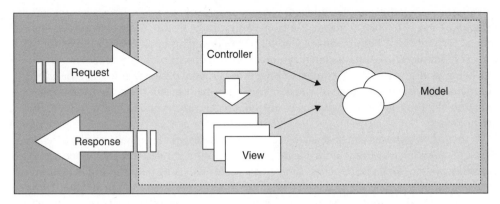

**Figure 14-3.** *In an MVC application, separate tiers handle display logic (view), data access (model), and business logic (the controller and the model).*

The next component, or set of components, used by the MVC architecture represents the **model**. There are a couple of broadly accepted definitions for the model components, but we like to think of them as the information that the controller uses to perform its processing. In other words, the controller contains the business logic, and the model represents the business/domain objects upon which that logic operates. If you've done any Swing programming, think of the model as the Swing model components that just provide a representation of the data being manipulated and displayed. Like Swing, model components are generally implemented as JavaBeans.

The final components in the MVC architecture are the **view** components. These are solely responsible for the presentation of information back to the user. Because all business logic is performed by the controller, the view components only have to present the information provided by the model to the user. Therefore, view components are typically implemented with JSP pages because these are most aligned to allow easy presentation of information back to the user (for example, using a markup language such as HTML).

Although this separation of concerns does seem slightly more complicated than simple page-centric designs, it gives you the ability to modify each of the three components in isolation. You can modify the data schema, the business logic, or the presentation separately. Not only is the application more maintainable because there is a centralized place for locating each specific type of code, but also the system as a whole is now much more extensible. Need to add a new flow of functionality? Simply add the logic into the controller component and add a new view to display the relevant information back to the user. Of course, it's still possible to build unmaintainable MVC web applications, and for this reason there is a collection of proven patterns that can be used during design and development.

# Design Patterns

A simple way to describe **design patterns** is that they're reusable solutions to common problems within a given context. In addition to this, and through the way that they're documented, patterns provide a common language with which to understand and use them.

Patterns really came into the limelight with the release of *Design Patterns: Elements of Reusable Object-Oriented Software* (Addison-Wesley, 1995) by the "Gang of Four" (Erich Gamma, Richard Helm, Ralph Johnson, and John Vlissides). This book details a large number of reusable solutions to common, language-independent design problems related to structural, behavioral, and creational contexts. Using these original design patterns as a basis, many people have extended this work to document new patterns for the design and implementation of Java EE systems, including many that are relevant to building Java-based web applications.

At first sight, patterns can be seen to complicate the design of a system, and to a degree this is true. After all, why implement a feature with a handful of related classes when just a single class will do? Well, the benefits come at several levels. Using patterns and the common language that they use allows us, as software developers, to easily communicate about how a particular part of the application works. For example, if we have a class that's responsible for creating other types of classes on demand, using the common name for this pattern (in this case, "factory") provides a certain level of common understanding. This is useful, as it helps other members of the project team, or anybody looking at the code, to come to grips with it easily.

The ability to use patterns also helps ensure that there's some consistency in the way that recurring problems are solved within the application. This practice subsequently promotes code reuse (and therefore quality) and maintainability, again because the design is easier to understand. Furthermore, because patterns have the ability to introduce a certain degree of structure to a design, the extensibility of that design is often greater than if the same functionality were built using a single class.

# Java EE Patterns and Web-Application Components

Probably the most well-known collection of Java EE patterns available to date is that cataloged by the Sun Java Center at `http://java.sun.com/blueprints/corej2eepatterns`. The patterns contained within this catalog cover all tiers of the Java EE 5 architecture, and if you're building multitier enterprise applications, they're well worth taking a look at. For the purpose of this chapter, you're interested in only those patterns that are relevant to building the web tier of Java EE applications. Let's take a look at some of these and see how they can help you build well-designed web applications.

## Front Controller

As you learned in the discussion of the MVC architecture, the controller component acts as the gateway into the web application and is the central place from which all requests are serviced. As it stands, the MVC architecture is programming language independent, and in translating this to the world of Java-based web applications, the Sun Java Center came up with the **Front Controller** pattern, a Java EE–specific version of the controller in MVC. Listing 14-1 shows a prototypical implementation of this pattern.

**Listing 14-1.** *FrontController.java*

```java
package com.apress.projsp;
import java.io.IOException;
import javax.servlet.RequestDispatcher;
import javax.servlet.ServletException;
import javax.servlet.http.*;
public class FrontController extends HttpServlet {
  protected void processRequest(HttpServletRequest request,
                                HttpServletResponse response)
      throws ServletException, IOException {
    // Step 1 - perform business logic and manipulate the model
    // someObject.someBusinessLogic();
    // Step 2 - dispatch to the appropriate view component
    RequestDispatcher dispatcher =
      getServletContext().
        getRequestDispatcher("name of a view component");
    dispatcher.forward(request, response);
  }
  protected void doGet(HttpServletRequest req, HttpServletResponse res)
      throws ServletException, IOException {
    processRequest(req, res);
  }
  protected void doPost(HttpServletRequest req, HttpServletResponse res)
      throws ServletException, IOException {
    processRequest(req, res);
  }
}
```

As this example implementation shows, a front controller can be as simple as a servlet that responds to HTTP GET and POST requests. Although the code doesn't actually show any real business logic being called, it does show the steps in servicing the request. First, you process the request by executing some business logic, and then you redirect to, or dispatch to, the view component that will be presenting the user with information. The main problem with this implementation is that if all business logic for an application is wrapped up inside a single controller, that controller will quickly become bloated and have a vast set of responsibilities. To overcome this problem, you can use the command and controller strategy.

## The Command and Controller Strategy

There are many ways in which the Front Controller pattern can be implemented, each of which is called a **strategy**. For example, in the previous example the front controller was implemented as a Java servlet, although there's nothing stopping that implementation from being a JSP page. To overcome the problem of the controller becoming bloated with all the application logic for a particular system, the command and controller strategy combines the controller servlet with classes that implement the **Command** design pattern. (The Command pattern is a more general object-oriented design pattern.) Essentially, the Command pattern says that the logic required to perform a specific task is wrapped up into a single class with a standard interface to execute that code. For example, you might wrap up the logic to locate a customer's details into a single class, inside a method called execute(). First, you might define a standard interface for all of the commands to be used by the front controller. Listing 14-2 shows an interface that does this.

**Listing 14-2.** *Action.java*

```
package com.apress.projsp;
import javax.servlet.ServletException;
import javax.servlet.http.HttpServletRequest;
import javax.servlet.http.HttpServletResponse;

public interface Action {
  public String execute(HttpServletRequest request,
                        HttpServletResponse response)
      throws ServletException;
}
```

This interface contains a single method with which to execute the logic that will be encapsulated within concrete implementations of this interface. Essentially, all you want to do is delegate the servicing of requests to an Action instance instead of putting that code inside the controller. Therefore, the method signature is defined to take references to the same request and response objects that are used when processing an HTTP request with a servlet. By using this interface, you can then supply an implementation that, given a customer ID, looks up that customer and places the corresponding domain object into the HTTP request to be displayed by the view component (see Listing 14-3).

**Listing 14-3.** *ViewCustomerAction.java*

```
package com.apress.projsp;
import javax.servlet.http.HttpServletRequest;
import javax.servlet.http.HttpServletResponse;
import javax.servlet.ServletException;
public class ViewCustomerAction implements Action {
  public String execute(HttpServletRequest request,
                        HttpServletResponse response)
      throws ServletException {
    String id = request.getParameter("id");
    Customer customer = CustomerFactory.getInstance().getCustomer(id);
    request.setAttribute("customer", customer);
    return "/view-customer.jsp";
  }
}
```

Assuming that all the necessary code to look up customers has been written, when a Customer instance is found, you can use the request object as an area in which to place any objects that are relevant for the lifetime of this request via the setAttribute() method. The final point to note about this implementation is that the value returned from the execute() method is the name of the JSP page representing the view component. In other words, this is the name of the JSP page that will be used to render, or present, the information back to the user.

With all the business logic then wrapped up inside Action instances, the front controller itself becomes very small and hence much more cohesive, as Listing 14-4 shows.

**Listing 14-4.** *FrontController.java*

```java
package com.apress.projsp;
import java.io.IOException;
import javax.servlet.http.*;
import javax.servlet.ServletException;
import javax.servlet.RequestDispatcher;
public class FrontController extends HttpServlet {
private ActionFactory actionFactory = new ActionFactory();
  protected void processRequest(HttpServletRequest request,
                                HttpServletResponse response)
      throws ServletException, IOException {
    Action action;
    try {
      action = actionFactory.getAction(request);
    } catch (ActionNotFoundException anfe) {
      throw new ServletException(anfe);
    }
    // Now process action, finding out which view to show the user next
    String nextView = action.execute(request, response);
    // and finally redirect to appropriate view,
    // remembering to prefix the path
    try {
      if (nextView != null) {
        RequestDispatcher dispatcher =
          getServletContext().getRequestDispatcher(nextView);
        dispatcher.forward(request, response);
      }
    } catch (Exception e) {
      e.printStackTrace();
      throw new ServletException(e);
    }
  }
  protected void doGet(HttpServletRequest req, HttpServletResponse res)
      throws ServletException, IOException {
    processRequest(req, res);
  }

  protected void doPost(HttpServletRequest req, HttpServletResponse res)
      throws ServletException, IOException {
    processRequest(req, res);
  }
}
```

In this version of the front controller, you're simply using a helper class to find which `Action` implementation should be used to service this particular request. How does the controller know which action to use? Well, there are various ways to communicate the name of the action to the controller. These range from using a named parameter within the query string to encoding the name of the action inside specially mapped URLs. One such example might be as follows:

```
http://www.mycompany.com/controller/ViewCustomer?id=123456
```

The key benefit of using the command and controller strategy is that it allows you to maintain a central place for accepting requests, while keeping the logic to actually service an individual request separate from that needed to service other types of requests.

### View Components

Before we move on to other patterns, we need to spend a little time discussing **View Components** within Java EE patterns. With the controller responsible for the business logic related to servicing a request, you may be asking how to implement the view components. In the simplest case, the views are implemented as JSP pages that are forwarded by the controller component. The job of the controller (or an action class if you're using that strategy) is to perform any processing and set up the environment for the view to present the information. In Chapter 9, you saw that it's quite possible for JSP pages to contain database code so that they can find the data they're supposed to display. However, the MVC architecture turns this on its head because it's now the responsibility of the controller to find that data. As you saw in the previous sample action implementation, it's possible to use the `request` object to store information that's required for the lifetime of the current request:

```
request.setAttribute("customer", customer);
```

Here, you're just placing a `Customer` instance into the map of objects maintained by the request. When it comes to presenting the information from the view, you can use the JSP EL to locate that `Customer` instance and display it. For example, you can use the following expression to display the name of the customer (assuming that a method called `getName()` exists):

```
${customer.name}
```

This separation of business and presentation logic gives you the ability to easily change one or the other independently if necessary. Should you need to change the way that the customer is presented to the user, this is no problem. You can just modify the JSP page without danger of breaking the existing business logic of locating that customer.

## View Helper

Although the front controller is responsible (possibly through delegation to commands) for executing the business logic required to service a given request, there is still often logic that is related to only the presentation of that information. View components such as JSP pages are great at displaying information, but sometimes some more code is needed. Perhaps a list of objects needs to be sorted prior to being displayed, or perhaps the information needs to be formatted in some specific way. Although that code can simply be embedded into the view components, the **View Helper** pattern describes a way to wrap up this code and make it reusable over multiple views.

You have already seen many examples of view helpers. If you look back to Chapter 7, one of the tags you saw filtered the domain of e-mail addresses, making it harder for spammers to obtain addresses. Although extremely useful, such logic isn't really classed as business logic. Instead, this is presentation logic—code that helps the view present information back to the users. Of course, such code could have been written and embedded into the JSP page, but this is considered bad practice for reasons of quality, maintainability, and so on. Instead, that code is wrapped inside a custom tag so that it can be used and reused throughout the pages of the web application. In effect, this custom tag is an implementation of the View Helper pattern. In this case, the tag is a component that the view uses to help it perform its task.

## Service to Worker

Each of the patterns that we've covered so far has tackled a different problem within the design of web applications. The front controller provides a single point of access for requests to centralize business logic, whereas views and view helpers separate the process of presenting information from the process of finding the information and manipulating it. To bring all these patterns together, the Java EE patterns catalog defines a macro pattern called Service to Worker, shown in Figure 14-4. By "macro pattern," we mean that this is really just a combination of other patterns—in this case, the front controller, views, and view helpers.

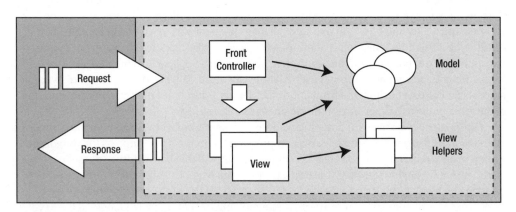

**Figure 14-4.** *The Service to Worker pattern is a combination of other patterns.*

Bringing all these patterns together is the basis for an extended MVC architecture and provides a common ground for web applications to be designed and easily understood. It also helps to emphasize the benefits of the individual patterns and demonstrates that they're much more useful if used with one another. As you'll see shortly, the Service to Worker pattern forms the basis of many web-application frameworks currently in use.

# Filter

Another useful, although not widely used, pattern worth briefly talking about is called **Filter**. The filter API that you saw in the previous chapters is an implementation of this pattern, so instead of looking at how to implement a filter, let's see how it can be used in the design of web applications and talk about some more typical uses.

Filters can play in important role in the design of web applications because they can have responsibilities unrelated to any particular JSP or servlet. Filters can be seen as channels through which all requests and responses can be passed.

One way I have used filters in web applications is to interpret user-friendly URLs. To help me keep my website up to date, I built some web-logging software—a simple date-based content management system to which I post short entries on a daily basis. The web log (abbreviated to "blog") then displays the most recent of these entries in reverse date order on the front page. In addition, when readers want to locate older entries, they can simply jump directly to a page containing all the entries for an individual day. In the past, such websites have been built of static pages, organized in such a way that made it easy to find the page for a specific day. For example, the blog entries for June 10, 2003, can be found at `http://www.simongbrown.com/blog/2003/06/10.html`.

With technologies such as JSP and servlets providing many benefits over writing static pages, I decided to write my web log as a Java-based web application. All the entries are stored separately on the filing system, and with the help of the Front Controller pattern, a couple of JSP pages are used to assemble the individual entries into a page that is presented back to the user. However, rather than show the user a URL such as `http://www.simongbrown.com/blog/servlet/ViewDailyBlog?year=2003&month=6&day=10`, I decided that I'd still like URLs such as the one shown previously to work. To implement this, I used a filter.

Because a filter can be set up to look at all incoming requests to a web application, all that the filter needs to do is look for a request matching `yyyy/mm/dd.html` and forward the request to the appropriate action via the front controller. The filter is being used to catch these requests for seemingly static content through user-friendly URLs and convert the requests into dynamic requests for content through the front controller. This is a simple yet powerful implementation of the Filter pattern that performs filtering on incoming requests.

Filters can also be used on outgoing responses. One example often cited is a filter that, after a request has been processed, uses compression techniques to compress the outgoing stream in an attempt to make more efficient use of the available bandwidth. Another example is a filter that highlights the usage of search terms in the page. Through the interfaces provided by the Servlet API, it's possible to find the complete URL of the website that the user came from to visit your site. For example, somebody might click a link in Google to get to your website. Using this information, you could write a filter to check for referrals from Google and highlight the occurrences of the search terms used before the response is subsequently sent back to the user. Again, this is another way that you can use filters to enhance the user's experience of your web applications.

# Other Web-Application Patterns

In addition to the Java EE patterns that we've just covered, there are other patterns or best practices that can help you to build web applications. Also, JSP 2.1 provides a much better and often easier way to implement some of these patterns, as we'll describe in this section.

## Including Standard Headers and Footers

Probably one of the most commonly used best practices when building JSP-based web applications is to separate out the common code used in headers and footers into JSP pages or fragments that are included wherever necessary. Such files might include all of the HTML tags to define well-formed HTML headers, the `<%@ taglib %>` directives to import common tag libraries, defining objects to be used in the page, and so on. Whatever it is you're trying to achieve, you'll typically implement this practice by using the JSP `include` directive to statically include the header on every page:

```
<%@ include file="header.jspf" %>
```

On translation of the JSP into a servlet, the JSP compiler inlines the included file into the source code of the generated servlet class. This is a useful way to make some of the content reusable, although it does rely on the page author remembering to include the header wherever possible. Also, often different headers are needed for different parts of the web application. For example, you might have a different file that is included when the JSP page is from a secure part of the site.

To address this, the teams behind the new JSP and Servlet specifications have come up with the idea of **preludes** and **codas**. The basic idea is that given any set of one or more JSP pages, it's possible to define one or more preludes or codas. Preludes are files that are included before the main body of JSP pages that match a given URL pattern; codas are files that are included after the main body of those JSP pages. So, instead of including a header and footer on every page, you can achieve the same result by using the following fragment within the `web.xml` deployment descriptor:

```
<jsp-property-group>
    <url-pattern>*.jsp</url-pattern>
    <include-prelude>/header.jspf</include-prelude>
    <include-coda>/footer.jspf</include-coda>
</jsp-property-group>
```

This is a great way to further increase the maintainability of your web applications and reduce the amount of duplicated content that they contain.

## Templating

Templating is another common implementation technique in web applications. A **template** is a predefined skeleton that you can customize at runtime by using parameters. If you look back to Chapter 6, one of the examples used to demonstrate tag files was a web page that contained a number of promotional notices on the homepage. Although the content contained within each tag was different, the actual structure and code to build them was the same. These are effectively templates that are being used and customized.

Before the introduction of tag files, templating was fairly hard to achieve with JSP because there was no easy way to express how templates should be customized. A couple of possible options included using short scriptlets or even custom tags to indicate where dynamic content should be inserted inside the body of the template. However, the problem with these was that all too often, using such methods introduced some Java code into the page. Perhaps objects needed to be set up or some presentation logic was needed. After code is introduced, many people stop calling those pages templates. After all, instead of simply indicating where dynamic content should be inserted, you basically have complete control over how the template works. Another option is to use a specific templating framework such as Velocity (discussed in the following "Frameworks for Building Web Applications" section).

With the introduction of EL in JSP 2.0, developers gained the ability to perform templating. Because the EL is an integral part of the JSP specification, templates are now much easier to build. Simply write the static content inside a JSP file and then insert EL expressions where the dynamic content is to be inserted. The expressions themselves can be fairly powerful, although they're still simple enough for people to understand, and they don't expose the inner workings of the template.

# Frameworks for Building Web Applications

So far you've looked at some proven ways of building web applications and a lot of patterns for translating these ideas into working code. Do you really have to write all of this every time you build an application?

## A Bespoke Framework

By combining the implementations of the Java EE patterns discussed previously, you basically have a bespoke framework on which to build an MVC-based web application. In fact, many of the web applications that we've worked on (open source and for clients) have used these simple implementations as a basis for a lightweight MVC framework used to service all of the requests throughout the application. We subscribe to the "keep it simple" approach to software design, and using such a lightweight framework has several benefits. The framework is easy to learn, easy to maintain, and, when necessary, easy to extend, one such example being to handle validation errors from HTML forms that users submit.

However, writing a bespoke framework isn't always the best option. The implementation of the Front Controller pattern presented here is fairly simple and straightforward, but many improvements can be made. Examples include a standard way to build HTML forms and perform validation, more sophisticated components to display information from the model, and so on. Although such work isn't particularly complex, it's time-consuming. Therefore, several third-party frameworks are available for developers to use as a starting point for their web applications.

## Struts

Struts from the Jakarta Project (http://jakarta.apache.org) is an open-source framework providing an implementation of not only a front controller, but also a complete implementation (or framework) of the MVC architecture. The key components are similar to those presented here, including, for example, a controller servlet (called `ActionServlet`), `Action` classes in which to place functionality for processing a request, and `ActionBean` classes in which to encapsulate data coming in from a request. In addition, Struts contains a comprehensive collection of JSP tag libraries for the easy assembly of HTML-based forms and JSP pages in general.

One of the most important features of Struts is that pretty much everything about it is externally configured through the `struts-config.xml` file. This includes the mappings between action names and `Action` classes (called `ActionMappings`), and also a concept called `ActionForwards`. For the simple implementation presented in Listing 14-3, the `Action` class returns a string representing the URI of the JSP page that should be displayed next. In Struts, however, the `Action` classes return a symbolic name (wrapped up in an `ActionForward` instance) representing which view component should be displayed next. As an example, consider a login form containing a username and password. On submission of the form, the login is either successful or unsuccessful. In this case, the `Action` class could return symbolic names such as `success` or `failure`. These symbolic names are then configured in the `struts-config.xml` file, and it's here that the physical URI to the appropriate JSP page is specified. The following snippet shows how two different flows through a login action might be handled:

```
<action path="/login" type="com.mycompany.myapp.LoginAction">
  <forward name="success" path="/index.jsp"/>
  <forward name="failure" path="/login-failed.jsp"/>
</action>
```

Here, we're saying that there are two possible outcomes for the login action. The first is that the login is successful, and if this is the case, the user is directed to the index page. Alternatively, a failed login takes the user to a page explaining that the user's login failed. Generally, this logic and the page names would have to be hard-coded into the actions. With Struts and its configuration file, the flows through an application can be easily changed, and it's another way that the flow and structure of the web application can be taken out of the code to increase maintainability. After all, if the structure of the site changes, only the configuration file needs to change. You will look at Struts in more detail in the next chapter.

# Spring

The Spring Framework (`http://www.springframework.org`) aims to be lightweight but powerful, and easy to use. Spring is a layered Java EE application framework, developed by Rod Johnson. Spring has a lot of features to make enterprise development easier for you.

---

**■Note**  If you want to learn more about Spring, beyond the short description here, we recommend *Expert One-on-One J2EE Design and Development* by Rod Johnson (Wrox Press, 2002), *Pro Spring* by Rob Harrop and Jan Machacek (Apress, 2005), or *Professional Java Development with the Spring Framework* by Rod Johnson and others (Wrox Press, 2005).

---

Spring can be used on its own to provide a complete enterprise application framework. The framework simplifies the work required to build and integrate the presentation tier, business tier, and data tier of your web application. Although Spring is powerful enough for enterprise applications, it does not force you to use Java EE. You can develop Spring components from plain old Java objects (POJOs) and use Spring to easily integrate those objects into a working application. The objects you build can easily be used in a Java EE environment or as part of stand-alone applications.

On the other hand, Spring is also flexible enough to work with other frameworks to provide enterprise solutions.

Spring has its own data abstraction layer for data persistence. But it can also integrate with other data abstraction technologies such as Oracle TopLink, Hibernate, and Java Data Objects (JDO). See Chapter 9 for more information about these and other data abstraction technologies.

Not only does Spring integrate well with the data tier, it also integrates well with other presentation tier technologies such as JSP, Velocity, and Tiles. So you can use Spring to develop the business objects, and use your favorite presentation-tier framework to provide the view in your MVC application.

Finally, Spring works well with other MVC frameworks such as Struts, WebWork, or Tapestry.

## WebWork

WebWork (`http://www.opensymphony.com/webwork/`) is another MVC framework that is often compared to Struts. It too uses the concepts of classes that implement the command pattern, although one of the key differences between Struts and WebWork is that WebWork is built on top of another framework (XWork) that isn't actually tied to the Web and concepts such as HTTP requests and responses. Therefore, it's possible to share implementations between web applications and other Java implementations such as a Swing client. In essence, the action classes are just JavaBeans, and in a web environment, parameters are simply mapped on to bean properties.

WebWork provides similar features to Struts in terms of user interface components for building views, customizable validation, an expression language for accessing information from the model, and so on. However, what makes WebWork more than just a Struts copy is that it doesn't rely on just JSP for the presentation tier. The view components themselves *can* be JSP, but they can also be written using other technologies, including XML and Velocity (see the next section for more information on Velocity).

A unique feature of WebWork is that it supports interceptors that can be used to execute logic before and/or after an action invocation. This is similar to the way that filters can be used to intercept incoming requests and outgoing responses. Like aspect-oriented programming (AOP), WebWork interceptors give you a way to insert cross-cutting concerns throughout your code base without having to open every action class and edit it. By "cross-cutting concerns," we mean logic that isn't specifically tied to the business function provided by the system, such as logging, security, caching, and so on. Typically, business logic can be seen as vertical in that in any application you have a collection of vertical slices providing business logic. With interceptors, you can build code that works across all of these vertical slices and, in WebWork, you can configure this declaratively.

In summary, WebWork is a simpler, although arguably more powerful, alternative to Struts that provides a quick way to build MVC-based web applications. Additionally, the simple interface provided by the action classes makes testing WebWork actions much easier than Struts, without the need for a testing framework such as Cactus. The only downside to using WebWork is that the user community is currently small and there isn't much information readily available. Hopefully, this will start to change.

## Velocity

Velocity (`http://jakarta.apache.org/velocity/`) is a Java-based templating engine that provides an alternative way to build the view components of web applications. In fact, Velocity is capable of much more than this, as it can be used outside of the context of a web application, perhaps for helping to generate reports or XML. Velocity has its own templating language (the Velocity Templating Language, or VTL) that provides a way to access pretty much anything that can be accessed through regular Java method calls. At the time that Velocity was created, JSP didn't include its own expression language, and Velocity was an attempt to fill this void and provide an easy way for developers to build true templates.

Although JSP now includes an EL, Velocity has a large following and has been deployed in many applications, particularly web applications. With frameworks such as WebWork providing easy integration with Velocity, it will still be a popular choice for web applications that are heavily based on dynamic content that can be easily templated.

# Testing

Testing plays an important role in the software development life cycle, although when time scales are short and deadlines loom, testing often doesn't get the attention that it should. Fortunately, new development methods such as Extreme Programming (http://www.xprogramming.com/) are doing a great job of promoting automated testing with tools such as JUnit, in which unit tests are actually written in Java. So then, how do these principles apply to testing web applications and what exactly can you test? Web applications are often complex by nature, and this can lead to confusion over exactly what can and should be tested. From an automated testing perspective, two types of testing generally take place: unit testing and functional testing. There are many tools available to help you perform unit and functional testing, such as JUnit, JUnitEE, Cactus, TagUnit, and HttpUnit. After looking at these tools, you will learn how to design your web applications for testing, what the guidelines for a testing strategy are, and why you would want to perform compatibility testing.

## Unit Testing Web Applications

**Unit testing** is the process of testing software from the perspective that you know how it works. It's also called **white box testing** because you can see how the software works—you can see inside the box. The opposite of this is **black box testing**, which we'll discuss shortly.

The idea behind unit testing is to ensure that all (or most) of the paths throughout the unit are sufficiently tested, including things such as boundary conditions on loops and method calls, correct and incorrect (for example, null) parameters into method calls, and so on. By doing this, you're making sure that the unit being tested is correct, does what it's supposed to do, and doesn't break when you throw inputs it just isn't expecting.

So, how can you apply unit testing to web applications? The simple answer is that you unit test all the classes and components that make up the web application—everything from the JavaBeans representing business objects to the servlets servicing requests. Although this sounds good in theory, in practice it's difficult to achieve because of the plumbing required by many of the Java EE components that live inside a server. With stand-alone Java classes, it's straightforward to write automated unit tests with the JUnit framework. Typically, such tests might create new instances of the class being tested, call methods on that instance, and subsequently perform assertions on the results to ensure that they were correct. However, with components such as servlets and JSP pages (which get compiled to servlets), this just isn't something that can be done in the same way. After all, these components need to be executed within the context of a server that supports the technologies. In essence, these components

rely heavily on the plumbing, infrastructure, and services provided by such servers. Fortunately, people have realized this and have come up with some ways of making unit testing
such components easier. However, there will generally be a cutoff point at which unit testing
becomes unfeasible and other testing methods must be used.

With these thoughts in mind, let's move on to look at what you can test and the tools you
can use to do so.

## JUnit

JUnit (http://www.junit.org), now the de facto standard for building automated tests within
the Java language, is widely used on projects ranging from desktop applications to enterprise-
scale distributed servers. JUnit provides a lightweight framework with which to write tests. At
a high level, you simply extend one of the provided classes and write one or more methods to
test each aspect of the class or classes that you wish to test. After you've compiled the test
classes, you then run the tests through one of the JUnit test runners, and it's this that keeps a
tally of the passes and fails, issuing a result at the end of the process.

Listing 14-5 illustrates how easy it is to write automated unit tests in JUnit by showing how
you might test a simple JavaBean representing a customer having two properties, firstName
and lastName. In this example, the class has an additional method called getFullName() that
simply joins the first and last names together with a space between them. With JUnit, you
might want to test that the various get methods function as expected by setting the appropriate properties and performing assertions on the results of accessing those properties.

**Listing 14-5.** *CustomerTest.java*

```java
import junit.framework.TestCase;
public class CustomerTest extends TestCase {
  public void testFirstName() {
    Customer customer = new Customer();
    customer.setFirstName("Simon");
    assertEquals("Simon", customer.getFirstName());
  }
  public void testLastName() {
    Customer customer = new Customer();
    customer.setLastName("Brown");
    assertEquals("Brown", customer.getLastName());
  }
  public void testFullName() {
    Customer customer = new Customer();
    customer.setFirstName("Simon");
    customer.setLastName("Brown");
    assertEquals("Simon Brown", customer.getFullName());
  }
}
```

All that you're doing here is extending one of the classes provided by JUnit and implementing testXXX() methods for the various pieces of functionality that you'd like to test. In
this case, you're testing the ability to set/get the first, last, and full names. Of course, this is a

simple example and it doesn't cover exceptional cases such as null values. However, it does demonstrate how easy it is to write unit tests with JUnit and shows its potential.

Getting started with JUnit can sometimes be tricky, particularly with respect to finding the motivation to write the tests in the first place. However, after they've gotten over the learning curve and experienced the benefit of JUnit, most people become hooked or, to use a phrase coined by the JUnit team, "test infected."

Seeing JUnit for the first time is a little daunting, especially when you start to think about how much more Java code you have to write for each and every class that you're building. However, based on our experience of using JUnit, we've found that after you use JUnit for a while you will start to appreciate the power of automated unit tests and the confidence that it can give you when refactoring or redesigning parts of a system. The feeling of confidence you get when you make a big design change and the tests still work is amazing!

When using JUnit, the types of classes that you can test include those representing the business domain, the business logic, MVC-style action classes, helper classes, and so on. Essentially, anything that stands alone can be tested using JUnit. In many web applications, this set of classes will cover the majority of the code being developed and should hopefully lead to a good level of confidence that the code works correctly. However, at times you may have stand-alone classes that still need to be run and therefore tested inside of a Java EE container environment. For these situations,  JUnitEE is useful.

## JUnitEE

JUnitEE (http://www.junitee.org) provides a way to run regular JUnit tests inside of a Java EE container. Why would you want to do this? Well, perhaps you have some classes that require the use of a database connection that is set up and made available to those classes through the container's JNDI tree. Or perhaps those classes need access to some other enterprise resource to function properly. With JUnitEE, you can bundle up all of your classes and their tests into a WAR file that you can then deploy onto a Java EE web container such as Tomcat. To execute those tests, you then point your web browser to the newly deployed web application and a servlet runs behind the scenes to execute the JUnit tests and presents the results back to you.

JUnitEE is effectively a lightweight test runner that allows you to execute tests within a server environment. However, it doesn't allow you to test components such as servlets and JSPs any easier than JUnit. For this you have to look at other options such as Cactus.

## Cactus

Cactus (http://jakarta.apache.org/cactus/) is an extension to JUnit that provides a mechanism for running unit tests inside of a running Java EE container. Although you're able to run regular JUnit tests within a server environment when using JUnitEE, you still don't have the complete infrastructure necessary to test those classes that depend on information delivered to them on a request-by-request basis. For example, to be able to truly test a servlet, you need to have a live request and response object available to you because the code inside the servlet might extract parameters from the request or push out information into the response. Cactus gives you the ability to test these types of components with the confidence that they're running within their real environment.

In Cactus, the testing functionality is broken into two halves. First is a client part. This looks just like a normal JUnit test and is used to initiate the test. The second part of Cactus lives on the server. Here, you can use Cactus-provided test classes to instantiate the components that you wish to test and invoke their methods. For example, you might choose to create a new instance of a servlet class and call the doGet() method. Of course, to actually call this method you need to have access to the HTTP request and response objects, so where do they come from?

The key here is a test redirector component that sits between the client and server test classes. When a test is initiated by the client, a request is made to the Java EE container and this is intercepted by a Cactus-provided servlet that must also be running on the server. This servlet (the test redirector) then determines which server-side test needs to be run and initiates the appropriate test class. As an actual HTTP request has been made to the Java EE container, Cactus simply wraps this up and passes it on to the server-side test class to use as necessary. The object representing the HTTP response is also wrapped up for use by the test class. With access to these, the server-side test class and the class being tested can extract parameters, write output to the response, and so on. Assertions can then be made that the class being tested works as expected, with the results of these assertions being passed back to the client for reporting.

As an example, consider the ViewCustomerAction class that we introduced during our discussion of MVC earlier in the chapter. Because this class relies on the server for a real request, it's a great candidate for testing with Cactus. Listing 14-6 shows how you might achieve this.

**Listing 14-6.** *ViewCustomerTest.java*

```java
import javax.servlet.ServletException;
import junit.framework.Test;
import junit.framework.TestSuite;
import org.apache.cactus.ServletTestCase;
import org.apache.cactus.WebRequest;
public class ViewCustomerTest extends ServletTestCase {

  public ViewCustomerTest(String theName) {
    super(theName);
  }
  public static Test suite() {
    return new TestSuite(ViewCustomerTest.class);
  }
  public void beginExecute(WebRequest webRequest) {
    webRequest.addParameter("id", "123");
  }
  public void testExecute() {
    Customer customer = CustomerFactory.getInstance().getCustomer("123");
    ViewCustomerAction action = new ViewCustomerAction();
    try {
      action.execute(this.request, this.response);
      assertEquals(customer, request.getAttribute("customer"));
    } catch (ServletException e) {
      fail();
    }
  }
}
```

In many ways, this class is similar to the JUnit tests that you saw in the previous section, except this time you subclass a Cactus-specific class. Again, you write a `testXXX()` method to test the functionality, but Cactus allows you to write a corresponding `beginXXX()` method that gets called before your test method. It's here that you can initialize request parameters and so on. The class that you've subclassed (`ServletTestCase`) provides you with access to a real request/response, and it's because of this that testing the server-side action is so straightforward.

Cactus provides a flexible way of testing those components that really do need to be tested inside a Java EE container, and it currently provides support for testing servlets, JSPs, custom tags, and filters. The biggest problem with Cactus is that it can seem complicated to begin with, particularly with respect to setting up the framework. The great thing about Cactus is that it provides a way to actually test all of those components that would otherwise be untested if you used JUnit on its own. On the flip side, Cactus tests do require you to write some of the code that would normally be executed automatically by the container. If you create a servlet instance, you should ideally also call the container-management methods such as `init()` and `destroy()`. In general, this isn't too much of a problem because the life cycle of servlets and filters is straightforward. Custom tags, however, are a slightly different story.

## TagUnit

One of the most complicated parts of custom tags (certainly before JSP 2.0 came along) was that the life cycle of tag handler instances seemed cryptic and hard to understand. JSP 2.0 addressed these features with the new `SimpleTag` interface, but before this the JSP specification placed some very strict rules around the life cycle and pooling of tag handler instances that were never widely understood. Because the code to implement these life cycle requirements is generally the responsibility of the Java EE container, this usually isn't a problem. To test custom tags with Cactus, however, the developer must write this code to accurately mimic the way that tags are used on the page. Unfortunately, this process can be error-prone, and therefore the TagUnit testing framework was created.

TagUnit (`http://tagunit.sourceforge.net/`) is a framework for testing custom tags. It differs from other testing tools in that it allows tags to be tested within the same environment where they'll eventually be used. In other words, the tests themselves are written as JSP pages with regular JSP syntax. To achieve this, TagUnit provides a tag library of its own that contains testing and assertion tags that mimic the `assertXXX()` methods found in JUnit. Therefore, testing custom tags becomes very easy. You just use your tags on the page and wrap them up within the TagUnit tags. Examples of assertions include comparing the generated content with some expected content, looking for the presence of scoped variables/attributes, and checking that exceptions are correctly handled.

Listing 14-7 is an example that tests the content generated from the e-mail address filter tag you saw in Chapter 7, in which you tested that the custom tag does in fact filter out the domain part of the e-mail address.

**Listing 14-7.** *TestEmailAddressFilter.jsp*

```jsp
<%@ taglib uri="http://www.tagunit.org/tagunit/core" prefix="tagunit" %>
<%@ taglib prefix="x" uri="/WEB-INF/tlds/myTags.tld" %>
<tagunit:assertEquals name="Simple filter test">
  <tagunit:actualResult>
```

```
    <x:emailAddressFilter>simon.brown@somedomain.com</x:emailAddressFilter>
  </tagunit:actualResult>
  <tagunit:expectedResult>simon.brown@...</tagunit:expectedResult>
</tagunit:assertEquals>
```

Unlike JUnit and Cactus, the tests for TagUnit are written as JSPs, with the assertions written using TagUnit-specific custom tags.

TagUnit tests are wrapped up as a WAR file and therefore can be deployed in any compatible Java EE container. As an additional benefit, this makes it easy to deploy the tests onto another server, which makes cross-vendor testing very easy, particularly when each test can implement aspects of the tag life cycle and pool in slightly different ways. Although Cactus provides a much richer framework for testing server-side components, TagUnit is ideally suited to testing custom tags, especially custom tags that will be reused by other people.

### Other Unit Testing Tools

The tools that we've mentioned in this chapter are just a sample of the wide variety of testing tools available. For more information on the tools available to unit test web applications, take a look at the JUnit web extensions page at `http://www.junit.org/news/extension/web/index.htm`.

Now that we've covered how to perform unit testing with respect to web applications, let's now switch gears and look at functional testing.

## Functional/Acceptance Testing Web Applications

The other key method to test web applications is **functional testing**. In contrast to unit testing, functional testing treats the application as a black box (you can't see inside it) and tests that the outputs are correct given a set of inputs. For example, this might include the request to add an item to your shopping cart in an online store. Here you're not interested in how the request works—you just want to know that it does work and that the desired result is achieved.

Functional testing is often broken down into two categories, with the tests being written by two types of people. The first category is written by developers in addition to the unit tests that they might write for the classes and components that they're writing. Unit testing classes in isolation is undoubtedly useful, but at times developers want to run some functional tests that span multiple classes and components. Typically, these tests are written with the internal flows of the application in mind and really help back up the unit tests in proving that the software works for a given set of inputs. The second category contains functional tests that are written by dedicated testing teams. Their responsibilities range from system testing (in which the end-to-end flows throughout the system are exercised) to writing tests that will be used to formally state that the functionality meets the requirements and will be accepted by the project sponsor or end users.

One of the problems associated with acceptance is that traditionally acceptance testing, sometimes called user acceptance testing, was performed manually following a textual script. Although this works and it's widely used, these manual tests must be reexecuted whenever a new version of the software is released for whatever reason. Although tools do exist that allow testers to capture the process of manually testing an application for automatic playback, many of these tools can be expensive and cumbersome to use. On the other hand, many open-source options are now available, although these tend to be oriented toward the developer community and require tests to be written with programming languages, scripting languages, or XML. This is an area of flux at the moment and it's worth bearing in mind your testing audience before you make a definitive tools selection. Let's see how functional level testing can be automated with another widely used open-source framework: HttpUnit.

## HttpUnit

HttpUnit (http://www.httpunit.org) is another extension to JUnit, but it's different from the others that we've discussed because it allows you to write tests at a slightly different level. Whereas you can use tools such as JUnit and Cactus to test that individual classes and components work correctly, HttpUnit is a framework that you can use to test the functionality provided by a web application. As you've seen, unit testing classes is easy, but how do you test the functionality of a web application?

The answer lies in the tools that HttpUnit gives you. The framework provides a collection of classes that allows you to simulate the process of a user using a web browser to connect to and use a website. Under the covers, it does this by making HTTP requests to the website, passing information that the user would typically type in manually. As far as the functionality available to you through the framework, HttpUnit allows you to access individual web pages and perform assertions that the web page contains certain elements. For example, if you're testing an online store, you might want to test that all pages contain the current total of your shopping cart. In addition to these basic features, HttpUnit provides a way to look for HTML forms on a page and programmatically fill out those forms to be sent back to the server, where the response can then be checked. Again, for an online store, you might want to test that a user can add an item to his cart and that the subsequent page shows the user the updated cart state.

HttpUnit provides a way to use Java code to programmatically test the functionality provided by a website, and the real benefit of this is that these tests can be rerun to regression test the web application when new versions are available. In fact, because HttpUnit uses the HTTP protocol, it can be used to test any other sort of HTML-based web application, including those written with Active Server Pages (ASP), Perl, PHP, and so on.

## Other Functional Testing Tools

To round off your look at functional testing tools, a couple of other frameworks are worth a quick mention. The first of these is jWebUnit (http://jwebunit.sourceforge.net), which is really an extension of HttpUnit. The team behind jWebUnit was using HttpUnit on a project and realized that many of the tests contained duplicate code to set up request objects and perform assertions. Therefore, the team built a collection of wrapper classes for HttpUnit that simplified the API for its purposes. This has been refined over time and released into the open-source community. Some people like the control that HttpUnit gives them, whereas others prefer the simpler interface provided by jWebUnit. At the end of the day, it's all up to personal preference.

The other framework worth mentioning is called Jameleon (http://jameleon. sourceforge.net). This framework provides a way to functional test an application, but from the perspective of the features that the application provides. Jameleon differs from HttpUnit and jWebUnit in that it breaks out testing of the features from the actual test cases. A feature can be something as fine-grained as logging in, and it might be something that has to happen before every test. With Jameleon, you write the feature tests separately and then script them together into a reusable test case. These test cases can then be made data-driven by associating them with a particular dataset at runtime, which provides an easy way of running specific tests on specific environments. Jameleon itself is not specifically designed to test web applications; instead, it has a plug-in architecture in which testing code can be plugged in and executed. At the time of this writing, Jameleon provides a plug-in for HttpUnit/jWebUnit; hence it can be used to functional test web applications. This is a great idea and is something that has typically been found only in commercial testing tools. As always, the open-source testing space is worth keeping an eye on as new tools and enhancements are released on a regular basis.

Now that we've presented the various ways that web applications can be tested, let's look at how the design can influence the ability to test web applications.

# Designing Web Applications for Testing

Although unit testing individual classes is straightforward, as we've hinted at, sometimes unit testing classes within web applications can be tricky. This is particularly true when the various flavors of business and presentation logic have all been mixed up with components such as servlets that need to be executed within a web server. To solve such problems, we must again turn to architecture and design.

## Architectural Layering

Although we haven't explicitly talked about architectural layering, we have talked about the MVC architecture and how it helps achieve a separation of concerns between the various components. For example, the controller is the overall component responsible for managing requests, the model represents the domain information being operated upon, and the views present information back to the user. Compare this with the Model 1 architecture, in which all of these responsibilities are embedded in a single component, and you can start to see how separating these responsibilities can lead to easier testing.

We've already said that the hardest part of unit testing web applications is testing those components that are reliant on the context of a Java EE web server, and one of the things that you can do to aid testing is to try to make these components as small and lightweight as possible. By making these components lightweight wrappers for functionality that's encapsulated within Java classes, you give yourself a much better chance of being able to unit test the application. For example, cast your mind back to the MVC architecture and, specifically, to the command and controller strategy in which the functionality to service incoming requests was split among individual command objects. Because each of these is just a stand-alone Java class, you can now use the same techniques for unit testing as you do with ordinary Java classes—you can use JUnit to create new instances and call methods on those instances.

One of the keys to being able to unit test web applications is to ensure that each of your classes has a well-defined role. In the MVC architecture, this involves breaking classes into one of the main categories of components: controller/action, model, and view/presentation. Furthermore, and regardless of whether or not you adopt an MVC architecture, certain types of classes are much easier to test than others. We've already alluded to this, but to recap, classes that can stand on their own are generally much easier to test—within a Java EE web application, this usually means classes that represent business/domain objects and those classes that encapsulate some level of business logic and processing.

On the projects that we've worked on, testing web-application components has always been one of the areas that has come up repeatedly as being difficult. At the end of the day, breaking components into distinct architectural layers really does improve your ability to test those components. In addition, it's often too much effort to try to achieve complete test coverage of all the components within your web application. If you've broken out the majority of the functionality into classes that can stand alone from the web server environment, testing these should provide a satisfactory level of confidence in the code that you're producing. The whole point of testing is to provide you with a certain level of confidence that the code will perform as expected rather than striving to achieve complete coverage.

## A Testing Strategy

When you're writing regular Java code (not Java EE related), a testing tool such as JUnit generally suits most of your needs. However, for Java EE applications, it isn't feasible to get by with just a single tool. For example, with JUnit and Cactus, it's possible to test only stand-alone classes. With TagUnit, it's possible to test only custom tags. With HttpUnit, you can test only the end-to-end functionality provided by the application. Because each of these tools provides a different angle on testing the software, you can't get away with using only one tool. The purpose of testing is to provide confidence that the software works, and this is just not possible with a single tool.

Testing can be performed at many layers, and this is also true of web-application testing. At the very bottom, you have the unit tests that can be performed with tools such as JUnit and Cactus. Moving up from this, you have slightly larger groups of interacting classes, or components. These can also be tested with JUnit and Cactus, although other tools such as TagUnit start to provide benefits. Moving further up, you start to test more functionality of the system, and this is where functional testing tools come into play. Testing one of these layers is great, but it doesn't guarantee that the system as a whole will work. After all, unit tests tend to be much more detailed and much more focused on robustness. Functional tests, on the other hand, tend to be more geared toward checking that the functionality works as expected. You should view all of these testing tools as complementary, and it's up to you to pick the ones that give you the confidence that your software works.

## Compatibility Testing Web Applications

As an additional level of testing, many developers test their applications for compatibility between servers. By writing to the Java EE platform, you are (at least in theory) guaranteed that your application will work on any other compliant or compatible Java EE implementation. For many people, this just isn't an issue because they'll run their applications on only a single type of Java EE server. For others, particularly those building products (regardless of whether those products are commercial or open source), testing compatibility can be essential to the success of their web applications.

A few years ago, Java EE compatibility was still very much something that was being worked on by the server vendors. This was especially true when the specifications were still maturing. Fortunately, this situation has improved considerably and now most web applications will run as is on any Java EE-compatible server. However, if you're building products, then there's still some mileage in testing that your web application does function as expected on some of the various implementations available. For example, small bugs in one vendor's implementation may stop your application from working completely. Other times, you may have been unknowingly relying on a specific implementation feature or just the way that a specification point has been implemented. As an example, the Tomcat team has recently changed some of the default security settings related to the way that servlets could be called directly through the servlet dispatcher. When upgrading to a newer version of Tomcat, many developers found that their web applications no longer worked because they had used this method of calling servlets within their JSP pages.

We were involved on a project in which we were responsible for the web tier of an enterprise application for a large investment bank. The licenses for the application server our team was using, BEA WebLogic, hadn't yet arrived, so we started building the web tier with Tomcat. When the licenses finally did arrive, we literally had to port some of the code between the servers because of incompatibilities in how the JSP/Servlet specifications had been implemented between the vendors. Thankfully, the implementations have matured a great deal and most code can be run as is on different Java EE servers.

The moral of the story is that it's beneficial to run your web applications on other Java EE–compatible servers, even if you aren't planning to use one from another vendor. For anybody building commercial products based on Java EE, Sun has a verification program consisting of a compatibility-testing suite that can test whether your application makes correct and standard use of the APIs provided by the Java EE specification. See `http://java.sun.com/j2ee/verified/avk_enterprise.html` for more details.

# Security

Although we covered security in Chapter 12, there are some security best practices worth recapping within the context of this chapter about web-application design and best practices.

## Using the Standard Security Model

Try to use the standard security model if possible. Many web applications use their own custom security model for authentication and authorization. Although this is sometimes necessary, perhaps because the standard model doesn't meet your requirements, many web applications don't even integrate with the standard security model. Apart from using the available technology, there are many reasons for using the standard security model.

The first of these reasons is related to how secure your web application is. Without the standard security model, every JSP page, servlet, and resource underneath your web application root is effectively public. When using bespoke frameworks, generally developers must insert scriptlet code into the top of their JSP pages that determines whether the request should be allowed or denied, perhaps by using the value of a session variable that indicates whether the user has logged in. But what happens if this code is omitted and users who aren't logged in are able to access those resources?

One of the projects that we provided some consultancy for implemented their own security model. Although the authorization of resources was complex, the actual authentication of users was nothing unusual. Rather than adopting the standard model, a bespoke solution was implemented for both authentication and authorization throughout the entire system. The system itself was built mostly around an MVC architecture, although parts were simply page centric. Therefore, and to ensure security, a custom tag was built to be inserted at the top of every page in order to determine whether the current user should be able to see the contents of the page. Although this works, and as we found by reviewing the application, there were pages where this custom tag hadn't been inserted and pages were left unsecured. Probably the worst of these was a page that allowed anybody to get a report of all the data within the system. Had the standard security model been used, every single JSP page could have easily been restricted to only authenticated users.

Not only does using the standard security model simplify the design of web applications, but it also really does provide an additional level of confidence in the security of your web applications.

## Securing View Components

Even if your web application doesn't require security in the sense of users logging in and authenticating themselves, there's still a need for ensuring that your application is secure and will work only as expected. For example, take an MVC-based web application. Typically, a request is serviced by the controller component, which in turn gets forwarded to a view component for presenting information back to the user. If the view components were simple JSP pages, what would happen if the user found out the name and location of that JSP page and tried to access it directly? In many cases, they would probably get a page containing no information or a nasty stack trace. Perhaps your JSP pages contain code that has other side effects on the system. If you're authenticating users, perhaps they'll be able to see somebody else's information because their request hasn't gone through the controller.

To get around this potential problem, one solution is to ensure that the view components (the JSP pages) are subjected to the standard security model. For example, if all the view components are placed within a directory called `view-components`, you can place the following code in the `web.xml` file to disallow all direct access:

```
<security-constraint>
    <web-resource-collection>
      <web-resource-name>No direct access</web-resource-name>
      <url-pattern>/view-components/*</url-pattern>
    </web-resource-collection>
    <auth-constraint>
      <role-name>some-nonexistent-role</role-name>
    </auth-constraint>
</security-constraint>
```

This code specifies that anything under that directory can be accessed only by users in the specified role. Therefore, if you don't map that role to any users, nobody can directly access the pages. Of course, the controller component can still forward to the JSP pages because it isn't subject to the same rules. Similarly, another option is to place all view components underneath the `WEB-INF` directory of your web application, which by definition doesn't have direct access. Either way, securing your view components can make your web application more secure and more resilient.

# Troubleshooting

A number of common problems can occur in JSP- and servlet-based applications. In this section, we'll review some of these problems and provide quick pointers to help you debug them.

## The Servlet Engine Runs Out of Memory

If the servlet engine or application server stops responding to requests and you find `OutOfMemoryError` messages in the log files, chances are that your application has consumed all available memory. This could be the result of a memory leak in the application code. Perhaps the application is holding references to a large number of objects and thus preventing them from being garbage collected. If this is the case, you'll need to resort to careful code reviews to understand where the problem is occurring. Some application servers provide a workaround for this problem: a feature called **server recycling**, whereby idle servlet engines are periodically restarted. Restarting a JVM is a sure way to clean up leaked objects.

Even if there isn't a memory leak in the code, it's still possible to run out of memory. Typically, a session object is created for each concurrent user of a JSP application. Session objects consume memory, and memory is a limited resource. Therefore, too many concurrent users can cause the servlet engine to run out of memory. When the server runs out of memory, it will need to be restarted. One way to address this problem is to configure the servlet engine for a shorter timeout period. Setting a shorter session timeout usually results in fewer concurrent sessions and lessens the chances of running out of memory. Other solutions to this problem are as follows:

- Add more memory so that each server can support more users.

- Add more application server instances to handle a larger total number of users.

- Keep the number and size of objects stored in the session to a minimum.

In addition to these solutions, if you have a completely stateless application, you can tell the container not to use sessions with the following JSP page directive and save yourself a great deal of memory:

```
<%@ page session="false" %>
```

The memory debugging tools built into commercial performance-tuning products such as Borland's Optimizeit (`http://www.borland.com/optimizeit`) and Quest Software's JProbe (`http://www.quest.com/jprobe/`) can be helpful in tracking down memory leaks, although such tools are moderately expensive. When you're running an application under one of these tools, you can pause the application and examine memory usage statistics for each class of object in memory, list methods responsible for largest number of object allocations, and determine where the objects currently in memory were allocated.

## The Database Connections Are Exhausted

If an application starts behaving strangely, emitting `database connections exhausted` or `cannot obtain database connection` errors, then it has consumed all database connections. The cause may be a database connection leak, meaning that database connections aren't being properly released after use. If the application is using database connection pooling, you may be able to turn on features of the connection pool so that you can locate the misbehaving code that's taking but not giving back connections. Failing this, careful code reviews and log files are probably the only options.

Even if an application isn't leaking database connections, it can still exhaust your connections. When using database connection pooling, you might be able to solve this problem by simply configuring the database connection pool to allow a larger number of maximum connections. If that doesn't work, talk to a database administrator about increasing the number of database connections allowed on the database server.

## The Servlet Engine Stops Responding

If the servlet engine or application server stops responding to HTTP requests and there are no instances of `OutOfMemoryError` messages in the log files, there are two other possible causes of this problem:

- There's a **thread deadlock**. Deadlock occurs in a multithreaded JSP when two or more threads can't continue because each is waiting on a lock held by the other.

- There's an **infinite loop** in application code. An infinite loop condition occurs when a thread becomes trapped in an improperly programmed `for`, `while`, or `do` loop.

Locating the exact location of the cause of the problem can be difficult. Usually, careful code reviews and examination of log files are the only options. This is one situation in which detailed debug logs can be very helpful.

## You Get a ClassCastException

Servlet engines use special class loaders to isolate web applications from each other and from the classes used internally by the servlet engine itself. These class loaders can cause problems that often appear to be incomprehensible. For example, you might get a `ClassCastException` that complains that you have incompatible versions of the same class. Often, these types of problems are caused when JARs that conflict with the JARs provided by the servlet engine are placed into the application's `WEB-INF\lib` directory, although in theory the class-loading mechanism should take care of this for you. Alternatively, redeploying your applications can also make this problem occur. Behind the scenes, although the web application reloads all of the classes, if you have references to objects residing in the session (and use the same browser instance), when the JSP container tries to cast these existing objects with the old class definition into the new definition, it will fail, throwing a `ClassCastException`. Simply restarting the container will solve the majority of such problems.

## The Page Runs Too Slowly

If a JSP page or a servlet is running too slowly, and the performance techniques described in this chapter haven't uncovered the cause of the problem, then try a **profiler**. A profiler will produce a report on the amount of time spent in each method of your application, allowing you to narrow your search for the cause of the performance problem. The commercial performance-tuning tools that we discussed earlier, Optimizeit and JProbe, include profilers. Also, under development at the time of this writing is a profiling plug-in called the Eclipse Profiler, for the Eclipse IDE. You can follow the progress of this project at `http://eclipsecolorer.sourceforge.net/index_profiler.html`.

# Debugging

Debugging is often the most difficult and frustrating aspect of programming. JSP- and servlet-based applications are often rather complex and therefore especially difficult to debug. Why are JSP applications so complex? Here are a few reasons:

- **JSP applications are distributed:** When deployed in a production environment, a JSP application can involve multiple distributed systems, including load-balancing routers, web servers, application servers, databases, and other back-end systems.

- **JSP applications include a mixture of different programming languages:** JSP applications can include HTML, JavaScript, Java code, SQL, XML, and other programming and markup languages. When you read a JSP page, it's often difficult to follow which parts of the page are executed on the server and which are executed on the client.

- **JSP applications run in a multithreaded environment:** JSP applications need to be thread-safe to achieve the best performance. Threading is a complex and confusing topic for many programmers, and threading problems can be difficult to debug.

- **JSP applications include many components:** A JSP application's technology stack typically includes a servlet engine, a JSP compiler, an MVC framework, a persistence framework, a JDBC driver, a database, and other back-end systems.

Learning how to solve problems in complex, distributed, and multithreaded programs takes time and often requires a lot of deep thought, so be prepared to think. If a particularly difficult problem arises, get some sleep and then think some more. Explain the problem to another, more experienced programmer. If no one is available, explain it to that plastic dinosaur sitting on top of your monitor. Often, simply explaining a problem in detail can spark the thought that leads to a solution.

If you can figure out how to explain your problem in simple terms, or you can isolate the problem in a simple code example, you might be able to get some help from a newsgroup, mailing list, or other online forum. Before you post a message to one of these forums, you should read the previous postings in the forum archive to see whether your problem or question has been asked before. Using a search engine such as Google may also be helpful for some problems.

# Logging

Logging is a best practice for any JSP application and is supported by the servlet API, application servers, and a wide variety of logging tools. There are many ways to perform logging, from using simple `System.out.println()` statements to using a full-featured logging API.

## Logging with the Servlet API

The Servlet API includes logging methods in the `javax.servlet.ServletContext` interface. The `ServletContext` interface's `log()` methods make it easy to write log messages and exception stack traces to your application server's logging system. The advantages of using the servlet API's built-in logging methods are as follows:

- Log messages are automatically prefixed with a timestamp string and written to log files. This means that you can access them after they scroll off the console and after the server is shut down.

- The application server manages log files and ensures that they never grow too big and consume all the disk space.

- Application servers generally provide an administration program so that you can easily view and search log files even if they're written to multiple remote servers.

All of this sounds good but, in fact, the servlet API provides only minimal support for logging. You can log a string message and you can log an exception. However, if you want to enable and disable logging, you need to add configuration properties and implement the conditional logic by adding a parameter to the web.xml file, for example. However, implementing your own ad hoc logging as shown previously isn't the best approach. There are many advantages to be had from instead using a full-featured logging system such as log4j or the Java logging API.

## Full-Featured Logging Systems

A full-featured logging system, such as the open-source log4j framework (http://logging. apache.org/log4j/docs/), offers several advantages over using System.out.println() calls or using the logging methods in the Servlet API:

- **Control over logging levels:** You can log messages at different severity levels. For example, log4j supports log levels of DEBUG, INFO, WARN, ERROR, and FATAL (listed in order of increasing severity). When you set a log level, the system will output messages for that log level and for all log levels above that. So, for example, the INFO-level logging will include messages at the INFO, WARN, ERROR, and FATAL levels. By simply changing a configuration parameter in the log4j properties file, you can enable DEBUG-level logging to help you debug a problem. When you've found and fixed the problem, you can set the log level back to ERROR so that only ERROR and FATAL log messages are recorded in the logs.

- **Multiple loggers:** You can use different logical loggers in different parts of your application. For example, you might use one logger named com.mydomain.ui in the presentation tier and another logger named com.mydomain.db in the data-access tier. This allows you to control the log level in only the part of the application that's experiencing a bug.

- **Multiple log destinations:** You can configure logging systems to send log messages to files, operating system logs, databases, message queues, remote systems via TCP/IP, and other destinations. This can be helpful in production in which an application may be running in a heterogeneous and distributed environment.

- **Better management of log files:** Log files can grow to large sizes very quickly, especially when DEBUG-level logging is enabled. You can configure a logging system to start a new log when the current log file grows too large. You can configure the logging system to delete or archive old log files so that your disk space isn't consumed.

- **Control over log formatting:** You can configure the format of the log messages produced by the logging system to suit specific needs.

Java now includes its own logging API under the `java.util.logging` package. This new logging API is a welcome addition to Java and is similar to the log4j API in many ways, but it isn't as powerful and flexible as log4j. For example, log4j can direct log messages to Unix system logs, the Microsoft Windows event log, Java Message Service (JMS) message queues, and e-mail. The Java logging API can log only to the console, files, and sockets. As in many aspects of development, people become attached to their favorite logging framework and this is often a problem when deciding which one to use. Also, there are some technical reasons for choosing one over another. Perhaps you need the functionality available in a specific API, or perhaps your Java EE server ships with log4j. Either way, to ensure that you retain the ability to freely switch between the two, Jakarta Commons Logging provides a solution.

### Jakarta Commons Logging

Jakarta Commons Logging (JCL, at `http://jakarta.apache.org/commons/logging/`) is a thin wrapper around both log4j and J2SE 1.4 logging, with the sole purpose of providing a common interface between the two. With the Commons Logging JAR file in your CLASSPATH, the framework will automatically locate either of the two logging frameworks and use whichever one it finds in your CLASSPATH. It will first look for log4j and, if it doesn't find log4j, it will check whether J2SE 1.4 logging is available. This is a simple trick, but it really works well. If you need to use log4j in your application, just make sure it's in the CLASSPATH.

Regardless of which logging framework you use, actually using JCL is easy, as demonstrated by the following code snippet:

```
Log log = LogFactory.getLog(MyClass.class);
```

Following this, and with the log initialized, you can write messages at the various levels with the following method calls:

```
log.fatal("Here is some useful information!");
log.error("Here is some useful information!");
log.warn("Here is some useful information!");
log.info("Here is some useful information!");
log.debug("Here is some useful information!");
log.trace("Here is some useful information!");
```

Like the framework that it ultimately delegates to, JCL has various levels of severity that map to those used by the underlying logging framework. If you need more control, perhaps JCL isn't for you. For many people, the sacrifice in control can easily be negated by the simplicity that JCL provides.

Jakarta Commons Logging has worked well on the projects we've used it on, and this is especially true for our open-source work. After all, you can never tell which logging library your users might prefer, or perhaps their Java EE server ships with log4j or isn't supported on J2SE 1.4. JCL gives you that extra degree of flexibility.

# General Guidelines

To wrap up this chapter, you'll look at some general guidelines for building web applications. Although these guidelines aren't specifically related to design, they can be just as important for building a successful website.

# Error Reporting

One of the things that we as developers like to see when errors happen are stack traces. After all, they're useful for tracking down the source and cause of a problem. Users, on the other hand, probably don't want to see them; they certainly don't add anything to the user experience.

Seeing stack traces or other forms of technical error messages on websites tends to put me off from returning to that site. For example, one particular e-commerce site that I visit regularly presents me with messages about how some Visual Basic component can't connect to their database. Though I don't confess to know anything about Visual Basic, seeing such messages does make me think twice about ordering from that site.

Unfortunately, even with the most tested of websites, errors will happen and therefore the JSP specification provides JSP error pages. You already saw these in Chapter 2 and, to recap, they're just pages that get forwarded to when an uncaught exception is encountered by the container. Setting your web application up to use these is a great way to ensure that you have a standard way to handle errors and that the user doesn't end up seeing a nasty stack trace in the process.

On a related note, another recommendation is to use a consistent exception-handling strategy and make sure that you handle and log all exceptions. This will help you to understand what went wrong and where it went wrong when an error occurs. Use the exception-handling facilities built into JSP where appropriate—they're there to help you. If you're using an MVC framework such as Struts, take advantage of its exception-handling facilities as well.

# I18n and l10n

Internationalization (I18n) and localization (l10n) are built into the Java platform, and there's nothing stopping you from using them within web applications, particularly if you intend to reach an international audience. Typically, and especially with public websites, a lot of effort is put into making the site both function correctly and look good. However, often little work is put into maximizing the appeal for international audiences. After all, the Internet is a global network and you can never tell exactly who will be using your site.

Putting in such features doesn't have to be a massive job, with tools such as JSTL supporting most of the functionality required to internationalize and localize a web application. For example, this can range from simply localizing dates and times to providing internationalized text and/or content. The overriding guideline here is to think about your audience.

# Adopting New Technologies and Standards

The Web has changed a great deal over the past few years, and some web applications have kept up with the changes better than others. Although there's an argument for not always adopting the latest and greatest technologies, there's a fine line between adopting those features that make most sense and never adopting at all. With technologies changing on almost a monthly basis, this provides an opportunity to try out new technologies and standards on every new web application that you work on. Most web developers have now taken up standards such as cascading style sheets (CSS), but you won't find many sites (relatively speaking) that use newer standards such as XHTML. This does have much to do with the expense of keeping existing sites up-to-date, but when you start a new web application, take a look around to see what's happening within the industry and use this to figure out if there are any new technologies or standards that can help you achieve your goals.

One of the projects that we worked on involved helping a team inside a client company build a web application for internal use. The system itself was replacing a "green screen" application, and this was the first time that the team had used Java, let alone built web applications. Although the first prototype of the system was functional, the user interface closely resembled that found on the original mainframe application. After just a day or so playing with the view components in conjunction with the team, we came up with something that matched the company's corporate image and was much closer to the sort of web applications that you find on the Internet. We showed them CSS and guided them through how some of the most popular websites on the Internet work. The result? Not only did the application look and feel much better, but also the business sponsors and users of the system suddenly became much more enthusiastic about the project. It's amazing what a little HTML and CSS can do!

To sum up, let your previous experiences of building web applications help you, but don't let them limit you.

## Adopting Existing Components

The final guideline worth talking about is the use of third-party components, particularly those that are open source. In the past couple of years, the open-source community has really moved on in terms of adoption and the sheer number of projects that are currently being undertaken. A quick look at websites such as the Jakarta Project (`http://jakarta.apache.org`), SourceForge (`http://sourceforge.net`), and java.net (`http://java.net`) confirms this. With project budgets and timescales decreasing, there's an opportunity here to take much of what has been built and use it in your own projects.

As I mentioned earlier in the chapter, I decided to build a blogging system implemented as a Java-based web application. In building the application, I used several open-source projects, including Jakarta Commons Logging and log4j for logging, Jakarta Commons FileUpload for uploading files to the website, Apache XML-RPC for accessing web services, and Lucene to provide a search facility for users. Implementing all these features myself would have taken an incredibly long time. As it was, each of these open-source tools took a maximum of a few hours to integrate, meaning that I could concentrate on the real purpose of the web application.

Let's take a quick look at some popular open-source tools currently available.

### Jakarta Commons

Jakarta Commons (`http://jakarta.apache.org/commons/`) is an umbrella project for all sorts of common functionality that developers build over and over again. You've already seen one component (Jakarta Commons Logging). Others include a servlet-based file upload component, an object pool implementation, an expression language, JavaBean utilities, and much, much more. This is an incredibly useful project, and new components and features are being added to it all the time.

### Lucene

Lucene (`http://lucene.apache.org/`) is an open-source implementation of a complete search engine. It's held in high regard throughout the Java open-source community because it's so robust, full-featured, and fast. The API is easy to pick up, and in just a few lines of code you can create an index for your data. Similarly, just a few lines are required to actually search that index. If you're looking to integrate a search facility on your website, look no further than Lucene.

# Summary

This chapter covered several topics related to web-application design and best practices, bringing together many of the topics you explored in the previous chapters. First, we discussed why design is important and we recapped the two major architectures for building web applications: page-centric (Model 1) and Model-View-Controller (Model 2). Then we showed how design patterns can help you design your application and described how some of the Java EE patterns can be used to build web applications based on the MVC architecture. These patterns included the following:

- Front controller

- View

- View Helper

- Service to Worker

- Filter

We then moved on to discuss some third-party frameworks such as Struts, WebWork, and Velocity.

After this, we showed how testing is an important part of web-application development and introduced unit testing and functional (or acceptance) testing. Automated testing has now really taken off with regard to web applications, and to illustrate this we discussed some of the testing tools that are now available. We then related testing back to the design aspects we presented earlier in the chapter by showing how the design of a web application can affect the ability to test it.

Finally, we covered some implementation topics, including logging, troubleshooting, and some general guidelines for building web applications.

# Using Struts, XDoclet, and Other Tools

**Y**ou can see from the previous chapters that there are many options for building a web application. If you develop a web application from scratch, you'll be a stronger programmer for it, but it'll (most likely) be a long and laborious process. In this chapter, we'll describe the tools to use for web development, and how to use them in developing this chapter's résumé-building application. By sharing our experiences and knowledge, hopefully you won't have to endure the same painful memorize-learn-develop progression that we've been through. To prepare you for the vast array of subjects in this chapter, let's first take a look at the various open-source tools and technologies that we'll be covering:

- **Ant**: A Java-based build tool for rapid compiling, deploying, and testing Java-based applications.

- **XDoclet**: A code-generation engine for creating Java classes and deployment descriptors. It requires the user to add @tags to Javadoc statements and produces files via Ant.

- **Struts**: A web application framework using a servlet-based Model-View-Controller (MVC) architecture.

- **Validator**: A validation framework integrated with Struts. Supports both client (JavaScript) and server-side validation.

- **Tiles**: A JSP-based templating framework integrated with Struts.

- **JUnit**: A Java-based regression-testing framework.

- **Cactus**: A Java-based testing framework for testing web applications.

- **StrutsTestCase**: An extension of Cactus for testing Struts's Action classes.

You were introduced to Struts in the previous chapter, and you might well have seen references to it scattered throughout the whole book. This is because since version 1.0 was released in June of 2001, it has gained wide acceptance and praise in the Java community. At the time of this writing, Struts is at version 1.2.7 and going strong.

The big advantage of using Struts to underpin your web applications is that it provides a set of ready-made services, and encourages you to structure your applications according to published standards and proven design patterns, which will make your applications highly extensible, flexible, and maintainable.

However, in this chapter we aren't going to teach you Struts from scratch: There are a lot of good books out there that teach you the basics of using Struts from scratch in far more depth than we could in one chapter! If you want a great Struts kickstart tutorial for free (and who doesn't want something great for free?!), check out the resources on Ted Husted's Struts website (`http://husted.com/struts/`).

Instead, in this chapter, we're going to assume that you have a basic understanding of how to use Struts, and focus upon enhancing Struts-based development through the use of third-party tools (including Ant, XDoclet, Validator, Tiles, StrutsGen, Struts Menu, Struts Console, Easy Struts, Hibernate, and StrutsTestCase). The idea is to show you how to use these tools to create your Struts-based applications more quickly, easily, and cost effectively. To do this, you'll use them to create an example application that can build and view résumés.

---

**■Note**  We don't have space to cover it here, but another third-party tool that you might find useful for Struts development is Struts Builder, a Java Swing-based development environment to assist in the rapid creation of Struts-based Web applications. It can be found at `http://sourceforge.net/projects/rivernorth/`.

---

Through the course of the chapter, you'll learn how XDoclet can generate the `web.xml` deployment descriptor and the `struts-config.xml` file. We'll also discuss the IDE tools for Struts, exception handling, built-in actions, modules, DynaFormBeans, and Struts tags (including the JSTL and JSP 2.1). We'll be using JSP pages for a view layer, because that is what we're familiar with (and this book is about JSP after all!). We'll also touch on good practices using XHTML and cascading style sheets (CSS).

However, let's start with a lightning-quick refresher on the Struts architecture.

# Struts Refresher

A **web framework** provides a set of services that can be used and reused across many different web applications. Struts is an open-source web framework that is based upon the tried-and-trusted MVC design pattern. Its core is made up of Java servlets, JavaBeans, resource bundles, XML, and tag libraries.

Struts provides the following services:

- A controller servlet

- Ready-made tag libraries

- A framework for internationalizing messages

- A generic error and exception-handling mechanism

- XML parsing

- File upload and logging utilities

Craig McClanahan originally wrote the Struts framework, mostly while on his Memorial Day vacation in 2000! The framework was subsequently donated by Craig to the Apache Software Foundation. The fact that it was mostly written in one weekend should suggest to you that it's a very simple framework. In our experience, not only is it simple, but it's also easy to work with once you get to know it.

---

**■Note**  If you'd like to read more about the web application frameworks, one of the best places to start is Craig McClanahan's blog at `http://blogs.sun.com/roller/page/craigmcc`.

---

You should also note that anything that can be done with JSP pages and servlets can still be done with Struts. So you can still write regular servlets that extend `HttpServlet` in your application or have JSP pages with whatever embedded scriplet code you want.

On the other hand, Struts does try to encourage certain better practices for coding web applications, and it does make it easier to write and deploy them. For instance, when using Struts, you don't need to write a whole slew of `request.getParameter()` calls in your servlet to get all your form's values. Struts does this for you with an `ActionForm`, which handles the population and grabbing of an HTML form's values.

## Struts Architecture

So how do these `ActionForms` fit into the overall Struts architecture? Figure 15-1 shows a schematic of a simple Struts application in general.

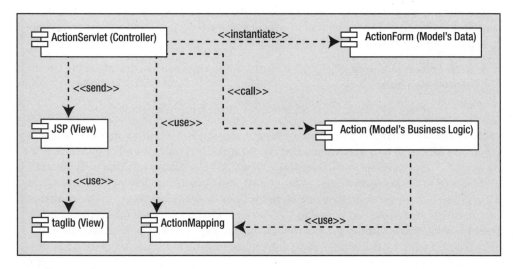

**Figure 15-1.** *This UML view of a Struts application shows how the primary components fit together.*

Let's quickly review the features of this diagram.

First, you can see that we've assumed that you're using JSP pages for the view, and that these are built using the Struts tag libraries. Each client request for the application to perform a particular **action** is passed to the controller servlet (known as the `ActionServlet`), which dispatches to an `Action` class.

Each `Action` class extends `org.apache.struts.action.Action`. Every `Action` provides application-specific implementation by overriding the `execute()` method. The business logic needed to perform each action (process each type of request) is present in this corresponding `Action` class in the `execute()` method. The `Action` classes represent the controller logic for your application. They control which view elements are presented to the user. For instance, if an error occurs, the action is responsible for displaying errors on an input page.

There also may be a corresponding `ActionForm` JavaBean class for each action. The `ActionForm` class extends `org.apache.struts.action.ActionForm` and overrides the `validate()` method. Each `ActionForm` validates user data and can be used by the `Action` class to retrieve user data. The `ActionForm` classes represent the data of the model. The model is your data and the code you write to retrieve, save, or delete that data.

So, as you would expect from the controller, the `ActionServlet` provides the link between the view and the `Action` and `ActionForm` model components. To do this it needs to map the request data to the appropriate `Action` and `ActionForm` classes, depending upon the action requested by the client. The correct mapping of request actions to `Action` and `ActionForm` classes is defined in a configuration file, `struts-config.xml` (defined by `http://struts.apache.org/dtds/struts-config_1_2.dtd`). This file defines a set of `ActionMapping` objects that each represents a mapping of an action to the appropriate model classes. Therefore, the `ActionServlet` checks this `struts-config.xml` file to find the appropriate mapping for the current request.

Finally, if the `Action` class processes the request correctly, it indicates to the `ActionServlet` where the user should be forwarded to (usually a JSP page), by passing the `ActionServlet` an `ActionForward` object.

For more in-depth information about the architecture and implementation of the Struts framework, you can refer to the books and article referred to in the introduction to this chapter, or try pointing your browser to the following links:

- `http://jakarta.apache.org/struts/`: Struts homepage (you can download the latest version from here)

- `http://struts.apache.org/userGuide/index.html`: Struts user guide

As you may have spotted already, a big benefit of using Struts is that you implement many proven Java EE design patterns without even knowing it. The Front Controller (`ActionServlet` and `Action`), View Helper (`Action`), Composite View (the `Tiles` framework that we'll discuss later), Service to Worker (`ActionServlet` to actions), and Dispatcher View (`ActionForward`) are all integrated into the Struts framework. From the book *Core J2EE Patterns*,[1] these are all the patterns mentioned in the "Presentation Tier Patterns" chapter, save the Intercepting Filter. The only reason that Struts doesn't incorporate the Intercepting Filter pattern is to maintain backward compatibility with the Servlet 2.2 specification (and for Struts 2.0, there is talk of replacing the `ActionServlet` with a filter).

---

1. Alur, Deepak, John Crupi, and Dan Malks, *Core J2EE Patterns: Best Practices and Design Strategies.* (Upper Saddle River, NJ: Prentice Hall, 2001)

## Struts Tag Libraries

Most Struts applications seem to use JSP pages for the view component of the application. This is most likely due to the rich set of tag libraries that are available to Struts developers. These tags make several things much easier. If you've ever developed a pure JSP or servlet application, you'll probably remember using JavaBeans, the `<useBean>` tag, or perhaps even writing a lot of `request.getParameter()` calls. Struts basically eliminates this need and easily populates forms using its controller and tag library architecture. Of course, other architectures, such as Velocity and XML, can be used. But since we've never implemented them on a project to date, we don't feel it's fair to comment on their usefulness.

---

**■Note**  More information on using Velocity and XML or XSL for rendering your view can be found at `http://jakarta.apache.org/velocity/index.html`.

---

At the time of this writing (Struts 1.2.7), there are six available tag libraries within the Struts framework. These libraries are listed in Table 15-1, coupled with a high-level definition of their function.

**Table 15-1.** *Struts Tag Libraries*

| Library | Function |
| --- | --- |
| Bean tags | Tags to interact with beans in any given scope. Uses include creating and rendering an `ActionForm`'s properties. Also used for internationalization with the `<bean:message>` tag. Many of these tags can be replaced with JSTL tags. |
| HTML tags | Tags to render HTML elements on a form. Also contains helpful tags for rendering context-sensitive URLs. No replacement in the JSTL. Using regular HTML tags and JSP 2.1 syntax may be easier though. |
| Logic tags | Tags to perform logic such as checking for the presence of roles, iteration of bean lists, and forward or redirects. Many of these tags can be replaced with JSTL tags. |
| Nested tags | These tags extend the basic Struts tags mentioned earlier, but allow them to relate to each other in a nested nature. No equivalent in the JSTL. |
| Tiles tags | Tags to perform JSP "templating" of your site. Very useful for creating applications from small, reusable components. We'll discuss this in more depth a little later. |
| Struts EL tags | A subproject that was recently created to use the expression language evaluation engine from the JSTL. Some of the Struts tags weren't ported, as their functionality already exists in JSTL. |

The online API documentation for these tags is excellent (refer to the links available from the Struts User Guide page at `http://struts.apache.org/userGuide/index.html`). Also, recent books (as mentioned earlier) have done a terrific job of documenting these tags thoroughly.

One significant feature of the Struts HTML tags is the ability to render XHTML-compliant tags. This means that if you add `xhtml="true"` to the top of your JSP or Tiles layout definition, all HTML tags will be well-formed XML (that is, closed with an end tag or trailing `/>`). To demonstrate, you can simply add the following tag to the top of a page, and then view the source in your browser:

```
<html:html xhtml="true"/>
```

If you're using JSP includes or Tiles, you'll likely have to use the `<html:xhtml />` tag at the top of your included pages to force rendering XHTML syntax. At the time of this writing, only XHTML 1.0 Transitional was supported as a DOCTYPE. This is because the name attribute is still rendered on a form. XHTML 1.0 Strict requires that only an id attribute be present.

You can give your Struts tags any prefix you want when importing them into your JSP pages. Let's take, for instance, the contents of this file:

```
<%@ taglib uri="http://jakarta.apache.org/struts/tags-bean" prefix="bean" %>
<%@ taglib uri="http://jakarta.apache.org/struts/tags-html" prefix="html" %>
<%@ taglib uri="http://jakarta.apache.org/struts/tags-logic" prefix="logic" %>
<%@ taglib uri="http://jakarta.apache.org/struts/tags-tiles" prefix="tiles" %>
<%@ taglib uri="http://java.sun.com/jstl/core" prefix="c" %>
```

You may well have already seen this de facto standard for Struts prefixes. There's really no reason to use these verbose prefixes though, and you may rather use single-letter prefixes like JSTL if you prefer, such as these:

```
<%@ taglib uri="http://jakarta.apache.org/struts/tags-bean" prefix="b" %>
<%@ taglib uri="http://jakarta.apache.org/struts/tags-html" prefix="h" %>
<%@ taglib uri="http://jakarta.apache.org/struts/tags-logic" prefix="l" %>
<%@ taglib uri="http://jakarta.apache.org/struts/tags-tiles" prefix="t" %>
```

We've come to know and love a couple of additional tag libraries that make developing web UIs a bit easier. The first is the **display tag library** (http://displaytag.sourceforge.net/) originally authored by Ed Hill, which facilitates column sorting and pagination of data and integrates nicely with Struts. All you need to do is create a List (or other collection) of ActionForms and pass those to the tag in the JSP. This tag library also supports exporting your table's data to Excel, CSV, and XML.

The second is the **Struts menu tag library**. This component is a Menu framework that can be used to declare your menu items in an XML file. It integrates with Struts as a plug-in, supports popular menu styles (for instance, CoolMenus and standards-compliant DHTML menus), and allows for hiding and showing menus and items based on roles. Currently, it supports absolute and context-relative links, as well as Struts forwards.

Both of these tag libraries are used in this chapter's application.

To reference the Struts tag libraries, you simply drop the struts.jar file into /WEB-INF/lib and match the URIs as specified in each library's tag descriptor (TLD) file. We've seen that some servlet containers require you to declare the location of your TLD in web.xml. This is also necessary if your TLD file doesn't declare a URI to map to. In our example struts-resume application, struts-resume.tld and struts-menu.tld require entries in web.xml for this reason.

JSP 2.1 helps keep the code concise by allowing a JavaBean's properties to be accessed directly in a JSP page. Previously, you had to use `<c:out value="${beanName.propertyName}"/>`, while now, JSP 2.1 lets you simply use ${beanName.propertyName}. We expect JSTL-type syntax to be around for a while, as will the Struts tags, if only for backward compatibility.

# Overview of the Example struts-resume Application

The struts-resume application we're going to use as an example throughout this chapter uses Ant (an open-source build tool) and XDoclet (an open-source code generation too) as its core engines. They will generate a significant portion of the application for you as well as run any JUnit and Cactus tests you may have.

## Screen Flow and Requirements

Let's explore the project's initial requirements and screen flow. The nice thing about this application is that we're our own customers, because we want to develop a better way to publish our résumés online. However, we're not the only people who will use this application, and therefore we're going to include administrator and user roles.

We're looking for a web-based system that supports the traditional résumé sections: user contact information, summary, objective, skill categories, skills, education, training, and extracurricular activities. Although we haven't completed all of these sections at the time of this writing, this is what we want the application to grow into. We want to be able to render our résumés in XML and use XSL to produce HTML, text, Word's rich text format, and PDF files. To demonstrate roles and security, we'll make this a multiuser system in which there are administrators and users. Administrators can see and do everything, while users can only view or change their own résumé. Figure 15-2 shows the application flow.

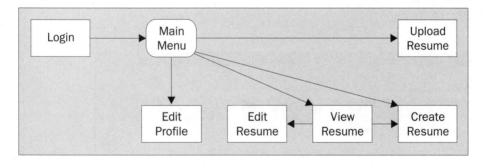

**Figure 15-2.** *From the main menu of the résumé application, you can upload, create, edit, and view a résumé.*

After users have signed in, they may choose to create, edit, view, and upload résumés. They can also edit their user details. Let's take a look at what each screen looks like by taking a quick walk through the application.

When you first access the application, you're presented with the Login page, as shown in Figure 15-3.

**Figure 15-3.** *The login page is the entry point to the résumé application.*

Filling in the appropriate username and password and clicking Login invokes the Main Menu page (Figure 15-4), the jumping-off point for the other pages.

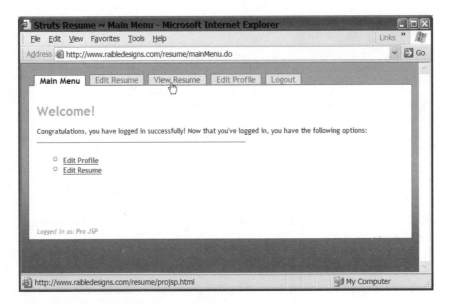

**Figure 15-4.** *The main menu page provides access to the functions of the application.*

If you click the View Resume link, you'll see the View Resumes page, shown in Figure 15-5.

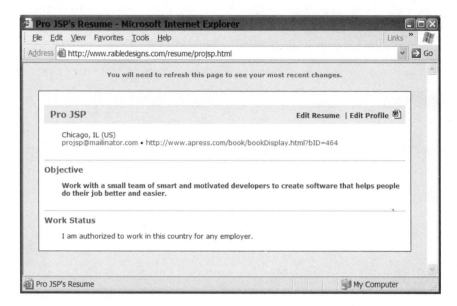

**Figure 15-5.** *The View Resumes page shows the user's résumé.*

This page allows you to view your résumé. This page has links for editing your résumé or editing your profile. Try clicking the Edit Resume link, and you'll see the page shown in Figure 15-6.

**Figure 15-6.** *When you click the Edit Resume link, you are directed to the Edit Resume page. In other words, you have the ability to modify the contents of existing résumés.*

Finally, go back to the Main Menu page. You'll see that there are various other options on this page. First, there are two links in the middle of the page: Edit Profile and Edit Resume. Edit Profile allows you to change your user profile, including your login name, password, and contact details (see Figure 15-7). Edit Resume allows you to edit your résumé. At the top of the page are various other links; the purpose of each should be obvious.

**Figure 15-7.** *The Edit Profile page allows you to modify your profile.*

## Directory Structure

To familiarize you with struts-resume's architecture, we'll start with the directory structure shown in Figure 15-8.

**Note** The code for struts-resume can also be downloaded from http://raibledesigns.com/ wiki/Wiki.jsp?page=Downloads. A CVS version is available at http://sourceforge.net/projects/ struts. A README.txt file is provided with the code download that gives full application deployment instructions.

**Figure 15-8.** *The directory structure for the résumé application development (not deployment)*

Let's go over what each file in the root directory is used for and what's in each subdirectory.

The app-settings.xml file allows you to easily customize your application. The Ant tool allows you to set properties from the command line using the -DpropertyName=propertyValue syntax. We separated these properties out of the main build file for readability. The main Ant build script, build.xml, at execution time includes this app-settings.xml file. The build.properties file contains application name settings and build directory settings. The database.properties file allows you to configure which database you want to talk to through Hibernate. Most databases are supported.

The lib directory contains all the third-party libraries (JARs) used by the project. We use several large third-party libraries, therefore this directory weighs in at approximately 11 MB. XDoclet, Cactus, Struts, and other libraries are contained in this directory. A lib.properties file within this directory will allow you to change version numbers for packages.

The metadata directory has a web subdirectory containing XML files that together make up web.xml and struts-config.xml. This is known as the **merge directory** in XDoclet terminology. If you were to add EJBs to this project, you could place any relevant XML fragments inside a new directory.

The properties.xml file loads all .properties files and environment variables. It then uses these values to set class path properties, database properties, and Tomcat deployment properties.

The src directory is (obviously) where all Java source files are kept. There are three directories underneath it: common, ejb, and web. Also, it makes sense to have an ejb directory for the persistence layer, because this makes the directory layout extensible for the future. XDoclet is used to generate a ValidatorForm, and the Hibernate Mapping XML file from a plain old Java object (POJO). The ValidatorForm is further marked up with @struts.validator XDoclet tags and used to generate a `validation.xml` file. The reason we've done it this way is because it allows new columns to be added to our tables easily. On our last project, we used validator forms, value objects, and DAOs, and if we added a new column to a table, we had to add getters and setters in two places (on the form and the POJO) and also change the SQL in the DAO. Using XDoclet and Hibernate eliminates this headache—especially since Hibernate generates a schema and can build your database for you. We've written a `db-create` Ant task to perform this table creation for you automatically.

The `tools` directory contains the StrutsGen tool written by Erik Hatcher. This tool uses Ant and XDoclet to generate a skeleton JSP and an associated properties file from an `ActionForm`, greatly speeding up application development.

The `web` directory contains all web-related files: images, JavaScript files, CSS files, properties files, and XML configuration files. It contains separate directories for most of these and also a `WEB-INF/classes` directory. The JSP files in the `pages` directory are copied to `WEB-INF` at deployment time.

---

**Tip**  By the way, this application was created using AppFuse (`http://raibledesigns.com/wiki/Wiki.jsp?page=Downloads`) as a baseline, and we recommend that you use it too when you develop your own Struts-based applications. It already has a directory layout built, a build script for compiling, testing, and deploying, and XDoclet fragments for generating your XML files. After downloading, simply execute `ant new -Dapp.name=yourAppName -Ddb.name=yourDBName`. Feel free to remove those files you don't find necessary.

---

# Struts Development Techniques and Tools

Now that we've reminded you of the architecture of a typical Struts application and provided an overview of an example `struts-resume` application, let's review some techniques, tools, and frameworks that you may not be aware of, which can enhance or speed up your Struts application development. We'll focus on Struts version 1.2 and mainly on its advanced features.

Struts has many great features, extensions, and plug-ins available for developers. Some of these plug-ins can seem intimidating at first, because they're very powerful and extremely configurable. When we first discovered some of them, we asked ourselves, "Who ordered the kitchen sink?" However, there's nothing wrong with using just a small piece of them if that's all you need.

We'll start off by looking at two open-source tools you can use to build and generate code respectively: Ant and XDoclet. Then we'll work through a series of techniques or tools you can use as you write code.

## Using Ant to Build Struts Applications

Apache Ant (available from `http://ant.apache.org/`) is a powerful Java-based build tool. Using Ant will make your compile, assemble, or deploy process much easier.

Ant is by far our favorite tool to use with Struts and Java as a whole. Yet we've met too many developers who either haven't heard of it or aren't using it. *JavaWorld's* readers voted it the "Most Useful Java Community-Developed Technology" of 2002. Also, in 2003, it won the *JavaPro* Readers' Choice Award for "Most Valuable Java Deployment Technology." In 2003 and 2004, it won the *Java Developer's Journal* Editors' Choice Award. Finally, in 2003, it won the *JavaWorld* Editors' Choice Award for "Most Useful Java Community-Developed Technology." It won't surprise us if it continues to win awards in the future. We used to be trapped within the confines of an IDE to compile our code, and now that we use Ant, we feel like we've been set free.

Ant is basically a technology that, at its very core, compiles your `.java` files into `.class` files using a build file (commonly named `build.xml`). Using Ant, it's much easier to configure your class path for compiling files, as illustrated by the following example:

```
<!-- Set a path reference that points to all Struts' JAR files -->
<path id="web.compile.classpath">
  <fileset dir="/lib/jakarta-struts-1.1" includes="*.jar"/>
</path>
<target name="compile" description="compiles .java files into .class files">
  <mkdir dir="${build.dir}/web/classes"/>
  <javac srcdir="src/web"
      destdir="${build.dir}/web/classes"
      debug="false"
      deprecation="true"
      optimize="true"
      classpathref="web.compile.classpath"
  />
</target>
```

The `<path>` element in the preceding snippet tells Ant to build a name-value pair with the name `web.compile.classpath`; the value is constructed as a list of all the JAR files in the `/lib/Jakarta-struts-1.1` directory. With a simple declarative statement, Ant creates the compile classpath for you.

For this chapter's example application, version 1.5.1 (or higher) of Ant is required. After downloading, you'll need to extract it to a location on your hard drive (for example, `c:\Tools\jakarta-ant-1.5.1` on Windows or `/usr/local/jakarta-ant-1.5.1` on Linux and Unix). After extraction, you'll need to set `ANT_HOME` as an environment variable that points to this extracted location and also add `$ANT_HOME/bin` to your `$PATH` environment variable.

## Ant Tasks

Executing `ant -projecthelp` will display the basic Ant tasks, but the following are ones you'll use most often:

- `ant deploy`: Generates and compiles everything, then deploys to Tomcat (if you have it installed).

- `ant compile-module`: Where `module` is `ejb`, `web`, or `common`.

- `ant ejbdoclet`: Generates `ValidatorForms` and Hibernate's XML-based mapping file.

- `ant webdoclet`: Generates `web.xml`, `struts-config.xml`, `validation.xml`, and the TLD.

- ant `test-module`: Where `module` may have the same values as for the `compile` option mentioned previously. This recursively runs all tests in the `test/module` directory. We recommend using ant `test-module -Dtestcase=ClassName`, where `ClassName` is the name of your test class.

- ant `test-cactus -Dtestcase=ClassName`: Starts Tomcat before tests are run and stops it once they're complete. Use ant `test-web -Dtestcase=ClassName` if Tomcat is already running.

Many third-party libraries in `struts-resume` require that you define a *task definition* for them to integrate with Ant. For instance, to use XDoclet to generate the Struts configuration file `struts-config.xml`, you must define the "webdoclet" task:

```
<taskdef name="webdoclet"
    classname="xdoclet.modules.web.WebDocletTask">
  <classpath>
    <path refid="xdoclet.classpath"/>
    <path refid="web.compile.classpath"/>
  </classpath>
</taskdef>
```

After defining this task, it can be used in your `build.xml` file, just like the `<javac>` task (see the previous example) is used. You can see the available attributes for this task in the section "Using XDoclet to Generate Configuration Files."

## Using Ant in the Example Application

Within `struts-resume`, Ant performs all of the following tasks:

- Generates Java code and XML files (via XDoclet)

- Builds (compiles) the entire source tree (`.java` files)

- Assembles the components into JAR and Web ARchive (WAR) files

- Deploys the WAR file to Tomcat

- Runs unit tests and in-container testing (via Cactus)

Ant is one of those technologies that we love because it *just works*. We've modeled the `build.xml` file in the `struts-resume` application to fit with the Ant Best Practices recommended by Erik Hatcher in his book *Java Development with Ant*.[2] We've used much of his architecture from his book's sample application and exchanged quite a few e-mails with him about it. The flexibility granted by having a test source-code directory (`test/src`) separate from the regular source-code directory (`src`) makes it easy to exclude test classes from a production deployment.

Finally, to us Struts has been an extremely stable framework—even the nightly builds. When you look at the Ant build file for your example application, you'll see we've created it so that you can easily switch versions of any third-party library, including Struts. All you need to do is download and extract a new version into the `lib` directory and change the version number given in `lib/lib.properties`. This really makes it easy to test a new version of a library and

---

2.  Hatcher, Erik and Steve Loughran, *Java Development with Ant* (Greenwich, CT: Manning Publications Co., 2002)

see whether your application still works. You can also override library directories from the command line using something like ant -Dstruts-dir=/ path/to/struts/jars.

## Using XDoclet to Generate Configuration Files

XDoclet is a code-generation engine. It enables **attribute-oriented programming** for Java. In short, this means that you can add more significance to your code by adding metadata (attributes) to your Java sources. This is done in special JavaDoc tags. XDoclet will parse your source files and generate many artifacts such as XML descriptors and/or source code from it. These files are generated from templates that use the information provided in the source code and its Javadocs tags. At the time of this writing, XDoclet can only be used as part of a build process utilizing Ant. Documentation and downloads for XDoclet are available from http://xdoclet.sourceforge.net/.

For the build process, you'll be using the power of Ant and XDoclet to generate the deployment descriptor (web.xml), the Struts configuration file (struts-config.xml), and even the form validation configuration file (validation.xml). To speed up the development process, you'll also use XDoclet to generate the Java code for the ValidatorForms from POJOs. Also, you'll generate Hibernate's XML-based mapping files to map POJOs to database tables.

Wow, that sounds like we're doing a lot doesn't it?! The truth is that before we found XDoclet, we were doing all of those activities manually, and it *was* a lot of work. Using XDoclet (which depends on Ant) has made it *much* easier to create all of the required XML artifacts for a web application and is a huge timesaver.

We like using XDoclet because we don't need to worry about editing our XML files as much when developing an application. It's simply a case of adding some tags to a class (or method) Javadoc, and then XDoclet generates these files for you. For example, we have the following normal Javadoc code at the top of our UserAction class:

```
/**
 * Implementation of <strong>Action</strong> that interacts with the {@link
 * UserForm} to retrieve/persist values to the database.
 *
 * @author Matt Raible
 * @version $Revision: 1.5 $ $Date: 2003/06/26 13:48:46 $
 *
 */
```

By adding some XDoclet tags to this Javadoc header, you can generate the <action-mappings> definition for the struts-config.xml file:

```
/**
 * Implementation of <strong>Action</strong> that interacts with the {@link
 * UserForm} and retrieves values. It interacts with the {@link
 * BusinessManager} to retrieve/persist values to the database.
 *
 * @author Matt Raible
 * @version $Revision: 1.5 $ $Date: 2003/06/26 13:48:46$
 *
 * @struts.action name="userForm" path="/editUser" scope="session"
 *         validate="false" parameter="action" input="mainMenu"
 */
```

When processed by XDoclet, the @struts.action tag will be transformed into an <action> element. In your Ant build file's (build.xml) webdoclet task, you use the following XML to generate the struts-config.xml file:

```
<target name="webdoclet" description="Generate web and Struts descriptors">
  <taskdef name="webdoclet"
      classname="xdoclet.modules.web.WebDocletTask">
    <classpath>
      <path refid="xdoclet.classpath"/>
      <path refid="web.compile.classpath"/>
    </classpath>
  </taskdef>
  <webdoclet destdir="${webapp.target}/WEB-INF"
      force="${xdoclet.force}"
      mergedir="metadata/web"
      excludedtags="@version,@author"
      verbose="true">
    <fileset dir="src/web"/>
    <fileset dir="${build.dir}/web/gen"/>
    <configParam name="cactusOn" value="${enable.cactus}"/>
    <deploymentdescriptor validatexml="true"
        servletspec="2.3" sessiontimeout="30"
        destdir="${build.dir}/web/WEB-INF"
        distributable="false">
      <configParam name="security" value="${security.mode}"/>
    </deploymentdescriptor>
    <jsptaglib validatexml="true"
      description="Tag Libraries for Security and Labels"
      validateXML="true"
      shortName="struts-resume"
      filename="struts-resume.tld"
    />
    <strutsconfigxml validatexml="true" version="1.1"/>
    <strutsvalidationxml/>
  </webdoclet>
</target>
```

That's all it takes to generate the following mapping in the resulting struts-config.xml file (we've prettied the XML up a bit to save space, but no text has changed):

```
<action path="/editUser" type="org.appfuse.webapp.action.UserAction"
    name="userForm" scope="session" input="mainMenu"
    parameter="action" unknown="false" validate="false">
</action>
```

Of course, you can still code your configuration files by hand, adding your own custom data by producing specifically named files known as **merge points**. These files are included in the main file when the items are produced. In the directory (also known as the **merge directory**) of struts-resume, a README.txt file lists available merge points for web.xml, struts-config.xml, and validation.xml. For example, to specify global forwards for your application, you can create a global-forwards.xml file that contains one or more <forward> elements. The global forwards file allows you to configure forwards that are used by multiple actions in a module, which makes it easy to configure forwards that are common to multiple pages.

```
<global-forwards>
    <forward name="mainMenu" path="/mainMenu.do"/>
</global-forwards>
```

This file will then be included in the generated file. XDoclet knows to look in this directory for these files by examining the mergedir attribute of the webdoclet task:

```
<webdoclet destdir="${webapp.target}/WEB-INF"
    force="${xdoclet.force}"
    mergedir="metadata/web"
    excludedtags="@version,@author"
    verbose="true">
```

XDoclet also works for producing form-bean entries in struts-config.xml as well as generating the validation.xml file for the Validator. For form beans, you can simply add the following in your class's Javadoc:

```
* @struts.form name="UserForm"
```

You can also use this tag to generate ActionForms from POJOs (or entity beans) by simply using @struts.form. However, if you want to include all the entity bean's fields, you'll need to add include-all="true". You can also add an optional extends attribute to specify that it extends ValidatorForm or your own base class. For instance, in struts-resume, the User.java file has the following in its Javadoc header:

```
/**
 * User class
 *
 * This class is used to generate the Struts Validator Form
 * as well as the Hibernate persistence later.
 *
 * @author Matt Raible
 * @version $Revision: 1.6 $ $Date: 2003/06/27 03:27:44$
 *
 * @struts.form include-all="true"
 *   extends="org.appfuse.webapp.form.BaseForm"
 *
 * @hibernate.class     table="app_user"
 */
```

Then you can add method-level tags to generate the validation.xml file. If you're adding XDoclet tags to an existing ValidatorForm, make sure to put these tags on your **setters**, as nothing will be generated otherwise!

```
* @struts.validator type="required" msgkey="errors.required"
```

If you're generating `ValidatorForms` from POJOs or entity beans, you'll need to put the `@struts.validator` tags on the class's get methods. In `struts-resume`, we've set up a custom XDoclet template for generating Struts's forms (in `metadata/templates/struts_form.xdt`), which will generate a `ValidatorForm`, complete with `@struts.validator` tags on the setters. Since this wasn't core functionality of XDoclet at the time of this writing, we were inspired to create a custom template to get it.

We don't know if we'd recommend coding your action-forwards into your classes. We've done it both ways and both seem comfortable. Of course, we've being working on a lot of one-person development teams lately, so that might skew our view a little. If you want to externalize your global forwards, you can put them in a merge-point file named `global-forwards.xml`. If you want to do it locally to the class, you can use the following syntax at the beginning of the class:

```
* @struts.action-forward name="list" path=".resumeList"
```

One great thing about XDoclet's integration with Ant is that you can specify Ant properties in your source code as well and these will be substituted at build time. Thus, you could configure all your values via Ant rather than hard-coding them. For example, in `LoginServlet`, we have the following XDoclet tags as part of the Javadoc header:

```
* @web.servlet-init-param
*     name="encrypt-password"
*     value="${encrypt-password}"
```

This value is set by default in the `app-settings.xml` file:

```
<property name="secure-login" value="false"/>
```

However, it can easily be overwritten by executing Ant with this parameter specified:

```
ant -Dsecure-login=true
```

This results in the following being generated in the deployment descriptor (`web.xml`) for the `LoginServlet`:

```
<init-param>
  <param-name>encrypt-password</param-name>
  <param-value>true</param-value>
</init-param>
```

If you already have a database schema and want to develop a Java EE-based application, you could use Middlegen (`http://boss.bekk.no/boss/middlegen/`). Middlegen is a database-driven code-generation engine based on JDBC, Velocity, Ant, and XDoclet. It can generate code for container-managed persistence (CMP), Enterprise JavaBeans (EJBs), Java Database Objects (JDO), and JSP or Struts—straight from a database! This is a great tool for rapid proto-typing. One drawback is that the Struts support appears very weak. When we first encountered Middlegen, it only supported Struts 1.0. At the time of this writing, the Middlegen web site still identified the Struts plug-in as being in alpha state.

### The StrutsGen Tool

There is a small, yet nimble, tool in the `struts-resume` application that Erik Hatcher originally wrote for his sample application in *Java Development with Ant*. It uses Ant and XDoclet to generate a JSP page and a `ResourceBundle` by inspecting a form's property files. The template used for both of these files is simple and customizable. This tool can be found in the `tools/strutsgen` directory of the `struts-resume` application. To use it, you first need to run the command `ant webdoclet` to generate your forms in the `build/gen/web` directory. Then navigate to `tools/strutsgen` and run `ant "-Dform.name=MyForm"` where `MyForm` is the name of the form you would like to generate files for.

This will result in two files being generated in the `tool/strutsgen/build` directory, one named `UserForm.jsp` and the other named `UserForm.properties`. You can also run the tool without specifying a form name, and it will generate these files for all your forms.

This tool uses a `TreeMap` for grabbing the properties from the form, so this means that the new files will contain the properties in alphabetical order. In most cases, you'll probably need to customize the order of your fields to make them user friendly anyway; this tool just speeds things up a bit. It also only supports generating `<html:text>` fields at this time, but since you'll have to get into the JSP to rearrange the order of fields anyway, it's not a big deal. We found it to be very useful during development of this application.

## Handling Persistence in Struts

In our opinion, Struts does a great job of giving you, the developer, great ways to implement your view and your controller, but it doesn't provide much for the model. `ActionForms` are great and `ValidatorForms` are even better, but if you want a database back end to your application, there isn't much in Struts that makes it easier to code it. Forms provide a nice interface to the back end, but Struts isn't in the business of providing data access, and therefore doesn't provide any classes for retrieving data. While there are many different ways to code your controller-to-database logic, we'll be telling you how we've done it and what's worked for us.

When we first started developing with Struts, our architecture had been predetermined and all we had to do was hook into it. We were using EJBs on the project and used RowSets for our list screens. It was fairly easy on our part, because all we had to do was call a particular session bean for each action and interact with it appropriately. We actually found it very easy to create accessors and mutators (getters and setters) for our data objects (or value objects or data transfer objects) on each form. We discovered later that this wasn't a recommended "design pattern"—our data objects should never make it to the presentation layer. However, it worked, and it worked great—and we were happy with it.

The topic of persistence options seems to grace the Struts user mailing list almost weekly. We believe this is because there are so many choices. In reality, you can use almost any Java-based persistence framework with Struts. It's all Java after all. It's tough to choose a framework when none has proved to be a dominant, well-used framework. This is an advantage of Struts in that it allows you to choose any framework—but we're guessing this is a big headache for many developers as well.

However, choosing a persistence framework for a Struts application can be easy if you stick to the technologies you know. If you're going to choose an open-source implementation, make sure the documentation is good, the development mailing list is active, and there are example applications. It's much easier to copy an existing example than to develop from scratch. It's worth your time to investigate code-generation tools that exist for databases, because this will save you a lot of time in the long run. Above all, learn and use XDoclet (we'll discuss this a little later) to help with your persistence layer. We expect you'll be very happy with it.

### Persistence Options

In Chapter 9, you spent a good bit of time evaluating the different persistence options available, so we won't bother to repeat that discussion here. Instead, we'll just let you know that we chose to use Hibernate on the example `struts-resume` project. We're very happy with it so far. It seems to have great documentation and also has XDoclet support. XDoclet support was a big seller for us, because we want to generate most of the database access code.

---

■**Note** The examples in `struts-resume` are modeled after Dave Johnson's examples (author of Chapter 9) in his sample application as well as help we've received from the Hibernate development mailing list.

---

## Enhancing Struts ActionForm Development

There are a few features of Struts that are often overlooked but may be useful when you come to develop your `ActionForms`. Let's take a look at them.

### Using DynaActionForms

The `DynaActionForm` was added as part of Struts 1.1. It basically allows you to declare your form's properties via XML, rather than writing a form using Java. The advantage for the developer is that you don't have to write and compile an `ActionForm`. However, if you're using XDoclet to generate an `ActionForm`, then you might not have a use for a `DynaActionForm`. They can be handy for providing simple forms that aren't persisted—for instance a `MessageForm` that is used to send e-mail. Let's use that as an example and look at its settings:

```
<form-bean name="messageForm"
            type="org.apache.struts.action.DynaActionForm">
  <form-property name="name" type="java.lang.String"/>
  <form-property name="email" type="java.lang.String"/>
  <form-property name="subject" type="java.lang.String"/>
  <form-property name="content" type="java.lang.String"/>
</form-bean>
```

Just like an `ActionForm`, all your properties should be strings for interaction with the web tier. Only object types (`String`, `Integer`, or `Boolean`) can be used as the `type` for the `<form-property>` element. Primitives aren't allowed. After specifying the form's properties, you can reference the form in an action mapping just like a regular `ActionForm` or `ValidatorForm`. A `DynaActionForm` can also utilize the Validator by using a type of `org.apache.struts.action.DynaValidatorActionForm`.

This form can then be retrieved in your `Action` class using the following code:

```
DynaActionForm msgForm = (DynaActionForm) form;
```

To retrieve values from the form, you must use the `form.get(propertyName)` syntax (similar to how values are retrieved from a `HashMap`):

```
String subject = (String) theForm.get("subject");
```

You can also create and initialize a `DynaActionForm` (or `DynaValidatorActionForm`) in an `Action` class:

```
DynaActionForm msgForm = (DynaActionForm) DynaActionFormClass
    .getDynaActionFormClass("messageForm").newInstance();
```

Then values can be set on the form using `form.set("propertyName", object)`. Just like a normal `ActionForm`, you'll need to place it into its assigned scope after you've populated it. If you plan on doing a lot of getting and setting of properties on a form, the `DynaActionForm` can be a bit of a pain, because of all the type casting you need to do, rather than the simple `form.getProperty()`. We suggest generating your `ActionForms` and `ValidatorForms` forms using XDoclet before using `DynaActionForms`. At the same time, there are good uses for it, as in the message form.

## Using Indexed Properties with Forms in Struts

Indexed properties are a feature of Struts that has been available since the beginning. If you've used it, you probably really like it, because it allows you to get and set lists of objects (such as an `ArrayList` of child forms on a parent form). In the `struts-resume` application, this might be something like getting/setting an `ArrayList` of `SkillForms` on a `ResumeForm`. Basically, the syntax involves tags like `<logic:iterate>` and `<c:forEach>` and setting an index on the form element's name:

```
<logic:iterate id="skill" name="userSkills" indexId="index">
```

Then you need to add get and set accessors to your form to allow these values to be retrieved and altered based on an index. Here is an example of how you might implement this in `struts-resume` on a `SkillGroup` form, where a user is assigning multiple `SkillForms`:

```
/**
 * The skill attribute.
 */
private ArrayList skill;
/**
 * Getter for skill. For the sake of the iterator
 * tags and the indexing of objects.
 */
public SkillForm getSkill(int index) {
  return (SkillForm) skill.get(index);
}
/**
```

```
 * Setter for the above getter.
 */
public void setSkill(int index, SkillForm skill) {
  this.skill.set(index, skill);
}
/**
 * Getter for ArrayList of skills
 */
public ArrayList getSkills() {
  return skill;
}
/**
 * Setter for ArrayList of skills
 */
public void setSkills(ArrayList skills) {
  this.skill = skills;
}
```

We haven't implemented indexed properties as yet, although we plan to, and may already have done so by the time you're reading this.

## Form Validation

Our favored method of performing form validation is to use Struts Validator. Validator was originally authored by David Winterfeldt to overcome the tediousness of writing validation logic in ActionForms. It can perform basic validations to check whether a field is required, or matches a regular expression, e-mail, or credit card, as well as server-side type checking and date validation. You can use the Validator in any JSP and servlet application, but it was originally designed for Struts and is therefore easiest to use within Struts. Since Struts 1.1, the Validation framework has been integrated into the core Struts library (struts.jar).

For detailed online information about Validator, go to http://struts.apache.org/userGuide/building_view.html#validator.

### Using Validator

The Validator framework relies on a validator-rules.xml file, which defines all of the pluggable Validator definitions. These definitions are basically Java classes for server-side validation and JavaScript functions for client-side validation. Let's look at the "required" pluggable Validator as an example:

```
<validator name="required"
          classname="org.apache.struts.validator.FieldChecks"
          method="validateRequired"
          methodParams="java.lang.Object,
                        org.apache.commons.validator.ValidatorAction,
                        org.apache.commons.validator.Field,
                        org.apache.struts.action.ActionErrors,
                        javax.servlet.http.HttpServletRequest"
          msg="errors.required">
  <javascript><![CDATA[
```

```
    ... insert JavaScript function here ...
  ]]>
  </javascript>
</validator>
```

We've left out the JavaScript function because it's 40 lines long and you're here to learn JSP, not JavaScript, right? In the previous definition, the FieldChecks is a class within the Validator framework, and it has a method named validateRequired() that takes the parameters listed. The <javascript> element defines the JavaScript function to do client-side validation. Having the definitions in this file makes the Validator framework easily configurable.

To enable the Validator in a Struts application, you first need to add the following XML into the struts-config.xml file. According to the Struts DTD, <plug-in> elements should appear toward the end of this file. If you're using XDoclet, you can put this XML into a file in your merge directory:

```
<plug-in className="org.apache.struts.validator.ValidatorPlugIn">
  <set-property property="pathnames"
                value="/WEB-INF/validator-rules.xml,/WEB-INF/validation.xml"/>
</plug-in>
```

You can see from this example that there are two files that the Validator is loading. These can be renamed to whatever you like; you just have to make sure your <plug-in> configuration is set correctly. Since these file names are the de facto standards for the Validator, we'll use these in our examples. The Validator also allows for extensions such as the following for validating that two fields match:

```
public static boolean validateTwoFields(Object bean, ValidatorAction va,
    Field field, ActionErrors errors, HttpServletRequest request,
    ServletContext application) {

  String value = ValidatorUtil.getValueAsString(bean, field.getProperty());
  String sProperty2 = field.getVarValue("secondProperty");
  String value2 = ValidatorUtil.getValueAsString(bean, sProperty2);

  if (!GenericValidator.isBlankOrNull(value)) {
    try {

      if (!value.equals(value2)) {
        errors.add(field.getKey(), ValidatorUtil.getActionError(
                   application, request, va, field));
        return false;
      }
    } catch (Exception e) {
      errors.add(field.getKey(), ValidatorUtil.getActionError(
                 application, request, va, field));
      return false;
    }
  }
  return true;
}
```

You can then add this class to the `validator-rules.xml` file by adding the following element:

```
<validator name="twofields"
           classname="com.mysite.StrutsValidator"
           method="validateTwoFields"
           msg="errors.twofields"/>
```

Then, in `validation.xml`, you can configure a field to use this validation rule:

```
<field property="password"
       depends="required,twofields">
  <arg0 key="typeForm.password.displayname"/>
  <var>
    <var-name>secondProperty</var-name>
    <var-value>password2</var-value>
  </var>
</field>
```

You could also easily add a JavaScript function to `validator-rules.xml` for client-side validation. This merely requires adding a `<javascript>` element inside the `<validator>` element.

Without the Validator, the easiest way to program validation logic into your application is to override the `validate()` method in your `ActionForm`. Its signature is as follows:

```
public ActionErrors validate(ActionMapping mapping, HttpServletRequest request);
```

This `ActionForm` method returns `null`, like the `ActionForm` `reset()` method, and similarly, overriding it isn't required if you don't want to.

```
public void reset(ActionMapping mapping, HttpServletRequest request);
```

The `reset()` method is designed to reset all your properties back to their default state. It is called before the bean is repopulated by the controller servlet and can be very helpful when using check boxes on your view forms. This is because neither the value nor the name of a check box is passed in the request when it's unchecked. This is the main reason the `reset()` method exists—to set the default state of check boxes so they behave like other form elements and are always passed along in the request as a name-value pair.

To be perfectly honest, we've only used the `validate()` method in any of our `ActionForms` when validating indexed properties, and we've only used `reset()` when we had check boxes on a form. We discovered the Validator framework about a month after we started working with Struts and haven't looked back since. The Validator is great for performing basic required field validation as well as more advanced functions such as regular expression matching, e-mail address syntax (not actual validation of addresses), credit card, and type checking (string, number, date). Furthermore, different validation rules can be defined for different locales. In order to make good use of the Validator, you do need to understand regular expression syntax fairly well, however.

To configure an `Action` to call the `validate()` method on an `ActionForm` or to use the `ValidatorForm`'s declarative validation, you don't need to do anything because validation is **turned on** by default. Personally, we like to specify `validate="true"` or `validate="false"` in our <action-mappings> element to avoid confusion. Also, you'll need to specify an input attribute for your <action-mappings>, or the Validator won't know where to return to for server-side validation. This is very important, especially when using the Tiles framework we'll discuss later—you'll get the blank screen of nothingness if you don't add the input attribute. Configuring this in XDoclet looks like the following example:

```
* @struts.action name="userForm" path="/saveUser" scope="session"
*   validate="true" parameter="action" input="editProfile"
```

This produces the following action mapping:

```
<action path="/saveUser" type="org.appfuse.webapp.action.UserAction"
  name="userForm" scope="session" input="editProfile" parameter="action"
  unknown="false" validate="true">
</action>
```

We're using inputForwards in the struts-resume application, so the value editProfile actually refers to a global forward.

We really like the Validator because it performs client-side (through JavaScript) as well as server-side validation. In our experience, most customers prefer client-side validation, as do developers. Why should the browser even attempt to submit the form if the required fields aren't populated? There are some larger organizations that discourage the use of JavaScript for the sake of compatibility, and it's a shame as it can help your web applications to behave more like traditional desktop applications. However, there are some HTML elements that require server-side validation—for instance, the <input type="file" ... /> element. It doesn't allow JavaScript manipulation or access, and therefore cannot be checked to see whether a value has been entered. This is for security reasons, because you wouldn't want a script to grab files from your hard drive without your consent.

When developing rich web clients with JavaScript, the most important things to remember are accessibility standards. Currently, there are two. In the United States, there is the federal government's Section 508 Initiative. Section 508 requires that federal agencies' electronic and information technology be accessible to people with disabilities. More information can be found at http://www.section508.gov.

The second standard, which is more worldwide, is the W3C's Web Accessibility Initiative (WAI). The World Wide Web Consortium's (W3C) commitment to lead the Web to its full potential includes promoting a high degree of usability for people with disabilities. WAI, in coordination with organizations around the world, pursues accessibility of the Web through five primary areas of work: technology, guidelines, tools, education and outreach, and research and development. More information can be found at http://www.w3.org/WAI/.

These accessibility standards are built on top of other standards, such as XHTML and CSS. If you follow these standards when developing your web application, you'll find that making your application accessible will be much easier. We've found that accessibility standards discourage the use of JavaScript to change pages on a <select>'s onchange event, but pop-up JavaScript alerts, like those used by the Validator, are fine. Most screen readers can understand and read them—the major accessibility concerns related to client-side JavaScript are 1) that the message is easy to understand, and 2) that messages are still given when JavaScript is turned off. Since the Validator provides both client and server-side validation, it satisfies many accessibility requirements.

### Generating validation.xml Using XDoclet

In the `struts-resume` application, XDoclet generates the `validation.xml` file from the
`ActionForms` and their subclasses, including the `ValidatorForm`. We created a `BaseForm` that
extends `ValidatorForm` and implements `Serializable` (for clustered environments), and then
all our forms extend it. The process by which `UserForm` and `validation.xml` are generated is
shown in Figure 15-9, where the arrows represent names of the Ant targets or tasks.

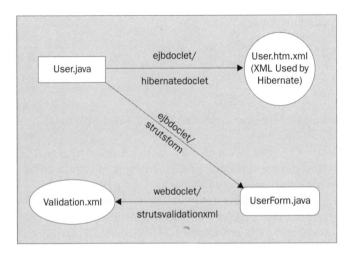

**Figure 15-9.** *XDoclet can generate forms and the validation descriptor for those forms.*

There are three method-level XDoclet tags you can use to generate values:

- `@struts.validator`

- `@struts-validator.args`

- `@struts.validator-var`

The simplest example of this is using the `required` Validator to generate an entry. We'll
use the `username` attribute that is generated on `UserForm` to illustrate. It starts, as illustrated in
the previous diagram, at the `User.java` file, and these tags are transferred to the generated
`ActionForm`. On the getter field for the username, you'll find the following tags:

```
/**
 * Returns the username.
 * @return String
 *
 * @struts.validator type="required" msgkey="errors.required"
 * @struts.validator type="email" msgkey="errors.email"
 * @hibernate.property
 *   column="username" type="string" not-null="true" unique="true"
 */
public String getUsername() {
  return username;
}
```

This code must be on the getter in order for the form generation to work correctly. At the time of writing, the strutsform task is a subtask of ejbdoclet, so we're still running it as an ejbdoclet task. When the ejbdoclet task is run, the <strutsform> subtask within it will generate the following entry in validation.xml:

```
<formset>
  <form name="userForm">
  ...
    <field property="username"
           depends="required,email">
      <msg name="required"
           key="errors.required"/>
      <msg name="email"
           key="errors.email"/>
      <arg0 key="userForm.username"/>
    </field>
  ...
  </form>
</formset>
```

We should point out that the <msg> elements aren't required; therefore you don't need to specify the msgkey attribute in the XDoclet tag. If you choose to eliminate this element, the Validator's default message from the validation-rules.xml file will be applied. This value is represented in validation-rules.xml by the msg attribute. For example, the required Validator has msg="errors.required". XDoclet creates msg entries for us in validation.xml, providing greater flexibility in the long run.

Now that you know how to generate validation.xml, let's examine what the parts actually mean. There are four different elements in the previous extract: <form>, <field>, <msg>, and <arg>.

The name attribute of the <form> element defines the name of your ActionForm, and this name should match the one defined in struts-config.xml. Since you're using XDoclet to generate the form and struts-config.xml file, you can be certain that these names will match.

The <field> element has two attributes, property and depends. The property attribute defines the name of the variable in UserForm.java to validate, while the depends attribute identifies which validation rules to apply.

There are two <msg> elements that signify which messages to use from the ApplicationResources.properties file or whatever the ResourceBundle is named in struts-config.xml. In struts-resume, these are defined as follows:

```
errors.required={0} is required.
errors.email={0} is an invalid e-mail address.
```

The last element, <arg0>, specifies the message key for the substitution value of {0} in each respective message. In struts-resume, this is defined as the following:

```
userForm.username=Username
```

If there is more than one argument you'd like to replace in your error message, you can add more arguments in ApplicationResources by incrementing the number, so {1} would signify the second argument. To add this argument's replacement value on your form, you could add another XDoclet tag to the original form:

```
@struts.validator-args arg1resource="username.lastName" arg1value="My Surname"
```

Of course, you would never use both of these attributes, because the first (arg1resource) is for looking up a resource key, and the second (arg2value) is for placing a literal string in your validation.xml. Running the previous code through the webdoclet task produces the following XML:

```
<arg0 key="username.lastName"/>
<arg0 key="My Last Name" resource="false"/>
```

Now that you've configured the form's validation, you should add some JavaScript to the JSP to enforce client-side validation. The first step is to use the <html:messages/> tag library to catch any server-side validation errors:

```
<logic:messagesPresent>
  <div class="error">
    <html:messages id="error">
      <bean:write name="error" filter="false"/><br/>
    </html:messages>
  </div>
</logic:messagesPresent>
```

In the struts-resume application, the previous code appears in a messages.jsp file. This file also contains code to catch regular messages (not error messages) and is located in the web/common folder. It's included in the Tiles template so we don't have to add it to every page that should use validation.

Secondly, you need to add an onsubmit event handler to your form:

```
<html:form action="/userSave" method="post" styleId="userForm"
    focus="password" onsubmit="return validateUserForm(this)">
```

While you're examining this form's syntax, we'd like to point out a couple of other things. By default, if you don't use a method attribute on your form, the <html:form> tag will render one for you. The problem with the one it renders is that it's not XHTML compliant. That is, it renders as method="POST", where XHTML requires that predefined attribute values be in lowercase. We usually add a styleId attribute to all our forms and form elements (such as <html:text> or <html:password>) so that they can be accessed via the Document Object Model (DOM) with document.getElementById(elementId). One thing you have to be aware of is that every Id must be unique within a page. Lastly, to increase the usability of the application, you should try to use the focus attribute on your forms but use it cautiously: if you hide fields based on a user's role or other logic, this may result in a JavaScript error.

After configuring the form, you need to add an onclick handler to the form's Submit and Cancel buttons to talk to the Validator's validateForm JavaScript function. This is so clicking the Cancel button won't invoke any validation:

```
<html:cancel styleClass="button" onclick="bCancel=true">
  <bean:message key="button.cancel">
</html:cancel>
<html:submit styleClass="button" onclick="bCancel=false">
```

```
    <bean:message key="button.submit">
</html:submit>
```

In the previous example, we've added the `styleClass` attribute to signify a CSS rule for our buttons. Lastly, you add the following to include the JavaScript necessary to perform the actual validation:

```
<html:javascript formName="userForm" cdata="false"
                 dynamicJavascript="true" staticJavascript="false"/>
<script type="text/javascript"
        src="<html:rewrite page="/scripts/validator.jsp"/>">
</script>
```

We always try to use `<html:rewrite />` when referencing JavaScript or CSS files, because this will render a URL that includes the application's context. That is, it will create a URL that is relative to the web server's root (/) directory. `validation.jsp` contains the following code in order to render all the JavaScript functions from the `validation-rules.xml` file:

```
<%@ page language="java" contentType="javascript/x-javascript" %>
<%@ taglib uri="http://jakarta.apache.org/struts/tags-html"
    prefix="html" %>
<html:javascript dynamicJavascript="false" staticJavascript="true"/>
```

### Testing the Validation

Now that you've configured everything, let's test it out! To do this, you'll need to log in to the `struts-resume` application and click the `Edit Profile` link. This will bring up your user information. If you clear the username field, you'll get the error dialog box shown in Figure 15-10.

**Figure 15-10.** *When the Validator detects an error, an error dialog box is displayed.*

When turning off JavaScript in your browser, the Validator will catch the error on the server side, and you'll get the message shown in Figure 15-11. So if you don't want to use JavaScript in your application, virtually no coding is necessary, save the XDoclet tags. If you aren't using XDoclet, you'll need to configure validation.xml manually—we like to refer to this as *declarative validation*.

**Figure 15-11.** *Even if JavaScript is disabled in the client browser, validation still occurs on the server side, and an error message will still be displayed.*

You can also use the Validator to perform validation based on variables, such as validating that a zip code matches a regular expression. This is possible with a mask that contains a regular expression as its value. For regular expressions that might be used more than once, it's a good idea to define them as constants in your validation.xml file. Since we're using XDoclet, this can be done in a validation-global.xml file, which lives in our merge directory. In the struts-resume application, this is metadata/web/.

```
<constant>
  <constant-name>zip</constant-name>
  <constant-value>^\d{5}\d*$</constant-value>
</constant>
```

This regular expression says that zip must be five characters long and all characters must be digits. To validate a zip code in the userForm, you'll need to configure validation.xml like so:

```
<field property="postalCode" depends="required,mask">
  <msg name="required" key="errors.required"/>
```

```
<msg name="mask" key="errors.zip"/>

<arg0 key="userForm.postalCode"/>
<var>
  <var-name>mask</var-name>
  <var-value>${zip}</var-value>
</var>
</field>
```

As mentioned earlier, the `<msg>` elements can be eliminated if you want to use the default values for the Validators. However, the default error message key for mask is `errors.invalid`, which is simply `{0}`, is invalid. To enhance usability of the application, a different key (such as `errors.zip`) with more information is probably better (such as The `{0}` field must be a 5-digit number). To configure this for the `postalCode` field is easy with XDoclet. All you need to do is add a tag to specify the rule and the variable's name-value pair:

```
* @struts.validator type="mask" msgkey="errors.zip"
* @struts.validator-var name="mask" value="${zip}"
```

### Advanced Validator Features

Other features of the Validator that we haven't mentioned yet include multipage validation, indexed property validation, conditional validation, and DynaFormValidation. Multipage validation allows you to spread your validation rules for a form across more than one page. This can be very helpful when you have a wizardlike form for gathering information in your application. To configure this, you need to add a hidden field to specify the page number in your JSP:

```
<html:hidden property="page" value="1"/>
```

This is complemented by adding a `page` attribute to the field's validation rule in `validation.xml`. In the examples you've seen so far, the fields have a `property` and `depends` attribute. Add the `page` attribute and now your form can contain validation that is invoked across different JSP pages!

```
<field property="firstName" depends="required,mask" page="1">
```

We really like this feature because it's so simple to configure.

Indexed property validation allows you to have forms contained within forms or subforms. For instance, in your application, a `ResumeForm` can contain one-to-many `SkillGroupForms`. `SkillGroups` describe a group of skills. On a technical résumé, a good `SkillGroup` might be "Java" or, at an even higher level, "Programming Languages." Furthermore, `SkillGroupForms` can contain one-to-many `SkillForms`. To elaborate on the Java example, you might have `SkillForms` such as "Swing," "JDBC," and "XML." A nice user interface for editing these would allow you to view all your résumé's `SkillGroups` and their subsequent `SkillForms`.

Displaying all this isn't a big deal, because you can use a `<logic:iterate>` tag or `<c:forEach>`. However, to save them, you have to know what row (or form) the user edited. This is where indexed properties come to the rescue. You can basically add a getter/setter to your form that allows for setting/getting nested form values. Please see the section "Using Indexed Properties with Forms in Struts" for more information. To configure the Validator

to validate an indexed property, you need to add an `indexedListProperty` attribute to your
`<field>` element:

```
<field property="groupName" depends="required" indexedListProperty="skills">
  <var>
    <var-name>field[0]</var-name>
    <var-value>name</var-value>
  </var>
  <var>
    <var-name>field-indexed[0]</var-name>
    <var-value>true</var-value>
  </var>
  <var>
    <var-name>field-test[0]</var-name>
    <var-value>NOTNULL</var-value>
  </var>
</field>
```

This states that the `skills` property contains a list, and the required field within this skills
list is the `name` property.

A new feature recently added to the Validator is an ability to conditionally require Validator
fields based on the value of other fields. It allows you to define logic such as "only validate this
field if field X is nonnull and field Y contains 'male'". The Validator has support for validating
indexed properties, indicated in the previous example by the `[0]` indicator. However, it doesn't
support dynamic indexed properties at the time of this writing. Which is to say that you must
know the number of child (indexed) properties and configure the Validator accordingly. Conditionally validating can be very useful, but since we haven't used it in `struts-resume`, we
recommend consulting the online documentation for more information.

### Using the Validator with DynaActionForms

The final feature of the Validator we would like to mention is that it can also be used with
`DynaActionForms`. As you saw earlier, `DynaActionForms` are forms that are created by specifying
the form's properties in `struts-config.xml`. This can save time when developing concrete
forms for an application. Personally, we prefer using concrete Java classes for our forms, rather
than cluttering up a configuration file with form properties. The main motivation behind
`DynaActionForms` was to speed up and facilitate Struts development so developers could
quickly create new forms. Using XDoclet to generate your forms is even faster, because it also
(in our example) creates the persistence layer. Using XDoclet also creates the form-bean
entries and `validation.xml` for you, while if you use `DynaActionForms`, you still need to manually create `validation.xml`. That said, creating a `DynaActionForm` that uses the Validator is as
simple as specifying which type of bean it is. A regular `UserForm` created as a `DynaActionForm`
might look as follows:

```
<form-bean name="userForm"
           type="org.apache.struts.action.DynaActionForm">
  ...
</form-bean>
```

To make this form Validator-enabled, all you need to do is change the `type` attribute:

```
<form-bean name="userForm"
           type="org.apache.struts.validator.DynaValidatorForm">
  ...
</form-bean>
```

Configuring the Validator might look like a lot of work; after all, you do have to add three different pieces of code to your JSP page: the form's `onsubmit` handler, the button's `onclick` handler, and the JavaScript declarations at the bottom of the form. However, it's easy to automate this process using the StrutsGen tool. We've simply modified the `ActionForm_jsp.xdt` file (located at `tools/strutsgen/src`) to include all of this Validator-specific code, and now our initial forms will be generated with Validator support! How sweet is that?

**Performing Validation on Indexed Tags**

The Validator is also capable of performing validation on indexed tags. You simply need to add a [#] to your `validation.xml` for the field you want to validate. As an example, if you wanted to configure the `ResumeForm` to require the first `SkillForm`'s name, you could configure the `validation.xml` file with something like the following:

```
<form name="resumeForm">
  ...
  <field property="skills[0]name"
         depends="required">
    <msg name="required"
         key="errors.required"/>
    <arg0 key="skillForm.name"/>
  </field>
```

# Using Built-In Struts Actions

If you've already built a Struts application, you might have found that you developed actions to follow an MVC pattern, but you really didn't need them. Or maybe you linked directly to JSP pages and bypassed the recommended "every link should go through a controller" model. We know we did—until we discovered the actions that Struts has built in. We now think of these as a bunch of eager benchwarmers saying, "Put us in coach, we promise we'll make you proud!" However, you might not realize they exist. Therefore, we'll introduce these well-conditioned actions now, so you'll get a taste of their potential and maybe even let them into the game.

There are five built-in actions with Struts and the first three (`ForwardAction`, `IncludeAction`, and `SwitchAction`) require no coding at all. The last two, `DispatchAction` and `LookupDispatchAction`, are designed to promote code reduction and reuse.

## ForwardAction

The `ForwardAction` can be used to redirect to a JSP page, but still utilize the built-in features of a controller—such as securing actions with the `roles` attribute. It can also be very useful when migrating a model 1 architecture (that is, JSP pages only) to Struts. In the example résumé application, a ForwardAction is used to direct users to the Main Menu page. To configure a ForwardAction, you simply specify the org.apache.struts.actions.ForwardAction class as the type, and the JSP page (or Tiles definition) as the parameter.

```
<action path="/mainMenu"
        type="org.apache.struts.actions.ForwardAction"
        parameter=".mainMenu"/>
```

We've also created a global forward to call this action:

```
<forward name="mainMenu"
         path="/mainMenu.do"/>
```

After configuring the action and forward, it can then be called in your application's start page (index.jsp):

```
<logic:redirect forward="mainMenu"/>
```

You should also note that the previous action and forward definitions are in the metadata/web directory in the files struts-actions.xml and global-forwards.xml, respectively. XDoclet grabs these fragments and merges them into the main struts-config.xml file when the strutsconfigxml task is executed. You'll need to define your actions and forwards in these files for all three of the "no-coding-required" actions.

### IncludeAction

IncludeAction was developed for the same reason as ForwardAction. It allows you to integrate servlet-based components that utilize RequestDispatcher.include(). Like ForwardAction, it only requires that you specify name, parameter, and type attributes. Personally, we've never used it, and we've never seen it in use, but here's how you might configure it:

```
<action path="/resumeComments"
        type="org.apache.struts.actions.IncludeAction"
        parameter="/path/to/servlet"/>
```

### SwitchAction

The SwitchAction was designed to allow switching of application modules. Please refer to the section "Using Modules in Team Development Environments" later for a full description and how to configure it.

### DispatchAction

DispatchAction and LookupDispatchAction are two great additions to the Struts framework. For the first application we developed, we ended up creating an Edit and Save action for each entity's Create, Retrieve, Update, and Delete (CRUD) classes. After writing the classes, we noticed that there was a lot of duplicate code in the Edit (used for retrieval and searching) and Save classes. DispatchAction, and its friendly sibling, LookupDispatchAction, allow you to create different methods in your action that are "dispatched" according to a parameter.

This means that rather than writing an execute() method in your action, you can write methods that detail your business logic (such as add(), save(), remove(), search()). Both dispatch action classes are subclasses of Action, so it's still possible to use the execute() method, but you'll have to build your own dispatching mechanism in this method if you want the dispatch behavior. These actions use reflection to choose and invoke the appropriate methods. Therefore, your methods must have a public modifier or you'll get the Struts white screen of death (or whatever background color you have your browser set to!).

To use the dispatch action, you simply have to extend it rather than Action in your Action class. We usually create a BaseAction for our applications and use that to extend the appropriate Action class. What advantages does this provide? By using a BaseAction, you only have to extend Struts's Action class in one location, and you can elect to switch to a DispatchAction or LookupDispatchAction at any time. Also, we've seen cases in which developers use BaseAction to process or dispatch, but we've never had the need to do things that way. Which is to say that there is an execute() method on the BaseAction class, and it's configured as the servlet for Struts in the web.xml. To do this in struts-resume, you could simply change the following line in metadata/web/servlets.xml

```
<servlet-class>org.apache.struts.action.ActionServlet</servlet-class>
```

to

```
<servlet-class>org.appfuse.webapp.action.BaseAction</servlet-class>
```

If you want to perform logic before dispatching to your methods, your best bet is to dig into the Struts code (good ol' open source!) and use DispatchAction or LookupDispatchAction as your base class. You can also use a preExecute() method in your base class (or in each class) that you call at the beginning of each method. We've had good success with simply using a BaseAction to hold common action methods. For instance, we've used our BaseAction to implement a convenience method, and getUserForm(session) to get a user's information from the session.

Once you've written your action, you then need to configure your <action-mappings> with a parameter appropriately named method or action—we use method to be consistent with the documentation, even though we prefer action:

```
<action path="/test" type="org.example.MyAction" name="MyForm" scope="request"
        input="/test.jsp" parameter="method"/>
```

Then you'll need to add a hidden field to your forms that call this action. For instance:

```
<html:hidden property="method" value="add"/>
```

You can also do this with a normal HTML tag if you aren't trying to grab the method property from your form:

```
<input type="hidden" name="method" id="method" value="add" />
```

It's also plausible that you won't always call your dispatch action with a form, say if editing an item from a list. For this, you can use a forward defined by the method already defined:

```
<forward name="editUser" path="/editUser.do?method=edit"/>
```

There are, however, issues with DispatchAction. For instance, if you have a form with a number of buttons (such as Add, Copy, Save, Delete) to perform different actions, you have to use JavaScript to manipulate the method hidden field. While JavaScript is a perfectly acceptable way to do this, there's an easier way—LookupDispatchAction.

## LookupDispatchAction

The LookupDispatchAction class is a subclass of DispatchAction that allows you to map button captions to method names. Furthermore, it reads the button captions from your Struts ResourceBundle (ApplicationResources.properties). This means that you can easily map the key button.save to the save() method.

To implement a LookupDispatchAction in your project, you must first extend the LookupDispatchAction in your class. Again, we recommend doing this in a BaseAction class, and then extending your project's actions from this one. You'll need to add a parameter to your <action-mappings>, which is very similar to DispatchAction:

```
<action path="/test"
        type="org.example.MyAction"
        name="MyForm"
        scope="request"
        input="/test.jsp"
        parameter="action"/>
```

You could set the parameter to method, but action is demonstrated in the LookupDispatchAction's Javadoc, so we've used it here to avoid confusion. The action request parameter will be used to locate the corresponding key in ApplicationResources. After configuring your struts-config.xml appropriately, or your XDoclet tags in your action class, you'll then need to implement the getKeyMethodMap() method in your subclass like so:

```
protected Map getKeyMethodMap() {
  Map map = new HashMap();
  map.put("button.add", "add");
  map.put("button.delete", "delete");
  return map;
}
```

Your ApplicationResources.properties file determines the text that appears on your buttons and therefore should contain entries for both of these keys:

```
button.add=Add Record
button.delete=Delete Record
```

Finally, you need to set the property attribute to action for your form's Submit buttons in order to pass the buttons' caption to your action:

```
<html:submit property="action">
  <bean:message key="button.add"/>
</html:submit>
```

```
<html:submit property="action">
  <bean:message key="button.delete"/>
</html:submit>
```

In the `struts-resume` application, the `BaseAction` extends `LookupDispatchAction`. We've also added our own little enhancement to the `getKeyMethodMap()` method, so that the key or value pairs are loaded from another property's file. This allows mapping new methods to buttons without recompilation. This might seem like overkill, but it only took a couple minutes to implement. One problem we've seen with this class is that if you use JavaScript to disable your Submit buttons after they've been clicked, the action parameter won't be sent.

---

■**Note**  More information on each of these built-in actions can be found in the Struts Javadocs at `http://struts.apache.org/javadoc.html`.

---

## Using the Tiles Framework to Assemble the View

**Tiles** is a Composite View framework for assembling presentation pages from component parts. Each part, or tile, can be reused as often as needed throughout your application. You can use Tiles in any JSP or servlet application, but it was originally designed for Struts and is therefore easiest to use within Struts. Since Struts 1.1, the Tiles framework has been integrated into the core Struts library (`struts.jar`). Tiles is often seen as a heavyweight, configuration-intensive plug-in, when in fact it offers the same simple functionality as the (now deprecated) `struts-template` tag library.

Tiles was developed by Cedric Dumoulin, and in our opinion is one of the best things that ever happened for JSP developers. Standards like CSS and XHTML are also awesome (and have provided more structure to develop web applications that work across browsers), but Tiles has made it so much *easier*. Tiles will reduce your development time in building web applications and will also make it relatively easy to change the entire application's look. It offers the best layout framework we know of, although there are others that have fervent supporters such as SiteMesh (`http://www.opensymphony.com/sitemesh`) from OpenSymphony.

We've developed several JSP applications over the past few years, and we've laid them out using many different techniques. The first technique was similar to how you would develop a static website, where each JSP page contained all the layout elements of a typical HTML page. This included the `<html>` declaration, the `<head>` element, `<body>`, and any `<div>` or `<table>` elements within the body as well as the actual content. While this is generally easier for HTML developers to grasp, it's definitely the hard way. If you ever need to carry out a site redesign, chances are you'll need to meddle with every JSP file to do so. Of course, HTML editors (such as Dreamweaver, BBEdit, and HomeSite) will make this easier with their global search-and-replace features, but you can easily mess up your HTML at the same time.

An easier way is to *include* elements that are common to all pages. Such elements include the `<head>` element, which contains your CSS and JavaScript references, or a menu that is common to all pages.

While this approach is much easier than the first approach, you're still duplicating code between all your pages to include these external elements. It might only be three or four lines of code, but nevertheless, if you forget to include the header, chances are you won't find out until you (or your users) run your page through a browser.

If you're using Struts, we'd recommend Tiles because it offers many built-in interoperability features with Struts. Just like the Validator, it can be used on its own by simply making a servlet entry in your application's web.xml. However, we won't explore this configuration because this chapter focuses on Struts-based solutions. We will illustrate the templating system used in the example résumé application and how we've implemented Tiles in this particular application. The architecture and techniques we'll be using have been tried and proven in production applications. Tiles can be used in many different ways for building portal sites and menuing systems as well as customization.

Detailed online documentation for Tiles can be found at http://www.lifl.fr/~dumoulin/tiles/.

## Using Tiles in the Example Application

First of all, let's see how to integrate Tiles into the Struts application. With Struts, it's much like the Validator and only needs to be registered as a plug-in in your struts-config.xml file:

```
<plug-in className="org.apache.struts.tiles.TilesPlugin" >
  <set-property property="definitions-config"
                value="/WEB-INF/tiles-config.xml" />
  <set-property property="moduleAware" value="true" />
  <set-property property="definitions-parser-validate" value="true" />
</plug-in>
```

If you're using XDoclet, this will need to go in a struts-plugins.xml file in your merge directory. There are basically two ways to use Tile:

- The first is through a JSP page that includes other pages as a template.

- The second is to use an XML file to define the different components in a given page, also known as a **definition**.

We highly recommend the XML-configuration route because it enables you to change page definitions in one location, rather than on a page-by-page basis. It also supports inheritance so you can define a base definition with the same header and footer, and then you don't need to specify these in the child definitions. The first property, definitions-config, points to the file you use to define your definitions. It also supports a comma-delimited list of file paths, which might be handy if you have many pages or definitions in your application. The second property, moduleAware, allows Tiles to recognize modules (formerly known as subapplications). We'll describe these further in an upcoming section.

The basis of Tiles is that it allows you to define a "template" for your entire application, or several templates depending on your needs. This template will generally look like a regular HTML file, with all the basic elements, such as <html>, <head>, <body>, and any layout elements, such as <div> or <table>. If you're still using tables for laying out your web applications, we implore you to try a tableless layout with <div> and CSS because it will make your pages much lighter and smaller for your clients. XHTML and CSS, and a modern browser of course, make this much easier. Listing 15-1 presents a very simple template for Tiles.

**Listing 15-1.** *template.jsp*

```
<!DOCTYPE html PUBLIC "-//W3C//DTD XHTML 1.0 Strict//EN"
    "http://www.w3.org/TR/xhtml1/DTD/xhtml1-strict.dtd">
<%@ taglib uri="http://jakarta.apache.org/struts/tags/struts-tiles"
    prefix="tiles" %>
<%@ taglib uri="http://jakarta.apache.org/struts/tags/struts-bean"
    prefix="bean" %>
<html:html xhtml="true" locale="true">
  <head>
    <%-- Push tiles attributes in page context --%>
    <tiles:importAttribute />
    <title><bean:message name="title.key"/></title>
  </head>
  <body>
    <div id="header">
      <tiles:insert attribute="header"/>
    </div>
    <div id="menu">
      <tiles:insert attribute="menu" ignore="true"/>
    </div>
    <div id="content">
      <%@ include file="/common/messages.jsp" %>
      <h1><bean:message name="heading.key"/></h1>
      <tiles:insert attribute="content"/>
    </div>
    <div id="footer">
      <tiles:insert attribute="footer"/>
    </div>
  </body>
</html:html>
```

In the previous template, you can see that there are attributes that you import and attributes you insert. Basically, the `<tiles:importAttribute>` is used for the `<bean:message/>` tags. When you configure the application to use this template, you can actually tell it which key from your `ApplicationResources.properties` file to use for the `title.key` and for the `heading.key`. The `<tiles:insert />` tag is used to insert or include a JSP page, but this could also be a URL to any component within your application.

If you're inserting JSP pages into your Tiles template, you'll need to configure your JSP pages so they can be executed independently of other pages. By this, we mean to say that they could be referenced with a dynamic include (`<jsp:include>`) rather than a static include (`<%@ include />`). Therefore, you must reference the appropriate tag libraries at the top of each page. To make development easier and faster, we usually create a JSP file with all our tag library declarations, and then use a static include to include them on every page. You can see an example of this in the `struts-resume` application. The template in Listing 15-1 will render a layout similar to the one shown in Figure 15-12.

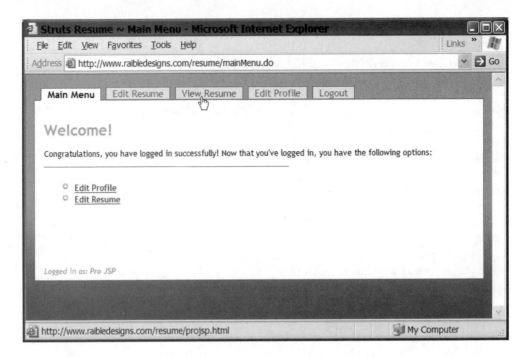

**Figure 15-12.** *The Tiles template shown previously renders this web page.*

Tiles templates, also known as layouts, can be referenced using two different techniques. The first is by using a JSP page. For example, you could put all the JSP pages in a pages directory. This technique comes in handy when using JSP pages to compose Tiles pages. You can simply put all your different page sections (or **tiles**) in the pages directory, and then reference them from the root directory. For instance, this is what a page might look like in the root directory:

```
<%@ include file="/common/taglibs.jsp"%>
<tiles:insert page="/layouts/simpleLayout.jsp" flush="true">
  <tiles:put name="title.key" value="login.title"/>
  <tiles:put name="heading.key" value="login.heading"/>
  <tiles:put name="header" value="/common/header.jsp "/>
  <tiles:put name="menu" value="/menu.html"/>
  <tiles:put name="content" value="/WEB-INF/pages/login.jsp"/>
  <tiles:put name="footer" value="/common/footer.jsp "/>
</tiles:insert>
```

The second option is to use an XML file and create **definitions** for each page. This is nice because definitions can extend each other as well as provide a central repository of your page composition information. Furthermore, definitions can still be references from a JSP page (when using a /do/* mapping) or as ActionForward paths in struts-config.xml. Let's look at how the previous JSP code might look in a tiles-config.xml file:

```
<definition name=".login" path="/layouts/simpleLayout.jsp">
  <put name="title.key" value="login.title"/>
  <put name="heading.key" value="login.heading"/>
```

```
  <put name="header" value="/common/header.jsp"/>

  <put name="menu" value="/menu.html"/>
  <put name="content" value="/WEB-INF/pages/welcome.jsp"/>
  <put name="footer" value="/common/footer.jsp"/>
</definition>
```

One of the principal advantages of using definitions is that you can inherit properties from each other. In this way, you can create a baseLayout definition that all definitions inherit from, and child definitions won't need to define certain properties, such as the header and footer. The previous definition can be refactored to something like this:

```
<definition name="baseLayout" path="/layouts/baseLayout.jsp">
  <put name="title.key"/>
  <put name="heading.key"/>
  <put name="header" value="/common/header.jsp"/>
  <put name="footer" value="/common/footer.jsp"/>
</definition>
<definition name=".login" extends="baseLayout">
  <put name="title.key" value="login.title"/>
  <put name="heading.key" value="login.heading"/>
  <put name="menu" value="/menu.html"/>
  <put name="content" value="/WEB-INF/pages/welcome.jsp"/>
</definition>
```

In the previous .login definition, you'll notice that we've prefixed the tile name with a period (.). This dot notation is the recommended practice for naming tiles. Since Tiles's definitions can be references in a forward's path attribute, this prefix makes them easier to recognize.

A definition can be referenced in a JSP page if you don't want to forward to it from an action. In struts-resume, we do this in the login.jsp page. We're protecting all *.do mappings with a <security-constraint>, so we're unable to access any action without authenticating. The content of the login.jsp page is short and simple:

```
<%@ include file="/common/taglibs.jsp"%>
<tiles:insert definition=".login" flush="true"/>
```

In the examples provided, you'll notice that messages come from ApplicationResources.properties for title and heading settings, but another option is available. This may be why Tiles seems so intimidating to some—there are so many options! However, we do want to show you some other options that might be more suitable for you. Rather than using the ApplicationResources.properties file to represent the title or heading, you can code the strings directly in your definition or JSP:

```
<put name="title" value="Login to Struts Resume"/>
```

Rather than using <tiles:importAttributes/> and <bean:message key="title.key"/>, you can use <tiles:getAsString name="title"/>. You might think you've lost the internationalization (I18n) support in this process, but Tiles allows for an alternative way of achieving I18n: creating separate XML definition files for each locale. Using this strategy, you would have a tiles_config_en.xml for English, tiles_config_ru.xml for Russian, and so on. Using the

ApplicationResources.properties file is an easier way to internationalize your application, because then all language changes are available in one file.

Earlier we mentioned that CSS stylesheets can be used to greatly improve your layout flexibility. We've worked on many projects where we used different stylesheets for different pages or even for different users. There are two approaches that we've used to switch stylesheets, the first being on a page basis, and the second for users. The first uses Tiles definitions to set the stylesheet for any given page. While you're at it, you might as well add this same feature for including JavaScript files. First of all, you can add the files you want to include in your baseLayout definition:

```
<definition name="baseLayout" path="/layouts/baseLayout.jsp">
  <put name="title.key"/>
  <put name="heading.key"/>
  <put name="header" value="/common/header.jsp"/>
  <put name="footer" value="/common/footer.jsp"/>
  <!-- Default JavaScript File -->
  <putList name="scripts">
    <add value="/scripts/global.js"/>
  </putList>

  <!-- Default Stylesheet File -->
  <putList name="styles">
    <add value="/styles/default.css"/>
  </putList>
</definition>
```

Then in the baseLayout.jsp file you can use Tiles tags and the JSTL to get these attributes and render them as follows:

```
<%-- Get JavaScript List --%>
<tiles:useAttribute id="scriptList" name="scripts"
                    classname="java.util.List" ignore="true"/>
<c:forEach var="js" items="${scriptList}">
  <script type="text/JavaScript"
          src="<%=request.getContextPath()%><c:out value="${js}"/>">
  </script>
</c:forEach>
<%-- Get List of Stylesheets --%>
<tiles:useAttribute id="styleList" name="styles"
                    classname="java.util.List" ignore="true"/>
<c:forEach var="css" items="${styleList}">
  <link rel="stylesheet" type="text/css" media="all"
        href="<%=request.getContextPath()%><c:out value="${css}"/>" />
</c:forEach>
```

We had to add the scriptlet <%=request.getContextPath()%> since the add value inside a putList only renders the literal value. We didn't want to hard-code the contextPath in the definitions file, so this was a simple solution. If you're using JSP 2.1, you can replace the `<c:out value="${variable}"/>` with `${variable}`. You can also replace the `<link>` tag for the stylesheet with the more modern method of importing stylesheets, using `@import`. Using this syntax, the stylesheet import would look as follows:

```
<style type="text/css" media="all">
  <c:forEach var="css" items="${styleList}">
    @import url(<%=request.getContextPath()%><c:out value="${css}"/>);
  </c:forEach>
</style>
```

This technique can be used to decrease the amount of HTML written as well as to disable stylesheets for older browsers (that is, Netscape 4.x). This may sound foolish, but why would you want to disable stylesheets for older browsers? The reason is simple. If your site is developed using CSS and `<div>` elements for layout, the chances are that viewing your site without stylesheets is still readable, but it's just plain text, in black and white, with no fancy layout. This allows older browsers to still see your content, and you don't have to worry about making your CSS compatible with old browsers. Of course, this luxury is purely dependent on your customers. Our advice is to drop support for older browsers—we guarantee that that alone will speed up your productivity. If you're willing to use a standards-compliant server (Java EE), why not expect a standards-compliant client? Surely most users have upgraded to newer browsers by now.

## BROWSERS—AN ALTERNATE VIEW

At least one author of this book, however, disagrees with the advice to arbitrarily drop support for older browsers. As of July 2005, 68% of web users were using Internet Explorer 6 (http://www.w3schools.com/browsers/browsers_stats.asp). But looked at from another point of view, 32% of your potential users are using some browser other than Internet Explorer 6. And when Internet Explorer 7 is released, you can expect that many people will stay with version 6 for many months before upgrading.

In addition to using older browsers, a great number of the users of your website may be using dial-up connections (41% according to http://www.websiteoptimization.com/bw/0506/).

As W3Schools says on their website:

"Global averages may not always be relevant to your website. Different sites attract different audiences. Some websites attract professional developers using professional hardware, other sites attract hobbyists using older low spec computers."

Part of your application design should be a consideration of the characteristics of the users of your site. If you determine that enough of them will be using bleeding edge technology, then your design decisions will be different from if you decide that many of them are older users with antiquated computers connecting through 56K dial-up modems.

In the `struts-resume` application, we're using the `<link>` syntax so we can use a stylesheet switcher in the future. Paul Sowden developed the stylesheet switcher we've implemented, and instructions on how to implement it are documented at http://www.alistapart.com/ stories/alternate/. Basically, it uses JavaScript and cookies to disable or enable your preferred stylesheets. We've used it on several projects and have found it very useful.

After you've set up the template and baseLayout definition to render multiple stylesheets, you can override the list in a child definition. One thing to note is <putList> doesn't allow extension, so you have to replace the entire thing. The means that if all you want to do is add an additional stylesheet, you also have to include the original (default.css) stylesheet. In the mainMenu definition, you're using the **Struts Menu** (http://www.sourceforge.net/projects/ struts-menu) as your menuing system. This menu requires an additional stylesheet file as well as an additional JavaScript file. Therefore, you should replace the original lists with new ones:

```
<putList name="scripts">
  <add value="/scripts/global.js"/>
  <add value="/scripts/menuExpandable.js"/>
</putList>
<putList name="styles">
  <add value="/styles/default.css"/>
  <add value="/styles/menuExpandable.css"/>
</putList>
```

Pretty slick huh? We've used this technique for the last year and it's worked great.

### Tiles, XDoclet, and Forwards

Using Tiles to assemble and define your pages can be quite handy, but how do you call these definitions? The easiest way to reference your Tiles definitions is using an ActionForward. When you add the Tiles plug-in to your Struts configuration file, a smart Tiles-aware processor is used to execute requests. This processor, named TilesRequestProcessor, subclasses the Struts default RequestProcessor to intercept calls to includes and forwards to see if the specified URI (path) is a definition name.

To configure Tiles definition forwarding in your application, all you need to do is match up the "path" attribute of a <forward> with the name attribute of a definition. For example, in struts-resume, the ResumeAction's search() method returns an ActionForward to a local <forward> named list:

```
return mapping.findForward("list");
```

This forward is defined in struts-config.xml for the ResumeAction class as follows:

```
<action path="/editResume" type="org.appfuse.webapp.action.ResumeAction"
        name="resumeForm" scope="request" input="viewResumes"
        parameter="action" unknown="false" validate="false">
  <forward name="edit" path=".resumeDetail" redirect="false"/>
  <forward name="list" path=".resumeList" redirect="false"/>
</action>
```

In `tiles-config.xml`, the ".resumeList" definition is a simple definition that defines a title, header, and content page.

```
<definition name=".resumeList" extends=".mainMenu">
  <put name="title.key"   value="resumeList.title" />
  <put name="heading.key" value="resumeList.heading" />
  <put name="content" value="/WEB-INF/pages/resumeList.jsp"/>
</definition>
```

In `struts-resume`, the `BaseAction` class extends `LookupDispatchAction`, and Tiles definitions are used extensively for assembling pages. The logic flow from a JSP's URL to an action's method to a Tiles definition can be somewhat confusing, especially when you bring XDoclet into the mix to define the action's mapping and local forwards. Figure 15-13 illustrates the logical flow of it all.

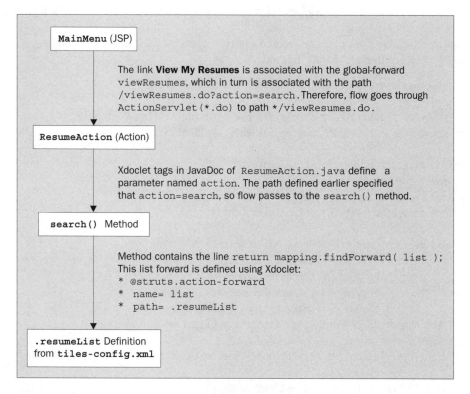

**Figure 15-13.** *The logical flow of control from JSP to Tiles*

In the previous diagram, the `ResumeAction` class extends `LookupDispatchAction`. Basically, it allows you to use a parameter (action) to specify which method to call in your `Action` class. The figure shows the XDoclet tags used to create the `ResumeAction`'s mapping in the Struts configuration file as well its local forward. All of these tags are written in the class's header Javadoc comments.

**Tiles Controllers**

Tiles controllers can be very helpful in improving the architecture of your Tiles-enabled application. They haven't received much press in current publications, but can be a very useful feature. At its core, a Tiles controller is designed to prepare data for presentation on a tile. You might think of it as a mini-action. However, these controllers aren't designed to determine application flow; that's the responsibility of the `ActionServlet`. If you're developing a portal site or you have tiles that require their own custom data, you should definitely considering using one.

Of course, it will be easier to understand if we give you an example. Therefore, we've created a feature for `struts-resume` that counts the current number of active sessions and displays it as "Current Users." We did this by first creating a `UserCounterListener` that implements `ServletContextListener` and `HttpSessionListener`. This listener increments an application-scoped variable when new sessions are created and decrements from the same variable when sessions are destroyed. This source file is located in `struts-resume` at `src/web/org/appfuse/webapp/listener`. We've used XDoclet's `@web:listener` tag to create a `<listener>` entry for this class in `web.xml`.

To implement a Tiles controller, we created a `UserCounterController` class that implements the `Controller` interface and its method:

```
public final class UserCounterController implements Controller {
    /**
     * This method illustrates a simple example of using a Tiles Controller
     * to get a "current users" counter for this application.
     *
     * @param tileContext Current tile context
     * @param request Current request
     * @param response Current response
     * @param servletContext Current Servlet Context
     */
    public void perform(ComponentContext tilesContext,
                        HttpServletRequest request,
                        HttpServletResponse response,
                        ServletContext servletContext)
                        throws ServletException, IOException {
        // Get the number of current users from the application's context
        String userCounter =
            (String) servletContext.getAttribute(UserCounterListener.COUNT_KEY);

        // Add this number to the request for display
        request.setAttribute(UserCounterListener.COUNT_KEY, userCounter);
    }
}
```

You can see that the `perform()` method's signature is similar to the `Action` class's signature—except there's no `ActionMapping` or `ActionForm`. The `ComponentContext` is a scope similar to that of a request or session; however, it's specific to Tiles and is used to store its configuration information.

The UserCounterController is simply grabbing an attribute out of the application scope and putting it into the request scope. However, you could easily add more complex logic in this method. In this example, you're storing the attribute in the request attribute for simplicity, but it could also be stored in the ComponentContext using the following code:

```
tilesContext.putAttribute(UserCounterListener.COUNT_KEY, userCounter);
```

This would ensure that the attribute was only available for this tile. To configure struts-resume to use this controller, we edited tiles-config.xml file (in web/WEB-INF). We decided we wanted to display this "Current Users" counter in the header of the page—and since we only defined the header in the "baseLayout" definition, this was an easy change. Before the change, the header tile was simply pointing to the header.jsp file:

```
<definition name="baseLayout" path="/layouts/baseLayout.jsp">
...
    <put name="header" value="/common/header.jsp"/>
...
</definition>
```

To make the *header* tile controller-enabled, we created a new definition for it and pointed to it from the baseLayout definition:

```
<definition name="baseLayout" path="/layouts/baseLayout.jsp">
...
    <put name="header" value=".header.userCount"/>
...
</definition>
<definition name=".header.userCount" path="/common/header.jsp"
            controllerClass="org.appfuse.webapp.action.UserCounterController" />
```

This means that for each page that the ".header.userCount" tile appears on, UserCounterController.perform() will be called. To display the counter in the header.jsp, we then added the following JSP code:

```
<%-- Check to ensure "userCounter" is in request, if not, don't display --%>
<c:if test="${requestScope.userCounter != null}">
<div id="activeUsers">
  <bean:message key="mainMenu.activeUsers"/>:
  <c:out value="${userCounter}" />
</div>
</c:if>
```

To test it, we logged in to the struts-resume application with two different browsers, which created two different sessions. After the sessions were created, the User Counter text in the header (see Figure 15-14) shows that there are currently two users active in the application. We realize this may not be a precise count, but it's about as accurate as it gets with web applications.

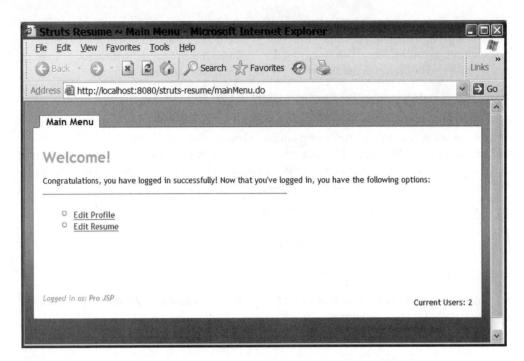

**Figure 15-14.** *Using a Tiles controller, the application can track the number of sessions and display that number in the header.*

You can see that the Tiles controller can be a very valuable asset in your Struts toolbox. You can reduce the amount of code needed in your actions and move specific logic to specific tiles. You might even eliminate the need to chain actions together, using multiple tiles and controller combinations instead. You're encouraged to consider using controllers because they can greatly help organize your code and view logic. By using controllers, actions can focus on page flow rather than preparing views.

If you're developing a very small and simple application, Tiles might not be necessary. The difficult part of Tiles is finding a good example to operate from and extend. We hope that these examples, in combination with the `struts-resume` application, will make your Struts development journey easier. You should be able to use the `basicLayout.jsp` and `tiles-config.xml` files to get up and running. If you already know Struts and aren't using Tiles, you owe it to yourself (and your deadlines) to try it out.

## Using IDEs and Struts Development Environments

We used to use Macromedia's HomeSite and vi for all our Java editing, because we hated the bloat and RAM wastage of an IDE. Furthermore, IDEs always seemed to complicate things more than they helped. With the maturity of tools like IDEA and Eclipse, using an IDE is fun again—and worth our time (a gig of RAM doesn't hurt either).

We've never felt the need to use an IDE to help us configure our `struts-config.xml` or `web.xml` file. However, this was probably because these tools didn't exist when we first started working with Struts and web application. Now we're glad we learned the DTDs and we feel that it's easier to do our job with this knowledge. If editing XML files by hand, we recommend XMLSpy (http://www.xmlspy.com). This is a great tool for any XML-related development because it validates your XML against a DTD or XML Schema and also performs auto-completion as you type. Another reason to learn the DTDs or Xml Schema is because tools like XDoclet assemble the struts-config.xml file from a number of XML fragments, and most IDE tools only support editing fully assembled struts-config.xml files.

There are also applications that have been created simply to provide a development environment for Struts's application development. Let's take a look at a couple of these now.

### Struts Console

Struts Console (found at http://www.jamesholmes.com/struts/) is a free application for managing Struts-based applications. Struts Console is a visual editor for JSP Tag Library, Struts, Tiles, and Validator configuration files. It can be used as a stand-alone Swing application or as a plug-in for your favorite IDE. Supported IDEs are JBuilder (v4.0+), Eclipse (v1.0+), IBM WebSphere Appl. Dev. (v4.0.3+), IDEA (v3.0, build 668+), NetBeans (v3.2), Sun ONE/Forte (v3.0+), and JDeveloper (v9i+). It has support for managing all your Struts-related XML files, such as struts-config.xml, tiles-config.xml, and validation.xml. When using this tool, as with many others, you'll lose any formatting you've applied to the document. However, it does allow formatting within the tool to "pretty up" your XML. It also has a wizard for converting JSP and HTML pages into Struts JSP pages—a very handy feature if you're converting an existing application to Struts.

### Easy Struts

The Easy Struts project (see http://easystruts.sourceforge.net/) provides a set of tools for Struts development, including a struts-config.xml editor, XSLT generation, tooltips from the Struts DTD, support for modules, and an input helper. Easy Struts is only available as an IDE plug-in; no stand-alone application is available. Supported IDEs are Eclipse (v2.0+) and JBuilder (v5.0+).

# Using Modules in Team Development Environments

Have you ever worked on a project where many developers were working on the same codebase? Many development teams work in this type of environment, while others allocate development roles to single individuals. Let's imagine two types of teams; the first has fifteen developers and the second has three individuals. We'll pretend that both teams are developing similar applications that use Struts and EJBs for handling credit card payments for a large bank. The large team will probably divide the work among tiers, where five people work on each tier—EJBs, ActionServlets, and business layer, and the web tier comprising JSP pages or Velocity templates. The second (smaller) team will simply assign one person to each tier.

In a team environment where many people are configuring and manipulating deployment descriptors, it can be difficult to keep your web.xml and struts-config.xml in sync. The simplest solution we've found is to use XDoclet to generate these configuration files, but there is another option—**modules**. When initially developed by the Struts development team, they were called subapplications, which is a more descriptive name. Modules allow you to separate different areas of an application out into different modules. Modules are a core feature of Struts 1.1 and can be very helpful for large projects as well as for creating pluggable features.

Since the development of modules is very similar to developing a standard Struts application, we'll show you how to set them up, and we've actually implemented an "upload" feature that uses them in the struts-resume application. The setup is rather simple, consisting of the following three steps:

1. Prepare a config file for your module.

2. Inform the controller of the module.

3. Use forwards or actions to switch to your new module.

We won't detail the first step here, because this is the same as creating a new Struts application. You could probably use XDoclet to create your configuration files for the different modules, but you would have to coax your Ant webdoclet task to output struts-config.xml to different directories. Of course, the purpose of submodules is to make development and configuration easier, and XDoclet already does this for you!

The second step involves adding a new init parameter to the ActionServlet's definition in the application's deployment descriptor, web.xml. In the struts-resume application, this configuration is located at metadata/web/servlets.xml:

```
<servlet>
  <servlet-name>action</servlet-name>
  <servlet-class>org.apache.struts.action.ActionServlet</servlet-class>
  <init-param>
    <param-name>config</param-name>
    <param-value>/WEB-INF/struts-config.xml</param-value>
  </init-param>
  <init-param>
    <param-name>config/upload</param-name>
    <param-value>/WEB-INF/struts-upload.xml</param-value>
  </init-param>
  <init-param>
    <param-name>debug</param-name>
    <param-value>2</param-value>
  </init-param>
  <init-param>
    <param-name>detail</param-name>
    <param-value>2</param-value>
  </init-param>
  <load-on-startup>2</load-on-startup>
</servlet>
```

This configuration indicates that there are two modules in this application—the default module, which has no forward slash (/) in its name, and the second, our "upload" feature. The configuration files for both modules are located in the WEB-INF directory. The recommended standard for naming module configuration files is struts-module.xml.

While you're looking at the ActionServlet's configuration, we want to point out a few changes between 1.0 and 1.1/1.2. In 1.0, it was common practice to specify the ResourceBundle for messages as an "application" init parameter. We used this setting, as well as the "nocache" init parameter. In Struts 1.1, these settings have been deprecated and moved to a `<controller>` element in the `struts-config.xml` file. The following setting can be found in `metadata/web/struts-controller.xml`:

```
<controller nocache="true"
            inputForward="true"
            maxFileSize="2M" />
```

The nocache setting tells the controller to add HTTP headers to prevent caching of content—it's off by default. You can also specify a `forwardPattern` attribute, such as `WEB-INF/pages/$M$P`, where the `$M` variable indicates the module prefix and `$P` indicates the path attribute of the selected `<forward>` element, although it isn't used here. The `inputForward` attribute allows you to use local or global forwards in the `input` attribute of an action mapping. This is a very handy and much needed feature.

---

■**Note** More information on optional values and their meanings can be found online at `http://struts.apache.org/userGuide/configuration.html`.

---

The application's ResourceBundle is now specified in a `<message-resources>` element in `struts-config.xml`. If you're using XDoclet, you can place this in a `struts-message-resources.xml` file. In the `struts-resume` application, this file is located in the same location as the rest of the Struts configuration fragments:

```
<message-resources parameter="ApplicationResources"/>
```

Since we keep this file (`ApplicationResources.properties`) directory under `WEB-INF/classes`, there is no need to specify a package name. You can also specify alternate resource bundles for the application by adding a second `<message-resources>` element and specifying a key attribute:

```
<message-resources parameter="CustomResources" key="custom"/>
```

This can be useful if, for instance, you're building a product using Struts and you only want to expose a minimal amount of options that customers may change. To use this ResourceBundle with the `<bean:message>` tag, you only need to specify a `bundle` attribute that matches the key:

```
<bean:message key="webapp.title.prefix" bundle="custom"/>
```

Now that you've seen how to set up modules for an application, let's see how to switch between them. For demonstration purposes, we've added an "upload" module to `struts-resume` for uploading résumés. This module doesn't demonstrate much more than file upload and module switching. It could be developed into a feature that allows for simple uploading of existing résumés, but not much more than that. At the time of writing, there are two basic techniques to switching modules. The first involves using a forward (global or local) with a contextRelative attribute set to true. This will tell the controller and request dispatcher to be module-sensitive, rather than simply context-sensitive:

```
<forward name="toUpload"
         contextRelative="true"
         path="/upload/index"
         redirect="true">
```

In this example, index is a definition in the tiles-upload.xml document. Adding redirect="true" is required to enable the switching to execute correctly. The second method is to use the built-in SwitchAction. Using the SwitchAction would result in an <action-mappings> such as the one you see here:

```
<action-mappings>
  <action path="/switchModule"
          type="org.apache.struts.actions.SwitchAction"/>
   ...
</action-mappings>
```

Then to change to the upload module, you could use a URL such as http://localhost:8080/ struts-resume/ switchAction.do?prefix=upload&page=index. We think it's much easier and cleaner to use the global-forward technique, and therefore we've configured the following forward in metadata/web/global-forwards.xml:

```
<forward name="uploadResume" contextRelative="true"
         path="/upload/index.do" redirect="true" />
```

One thing we noticed when building the "upload" module for struts-resume was that it was possible to share configuration settings between the applications. For instance, we've shared the same basicLayout.jsp template that we used for Tiles. The one problem we encountered was that any messages (in ApplicationResources) and any forwards that you include in your submodule have to be defined in their respective files. For instance, we had to define the error page messages, button labels, and Validator messages. We expected this, so it wasn't an issue. It's nice to see that there is clean separation of modules, but you're also allowed to share pieces of each.

Hopefully, you'll find this simple enough to consider using if you think you have need for modules in an application. The one limitation of modules at this point is that they're only supported when using extension mapping of your ActionServlet. Which is to say that *.do is supported, but /do/* isn't; but consult the Struts site (http://struts.apache.org/) or mailing lists for the current status of this issue.

## Testing Struts Applications

Like any good Java programmer, you will have heard of testing frameworks and you've probably used **JUnit** before. JUnit version 3.8.1 (required by struts-resume) can be downloaded from http://www.junit.org. Ant can be a very powerful tool for running JUnit tests. To run them, you need to have JUnit's JAR file (junit.jar) in the $ANT_HOME/lib directory.

JUnit works great for testing classes outside a servlet container, but doesn't provide the needed structure for testing what a user will actually do. For this, you've been blessed with **Cactus** from the Jakarta project. Cactus is a simple test framework for unit testing server-side Java code such as servlets, EJBs, tag libraries, and filters. It supports both in-container testing and out-of-container testing via *mock objects*. It's pretty slick in that you can run a test (for instance, ant test-cactus -Dtestcase=ActionFilterTest for the struts-resume application), and it will start Tomcat, run the test, and then stop Tomcat. It also integrates with **HttpUnit** for testing your JSP pages and validating that the resulting HTML is correct. More information on Cactus can be found at http://jakarta.apache.org/cactus. You can find the HttpUnit website at http://httpunit.sourceforge.net.

The struts-resume example uses a tool called **JUnitDoclet** (http://www.junitdoclet.org) to generate JUnit-based skeleton test cases and test suites of all your Java source files. All you need to do is execute ant gen-test-module where module is common, web, or ejb.

JUnitDoclet is a pretty slick tool in that it will update your test cases if you add new methods, and it won't overwrite any custom code you've added to the test case. We're saying this to warn you that there may be some test cases without any "meat in the methods." In most cases, this is because we've used the class before and we know it works, so we don't care to test it. Is this a bad practice? Maybe, but it will sure help our development time.

We're using a different source tree for test cases, and it works really well with this approach. Unfortunately, once you've changed a test case to extend something other than JUnit (that is, Cactus's ServletTestCase), it won't update that class anymore. It will simply ignore it, which is fine with us.

Another testing framework, specific to Struts, was introduced in late 2001. Known as **StrutsTestCase for JUnit** (see http://strutstestcase.sourceforge.net/), it's an extension of the standard JUnit test case. By providing both a mock object and a Cactus approach to run the ActionServlet, StrutsTestCase allows testing of Struts code with or without a running servlet engine. Since it uses the controller to test code, it tests not only the implementation of Action objects, but also mappings, ActionForms, and ActionForwards.

StrutsTestCase is compliant with both the Java Servlet 2.5 specifications and supports Struts 1.2, Cactus 1.6.1, and JUnit 3.8.1.

StrutsTestCase already provides validation methods, so it's simple to create unit test cases, as demonstrated by the following code snippet:

```
public void testEditUser() {
  setRequestPathInfo("/editUser");
  setRequestParameter("action", "edit");
  addRequestParameter("email","tomcat");
  actionPerform();
  verifyForward("success");
  assertTrue(getSession().getAttribute(Constants.USER_KEY) != null);
}
```

You could run a very comprehensive test of your application using Cactus and HttpUnit to verify your action classes and whatever view technology you happen to use in rendering your UI (JSP, XML, or Velocity). An HttpUnit test is also pretty simple, as demonstrated in the following example:

```
WebConversation wc = new WebConversation();
WebResponse resp = wc.getResponse(
                  "http://www.httpunit.org/doc/Cookbook.html");
WebLink link = resp.getLinkWith("response");
link.click();
WebResponse jdoc = wc.getCurrentPage();
```

HttpUnit also supports testing of JavaScript, and their site carries the warning that it's "very basic at present" (see http://www.httpunit.org/doc/javascript-support.html). If you're looking for a more robust JavaScript testing framework, we recommend **JsUnit** (http://www.jsunit.net). JsUnit is a unit testing framework for client-side testing of JavaScript. JsUnit tests are written in JavaScript: it's essentially a JavaScript port of JUnit, so you name your methods and such accordingly. It's important to note that these languages are drastically different, and whoever writes the JavaScript should probably also write the tests.

The last testing framework we want to cover is the **WebTest** tool (http://webtest.canoo.com) from Canoo. This is a much easier testing framework to develop with because everything is simply configured in an XML file. Similar to the other testing frameworks, WebTest is run with Ant. However, the main difference is that the entire test is configured in an Ant task. For instance, this might be how you create a test for a user logging into your application:

```
<target name="login">
  <testSpec name="tomcat-login">
    <config host="${tomcat.server}" port="${tomcat.port}"
            protocol="http" basepath="${webapp.name}" verbose="true"
            resultpath="." resultfile="web-test-result.xml" summary="true"
            saveresponse="true"/>
    <steps>
      <invoke stepid="get Login Page" url="/"/>
      <verifytitle stepid="we should see the login title" text="Login"/>
      <setinputfield stepid="set user name"
                     name="j_username" value="tomcat"/>
      <setinputfield stepid="set password"
                     name="j_password" value="tomcat"/>
      <clickbutton label="Login" stepid="Click the submit button"/>
      <verifytitle text="Main Menu"
                   stepid="Home Page follows if login ok"/>
    </steps>
  </testSpec>
  <loadfile property="web-test.result"
            srcFile="web-test-result.xml"/>
  <echo>${web-test.result}</echo>
</target>
```

WebTest is a great framework for web developers, because you can easily test the path a user takes without writing any code, just XML. It also appears to use HttpUnit, so it isn't reinventing the wheel, rather just providing an easier way to develop it.

For testing your application's interactions with a database, you might want to take a look at **Dbunit** (http://www.dbunit.org). Dbunit is a JUnit extension that sets up your database in a known state so you can execute your tests with expected data. It uses XML datasets, or collections of data tables, and performs database operations before and after each test. Of course, you can also do this in your test cases, where you can insert, update, or delete an object, but since there's no guarantee of the order that these will execute, Dbunit is probably a good idea. We've had good luck with putting our tests in a particular order in a class, and then having these methods get executed in that order, but an ideal test method is autonomous.

We've included examples of Cactus tests, Struts Action tests, HttpUnit tests, and even a simple Canoo WebTest example. Table 15-2 indicates which classes you can use for these and how to run them. Run `test-cactus` instead of `test-web` if you want to run these tests while Tomcat is already running.

**Table 15-2.** *Testing struts-resume with Various Testing Frameworks*

| Test Type | File Location | Ant Command |
|-----------|---------------|-------------|
| Cactus | test/org/appfuse/webapp/action/UserAction | ant test-web -Dtestcase=LoginActionTest |
| Struts | test/org/appfuse/webapp/action/ResumeAction | ant test-web -Dtestcase=ResumeActionTest |
| HttpUnit | test/org/appfuse/webapp/action/MainMenuTest | ant test-web -Dtestcase=MainMenuTest |
| Canoo | web-tests.xml | ant test-canoo -Dtestcase=login |

Using servlet testing frameworks like StrutsTestCase and Cactus will make testing your actions much easier. It's either that or testing them through your browser, which may take you five clicks to get to. There's no need to wait for your JSP pages to compile if you really only want to hit a servlet. The `struts-resume` application makes it easy to develop and run new tests. We encourage you to use it and learn from it.

A real timesaver with JSP development is precompiling the JSP pages prior to deploying them to your servlet container. This can be done with Ant's `<jspc>` task, which uses Tomcat's Jasper compiler to generate `.java` source files. While it's great for testing, you would like to use this tool to precompile your JSP pages for production use too, right? Unfortunately, to do this, you need to make an entry for every JSP in your `web.xml` file, and boy would that be a long and laborious process. If you don't do this step, Tomcat will just recompile over the top of the pages you've already compiled. Some application servers, such as WebLogic and SunONE, allow you to configure precompilation of JSP pages once the application has been deployed. We'd love it if other vendors would copy this feature.

Another nice thing to do when developing JSP pages is to check that your CSS and HTML is correct. Of course, you won't be able to do this until the JSP has compiled and displayed. If you're using WebTest, it actually generates an HTML file for each request it makes, thereby recording the last viewed request. In the `struts-resume` application, these can be found in `build/test/data`. If you aren't using WebTest, you can just view source in your browser and save the HTML to a directory. Then you can upload it to the W3C's Validator (`http://validator.w3.org`) to ensure the HTML complies with the specified DOCTYPE. We usually create a "sandbox" directory in our project's directory where we can put these HTML files for validation and other quick fixes. Sometimes it's nice to work with a static HTML version. What we do is change the absolute path for all our stylesheets, JavaScript, and images in order to use a relative path. In the `struts-resume` project, this would entail changing `/struts-resume/` to `../web/`.

Once you've validated your application and tested it thoroughly, you'll be much more confident that it works and therefore more likely to produce quality software. Hopefully, with the examples we've put together, the hard work of writing tests is over. Writing tests might seem like a pain, but that's only if you're writing your actual code first. Try writing your test cases first next time, we think you'll find them most enjoyable. There's nothing like writing an application that works the first time you run it in a browser (thanks to the unit tests, of course).

## Handling Exceptions in Struts Applications

Struts 1.1 made it much easier to handle exceptions in a Struts application. A popular rule in software development is that "if something goes wrong, you should tell the user about it." This can become quite complicated in a web application that uses MVC and business objects to talk to a database. Exceptions can be thrown at any level, in your data access code, in your Action classes, in your business objects, or even in your JSP pages.

What we've done in the past was to use a try...catch in both our Action classes and in our business objects and then "bubble" any exceptions up to the top. This is ugly and can result in the user being presented with a message such as column street_address not found. Furthermore, in our Action classes, we've caught our business-level exceptions, wrapped them in a ServletException, and thrown them to the client. We have an error page configured in web.xml as well as on our JSP pages, which the client is directed to in the event of an error.

Even though we're going to show you a better way to handle exceptions with Struts, we still think it's important to configure your JSP pages and web.xml to deal with uncaught exceptions. You should add an entry to web.xml for when the server throws a HTTP Status Code 500, the dreaded Internal Server Error:

```
<error-page>
  <error-code>500</error-code>
  <location>/error.jsp</location>
</error-page>
```

Alternatively, you can use <exception-type> rather than an HTTP status code or error code:

```
<error-page>
  <exception-type>java.lang.Throwable</exception-type>
  <location>/error.jsp</location>
</error-page>
```

You can also add both of them, just to be safe. When using XDoclet, you can specify these entries in an error-pages.xml file in your merge directory. We usually declare an errorPage in our JSP pages as well:

```
<%@ page language="java" errorPage="/error.jsp" %>
```

In the struts-resume example application, this line only exists in the common/taglibs.jsp file. Adding these entries will basically prevent users from ever seeing a stack trace of the exception—providing that you've written your error.jsp appropriately. For an advanced error page, you might even configure it to e-mail an administrator when it's displayed to users (or use log4j's SMTP Logger). We've seen the 500 Internal Server Error more than we've seen the classic 404 error in recent years. Adding a pretty face onto these errors can make everyone's life a little more pleasant.

The real hope is that an error page will never be displayed. As a savvy web user, if it does get displayed, we'd like to see exactly what went wrong—the SQL details. Of course, this will depend on your application's security requirements. If your application is open for attack (resides on the Internet rather than an intranet), you might want to suppress messages that give any database information. At the same time, not all your users will want to see the nitty-gritty details of exceptions, and therefore, we recommend you aim for more user-friendly messages.

## Chained Exceptions

In our opinion, a well-developed application should catch error messages, turn them into friendly messages, and then return the user to the last page they viewed successfully. At the same time, it would be nice to add a technical message as well, for those savvy users (or developers) who want to know the exact cause of the problem and may be able to avoid it. To achieve this, the first thing you can do is to use **chained exceptions**. The traditional Java exception mechanism only allows you to throw one exception. This presents a problem in a layered architecture where exceptions can occur at each layer.

Of course, you can wrap exceptions, as we've done with a ServletException, but this might result in a loss of detail in the end. Ted Husted described the solution best in one of his Struts Tips. Rather than trying to manipulate his words to sound like we came up with the idea, it's easiest to quote him (see http://husted.com/struts/tips/015.html):

> *What we really need to do is "stack" or "chain" the exceptions, so that each layer can add its own viewpoint to the incident. Then, at the end, display them all, with the originating exception at the bottom of the list.*

> *This approach works surprisingly well in a layered architecture. The "topmost" layer is "closest" to the user, and so throws the most "user-friendly" exceptions. The "lowest" layer throws the "geek-friendly" errors that we need to solve the problem. When we chain exceptions by linking them together, the user-friendly message comes first, followed by the more detailed messages. The user is told what they need to know first, and can leave the rest to the system administrators.*

Starting with JDK 1.4, the java.lang.Exception class has a getCause() method that allows you to find the original cause of each exception. To use this properly, you'll need to throw the exceptions that occurred from each tier, rather than just catching an exception and throwing it with a message. By this, we mean to say that it's better to have this:

```
try {
    ...
} catch (Exception e) {
    throw new DAOException("Error occurred connecting to database", e);
}
```

rather than just throwing the message:

```
try {
    ...
} catch (Exception e) {
    throw new DAOException("Error occurred connecting to database");
}
```

We're using this functionality in the struts-resume application, in the ActionFilter.java class to be precise. If you're using a JDK less than 1.4, we invite you to take a look at the Scaffold package, which includes a ChainedException class that works with older JDKs. The following snippet illustrates how we've implemented this functionality in the ActionFilter.java class (located in src/web/org/appfuse/webapp/filters/):

```java
// User authenticated, empty user object
if (username != null && userForm == null) {
  try {
    UserManager mgr =
      new UserManagerImpl(
        (String) ctx.getAttribute(Constants.DAO_TYPE));
    UserForm user = mgr.getUser(username);
    session.setAttribute(Constants.USER_KEY, user);
  } catch (Exception e) {

    // Log the message so we can read the logs and see
    //   what went wrong
    log.error("Error getting user's information " + e);
    // Print a StackTrace, always a good idea
    e.printStackTrace();
    // Set up an empty ActionErrors collection to add all
    //   the exception messages to
    ActionErrors errors = new ActionErrors();

    // Add a general message that says "The process did not complete."
    errors.add(ActionErrors.GLOBAL_ERROR,
          new ActionError("errors.general"));

    StringBuffer sb = new StringBuffer();

    // JDK 1.4 ONLY - if there are causes, loop through them and get
    //   all their messages
    if (e.getCause() == null) {
      sb.append(e.getMessage());
    } else {
      while (e.getCause() != null) {
        sb.append(e.getMessage());
        sb.append("\n");
        e = (Exception) e.getCause();
      }
    }

    // Add all the errors to a resource bundle key, defined as:
    //   errors.detail={0}
    errors.add(
      ActionErrors.GLOBAL_ERROR,
      new ActionError("errors.detail", sb.toString()));
```

```
    // Add the errors to the request so we can display them for the user
    request.setAttribute(Globals.ERROR_KEY, errors);
    // Dispatch to the error messages page
    RequestDispatcher dispatcher =
      request.getRequestDispatcher("/error.jsp");
    dispatcher.forward(request, response);
    return;
  }
}
```

The end result is a series of error messages as follows:

- A required resource is not available.

- The process did not complete. Details should follow.

- Cannot connect to MySQL server localhost:3307. Is there a MySQL server running the machine/port you're trying to connect to? (java.net.ConnectException)

It's easy to see how chained exceptions can give you messages that will satisfy all your users. It might even be possible to use the previous error-looping code in a declared exception for Struts, but we haven't tried this yet. After you've built all your errors, you need to direct the user to a friendly page. When using this code in an `Action` class, you'll most likely direct them back to where they came from.

```
return (new ActionForward(mapping.getInput()));
```

This can be problematic if you access the same `ActionMapping` from several different pages. We've seen this solved in a couple of different ways. The first way is to add an extra parameter to the form or URL that called the action, and then use that value to forward appropriately. The other method is one used by the Roller Weblogger open-source project (http://www.rollerweblogger.org). It uses a `BreadCrumbFilter` to hold a stack of the last URLs accessed by the application. This is nice in that you can simply grab the last URL off the stack and so forward back to the last viewed page.

## Declaring Exceptions

Struts 1.1 introduced the concept of configurable exceptions. That is, you can declaratively specify exceptions on a global level in `struts-config.xml` as well as on an `ActionMapping` level. This concept is similar to the one you see with global forwards and with local forwards. It's easy to register an exception—the only attribute that is required is `type`, which states the type of the exception. Optionally, you can specify a key (to a message in your resource bundle) and the path to direct the response to. The following is an example that might be used to handle `UserNotFoundException`:

```
<exception key="missing.user"
           type="org.appfuse.webapp.services.UserNotFoundException"
           path="addUser"/>
```

In this example, `addUser` is a forward whose path references a tile's definition (in `tiles-config.xml`). You could easily change this to redirect to a JSP page (for instance, `/addUser.jsp` or perhaps /editUser?action=add). Exceptions are best used at the `ActionMapping` level, without a defined path. If you don't define a path, Struts is smart enough to redirect to your `ActionMapping`'s input value. Of course, if you don't have an input defined, you should probably specify the path for your exception, or you'll get the dreaded blank screen of Struts. The key in this example is used to override the key used by the exception itself.

Struts makes it easier to develop exceptions and provides built-in internationalization. Let's take a look at the code for the `UserNotFoundException`:

```
import org.apache.struts.util.ModuleException;
public class UserNotFoundException extends ModuleException {
  /**
   * Construct a new instance of this exception for the specified username.
   * @param username Username that was not found
   */
  public UserNotFoundException(String username) {
    super("error.user.missing", username);
  }
}
```

The String `error.user.missing` refers to a key in the default ResourceBundle, as defined in `struts-config.xml`. In the `struts-resume` application, this bundle is `ApplicationResource.properties`, where the key is defined as follows:

```
error.user.missing=Could not find user information for username '{0}'
```

Of course, you can change your exception's constructor to handle as many parameters as you have in your message key. If you specify a key for this exception in `struts-config.xml`, it will override the message that is spit out by the exception. One disadvantage to this is that you lose the ability to substitute parameters, but it can be useful for exceptions that don't use the Struts's message bundle.

A nice feature of Struts's exception handling is that messages are easily externalized in a properties file. That is, you get I18n built right into your exception handling. Furthermore, you can specify a separate `ResourceBundle` for your error messages by specifying the bundle attribute on your exception. Of course, you could use a `ResourceBundle` on your business and persistence layers with properties file, but it might not be needed if these exceptions never bubble up to the UI.

The beauty of using declared exceptions in your application is that you don't have to catch them in your `Action` classes. The Struts `execute()` method throws a top-level `Exception`. Since all exceptions extend `Exception` somewhere along the line, this makes it easy to write and throw your exceptions:

```
public ActionForward execute(ActionMapping mapping,
                             ActionForm form,
                             HttpServletRequest request,
                             HttpServletResponse response)
                       throws Exception {
```

When a registered exception is caught by Struts, it will actually create an errors object for you that can then be displayed using `<html:errors/>` or a syntax like that in `struts-resume`.

The following is what the messages.jsp file uses that is included in the struts-resume application's main Tiles template:

```
<%-- Error Messages --%>
<logic:messagesPresent>
  <div class="error">
    <html:messages id="error">
      <bean:write name="error" filter="false"/><br />
    </html:messages>
  </div>
</logic:messagesPresent>
<%-- Success Messages --%>
<logic:messagesPresent message="true">
  <div class="message">

    <html:messages id="message" message="true">
      <bean:write name="message" filter="false"/><br />
    </html:messages>
  </div>
</logic:messagesPresent>
```

This could also be done with the JSTL, but we prefer the shorter method with less typing, so we're using Struts tags. You'll notice the second half of this page is used to display success messages. We think it's important to know how to create and display success messages in an application, so we'll show you how easy it is. Essentially, all you need do is create a new messages object and add one or more messages to it. It's very similar to the ActionErrors class (it's actually its superclass), so the creation process is pretty much the same:

```
ActionMessages messages = new ActionMessages();
// execute business logic to add a new record
// add success message to the request
messages.add(ActionMessages.GLOBAL_MESSAGE, new ActionMessage("record.added"));
```

While we haven't yet used declarative exception handling with Struts on any real-world projects, we've implemented it in the struts-resume application where it was very useful. If you have an exception framework that works for your Struts-based application, we also invite you to chime in on the struts-dev mailing list and suggest improvements. The struts-resume application gives an example of using declared exceptions, and you can also find an example in the struts-example application that ships with Struts.

# Summary

One of the most frustrating things we've experienced in software development is reading about how to do something, but not having any examples. Design patterns are good only if they work when implemented. We believe in keeping it simple, and we believe that Struts makes JSP and servlet development simpler. We know that Struts can be overwhelming at first, but its rewards are awesome. Using Struts will ultimately lead you to understand web applications better and will reduce your development time as you use it more.

Using the tools and sample applications available for Struts can also be overwhelming. The only way to truly learn what is best is to try them and learn what is best for you. If you send a message to the Struts user mailing list about something non-Struts-related (for example HTML, JavaScript, persistence), chances are you'll get a whole gamut of different responses and opinions. However, it's a very active community, and chances are you'll get your questions answered. Hopefully, we've given you some guidance in what works well with Struts, and perhaps our sample application will show you how XDoclet makes generating code and other items much easier. We also invite you to download and use Dave Johnson's Roller Weblogger software—it's open source and has a lot of good Struts code in it. It also uses XDoclet and is a fairly robust application. More information on Roller can be found at `http://www.rollerweblogger.org`.

Above all, we advise not trying to reinvent the wheel with anything related to web applications. Chances are that someone has already tried to do what you're doing. Spending the time to research your problem and solutions may save you a lot of time down the road. Using mailing list archives and Google can solve a great number of problems. Open-source projects are great because you get a whole team of developers working with you and helping you use their frameworks. It helps to get involved with the technology you're using as well. If you're using Struts, subscribe to the `struts-user` mailing list and watch your inbox fill up, or subscribe to the digest list for only a couple of e-mails per day. Remember that anything possible in a simple JSP and servlet application is possible when using Struts. Struts just makes it easier, as we're sure any web-based MVC framework does. Likewise, anything that is possible on an HTML page or with a servlet is possible in a JSP page.

Another reason we really like using Struts is because of the tools that have appeared to automate the development process. We're comfortable enough with developing all the components that we can check the generated code to make sure everything is fine. You wouldn't want to use a code-generator that produces spaghetti code! The Struts Roadmap includes enhanced support for these tools as well as embraces newer technologies such as JSF and the JSTL.

We'll just note a few tips here as gentle reminders of what we covered in the chapter:

- If you need validation in your Struts application, use the Validator. If you're using the Validator, use XDoclet to generate your `validation.xml`.

- If you need templating in a Struts application, use Tiles. If you're using Tiles, use definitions and use them as forwards in your `struts-config.xml`.

- Use container-managed authentication for login—then you'll have roles available to show or hide tiles and to limit access to certain actions and links.

- Use CSS rather than tables for page layout. It will reduce the size of your pages, and it's easier to develop with in the long run.

# JavaServer Pages
# Syntax Reference

This appendix describes the syntax for JavaServer Pages 2.1. The intention is to provide you with a reference that is complete and useful, but more compact than the specification. JSP specifications are available by visiting `http://java.sun.com/products/jsp/`.

This appendix looks in turn at the following:

- Various preliminary details: the notation we're using, how URLs are specified in JSP code, and the various types of commenting you can use.

- The JSP **directives**: the `page`, `taglib`, and `include` directives.

- JSP **scripting elements**: declarations, scriptlets, and expressions.

- JSP's **standard actions** including the `<jsp:useBean>`, `<jsp:setProperty>`, `<jsp:getProperty>`, `<jsp:include>`, and `<jsp:forward>` actions.

- A brief review of the syntax for using **tag libraries**.

- The **implicit objects** that are available within a JSP such as `request`, `response`, `session`, and `application`. You'll examine these in more detail in Appendix B.

- Various predefined request and application **attributes** that you may find useful.

## Preliminaries

Before you get stuck in the details, here are a few miscellaneous observations.

### Notation

A word on the notation used in this appendix:

- Attribute names are shown in regular text. These names are used exactly as shown.

- **Bold** shows the default value of an attribute. Attributes with default values are optional, if you're using the default. Sometimes, where the default value is a little complicated, we use **default** to indicate that the default is described in the following text.

- When an attribute has a set of possible values, those are shown delimited by "|".

- Nondefault attribute values are shown in regular text. In general, if several possible values are shown, these are the values to use in your JSP. In the following snippet, true or false are the only valid values for session. In other cases, the value shown is a sample that you would replace with the appropriate value. For example, the sample value used with import would be replaced with the actual classes to be imported, such as java.util.Vector or java.io.*. You should have little difficulty distinguishing which values are actual values and which are samples.

```
import="package.class, package.*, ..."
session="true|false"
```

## URL Specifications

URLs specified within JSP tags can be of two sorts:

- **Context-relative** paths start with a "/"; the base URL is provided by the web application to which the JSP belongs. For example, in a web application hosted at http://localhost:8080/projsp-appendixA/, the URL /pageurl.jsp would be equivalent to http://localhost:8080/projsp-appendixA/pageurl.jsp.

- **Page-relative** paths are relative to the JSP page in which they occur. Unlike context-relative paths, page-relative paths don't start with "/". For instance, a page application hosted at http://localhost:8080/projsp-appendixA/morespecs/urlspec.jsp might give a page as subfolder/urlspec.jsp, which would be equivalent to http://localhost:8080/projsp-appendixA/morespecs/subfolder/urlspec.jsp.

## Comments

Two sorts of comments are allowed in JSP code—JSP and HTML:

```
<!-- HTML comments remain in the final client page.
     They can contain JSP expressions, which will be ignored by the JSP
     container.
-->
<%-- JSP comments are hidden from the final client page --%>
```

Remember too that within scriptlets (inside <% %>, <%! %>, or <%= %> tags), you can use standard Java comments:

```
<%
  /* This Java comment starts with a slash asterisk and continues
     until you come to a closing asterisk slash.
  */
  // Comments starting with a double slash continue to the end of the line.
%>
```

# Directives

Directives are instructions to the JSP container regarding page properties, importing tag libraries, and including content within a JSP. Because directives are instructions rather than in-out processes, they cannot produce any output via the out stream.

## The page Directive

The page directive specifies attributes for the page—all the attributes are optional, because the essential ones have default values, shown in bold.

```
<%@ page language="java"
        extends="package.class"
        import="package.class, package.*, ..."
        session="true|false"
        buffer="none|default|sizekb"
        autoFlush="true|false"
        isThreadSafe="true|false"
        info="Sample JSP to show tags"
        isErrorPage="true|false"
        errorPage="ErrorPage.jsp"
        contentType="TYPE|
                    TYPE; charset=CHARSET|
                    text/html; charset=ISO-8859-1"
        pageEncoding="default"
        isELIgnored="true|false"
        deferredSyntaxAllowedAsLiteral="true|false"
        trimDirectiveWhitespaces="true|false"
%>
```

- The default buffer size is defined to be at least 8 KB.

- The errorPage attribute contains the relative URL for the error page to which this page should go if there's an unhandled error on this page.

- The specified error page file must declare isErrorPage="true" to have access to the Exception object. This is an example of the code that may be used for an error page:

```
<%@ page language="java"
        isErrorPage="true" %>
<html>
  <body>
    <!-- This displays fully-qualified name of the exception -->
    <%= exception.toString() %>
    <br>
    <!-- This displays the exception's descriptive message -->
    <%= exception.getMessage() %>
  </body>
</html>
```

The page will print out the error message received.

- The `contentType` attribute sets the MIME type and the character set for the response. The default value is `text/html` when defining JSP Pages standard syntax and `text/xml` when implementing JSP Documents in XML format.

- The `pageEncoding` attribute defines the character encoding for the JSP page. The default is that specified in the `contentType` attribute, or `"ISO-8859-1"` if none was specified there.

- `isELIgnored`: Sets EL support. The default is false, meaning EL is enabled in the page. The value for this attribute overrides the value specified in `web.xml`.

- The `deferredSyntaxAllowedAsLiteral` attribute configures whether #{ is treated as the beginning of a deferred EL statement or a literal.

- The `trimDirectiveWhitespaces` attribute configures whether whitespace is trimmed from template text.

## The taglib Directive

A tag library is a collection of tags used to extend a JSP container functional model. The `taglib` directive defines a tag library namespace for the page, mapping the URI of the tag library descriptor (TLD) to a prefix that can be used to reference tags from the library on this page.

```
<%@ taglib uri|tagdir="/WEB-INF/taglib.tld" prefix="tagPrefix" %>
<tagPrefix:tagName attributeName="attributeValue" >
  JSP content
</tagPrefix:tagName>
<tagPrefix:tagName attributeName="attributeValue" />
```

You should assume that the tag library descriptor defines a `tagName` element. The `tagdir` attribute indicates this prefix is to be used to identify tag extensions installed in the `/WEB-INF/tags/` directory or a subdirectory. If a `tld` is present in the specified directory, it's used. Otherwise, an implicit tag library is used. A translation error must occur if the value for the `tagdir` attribute doesn't start with `/WEB-INF/tags/`. A translation error must occur if the value doesn't point to a directory that exists. A translation error must occur if used in conjunction with the `uri` attribute.

## The include Directive

There are two include tags—the `include` directive and the `jsp:include` action. The `include` directive includes a static file at translation time, adding any JSP in that file to this page for runtime processing:

```
<%@ include file="header.html" %>
```

# Tag Files

The directives available in tag files differ from that used in a JSP page. The page directive is not allowed in a tag file. The `taglib` and `include` directives can be used in a tag file. There are three directives that are only valid in tag files, and these are listed here:

- `tag`

- `attribute`

- `variable`

## The tag Directive

Note that the page directive itself isn't used in a tag file, and instead you use the `tag` directive, which may only be used in tag files. The `tag` directive looks like this:

```
<%@ tag
        display-name="display-name"
        body-content="scriptless|tagdependent|empty"
        dynamic-attributes="name"
        small-icon="small-icon"
        large-icon="large-icon"
        description="description"
        example="example"
        language="scriptingLanguage"
        import="importList"
        pageEncoding="peinfo"
        isELIgnored="true|false"
        deferredSyntaxAllowedAsLiteral="true|false"
        trimDirectiveWhitespaces="true|false"
%>
```

Here's an example tag directive:

```
<%@ tag name="msg"
    display-name="Message"
    body-content="scriptless"
    dynamic-attributes="true"
    small-icon="/WEB-INF/small-icon.jpg"
    large-icon="/WEB-INF/large-icon.jpg"
    description="Simple usage of a tag directive"
%>
```

### The attribute Directive

The attribute directive is analogous to the <attribute> element in the tag library descriptor, and allows for the declaration of custom action attributes.

```
<%@ attribute
          name="attribute-name"
          required="true|false"
          fragment="true|false"
          rtexprvalue="true|false"
          type="type"
          description="description"
          deferredValue="true|false"
          deferredValueType="type"
          deferredMethod="true|false"
          deferredMethodSignature="signature"
%>
```

### The variable directive

The variable directive is analogous to the <variable> element in the tag library descriptor, and defines the details of a variable exposed by the tag handler to the calling page.

```
<%@ variable
          ( name-given="output-name" |
          (name-from-attribute="attr-name" alias="local-name" ) )
          variable-class="output-type|String"
          declare="true|false"
          scope="AT_BEGIN|AT_END|NESTED"
          description="description"
%>
```

# Scripting Elements

Scripting elements are used to include snippets of Java code within a JSP: to declare variables and methods, execute arbitrary Java code, and display the result of Java expressions.

## Declarations

The following syntax allows you to declare variables and methods for the page. These are placed in the generated servlet outside the _jspService() method; in other words, variables declared here will be instance variables of the servlet, and methods declared here will be instance methods of the servlet. Declarations don't produce any output.

Here's an example of declaring a variable:

```
<%! String  message; %>
```

The following code declares a variable and initializes it:

```
<%! String message = "variable declared"; %>
```

You can define a method for use on the global page like so:

```
<%! public String showMessage() { return message; } %>
```

Declaration tags are mainly used in conjunction with scriptlets.

## Scriptlets

Scriptlets enclose Java code (on however many lines) that is evaluated within the generated servlet's _jspService() method to generate dynamic content:

```
<%
  // Java code
%>
```

Take care when using adjacent scriptlet blocks; the following code

```
<% if(user.isLoggedIn) { %>
    <p>Hi!</p>
<% } %>
<% else { %>
    <p>Please log in first...</p>
<% } %>
```

isn't legal because we've broken the else block into two scriptlets with embedded whitespace between the scriptlets.

## Expressions

Expressions return a value from the scripting code as a String to the page:

```
<p>Hello there,
<%= userName %>
Good to see you.</p>
```

Expressions are not complete Java statements, so you do not terminate an expression with a semicolon as you would with a line of code in a scriptlet.

# Standard Actions

The standard actions provide various facilities for manipulating JavaBeans components, including and forwarding control to other resources at request time and generating HTML to use the Java plug-in.

## <jsp:useBean>

The <jsp:useBean> tag checks for an instance of a bean of the given class and scope. If a bean of the specified class exists, it references it with the id; otherwise it instantiates it. The bean is available within its scope with its id attribute.

You can include code between the `<jsp:useBean>` tags, as shown in the second example—this code will only be run if the `<jsp:useBean>` tag successfully instantiates the bean:

```
<jsp:useBean id="aBeanName"
             scope="page|request|session|application"
             typeSpecification
/>
```

or

```
<jsp:useBean id="anotherBeanName"
             scope="page|request|session|application"
             typeSpecification>
  <jsp.setProperty name="anotherBeanName"
                   property="*|propertyName" />
</jsp:useBean>
```

There is a lot of flexibility in specifying the type of the bean (indicated by typeSpecification). You can use

- `class="class_name"`

- `type="typeName"`

- `class="package.class" type="typeName"` (and with terms reversed)

- `beanName="beanName" type="typeName"` (and with terms reversed)

where

- `typeName` is the class of the scripting variable defined by the `id` attribute; that is, the class that the bean instance is cast to (whether the class, a parent class, or an interface the class implements).

- `beanName` is the name of the bean, as used in the `instantiate()` method of the `java.beans.Beans` class.

## `<jsp:setProperty>`

The `<jsp:setProperty>` tag you used previously sets the property of the bean referenced by name using the value:

```
<jsp:setProperty name="anotherBeanName"
                 propertyExpression
/>
```

The `propertyExpression` can be any of the following:

- `property="*"`

- `property="propertyName"`

- `property="propertyName" param="parameterName"`

- `property="propertyName" value="propertyValue"`

where

- The * setting tells the tag to iterate through the request parameters for the page, setting any values for properties in the bean whose names match parameter names.

- The param attribute specifies the parameter name to use in setting this property.

- The value attribute can accept a request-time attribute expression.

- Omitting value and param attributes for a property assumes that the bean property and request parameter name match.

- The value attribute String can be automatically cast to boolean, byte, char, double, int, float, long, and their class equivalents. Other casts will have to be handled explicitly in the bean's setPropertyName() method.

## <jsp:getProperty>

The final bean-handling action is <jsp:getProperty>, which gets the named property and outputs its value for inclusion in the page.

```
<jsp:getProperty name="anotherBeanName" property="propertyName" />
```

## <jsp:include>

The <jsp:include> action includes a static or dynamically referenced file at runtime:

```
<jsp:include page="relativeURL" flush="true|false" />
```

or

```
<jsp:include page="relativeURL"
             flush="true" >
  <jsp:param name="parameterName" value="parameterValue"/>
</jsp:include>
```

where

- The page attribute can be the result of a request-time expression.

- The optional flush attribute determines whether the output buffer will be flushed before including the specified resource. The default value is "false".

- The jsp:param tag allows parameters to be appended to the original request, and if the parameter name already exists, the new parameter value takes precedence in a comma-delimited list.

## <jsp:forward>

To forward the client request to a static resource, whether it be an HTML file, a JSP page, or a servlet class in the same context as the page, use the following syntax:

```
<jsp:forward page="relativeURL" />
```

or

```
<jsp:forward page="relativeURL" >
  <jsp:param name="parameterName" value="parameterValue" />
</jsp:forward>
```

where

- The page attribute for `<jsp:forward>` can be a request-time expression.

- The `jsp:param` tag allows parameters to be appended to the original request, and if the parameter name already exists, the new parameter value takes precedence in a comma-delimited list.

# \<jsp:param\>

The `<jsp:param>` action is used within the body of `<jsp:forward>`, `<jsp:include>`, and `<jsp:plugin>` to supply extra name-value parameter pairs. It has the following syntax:

```
<jsp:param name="parameterName" value="parameterValue" />
```

# \<jsp:plugin\>

The `<jsp:plugin>` action enables the JSP to include a bean or an applet in the client page. It has the following syntax:

```
<jsp:plugin type="bean|applet"
            code="objectCode"
            codebase="objectCodebase"
            name="instanceName"
            title="title"
            archive="archiveURI"
            align="bottom|top|middle|left|right"
            height="inPixels"
            width="inPixels"
            hspace="leftRightPixels"
            vspace="topBottomPixels"
            jreversion="1.2|number"
            nspluginurl="pluginURL"
            iepluginurl="pluginURL"
            mayscript="true|false" >
  <jsp:params>
    <jsp:param name="parameterName" value="parameterValue">
  </jsp:params>
  <jsp:fallback>arbitrary text</jsp:fallback>
</jsp:plugin>
```

Most of these attributes are direct from the HTML spec (http://www.w3.org/TR/html4/), with the exceptions being type, jreversion, nspluginurl, and iepluginurl.

- The name, archive, align, height, width, hspace, vspace, jreversion, nspluginurl, and iepluginurl attributes are optional.

- The <jsp:param> tag's value attribute can take a runtime expression.

- The jreversion is the Java Runtime Environment specification version that the component requires.

- nspluginurl and iepluginurl are the URL where the Java plug-in can be downloaded for Netscape Navigator and Internet Explorer.

## <jsp:params>

Only valid as part of a <jsp:plugin> action. Contains zero or more <jsp:param> actions.

## <jsp:fallback>

Only valid as part of a <jsp:plugin> action. Provides content for the client browser if the plug-in cannot be started.

## <jsp:attribute>

Used to define one or more attributes for a standard or custom action. Can also be used as part of the body of a <jsp:element> standard action. It has the following syntax:

```
<jsp:attribute
          name="attributeName"
          trim="true|false"
</jsp:attribute>
```

- name is required and is the name of the attribute being defined.

- trim is optional and specifies whether whitespace should be trimmed from the body of the action.

- The body of the action is the value of the attribute being defined.

    For example, this use of the <jsp:attribute> action:

```
<jsp:getProperty>
  <jsp:attribute name="name">anotherBeanName</jsp:attribute>
  <jsp:attribute name="property">propertyName</jsp:attribute>
</jsp:getProperty>
```

is equivalent to

```
<jsp:getProperty name="anotherBeanName" property="propertyName" />
```

## <jsp:body>

Defines the body of a custom or standard action. Required if one or more <jsp:attribute> elements appear in the body of the tag. This action has no attributes.

# \<jsp:invoke>

This tag is valid only in tag files. It takes the name of an attribute that is a fragment, and invokes the fragment, sending the output of the result to the JspWriter, or to a scoped attribute that can be examined and manipulated. If the fragment identified by the given name is null, `<jsp:invoke>` will behave as though a fragment was passed in that produces no output. It has the following syntax:

```
<jsp:invoke
            fragment="fragmentName"
            var="varName"
            varReader="varReaderName"
            scope="page|request|session|application"
</jsp:invoke>
```

- `fragment` is the name of the fragment being invoked.

- `var` is optional and is the name of the attribute that stores the result. Only one of `var` or `varReader` can be used.

- `varReader` is optional and is the name of the attribute of type `java.io.Reader` that stores the result. Only one of `var` or `varReader` can be used.

- `scope` is optional and is the scope in which `var` or `varReader` is stored.

Suppose you had a tag that looked like this:

```
<projsp:copyright>
  <jsp:attribute name="frag">
    fragment template text ${var1}
  </jsp:attribute>
</projsp:copyright>
```

You would access the fragment in a tag file like this:

```
<%-- /WEB-INF/tags/copyright.tag --%>
<%@ attribute name="frag" fragment="true" %>
Some template text.
<jsp:invoke fragment="frag" />
```

# \<jsp:doBody>

The `<jsp:doBody>` standard action can only be used in tag files. It invokes the body of the tag, sending the output of the result to the JspWriter, or to a scoped attribute that can be examined and manipulated. It has the following syntax:

```
<jsp:doBody
            var="varName"
            varReader="varReaderName"
            scope="page|request|session|application"
</jsp:doBody>
```

- var is optional and is the name of the attribute that stores the result. Only one of var or varReader can be used.

- varReader is optional and is the name of the attribute of type java.io.Reader that stores the result. Only one of var or varReader can be used.

- scope is optional and is the scope in which var or varReader is stored.

# <jsp:element>

The <jsp:element> action is used to dynamically define the value of the tag of an XML element. This action can be used in JSP pages, tag files, and JSP documents. This action has an optional body; the body can use the <jsp:attribute> and <jsp:body> actions. A <jsp:element> action has one mandatory attribute, name, of type String. The value of the attribute is used as that of the tag of the element generated. Its syntax is

```
<jsp:element name="elementName"
  <jsp:attribute name="attributeName">attribute value</jsp:attribute>
  <jsp:body>arbitrary text</jsp:body>
</jsp:element>
```

So, for example, this <jsp:element> tag

```
<jsp:element name="projsp:copyright"
  <jsp:attribute name="year">2005</jsp:attribute>
  <jsp:body>copyright body</jsp:body>
</jsp:element>
```

is equivalent to

```
<projsp:copyright year="2005" >
  copyright body
</projsp:copyright>
```

# <jsp:text>

A <jsp:text> action can be used to enclose template data in a JSP page, a JSP document, or a tag file. A <jsp:text> action has no attributes and can appear anywhere that template data can. Its syntax is

```
<jsp:text>arbitrary text</jsp:text>
```

The <jsp:output> action can only be used in JSP documents and in tag files in XML syntax, and a translation error must result if used in a standard syntax JSP or tag file. This action is used to modify some properties of the output of a JSP document or a tag file. Its syntax is

```
<jsp:output omit-xml-declaration="yes|no|true|false" doctypeDecl />
```

where docTypeDecl can be

```
doctype-root-element="rootElement"
doctype-public="PubidLiteral"
doctype-system="SystemLiteral"
```

or

```
doctype-root-element="rootElement"
doctype-system="SystemLiteral"
```

- omit-xml-declaration is optional, and it indicates whether to omit the generation of an XML declaration. Acceptable values are true, yes, false, and no.

- doctype-root-element is optional, and it indicates the name that is to be output in the generated DOCTYPE declaration.

- doctype-system is optional, and it specifies that a DOCTYPE declaration is to be generated and gives the value for the system literal.

- doctype-public is optional, and it gives the value for the public ID for the generated DOCTYPE.

## Tag Libraries

The syntax for using tag libraries is very similar to that for the standard actions, except of course that the tag names and attributes are defined in the tag library itself rather than by the JSP standard. Each tag library is associated with a **prefix** by using the taglib directive to map the prefix to a URI identifying the tag library. For example, to use the IO tag library from the Jakarta Taglibs project (http://jakarta.apache.org/taglibs/doc/io-doc/intro.html), you would insert the following taglib directive at the top of a page:

```
<%@ taglib uri="http://jakarta.apache.org/taglibs/io-1.0"
           prefix="io"  %>
```

Within the JSP, tags from the library can then be used by including the prefix defined in the taglib directive and the tag's name. For example, the <request> tag can be used to access a web resource and include it in the JSP page:

```
<io:request url="http://www.apress.com">
</io:request>
```

The mapping between a particular URI (as used in the taglib directive) and the TLD can be set up in one of two ways. In JSP 2.1, it's possible to package tag libraries so that the mapping is automatic, based on settings contained in the TLD file. Alternatively, an entry can be made in the web.xml file to map a URI to a TLD file:

```
<taglib>
  <taglib-uri>http://jakarta.apache.org/taglibs/io-1.0</taglib-uri>
  <taglib-location>/WEB-INF/request.tld</taglib-location>
</taglib>
```

# Implicit Objects

JSP defines a number of implicit objects that JSP scripting elements can make use of:

- request, of type javax.servlet.http.HttpServletRequest

- response, of type javax.servlet.http.HttpServletResponse

- out, of type javax.servlet.jsp.JspWriter

- session, of type javax.servlet.http.HttpSession

- application, of type javax.servlet.ServletContext

- exception, of type java.lang.Throwable

- config, of type javax.servlet.ServletConfig

- page, a reference to the implementing servlet class for the JSP

- pageContext, of type javax.servlet.jsp.PageContext

Appendix B gives details of these objects and the methods that each makes available. There are many more classes and interfaces defined by the JSP and Servlet specifications.

# Predefined Attributes

The Servlet and JSP specifications define a number of special request and context (application) attributes. You access these through the getAttribute() and getAttributeNames() methods of the request object.

## SSL Protocol Attributes

These attributes are only available when a request has been made over the Secure Sockets Layer (SSL). SSL allows you to set up secure communications between the server and a client.

### javax.servlet.request.cipher_suite

javax.servlet.request.cipher_suite is a request attribute of type String containing the **cipher suite** used for an SSL request.

### javax.servlet.request.key_size

javax.servlet.request.key_size is a request attribute of type Integer containing the bit size that was used for an SSL request. Here's an example:

```
public boolean isOver128bit(HttpServletRequest request) {
  Integer reqSize = (Integer) request.getAttribute(
                        "javax.servlet.request.key_size");
  if(reqSize != null) {
    if (reqSize.intValue() < 128) {
      return false;
```

```
      } else {
        return true;
      }
    }
  }
}
```

### javax.servlet.request.X509Certificate

`javax.servlet.request.X509Certificate` is a request attribute that contains an array of objects of type `java.security.cert.X509Certificate` containing any certificate associated with an SSL request.

## Inclusion- and Forward-Related Attributes

These attributes apply when a servlet or JSP is accessed via a `<jsp:include>`, `RequestDispatcher.include()`, or `RequestDispatcher.forward()` like so:

```
request.getRequestDispatcher("servlet_path/myservlet").forward(req, res);
```

### javax.servlet.include.request_uri

`javax.servlet.include.request_uri` is a request attribute of type `String` containing the URI under which this included servlet or JSP is being accessed.

```
String reqURI = (String) request.getAttribute(
                          "javax.servlet.include.request_uri");
```

### javax.servlet.include.context_path

`javax.servlet.include.context_path` is a request attribute of type `String` containing the context path of the URI under which this included servlet or JSP is being accessed.

```
String contextPath = (String) req.getAttribute(
                              "javax.servlet.include.context_path");
```

### javax.servlet.include.path_info

`javax.servlet.include.path_info` is a request attribute of type `String` containing the path info of the URI under which this included servlet or JSP is being accessed.

```
String pathInfo = (String) req.getAttribute(
                           "javax.servlet.include.path_info");
```

### javax.servlet.include.servlet_path

`javax.servlet.include.servlet_path` is a request attribute of type `String` containing the servlet path of the URI under which this included servlet or JSP is being accessed.

```
String pathInfo;
if(req.getAttribute("javax.servlet.include.servlet_path") != null) {
  pathInfo = (String)req.getAttribute("javax.servlet.include.path_info");
}
```

### javax.servlet.include.query_string

`javax.servlet.include.query_string` is a request attribute of type `String` containing the query string of the URI under which this included servlet or JSP is being accessed.

```
String reqQueryString = req.getAttribute(
                    "javax.servlet.include.query_string");
```

## Servlet Error Page Attributes

These attributes are only available within an error page declared in `web.xml`.

### javax.servlet.error.status_code

`javax.servlet.error.status_code` is a request attribute of type `Integer` containing the status code of the servlet or JSP that caused the error.

```
Integer statusCode = (Integer) req.getAttribute(
                            "javax.servlet.error.status_code");
String error = "HTTP Status Code - " + statusCode.intValue();
return error;
```

### javax.servlet.error.exception_type

`javax.servlet.error.exception_type` is a request attribute of type `Class` that contains the type of the exception thrown by the servlet or JSP. It's now redundant with the introduction of the `javax.servlet.error.exception` attribute.

```
Exception e = (Exception) req.getAttribute(
                        "javax.servlet.error.exception_type");
```

### javax.servlet.error.message

`javax.servlet.error.message` is a request attribute of type `String` containing the message contained within the exception thrown by the servlet or JSP. It's now redundant with the introduction of the `javax.servlet.error.exception` attribute.

```
String statusCode = (String) req.getAttribute(
                            "javax.servlet.error.status_code");
String message= (String)req.getAttribute("javax.servlet.error.message");
if message == null) {
  message = "Unknown error";
}
```

### javax.servlet.error.exception

`javax.servlet.error.exception` is a request attribute of type `Throwable` containing the exception thrown by the servlet or JSP.

```
public void doGet(HttpServletRequest req, HttpServletResponse res)
                            throws ServletException, IOException {
  PrintWriter out = res.getWriter();
  Throwable throwable = (Throwable) req.getAttribute(
                        "javax.servlet.error.exception");
  if (throwable != null)
    throwable.printStackTrace(out);
}
```

### javax.servlet.error.request_uri

`javax.servlet.error.request_uri` is a request attribute of type `String` containing the URI of the request that caused the servlet or JSP to throw an exception.

```
String reqErrorUri = (String) req.getAttribute("
                        javax.servlet.error.request_uri");
```

### javax.servlet.error.servlet_name

`javax.servlet.error.servlet_name` is a request attribute of type `String` containing logical name of the servlet in which the error occurred.

## JavaServer Pages Error Page Attribute

This attribute is available within error pages declared in a JSP page directive.

### javax.servlet.jsp.jspException

`javax.servlet.jsp.jspException` is a request attribute of type `Throwable` containing the exception thrown by the JSP page.

```
<%
  try {
    InputStream in = pageContext.getServletContext()
                    .getResourceAsStream(fileName);
    if(in == null) {
      throw new JspException( "Error while opening file: '"+ fileName + "'");
    }
  } catch(Exception ex ) {
    //handle exception
  }
%>
```

# Temporary File Directory Attribute

This attribute allows a web application to make use of a temporary working directory.

## javax.servlet.context.tempdir

`javax.servlet.context.tempdir` is a `context` attribute of type `java.io.File` referencing a temporary working directory that can be used by the web application.

```
File tempDir = (File) getServletContext()
                   .getAttribute("javax.servlet.context.tempdir");
```

# JSP Implicit Objects

**J**SP defines a number of implicit objects that scripting elements can make use of. These implicit objects are Java objects that implement interfaces in the Servlet and JSP API and that the JSP container makes available to developers in each page. These objects may be accessed as built-in variables via scripting elements and can also be accessed programmatically by custom and standard actions. This appendix gives details of these objects and the methods that each of them exposes. There are many more classes and interfaces defined by the JSP and Servlet specifications.

---

**■Note**  Apart from the page, `pageContext`, and exception implicit objects, this appendix lists all the methods available for each object (except those defined in `java.lang.Object`), irrespective of which class or interface defines the methods.

---

The implicit objects are as follows:

- `request`
- `response`
- `out`
- `session`
- `application`
- `exception`
- `config`
- `page`
- `pageContext`

# The request Object

The request object is an instance of a class that implements the javax.servlet.http. HttpServletRequest interface. The most common use of the request object is to obtain request parameters, request attributes, and query string values. It represents the request made by the client, and makes the following methods available:

public Object **getAttribute**(String name)

getAttribute() returns the value of the specified request attribute name. The return value is an Object or subclass if the attribute is available to the invoking ServletRequest object or null if the attribute isn't available.

public java.util.Enumeration **getAttributeNames**()

getAttributeNames() returns an Enumeration containing the attribute names available to the invoking ServletRequest object.

public String **getAuthType**()

getAuthType() returns the name of the authentication scheme used in the request or null if no authentication scheme was used. It returns one of the constants BASIC_AUTH, FORM_AUTH, CLIENT_CERT_AUTH or DIGEST_AUTH or null if the request was not authenticated.

public String **getCharacterEncoding**()

getCharacterEncoding() returns a String object containing the character encoding used in the body of the request or null if there is no encoding.

public int **getContentLength**()

getContentLength() returns the length of the body of the request in bytes or –1 if the length is not known.

public String **getContentType**()

getContentType() returns a String object containing the MIME type (text/plain, text/html, image/gif, etc.) of the body of the request or null if the type isn't known.

public String **getContextPath**()

getContextPath() returns the part of the request URI that indicates the context path of the request. The context path is the first part of the URI and always begins with the "/" character. For servlets running in the root context, this method returns an empty String. For example, if there is an incoming request for http://localhost/guide/suburbs/index.jsp, then getContextPath() would return /guide.

public Cookie[] **getCookies**()

getCookies() returns an array containing any Cookie objects sent with the request or null if no cookies were sent.

`public long` **`getDateHeader`**`(String name)`

getDateHeader() returns a long value that converts the date specified in the named header to the number of milliseconds since midnight January 1, 1970, Greenwich Mean Time (GMT). This method is used with a header that contains a date and returns –1 if the request doesn't contain the specified header.

`public String` **`getHeader`**`(String name)`

getHeader() returns the value of the specified header expressed as a String object or null if the request doesn't contain the specified header. (See also the getHeaderNames() method next.) Here is an example HTTP request:

```
GET /search?index=servlets+jsp HTTP/1.1
Accept: image/gif, image/jpg, */*
Accept-Encoding: gzip
Connection: Keep-Alive
Cookie: userID=id66589
Host: www.mycompany.com
Referer: http://www.mycompany.com/getproducts.html
User-Agent: Mozilla/4.6 [en] (WinXP; U)
```

For example, if the usage is getRequest("Connection"), it would return Keep-Alive:

`public java.util.Enumeration` **`getHeaderNames`**`()`

getHeaderNames() returns an Enumeration containing all of the header names used by the request.

`public java.util.Enumeration` **`getHeaders`**`(String name)`

getHeaders() returns an Enumeration containing all of the values associated with the specified header name. The method returns an empty enumeration if the request doesn't contain the specified header.

`public ServletInputStream` **`getInputStream`**`() throws java.io.IOException`

getInputStream() returns a ServletInputStream object that can be used to read the body of the request as binary data.

`public int` **`getIntHeader`**`(String name)`

getIntHeader() returns the value of the specified header as an int. It returns –1 if the request doesn't contain the specified header and throws a NumberFormatException if the header value cannot be converted to an int. This method was made for convenience when the header type is known to be an integer.

`public String` **`getLocalAddr`**`()`

getLocalAddress() returns the Internet Protocol (IP) address of the interface on which the request was received.

public java.util.Locale **getLocale**()

getLocale() returns the preferred locale of the client that made the request.

public java.util.Enumeration **getLocales**()

getLocales() returns an Enumeration containing, in descending order of preference, the locales that are acceptable to the client machine.

public String **getLocalName**()

getLocalName() returns the host name of the IP interface on which the request was received.

public int **getLocalPort**()

getLocalPort() returns the IP port number of the interface on which the request was received.

public String **getMethod**()

getMethod() returns the name of the HTTP method used to make the request. Typical return values are "GET", "POST", or "PUT".

public String **getParameter**(String name)

getParameter() returns a String object containing the value of the specified parameter or null if the parameter doesn't exist.

public java.util.Map **getParameterMap**()

getParameterMap() returns a Map containing the request parameters. Each parameter name is a key in the map; parameter values are stored as String arrays.

public java.util.Enumeration **getParameterNames**()

getParameterNames() returns a Enumeration of String objects containing the names of the parameters that are part of the current request.

public String[] **getParameterValues**(String name)

getParameterValues() is used when a parameter may have more than one value associated with it. The method returns a String array containing the values of the specified parameter or null if the parameter doesn't exist.

public String **getPathInfo**()

getPathInfo() returns any additional path information contained in the request URL. This extra information will appear after the servlet path and before the query string. It returns null if there is no additional path information. For example, if a request URL had the form http://localhost/guide/suburbs/innersuburbs/ where guide is the context and suburbs identifies a resource in the application, then getPathInfo() would return /innersuburbs.

public String **getPathTranslated**()

getPathTranslated() returns the same information as the getPathInfo() method, but translated into a real path.

public String **getProtocol**()

getProtocol() returns the name and version of the protocol used by the request. A typical return String would be "HTTP/1.1".

public String **getQueryString**()

getQueryString() returns the query string that was contained in the request URL without any decoding from the container or null if there was no query string.

public java.io.BufferedReader **getReader**() throws java.io.IOException

getReader() returns a BufferedReader object that can be used to read the body of the request as character data.

public String **getRemoteAddr**()

getRemoteAddr() returns a String object containing the IP address of the client machine that made the request.

public String **getRemoteHost**()

getRemoteHost() returns a String object containing the name of the client machine or the IP address if the name cannot be determined.

public int **getRemotePort**()

getRemotePort() returns the IP source port of the client or last proxy that sent the request.

public String **getRemoteUser**()

getRemoteUser() returns the login of the user making the request or null if the user hasn't been authenticated.

public RequestDispatcher **getRequestDispatcher**(String path)

getRequestDispatcher() returns a RequestDispatcher object that acts as a wrapper around the resource located at the specified path. The path must begin with "/" and can be a relative path.

public String **getRequestedSessionId**()

getRequestedSessionId() returns the session ID that was specified by the client or null if the request didn't specify an ID.

public String **getRequestURI**()

getRequestURI() returns a subsection of the request URL, from the protocol name to the query string.

public StringBuffer **getRequestURL**()

getRequestURL() reconstructs the URL used to make the request including the protocol, server name, port number, and path, but excluding the query string.

public String **getScheme**()

getScheme() returns the scheme ("http", "https", "ftp", and so on) used to make the request.

public String **getServerName**()

getServerName() returns a String object containing the name of the server that received the request.

public int **getServerPort**()

getServerPort() returns the port number that received the request.

public String **getServletPath**()

getServletPath() returns the part of the request URL that was used to call the servlet, without any additional information or the query string.

public HttpSession **getSession**(boolean create)
public HttpSession **getSession**()

getSession() and getSession(true) return the HttpSession object associated with the request. If the request doesn't currently have a session, calling either method will create one. Setting the boolean parameter create to false overrides this.

public Principal **getUserPrincipal**()

getUserPrincipal() returns a java.security.Principal object containing the name of the current authenticated user. If the user has not been authenticated, the method returns null.

public boolean **isRequestedSessionIdFromCookie**()

isRequestedSessionIdFromCookie() returns true if the session ID came in from a cookie.

public boolean **isRequestedSessionIdFromURL**()

isRequestedSessionIdFromURL() returns true if the session ID came in as part of the request URL.

public boolean **isRequestedSessionIdValid**()

isRequestedSessionIdValid() returns true if the session ID requested by the client is still valid.

public boolean **isSecure**()

isSecure() returns true if the request was made using a secure channel, for example HTTPS.

`public boolean `**`isUserInRole`**`(String role)`

   `isUserInRole()` returns `true` if the authenticated user has the specified logical role or `false` if the user isn't authenticated.

`public void `**`removeAttribute`**`(String name)`

   `removeAttribute()`makes the specified attribute unavailable to the invoking `ServletRequest` object. Subsequent calls to the `getAttribute()` method for this attribute will return `null`.

`public void `**`setAttribute`**`(String name, Object o)`

   `setAttribute()` binds a value to a specified attribute name. Note that attributes will be reset after the request is handled.

`public void `**`setCharacterEncoding`**`(String env) ➡`
   `throws java.io.UnsupportedEncodingException`

   `setCharacterEncoding()` overrides the character encoding used in the body of this request.

`public static final String `**`BASIC_AUTH`**
`public static final String `**`FORM_AUTH`**
`public static final String `**`CLIENT_CERT_AUTH`**
`public static final String `**`DIGEST_AUTH`**

   These `String` constants are used to identify the different types of authentication that may have been used to protect the servlet. They have the values `BASIC`, `FORM`, `CLIENT_CERT`, and `DIGEST`, respectively.

`public String `**`getRealPath`**`(String path)`
`public boolean `**`isRequestedSessionIdFromUrl`**`()`

   These methods are deprecated and should not be used in new code—they exist for compatibility with existing code. Use `ServletContext.getRealPath(java.lang.String)` instead of `getRealPath(String path)` and use `isRequestedSessionIdFromURL()` instead of `isRequestedSessionIdFromUrl()`.

# The response Object

The `response` object is an instance of a class that implements the `javax.servlet.http.HttpServletResponse` interface. It represents the response to be made to the client and makes the following methods available:

`public void `**`addCookie`**`(Cookie cookie)`

   `addCookie()` adds the specified cookie to the response. It can be called multiple times to set more than one cookie.

```
public void addDateHeader(String name, long date)
```

addDateHeader() adds a response header containing the specified header name and the number of milliseconds since midnight January 1, 1970, GMT. This method can be used to assign multiple values to a given header name.

```
public void addHeader(String name, String value)
```

addHeader() adds a response header with the specified name and value. This method can be used to assign multiple values to a given header name.

```
public void addIntHeader(String name, int value)
```

addIntHeader() adds a response header with the specified name and int value. This method can be used to assign multiple values to a given header name.

```
public boolean containsHeader(String name)
```

containsHeader() returns true if the response header includes the specified header name. This method can be used before calling one of the set() methods to determine whether the header value has already been set.

```
public String encodeRedirectURL(String url)
```

encodeRedirectURL() encodes the specified URL with session tracking data or returns it unchanged if encoding isn't required. This method is used to process a URL before sending it to the sendRedirect()method.

```
public String encodeURL(String url)
```

encodeURL() encodes the specified URL by including the session ID or returns it unchanged if encoding isn't needed. All URLs generated by a servlet should be processed through this method to ensure compatibility with browsers that don't support cookies.

```
public void flushBuffer() throws java.io.IOException
```

flushBuffer() causes any content stored in the buffer to be written to the client. Calling this method will also commit the response, meaning that the status code and headers will be written.

```
public int getBufferSize()
```

getBufferSize() returns the buffer size used for the response or 0 if no buffering is used.

```
public String getCharacterEncoding()
```

getCharacterEncoding() returns a String object containing the character encoding used in the body of the response. The default is "ISO-8859-1", which corresponds to Latin-1.

```
public String getContentType()
```

getContentType() returns the content type used for the MIME body sent in this response.

`public java.util.Locale `**`getLocale`**`()`

`getLocale()` returns the locale that has been assigned to the response. By default, this will be the default locale for the server.

`public ServletOutputStream `**`getOutputStream`**`() throws java.io.IOException`

`getOutputStream()` returns a `ServletOutputStream` object that can be used to write the response as binary data.

`public java.io.PrintWriter `**`getWriter`**`() throws java.io.IOException`

`getWriter()` returns a `PrintWriter` object that can be used to write the response as character data.

`public boolean `**`isCommitted`**`()`

`isCommitted()` returns `true` if the response has been committed, meaning that the status code and headers have been written.

`public void `**`reset`**`()`

`reset()` clears the status code and headers and any data that exists in the buffer. If the response has already been committed, calling this method will cause an exception to be thrown.

`public void `**`resetBuffer`**`()`

`resetBuffer()` clears the content of the response buffer without clearing the headers or status code. It will throw an `IllegalStateException` if the response has been committed.

`public void `**`sendError`**`(int sc, String msg) throws java.io.IOException`
`public void `**`sendError`**`(int sc) throws java.io.IOException`

`sendError()` sends an error response back to the client machine using the specified error status code. A descriptive message can also be provided. This method must be called before the response is committed (in other words, before the status code and headers have been written).

`public void `**`sendRedirect`**`(String location) throws java.io.IOException`

`sendRedirect()` redirects the client machine to the URL specified by the location parameter. This method must be called before the response is committed (in other words, before sending it to the client).

`public void `**`setBufferSize`**`(int size)`

`setBufferSize()` requests a buffer size to be used for the response. The actual buffer size will be at least this large.

`public void `**`setCharacterEncoding`**`(String charset)`

Sets the character encoding (MIME charset) of the response being sent to the client, for example, to UTF-8.

public void **setContentLength**(int len)

    setContentLength() sets the length of the response body.

public void **setContentType**(String type)

    setContentType() sets the content type of the response sent to the server. The String argument specifies a MIME type and may also include the type of character encoding, for example, "text/plain; charset=ISO-8859-1".

public void **setDateHeader**(String name, long date)

    setDateHeader() sets the time value of a response header for the specified header name. The time is the number of milliseconds since midnight January 1, 1970, GMT. If the time value for the specified header has been previously set, the value passed to this method will override it.

public void **setHeader**(String name, String value)

    setHeader() sets a response header with the specified name and value. If the value for the specified header has been previously set, the value passed to this method will override it.

public void **setIntHeader**(String name, int value)

    setIntHeader() sets a response header with the specified name and int value. If the int value for the specified header has been previously set, the value passed to this method will override it.

public void **setLocale**(java.util.Locale loc)

    setLocale() specifies the locale that will be used for the response.

public void **setStatus**(int sc)

    setStatus() sets the status code and should be one of SC_ACCEPTED, SC_OK, SC_CONTINUE, SC_PARTIAL_CONTENT, SC_CREATED, SC_SWITCHING_PROTOCOLS, or SC_NO_CONTENT.

```
public static final int SC_CONTINUE
public static final int SC_SWITCHING_PROTOCOLS
public static final int SC_OK
public static final int SC_CREATED
public static final int SC_FOUND
public static final int SC_ACCEPTED
public static final int SC_NON_AUTHORITATIVE_INFORMATION
public static final int SC_NO_CONTENT
public static final int SC_RESET_CONTENT
public static final int SC_PARTIAL_CONTENT
public static final int SC_MULTIPLE_CHOICES
public static final int SC_MOVED_PERMANENTLY
public static final int SC_MOVED_TEMPORARILY
public static final int SC_SEE_OTHER
public static final int SC_NOT_MODIFIED
public static final int SC_USE_PROXY
```

```
public static final int SC_TEMPORARY_REDIRECT
public static final int SC_BAD_REQUEST
public static final int SC_UNAUTHORIZED
public static final int SC_PAYMENT_REQUIRED
public static final int SC_FORBIDDEN
public static final int SC_NOT_FOUND
public static final int SC_METHOD_NOT_ALLOWED
public static final int SC_NOT_ACCEPTABLE
public static final int SC_PROXY_AUTHENTICATION_REQUIRED
public static final int SC_REQUEST_TIMEOUT
public static final int SC_CONFLICT
public static final int SC_GONE
public static final int SC_LENGTH_REQUIRED
public static final int SC_PRECONDITION_FAILED
public static final int SC_REQUEST_ENTITY_TOO_LARGE
public static final int SC_REQUEST_URI_TOO_LONG
public static final int SC_UNSUPPORTED_MEDIA_TYPE
public static final int SC_REQUESTED_RANGE_NOT_SATISFIABLE
public static final int SC_EXPECTATION_FAILED
public static final int SC_INTERNAL_SERVER_ERROR
public static final int SC_NOT_IMPLEMENTED
public static final int SC_BAD_GATEWAY
public static final int SC_SERVICE_UNAVAILABLE
public static final int SC_GATEWAY_TIMEOUT
public static final int SC_HTTP_VERSION_NOT_SUPPORTED
```

These constants represent the status codes defined in the HTTP specification. (Go to http://www.w3.org/TR/html401/ for more information.)

```
public String encodeUrl(String url)
public String encodeRedirectUrl(String url)
public void setStatus(int sc, String sm)
```

These methods are deprecated and should not be used in new code—they exist for compatibility with existing code.

# The out Object

The out object is an instance of the javax.servlet.jsp.JspWriter class. It's used to create the content returned to the client and has the following useful methods available:

```
public abstract void clear() throws java.io.IOException
```

clear() clears the contents of the buffer; it throws an exception if some data has already been written to the output stream.

```
public abstract void clearBuffer() throws java.io.IOException
```

clearBuffer() clears the contents of the buffer, but doesn't throw an exception if some data has already been written to the output stream.

public abstract void **close**() throws java.io.IOException

close() flushes and then closes the output stream.

public abstract void **flush**() throws java.io.IOException

flush() flushes the output buffer and sends any bytes contained in the buffer to their intended destination. flush() will flush all the buffers in a chain of Writers and OutputStreams.

public int **getBufferSize**()

getBufferSize() returns the size in bytes of the output buffer.

public abstract int **getRemaining**()

getRemaining() returns the number of bytes still contained in the buffer. It will return 0 if output is unbuffered.

public boolean **isAutoFlush**()

isAutoFlush() returns true if the buffer flushes automatically when an overflow condition occurs.

public abstract void **newLine**() throws java.io.IOException

newLine() writes a newline character to the output stream.

```
public abstract void print(boolean b) throws java.io.IOException
public abstract void print(char c) throws java.io.IOException
public abstract void print(int i) throws java.io.IOException
public abstract void print(long l) throws java.io.IOException
public abstract void print(float f) throws java.io.IOException
public abstract void print(double d) throws java.io.IOException
public abstract void print(char[] s) throws java.io.IOException
public abstract void print(String s) throws java.io.IOException
public abstract void print(Object obj) throws java.io.IOException
```

The print() method prints the specified primitive data type, the specified Object, or the specified String to the client.

```
try {
  boolean b = false;
  out.print(b);
  JspWriter out = pageContext.getOut();
  out.print(b);
} catch(IOException ioe) {
  // Catch error.
}
```

The output of the preceding code is as follows:

```
false
```

```
public abstract void println() throws java.io.IOException
public abstract void println(boolean x) throws java.io.IOException
public abstract void println(char x) throws java.io.IOException
public abstract void println(int x) throws java.io.IOException
public abstract void println(long x) throws java.io.IOException
public abstract void println(float x) throws java.io.IOException
public abstract void println(double x) throws java.io.IOException
public abstract void println(char[] x) throws java.io.IOException
public abstract void println(String x) throws java.io.IOException
public abstract void println(Object x) throws java.io.IOException
```

println() prints the specified primitive data type, the Object, or the String to the client, followed by a newline character at the end. The no-argument version simply writes a newline character. For example:

```
try {
  JspWriter out = pageContext.getOut();
  out.println("<html><title>Page Title</title></html>");
} catch(IOException ioe) {
  // Catch error.
}
```

```
public void write(char[] cbuf)
public abstract void write(char[] cbuf, int off, int len)
public void write(int c)
public void write(String str)
public void write(String str, int off, int len)
```

The write() method writes the given data to the client.

# The session Object

The session object is an instance of a class that implements the javax.servlet.http. HttpSession interface. It can be used to store session state for a user and makes the following methods available:

```
public Object getAttribute(String name)
```

getAttribute() returns the Object bound to the specified name in this session or null if it doesn't exist.

```
public java.util.Enumeration getAttributeNames()
```

getAttributeNames() returns an Enumeration of String objects containing the names of all the objects bound to this session.

```
public long getCreationTime()
```

getCreationTime() returns the time when the session was created in milliseconds since midnight Jan 1, 1970 GMT.

public String **getId**()

getId() returns a String object containing a unique identifier for this session.

public long **getLastAccessedTime**()

getLastAccessedTime() returns the last time a client request associated with the session was sent. The return value is the number of milliseconds since midnight Jan 1, 1970, GMT.

public int **getMaxInactiveInterval**()

getMaxInactiveInterval() returns the number of seconds the server will wait between client requests before the session is invalidated. A negative return value indicates the session will never time out.

public ServletContext **getServletContext**()

getServletContext() returns the ServletContext to which this session belongs.

public void **invalidate**()

invalidate() invalidates the session and unbinds any objects bound to it.

public boolean **isNew**()

isNew() returns true if the server has created a session that hasn't yet been accessed by a client.

public void **removeAttribute**(String name)

removeAttribute() removes the Object bound to the specified name from this session.

public void **setAttribute**(String name, Object value)

setAttribute() binds an Object to the specified attribute name in this session. If the attribute name already exists, the Object passed to this method will replace the previous Object.

public void **setMaxInactiveInterval**(int interval)

setMaxInactiveInterval() specifies the number of seconds the server will wait between client requests before the session is invalidated. If a negative value is passed to this method, the session will never time out.

public HttpSessionContext **getSessionContext**()
public Object **getValue**(String name)
public String[] **getValueNames**()
public void **putValue**(String name, Object value)
public void **removeValue**(String name)

These methods are deprecated and should not be used in new code—they exist for compatibility with existing code.

# The application Object

The application object is an instance of a class that implements the javax.servlet. ServletContext interface and allows the page to obtain and set information about the web application in which it is running. It makes available the following methods:

public Object **getAttribute**(String name)

getAttribute() returns the value of the specified attribute name. The return value is an Object or subclass if the attribute is available to the invoking ServletContext object or null if the attribute isn't available.

public java.util.Enumeration **getAttributeNames**()

getAttributeNames() returns an Enumeration containing the attribute names available to the invoking ServletContext object.

public ServletContext **getContext**(String uripath)

getContext() returns the ServletContext object for the resource at the specified path on the server. The path argument is an absolute URL beginning with "/".

public String **getInitParameter**(String name)

getInitParameter() returns a String object containing the value of the specified initialization parameter or null if the parameter doesn't exist.

public java.util.Enumeration **getInitParameterNames**()

getInitParameterNames() returns an Enumeration containing the initialization parameter names associated with the invoking ServletContext object.

public int **getMajorVersion**()

getMajorVersion() returns the major version of the Java Servlet API that the server supports. For servers supporting version 2.5 of the Servlet specification, this method will return 2.

public String **getMimeType**(String file)

getMimeType() returns the MIME type of the specified file or null if the MIME type cannot be ascertained. Typical return values will be "text/plain", "text/html", or "image/jpg".

public int **getMinorVersion**()

getMinorVersion() returns the minor version of the Java Servlet API that the server supports. For servers supporting version 2.5 of the Servlet specification, this method will return 5.

public RequestDispatcher **getNamedDispatcher**(String name)

getNamedDispatcher() returns a RequestDispatcher object that will be wrapped around the named servlet.

public String **getRealPath**(String path)

getRealPath() returns a String object containing the real path, in a form appropriate to the platform on which the servlet is running, corresponding to the given virtual path. An example of a virtual path might be "/blah.html".

public RequestDispatcher **getRequestDispatcher**(String path)

getRequestDispatcher() returns a RequestDispatcher object that acts as a wrapper around the resource located at the specified path. The path must begin with "/" and is interpreted relative to the current context root.

public java.net.URL **getResource**(String path)
        throws java.net.MalformedURLException

getResource() returns a URL object that is mapped to the specified path or null if there is no resource mapped to the path. The path must begin with "/" and is interpreted relative to the current context root.

public java.io.InputStream **getResourceAsStream**(String path)

getResourceAsStream() returns the resource at the specified path as an InputStream object.

public java.util.Set **getResourcePaths**()

getResourcePaths() returns all the paths to resources held in the web application as Strings beginning with a "/".

public String **getServerInfo**()

getServerInfo() returns a String object containing information on the server on which the servlet is running. At a minimum, the String will contain the servlet container name and version number.

```
<% out.print(application.getServerInfo()); %>
```

The output is as follows:

```
Apache Tomcat/5.5.9
```

public String **getServletContextName**()

getServletContextName() returns the name of the web application, as specified in the <display-name> element in web.xml.

public void **log**(String msg)
public void **log**(String message, Throwable throwable)

log() is used to write a message to the servlet engine's log file. The second version writes both an explanatory message and a stack trace for the specified Throwable exception to the log file.

```
public void removeAttribute(String name)
```

removeAttribute() makes the specified attribute unavailable to the invoking ServletContext object. Subsequent calls to the getAttribute() method for this attribute will return null.

```
public void setAttribute(String name, Object object)
```

setAttribute() binds a value to a specified attribute name.

```
public Servlet getServlet(String name) throws ServletException
public java.util.Enumeration getServlets()
public java.util.Enumeration getServletNames()
public void log(Exception exception, String msg)
```

These methods are deprecated and should not be used in new code—they exist for compatibility with existing code.

# The exception Object

The exception object is an instance of the java.lang.Throwable class. It's available in error pages only and represents the exception that occurred that caused control to pass to the error page. Its most useful methods are as follows:

```
public String getLocalizedMessage()
```

getLocalizedMessage() returns a localized description of this Throwable object. In many cases, this will return the same result as getMessage().

```
public String getMessage()
```

getMessage() returns the error message string of this Throwable object.

```
public void printStackTrace()
public void printStackTrace(PrintStream ps)
public void printStackTrace(PrintWriter pw)
```

printStackTrace() prints information about this Throwable object, along with a listing of the method calls that led to the error condition arising. The output can be directed to the standard error stream or to a specified PrintStream or PrintWriter object.

```
public String toString()
```

toString() returns a short description of this Throwable object. If an error message was supplied when the object was created, the result is the Throwable class's name, followed by a colon and a space, followed by that message. For example:

```
<%
  try {
    throw new Exception("Here's my Exception");
  } catch(Exception e) {
    out.print(e.toString());
  }
%>
```

The output is as follows:

```
java.lang.Exception: Here's my Exception
```

# The config Object

The config object is an instance of the javax.servlet.ServletConfig interface. It's used to make initialization parameters available and has the following methods:

public String **getInitParameter**(String name)

getInitParameter() returns the value of the specified initialization parameter or null if the parameter doesn't exist.

public java.util.Enumeration **getInitParameterNames**()

getInitParameterNames() returns an Enumeration of String objects containing the names of all of the servlet's initialization parameters.

public ServletContext **getServletContext**()

getServletContext() returns the ServletContext object associated with the invoking servlet. A ServletContext object contains information about the environment in which the servlet is running.

public String **getServletName**()

getServletName() returns the name of the servlet. If the servlet is unnamed, the method will return the servlet's class name.

# The page Object

The page object is of type java.lang.Object and is a reference to the servlet object that implements this JSP page. JSP page authors don't often use this object, because it's very expensive memory-wise.

# The pageContext Object

The pageContext object is an instance of the javax.servlet.jsp.PageContext class and is used by the container-generated servlet code for your JSP page to access the various scopes available within the JSP page. JSP page authors don't often use this object, because it was intended to be generated by the container; it's important when writing tag libraries.

# Index

# forums.apress.com

JOIN THE APRESS FORUMS AND BE PART OF OUR COMMUNITY. You'll find discussions that cover topics of interest to IT professionals, programmers, and enthusiasts just like you. If you post a query to one of our forums, you can expect that some of the best minds in the business—especially Apress authors, who all write with *The Expert's Voice*™—will chime in to help you. Why not aim to become one of our most valuable participants (MVPs) and win cool stuff? Here's a sampling of what you'll find:

## DATABASES

**Data drives everything.**

Share information, exchange ideas, and discuss any database programming or administration issues.

## INTERNET TECHNOLOGIES AND NETWORKING

**Try living without plumbing (and eventually IPv6).**

Talk about networking topics including protocols, design, administration, wireless, wired, storage, backup, certifications, trends, and new technologies.

## JAVA

**We've come a long way from the old Oak tree.**

Hang out and discuss Java in whatever flavor you choose: J2SE, J2EE, J2ME, Jakarta, and so on.

## MAC OS X

**All about the Zen of OS X.**

OS X is both the present and the future for Mac apps. Make suggestions, offer up ideas, or boast about your new hardware.

## OPEN SOURCE

**Source code is good; understanding (open) source is better.**

Discuss open source technologies and related topics such as PHP, MySQL, Linux, Perl, Apache, Python, and more.

## PROGRAMMING/BUSINESS

**Unfortunately, it is.**

Talk about the Apress line of books that cover software methodology, best practices, and how programmers interact with the "suits."

## WEB DEVELOPMENT/DESIGN

**Ugly doesn't cut it anymore, and CGI is absurd.**

Help is in sight for your site. Find design solutions for your projects and get ideas for building an interactive Web site.

## SECURITY

**Lots of bad guys out there—the good guys need help.**

Discuss computer and network security issues here. Just don't let anyone else know the answers!

## TECHNOLOGY IN ACTION

**Cool things. Fun things.**

It's after hours. It's time to play. Whether you're into LEGO® MINDSTORMS™ or turning an old PC into a DVR, this is where technology turns into fun.

## WINDOWS

**No defenestration here.**

Ask questions about all aspects of Windows programming, get help on Microsoft technologies covered in Apress books, or provide feedback on any Apress Windows book.

**HOW TO PARTICIPATE:**

Go to the Apress Forums site at **http://forums.apress.com/**.
Click the New User link.